D1131364

McGRAW-HILL SERIES IN HEALTH SCIENCE

Amos Christie, M.D., *Consulting Editor*

RURAL HEALTH AND MEDICAL CARE

The quality of the materials used in the manufacture of this book is governed by continued postwar shortages.

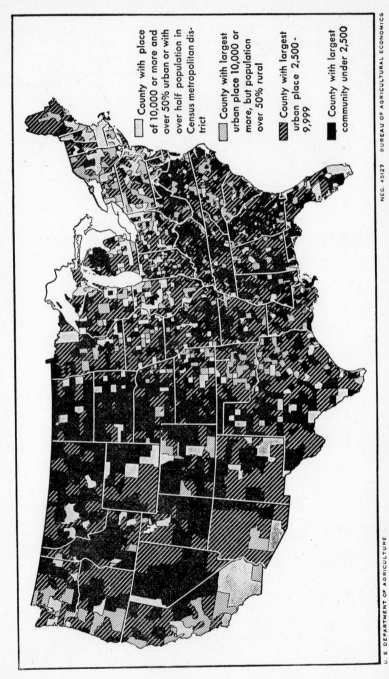

U. S. DEPARTMENT OF AGRICULTURE

NEG. 45127   BUREAU OF AGRICULTURAL ECONOMICS

Rural America: Counties of the United States by rural-urban character, 1940.

County with place of 10,000 or more and over 50% urban or with over half population in Census metropolitan district

County with largest urban place 10,000 or more, but population over 50% rural

County with largest urban place 2,500 - 9,999

County with largest community under 2,500

RURAL HEALTH

AND MEDICAL CARE

by FREDERICK D. MOTT, M.D.

and MILTON I. ROEMER, M.D., M.P.H.

FIRST EDITION

———

NEW YORK TORONTO LONDON

McGRAW-HILL BOOK COMPANY, INC.

1948

614.0973

M321

RA427
M73

RURAL HEALTH AND MEDICAL CARE

Copyright, 1948, by the McGraw-Hill Book Company, Inc. Printed in the United States of America. All rights reserved. This book, or parts thereof, may not be reproduced in any form without permission of the publishers.

PREFACE

FACTS and issues concerning the distribution of medical care have won the increasing attention of the nation over the last twenty or thirty years. They are an aspect of the problem of what Ogburn called "cultural lag," the problem of social organization falling far behind technological advances. The extent of the lag in medicine seems to have become particularly wide on the American scene where scientific advances have been especially great and social adjustments particularly slow.[1]

While this divergence of the lines of organization of medical care from those of medical science has characterized America as a whole, it has been most extreme in the rural sections of our country. The forces of social organization necessary to bring to the average citizen the benefits of applied medical science have been strongest in the cities; the country dweller is the last to be served. It is this that has made rural medicine a special social problem and that has stimulated this account of rural health and medical care.

The definition of rural medicine is, of course, relative. In the villages of Massachusetts the volume and quality of medical service are perhaps to be compared favorably with the levels of service in the urban communities of certain other states or nations. By the same token, on a time scale, the urban medicine of colonial America was far more "rural" in character than that of the most isolated county of Wyoming today. In a sense all American medicine, not too many years ago, was what we today consider rural.

Yet the recognition of rural health and medical care as a special problem is not new with the era of penicillin and atomic energy. In 1837 Dr. Benjamin W. McCready could write, "Agriculture is the oldest, the healthiest, and the most natural of all employments. The

---

[1] OGBURN, WILLIAM F., *Social Change with Respect to Culture and Original Nature*. New York: B. W. Huebsch, 1922. See also MOORE, HARRY H., *American Medicine and the People's Health*. New York: D. Appleton-Century and Company, Inc., 1927; and SIGERIST, HENRY E., *Medicine and Human Welfare*. New Haven: Yale University Press, 1941.

v

66423
AUG 29 1951

husbandman, in general, enjoys pure air, and varied and moderate exercise. In this country his diet is always abundant and nutritious, and his habits much more temperate than those of the manufacturing or laboring classes."[2] Only 25 years later, however, Dr. W. W. Hall of New York City wrote in a paper included in the first annual report of the Commissioner of Agriculture, submitted to President Lincoln in 1862:

The impression pervades all classes of society that the cultivation of the soil is the most healthful mode of life, and gives the highest promise of a peaceful, quiet, and happy old age. Dwellers amid brick and mortar, looking on from a distance, have visions in which it is a luxury to indulge, of independence, of comfort, of repose, and of overflowing abundance, as inseparable from a farm-house; and under the influence of these, with the bewitching and sweetly sad memories of blossoms and budding trees, of green pastures and waving meadows and birds of spring, of fishing and hunting, of shady woods and cool, clear waters dashing briskly over pebbled bottoms, they pine for the country with deep and abiding longings. It may, therefore, be practically useful to inquire as to the correctness of these views, whether they are not materially modified by incidental circumstances which do not necessarily exist, and if so, what may be the best remedy for their prevention or removal. To do this properly, we must look whole facts full in the face and take our departure from what is, and not from what we may think ought to be.[3]

Hall then proceeds to discuss the excessive burden of insanity, the shortened life expectancy, and the general hardships of agricultural existence which may make of the farmer's wife a "vision, not of youth and beauty, innocence and exuberant health, but that of the pale and wan and haggard face." In the following year's report, Hall discusses the disease hazards created by the miasms arising near farmhouses, the difficulties of obtaining pure water, and the inconvenience of outdoor privies which eventually leads to a variety of

[2] McCready, Benjamin W., *On the Influence of Trades, Professions, and Occupations in the United States, in the Production of Disease*. Baltimore: Johns Hopkins University Press, 1943, pp. 33-38. (Reprinted from *Transactions of the Medical Society of the State of New York*, Vol. 3, Albany, 1837, pp. 91-150.)

[3] Hall, W. W., "Health of Farmers' Families," *Report of the Commissioner of Agriculture for the Year* 1862, Washington, pp. 453-470.

intestinal and related ailments.[4] It is evident that a recognition of the special problems of rural health is not new.

Likewise, a consciousness of the special problems of rural medical practice is not new with the current period. In Colonial times and through most of the nineteenth century, urban and rural medicine may perhaps have been largely indistinguishable. With the era of Pasteur and Koch, however, when modern science began to flower, medical practice soon outgrew the confines of the little black bag. The wealth brought by industrialization became accumulated in the cities, and hospitals and centers of learning came to be highly developed in them. Physicians accordingly began to concentrate in the cities and a recognition of special disadvantages in rural medicine appeared. Evidence of this is found in the appearance in the last quarter of the nineteenth century of at least three journals designed specifically for the country doctor. The earliest of these, entitled *The Country Practitioner or New Jersey Journal of Medical and Surgical Practice* was issued in 1879.[5] Since this period, as general cultural disparities between city and country have increased, recognition of the special problems of rural medicine has heightened.

No clear-cut line of demarcation, of course, separates rural health problems from urban health problems or rural medical care from urban medical care. Disease knows no corporate limits, no definitions of residence. The automobile and the telephone, moreover, have shortened the lines of science. The farmer may be hospitalized in a near-by city; the city specialist may be called out to the country in consultation. And yet the farmer as a rule is not hospitalized in a modern urban hospital, and the city specialist views the country chiefly as a recreation area. It is facts like these that have made rural health and medical care a special issue.

Any description of health conditions and medical service becomes rapidly outdated. The study of rural medical care is as dynamic as

[4] HALL, W. W., "Farmers' Houses," *Report of the Commissioner of Agriculture for the Year* 1863, Washington, pp. 313-337.

[5] This journal was edited by Dr. E. P. Townsend of Beverly, New Jersey. For a fuller discussion, see ROEMER, MILTON I., "Historic Development of the Current Crisis of Rural Medicine in the United States," in *Victor Robinson Memorial Volume: Essays on History of Medicine.* New York: Froben Press, 1948.

the myriad social and economic forces that shape its character. With the Second World War, these forces have been particularly complex and their effects on rural medicine especially severe. While we shall never return precisely to the "normalcy" of the prewar years, the picture of rural medicine in America during the war and early postwar years 1941-47 is admittedly quite atypical. For this reason, it has been considered appropriate to regard 1940 as a more normal base line, and most of the statistical material in this volume describes experience in that year and the trends leading up to that year. From time to time the special effects of the war are considered, and more recent data are given on the new and significant programs for health improvement. The disruption of the war years appears to have had some lingering effects on rural medicine, especially on the supply of personnel, so that present rural needs are, in general, even more serious than those portrayed.

Much information on general health conditions and medical care has been assembled in the last 20 years. The nation-wide studies of the Committee on the Costs of Medical Care (1928-31) and the National Health Survey (1935-36) have provided a firm foundation; reports of the U.S. Public Health Service, the Social Security Board, the American Medical Association, the Bureau of the Census, the Department of Agriculture, and numerous other governmental and voluntary agencies have yielded rich bodies of information. Definitions of "rural" have been by no means identical in different studies and much valuable material has been published without rural-urban breakdowns. It has been frequently necessary, therefore, to make new types of computations of published data or to consult unpublished material in order to present throughout a reasonably consistent picture of rural health problems. Drawing freely from all sources at our disposal, we have attempted to paint the panorama of American medicine as it relates to the farmer and village dweller.[6]

Much of the basic statistical information on rural health and medical care, as compared with urban, may appear sadly out of date as of 1948. Data of the Committee on the Costs of Medical Care may

[6] This study deals essentially with the continental United States. There is little doubt that the rural health problems of Puerto Rico, Hawaii, Alaska, and other territories represent an aggravated expression of what is found in the states.

appear like past history to the current reader. It should be recognized, however, that our use of such data is primarily for their comparative urban-rural value rather than for the absolute figures. In the years since this and other monumental studies, it is evident that the urban health situation has improved more than the rural, so that rural-urban discrepancies today are, if anything, greater.

This work attempts to portray the real situation as it confronts us today in rural areas without theoretical "correction" for certain background factors. Thus, some who would minimize rural needs may point out that rural areas have a high incidence of communicable disease merely because they have more children, that rural infant mortality is high because of the racial composition of the population, that the supply of rural physicians is low because of economic rather than rural causes, and so on. Such an approach, of course, has its theoretical foundation and occasionally it is used where hypothetical comparisons are appropriate. In general, however, our interest is not with a statistical abstraction of "rurality." It is focused on the actual rural health situation and the corrective action it demands.

Problems of rural health and medical care are attracting the increasing attention of thoughtful persons — in the health professions, in agriculture, and among the general public — in rural and urban areas alike. In a sense, the various expressions of this interest, in words and deeds, have acquired the aspect of a real social movement. It is a movement which here and there may get off the main path toward its goal, because of lack of accurate information or clouded vision. But there can be no lack of assurance that the ultimate goal of adequate rural health services will be reached. If this volume will in some small measure serve as a handmaiden to that movement, as a source of facts and figures and some evaluations of what things come first and what things come second, the generous contributions of all those who, by their writing or their personal assistance and counsel, made this study possible will perhaps be rewarded.

FREDERICK D. MOTT
MILTON I. ROEMER

WASHINGTON, D.C.
1947

ACKNOWLEDGMENTS

IN A very real sense this study has been the result of the cooperative efforts of many persons and agencies. A listing of those who
have played some part is bound to be incomplete. For generous
financial assistance in supporting the research on which the main
body of the volume is based, grateful acknowledgment is extended
to the Rockefeller Foundation and the Farm Foundation. The en-
couragement and backing of Drs. Alan Gregg and Henry C. Taylor,
and of Frank Peck of these organizations is deeply appreciated.

For painstaking collection of data and information of every sort
around which the story of rural health and medical care is built,
major credit must go to Mrs. Rose Ehrlich and to Mrs. Katharine G.
Clark. As great as their help in assembling facts and figures was their
contribution in the way of critical suggestions at all stages of development of the manuscript. Additional technical assistance in countless
ways was rendered by Jesse B. Yaukey, and also by Leah Resnick,
Cozette Hapney, and Ruth Bunker, to all of whom is extended gratitude. Especially great is the indebtedness to Miss Carol F. Hobbs
whose devotion to the task of checking references and shepherding
the manuscript through to its final typing was of an order that only
the authors can appreciate.

For the assemblage of material in a number of special fields, the
authors are under obligation to many colleagues in the U.S. Department of Agriculture. To Drs. Olen E. Leonard and J. Douglas Ens-
minger go thanks for assistance in preparation of the account on
rural economics and sociology. To Dr. Henry B. Makover go thanks
for assistance in this connection, as well as in analysis of certain
phases of rural health status, and to Dr. S. J. Axelrod for help in
developing the account of other phases of rural health. Thanks are
extended to Drs. Philip W. Woods and Edward W. Neenan for preparation of much material on dental health and dental personnel, to
Kenneth E. Pohlmann for work on the contributions to rural health
improvement of the major farm organizations, to Robert Van Hyning

for work on welfare medical services, to Henry C. Daniels for work on farm-labor health services, and to Zella Bryant for work on the analysis of nursing problems. Special assistance was rendered by Ivan F. Shull on problems of rural sanitation, by Wallace C. Crozer on farm accidents, and in various other ways by Jean Pennock, Josiah C. Folsom, Mildred Gilbert, Mrs. Beth M. Siegel, and Mrs. Madeline Donner.

Outside the Department of Agriculture advice or assistance of various kinds was received from Drs. Lester J. Evans, Leslie A. Falk, C. Horace Hamilton, Gertrude Sturges, Dean A. Clark, Louis S. Reed, Michael M. Davis, O. W. Hyman, George M. Mackenzie, and Elizabeth McNaughton, from Martha Luginbuhl, and from a number of others. The entire list of those inside and outside the Department of Agriculture consulted on specific points is too long to recite; many of their names will be found among the references.

Deep gratitude is extended to a number of authorities in different agencies of the Federal Government who gave the benefit of their critical review. The authors are indebted for comments on the discussion of the rural economy and rural life to Drs. John M. Brewster, Edgar A. Schuler, and Arthur F. Raper of the Bureau of Agricultural Economics; for invaluable criticism of the material on rural health status, to Dr. Selwyn D. Collins of the Public Health Service; and for critical review of the material on health personnel and facilities to Elliott H. Pennell of the Public Health Service. The authors are also indebted for review and most helpful suggestions concerning the sections on health services and expenditures to Margaret C. Klem of the Social Security Administration; to Dr. Joseph W. Mountin of the Public Health Service for review of the section on public health; to Mrs. Lucille Smith and associates of the Social Security Administration for review of the section on welfare medical services; for review of the section on nutrition, to personnel of the Bureau of Human Nutrition and Home Economics; and for review of the section on housing to personnel of the Bureau of the Census. Special gratitude goes to Dr. Barkev S. Sanders of the Social Security Administration for critical review and helpful suggestions on a number of chapters.

CONTENTS

FOREWORD

Rural Health and Medical Care is an unusually comprehensive analysis of a subject that has been of growing concern to the nation for many years. In bringing together for the first time a wealth of material on rural health problems, the book admirably meets an insistent demand for information from both professional and lay groups.

The essence of current knowledge on virtually every aspect of rural health status and medical care has been condensed into these pages. Yet the volume is by no means limited to facts and figures. With broad social perspective it describes the economic and historical developments out of which arise present difficulties in rural medical services. It presents an integrated story of health conditions, medical resources and services, and organized efforts for health improvement in rural areas. In conclusion, it offers recommendations for future action which merit careful study.

The authors are to be commended on the timeliness of their study and on their interpretation of the facts of rural medicine against a background of the national scene. For the problems of rural health are, in large measure, the most extreme expression of the problems of national health. Therefore, while of first interest to those concerned with rural life, the book deserves the attention of all persons who work to improve public health and medical services throughout the nation. I regard *Rural Health and Medical Care as* a valuable addition to the literature on the general field of health services in the United States.

THOMAS PARRAN

PART I: RURAL AMERICA

THE VAST SURFACE of the United States is predominantly rural. The traveler by air is struck with the way cities fall rapidly behind as the plane soars from the airport. Miles upon miles of farms and wooded stretches unfold, dotted only occasionally by villages and towns.

Tens of millions of our nation live on this vast rural surface of America. Here they grow up, marry, work, and live out their days. Here, too, they give birth, suffer accidents, endure sicknesses, and die.

Though they may be remote, the cities of America affect directly the everyday lives of farm and village people. For the most part the influence is beneficial. Cities furnish markets for food and cotton and lumber and tobacco. In turn they sell a multitude of products that lessen the burdens of rural life and add to its conveniences. Urban culture, urban science, and urban wealth are diffused widely if somewhat unevenly beyond city borders.

For a century and more, however, the industrialization and urbanization of our nation have exerted pulls drawing much that is best from rural life. Wealth has become increasingly concentrated in the cities. In a very real sense much of rural America has become a casualty of the industrial revolution. Perhaps no better illustration of this is to be found than the grossly inadequate health resources available to many millions of underserved rural people. It is small comfort to those bearing the burden and anguish of needless sickness and preventable death to know that the United States has become the wealthiest nation in the world and that American medicine at its best is unsurpassed.

Rural America is rooted in the soil. Over half the rural population is found on farms, pursuing "the most fundamental occupation of all civilization."[1] Most of the other millions of rural people are largely dependent on our basic agricultural economy for their livelihood; the great majority of our small towns are trade and service centers for the surrounding farm population. Even so, large numbers of rural people have little or no connection with agriculture. Many are on the fringes of large urban communities and look to them for em-

[1] TAYLOR, CARL C., *Rural Sociology*. New York: Harper & Brothers, 1933, p. 110.

3

ployment and the many benefits they provide. Others are in small
mining or mill towns, or in lumbering or fishing centers.

There is no lack of diversity in our farm population or in the
way they wrest a living from the soil. There are those whose ances-
tral roots go back to the first English, Spanish, and French settlers.
There are those of Anglo-Saxon, Southern European, and Slavic
descent. Several million Negroes are on farms, and many thousand
Japanese-Americans and Indians. There are large landholders and
small owners, tenants, sharecroppers, hired hands, and migratory
seasonal workers. From California's factories in the field to the
dairy farms of New England, from the corn and hog farms of the
Midwest to the cotton plantations of the Mississippi Delta, from the
Wyoming ranch to the truck farm of the Eastern Shore of Maryland,
there is endless variety in types of land, kinds of farming, size of
holdings, extent of ownership, and degree of mechanization. The
mosaic of socio-economic patterns of rural life finds its origin in the
pages of history from the early Colonial days and the slave economy
of the old South through the winning of the West and up to recent
times. Chapters are still being added, and future history will doubtless record far-reaching changes we little imagine.

There are wide variations, too, in the health problems confronting
rural people in different areas, and in the difficulties to be overcome
in obtaining health services. Underlying these varying problems,
however, are basic geographic and economic factors, and social
attitudes associated with them, that have led to the recognition of
rural medicine as an entity demanding special attention.

Any definition of rural people or rural territory must be arbitrary.
With unimportant exceptions, the Bureau of the Census considers
the population as rural when residence is in the open country or in
communities of less than 2,500. Thus defined there was a rural population of 57 million persons in 1940, or 43.5 per cent of the total
population of the United States. In general this definition may be
accepted when we deal with the health status of rural people — with
their death and sickness rates, their disabilities and impairments —
and when we consider the services they receive and the costs incurred. When the health personnel and facilities available to the
rural population are studied, however, we must inevitably broaden
our consideration to include those resources in urban communities
that serve rural people. The health resources on which large num-

bers of rural families must depend are found in smaller urban centers, typically towns of 2,500 to 10,000 population. In this sense, these communities must be considered part and parcel of the general problem of rural medicine.

For an essential background to our study of rural health and medical care, we must first review the main features of the population, the economic organization, and the general characteristics of life in rural America.

CHAPTER 1

THE POPULATION

A T THE TIME of the first census, in 1790, the population of
the United States — numbering less than 4 million in all — was
almost entirely rural. There were only six cities of over 8,000 persons.
Fifty years later, in 1840, the rapidly growing population — already
over 17 million — was still 89 per cent rural. During the past century,
however, with industrial development and rapid urbanization of the
nation, the constantly increasing population has become progres-
sively less rural (Figure 1). By 1900 the population of over 75 million

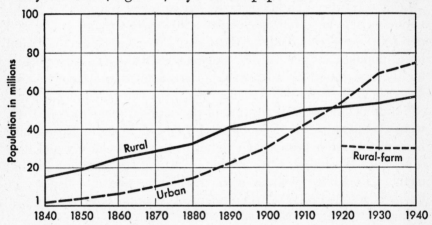

FIG. 1. Population Trends: Urban and rural population, the United States,
1840-1940. Source: U. S. Bureau of the Census, Sixteenth Census of the United
States, 1940. *Population.* Vol. 2, *Characteristics of the Population.*

was two-fifths urban, and by 1920 the nation had become over half
urban. As of 1940, although more people were living in rural communities and areas than ever before, they made up just 43.5 per
cent of our total population.[1]

The great majority of our 57,245,573 rural residents live in small
unincorporated towns and villages or in the open country. Only

[1] Except when some other reference is given, all population data used in this
chapter are from the Population Series of the 1940 Census. U. S. Bureau of the
Census, Sixteenth Census of the United States, 1940. *Population.* Vol. 1, *Num-*

about 9,300,000, or 16 per cent, live in incorporated places of under 2,500 population, and almost half of these are in towns of under 1,000.

Closely related to our strictly rural population, as defined by the Bureau of the Census, are the 11,600,000 people living in towns of 2,500 to 10,000. In general they share common medical and related resources with rural people in the surrounding countryside. From the viewpoint of rural medicine, therefore, we are concerned to a greater or lesser extent with about 68,850,000 people, or over half the 1940 total United States population of 131,669,275.

Farm and Rural Nonfarm People and Their Distribution

Over a century ago about eight out of every ten persons in the nation were living on farms. In 1940 a little over two out of ten, 22.9 per cent, were classified by the Census as comprising the "rural farm" population of 30,216,188. Between 1910 and 1920 there began for the first time a trend toward an absolute as well as a relative decrease in the farm population (Figure 1). The remaining 27,029,-385 rural people, or 20.6 per cent of the national population in 1940, were classified as "rural nonfarm." While not living on farms, millions of this latter group have homes in the open country and thus experience the farmer's geographic isolation from readily available medical resources. Millions more, of course, live in villages and towns of less than 2,500, where medical isolation is frequently just as real.

In 1940, almost half of our entire rural population — over 26 million people — and 54 per cent of our entire farm population — over 16 million people — lived in the sixteen South Atlantic and South Central states. It is small wonder that so many of the health characteristics of rural America as a whole are heavily influenced by the conditions found in the South.

In the North Central region about one-fourth of the rural population and 31 per cent of the farm population are found. The remaining fourth of the rural population and the remaining 15 per cent of the

ber of Inhabitants; Vol. 2, Characteristics of the Population; Vol. 3, The Labor Force; Vol. 4, Characteristics by Age; Population, Comparative Occupation Statistics for the United States, 1870-1940. Washington: Government Printing Office, 1943 (Vol. 1, 1942).

farm population are about evenly distributed between the Northeast
and the West.[2]

In dealing with rural health problems it is often convenient to
consider rurality on a broad regional rather than a community basis.
The South, for example, is typically rural. It is almost half again more
rural than the nation as a whole, and its 63.3 per cent rural population certainly justifies the concept of "the rural South." It is natural,
too, to speak of the Northeast as "urban," considering that only 23.4
per cent of its population is rural. Close to the national average of
43.5 per cent rurality are the North Central region and the West,
with almost identical rural population percentages of 41.6 and 41.5,
respectively.[3]

A somewhat wider range in degrees of population rurality is found
in the nine Census geographic divisions.[4] The greatest variation in
rurality, however, is found in the case of the individual states. Mississippi was 80.2 per cent rural in 1940, and North Dakota 79.4 per
cent. At the other extreme were Massachusetts and Rhode Island
with populations only 10.6 and 8.4 per cent rural (Figure 2).
Although there is a tendency for the more rural states to be grouped
geographically, there are wide variations within general regions.
Thus one finds a state like Vermont with about two-thirds of its population rural in a Census division — New England — which is over
three-fourths urban.[5]

Of course even the most urban states have their rural areas and

2 The proportion of rural people living on farms — 52.6 per cent for the
whole nation — varies markedly from region to region. Whereas in the South
62 per cent of all rural people were on farms, and in the North Central region
55 per cent, in the West just 40 per cent were on farms, and this was true of
only 27 per cent of rural residents in the Northeast.

3 The Bureau of the Census generally refers to three major regions rather
than four — the North, the South, and the West; the North, which includes the
Northeastern and North Central states, is 33 per cent rural.

4 Among the nine Census divisions the percentage of rurality ranges from
70.6 in the East South Central division to 23.2 per cent in the Middle Atlantic.
The South Atlantic and West South Central divisions are over 60 per cent rural,
and close behind are the Mountain and West North Central divisions, each
over 55 per cent rural. Predominantly urban, on the other hand, are the New
England, East North Central, and Pacific divisions, as well as the Middle
Atlantic — all of which are over 60 per cent urban.

5 A device to permit valid comparisons of data from states of differing rural
character is often useful. Vermont, for example, may be taken away from its

pressing problems of rural medicine. The highly urban state of New York actually has an absolute number of rural people exceeding the combined rural populations of North and South Dakota, Nebraska, Wyoming, and Montana. That highly rural counties are found in virtually every state is illustrated in the frontispiece. There are 1,226 counties in which the largest community is under 2,500. There are 1,141 more with the largest town from 2,500 to 10,000, and these, as already noted, are hardly less rural from the point of view of medical care. These 2,267 counties in which most of our rural population lives — almost three-fourths of the 3,071 counties in the United States — present the most challenging problems in the whole field of personal and public health services.

There are only 704 counties in the United States with urban places of 10,000 or more, or which — without having such places — have at least half their population in a Census metropolitan district. Of these, 303 with places of over 10,000 actually are predominantly rural in the sense of having total populations over 50 per cent rural. Thus according to this classification there are only 401 clearly urban counties in the nation.[6]

Where the population is sparsely settled, the problems of rural medical care and sanitation are intensified. Agriculture is unique among occupations in requiring large amounts of land surface. Where climate and soil prescribe types of agriculture calling for very extensive land holdings, the density of the farm population drops to amazingly low levels. In the Great Plains states, for example — Montana, Wyoming, the Dakotas, Nebraska, and Kansas — there is actually less than one family per square mile west of the more populated belt along the eastern border of the region. Throughout vast stretches towns of any size are few and far between, and the professional isolation of the physician is almost as great a drawback to proper medical service as the isolation of the rancher or the wheat farmer.

---

urban neighbors and grouped with all other states from 60 to 69 per cent rural. Six groups of states, from the group 70 per cent or more rural to the group less than 30 per cent rural, may thus be used to bring out important rural-urban comparisons.

[6] U. S. Bureau of Agricultural Economics, *County Classifications: By Size Of Largest City, April,* 1940. Washington: U. S. Department of Agriculture, 1944, Processed.

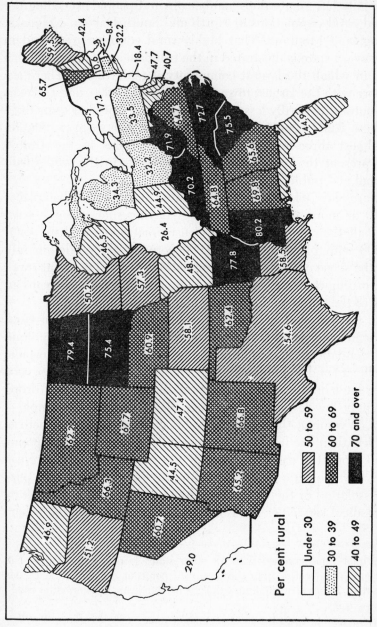

Fig. 2. Rural Population: Percentage of the total population in rural areas, by states, 1940.
Source: U. S. Census, 1940. *Population.* Vol. 1, *Number of Inhabitants.*

Mountain ranges, forests, and arid areas naturally affect population density, too, and erect their own barriers between patients and medical facilities. In the Mountain states as a whole there are only 4.8 persons per square mile, in marked contrast to 274 persons per square mile in the Middle Atlantic states. Distance and isolation factors influence rural medicine everywhere, but in sparsely settled areas they are of major importance.

The Composition of the Rural Population

The origins of our rural population are as diverse as the streams of colonists, indentured labor, slaves, refugees from foreign oppression, and immigrants seeking new and undreamed-of opportunities, that for four centuries have converged on our soil and built a united nation. About seven-eighths are native-born whites. Northern European stock forms the predominant element of the farm population.

Negroes constitute an important part of the rural population, particularly in the South. They made up only 8.4 per cent of the nation's urban population and 9.8 per cent of the total population in 1940, but the 6,611,930 rural Negroes comprised 11.4 per cent of the rural population. In the South, where 77 per cent of all Negroes were located, they made up 23.8 per cent of the rural population. The farm population on a nation-wide basis, moreover, was 14.9 per cent Negro, and in the South it was over one-fourth Negro — 27.1 per cent. In Mississippi and South Carolina, Negroes outnumbered whites on farms.

The most rural racial group in the United States happens to be our Indian population. In 1940, 92 per cent of the one-third of a million Indians lived in rural territory, and over three out of five of these were on farms. The great majority were in the Mountain and West Central states. The small remainder of the rural population is mostly of Japanese racial origin. The 61,000 rural people of Japanese origin in 1940 — four out of five on farms — were mostly in the Pacific states where they filled an important place in agriculture.

Certain striking characteristics in the age and sex groupings of the rural population have implications not only for rural health but for the whole nation. Foremost in significance is the proportionately large number of children in rural families, children destined not only to take the places of their elders on the farms and in the villages, but to pour into the cities and bolster dwindling urban populations.

The birth rate is high in rural America. Some of the most rural states have birth rates about one-third higher than the most urban states. A measure of population change which takes both birth and death rates into account and points up the drama of America's rural nursery is the so-called net reproduction rate.[7] As of 1940 the rate of 96 for the United States as a whole indicated a general decline in reproduction rate — a trend reversed for the time being by the war. There were sharp differences, however, between rural and urban net reproduction rates. The rural rate was 130 in contrast to the urban rate of 76. The rate of 145 for the farm population was almost double the urban rate.[8] If the 1940 birth and death rates were to prevail, following the temporary wartime rise in birth rates, the urban population would decline about 24 per cent in a generation. Clearly our cities must depend increasingly on the flow of young people from the country for their life and growth.

In urban places of over 10,000 inhabitants 10 adults are raising 7 children; on farms 10 adults are raising 14 children. Children under 15 make up 30 per cent of the entire rural population, but only 21 per cent of the urban population (Figure 3). Although only 43.5 per cent of the whole population is rural, 51.6 per cent of all children in the United States under 15 years of age are in rural communities. Surely children are rural America's most important product, far outweighing in significance for the nation's welfare its basic contribution of food and fiber.

The perennial bumper crop of farm children and the harvesting of nearly half that crop by our cities result in a disproportionately low number of persons in the prime of life in rural areas (Figure 3). While 48.7 per cent of the urban population is in the age group 20 to 50, only 40.6 per cent of the rural population is in this most productive group. The proportion of persons from 50 to 65 years of age is also smaller in rural areas, but after 65 years the rural proportion is somewhat higher. Thus the relatively small rural adult population in the ages of maximum productivity must support an

[7] The net reproduction rate is a measure of the potential increase or decrease of a population over a generation, under the assumption that current birth and death rates at different age levels continue unchanged.

[8] U. S. Census, 1940. *Population, Special Reports, Differential Fertility* 1940 *and* 1910.

excessively large proportion of children and a slightly greater complement of the aged.

The rural and urban populations also differ greatly in sex distribution. There were 101.1 males for every 100 females in the United States in 1940. The rural nonfarm population, however, consisted of 104.2 males to 100 females, and the farm population had a ratio of 112.1 to 100. In contrast there were 95.8 males to 100 females in the urban population. Obviously the farmer's daughter can leave for the city more readily than the farmer's son, who is more likely to be needed and to remain in the rural economy. Reverse migration to

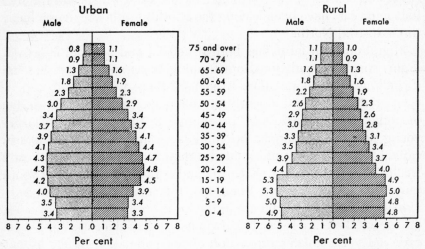

Fig. 3. Age and Sex: Percentage distribution of the urban and rural population of the United States by age and sex, 1940. Source: U. S. Census, 1940. *Population*. Vol. 4, *Characteristics by Age*.

the farm, moreover, brings more men than women into agriculture. There have never been sufficient economic opportunities in agriculture to attract and hold all the young people growing up on farms. Since Colonial days there has been a farm-to-city movement, accelerated since we reached the limits of the frontier at about the turn of the century. But the movement is not all one way. Its flow is governed in large degree by the extent of economic opportunities in the cities. The size of the farm population, in fact, has tended to vary inversely with the level of nonagricultural employment. For a quarter-century, however, net migration from farms has tended to exceed the average annual rate of natural increase in the farm population of about 430,000 persons a year.[9] Despite the high rural birth rate, therefore, the net result has been a decline in the farm population.

With vastly increased economic opportunities associated with all-out war production, it has been estimated that over 4½ million persons (not including those entering the armed forces) left the farms during the 1940-45 war years, or more than twice the number at the prewar migration rate.[10] These movements not only create communicable disease hazards but also problems involving the overtaxing of urban medical facilities. Since 1940 some 750,000 Negroes have migrated from the rural South, some to Southern cities but most to congested centers in the North and West.[11] Both whites and Negroes for some years have been leaving the South for other regions, chiefly the industrial North.

Migration from farms has both beneficial and harmful effects. It drains surplus population from farming areas and replenishes the dwindling urban population. In general those who migrate experience greater economic opportunity for having made the move. On the other hand, the loss of productive manpower — the majority young people entering the prime of life — means a distinct loss in capital for rural communities and a gain in capital for the already wealthier cities; the cost of rearing and educating these rural youth represents a tangible loss. Then, too, the small proportion of individuals in rural areas who are in the most productive years of adult life means there are fewer breadwinners to pay the costs of medical care and yet a greater proportion of the population in age groups likely to need such care.

Farm-to-city migration has an even more important implication for both rural and urban health. If tomorrow's urban citizens are to have the opportunity to build sound bodies and alert minds in infancy and childhood, the benefits of scientific health care must be extended to the country as well as the city. The health of children everywhere must be a matter of national concern.

[9] DUCOFF, LOUIS J., *Wages of Agricultural Labor in the United States.* Washington: U. S. Bureau of Home Economics, September, 1944, Processed, pp. 188, 190.

[10] U. S. Department of Agriculture, Interbureau Committee on Postwar Agricultural Programs, *Farm Opportunities in the United States: Outlook, Problems, Agricultural Policies.* Washington, July, 1945, Processed, p. 3.

[11] Julius Rosenwald Fund, *Review for the Two-year Period 1942-1944.* Chicago, 1944, p. 4.

CHAPTER 2

THE ECONOMY

THE ECONOMY of rural America is of course primarily agricultural. Over half the rural population is found on farms, and almost half of those working in rural areas are engaged directly in farming. The great majority of rural people depend either directly or indirectly on agricultural enterprises as their principal source of support. Those engaged in rural enterprises other than farming are part of a diverse economy with income returns more like those of agriculture than those characteristic of the urban economy.

Agriculture in Transition

During the last century the position of agriculture in relation to the national economy has undergone vast changes. As we have seen, the population of the United States in 1840 was almost 90 per cent rural; by 1940 it was only 43.5 per cent rural. In the course of this change, agriculture has not enjoyed its equitable share of the growing wealth of the nation. Although persons living on farms made up 23 per cent of the nation's population in 1940, they received only 10 per cent of the national income. The average annual net farm income of persons engaged in agriculture was $531 in 1940, while the average annual wage of industrial workers was $1,273.[1]

The whole structure of our national economy has changed markedly during this hundred years. The process has been mainly one of industrialization resulting from technological development in machines, transportation, and communications. The applications of science have brought about a spectacular increase in the volume of manufactured products. Through the years there has been a continuous elevation in our standard of living. We have come to accept as nonluxury essentials such goods and services as ready-made

[1] U. S. Bureau of Agricultural Economics, *Net Farm Income and Parity Report: 1943, and Summary for 1910-42.* Washington, July, 1944, Processed, pp. 4, 14.

clothing, electric lights, the telephone, running water in the house, and refrigeration.

Our economy is based on the exchange of goods and services through the medium of money. It takes cash income to enable people to buy the products of farm and factory and to avail themselves of the services that make up our standard of living. Over the years, therefore, it became clear that the farmer, like the businessman, had to sell his products in the market for cash in order to be able to purchase the goods and services that would enable him to approach the living standards customary in the cities.

Thus farming for the market gradually became the predominant pattern for successful agriculture. The rather distinct areas of commercial farming throughout agricultural America are familiar to all of us — the cotton South, the corn and hog belt of the Midwest, the wheat belt of the Great Plains, the cattle country of the West, and so throughout the land from border to border. To this specialization of crops by regions the nature of the soil and climate and physical terrain is fundamental, and almost equally so the railroad and highway, the refrigerator car, and the truck.

Farming has become dependent on markets, national and international. Farm incomes rise and fall with city payrolls and with exports. This is the core of the "farm problem." Unfortunately, for many years, except in wartime with its abnormal demands, the effective demand for agricultural products has been generally far below the capacity for production.

Competition for agricultural markets has affected the farm economy in much the same way that competition for markets for manufactured goods has affected the industrial economy. The larger or more efficient producers tend to dominate the markets, leaving their less efficient competitors to struggle for their very existence. As in industry, efficiency and volume of agricultural production depend upon a variety of factors which differ in importance with the type of product. Perhaps the most basic factor is the nature and extent of landholdings. For many types of farm operations, moreover, large capital investments are essential to successful competition. To operate a dairy farm in Wisconsin with an inferior herd, or to cultivate wheat in North Dakota with a plow and a mule, is as much economic suicide as to weave cloth on a hand loom in price competition with a modern textile mill. There must be a logical balance, too, between the size and type of holdings and the economic efficiency of the mechanized equipment necessary to produce the maximum crop per acre. Again, there may be need for liberal and long-term credit for operating capital, suited to the particular needs of agriculture. And, finally, the farmer must know how to apply scientific knowledge to production, taking full advantage of agricultural research in improved varieties of crops, better livestock, soil conservation, fertilization, and disease and insect control.

Income of Farm Families

Where the farm unit, for whatever reason, is not economically effective, the farmer is not able to secure enough cash return from his products to obtain a reasonable standard of living. How many of the 6 million farm units in the United States are economically effective? With the wide variation in requirements for successful farming in terms of land and other resources, we must set some arbitrary standard of adequacy. One quite conservative measure sets the level of adequacy, under 1939 conditions, at a gross farm income of at least $1,500.[2] This does not mean that every farm falling below this standard was necessarily inadequate, nor that every farm exceeding it was adequate. Taking the country as a whole, however, this appears to be a reasonable measure.

What does this suggested $1,500 gross income level of adequacy mean in terms of purchasing power and living standards? It represents the total value of the products of the farm, that is, the value of products sold, traded, or used by the farm family. After the value of home-used products and the cost of farm operation are deducted from a $1,500 income, there remains on the average a net cash income of about $750. From this net cash income must come payments on the farm mortgage and reserves for the following year's operations, leaving the dwindling balance to meet all family living expenses.

It is difficult indeed to see how a farm family can maintain any sort of decent standard of living, including medical and dental care, with a net cash income of less than $750, derived from a gross

[2] ELLICKSON, JOHN C., and JOHN M. BREWSTER, "Manpower and the American Farm Plant," *Land Policy Review* (U. S. Department of Agriculture), 5:17-22, May, 1942.

farm income of less than $1,500.[3] And yet in prewar 1939 little
more than one in every five farms the country over attained even
this modest standard of adequacy. These units, comprising only
22.6 per cent of the total number of farms, raised products valued
at 68 per cent of the nation's total farm production (Figure 4). The
other 77 per cent of the total number of farms, all of which must be

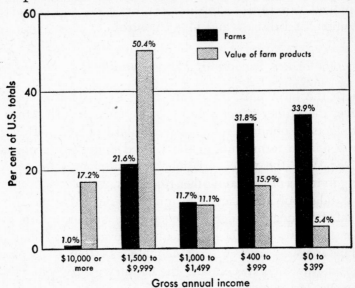

FIG. 4. Farm Income: United States farms classified by gross farm income
ranges (total value of products sold, traded, or used), 1939. Based on 6,057,257
classified farms. Source: U. S. Census, 1940. *Agriculture*. Vol. 3, *General
Reports*.

classed as inadequate, were responsible for only 32 per cent of total
farm production. Relatively few of these, only 11.7 per cent of all
farms, could even be classed as borderline in the sense of approaching adequate standards. Practically two-thirds of all the farms in
the United States produced gross returns valued at under $1,000,
and one-third raised products valued at less than $400 and aver-
aging only $215. If we consider just the portion of gross farm in-
come representing products sold in the market, an even greater
disparity is revealed as between farms of large and small produc-

[3] Professor Black of Harvard University sets as a farm family income of minimum adequacy $60 a month, or $720 a year, in addition to the use of the farm
dwelling and food and fuel obtained from the farm. BLACK, JOHN D., "Postwar
Soldier Settlement," *Quarterly Journal of Economics*, 59:1-35, November, 1944.

tive capacity. The top 2 million farms marketed 84 per cent of all products sold in 1939, the middle 2 million about 13 per cent, and the bottom 2 million only 3 per cent.[4]

What do these gross income figures mean in terms of the net cash income with which farm people must purchase goods and services for family living? It is clear that in 1939 well over 4 million families operated farms which yielded less than $750. Even in 1941, when farm income was higher than in any year since 1920, one of every two farm operator families earned an annual net cash farm income of less than $440, and as a group they received only an 8 per cent share of the net cash farm income of the nation.[5]

Under such circumstances off-farm employment is naturally sought as a means of supplementing meager farm earnings. It constitutes a substantial source of support for many farm families. In 1941, however, income of persons on farms from all nonagricultural sources, including off-farm employment, pensions, and other income, amounted to only 27 per cent of total net income including products consumed on farms.[6] Nevertheless, outside sources of cash income are a boon particularly to the small farmer. Taking them into account raises the median net cash income of farm operators in 1941 from $440 to $760.[7] Thus the various effects of the war, including the rapidly rising prices of farm products, stepped-up farm production, and increased off-farm employment, meant that just half of all farm operators had attained incomes by 1941 that were presumably above a minimal level of adequacy. Actually their real income in terms of purchasing power was lower than this because of the higher prices of practically all commodities and, for that matter, services like medical care. Even under prosperous conditions, it is obvious how a major medical expense can wreck the budgetary plans of most farm families and can be met, if at all, only at the expense of foregoing the essentials of family living or even of farm production.

[4] U. S. Department of Agriculture, Interbureau Committee on Postwar Agricultural Programs, *op. cit.*

[5] BRADY, DOROTHY S., and MARGARET J. HAGOOD, "Income of Farm Families," *The Agricultural Situation* (U. S. Department of Agriculture), 27:9-11, August, 1943.

[6] U. S. Bureau of Agricultural Economics, *Net Farm Income and Parity Report: 1943 and Summary for 1910-42*, p. 4.

[7] BRADY and HAGOOD, *op. cit.*

Farm income rocketed to unprecedented heights under wartime conditions, with the prices farmers received rising much higher than the prices they had to pay.[8] Nevertheless, the war boom fell far short of eliminating the disparity between farm and city income levels. The total net income in 1943 of persons on farms from all sources, amounting to 17½ billion dollars, was only 12 per cent of the national income of 148 billion dollars, although farm people made up 20.5 per cent of the population that year. The per capita net income of persons not on farms, moreover, was twice as high as per capita net income of persons on farms.[9] Neither did the war wipe out rural poverty even temporarily. In 1942, with farm income almost as high as in 1943, the top 10 per cent of all farm operator families received 37 per cent of the aggregate net cash income derived from farming, while the bottom 10 per cent received only 0.6 per cent.[10]

By 1945, the realized net income of farm operators per farm had risen to the unprecedented peak of $2,251. In this year the net per capita income of persons living on farms (including income from nonfarm employment) was up to $743. This still remained considerably below the average net per capita income of persons not on farms, however, which was $1,259.[10a] A great share of the rise of farm and nonfarm income alike, moreover, was consumed in a spiraled cost of living. In early 1947 signs of an eventual decline in farm income were already becoming evident.

It should be no surprise that much rural poverty persists despite unparalleled general prosperity. By and large the farmer is dependent on the yield of his acreage. And yet in 1939 one-third of all farms averaged only 11 acres of harvested cropland, encompassed only 7 per cent of all such land, and had only 10 per cent of the value of all machinery and equipment.[11] The story is one of too little land, too poor soil, too little machinery, and farmers with too little training. No business could survive under comparable circum-

[8] U. S. Office of Price Administration, *Farmers in the War*. Washington: Government Printing Office, December 1944, p. 5.

[9] U. S. Bureau of Agricultural Economics, *Net Farm Income and Parity Report: 1943 and Summary for 1910-42*, p. 12.

[10] BRADY and HAGOOD, *op. cit.*

[10a] U. S. Bureau of Agricultural Economics, *Farm Income Situation*. Washington, June 1946, Processed, pp. 22, 24.

[11] ELLICKSON and BREWSTER, *op. cit.*

stances. Farm families, however, can actually eke out an existence on farms largely removed from any place in the national economy, either as producers or consumers. Too many farm families tend to stay on the land as long as basic sustenance, if nothing more, can be wrested from the soil. Tens of thousands of families are dammed back on farms largely because in ordinary times the urban economy cannot offer them employment. Evidence of this is seen in the greatly accelerated farm-to-city migration of the war years when there was ample opportunity for industrial employment.

In effect, there is a parallel between these farmers who cannot sell an adequate volume of products in the national market and unemployed urban workers who cannot sell their labor. The chief difference lies in society's reaction to these parallel situations. On the farms this economic unemployment or underemployment is very largely concealed or overlooked; in urban communities, on the other hand, it is apparent, and social security and other social welfare measures have been adopted with a view to providing unemployment benefits, "free" medical care, and other necessities of life on an emergency basis.

In generalizing about American agriculture as a whole, one must not forget the vast differences between and within regions. From early Colonial days economic and geographic factors have influenced regional developments in socio-economic and political structure. In order to make profits in the South from tobacco and cotton, a much larger labor force was needed than on the farms of less sunny New England. As a result thousands of laborers, indentured servants, and later slaves were brought into the Southern economy. Centuries later we still have the small independent farmer of New England and virtually the plantation system of the old South. The Midwest, with its corn and wheat belts, and the West, with its large-scale farming enterprises, have been more directly affected so far by the revolutionary technological changes and industrializing forces within agriculture.

In terms of average production of farms, reflecting the ability of farm families to pay for goods and services, there are wide differences between regions. Taking the major Census regions only, we find a sharp contrast between the South, with only 10.3 per cent of its classified farms raising products valued at $1,500 or more in 1939, and the North and West, each with 35 per cent of its farms attaining this minimum standard of adequacy. An appalling number of Southern farms— 80.6 per cent of the total of 2,995,000 — raised products valued at less than $1,000, an utterly inadequate gross income from farming.[12] In the North one farm of every two — 50.5 per cent of 2,556,000 farms — was similarly inadequate, and in the West 54.4 per cent of 506,000 farms were in the same class.[13] Marginal and submarginal farming are confined to no one region or state.

Other characteristics of farm income have a special bearing on ability to purchase medical services and may affect health in other ways. Years of drought and soil erosion spell bankruptcy for farmer and country doctor alike. Too much rain or a sudden wind or hailstorm or an insect pest may wipe out most of a year's income in a matter of days — or minutes. Even in good years the cash-crop farmer tends to have cash in hand only for a time after selling the crop, and he is forced to live on credit the rest of the year. Natural reluctance to seek medical attention for which he cannot pay often results; where it is sought, credit and barter are an old story to the doctor.

Owners, Tenants, Croppers, and Hired Workers

We have seen how the relatively few economically efficient farms have largely captured the existing market for agricultural products, and how there remain a great number of inadequate farming units. The small share of the national income derived from agriculture as a whole, and the extremely low purchasing power of the majority of farmers, are central facts to be borne in mind in studying the problems of rural medicine. Certain other aspects of concentration of farming wealth should be mentioned, however, in so far as they bear on these problems.

Ownership of his land by the farmer is commonly recognized as desirable. Extent of ownership is one gauge of rural well-being, not so much because it is an absolute good per se, but because it tends to be associated in America with social and human values. By this

[12] The Bureau of the Census counts as a separate farm each tract of 3 acres or more in agricultural production handled by a separate farm operator, whether he be owner, cash tenant, or sharecropper. Thus large holdings, common in the South, may be counted as several farms each.

[13] U. S. Census, 1940. *Agriculture,* Vol. 3, *General Reports.*

criterion, rural welfare is hardly on the upgrade, for prior to the war about 40,000 farm owners were losing their land and slipping into tenancy each year.[14] In 1940 only 50.6 per cent of farm operators were sole owners of the farms they were operating.[15] Outright and unfettered ownership is relatively rare, moreover, with heavy mortgage indebtedness almost the rule.[16]

With the increasing commercialization of agriculture there is growing concentration of wealth in large landholdings. Since 1910 the proportion of farms of 500 acres and over has been increasing, and the portion of all farm land in such farms had risen from 28 to 45 per cent as of 1940. Only 4.3 per cent of over 6 million farms thus controlled almost half of the nation's total farm acreage in 1940.[17] This consolidation of landholdings was accelerated by the recent war, as thousands of farmers left agriculture to seek industrial employment. While bringing large tracts of semi-arid land into production plays a part, it seems clear that concentration of agricultural wealth is the dominant force in this entire trend.

The concentration of ownership of farming land is illustrated also by multiple farm ownership. In connection with the corn-hog program of the Agricultural Adjustment Administration in 1934, it was reported that 124 owners (each of whom owned 100 or more farms) owned a total of 97,618 farms comprising almost 19 million acres.[18] Obviously multiple owners, whether banks, insurance companies, other corporations, or individuals, are as a rule absentee landlords. The extent of interest of such owners in the health and welfare of the workers producing their profits is perhaps best illustrated by the steps, described later, which the government has been

[14] MARIS, PAUL V., "Farm Tenancy," *Farmers in a Changing World (Yearbook of Agriculture,* 1940) Washington: Government Printing Office, 1940, pp. 887-906.

[15] U. S. Census, 1940. *Agriculture,* Vol. 3, *General Reports.*

[16] In 1940 farm mortgage indebtedness for the United States as a whole amounted to 42.6 per cent of total farm value. The highest proportion of mortgage debt was 51.3 per cent in the West North Central states. On the other hand, mortgage debt was lowest in those farming areas of the South where the farmer's credit is too poor even to sustain a mortgage and tenancy or farm-labor status is the usual alternative to outright ownership.

[17] *Ibid.* Also, Temporary National Economic Committee, 76th Cong., 3d Sess., *Agriculture and the National Economy* (Monograph 23). Washington: Government Printing Office, 1940, p. 10.

[18] Temporary National Economic Committee, *op. cit.,* p. 12.

forced to take to relieve distress and combat disease among migrants in California.

The reverse side of the picture of concentration of ownership is tenancy. Cash and share tenants operated 38.7 per cent of all farms in 1940 as against 25.6 per cent in 1880.[19] Tenancy has long been a characteristic of the cotton South, but less well known is its prevalence in the corn and wheat belts. In both Nebraska and South Dakota, for example, 52 per cent of the farms were operated by tenants in 1940, and 45 per cent of the farms in Iowa and North Dakota.[20] As a matter of fact, tenancy is by no means associated only with small and unproductive farms; throughout the nation as a whole tenants other than sharecroppers operate about the same proportions of farms of high, middle, or low gross income classes as do owners.[21] Tenancy in one region, in fact, may represent a more favorable social and economic status than ownership in another. Within any one region, however, tenancy usually means insecurity, frequent moves, lack of farm and home improvements, poor sanitation facilities, and chronic exploitation of land resources and dilapidation of buildings. It presents issues of deep social, political, and economic significance.

It is chiefly in the South, with almost half its farms operated by tenants and with over a million share tenants and croppers in 1939, that one finds associated with tenancy miserably low standards of housing, sanitation, nutrition, and health. In the essentially feudalistic plantation communities of the deep South,[22] one finds that sharecroppers actually decreased in number from 1930 to 1940 — not because they climbed the "agricultural ladder" to cash tenancy, on the way up to ownership, but largely because they slipped down to the bottom rung as hired workers.[23]

Among the most disadvantaged of all occupational groups are hired farm workers. In prewar years there were from 1 to 1½ million regularly employed for most of the year, and from 2 to 3 million seasonal workers employed for varying periods during the year. Of this latter group from ½ to 1 million were migrants, while from 1½ to 2 million were nonmigratory seasonal workers. The importance

[19] U. S. Census, 1940. *Agriculture*, Vol. 3, *General Reports*.

[20] *Ibid.*

[21] DUCOFF, *op. cit.*, p. 14.

[22] RAPER, ARTHUR, and IRA DEA. REID, *Sharecroppers All*. Chapel Hill: University of North Carolina Press, 1941.

[23] DUCOFF, *op. cit.*, p. 35.

of hired workers varies greatly in different parts of the country. In the Pacific states they made up almost half the total number of all persons engaged in farming in 1943, while in the East South Central states they comprised only about one-sixth of the total. For the country as a whole the annual average was 23.4 per cent. Associated as they are with large-scale and commercial farming, hired laborers are employed by only a minority of all farm operators.[24]

The year-round hired man of the Northern states, who may be practically a member of the family and may have his own farm someday, has very different status from that of the Southern plantation laborer, who is pushed back and forth from sharecropping to working for wages, or the homeless migratory worker who follows the crops. In terms of income, however, all hired farm workers are virtually poverty-stricken and far worse off than industrial workers. Half of all farm laborer families had annual incomes of less than $363 in 1939. Regional differences were striking — median family incomes of $674 and $655 in the Northeast and the West, $408 in the North Central region, and $295 in the South. Even in 1943, with farm wages far higher than before the war, hired workers earned an estimated average income of $803 including the value of perquisites, or only 37 per cent of the average income of industrial workers.[25] Despite the wearing and often hazardous nature of their work, moreover, farm laborers are generally excluded from the benefits of legislation protecting industrial workers, such as workmen's compensation, wage and hour laws, unemployment compensation, and other welfare and social security legislation.

The social and economic plight of migratory farm workers has been such as to evoke a stirring and timely literature and to demand the attention of congressional committees.[26] This group has perhaps felt the effects of the agricultural revolution more than any other. Uprooted from their home communities — often "tractored out" — and merging in the streams of migration along well-traveled routes, the migrants suffer not only from the ills common to most farm laborers but also from the most primitive housing and sanitation and

[24] *Ibid.*, pp. 6, 28, 29, 31.

[25] *Ibid.*, pp. 139, 152.

[26] See, for example, John Steinbeck's *The Grapes of Wrath*, Carey McWilliams's *Factories in the Field* and *Ill Fares the Land*, and the hearings of the Tolan Committee to Investigate Interstate Migration and the LaFollette Civil Liberties Committee.

from the general discrimination that is practiced against nonresi-
dents. Settlement laws that can be traced back to feudal England
tend to shut the doors of clinics, hospitals, sanatoriums, and public
assistance agencies to the migrant and his family.[27] Thus disease
jeopardizes not only the migrants themselves but also the communities through which they pass and in which they work.

Child labor is virtually a characteristic of migratory farm labor.
Wages are so low and uncertain that, when opportunity offers,
usually whole families must go to the fields. Long hours in "stoop
crops," exposure and malnutrition, lack of regular schooling and
recreation, are hardly conducive to the normal physical and mental
development of children. Progress in controlling industrial child
labor has no effective counterpart with respect to agricultural child
labor, which is for the most part unregulated by either federal or
state legislation.[28] According to the 1940 Census, there were almost
half a million children from 14 through 17 years of age gainfully
employed in agriculture, or 52 per cent of all employed children of
that age group. The number under 14 years of age was not reported,
and the figures do not include children working on home farms, who
make up a large part of the total of 1½ to 2½ million "family helpers"
receiving no wages. The war, with its shortages of farm labor in
many areas, led to a vast increase in child labor and a general relaxation of such regulations as do exist. The educational and other
problems thus intensified continue to make postwar readjustments
highly difficult.[29]

The economic situation of Negroes in America has been aptly

[27] BLANKENSHIP, C. F., and FRED SAFIER, A Study of Medical Problems
Associated with Transients (U. S. Public Health Service Bull. 258). Washington: Government Printing Office, 1940, pp. 33-43.

[28] The Federal Fair Labor Standards Act of 1938 does not extend protection
to children working in agriculture, except when they are legally required to
attend school. Only nine states, moreover, have child labor laws definitely
covering the employment of children in industrialized agriculture. In eighteen
other states general minimum-age provisions apply to all employment during
school hours, but enforcement for agriculture is weak and does not affect
vacation periods when most farm work is done. SIMONS, SAVILLA M., "Child
Labor in Industrialized Agriculture in Hidalgo County, Texas," Social Service
Review, 16:414-435, September, 1942.

[29] ZIMAND, GERTRUDE F., "The Changing Picture of Child Labor," The Annals
of the American Academy of Political and Social Science, November, 1944, pp.
83-91.

described as pathological.[30] The Negroes in Southern agriculture are the worst off of all. In 1940 only one-twelfth of the South's over-populated farm land [31] was operated by Negro owners, tenants, and croppers, although over one-fourth of the South's farm population was Negro. Beyond that, the place of Negroes in the Southern agricultural economy is that of hired laborers with pitifully low wages and no assurance of year-round employment.[32] The median income in wages of Negro farm laborer families in the South in 1939 was $254, with over 40 per cent of them hitting rock bottom with less than $200.[33]

The Rural Nonfarm Economy

The 27 million people who live in rural communities and areas but not on farms are practically as diverse in their means of earning a livelihood as is our entire population. Storekeepers, clerks, bankers, lawyers, carpenters, laborers, teachers, miners, fishermen, lumbermen, doctors — all are represented, active and retired, in small towns or the open country, and they even include a considerable number of farm managers and laborers living away from the farm. Despite all this diversity, however, and the approach of the towns-folk toward urban life, most of these nonfarm rural people are very closely associated with the agricultural economy. Naturally the fortunes of rural trade centers and the people who serve or sell to farmers rise and fall with the fluctuations in farmers' spending power.

To an extent, of course, this relationship is reciprocal. Prosperity in the town means sales for the farmer. Textile mills, sawmills, food processing plants — all mean payrolls and a demand for farm products. Seventy-three per cent of all miners, 88 per cent of all lumbermen, and 67 per cent of all fishermen live in rural communities or reside on farms, and they swell the local market for the

[30] MYRDAL, GUNNAR, RICHARD STEINER, and ROSE ARNOLD, *An American Dilemma: The Negro Problem and Modern Democracy.* New York: Harper & Brothers, 1944, p. 205.

[31] The South had over half the nation's farm population in 1940 but only 35 per cent of all land in farms, and the value of this land together with buildings and farm machinery was only 28 per cent of the national figure.

[32] *Ibid.*

[33] DUCOFF, *op. cit.,* pp. 150, 152.

products the farmer sells. By and large, however, it is the large towns and cities that offer a market for cash crops, and the income of the farmer — and the miner, the lumberman, the fisherman, the local processor — depends on industrial activity and urban employment. Thus the economic fortunes of the farm and the small town run parallel, and jointly they depend on the larger urban centers.

The incomes of rural nonfarm people, in fact, are not very different from those of farmers. The net money income of nonfarm families and single persons was somewhat higher than that of farm operators in 1941, but when full account is taken of home-produced items and non-money income in general, the average income of farm operators, according to an official study, was actually higher than that of rural nonfarm people.[34] It must be noted that this applies only to farm operators, since this study classified hired laborers (and farm managers) as part of the rural nonfarm group. The chances are, therefore, that the average income of rural nonfarm people in the strict sense was somewhat higher in 1941 than that of all rural farm people, although surprisingly close to the same generally low level.

The greater the proportion of rural people in a state, the poorer is that state in terms of the average income of all its citizens. The more urban a state, the higher its per capita income. There is a strikingly close correlation between degree of rurality and per capita income in the great majority of our 48 states. It may be seen in Figure 5 that of the 12 states more urban than the national average, 11 are likewise higher than average in per capita income; of the 36 states less urban than the national average, 31 are likewise lower than average in per capita income. One might almost say that as of 1940 each 10 per cent by which a state was more rural than other states meant in effect a reduction of about $100 in the per capita income of its citizens.

The few deviations from the general correlation that are seen in Figure 5 reflect over-all regional variations in wealth or special conditions within individual states. Thus among the most rural states, those in the South have even lower per capita incomes than equally rural states like the Dakotas, West Virginia, and Vermont.

[34] U. S. Department of Agriculture, *Rural Family Spending and Saving in Wartime* (Misc. Pub. 520). Washington: Government Printing Office, June, 1943, pp. 26-27.

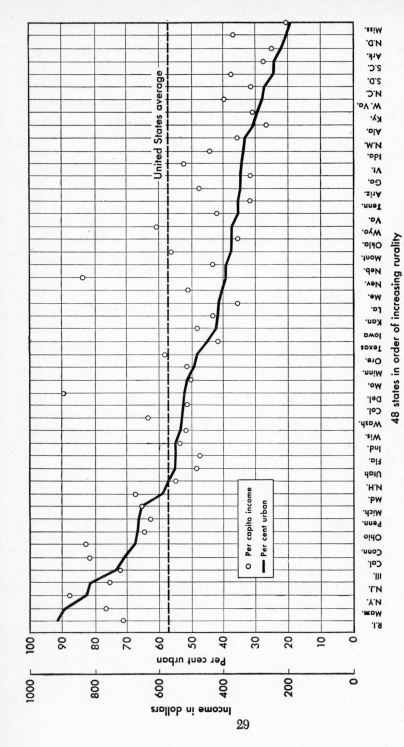

FIG. 5. Income and Rurality: Per capital income and rural-urban composition of the population, by states, 1940. Sources: U. S. Census, 1940. *Population.* Vol. 2, *Characteristics of the Population;* U. S. Department of Commerce, Bureau of Foreign and Domestic Commerce, *Current Business,* 24:19, August, 1944. Note: The line "United States average" refers to both per capita income and per cent urban.

By and large, however, the degree of rurality of the various states is a much more significant determinant of prosperity than geographic location or special conditions affecting the rural or urban economy of individual states. In later chapters we shall see just what this means in terms of the health resources and services available to rural people.

CHAPTER 3

CHARACTERISTICS OF RURAL LIFE

THE NATURAL conditions of rural life favorable to health have been appreciated ever since urbanization created some of the ugliness and the hazards of congested living. Supported by the "back to nature" philosophy as expounded by Thoreau a century ago, the notion has long prevailed that the rural landscape is the site of all things good for the health of body and mind.[1]

Certain of the natural features of life in the open country are, indeed, favorable to health. Fresh air and sunshine and the "hardening" effects of physical work undoubtedly have their value. Vigorous exercise with long hours of sleep coupled with a slower general tempo of living fosters a certain robustness, it would seem, much more than does the sedentary, high-tension living of city dwellers. Access to garden-fresh food and abundant quantities of fresh eggs and dairy products in many areas would certainly imply nutritional advantages. The mere lack of congestion would suggest less likelihood of contracting communicable disease.

Many of these advantages are greatly exaggerated, however, for the great majority of the rural population, even for families living right on farms. But more important, even to the extent that they are valid, they tend to be counteracted by lacks in those amenities of civilization which play a direct part today in the promotion or preservation of health. For the generally low-income levels of the rural areas mean not only great lacks in medical personnel and facilities but also deficiencies in other technical resources and cultural advantages which, in turn, exert a profound influence on the public health. The thin dispersion of the rural population, moreover, makes the delivery of any technical service far more expensive.

[1] See, for example, BORSODI, RALPH, *This Ugly Civilization*. New York: Simon and Schuster, Inc., 1929.

Rural Housing

Few environmental factors are more basic to the maintenance of health than good housing.[2] Yet, despite the abundance of space in the country and, for that matter, labor and often timber and other materials, rural housing in the United States is all too frequently crowded, of poor quality, and in a state of disrepair. In 1940 the average value of all owner-occupied urban houses was $4,131, while the corresponding average value of rural nonfarm houses was $2,408 and of rural farmhouses hardly more than one-third of the urban value, or $1,419.[3] That this differential was not due merely to the influence of a small number of urban mansions is indicated by an even greater differential between the median values of $3,501 for urban dwellings and $1,028 for farmhouses. Despite their much lower value, farm dwellings had to accommodate on the average 4.3 persons in 1940, compared with 3.6 in urban. While 6 per cent of urban dwelling units were seriously overcrowded (having more than 1.5 persons per room when the minimum standard is 1.0 per room), 16 per cent of all farmhouses were so listed.[4]

We are accustomed to thinking of shabby slums as being a part of big cities only, because there they are concentrated in blighted districts and may be readily seen. The state of dilapidation of a large proportion of rural houses both in the open country and in small towns, nevertheless, is reflected by a Census Bureau report that 21.4 per cent of rural nonfarm and 33.9 per cent of all rural farm dwellings were in need of major repairs in 1940, compared with 11.5 per cent of all urban dwellings.[5] The Bureau of Agricultural Economics, moreover, points out that in 1940 over one-third of the nation's 5,760,000 occupied farm operator dwellings on farms were hopelessly beyond repair and almost another third were in need of

[2] POND, M. ALLEN, "How Does Housing Affect Health? *Public Health Reports*, 61:665-672, May 10, 1946.

[3] The estimates on farmhouse value are probably less satisfactory than those on nonfarm units. Since it is obviously difficult to determine what portion of total farm land value to assign to the dwelling unit, the value of the land is excluded. This is the method of evaluation used by the Census Bureau. U. S. Census, 1940. *Housing*. Vol. 2, *General Characteristics*. 1943.

[4] *Ibid.*

[5] *Ibid.*

major structural alterations.[6] Rural slum housing frequently fails to provide even basic shelter from the elements. Farms are purchased or leased primarily for their land assets and the farmhouse gets scant consideration in the negotiation.

The situation is worst for tenant-occupied houses, some 51 per cent of which were estimated as beyond repair.[7] The entire basis of farm tenancy is such as to lead to progressive deterioration of housing and sanitation. The tenant, knowing he may move in a year or two, allows the place to run down; the landlord, knowing he can get another tenant with little difficulty, rarely makes any repairs or improvements. Migratory farm-labor families, stopping by on a grower's premises only for the duration of the harvest, must usually tolerate the most miserable housing of all. Old barns and chicken coops and tool sheds are commonplace abodes for these families at the bottom of the agricultural ladder. Leaky roofs, broken stairs, and even the absence of floors obviously form a favorable environment for accidents, respiratory illness, and generally lowered resistance.

Sanitation and Public Utilities

With regard to the basic facilities for sanitation — water supply and sewage disposal — rural deficiencies are more striking still. These facilities are so intimately related to health and the prevention of filth-borne diseases that they will be considered in some detail in the discussion on health facilities. But beyond these elementary requirements, millions of farmhouses are without benefit of screens on their windows, refrigeration, proper heating systems, or any of the numerous conveniences in the kitchen or bathroom that help to emancipate the urban housewife from drudgery.

Many of the conveniences making for more healthful modern living call for the delivery of public utilities, like gas, water, and electricity, from central sources. While wood fuel may be substituted for gas, though with more labor and less efficacy, and water may be

[6] U. S. Department of Agriculture, Interbureau Committee on Postwar Agricultural Programs, *The Farm Housing Problem*. Washington, January, 1945, Processed.

[7] *Ibid.*

derived from a local source, electricity provided independently on individual farmsteads is beyond the ability of all but quite well-to-do farmers. The cost of constructing power lines to individual farmhouses, moreover, is beyond the means of most farm families, so that commercial utility companies have seldom found the venture profitable enough to be worth their while. Largely for these reasons, the majority of farm dwellings are without electric service. Of all farm housing units in 1940, about 69 per cent were without electric lighting; the figure was about 22 per cent even among nonfarm rural dwellings, as against only 4 per cent of urban units.[8]

The effects of lack of electricity on health are evident on a moment's consideration. Faulty lighting is a frequent cause of accidents and fires. Poor illumination, moreover, causes eyestrain and discourages reading. Radios, which like reading are an effective medium of both general and health education, are difficult to maintain without electricity. Lack of adequate refrigeration has more serious implications for health. Only 15 per cent of farmhouses enjoyed mechanical refrigeration in 1940 and only an additional 18 per cent, for that matter, had equipment for ice.[9] In the warm climate of the South, where the dangers of food spoilage are greatest, refrigeration is least adequate of all. The effective operation of community facilities involving health directly, like hospitals or clinics, or indirectly, like schools or community centers, depends on electrification and other public utilities.

Communications and Transportation

The same factors making electric power unavailable to most farm people operate even more disadvantageously with respect to telephone service. In fact, the effect of economic pressure associated with the consolidation of telephone companies and rising rates has

[8] U. S. Census, 1940. *Housing.* Vol. 2, *General Characteristics.*

If it had not been for the farmers' cooperatives sponsored and financed by the Rural Electrification Administration since 1935, the situation would have been even worse in 1940. This program deserves credit for notable progress and promises much for the future, but as of 1944 little more than 40 per cent of our farms were electrified. U. S. Department of Agriculture, Interbureau Committee on Postwar Agricultural Programs, *Rural Electrification after the War.* Washington: Government Printing Office, February, 1945, p. 2.

[9] U. S. Census, 1940. *Housing.* Vol. 2, *General Characteristics.*

been such that since 1920 the number of farms with telephone service has declined sharply.[10] In 1920 there were 2,498,000 farms with telephones and in 1940 there were only 1,527,000, or only one-fourth of all farms. Less than 10 per cent of all farms in the South had telephones in 1940.[11] How this affects the ability of the farm family to reach the doctor or seek help of other kinds is obvious. Lack of telephone communication with his patients is also a serious handicap to the hard-driven rural practitioner.

It is not as though the lack of telephone service were compensated for by other means of communication and transportation. For, despite the greater distances they have to cover to reach the nearest trade center or the doctor or hospital, farm families are very poorly supplied with automobiles. In 1940, 42 per cent of all farm operators had no cars, while 51 per cent of tenants and 85 per cent of all non-white tenants had none.[12] Most farmers' cars or pickup trucks are characteristically in a state of disrepair, and the ramshackle jalopy which we associate with the migrating Joads of the nation is more picturesque than it is effective as a means of transportation.

Even with a car the farmer's handicaps are not overcome, for country roads are still largely unpaved. While through highways or surfaced roads may link many small country towns, the isolated farm family is often forced to use roads that in the winter may be snowbound or in the spring a bed of mud. Less than half of all farms are located on all-weather roads.[13]

Education

Facilities for education in widespread rural areas are in a state of backwardness such as characterized the nation as a whole many decades ago.[14] Yet rural America, with 43.5 per cent of the nation's

[10] U. S. Federal Communications Commission, *Preliminary Studies on Some Aspects of the Availability of Landline Wire Communications Service*. Washington, October, 1944, Processed, pp. 23-30.

[11] U. S. Census, 1940. *Agriculture*. Vol. 3, *General Reports*.

[12] *Ibid.*

[13] Association of Land-grant Colleges and Universities, *Postwar Agricultural Policy* (Report of Committee on Postwar Agricultural Policy). October, 1944, p. 6.

[14] For a general discussion of rural education, see WORKS, GEORGE A., and SIMON O. LESSER, *Rural America Today: Its Schools and Community Life*. Chicago: University of Chicago Press, 1942.

population, has over half the nation's children to be educated. To the rural child are imparted only meagerly the fundamentals of good hygiene and the general cultural development that lead to living more intelligently with respect to health and general social well-being. The nature of the problem of poor rural education is reflected in school financing. The estimated value of school property in rural areas is only $185 per pupil compared with $405 in urban areas.[15] For each urban pupil enrolled, the school system of the nation spends annually $105, but only $70 for each rural pupil.[16] Expenditures by states find nearly all the urban states at the top of the list and nearly all the rural states at the bottom. For the school year 1939-40, for example, New York, New Jersey, California, and the District of Columbia made median expenditures of more than $3,000 per classroom unit. The rural states, on the other hand, appear to try to do as much, spending about the same proportion of total state income on education as the urban states. Yet the median expenditures per classroom unit for Virginia, Georgia, Tennessee, Alabama, Kentucky, Arkansas, and Mississippi were all $750 or less.[17]

With such low expenditures in most rural sections, obviously schools are poorly equipped and teachers are greatly underpaid. Naturally the most competent men and women are seldom attracted into rural teaching and the turnover among all teachers is high. The rural child has a shorter school year — averaging 8 months compared with 9½ months in urban schools — and bad weather, farm chores, or the demands of seasonal crops for all available labor make for a high rate of absence and retardation as well as early dropping out from school. The commonest pattern is the one-room or one-teacher schoolhouse, without benefit of any specialized instruction by teachers of music, art, handicrafts, home economics, or physical education. Despite the movement toward consolidated schools, rural areas are still served by about 108,000 one-teacher

[15] DAWSON, HOWARD A., "Trouble at the Crossroads," *The White House Conference on Rural Education.* Washington: National Education Association, 1944, p. 30.

[16] STUDEBAKER, JOHN W., "Better Rural Education Opportunities — A National Need," *The White House Conference on Rural Education,* p. 54.

[17] NORTON, J. K., Testimony before the Committee on Education and Labor, U. S. Senate, 79th Cong. 1st Sess., S. 181, "Education Finance Act of 1945," Jan. 29, 1945, *Federal Aid for Education,* Part 1, pp. 9-96.

units.[18] Clearly very few rural schools can make special provision for the blind, deaf, mentally deficient, or other handicapped children. All things considered, it should be no surprise that 3 million adults in the United States have never attended school and that 10 million, mostly rural, are virtually illiterate.[19] The war intensified the crisis in rural education; it hit rural schools far harder than urban, as thousands of teachers went into direct war service or industry — or were recruited for urban schools.[20]

Other cultural institutions available for adult education are rare in rural areas, and the only programs of any importance are confined largely to those of the agricultural extension services and the major farm organizations. Some 57 per cent of the rural population live in areas without any public library service.[21]

Rural Community Organization

Despite the way the rural population is spread out, the lines of social interaction are stronger than might appear evident from the rural panorama. Rural people may be essentially individualistic, but many social institutions tie them together into organic communities. The effort to satisfy human needs for religion and for recreation helps to build these social groups. Economic needs exert a strong influence, and the political structure, of course, is developed to provide for law and order and to some extent for social improvement. Beyond these formal lines, the social structure of rural communities naturally grows out of physical proximity and such motivations as friendship and common interests.

The rural community is usually characterized by a small town or village as a trade center, with lines of trade and social interaction radiating into the surrounding countryside. Within the community, typically, there are so-called neighborhood groups in which special interfamily bonds are developed not only by reason of locality but also by the unifying leadership of particular families. There are

[18] DAWSON, op. cit., p. 30.

[19] Council for Social Action of the Congregational Christian Churches, The Washington Report, 1:2, June, 1945.

[20] DAWSON, op. cit., pp. 31-32.

[21] BATCHELDER, MILDRED L., "Building Rural Schools and Communities to Cope with the Problems of Tomorrow," The White House Conference on Rural Education, p. 103.

said to be some 45,000 such rural communities in the nation and some 250,000 functioning neighborhoods. With greatly improved transportation and the consequently widened range of social inter-relationship, however, the neighborhood has lost many of its functions to the larger community.[22] It is clear that the rural community, like the urban, is dynamic and is defined more by lines of common interest than by mere location.

The church is one of the strongest forces in rural society and is often the principal center of community social life. It is a tribute to the force of religion that so many small towns, whether in prosperous or needy areas, are served by churches. Yet the number of towns that have well-kept churches but are utterly lacking in even a minimum hospital unit or health center cannot but win the attention of the student of rural health. There are encouraging signs that some rural church leaders are taking the initiative in general social betterment, including the movement toward vastly improved economic and health conditions for rural people.

If recreation is defined as diversion from the usual occupation, we must recognize that many rural people get less than their share. Though farm and village people often enjoy such varied activities as church or school socials, hunting, fishing, or square dancing, it is still true that great numbers of rural families live in monotonous and dulling isolation. The consequences of such isolation are reflected in a burden of psychological maladjustments and even psychiatric disorders, the full extent of which has only recently been recognized.

The significant governmental unit in most rural sections is the county rather than the municipality, although in New England, for example, the town, and in parts of the Midwest, the township, is an important political subdivision. With county government getting its funds almost entirely from property taxes, it is inevitable that the largest property owners should come to have the strongest voice in local political affairs. This being the case, pressure is strong to keep county government expenditures to a minimum. Since rural public health work and medical assistance to the needy depend largely on county expenditures, they necessarily suffer from this pattern. As a matter of fact, the taxable wealth of most rural counties, rela-

[22] SANDERSON, EZRA DWIGHT, and ROBERT A. POLSON, *Rural Community Organization*. New York: John Wiley & Sons, Inc., 1939.

tive to highly industrialized counties, tends to be so low that funds for all types of health and welfare services, even under the most enlightened county leadership, are sparse.

Federal programs of social welfare, nevertheless, are not generally available to meet the need. The extensive national social security program of old age and survivors' insurance and the federal-state program of unemployment compensation, initiated in 1935, specifically bar from coverage farmers and agricultural workers. While social security coverage does not, of course, provide health services, the cash benefits may enable a family to purchase private medical services that might otherwise be foregone. Although changes are contemplated in "cradle to grave" security legislation, up to now the farm population has simply not been under the umbrella of social insurance protection.

At the same time, a number of federal agricultural agencies, dealing with such vital matters as planned production, crop insurance, rural rehabilitation, credit, soil conservation, and rural electrification, do carry their programs down into the counties directly to farm people. These programs represent important instruments for change in all rural life. Through these activities, the farmer may actually have closer everyday ties with the national government than the city dweller. These relationships will doubtless influence the farmer's attitude toward federal legislation concerning medical care.

In general, the structure and functions of local governmental units tend to be so relatively circumscribed that numerous other rural organizational forms are developed on a voluntary basis to accomplish particular ends. Many are set up entirely through local initiative, while others have been promoted by federal farm agencies. Most functions of agricultural production or distribution calling for group action are maintained largely as voluntary endeavors.

Faced with the common hazards or trials of bad weather, droughts, soil erosion, economic depression, urban monopolistic practices, or other stresses and strains, farmers have learned to band together in cooperative associations, many of which extend beyond counties and districts into large regional organizations. In 1945 more than 3 million farmers were said to hold memberships in over 19,000 farmer-owned and farmer-controlled cooperative associations and mutual companies. The total volume of business of marketing and purchasing associations alone aggregated more than 5 billion dollars in 1943.[23] Increasing recognition has been given to the propriety of cooperatives in state legislation, ever since the first such statute enacted by Michigan in 1865.

Many cooperative organizations and other groups organized among farm people for civic or social purposes offer the organizational structure through which the provision of medical service or the payment of its costs may be undertaken. Geographic units like irrigation or soil conservation districts, likewise, lend themselves to health purposes, such as community organization into "sanitary districts" for improved water supply or sewage disposal facilities.

Special importance attaches to the national farm organizations developed largely to give a political voice to the farmer. The most important of these are the Grange, the Farm Bureau Federation, and the Farmers Union. The role each of these bodies has played in the articulation of farm opinion on health matters and in promoting measures to improve rural health will be considered in a later chapter.

With the variety of organizational forms operating to meet the farmer's needs through nonofficial or through federal channels, it is evident that local governmental boundaries have relatively little functional significance. Most county lines were marked out on an arbitrary, somewhat geometrical basis, and only rarely do the boundaries of rural community life happen to fall precisely within these limits. This situation obviously creates numerous problems in any field of public administration — such as public health — restricted by county legal structure. The soundest organization of any public health or public medical care service would clearly be in conformity with natural trade channels, whether they cross county lines or not. The number of people in many rural counties, furthermore, is too small to be able to finance effectively a technical service such as public health of the modern type. These problems of political jurisdiction seriously complicate the task of developing sound public health and medical administration for rural people, and they call for solutions for which there is little precedent and which generally must break rather sharply with tradition.

[23] U. S. Department of Agriculture, Interbureau Committee on Postwar Agricultural Programs, *Agricultural Cooperatives in the Postwar Period.* Washington, July, 1945, Processed, p. 3.

Living Habits and Attitudes

The occupational character and the social organization of rural life establish among rural people habits and attitudes quite different from those of urban people. The pattern of family spending, for example, tends to be different not only because of marked differences in total income, but also because of varying needs and desires. Comparing farm family with nonfarm (urban and rural) family

Table 1. Expenditures for Family Living: *Amount and distribution of expenditures of median farm and nonfarm families and single consumers for major items of family living*, 1941

Expenditures	Farm		All other	
	Money expenditures	Per cent	Money expenditures	Per cent
Total family living	$710	94.7	$1,552	94.6
Food	229	30.5	518	31.6
Housing, fuel, light, and refrigeration .	68	9.1	304	18.6
Household operation	28	3.7	63	3.8
Furnishings and equipment	51	6.8	89	5.4
Clothing	119	15.9	173	10.5
Medical care	50	6.7	76	4.6
All other	165	22.0	329	20.1

Source: U. S. Bureau of Home Economics and U. S. Bureau of Labor Statistics, Study of Family Spending and Saving in Wartime, *Estimates of the Expenditures of American Consumers* 1941 *and the First Quarter of* 1942. Washington: U. S. Department of Agriculture, August, 1942, Processed.

spending, we find smaller proportionate expenditures by farm families for housing, fuel, light, and refrigeration, and higher proportionate expenditures for furnishings and equipment and, for that matter, medical care (Table 1). But it is evident that while the farm family spends about a 50 per cent higher proportion of its income on medical care than other families, its actual money expenditures are about 50 per cent less. The consequences of this fundamental economic fact will be found running through the entire story of rural medical services.

It may be surprising to observe that farm families spend nearly as high a proportion of their income on food as other families. It is evident that in many sections, under current patterns of cash crop farming, only a small share of the average farm family's food is home-produced. Few popular misconceptions, as we shall see, are more prevalent than those about the adequacy of nutrition of families living on the land.

While the average farm family spends a higher proportion of income on clothing than the nonfarm family, the absolute money expenditure is much lower. Although occupational and isolation factors must be borne in mind, there are significant numbers of ill-clad farm people in most farming districts and in some areas this is true of the large majority. The effects of inadequate clothing on morale and social adjustment are commonly recognized. But bearing even more directly on health are such conditions as the lack of shoes among children in hookworm-infested areas and the lack of heavy clothing in severe winter weather.

The demands of an agricultural existence tend to give the farmer a psychological make-up quite distinct from that of the city resident. Typically, his contacts with people tend to be fewer and he is thrown more completely on his own resources. All too frequently isolation prevents his exposure to new ideas. In general, he tends to be more individualistic and slower to accept novel viewpoints or unaccustomed ways. He is more attached to the traditional, the "tried and true" way of doing things. His closeness to nature and his relative helplessness against the ravages of drought or flood or windstorm make him somewhat fatalistic and, at the same time, rather stoical about the misfortunes of life.

Obviously these attitudes have a bearing on the farm family's reaction to illness, injuries, or impairments and to the need for medical services. They tend to make the rural family less alert to the need for medical care and less demanding of medical attention than the city family. Thus the rural family, at least up to very recent years, has tended to be more or less satisfied with — or at least tolerant of — the old country doctor or the old dug well. As Harry S. Mustard points out, almost every rural health worker has found it necessary to hurdle the attitude bound up in the expression "what was good enough for my grandfather is good enough for me." [24]

Farming is a wearing occupation, and the long hours of toil of

[24] MUSTARD, HARRY S., *Rural Health Practice*. New York: The Commonwealth Fund, 1936, p. 7.

the farmer in the field or of his wife in the farmhouse and garden exact their physical and psychological toll. Compared with the city dweller, the farmer tends to "look old for his age," reflecting years of hard work and exposure, and the farmer's wife is too often characterized by a weary and worn demeanor. For many, low income combined with a low educational level and lack of social contacts results in a loss of pride in their personal appearance and the upkeep of the farmstead. A drab and meagerly furnished home within dilapidated, insanitary, and unsightly surroundings does little to encourage sound habits of mental or physical hygiene. Farm children and youth reared in such an environment and under such depressed circumstances tend to perpetuate these low living standards. Thousands are caught in this vicious circle that, with the years, becomes increasingly hard to break. The result in human erosion is even more significant than the widely recognized gullies and washes of millions of acres of eroded farm land.

While the social contacts of the farmer or the villager may be fewer than those of the city dweller they tend, on the other hand, to be on a deeper level. He knows his neighbor intimately and, more than the city dweller, shares his joys and sorrows with him — as well as wheelbarrows and baby cribs.

There tends to be a relative homogeneity throughout a given rural community with respect to national origins, religion, and attitudes, and by the same token greater resistance to "foreign ideas." Class differences are less marked than in the industrialized cities. The dependence of farm operators on the soil, whether they are renters or owners, tends to give them all a somewhat middle-class psychology. The sons of farmers tend to follow in their fathers' occupational footsteps more frequently than do those of other principal groups.[25] Family bonds, in general, tend to be stronger, especially because the farm family is more of an interdependent psychological and economic unit than the city family.

It must be recalled, nevertheless, that the sharpest caste system ever known to American life, slavery, was a rural institution. Class lines based on color or national origin are still an extremely powerful force, often splitting rural communities into various social levels.

[25] SOROKIN, PITIRIM, and CARLE C. ZIMMERMAN, *Principles of Rural-urban Sociology.* New York: Henry Holt and Company, Inc., 1929, p. 26.

The increasing industrialization of agriculture, moreover, tends to accentuate rural class lines, with rising farm-labor and tenant groups.[26]

It is impossible to generalize validly about the psychology of all rural people. Yet certain broad traits are commonly attributed to the farmer. They boil down to what some consider the consequences of a large volume of "direct experience" and a limited volume of "indirect experience." The farmer's experience is such as to make him thoroughly competent with respect to the practical everyday problems with which he deals. Yet in fields outside his direct experience, he is too often subject to ignorance, prejudice, even superstition, and consequently fallacious judgment.[27] The fact that modern scientific medical care falls largely outside his field of actual experience creates one of the special psychological problems that must be met in getting better medical services to rural people.

These general characteristics obviously do not apply to every farm family in the nation, and in the more prosperous rural sections they are applicable only to a limited extent. There tends to be variation in farmers' attitudes along with varying nearness to urban centers, differences in types and size of farm holdings, tenure status, degree of mechanization, and so on. The attitudes of the marginal cotton sharecropper, for example, are obviously different from those of the substantial dairy farmer. In general, however, the observations are probably valid. The thinking of village people, moreover, has much in common with that of farmers and is, in fact, often strongly colored by that of farmers who have retired to live in town.

Traditional rural attitudes are changing, nevertheless, as technology and industrialization exert a growing influence on the agricultural economy and as city and country are drawn closer together. As farmers have experienced the consequences of economic stresses, they have learned increasingly to band together for their common good, and membership in all types of farm organizations has expanded. Through their organization leaders such groups are exerting increasing political pressure for agricultural and other legislation.

[26] On the other hand, it must be recognized that in certain sections, like the wheat belt, mechanization has to some extent strengthened the independent family-sized unit.

[27] SMITH, T. LYNN, *The Sociology of Rural Life.* New York: Harper & Brothers, 1940, pp. 127-128.

Even the farmer's age-old mistrust of the "city slicker" or the urban worker is diminishing in the face of his growing recognition of the dependence of farm prosperity on a high level of well-paid employment in the cities. This awakening of the farm population has its direct bearing on rural medicine, through a steadily mounting demand for improved rural medical facilities and services.

IN THIS SETTING rural medicine is found. In this setting hospitals are operated and doctors practice. The composition of the rural population, their manner of making a living, and their way of life are the essential components of the background against which a picture of rural health and medical care must be drawn. Again and again the sources of problems in rural medical care will be found in such factors as the dispersion of the rural population, their generally low economic level, their social psychology, and other cultural characteristics. Ultimate solutions must strike at these basic causes.

PART II: PRESENT-DAY LEVELS AND
TRENDS OF RURAL HEALTH

WHAT IS THE health status of that large section of our population living on farms and in rural communities? How does it compare with the health of our urban population? What heritage or endowment of health do our rural youth take with them as thousands leave their home communities to become tomorrow's urban citizens? The answers to these questions are not simple. Dogmatic answers cannot be given. And yet, despite gaps in our knowledge, information is available from many sources that reveals trends in rural health and permits valid comparisons with urban health status.

Cities were once the virtual breeders of disease. Even the cities of today, with their organized public health programs and vastly improved sanitation, have their congestion and their slums, their clatter and their dust-ridden, sunless alleys. People in cities have long looked on rural life as the healthful life, and 40 years ago in this country they were close to the truth. Rural people were then healthier as a group; the toll of fatal disease and premature death was much lower among them. But movements were already afoot and trends taking shape that were to mean progressive and rapid improvement in urban health, a dramatic advance only feebly reflected and far from paralleled by the lagging betterment of rural health during the same decades.

It is not easy to measure health. Most of the specific information available on rural health today is confined to measurements of rather marked deviation from good health. Thus we must rely for the most part on three principal types of information — data on deaths and their causes, on the amount and kinds of sickness, and on physical and mental impairments. In general, disease processes have had to result in disability, chronic handicapping conditions, or death, before they won the attention of the examiner, the investigator, and the vital statistician. And yet a review of currently available data gives us much information on the relative status of rural health and the dimensions of the problem with which rural medicine must deal.

CHAPTER 4

DEATHS AND THEIR CAUSES

DEATH IS A final, ultimate event which, if reported accurately, furnishes certain undebatable information about population groups. While this information gives little indication of the total amount of illness and disability prevailing, taken together with studies of sickness and physical impairments it helps to reveal fundamental trends in the nation's health.

Unfortunately the usefulness of annual mortality records for rural-urban comparisons is seriously diminished by several factors. It was not until 1933, for example, that mortality records became available for the entire United States. Then, too, there has long been a confusing lack of uniformity in the definition of rural territory. Any definition must necessarily be arbitrary. From the point of view of rural medical resources in facilities and personnel, the most appropriate definition would be that long used by the Division of Vital Statistics of the Bureau of the Census, namely, that places with less than 10,000 population are rural. The health resources of such places typify rural medicine, even though rural people as such are now generally defined as those living in places of under 2,500 population and mortality data are ordinarily presented on that basis.[1]

A more serious drawback to the use of mortality data in gauging rural health has been the policy of the Division of Vital Statistics in tabulating mortality statistics by the place of occurrence of the death rather than by the place of residence of the deceased. This obviously increases urban death rates and at the same time lowers rural rates, as reported, since the deaths of rural residents frequently occur in hospitals and other institutions in urban places. As Harold F. Dorn points out, rates computed from such tabulations may be as

[1] Before 1930 the Division of Vital Statistics of the Bureau of the Census referred to places with less than 10,000 population as rural, whereas the Division of Population used as its definition places with less than 2,500 population. Since 1930 the Division of Vital Statistics has been using both definitions, leading to considerable confusion in analyzing mortality data, although use of the "less than 2,500" definition has been the general rule since 1942.

much as 20 to 25 per cent in error.[2] The Bureau of the Census has belatedly commenced to tabulate certain mortality statistics by place of residence, starting with 1939 and 1940 data. It is naturally difficult to define with any precision certain long-range trends in the mortality rates of the rural population.[3]

Another factor seriously affecting the reliability of mortality data is the incomplete registration of deaths in many rural areas. It has been reliably estimated that for the country as a whole as many as 10 per cent of the deaths of rural residents may be unregistered.[4] The Bureau of the Census stresses the under-reporting of deaths in rural areas, pointing out that it applies especially to a number of Southern and Western states where death registration is more recent and less well established.[5]

These various factors which impair the usefulness of rural-urban mortality records and almost certainly understate the extent of fatal illness in rural areas must be borne in mind as life expectancy and death rates are reviewed in an attempt to evaluate the present-day status of rural health.

Life Expectancy and Mortality Trends

The years since the turn of the century have been notable for the tremendous advances made in man's conquest of disease. As our knowledge has increased, particularly on the prevention and control of infectious diseases, along with generally rising living standards, man's average life span has stretched almost to the psalmist's three score years and ten. In just four decades the average length of life in the United States increased nearly one-third, or by about 15 years.

[2] DORN, HAROLD F., "Rural Health and Public Health Programs," *Rural Sociology*, 17:22-32, March, 1942.

[3] The attempt to record deaths by place of residence, while the only logical course to pursue, can seldom be wholly successful. Inevitable errors tend to result in the recording of relatively more urban deaths. Just the main post office address may be given, for example, rather than the R.F.D. route. Then, too, when certain kinds of critical illness strike, there is a movement toward the better medical facilities of urban places, and the home of a relative frequently comes to be recorded as the decedent's residence.

[4] DORN, *op. cit.*

[5] U. S. Bureau of the Census, *United States Abridged Life Tables*, 1939. Washington: U. S. Department of Commerce, June 23, 1943, p. 5.

People living on farms and in small towns had a big head start in 1900 in this running battle with Father Time. In our white population the average length of life of rural males was then 10 years longer, and of females 7½ years longer, than corresponding life durations in cities (Table 2). If rural people could have shared equally the remarkable increase in average length of life over the next four decades, their newborn could now look forward to average life spans of approximately 70 years. But during this period the

Table 2. Life Expectancy: *Average duration of life (in years) of white persons in the United States by sex, and by rural and urban place,** 1901 *and* 1939

	Males		Females	
	Urban	Rural	Urban	Rural
1901	44.0	54.0	47.9	55.4
1939	61.4	64.1	66.2	67.5
Increase	17.4	10.1	18.3	12.1

Source: U. S. Census, *United States Abridged Life Tables*, 1939, p. 5.

*Rural in 1901—places under 8,000; rural in 1939—places under 2,500. Urban in 1901—places 8,000 or more; urban in 1939—places 2,500 to 100,000; (expectancy for places of 100,000 or more was even higher: males—61.6; females—66.3).

average duration of life of urban white males increased by 40 per cent whereas the increase for rural males was only 19 per cent, and the figures for white females are almost as striking.[6] Here was proof that not only health but life itself was in a sense purchasable, for the period witnessed an outpouring of funds making our cities more habitable, an expenditure for expanding public health activities and medical services that was not paralleled in the rural districts.

As of 1939 our rural white population still had a slight edge on urban residents in life expectancy at birth, as seen in Table 2. For males, however, there was only a 2.7-year advantage and for females slightly over 1 year. The Bureau of the Census, moreover, points out that taking account of under-registration of deaths in rural areas would tend to reduce the rural figures and bring them even closer

[6] Doubtless the smaller increase in life expectancy in the rural population is due in part to the fact that this population is somewhat closer to the maximum expectation of life attainable with present knowledge. With thousands of individuals now living to be centenarians, however, it would seem inappropriate to stress this factor unduly.

to the corresponding urban figures.[7] It seems not improbable that unless present trends are modified through vigorous measures to reduce the toll of preventable rural deaths, the average life span of city dwellers will soon come to exceed that of the rural population.

Although the average length of life in our Negro population has been increasing rapidly in recent years, in 1940 their average life expectancy was still about 11 years less than for white persons. It was, moreover, little better than that of the white population 40 years before.[8] In general, the average life span of rural Negroes was somewhat longer than that of urban, as in the case of the white population.[9]

The number of deaths per 1,000 population in the United States was 10.8 in 1940, a remarkable figure measured against the death rate in 1900 of 17.2, though not a matter for smugness when compared to recent death rates in several other nations like the Netherlands and the British Dominions.[10] Among residents of cities of 100,000 or more population the 1940 crude death rate was 11.3; in cities of 10,000 to 100,000 the rate was 11.4; in towns of 2,500 to 10,000 it was 12.4; and in rural territory it was 9.8.[11]

General trends in death rates for rural and urban populations from 1900 to 1940 are presented in Table 3.[12] These data illustrate in another way the decidedly greater relative improvement in urban health since the beginning of the century, as revealed by mortality rates. In the 40-year period the urban death rate was reduced 45 per cent while the decrease in the rural rate was only 29 per cent. The percentage decline in urban rates, in fact, exceeded the rural decline for every age group. Nevertheless, age-specific mortality

[7] U. S. Census, *United States Abridged Life Tables,* 1939, p. 5.

[8] DORN, HAROLD F., "Changes in Mortality Rates, 1930 to 1940," *Public Health Reports,* 57:1858-1868, Dec. 4, 1942.

[9] U. S. Census, *United States Abridged Life Tables,* 1939, p. 4.

[10] Special Committee on Social Security (Canada). *Health Insurance* (Report of the Advisory Committee on Health Insurance). Ottawa: King's Printer, 1943, p. 296.

[11] U. S. Census, "Mortality Summary for Registration States: All Causes of Death," *Vital Statistics — Special Reports,* 16:9, July 8, 1942.

[12] The percentages of decrease in death rates from 1900 to 1940 must be viewed as approximations only, for the table lacks uniformity at different periods with respect to the number of death registration states, the definition of rural territory, and the reporting of nonresident deaths.

rates in urban places were still generally higher than in rural communities in 1940, particularly in the older age groups. In the age groups from 15 to 29, the rural rates were actually higher than the urban.

Table 3. Mortality Trends: *Number of deaths per 1,000 population by age in urban and rural communities and the percentage decrease in death rates, 1900–02 to 1940**

Age	Urban		Rural		Percentage decrease 1900–02 to 1940	
	1900–02	1940	1900–02	1940	Urban	Rural
0–4	55.5	13.5	32.1	12.3	76	61
5–9	5.2	1.1	3.2	1.0	79	69
10–14	2.9	1.0	2.5	0.9	66	64
15–19	4.8	1.7	4.2	1.8	65	57
20–24	7.1	2.3	5.8	2.6	68	55
25–29	8.4	2.7	6.2	2.9	68	53
30–34	9.8	3.4	6.4	3.3	65	48
34–44	12.5	5.5	7.3	4.7	56	36
45–54	18.9	11.7	10.6	8.9	38	16
55–64	35.0	24.8	20.6	18.6	29	10
65–74	68.6	52.1	47.8	42.7	24	11
75 and over	155.4	132.0	133.6	126.9	15	9
All ages: Crude . .	18.4	11.5	14.2	9.8	38	31
Standard- ized . .	20.8	11.4	13.9	9.9	45	29

Source: Adapted from Dorn, Harold F., "Rural Health and Public Health Programs," *Rural Sociology,* 7:25, March, 1942. Data for 1940 from U. S. Census, *Special Reports, Vital Statistics of the United States,* 1940.

*The rates for 1900–02 are for the original registration states; those for 1940 are for the total United States. The 1940 rates are by place of residence rather than place of occurrence of the death. Rural in 1900–02—places under 8,000 population; rural in 1940—places under 2,500. The total United States population for 1940 was used as the standard population.

It appears that the urban death rate was 50 per cent higher than the rural rate in 1900, while in 1940 it was only 15 per cent higher. It is probable, however, that in 1940 the actual difference was considerably less than 15 per cent, when one takes account of factors such as the seriously incomplete recording of deaths in rural areas. Presumably the urban death rate actually exceeded the rural rate by little more than 10 per cent in 1940, and by the present time the

difference is probably even less. It is stressed by some, in fact, on
the basis of on-the-spot studies, that rural under-registration of
deaths may be so great as to eliminate entirely any apparent differential between over-all country and city rates.

In Table 3 the urban death rates for different age groups in
1940 are combined rates for residents of urban places of all sizes,
including small towns of 2,500 to 10,000, which in general show the
highest death rates. As a result, the corresponding rural rates appear

Table 4. Rural-Urban Mortality: *Death rates* by age groups and by residence in
large and small urban communities and in rural areas, 1940*

Size of community	Age in years						
	Under 1	1–4	5–14	15–24	25–44	45–64	65 and over
Cities of 100,000 or more . .	39.3	2.3	1.0	1.8	4.2	17.4	74.6
Towns of 2,500–10,000 . . .	53.4	3.7	1.4	2.5	4.5	16.4	77.1
Rural territory	50.1	3.0	1.0	2.1	3.8	13.0	67.6

Source: U. S. Census, *Special Reports, Vital Statistics of the United States,* 1940.

*Under 1 year, death rates are per 1,000 live births; all other death rates are per 1,000
population.

more favorable than the facts justify. Towns of 2,500 to 10,000, most
of which we ordinarily regard as semirural, show the highest death
rates for all age groups, except that of 45–64 years. It has been
concluded by some that these smallest urban communities ". . . have
sacrificed the healthful environment of the rural area without having
attained the superior facilities of the city."[13]

To obtain a more realistic comparison of rural and urban health,
we may study the relationship between rural death rates and those
of residents of large cities. It is in the cities of 100,000 or more population that we find the most typically urban medical and public
health facilities and the financial resources to provide health services
for the medically needy. Accordingly Table 4 is presented to permit
review of 1940 death rates for different age groups in large cities
and in rural areas. The rates for residents of towns of 2,500 to 10,000
are shown separately so that their influence on the over-all urban
rates in the previous table can be gathered.

[13] SOMMERS, HERBERT J., "Infant Mortality in Rural and Urban Areas,"
Public Health Reports, 57:1494-1501, Oct. 2, 1942.

As illustrated in Table 4, the mortality rates in 1940 for infants
(under 1 year), preschool children (1–4 years), and youths
(15–24 years) are actually higher in rural areas than in large cities,
with the rate for school children (5–14 years) being the same. On
the other hand, the rural death rates appear lower for adults of all
age groups. As the Bureau of the Census has summarized it: "Mortality at the older ages appears to be lowest generally in rural areas.
In the earlier years of life, large cities seem to offer the most favorable conditions for survival."[14] The development of far-reaching
public health programs and the availability of medical services in
large cities have had their greatest effect in reducing the number of
deaths among babies, children, and youth. The healthful effects of
the rural environment, on the other hand, seem mostly to benefit
persons in the older age groups.[15]

It is obvious that everywhere death rates in the later years of
life are higher than in children beyond infancy. To the extent that
rural states or counties have a higher proportion of the young, therefore, it will be found that their over-all crude death rates tend to
be lower; adjustment for age will, of course, tend to reduce these
differentials.

Negro death rates exceed white in rural and urban areas alike.
While they have declined more rapidly in recent years than the
rates for the white,population, they are still considerably higher.
From 1930 to 1940 the death rate for white persons declined from
10.8 per 1,000 to 10.4, a reduction of 3.7 per cent. During the same
decade the Negro mortality rate dropped from 16.5 to 13.9, a reduction of 15.8 per cent. The death rate for rural Negroes was 12.2 in
1940, a figure substantially lower than the rate for urban Negroes

[14] U. S. Census, *United States Abridged Life Tables*, 1939, p. 1.

[15] It has been pointed out, however, that to a considerable extent the apparent
lower death rates among persons in older age groups in rural areas may be an
artifact. Since it is a social distinction to be well along in years in rural communities, country dwellers past middle age have a strong tendency to exag-
gerate their age and, since birth registration came along relatively recently,
their memory is not reenforced by official records. With the age-specific
population base artificially raised, the computed rural death rates would often
tend to be unduly low. In the cities, on the other hand, the handicap of
advanced age in securing industrial employment tends to exert the opposite
effect, not to mention the more frequent occasions for a city dweller to record,
and thus to remember, his exact age.

but still 24 per cent higher than the rate for the rural population as a whole.[16]

The Principal Causes of Death

An examination of the principal causes of rural deaths — the first fifteen such causes accounting for 83 per cent of all rural deaths — will help to reflect the special nature of the disease problems facing rural medicine. In Figure 6, one may compare the mortality experience of strictly rural territory with that of large cities, as well as the corresponding death rates of small towns of 2,500 to 10,000 persons. Deaths of persons in these small towns are, as we have noted, conventionally recorded as urban deaths, but from the standpoint of medical resources these towns are far more like strictly rural communities than like cities. Their hospitals and doctors and nurses and health departments, in fact, tend to be the common health resources for town and country alike. The mortality rates of their residents necessarily reflect not only the environmental disadvantages of such places, noted previously, but also the inadequate preventive, diagnostic, and therapeutic services which they share with surrounding rural people.

Proper perspective on causes of death in rural and urban sections must first stress that by and large the main mortality burden is quite similar. Diseases of the heart and cancer are the two leading causes of death in communities of all sizes. The other principal degenerative diseases, intracranial lesions and nephritis, are likewise of greater rural importance than the other causes of death, just as they are of greater urban importance. In fact, the ten or fifteen main killers of rural people are about the same as the main killers of urban people. It is chiefly by comparing actual rates or age-adjusted rates for each cause separately that we can discern a slightly but significantly different pattern in the relative magnitude of the disease problems.

There are pitfalls in any attempt to make an analysis of this kind. Even a comprehensive analysis, using all available knowledge, would entail some speculation. The under-registration of rural deaths — where the family may have a quiet burial on the farm with-

[16] U. S. Census, "Mortality Summary for Registration States: All Causes of Death," p. 11.

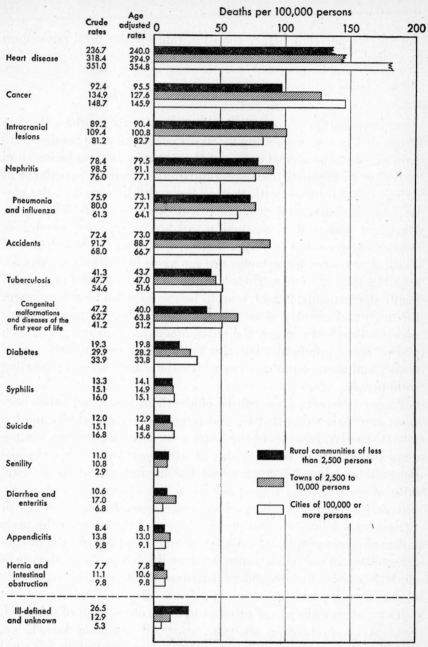

	Crude rates	Age adjusted rates
Heart disease	236.7 318.4 351.0	240.0 294.9 354.8
Cancer	92.4 134.9 148.7	95.5 127.6 145.9
Intracranial lesions	89.2 109.4 81.2	90.4 100.8 82.7
Nephritis	78.4 98.5 76.0	79.5 91.1 77.1
Pneumonia and influenza	75.9 80.0 61.3	73.1 77.1 64.1
Accidents	72.4 91.7 68.0	73.0 88.7 66.7
Tuberculosis	41.3 47.7 54.6	43.7 47.0 51.6
Congenital malformations and diseases of the first year of life	47.2 62.7 41.2	40.0 63.8 51.2
Diabetes	19.3 29.9 33.9	19.8 28.2 33.8
Syphilis	13.3 15.1 16.0	14.1 14.9 15.1
Suicide	12.0 15.1 16.8	12.9 14.8 15.6
Senility	11.0 10.8 2.9	
Diarrhea and enteritis	10.6 17.0 6.8	
Appendicitis	8.4 13.8 9.8	8.1 13.0 9.1
Hernia and intestinal obstruction	7.7 11.1 9.8	7.8 10.6 9.8
Ill-defined and unknown	26.5 12.9 5.3	

Deaths per 100,000 persons

Legend:
- Rural communities of less than 2,500 persons
- Towns of 2,500 to 10,000 persons
- Cities of 100,000 or more persons

FIG. 6. Principal Causes of Death: Death rates for the 15 most common causes of death for rural communities and corresponding rates for small towns and large cities, 1940. Source: United States Bureau of the Census. "Mortality Summary for Registration States," *Vital Statistics — Special Reports,* 16:29-221, July 16-October 12, 1942.

out benefit of legal sanction — introduces, as we have seen, as much as a 10 per cent error. The generally lower diagnostic acumen of rural physicians, as revealed in the relatively high rate of "ill-defined and unknown" causes of death, is a further limitation on comparative analysis.

It is of interest to note at the outset that the differential in age-specific death rates between rural communities and large cities in a sense reflects the differentials found to prevail by examination of the actual causes of death. Thus the degenerative diseases as a group, taking their toll in the later years of life, tend to have higher mortality rates in the cities where we have noted general death rates in the older age groups to be higher than rural rates. On the other hand, the infectious and more or less preventable causes of death, taking larger tolls during the younger years, tend to have higher mortality rates in the small towns and rural areas, where we have noted general death rates in the younger age groups to be higher as a rule than the rates found in large cities.

For heart disease, the age-adjusted rural death rate is far below the big-city rate, and the small-town rate is intermediary. While the problem of heart disease is complex and must be considered in relation to its different causes, it seems fair to assume that this differential is due mainly to the oft-described stresses and strains of urban life and occupations. Whatever may be the actual pathogenesis of arteriosclerotic or hypertensive heart disease, the most common types found, there is much evidence to point to a relationship with the nervous strains more typically a part of urban than of rural life.[17]

For other components of the cardiovascular-renal group of diseases — nephritis and intracranial lesions — big-city experience is recorded as slightly lower than rural, with small-town experience somewhat higher than either. While to some extent the higher reported death rate from cerebral accidents in small towns and rural sections may be due to cases with hypertension going undetected (and hence without benefit of a cautious living regime), these differentials

[17] A considerably higher urban death rate from peptic ulcer (8.2 per 100,000 urban and 5.5 rural) offers evidence of other possible consequences of the nervous strains of urban life. U. S. Census, "Mortality Summary for Registration States: Ulcers of Stomach or Duodenum," *Vital Statistics — Special Reports,* 16:126, Sept. 10, 1942.

more likely reflect differences in average accuracy of diagnosis in communities of different sizes. A death diagnosed as due to coronary thrombosis in the city may too readily be recorded on the rural death certificate as due to a "stroke," and a cardiac death is liable to be recorded as nephritis when the urine contains albumen. If we group all cardiovascular-renal deaths, to allow for inaccurate diagnoses within the group, we find the rural rate to be 410 deaths per 100,000, the small-town rate to be 487, and the city rate to be 515.

The causes of an age-adjusted death rate from cancer which is higher in proportion to size of community are not clear, though here again inaccurate diagnosis — without benefit of modern diagnostic equipment in most rural sections — may play a part. It has been claimed that cancer increases with the degree of "civilization." Whether or not this is true, the specific factors involved are not clear. As for the occurrence, rather than mortality, of cancer, it has been found that the rural South has the highest rate, due mainly to a high occurrence of cancer of the skin. Exposure to the sun very likely plays a part in this.[18]

Death rates for pneumonia and influenza in 1940 were higher in rural areas and small towns than in large cities. Exposure to cold weather, meager housing, and poor heating systems probably contribute to this, but deficiencies in medical care are certainly a related factor. It seems clear that modern therapeutic advances against pneumonia reach the rural and small-town patient less often and that hospitalization for the condition, frequently involving long rides over country roads, is less often attempted. Serum therapy for pneumonia in the 1930's was almost unavailable to the average rural pneumonia case; even the sulfa drugs were introduced only after a lag. Between 1930 and 1940, the decade that saw so many advances in the treatment of pneumonia, death rates from pneumonia and influenza — once higher in the cities — reversed their order.[19]

[18] DORN, HAROLD F., "Illness from Cancer in the United States," *Public Health Reports*, 59:97-115, Jan. 28, 1944.

[19] While one factor contributing to this reversal was probably the change to reporting of deaths by place of residence, there seems every likelihood that the major factor was the prior and more intensive application of new techniques of therapy in the cities. (Deaths attributed to "influenza" are actually so generally due to a complicating bacterial infection of the lungs that it is proper to consider them along with frank pneumonias, as amenable to the

It may be surprising that deaths due to accidents are more frequent in rural areas and small towns than in large cities, despite the urban character of our machine culture. The point is that the most frequent types of rural as well as urban accidental deaths are those occurring from accidents in the home, rather than at the job or on the street.

Even with respect to occupational accidents, moreover, rural rates are high; work accidents in agricultural employment killed 54 per 100,000 in 1943 compared with 20 per 100,000 in manufacturing. The highest occupational death rate from accidents is found in mining and petroleum industries, 211 per 100,000, and workers in these fields are predominantly rural residents. Even motor vehicle death rates are higher among rural people. In all, there were in 1943, for example, 17,200 accidental deaths among members of farm families of which 7,500 occurred in the home, 4,500 while at work, 3,700 due to motor vehicles, and 1,500 in other public places.[20] It is evident that rural life is far more hazardous than it appears. The farm house with the broken front stoop, the unguarded threshing machine, the shaky car speeding along a country road, the kerosene lantern in a barn filled with dry hay, do not spell safety.[20a]

The major chronic infectious diseases in the United States, tuberculosis and syphilis, cause higher death rates in the large cities than in the small towns or rural areas. Considering the element of exposure in the spread of these diseases associated with population congestion and epidemiological contacts, however, the surprise is that the differentials are not greater. The diagnostic problem with respect to attributing a death to syphilis, moreover, may conceal more rural than urban cases.

While the rural death rate from tuberculosis is lower than the urban, it is important to recognize that over the years the rural

newer forms of therapy.) U. S. Census, *Mortality Statistics*, 1930-36. Also U. S. Census, *Vital Statistics of the United States*, 1937-42. Part 2, *Natality and Mortality Data for the United States Tabulated by Place of Residence.* Washington: Government Printing Office, 1937-42.

[20] National Safety Council, *Accident Facts*, 1944. Chicago, pp. 50-51.

[20a] For a clinical discussion of serious farm accidents, see YOUNG, H. HERMAN, and RALPH K. GHORMLEY, "Accidents on the Farm," *Journal of the American Medical Association*, 132:768-771, Nov. 30, 1946.

improvement has on the whole been much less impressive. Thus in 1890 the urban death rate from tuberculosis was over 60 per cent higher than the rural rate in the registration states, in 1910 it was 45 per cent higher, in 1920 only 5 per cent higher, and by 1930 the urban rate as reported had actually become 5 per cent lower than the rural.[21] These rural-urban trends are somewhat distorted by the fact that during this period deaths were being recorded not by place of residence but by place of occurrence, which was increasingly becoming the tuberculosis sanatorium in a country district. Yet this certainly cannot account for the entire direction of the trends. In 1940, when deaths were for the first time recorded by place of residence, the urban rate is found to be higher than the rural, though clearly less so than at the turn of the century, when death records by place of occurrence probably give a valid rural-urban comparison — since tuberculosis sanatoria had hardly come into widespread use.

The application of new techniques of mass diagnosis in the cities, with treatment of cases, may eventually create a situation where tuberculosis, like typhoid fever, will be predominantly a rural affliction. In fact, considering the weight of tuberculosis in the total toll of deaths, we find that in 1940 it accounted for 4.8 per cent of big-city mortality and almost as much, or 4.2 per cent, of rural mortality.[22] If we consider women alone, we find that in 1940 their death rates from tuberculosis in the small towns and rural areas were 39.7 and 37.5 per 100,000, respectively, compared with 39.1 in cities of over 100,000 and only 34.2 in cities of 10,000 to 100,000.[23] Tuberculosis deaths among white women, of all age groups over 25 years, show a striking and consistent increase with decreasing size of community.[24]

Diabetes death rates are clearly higher in urban centers. While this again may have a diagnostic component, it is most likely related to

[21] MUSTARD, HARRY S., *Rural Health Practice*. New York: The Commonwealth Fund, 1936, p. 481.

[22] U. S. Census, "Mortality Summary for Registration States: Tuberculosis (All Forms)," *Vital Statistics — Special Reports*, 16:29, July 16, 1942.

[23] U. S. Census, *Vital Statistics Rates in the United States*, 1900-1940. Washington: Government Printing Office, 1943, pp. 534-553.

[24] YERUSHALMY, JACOB, and CHARLOTTE SILVERMAN, "Tuberculosis Mortality in Communities of Different Size," *American Review of Tuberculosis*, 51:413-431, May, 1945.

the more prevalent obesity in the cities associated with higher incomes and a more sedentary life.[24a]

Deaths due to hernia and intestinal obstruction, and also those due to appendicitis, are most frequent in the small towns, while they are slightly lower in the strictly rural areas than in the large cities. These conditions are, of course, treated mainly by surgical intervention and, in view of lower rates of surgical operations among open-country people, it is difficult to explain the relationship. Some might speculate that the farmer is less subject to being stricken by appendicitis or intestinal obstruction or that the higher urban tolls represent excessive surgical interference and, in the small towns, a generally poorer quality of surgical work. Any analysis is certainly complicated by the fact that between 1900 and 1940 over-all death rates from appendicitis have not declined, but with urbanization and despite advances in surgery, have risen from 8.8 per 100,000 to 9.9.[25]

Many pages have been written on the relation of suicide to urbanization. Suffice it to say here that the higher rate in relation to size of community may simply reflect the more complex social and incomes and a more sedentary life.[24a]

For the remaining diagnoses among the fifteen principal causes of death, big-city death rates are lower than either rural or small-town rates or both. For deaths due to congenital malformations and diseases peculiar to the first year of life (not to be confused with "infant mortality," to be discussed), small-town experience is highest, while the reported rural rate is lower than that for cities. Birth rates are not involved since the computed death rates are age-adjusted to a common standard. In fact, when the actual non-age-adjusted rates from this cause are considered, the death rate in rural areas is 47.2 per 100,000 persons compared with 41.2 in large cities.

Deaths due to diarrhea and enteritis, occurring mainly in the earliest years of life, are significantly higher in both rural areas and small towns than in large cities. The relationship of these conditions to improper environmental sanitation needs only to be mentioned.

[24a] DUBLIN, LOUIS I., and ALFRED J. LOTKA, *Twenty-five Years of Health Progress.* New York: Metropolitan Life Insurance Company, 1937, pp. 319-342.

[25] U. S. Census, "Mortality Summary for Registration States: Appendicitis," *Vital Statistics — Special Reports,* 16:133, Sept. 12, 1942.

Finally, it is highly significant that death rates recorded as due to "senility" and rates from ill-defined and unknown causes are considerably higher in rural areas and small towns than in large cities. For every death in cities of 100,000 or over attributed to the ambiguous catch-all of "senility," there are four so recorded in rural areas, and for every big-city death signed out as due to an ill-defined or unknown cause, there are five in rural areas. This reflection of careless or even missing diagnosis is due not only to a generally inferior quality of medicine in most rural sections but also to the fact that a large number of rural deaths are completely unattended by a physician, with the death certificate filled out by a local lay registrar and countersigned later by a health official who never saw the patient.

With relation to the general picture of mortality in the last several decades, there can be no doubt that the pattern in the nation as a whole is changing markedly. As the infectious diseases have gradually come to be conquered, the degenerative disease group — the cardiovascular-renal diseases and malignant tumors — have acquired increased importance. In 1940, in fact, only 1 death in 22 was due to those preventable diseases which are traditionally regarded as a public health responsibility.[26] This general situation holds in rural areas as well as urban, so that we are forced to the conclusion that the preventive medicine of the future must be directed increasingly against this noninfectious disease group. Since our methods of environmental control over these major maladies are as yet limited, the primary efforts at control must be through early diagnosis and prompt treatment. In other words, the progress of preventive medicine in the future will rest in large measure upon a basis of adequate medical care for the general population.

Relative to urban experience, however, the change in the disease picture over the years has significantly been less striking in the country and small towns. In such places deaths today are closer to the general pattern of deaths in the nation as a whole a half-century ago than are city deaths. Taking the main degenerative causes of death together (cardiovascular-renal disease, cancer, diabetes, and senility), we find the rural and small-town death rates to be 536.2 and 653.4 per 100,000, respectively, compared with 697.2 for the

[26] FALK, I. S., "Unmet Health Needs," *American Journal of Public Health*, 34:1223-1230, December, 1944.

big cities. For all the remaining conditions among the first fifteen causes of rural death, however, the rural and small-town rates are 283.3 and 346.9 per 100,000, respectively, compared with 290.0 in the big cities. It would seem evident that much as the rural areas and semirural towns are in need of improved facilities and personnel for medical care, their deficiencies in public health and preventive services — in relation to big-city resources — are even greater.[27]

Preventable Deaths

Other reflections of the relatively large preventable component in the rural mortality picture are found among several diseases not among the first fifteen causes of death. We have considered deaths from tuberculosis, syphilis, pneumonia, diarrhea, enteritis, and accidents. Beyond these are a number of infectious or nutritional diseases for which death rates are not high but which are, in a real sense, inexcusable in this day and age because they are readily preventable by the application of known techniques.

Thus, typhoid and paratyphoid fevers have been almost eradicated in large cities, where the death rate in 1940 was 0.4 per 100,000; in rural areas and small towns the death rates were 1.5 and 1.7 per 100,000, respectively, or about four times as high. Malaria in the large cities kills only 0.2 per 100,000 by death records, but in rural districts the death rate is 1.9. Diphtheria kills only 0.5 per 100,000 in the large cities, compared with 1.5 in rural sections. Pellagra is typically rural in its occurrence, with a death rate of 0.5 per 100,000 in the large cities and 2.4, or nearly five times as high, in the rural sections.[28]

The important infectious diseases of childhood take higher tolls in rural districts, despite fewer means of contact. The measles death rate in large cities is only 0.2 per 100,000 compared with 0.7 and 0.9 in rural areas and small towns, respectively. Scarlet fever kills 0.4 per 100,000 in large cities compared with 0.6 in both rural and small-

[27] For a description of the role of organized public health services in the general reduction of mortality in the United States between 1900 and 1940, see "Who Killed Cock Robin?" editorial, *American Journal of Public Health*, 34:658-659, June, 1944.

[28] U. S. Census, "Mortality Summary for Registration States," *Vital Statistics — Special Reports*, 16:13, 25, 41, 73, July 11, 15, 20, and Aug. 6, 1942.

town sections. Whooping cough has a death rate of 1.0 per 100,000 in the large cities, compared with 3.2 in rural areas.[29]

The critical point is that practically all these deaths are preventable by proper environmental sanitation, immunization, isolation of cases, or improved nutrition. Even after these diseases are contracted, fatalities can ordinarily be averted by proper medical care. Of course, noncommunicable disease deaths of many kinds are also preventable or postponable by the application of medical science. It has been computed that in North Carolina, for example, 16,600 lives could be saved each year if the age-specific death rate for each age group were as low as that in the state with the best record.[30] Over 50 per cent of North Carolina's deaths in 1940 could have been prevented under such circumstances, and a corresponding "saving" of lives would, of course, apply to all the states.

Many of these preventable diseases and preventable deaths are becoming so rare in urban centers and, with several other uncommon afflictions, are becoming so characteristically associated with rural life that today they may almost be regarded as "rural diseases." It will be helpful to review these later in some detail, but before discussing morbidity we must consider a final important group of deaths that are largely preventable: the mortality of infants and of mothers in connection with childbirth.

Infant and Maternal Mortality

In the continuing offensive against disease and premature death, one of the most dramatic advances has been in the field of infant hygiene. In 1915 there were 100 deaths among infants under 1 year of age for every 1,000 live births. By 1940 the figure had been cut to 47. The rate has continued to decline — to 45.3 in 1941, to 40.4 in both 1942 and 1943,[31] and down to 38.3 in 1945 — quite a remarkable accomplishment during a war period.[32] The stillbirth rate has

[29] *Ibid.*, pp. 17, 21, 49, July 13, 14, and 22, 1942.

[30] MAYO, SELZ C., *Preventable Deaths in North Carolina*. Raleigh: North Carolina Agricultural Experiment Station (Prog. Rep. RS-6), September 1945, Processed, p. 3.

[31] U. S. Census, "United States Summary of Vital Statistics, 1943," *Vital Statistics — Special Reports*, 22:5, Feb. 28, 1945.

[32] U. S. Census, "Infant Mortality by Race and by Urban and Rural Areas, United States, Each Division and State, 1945," *Vital Statistics — Special Reports*, 27:53, Aug. 19, 1947.

also been declining, reaching 28.2 per 1,000 live births in 1942, compared with 31.3 in 1940, 35.8 in 1935, and 39.2 in 1930. Throughout these years, however, the rate of rural decline in infant deaths has been definitely slower than the rate of urban decline. In 1915, urban infant mortality was clearly in excess of rural. As both rates declined, the rural more slowly than the urban, the differential gradually lessened so that in 1928 the rates became reversed[33] and the rural rate became higher, where it remains today.[34]

Public health workers look on infant mortality as a highly sensitive measure of general welfare as well as a significant index of accomplishments in the health field. The dramatic reduction in infant deaths in recent years has been the direct result of the application of expanding knowledge in preventive and therapeutic medicine and the control of man's environment. The picture, however, is not wholly bright by any means. Infants born in rural New Mexico, for example, had less chance of survival in 1942 than infants in the nation as a whole had in 1915, when 1 of every 10 died. In rural areas 9 more babies out of every 1,000 died than among those from large cities.[35]

In most countries infant mortality is lowest or fast becoming so in the larger urban centers, where modern facilities for good obstetrical care and hospitalization are within reach of those who can afford to pay for them and free clinics are available to others.[36] In the United States the lowest infant mortality rate by size of community in 1942 was the rate of 34.3 for cities of 100,000 or more. The highest rate, 44.6 deaths for every 1,000 infants born alive, was that for towns of 2,500 to 10,000; almost as high was the 43.3 rural infant mortality rate.[37] If there were complete registration of both births and infant

[33] It is noteworthy that this reversal in rates came about when deaths were still being recorded by place of occurrence — tending to understate the rural rate — and twelve years before they came to be recorded by place of residence. Before 1930, it is to be recalled, "rural" was defined as places with population under 10,000.

[34] U. S. Children's Bureau data presented in WORKS, GEORGE A., and SIMON O. LESSER, *Rural America Today, Its Schools and Community Life.* Chicago: University of Chicago Press, 1942, p. 193.

[35] U. S. Census, "Infant Deaths and Death Rates, United States, 1942," *Vital Statistics — Special Reports,* 19:16, Jan. 7, 1944.

[36] Special Committee on Social Security (Canada), *op. cit.,* p. 233.

[37] U. S. Census, "Infant Deaths and Death Rates, United States, 1942."

deaths in rural areas, the rural rate, as the Census points out, might exceed that for small towns.[38] One price of today's rural and small-town inadequacies is the loss of thousands of babies who have the bad luck not to be born in large cities.

Babies born in some rural areas, nevertheless, have an excellent chance of survival. There are striking differences betwen states in this respect, as illustrated by Figure 7. The lowest rural infant mortality rates in 1942 — a challenge to the whole nation — were in Connecticut and Minnesota, 26.7 and 27.1 per 1,000 live births, respectively, with Iowa the third state with a rate under 30.[39] Moreover, 11 other states had rural rates lower than the nation-wide rate for large cities, and a total of 25 states had rural rates lower than the national infant mortality rate of 40.4. But 14 states had rural rates between 40.4 and 50, 7 were between 50 and 60, and Arizona and New Mexico had deplorable rural rates of 90.4 and 111.2, respectively. The states with the worst records are found largely among the Southern and Mountain states. Of the 50,716 babies under 1 year of age who died in rural America in 1942, almost 20,000 would have been saved if the rural infant mortality rate had been as low as the rates for rural Connecticut and rural Minnesota. Only two Southern states had rural rates lower than the national average — Arkansas and Oklahoma — although the greatest relative reduction in infant mortality in recent years has been in the South.

Negro infant mortality rates are a large factor in the general rural record, due mostly to conditions in the South. While Negro infant deaths fell sharply from 180.6 for every 1,000 live births in 1915 [40] to a rate of 64.2 in 1942, the 1942 rate was still 72 per cent higher than the rate for white infants. In Maryland, Virginia, and South Carolina the infant mortality rates among Negroes were more than double the rate for white infants for the nation as a whole.[41] The stillbirth rate for Negro infants in 1942, moreover, was 50.5 per 1,000 live births, a rate double the white infants' rate of 25.5 despite the especially incomplete reporting in the case of Negroes.[42]

[38] U. S. Census, *United States Abridged Life Tables,* 1939, p. 6.

[39] U. S. Census, "Infant Deaths and Death Rates, United States, 1942."

[40] U. S. Census, "A Review of Vital Statistics, United States, 1941," *Vital Statistics — Special Reports,* 17:539, Aug. 6, 1943.

[41] U. S. Census, "Infant Deaths and Death Rates, United States, 1942," p. 14.

[42] U. S. Census, "United States Summary of Vital Statistics, 1942," *Vital Statistics — Special Reports,* 20:8, Jan. 8, 1944.

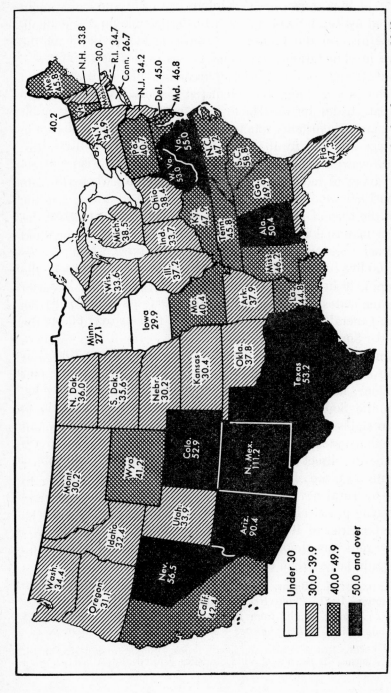

FIG. 7. Rural Infant Mortality: Number of rural deaths under 1 year per 1,000 live births, by states, 1942. Source: U. S. Bureau of the Census, "Infant Deaths and Death Rates, United States, 1942," *Vital Statistics — Special Reports*, 19:16, January 7, 1944.

The most important causes of infant deaths are premature birth, congenital malformations, injury at birth, pneumonia and influenza, and enteritis. All the prenatal, obstetrical, and pediatric services effective in eliminating these chief causes of deaths in infants are provided far less in rural districts than in most of our cities.

Turning to a consideration of maternal mortality, we again find that great strides forward have been made in recent years. The lowest maternal mortality rate recorded up to that time in the United States was attained in 1942 — 25.9 deaths per 10,000 live births. This rate was 62 per cent lower than in 1930, and it is equivalent to the saving of more than 11,600 lives annually when compared with the 1930 rate.[43]

As in the case of infant mortality, however, there are great variations in maternal mortality between regions, states, communities of different sizes, and races. In 1942 the rates ranged from 7 deaths per 10,000 live births in Nevada, and 12 in New Hampshire, to 44 in Mississippi, 48 in New Mexico, and 53 in South Carolina.[44] Each of these three states with the highest death rates is over 65 per cent rural. In general the highest rates were in regions over 60 per cent rural — the South and the Southwest.

The maternal mortality among Negroes was 55 per 10,000 live births in 1942, a rate 2½ times the rate of 22 for whites. The racial factor alone, however, was not responsible for the generally high rates in the South. The maternal death rates for whites in the Southern states were substantially higher than corresponding rates for the other states.[45]

Considering direct rural-urban comparisons, in 1941 the maternal death rate by place of residence was highest — 35.1 per 10,000 live births — for rural territory, with the 34.8 rate for towns of 2,500 to 10,000 being practically as high. The "total urban" rate was 29, and the rate for cities of 100,000 or more was 26.4.[46] Thus the maternal mortality rate was almost one-third higher in rural communities in 1941 than in large urban centers.

[43] YERUSHALMY, J., "Births, Infant Mortality, and Maternal Mortality in the United States — 1942," *Public Health Reports*, 59:797-804, June 23, 1944.

[44] U. S. Census, "Deaths from Puerperal Causes by Race and by State, United States, 1942," *Vital Statistics — Special Reports*, 19:65, Mar. 6, 1944.

[45] *Ibid.*

[46] U. S. Census, "A Review of Vital Statistics, United States, 1941."

Of the deaths associated with pregnancy and childbirth 9 out of every 10 are due to septicemia, toxemia, or the group of conditions comprising hemorrhage, trauma, or shock[47] — all largely controllable. Maternal mortality may be influenced directly, almost mathematically, by thorough prenatal care, hospitalization in an up-to-date facility, and competent medical attendance during and after childbirth. Some of our large cities are showing what can be done. Bearing in mind South Carolina's maternal death rate of 53.0 per 10,000 live births, we may note the remarkable rates of 3.0 and 4.0 deaths per 10,000 live births in Portland, Oregon, and in Albany, New York, respectively.[48] One wonders how long we will tolerate such contrasts within our borders.[49]

Mortality and Economic Status

Some of the factors accounting for differentials in mortality rates operate not only between rural and urban areas but also within rural areas themselves. The most important of these is probably economic status.

The general relationship between income level and death rates is well-known; the poor die at greater rates than the well-to-do. As one might expect, the differentials are most striking for those diseases amenable to control by medical and sanitary science, that is, chiefly the infectious disease group.[50] The relationship holds true in rural areas, as elsewhere.

Data on the question are actually sparse, but one detailed study of rural death rates in Ohio, classified according to the prosperity of the county of residence, showed that the rural residents of poor economic areas had a standardized death rate about 10 per cent higher than that of residents of prosperous economic areas.[51] The difference was referable chiefly to deaths in the younger and middle-

---

[47] YERUSHALMY, op. cit., p. 807.

[48] U. S. Census, "Deaths from Puerperal Causes by Race and by State, United States,1942," p. 66.

[49] For a general discussion, see GOOCH, MARJORIE, "Maternal and Infant Mortality in the United States, 1942," The Child, 8:179-185, June, 1944.

[50] COOMBS, L. C., "Economic Differentials in Causes of Death," Medical Care, 1:246-255, July, 1941.

[51] DORN, HAROLD F., "Mortality Rates and Economic Status in Rural Areas," Public Health Reports, 55:3-12, Jan. 5, 1940.

age groups and deaths due to medically manageable diseases. Thus
for the communicable diseases of childhood, death rates were two to
three times higher in the depressed areas. Infant mortality, the social
index par excellence, was 75 per 1,000 live births in the poor economic areas as against 52 per 1,000 live births in the good economic
areas. For tuberculosis, diarrhea and enteritis, accidents, and pneumonia and influenza, corresponding though smaller differences were
found.

After age 55, however, it is surprising to learn that in this study
death rates were reported as slightly higher in the more prosperous
rural areas. It is in this age group, of course, that the degenerative
diseases less responsive to prevention and therapy take their toll.
Accordingly death rates from cancer and from the cardiovascular-
renal group of diseases were found higher in the better economic
areas. One may hazard a guess that some of this presumable advantage of lower income areas is only apparent and referable perhaps to
poor reporting of deaths as well as faulty diagnosis. Perhaps more
obesity in the prosperous sections contributes to a higher occurrence
of the degenerative diseases of later life. If, as has been suggested,
the preservation of the "unfit" in early life, through medical and
public health science, leads to a weaker stock in later years among
the more well-to-do, the thesis is certainly without any direct scientific evidence.

The implications of rural mortality rates by economic status in
relation to other sociological factors like rural occupational status
(farm owner, farm laborer, rural storekeeper, and so on), race, and
region are obvious. One would expect to find higher age-adjusted
mortality rates at the lower rungs of the agricultural ladder, among
Negroes and Spanish-Americans and Indians, and in generally depressed rural areas like the cotton South, the cutover regions of
northern Michigan, or arid sections of the Southwest. We have seen,
for example, that the rural infant mortality rate in New Mexico was
111.2 per 1,000 live births in 1942, while the corresponding rural
rate was 26.7 in Connecticut, a state with more than double the per
capita income, with relatively prosperous rural enterprises, and
with fewer members of economically depressed racial groups. For
the 14 Southern states, general death rates are higher than the
national average at all ages up to 55 years, after which the lower
rural mortality from cardiovascular disease seems to account for an

apparent Southern advantage.[52] But poverty in the rural areas actually exerts its ill effects less impressively through deaths than it does through the tedious burden of illness and physical impairment.

[52] ROEMER, MILTON I., "Present-day Levels of Health in the South," Hearings before Special Subcommittee on Cotton of the Committee on Agriculture, House of Representatives, 80th Cong., 1st Sess., *Study of Agricultural and Economic Problems of the Cotton Belt,* Washington: Government Printing Office, 1947, pp. 812-817.

CHAPTER 5

THE BURDEN OF SICKNESS

T HE NEED for health services cannot, of course, be measured by deaths alone. It was long ago pointed out that the causes of death, which we have discussed, give very little reflection of the main causes of illness and disability.[1] To obtain a better idea of the need for medical and related services among rural people, it is necessary to explore the amount and kind of illness that strikes them as well as the extent of physical defects and impairments with which they are burdened.

The Volume of Illness

The number and duration of illnesses afflicting a population group are actually quite difficult to measure. The old family doctor who served the members of a family through one or two generations may have been able to give some notion of the burden of illness in the family, or at least that share of it which he was called on to handle. To develop accurate statistical data on illness, however, suitable for comparison of the experience of different income groups, for example, or of rural and urban areas, ordinarily requires detailed house-to-house surveys and skillful questions. Definition of what constitutes illness must be crystal-clear, and the frailties of human judgment, memory, and expression must be taken into careful account. Despite these difficulties certain studies of the incidence of illness have been made. Most of these have been urban studies, however, and it must be acknowledged that rural data are relatively sparse — a reflection perhaps of lack of sufficient concern for the problems of rural health.

During the period 1928 to 1931, the Committee on the Costs of Medical Care undertook a study of illnesses in communities of different sizes. Illness was defined as any symptom, disorder, or affection which persisted for one or more days, or for which medical

[1] McKENZIE, SIR JAMES, *The Future of Medicine*. London: Oxford Medical Publications, 1919.

74

service was received (exclusive of dental service, eye refractions, immunizations, or routine physical examinations), or medicine costing at least 50 cents was purchased. Under this definition it is evident that many minor conditions such as upper respiratory tract infections, small injuries, or digestive upsets would go unrecorded. The data were gathered by making periodic visits to certain households every two to four months for one year and recording the family's testimony of illnesses, given usually by the housewife. While this method was intended to minimize errors caused by poor memory of minor ailments, it is apparent from the results that many small but economically important illnesses must have gone unreported.

The Committee found that in cities of 100,000 or over there occurred 790 cases of illness annually per 1,000 persons (age-adjusted); in places of 5,000 to 100,000 there were 830 such cases; and in small towns of less than 5,000 and rural areas there were likewise 830 illnesses per 1,000 persons per year.[2] The average duration of these illnesses was not tabulated by size of community, but the average annual number of days in bed on account of illness for persons in cities of over 100,000 was 4.0 days, in places of 5,000 to 100,000, 3.2 days, and in small towns of 5,000 or less and rural areas, 3.1 days.[3] This suggests that rural people are ill about as often as residents of medium-sized cities and more often than residents of big cities, but that when they get sick they tend to stay in bed for shorter periods of time, perhaps because of fewer instructions from physicians and because of the insistent day-to-day demands of farming, the predominant rural occupation.

Further analysis of a somewhat different sample of these data of the Committee on the Costs of Medical Care, in which the illness rates are broken down to distinguish residents of small towns and villages of under 5,000 population from persons living in the open country, might lead one to believe that the farmer is the healthiest citizen of all. Such analysis yields an age-adjusted annual rate of 937 illnesses per 1,000 persons in small rural and semirural towns

[2] FALK, I. S., MARGARET C. KLEM, and NATHAN SINAI, *The Incidence of Illness and the Receipt and Costs of Medical Care among Representative Families* (Publication of the Committee on the Costs of Medical Care No. 26). Chicago: University of Chicago Press, 1933, p. 265.

[3] *Ibid.*, p. 276.

under 5,000 population — the highest rate of all — in comparison with 909 cases in places of 5,000 to 100,000, 803 cases in cities of over 100,000, and 771 cases — the lowest rate of all — in the open country. For disabling illnesses severe enough to keep the individual from his usual occupation or from school, corresponding age-adjusted rates were found to be 502 cases per 1,000 persons per year in cities of over 100,000 population, 578 such cases in places of 5,000 to 100,000, 578 cases likewise for towns of under 5,000, and 467 disabling cases in the open country.[4]

Thus these data show a wide variation between the illness rates in small towns and those in unincorporated territory. In the predominantly rural incorporated towns of under 5,000 (their 1930 population 66 per cent in places under 2,500) the illness rate was the highest found and the rate for disabling illness was not exceeded in places of any other size. On the other hand, the rates for predominantly "open country" people were reported as the lowest of all.

There are several factors, however, that cast grave doubt on the validity of findings so much at variance with numerous other findings relating to ill-health in the farm population. Since the field studies were made almost entirely by public health nurses, the areas coming under study were generally those with organized health departments. And since the most prosperous rural sections tended to be served by health departments more than the depressed sections (even more the case 15 years ago than now), one may suspect that more prosperous country districts, where illness is probably less, weighed heavily in the sample under investigation. Moreover, the sample studied included relatively few open country residents; it under-represented certain regions, notably the South where rural health needs are probably greatest; and it excluded all except white families.[5]

Beyond these facts are reasons for suspecting significant under-reporting of illnesses by farm families in any section. In contrast to the worker in the industrialized city, the memory of the farmer or his wife for illness is not fortified by the clear-cut experience of work time or wages lost and less often fortified, for that matter, by the

[4] Dorn, Harold F., "The Relative Amount of Ill Health in Rural and Urban Communities," *Public Health Reports,* 53:1181-1195, July 15, 1938.
[5] *Ibid.*

memory of a doctor's care. The lower general educational level of farm people, moreover, tends to make them less health conscious, less likely to recognize the signs of illness. Furthermore, there are daily chores on a farm that must be done rain or shine, and there are critical seasons when the whole year's livelihood is at stake. Thus farm people often simply cannot take time off to be sick and they are apt to ignore all but serious illness. Finally, the somewhat stoical psychology of farm people, discussed previously, creates an attitude which would minimize their statement of complaints in the course of any canvassing of illness.

There are presumptive reasons, in fact, for expecting that among all rural people as a group the volume of illness would be at least as high if not higher than among urban. Entirely aside from the lack of medical and sanitation resources, demographic factors like the age distribution, the birth rate, the racial composition, and the income levels of rural people are such as to suggest theoretically a higher volume of illness and disability.

Thus we have noted that the rural areas have a much higher percentage of children than the cities, a considerably lower percentage of middle-aged adults, and a slightly higher percentage of aged persons. The incidence of illness, according to the Committee on the Costs of Medical Care, is surprisingly parallel, as indicated in Figure 8, to the curve of age distribution in rural areas. It is among small children and very aged persons that illness strikes most often, and it is just these groups that predominate in rural areas, while the middle-aged group in which illness strikes least often is found in smallest proportion in the rural sections. The Committee on the Costs of Medical Care data cited above are "age-adjusted" to a common national population standard, so that these actual features of the rural health problem have been, somewhat unrealistically, eliminated.

The higher birth rate in rural areas would contribute toward a higher incidence of illness, not because pregnancy is an illness but because it does represent a physiological hazard with many potential complications or sequelae in later years. In any event, high pregnancy rates obviously imply greater needs for medical care despite the smaller percentage of women in rural areas. As for race, there are many indications of a higher incidence of illness

among Negroes,[6] albeit for environmental or economic reasons. As
we have noted, the rural population contains 11.4 per cent Negroes
while the urban population is only 8.4 per cent colored.

Finally, the basic fact of rural poverty would *ipso facto* suggest
a higher incidence of rural illness than urban. We have observed the

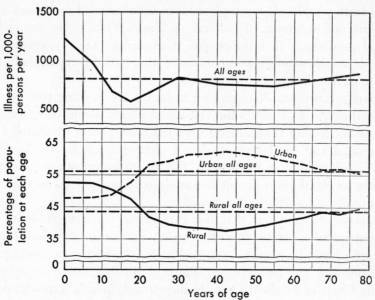

Fig. 8.   Illness and Age: Frequency of illnesses at each age in the general
population and percentage of total population in each age group in rural and
urban areas. Source: Illness curve from Falk, I. S., Margaret C. Klem, and
Nathan Sinai, *The Incidence of Illness and the Receipt and Costs of Medical
Care Among Representative Families*. Chicago: University of Chicago Press,
1933, p. 264. Age curves from U. S. Bureau of the Census, Sixteenth Census,
1940, *Population*. Vol. 4, *Characteristics by Age*.

generally much lower income level in the rural sections than in the
cities. The most extensive study of illness ever made in the United
States discloses that both the frequency and duration of illness bear
a striking relation to income. As one considers illnesses of greater
severity, the relationships become more striking. Thus in the National
Health Survey of 1935-36 the frequency of illnesses disabling for
seven days or more followed this relation to annual family income:
$3,000 and over, 146 cases per 1,000 persons per year; $2,000 to

[6] DUBLIN, L. I., *The Health of the Negro*. New York: Metropolitan Life
Insurance Co., 1937.

$3,000, 145.9 cases; $1,000 to $2,000, 152.3 cases; under $1,000, 180.3 cases; relief groups, 238.4 cases. In terms of days of disability from such illnesses the corresponding rates per person per year followed the same course in relation to descending incomes: 6.8 days, 6.9 days, 7.5 days, 12.2 days, and 16.2 days, in that order.[7] While this represents an urban study, there is little reason to doubt its general applicability to the nation as a whole, especially in view of comparable findings within rural sections taken alone, to be considered below, and in view of substantial confirmation through parallel findings in other nations over many years.[8] It would seem reasonable to expect rural illness, therefore, to be in excess of urban in both frequency and duration — particularly the latter, in view of poor medical services — if it were accurately measured.

The largest sample of rural families studied in this country was actually in connection with the National Health Survey of 1935-36 in the states of Michigan, Missouri, and Georgia.[9] The study in Georgia was made under instructions and supervision somewhat different from those of the rest of the nation-wide survey, so that its results are not comparable, but the schedules and supervision of the study in representative rural counties of Missouri and Michigan were identical with those of the general urban study. This hitherto unpublished rural study carried out in Michigan and Missouri was, of course, not broadly representative of the whole country as was the urban study. Inasmuch as the South is not represented, however, there is some reason to believe that the rural illness rates presented may actually be unduly favorable. In order to learn what we can from this extensive study of about 86,000 predominantly rural persons, the data, with corresponding urban data, are presented in Table 5.

[7] PERROTT, G. ST. J., and DOROTHY F. HOLLAND, "Health as an Element in Social Security," *The Annals of the American Academy of Political and Social Science,* 202:116-136, March, 1939.

[8] STERN, BERNHARD J., *Society and Medical Progress.* Princeton: Princeton University Press, 1941, pp. 126-141.

[9] This study covered 37,000 households, or about 140,000 persons in these three states. The major urban section of the National Health Survey covered 2,300,000 persons. PERROTT, G. ST. J., CLARK TIBBITTS, and R. H. BRITTEN, "The National Health Survey, Scope and Method of the Nation-wide Canvass of Sickness in Relation to Its Social and Economic Setting," *Public Health Reports,* 54:1663-1687, Sept. 15, 1939.

From these comparisons it appears that rural people, according
to the most conventional definition (residents of towns of under
2,500 population and open country), are probably sick as often or

Table 5. Incidence of Illness: *Frequency of disabling illnesses on day of survey, and
frequency and duration of illnesses causing seven or more days of
disability, in rural and urban communities, 1935–36*

Type or duration of illness	Urban popula-tion (83 cities)	Rural counties in Michigan and Missouri		
		Towns 2,500 to 5,000*	Villages under 2,500 and open country	Open country only
Disabling illness on day of survey (Cases per 1,000)	45	41	49	46
Disabling illness of seven days of more (Cases per 1,000 per year)	171	233	250	246
Disabling acute illness of seven days or more† (Cases per 1,000 per year) . .	124	182	191	189
Disabling chronic illness of seven days or more‡ (Cases per 1,000 per year) .	47	51	59	57
Days of disability per case of illness of seven days of more	57	46§	49§	48§
Days of disability per person from ill-ness of seven days or more . . .	9.8	10.7‖	12.0‖	12.0‖

Source: U. S. Public Health Service, National Institute of Health, "An Estimate of the
Amount of Disabling Illness in the Country as a Whole," *National Health Survey* 1935–36,
Preliminary Reports, Sickness and Medical Care Series, Bull. 1, Washington, 1939; unpublished data from the same source on rural health study of about 86,000 persons in representative counties of Michigan and Missouri.

* One town with a population of 5,120 is included.
† Defined as illness disabling for seven days or more, with total duration of symptoms
less than three months.
‡ Total duration of symptoms three months or more.
§ Based on rural counties of Missouri; Michigan data unavailable.
‖ Based on incidence of illness in all counties and duration of illness in Missouri only.

more often than urban people. With respect to illnesses of a more
serious nature, causing disability for seven days or longer, the disadvantage of rural people as reported is rather striking, with the
rate of such cases being 45 per cent higher than in cities. When this
experience is broken down according to the duration of such ill-

nesses, it is seen that the rural disadvantage is most severe for acute illnesses of over one week but with symptoms lasting less than three months, for which rural experience appears to be over 50 per cent higher than urban. As for days of disability per case of seven-day-or-more illness, rural people appear to have an advantage. This may be due to the fact that the rural county resident is less likely to be "kept disabled" or in bed under the instructions of a physician at home or in the hospital, merely because physicians and hospitals are less available. For average per capita days of disability from seven-day-or-more illness, nevertheless, the general frequency of rural cases reported in this study is so great that we find the rural manpower loss due to illness significantly higher than the urban.

It is rather impressive, in view of the contrary findings of the Committee on the Costs of Medical Care study, that illness rates within the rural counties studied are uniformly higher in the open country than in the small towns of 2,500 to 5,000. This would tend to confirm some of the suspicions expressed about the validity of the rural sample of the Committee on the Costs of Medical Care. The rates for towns of under 2,500 exclusive of open country, not shown in the table, were indeed slightly higher than the rates for open country alone. Nevertheless, the significant point is that open country illness rates alone are still appreciably higher than those for all urban areas combined, contrary to the findings of the Committee on the Costs of Medical Care.

Further evidence suggestive of a greater total burden of disabling illness in rural communities is found by analysis of the findings even among the 83 cities studied in the National Health Survey. When the data for these cities are broken down according to their size, a consistent increase in the annual days of disability per person, from illnesses of a week or more, is found as the size of community decreases. Thus for cities of 500,000 and over, the disability rate is 9.0 days per year; for cities of 100,000 to 500,000, it is 9.7 days; for cities of 25,000 to 100,000, it is 9.8 days; and for cities and towns of under 25,000, it reaches the level of 11.0 days per person per year. This same relationship is found for all regions of the nation except the Northeast, where there is a slight irregularity (and yet with smallest size city rates still exceeding largest size city rates).[10] It may

[10] Unpublished data from the National Health Survey furnished by the U. S. Public Health Service.

be noted in Table 5 that the rate for purely rural communities in Michigan and Missouri was 12.0 days of disability per person per year. While some question has been raised about the reliability of these data by size of community, because of such factors as differences among enumerators in different places,[11] the trend of the rates seems almost unmistakable.

Aside from rural-urban comparisons, a few isolated studies reveal the high burden of illness among the rural population. In 1938 the Standard Umsted Community in Arkansas, for example, was shown to have a burden of illness amounting to between 9.1 and 15.5 days per person per year, depending on the income level.[12] An unpublished study of Farm Security Administration borrower families in Aroostook County, Maine, in 1940 revealed 189 cases of illness of seven days or more per 1,000 persons per year, with an average disability per case of 45 days.[13] Special studies have been made in Missouri, Arkansas, Mississippi, South Carolina, and other states.[14] The study in rural Missouri, for example, found 16 per cent of the population suffering from some chronic illness (not necessarily dis-

[11] There seems to be some evidence that enumerators with lower intelligence quotients reported smaller rates of illness. LIENAU, C. C., "Selection, Training and Performance of the National Health Survey Field Staff," *American Journal of Hygiene*, 34:110-132, July-September-November issue, 1941.

In view of the well-known relation, however, between I.Q. test performance and educational background, there is little reason to expect that such poorer enumerators were to be found more frequently in the large cities than in the smaller-sized communities. The opposite, in fact, seems more likely.

[12] WILSON, ISABELLA C., *Sickness and Medical Care among the Rural Population in a Petroleum-producing Area of Arkansas,* 1938. Fayetteville: University of Arkansas Agricultural Experiment Station (Bull. 413), June, 1941.

[13] STEIN, MARGARET I., *Survey of Health among a Representative Group of FSA Clients in Aroostook County, Maine, by House-to-house Canvass.* Unpublished study, 1940.

[14] See, for example, KAUFMAN, HAROLD F., and WARREN W. MORSE, *Illness in Rural Missouri.* Columbia: University of Missouri Agricultural Experiment Station (Research Bull. 391), August, 1945; ALMACK, R. B., *The Rural Health Facilities of Lewis County, Missouri.* Columbia: University of Missouri Agricultural Experiment Station (Res. Bull. 365), May, 1943; WILSON, I. C., *Sickness and Medical Care among the Negro Population in a Delta Area of Arkansas.* Fayetteville: Arkansas Agricultural Experiment Station (Bull. 372), 1939; WIEHL, DOROTHY, and EDGAR SYDENSTRICKER, "Disabling Sickness in Cotton Mill Communities of South Carolina in 1917," *Public Health Reports,* 39:1417-1443, June 13, 1924.

abling) lasting three months or longer. Although these studies use different definitions and methods, they all tend to reveal a high burden of rural illness.

In 1942-43 in six special prepayment health programs in rural counties sponsored by the United States Department of Agriculture, with a total membership of over 35,000 persons, an annual rate of 1,324 cases of illness per 1,000 persons was recorded.[15] This did not represent the outcome of a house-to-house survey but rather the actual number of cases of illness for which farm people sought medical attention with the financial barrier removed.[16] While this was not necessarily an unselected group (since membership in this program was voluntary and also overrepresented the South), and while not all cases of illness can be expected to reach medical attention even with financial restrictions removed, this method does eliminate the factor of poor memory encountered in the usual incidence of illness studies. The rate yielded on this basis points up the probable understatement in the rural findings of the Committee on the Costs of Medical Care, particularly the rate of 771 illnesses per 1,000 persons per year for open country residents.

Illness Variations within Rural Areas

Within rural areas there are, of course, great differences in the incidence of illness depending on income level and other factors. The rising incidence of illness with lower income, both as to frequency and duration, found to hold for all urban communities in the National Health Survey is characteristic of rural areas also, although certain irregular features occur. In the rural Michigan-Missouri section of the National Health Survey, nonrelief families experienced 44 illnesses per 1,000 on the day of visit and 234 cases of seven-day-or-more illness per 1,000 persons per year; the corresponding rates for families on relief, on the other hand, were 63 illnesses and

[15] Derived from YAUKEY, JESSE B., *Activities of an Experimental Rural Health Program in Six Counties during Its First Fiscal Year, 1942-43.* Washington: Farm Security Administration, March, 1945, Processed, p. 17.

[16] This rate is exclusive of 84 cases per 1,000 representing immunizations or health examinations. Office calls held a ratio to home calls of 12 to 1, so that — by this index of patient "abuse" — unnecessary demand for service was probably negligible.

308 cases, respectively.[17] The relationship of illness to income demonstrated in other rural studies is shown in Figure 9.

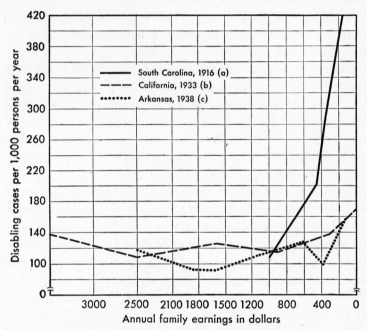

FIG. 9. Illness and Rural Income: Cases of disabling illness per 1,000 persons per year, in relation to family earnings; selected rural studies, 1916, 1933, and 1938. Sources: Adapted from (a) Sydenstricker, Edgar, G. A. Wheeler, and Joseph Goldberger, "Disabling Illness Among the Population of Seven Cotton-mill Villages of South Carolina in Relation to Family Income," *Public Health Reports*, 33.2038-2051, Nov. 22, 1918. (b) Klem, Margaret C., *Medical Care and Costs in California Families in Relation to Economic Status.* San Francisco: State Relief Administration, 1935, Processed. (c) Wilson, Isabella C., *Sickness and Medical Care Among the Rural Population in a Petroleum-Producing Area of Arkansas.* Fayetteville, Arkansas: University of Arkansas Agricultural Experiment Station, June 1941.

It may be surprising that, despite the general correlation between illness and low income, the very lowest incidence is not always recorded for the very highest income rural group, but rather for an income group somewhat short of the top. This may well be because of the likelihood of increased recognition of, and attention toward,

[17] Based on unpublished data from the National Health Survey furnished by the U. S. Public Health Service.

illness among families in the most comfortable circumstances, a factor discernible quite strikingly in other studies.[18] In all these rural studies, however, the highest illness burden is found in the lowest income group. That illness itself is often the cause of low income is well known, although the consensus is that the converse relationship is more significant.[19]

In all income groups, rural as well as urban, the burden of illness — particularly serious disabling disorders — is characterized by its highly uneven incidence. In any one year, a large proportion of rural persons suffer no illness incapacitating the individual for as much as one day. At the same time, an unfortunate minority suffer one or more illnesses confining them to bed for long periods of time. Thus, the Committee on the Costs of Medical Care reported that 68.7 per cent of residents of towns under 5,000 population and rural areas experience no bed-confining illness in the course of a year, while 8.5 per cent experience one or two days of bed illness, 13.9 per cent experience three to eight days of bed illness, 5.9 per cent experience nine to seventeen days, 2.8 per cent experience eighteen to eighty days, and 0.2 per cent are invalided for a period of from eighty days to the entire year.[20] These figures omit consideration of many cases of institutionalized chronic disease which may confine patients to mental or tuberculosis hospitals for more than an entire year. It is obviously impossible to predict at the beginning of a year in which group an individual will fall, though over a large group fairly accurate predictions can be made. The manifest implications

[18] The Committee on the Costs of Medical Care, for example, showed the highest incidence of illness in upper income groups, but the sample of families was so much smaller than that of the National Health Survey and the findings so different from all subsequent studies that authorities feel that the conclusion of the Committee on the Costs of Medical Care on this particular matter may be discounted. With respect to days of disabling illness in gainfully occupied persons, the data of the Committee on the Costs of Medical Care did, in fact, show higher rates in lower income groups. For discussion of the probable fallacies in this study, see HOLLINGSWORTH, HELEN, and MARGARET C. KLEM, *Medical Care and Costs in Relation to Family Income: A Statistical Source Book.* Bureau of Research and Statistics, Social Security Board. Washington: Federal Security Agency (Bur. Mem. 51), March, 1943, pp. 20-21.

[19] COLLINS, SELWYN D., and CLARK TIBBITTS, *Research Memorandum on Social Aspects of Health in the Depression.* New York: Social Science Research Council (Bull. 36), 1937, pp. 1-2.

[20] FALK, KLEM, and SINAI, *op. cit.,* p. 277.

of this in terms of the cost of purchasing medical services will be explored in detail in a later chapter.

Whether the degree of unevenness in the incidence of illness is greater in rural than in urban sections and whether it is more exaggerated in low- than in high-income rural groups is not clear. Consideration later of actual expenditures for health services, however, suggests that both these relationships hold true.

All these estimations of over-all morbidity probably fall short of defining the real extent of the problem. Consideration of the simple fact, for example, that residents of the United States are estimated to be afflicted with from one to five cases of the common cold alone each year (with a probable average of about three)[21] casts serious doubt on any report for *total* illnesses suggesting only about one case per person per year or less. Yet most of the studies we have considered have actually yielded rates of only this order of magnitude.

Beyond this, thousands of rural people, particularly in the South, are afflicted with certain chronic, enfeebling diseases like hookworm infestation, malaria, or pellagra, of which they may be quite unaware, considering their usual state of ill-being as normal and natural. This is not to mention the myriad functional and ill-defined ailments burdening rural and urban people alike. Obviously only the performance of systematic medical investigations, with medical histories, physical examinations, and laboratory studies, repeated periodically over the course of a year or more on a large and representative population group, could tell the true story. Even without such studies and considering only illnesses recognized by the individual himself, it is clear that the problem is of tremendous proportions. On the basis of the rural sample of the National Health Survey (Table 5) it may be estimated that on an average day some 2,750,000 rural persons are consciously sick and that in the course of a year some 720,000,000 days are lost from usual occupations due solely to illnesses disabling rural people for one week or more.

[21] FABRICANT, NOAH D., *The Common Cold and How to Fight It*. New York: Ziff-Davis Publishing Co., 1945. Also VAN VOLKENBURGH, V. A., and W. H. FROST, "Acute Minor Respiratory Diseases Prevailing in a Group of Families Residing in Baltimore, Maryland, 1928-30," *American Journal of Hygiene*, 17:122-153, January, 1933; FROST, W. H., and MARY GOVER, "The Incidence and Time Distribution of Common Colds in Several Groups Kept under Continuous Observation," *Public Health Reports* (Reprint 1545), 47:1815-1841, Sept. 2, 1932.

The Main Causes of Rural Sickness

By and large rural people appear to get sick from the same causes as urban people. Whatever may be the actual comparative total burden of illness in rural and urban sections, the relative importance of different illnesses is quite similar. Detailed information on the actual rates of specific illnesses of all durations in rural areas is sparse. Studies which have explored the matter thoroughly have been confined largely to urban locations.

Certain information, however, on the proportionate distribution of rural illness — the composition of the total sickness burden — can be gathered from previously unpublished data of the Committee on the Costs of Medical Care and from the experience of certain organized health programs serving rural people. From the latter, records of diagnosis are available on persons seeking medical service with financial barriers removed. The deficiencies of this measurement of illness may be compensated by the fact that this approach eliminates the errors of memory or lay judgment of disease that are inherent in the orthodox illness study. Data on the proportionate distribution of cases of illness of any duration are presented for selected rural and urban groups in Table 6.

The most striking feature of the comparative rural and urban patterns of illness is their similarity. It is likely that most of the differentials are due less to differences in actual morbidity than to variations in the definition of illness, the manner of collecting the data, and the geographic location of the groups studied. For both rural and urban groups respiratory disease is by far the most frequent cause of day-to-day illness. Digestive tract disorders are, by and large, the next highest cause, although in the farm workers of California and Arizona they are exceeded by conditions related to pregnancy. It is important to recognize that conditions so readily preventable as injuries and poisonings rank high in both groups and that infectious diseases likewise rank high. The low proportionate importance of infectious diseases reported among farm workers and their families may be due to a program of active preventive medicine covering this particular group. The higher proportion of diseases of the nervous system reported for these workers is difficult to explain, but the higher proportion of diseases of the genito-urinary system among these persons and the Texas plan members may reflect

Table 6. Types of Illness. *Proportionate distribution of all cases of illness, disabling and nondisabling, by diagnosis groups in urban and rural areas,* 1928-1943

General diagnosis group	Urban		Rural		
	Nation-wide*	Hagers-town, Mary-land	Nation-wide†	Cass County, Texas‡	Cali-fornia-Ari-zona§
Diseases of the respiratory system	41.7	61.5	40.7	30.1	29.0
Diseases of the digestive system .	10.7	10.7	12.0	10.5	10.9
Infectious diseases	9.5	8.1	11.7	10.4	5.3
Injuries and poisonings	8.8	3.7	8.6	4.7	7.9
Diseases of the nervous system .	5.5	5.8	4.4	4.5	10.6
Diseases of the skin	5.1	1.6	5.3	9.0	5.6
Diseases of the puerperal state .	4.8‖	2.2	4.4‖	1.5	11.9
Other and ill-defined diseases . .	4.7	1.0	5.2	7.3	4.5
Other general diseases	2.8	2.0	2.2	5.0	3.2
Diseases of the circulatory system	2.6	1.7	2.1	4.5	2.1
Diseases of the genito-urinary system	2.3¶	1.0	2.4¶	10.4	6.8
Diseases of the bones and organs of locomotion	1.2	0.6	0.6	2.0	1.3
Malformations	0.3	0.1	0.3	0.1	0.9
All diagnoses	100.0	100.0	100.0	100.0	100.0
Number of cases	20,264	17,847	5,373	17,270	42,685

Sources: Falk, I. S., Margaret Klem, and Nathan Sinai, *The Incidence of Illness and the Receipt and Costs of Medical Care among Representative Families* (Committee on the Costs of Medical Care). Chicago: University of Chicago Press, 1933.

Sydenstricker, Edgar, "The Causes of Illness at Different Ages," *Public Health Reports*, 43:1067–1074, May 4, 1928. (Hagerstown Morbidity Studies No. VII.)

Unpublished data for rural rates furnished by the U. S. Public Health Service and the Farm Security Administration.

* Committee on the Costs of Medical Care, 1928–31, places of 5,000 population and over.

† Committee on the Costs of Medical Care, 1928-31, places of under 5,000 and rural areas.

‡ Based on cases seeking medical attention from membership of prepayment plan composed of farm families of all incomes, 1942-43.

§ Cases seeking care; seasonal farm workers in California and Arizona eligible for free care through Agricultural Workers Health and Medical Association, 1942.

‖ Includes female genital.

¶ Excludes female genital.

the true state of affairs, which tends to be concealed in illness studies conducted by questioning from nonmedical investigators. The high proportion of puerperal conditions tabulated for the seasonal farm workers may well be an artificial effect of a program in which women are provided with prenatal care on an organized basis. In all groups, diseases of the circulatory system and "general diseases" play a small part in the accounting of cases of illness, despite their major part in the causes of death.

Actual rural-urban disease rates are available from the National Health Survey for the more serious illnesses of at least seven days' duration.[22] It may be seen from Table 7 that the higher rural incidence of these diseases, as reported, is not referable merely to all diseases proportionately down the line. Although in nearly all the major disease groups the rural rates are higher, much the greatest differential is noted for respiratory diseases causing seven or more days' disability. For these the rural rate of 100.4 cases per 1,000 persons per year is more than twice the city rate. This may well be referable to greater lack of proper medical attention for minor respiratory tract complaints which, in the cities under more accessible medical surveillance, tend to cause disability for only a few days. Exposure to the elements and poor housing must play a part and the relationship to a higher rural death rate for pneumonia and influenza is evident. It is significant that the rural respiratory system disease rate is lower for "tonsillitis including tonsillectomy," reflecting lower elective surgery in rural areas,[23] but is higher for pneumonia and for "other diseases of the respiratory system."

The higher rate of communicable disease causing disability of a week or more in the rural sample may be related slightly to the occurrence of diseases like undulant fever or typhoid fever, but it is mainly referable to the common communicable diseases of childhood. The rural rate for these is obviously influenced by the higher

[22] As noted previously, the data are comparable in that identical survey methods were employed for both rural and urban communities, but the rural sample was much less representative, being confined to two states and omitting the rural South. Any analysis must be made, and accepted, with caution.

[23] Although current medical opinion frowns on indiscriminate tonsillectomies, the retention in rural patients of defective tonsils, the removal of which is medically indicated, is doubtless the greater problem. The tonsillectomy rate, moreover, still serves as a useful index of general elective surgery.

Table 7. Types of Disabling Illness: *Number of cases of illness disabling for seven days or more per 1,000 persons per year by diagnosis in urban and rural areas,* 1935-36

Diagnosis groups	Urban (83 cities)		Rural (Michigan and Missouri)	
All causes		171.4		250.0
Communicable diseases		30.3		41.7
Common communicable diseases of childhood	—		37.9	
Other infectious and parasitic diseases . . .	—		3.8	
Diseases of the respiratory system		50.0		100.4
Pneumonia	4.6		7.5	
Tonsillitis (including tonsillectomy)	10.2		7.8	
Other diseases of respiratory system	35.2		85.1	
Diseases of the digestive system		12.6		16.5
Appendicitis	5.2		4.4	
Other diseases of digestive system	7.4		12.1	
Puerperal state—live births only		13.9		18.5
Accidents		15.6		15.5
Tuberculosis—all forms		1.3		1.4
Neuroses and mental diseases		5.5		5.6
Rheumatism		5.6		9.1
Degenerative diseases		14.4		20.1
Cancer and tumors	1.0		3.2	
Diabetes	0.9		1.0	
Cardiovascular-renal	12.3		14.4	
Bladder and male genito-urinary	—		1.5	
Orthopedic impairments		2.9		2.5
Diseases of ear and mastoid		1.9		1.5
Hernia		1.0		0.7
Teeth, mouth, and gums		0.5		0.9
Thyroid		0.6		0.6
Hemorrhoids		0.7		0.7
Skin diseases		2.1		2.4
All other		12.5		11.9

Source: U. S. Public Health Service, National Institute of Health, "An Estimate of the Amount of Disabling Illness in the Country as a Whole," *National Health Survey* 1935-36, *Preliminary Reports,* Sickness and Medical Care Series, Bull. 1, Washington, 1939; unpublished data from the same source on rural health study of about 86,000 persons in representative counties of Michigan and Missouri.

proportion of children in the rural population, but it may also be influenced by the inadequacy of isolation facilities and the tardiness in recognizing cases in the country schoolhouse. As for diseases of the digestive system, it is significant that the urban rate for appendicitis is higher than the rural, corresponding with a higher urban death rate for this disease; it is "other diseases of the digestive system" which accounts for the general differential and this includes the high rural occurrence of "diarrhea and enteritis" doubtless related to inadequate sanitation and refrigeration of foods. The higher rural disability rate reported for puerperal causes is obviously related to the higher rural birth rate.

Comparative analysis of other conditions, particularly those of low incidence, calls for special caution. Rural-urban differentials do not appear to be significant with respect to disabling accidents, tuberculosis, nervous and mental diseases, thyroid conditions, or skin diseases. For orthopedic impairments, diseases of the ear and mastoid, and hernia, urban experience appears to be slightly higher and for rheumatism and diseases of the teeth, mouth, and gums, on the other hand, rural experience appears to be slightly higher, but it is hard to say what significance these findings hold.

The higher rural experience for the so-called degenerative diseases is difficult to explain in view of the opposite finding for death rates. The higher reporting of disabling cases of cancer and tumors in rural areas may represent mistaken diagnoses or possibly a high incidence of tumors in women, such as fibroids of the uterus, or cancer of the cervix occurring more frequently in the multiparous rural woman. The urban-rural rates of disabling cases attributed to diabetes are not significantly different, but the higher rate for cardiovascular-renal diseases reported for rural areas may possibly indicate that the actual occurrence of these disorders in rural communities is as high as in cities, although the somewhat less strained life for the rural adult in later years leads to lower case fatality rates.

All in all, the composition of the practice of a rural physician may not be very strikingly different from that of a city practitioner, except for the management of certain relatively uncommon conditions which, as we shall see, have come to be rather characteristic of rural life. Perhaps the most important distinction is that the rural physician sees ailments of a somewhat more serious nature mainly because the rural family tends to call him only when it feels the need is critical. Further information on the nature of rural sickness, nevertheless, may be gathered from a review of the records of the legally notifiable diseases.

Reportable Diseases

We have observed the higher death and disability rates from many preventable diseases in rural areas. Another reflection of this may be gathered from a consideration of the record of the "reportable diseases," that is, those diseases for which notification of the official department of health is customarily required. The reported rates for the principal communicable diseases in a recent year are indicated in Table 8, according to the state of origin.

Although strictly rural-urban data are not available, certain comparisons become evident by considering rates reported by states of certain degrees of rurality. In order to eliminate the influence of certain strictly geographic or regional distributions of certain of these diseases and to elicit the effect of rurality, a combination of the rates for the single most urban and the single most rural states reporting a given disease in each of the nine geographic Census divisions has been computed. One hardly need mention that reporting of most communicable diseases in the United States is far from complete, that it tends to be less complete for the more common diseases and in ordinary (as distinguished from epidemic) periods, and that it tends to be least complete at all times in rural areas. This being the case, one would expect the communicable disease case rates reported in rural states to be more of an understatement than the rates in urban states.

Despite these qualifications, the reported incidence of common communicable diseases of childhood like mumps, chickenpox, whooping cough, and scarlet fever is appreciably higher in the more rural states than in the urban. The higher prevalence of diseases of this type, of course, must be related to the higher rural proportion of children, but this is simply part of the picture of rural America. The greater contacts among children in cities seem to yield a higher urban rate only for rampantly communicable measles. The rural-urban ratio of over 10 to 1 for malaria is probably an understatement of the true relationship, since even in the more urban states of the

South reporting it the disease is obviously rural in occurrence. On the other hand, the higher urban rates for tuberculosis and meningococcus meningitis undoubtedly reflect the epidemiologic liabilities of urban crowding.

The significantly higher reported rate in the more rural states for bacillary dysentery would be expected in view of rural sanitation

Table 8. Communicable Diseases: *Case rates reported in the most rural and most urban states of all regions, 1942**

Diagnosis	Cases per 100,000	
	Urban states	Rural states
Measles	522.8	477.8
Mumps	325.8	365.2
Chickenpox	229.7	278.6
Whooping cough	139.8	197.9
Malaria	18.6	191.9
Scarlet fever	78.1	120.9
Tuberculosis	106.8	66.2
Dysentery, bacillary	17.6	55.9
Diphtheria	10.6	18.3
Septic sore throat	4.1	6.3
Typhoid and paratyphoid fever	4.8	5.5
Poliomyelitis	3.3	3.0
Meningitis, meningococcus	3.1	2.9
Undulant fever	2.4	1.8
Tularemia	0.7	1.1
Smallpox	0.7	1.1
Encephalitis, infectious	0.7	0.4
Rocky Mountain spotted fever	0.3	0.2

Source: U. S. Public Health Service, *The Notifiable Diseases: Prevalence of Certain Important Communicable Diseases, by States,* 1942, Supp. 174 to the Public Health Reports.

* Rates computed for a combination of the single most rural states and the single most urban states reporting the indicated disease in each of the nine Census divisions. With certain exceptions, the "rural" states are Vermont, Pennsylvania, Wisconsin, North Dakota, South Carolina, Mississippi, Arkansas, New Mexico, and Oregon; the "urban" states are Rhode Island, New York, Illinois, Missouri, Maryland, Tennessee, Texas, Utah, and California. Where data were not available for any of these states, the next most "rural" or the next most "urban" state in which the disease was reportable was used.

deficiencies. The relatively slight excess for rural as against urban rates for typhoid and paratyphoid fever can probably be attributed largely to the inadequacies of comparisons between whole states, since comparative death rates show a marked rural preponderance.

The higher rural rate reported for septic sore throat suggests a relationship to the lack of milk pasteurization in rural districts. The lower rural rate for undulant fever — a disease which other evidence strongly suggests is predominant in rural sections — can be explained not only by inadequate reporting, but particularly by difficulties in recognizing and diagnosing the disease in the first place. The higher rural occurrence reported for diphtheria may well be explained by less immunization among rural people as well as a higher proportion of natural susceptibles than in the cities, where frequent subclinical exposure induces a certain degree of natural immunity.

With little certain knowledge on the epidemiology of poliomyelitis it is difficult to interpret the slight urban excess for this infectious disease.[24] The insect-borne and animal-borne epidemiologic features of tularemia and Rocky Mountain spotted fever and the probable mosquito transmission of infectious encephalitis, by the same token, imply a rural predominance. This is found reported for tularemia, but for spotted fever and encephalitis the opposite is found.[25] The higher smallpox rate reported for the rural states is undoubtedly related to their less rigorous vaccination laws or regulations.[26]

Certain other communicable diseases having a rather limited geographic distribution were not subject to the type of analysis given in Table 8. Among those tending to occur in predominantly rural sections are dengue fever, reported in South Carolina, Texas, and Mississippi, and endemic typhus fever concentrated in the rural South.[27] Uncommon diseases associated with animals or animal products, like anthrax and psittacosis, appear to have the preponder-

[24] As judged by mortality, in fact, the rate of poliomyelitis deaths for 1940-41 was higher in small towns and rural areas than in larger cities in all regions except the West. COLLINS, SELWYN D., "The Incidence of Poliomyelitis and Its Crippling Effects, As Recorded in Family Surveys," Public Health Reports. 61:327-355, Mar. 8, 1946.

[25] Aside from the factor of poor reporting, it is found that the higher rate among urban states for spotted fever is referable to an excessive number of cases in 1942 reported from Maryland. Most of these Maryland cases were presumably from the rural districts of that "urban" state.

[26] HAMPTON, BROCK C., "Smallpox in Relation to State Vaccination Laws and Regulations," Public Health Reports. 58:1771-1777, Dec. 3, 1943.

[27] U. S. Public Health Service, The Notifiable Diseases: Prevalence of Certain Important Communicable Diseases, by States, 1942, Supp. 174 to the Public Health Reports. Washington: Government Printing Office, 1944.

ance of cases reported in a few urban states. Human rabies appears to be spotted about equally between a few rural and a few urban states, although from 1931 to 1940 the highest number of cases was reported in rural states like Tennessee, West Virginia, and Texas.[28] The venereal diseases, although they are notifiable, will be considered below as types of physical impairment.

[28] WEBSTER, LESLIE T., *Rabies*. New York: The Macmillan Company, 1942, pp. 45-54.

CHAPTER 6

DISEASES OF RURAL LIFE

A NUMBER of diseases and disorders that play no great part in the over-all burden of rural sickness afflict rural people more than urban. Either because they are typically associated with the rural environment or because they have become largely eliminated from the cities — remaining chiefly in the country — they constitute a group of conditions that may be considered "diseases of rural life." As with industrial diseases in urban practice, on which the literature is extensive, they are important less because of their total volume than because they present special problems to rural medical practice and public health. A few of these diseases, like malaria, hookworm disease, or pellagra, have come to be regarded generally by American medicine as rural problems. Many others become evident, however, on further consideration.

The diseases of rural life tend to fall under half a dozen categories of "social etiology" in so far as they relate to (1) the geographic characteristics of rural areas, (2) association with plants and animals, (3) rural housing and sanitation, (4) occupational patterns of farming, (5) general rural poverty, and (6) rural lacks in the application of modern medical science. These groupings range by degrees from the effects of "nature in the raw" toward the influences of socioeconomic conditions. As in most classifications of complex phenomena, the categories are not entirely mutually exclusive, but it will be convenient to consider each disease under the "epidemiological" heading where it appears predominantly to fall.

Rural Geography

Certain diseases are associated with the character of the land on which rural people live. The relationship between colloid goiter and the iodine content of water and food is well known.[1] While nothing about low iodine content in the soil is intrinsically rural, in the United States this condition happens by chance to be found prin-

[1] SYDENSTRICKER, EDGAR, *Health and Environment.* New York: McGraw-Hill Book Company, Inc., 1933, pp. 49-51.

cipally in rural districts such as the Northwest and the upper Mississippi Valley, as well as in the Great Lakes Basin. Colloid goiter was found in 21 to 27 men per 1,000 examined in the First World War from the Northwestern states, although since then the wide use of iodized salt and water in the endemic regions has cut down its prevalence.[2] Even in goiter belts, city populations tend to be better protected because they enjoy a food distribution system that brings iodine-containing foods from far and wide.

Fluorosis causing mottled tooth enamel, a condition related to high fluorine content in the soil and drinking water, likewise happens to be most widespread in rural sections. The use of ground water, with generally high mineral content, aggravates the problem. Fluorosis occurs most commonly in rural territory like the Texas panhandle region, Colorado, South Dakota, Arizona, and southern Illinois.[3] Recent experiments with carefully controlled fluorination of the water supply as a preventive for dental caries are based on discoveries in whose making thousands of rural people have been unwitting guinea pigs for years.

The chemical content of the soil appears also to exert certain systemic effects. Rural families in certain sections of Wyoming, South Dakota, and Nebraska seem to suffer gastro-intestinal and other disturbances due to ingestion of food containing selenium, raised in the local seleniferous soil.[4] Soil composition appears to some extent to govern the vitamin content of food raised in that soil. In Maine, for example, it has been shown that tomatoes raised in certain sections tend to have a below-par vitamin C content — with associated vitamin deficiency among the farm families living off this soil.[5]

[2] DuBois, Eugene F., "Colloid Goiter," A Textbook of Medicine, Russell L. Cecil, ed., 6th ed. Philadelphia: W. B. Saunders Company, 1943, p. 1206.

[3] American Dental Association, Bureau of Public Relations, "Endemic Dental Fluorosis or Mottled Enamel," Journal of the American Dental Association, 30:1278, August, 1943.

[4] Smith, M. I., and R. B. Westfall, "Further Field Studies on the Selenium Problem in Relation to Public Health," Public Health Reports, 52:1375-1384, Oct. 1, 1937; Smith, M. I., "Chronic Endemic Selenium Poisoning," Journal of the American Medical Association, 116: 562-567, Feb. 15, 1941.

[5] Kellogg, Charles E., "Soils and Nutrition," Annals of the American Academy of Political and Social Science, 225:17-19, January, 1943. Also Murphy, E. F., "The Ascorbic Acid Content of Different Varieties of Maine-grown Tomatoes and Cabbage as Influenced by Locality, Season, and Stage of Maturity," Journal of Agricultural Research, 64:483-502, May, 1942.

The relationship of soil composition to nutrition is currently under study by several state agricultural experiment stations.[6]

Lightning, tornadoes, dust storms, and general exposure to the elements doubtless contribute greater health and accident hazards to the farm family than to the protected city dweller.

Plants and Animals

Association with plants and animals on a relatively intimate basis in rural life naturally exposes country dwellers to certain diseases.

By direct contact with plants, rural people are bound to get more than their share of the Rhus dermatitis group of skin reactions due to poison ivy, poison oak, poison sumac, or other plants.[7] Whatever rare gastrointestinal or central nervous system poisonings come from inedible mushrooms or other poisonous plants also probably occur more commonly among rural people, who get a smaller proportion of their food through commercial marketing channels.[8]

Certain serious fungous infections are transmitted to man from plants or animals, directly or indirectly. Actinomycosis is the best known and perhaps the most widely disseminated of the serious mycotic infections in this country, caused by the ray fungus or *Actinomyces bovis*. The disease is found most often in farmers and cattlemen, in whom it usually takes the form of a granulomatous lesion of the jaw, presumably from chewing on infected straw or grain.[9] Cases have been reported from every state, although it is said to be most prevalent in the upper Mississippi Valley and the Northwest.[10]

[6] CARPENTER, C. C., "Riboflavin-Vitamin B_2 in Soil," *Science*, 98:109, 110, July 30, 1943.

[7] For a further discussion of poisonous plants, see SCHWARTZ, LOUIS, and LOUIS TULIPAN, *Occupational Diseases of the Skin*. Philadelphia: Lea & Febiger, 1939, pp. 430-456.

[8] It may be that adults in the open country, by virtue of their experience, acquire a recognition of these poisonous plants which guards them from contact even more than the city dweller on his Sunday outings, but this probably cannot be said for rural children. For a general discussion, see DACK, G. M., *Food Poisoning*. Chicago: University of Chicago Press, 1943, pp. 22-35.

[9] LEWIS, GEORGE M., and MARY E. HOPPER, *An Introduction to Medical Mycology*. Chicago: Year Book Publishers, Inc., 1939, p. 158.

[10] SANFORD, A. H., "Distribution of Actinomycosis in the United States," *Journal of the American Medical Association*, 81:655-659, Aug. 25, 1923.

While anthrax is best known as an occupational disease of tannery workers or wool sorters, it is, of course, an occupational hazard of cattlemen or sheep herders as well. Fortunately, it occurs only sporadically in the United States, with about 100 cases reported annually.[22] Close contact with hogs exposes farm people to balantidiasis, or balantidial dysentery due to the protozoan *Balantidium coli*, a harmless parasite in the pig.[23] Erysipeloid is another hog-borne disease creating an occupational hazard to persons in close contact with swine.[24]

Rare infections with the *Echinococcus granulosus*, the dog tapeworm causing hydatid disease, have occurred in cattle herders or other farm workers coming in close contact with dogs which have been associated with hogs, oxen, horses, or sheep.[25] Other common helminthic diseases like trichinosis, or uncommon ones like infestations with the beef tapeworm (*Taenia saginata*) or the pork tapeworm (*Taenia solium*), occur in rural and urban persons alike since they are spread by ingestion of improperly cooked, infested meat.[26] Contact with chickens exposes farmers and their families to the virus of psittacosis (ornithosis) more than is generally recognized.[27]

Proximity to animals exposes rural people to certain diseases carried from animals to man by insect vectors. Rocky Mountain spotted fever, carried to man from wild rabbits and other smaller animals by the tick (*Dermacentor andersoni* or *Dermacentor variabilis*) has become increasingly familiar in recent years. The disease is a rickettsial infection resembling typhus and frequently has a high case fatality rate, averaging for the United States about 20 per cent.[28] While "tick fever" is widespread throughout the United States, it is particularly prevalent in the tick-infested sections of

[22] *Ibid.*, pp. 37-65.

[23] *Ibid.*, pp. 219-220.

[24] KLAUDER, J. V., "Erysipeloid as an Occupational Disease," *Journal of the American Medical Association,* 111:1345-1348, Oct. 8, 1938.

[25] STRONG, RICHARD P., *Stitt's Diagnosis, Prevention, and Treatment of Tropical Diseases.* Philadelphia: The Blakiston Company, 1944, p. 1475.

[26] *Ibid.*, pp. 1238 ff. and pp. 1463 ff.

[27] MEYER, KARL F., "Ecology of Psittacosis and Ornithosis," *Medicine,* 21:175-206, May, 1942.

[28] BAKER, GEORGE E., "Rocky Mountain Spotted Fever," *Journal of the American Medical Association,* 122:841-850, July 24, 1943.

the Great Plains and the Northwest, where it has the highest case fatality rate and is a definite hazard to workers in the fields. In 1942 about 500 cases of tick fever were reported, the greatest number of cases occurring in Montana, Wyoming, Maryland, and Virginia, with the peak period being in the spring and summer.[29]

Tularemia is another animal disease that may be transmitted directly to man from a number of wild animals, especially rabbits and squirrels, or through several insects such as the tick or deer fly as intermediary hosts. While in urban practice it is likely to be seen most frequently during the hunting season when the city dweller goes out into the fields, in rural practice it is a year-round phenomenon.[30] It has been reported in almost every state, but in 1942 was most numerous in Arkansas, Georgia, and Tennessee.[31]

Equine encephalomyelitis is manifestly a hazard to farm people living in proximity to horses and barnyard fowl, from which it may be transmitted by the *Aedes aegypti* and other mosquitoes. Both the eastern and western types of this virus disease have appeared to be on the increase since their first description a few years ago.[32] While these infections almost certainly have a higher incidence in rural areas, the distribution of other neurotropic virus diseases, such as the St. Louis type of encephalitis or infantile paralysis, is not clear. It has been claimed by some, however, that they are particular liabilities in rural areas, associated possibly with insect transmission of the viruses from other cases, animal reservoirs, or from exposed excreta.[33] In recent years, the administration of vaccines to animals by farmers themselves has created a hazard of accidental human inoculation with live viruses used in veterinary medicine.

[29] U. S. Public Health Service, *The Notifiable Diseases: Prevalence of Certain Important Communicable Diseases by States,* 1942.

[30] HULL, *op. cit.,* pp. 265-276.

[31] U. S. Public Health Service, *The Notifiable Diseases: Prevalence of Certain Important Communicable Diseases by States,* 1942.

[32] HAMMON, W. McD., W. C. REEVES, S. R. BENNER, and B. BROOKMAN, "Human Encephalitis in the Yakima Valley, Washington, 1942," *Journal of the American Medical Association,* 128:1113-1139, Aug. 18, 1945.

[33] AYCOCK, W. L., "The Epidemiology of Poliomyelitis," *Virus and Rickettsial Diseases,* Harvard School of Public Health Symposium. Cambridge: Harvard University Press, 1940, p. 560; HAMMON, W. McD., and W. C. REEVES, "Recent Advances in the Epidemiology of the Arthropod-borne Virus Encephalitides," *American Journal of Public Health,* 35:994-1004, October, 1945.

Rural Sanitation and Housing

While some of the above diseases are related indirectly to improper hygiene in man's relations to the animals or plants in the rural environment, other rural diseases are directly caused by improper environmental sanitation. The most prevalent of the "diseases of rural life" — hookworm disease — is related to this.

Spread from man to man, through frank contamination of the soil with ova-infested excreta, hookworm infestation has been one of the most prevalent disorders of the rural South.[34] The etiologic agent in the United States is nearly always *Necator americanus*, which typically penetrates the bare feet of children, whites more frequently than Negroes. Studies in eight Southern states during 1930-38 showed prevalence rates averaging 11.2 per cent of the population, with the highest rates being in Mississippi, South Carolina, and Alabama.[35]

Hookworm disease is important because of its systemic effects of stunted growth, anemia, and general debility, which increase susceptibility to other infections like pneumonia or tuberculosis. Recent studies, however, stress the importance of associated malnutrition in producing the typical picture of "hookworm disease."[36] During the last 20 or 30 years, the disease has declined in prevalence because of the widespread construction of sanitary privies and the mass treatment of thousands of cases. The crusade to eliminate hookworm infestation has given the impetus to the establishment of many full-time departments of public health in the South.

Another prevalent helminthic infestation, though less common in the United States, is ascariasis, due to the large intestinal roundworm *Ascaris lumbricoides*. Its propagation is ordinarily dependent on extravagant fecal pollution of the soil, in which children play and from which they may carry the ova from their dirty fingers to their mouths. Such environmental conditions are often found among the mountain people of the Appalachian plateau.[37]

[34] STRONG, *op. cit.*, pp. 1251-1272.

[35] KELLER, A. E., W. S. LEATHERS, and P. M. DENSEN, "The Results of Recent Studies in Hookworm in Eight Southern States," *American Journal of Tropical Medicine*, 20:493-509, July, 1940.

[36] ANDREWS, J., "New Methods of Hookworm Disease Investigation and Control," *American Journal of Public Health*, 32:282-288, March, 1942.

[37] STRONG, *op. cit.*, pp. 1221-1229.

Because of the deficiencies of rural excreta disposal and water supply and the advances in urban sanitation, we have arrived at a situation in which the enteric fevers — typhoid and paratyphoid fevers and bacillary dysentery — are essentially rural diseases. We have already noted that the death rates from these diseases are highest in the rural areas. Recent studies have shown a considerably higher prevalence of carriers of bacillary dysentery (*Shigella paradysenteriae*) as well as a higher occurrence of all acute diarrheal diseases in rural than in urban districts investigated.[38] Epidemics of typhoid fever are now practically a thing of the past, but the sporadic occurrence of cases in rural sections probably is evidence of continuing transmission of the disease by occasional carriers, contaminated water supplies, and by flies from improperly protected outdoor privies. In many rural counties typhoid fever is virtually endemic, with cases being seen every year. Cheese-borne outbreaks of the disease have recently been reported in rural districts of Indiana[39] and in California.

To the mere necessity of using outdoor privies, with all their inconveniences, may possibly be attributed much of the constipation which is evidently widespread among rural people, despite their nonsedentary life. As Dr. W. W. Hall claimed in the Report of the Commissioner of Agriculture in 1862, the lack of easy accessibility of a toilet naturally discourages the formation of good bowel habits, with resultant intestinal dysfunction.[40] In this sense, the rectal lesions or aggravated hernias, associated with long-standing constipation and wide overindulgence in laxatives, represent basic problems in modern rural sanitation.

The lack of pasteurization for a great part of the rural milk supply is responsible for the continued occurrence in rural areas of undulant fever, much of which, of course, goes undiagnosed and disguised as

[38] WATT, J., and A. V. HARDY, "Studies of the Acute Diarrheal Diseases: XIII. Cultural Surveys of Normal Population Groups," *Public Health Reports,* 60:261-273, Mar. 9, 1945.

[39] U. S. Public Health Service, "Typhoid Epidemic in Indiana due to Eating Green Cheese Made from Unpasteurized Milk," *Public Health Reports,* 59:527, Apr. 21, 1944.

[40] HALL, W. W., "Health of Farmers' Families," *Report of the Commissioner of Agriculture,* Washington, 1862, p. 329.

unexplained malaise, aches, or slight fevers. The same applies to the rare case of bovine tuberculosis which still occurs, causing bone, joint, or intestinal lesions. The relatively few milk-borne epidemics of septic sore throat or diphtheria or the enteric fevers that still occur have almost invariably been in small villages or rural areas served by unpasteurized milk or milk products.[41] "Milk sickness," a disease caused by plant toxins in cow's milk, is a hazard to the farm family getting milk directly from a single cow. While not destroyed by pasteurization, the toxin is so diluted in ordinary milk on the urban market that it is no hazard to the city dweller.[42]

Diseases associated with poor housing and slums have been recognized in the cities for years,[43] but the rural areas also have their "slum diseases." In fact, in so far as rural housing is more crowded than urban, more frequently in disrepair, and more often lacking in sanitary conveniences, it may be assumed to contribute to the spread of many communicable diseases and the high accident rate in rural areas.[44] Beyond these are specific diseases spread by rats, associated with the prevalence of rats on farms and in the villages and small towns.

Most important of the rat-borne diseases in this country is typhus fever of the murine or endemic type, spread to man by the rat flea *Xenopsylla cheopis* and occurring primarily in the rural states of the South. There seems to have been an increase of endemic typhus in the South in recent years, with the majority of the approximately 4,000 cases reported annually in the nation occurring in Texas, Alabama, and Georgia. While typhus has had its origins in the large cities, it has spread to the rural areas and small towns where, with ineffective rat control, it has increased rapidly.[45] In Georgia, Alabama, and North Carolina analysis shows the highest rates to be in

[41] ANDREWS, JOHN, and A. W. FUCHS, "National Inventory of Needs for Sanitation Facilities: II. Milk Pasteurization Facilities," *Public Health Reports*, 59:189-204, Feb. 11, 1944.

[42] HULL, *op. cit.*, pp. 101-108.

[43] MARQUETTE, BLEECKER, "Housing and Health Relationships Reexamined," *Public Health Reports*, 55:547-554, Mar. 29, 1940.

[44] BRITTEN, ROLLO H., "New Light on the Relation of Housing to Health," *American Journal of Public Health*, 32:193-199, February, 1942.

[45] BAKER, J. N., J. G. McALPINE, and D. G. GILL, "Endemic Typhus in Alabama," *Public Health Reports*, 50:12-21, Jan. 4, 1935.

the small towns under 5,000 and in rural areas.[46] Rat-bite fever[47] and
Weil's disease (spirochetosis icterohaemorrhagica)[48] are other diseases carried to man directly or indirectly by rats that may be considered among the problems of rural medicine. Human plague has
fortunately been almost nonexistent in the United States for many
years, although rats infected with *Bacillus pestis* have recently been
discovered increasingly in the West.[49]

Finally, intimately related to the inadequate sanitation and housing in rural areas is the continuation of malaria as a problem in the
United States. The disappearance of malaria in many sections of the
country in which the anopheline mosquito vectors still abound can
hardly be explained except by improvements in environmental
hygiene. While in the 1880's the disease was known as far north as
New York and Michigan, it is today practically confined to the
Southeast, especially concentrated in the rural districts of the Mississippi delta region, South Carolina, and northern Florida. During
1933-37 there were 200 southern counties reporting a malaria death
rate of 25 per 100,000 or more.[50]

The actual prevalence of malaria in the South is not known,
although it is estimated by the United States Public Health
Service to be something under 1 per cent, based on mass studies of
blood smears. Discussions on the prevalence of the disease are often
based on mortality statistics (assuming several hundred cases per
death), which are notoriously unreliable. Not only are many unattended or scantily attended rural deaths (particularly among Negroes) registered carelessly as malaria, which gives an unduly high

[46] MELENEY, HENRY E., "Recent Extension of Endemic Typhus Fever in the
Southern United States," *American Journal of Public Health*, 31:219-227,
March, 1941.

[47] BROWN, THOMAS McP., and J. C. NUNEMAKER, "Rat-bite Fever," *Bulletin
of the Johns Hopkins University School of Medicine*, 70:202-230, March, 1942.

[48] MOLNAR, J. G., and J. A. KASPER, "Epidemiology and Laboratory Diagnosis
of Infectious Jaundice (Weil's Disease)," *American Journal of Public Health*,
31:945-950, September, 1941.

[49] CREEL, R. H., "Plague Situation in the Western United States," *American
Journal of Public Health*, 31:1155-1162, November, 1941. Also, U.S. Public
Health Service, "Plague Infection Reported in the United States in 1946,"
Public Health Reports, 62:1336-1340, Sept. 12, 1947.

[50] STRONG, *op. cit.*, pp. 7-9.

rate in certain areas, but undoubtedly many more cases, not dying or even seeing a physician, are never reported.[51] As a matter of fact, the benign tertian form of malaria occurring in this country (caused by *Plasmodium vivax*) is seldom fatal, although its effects are enervating and debilitating for long periods.

For the "chills and fever" correctly or incorrectly associated with malaria in the South, a whole industry of patent medicines has developed. The saga of cure-alls like "666" and a host of other potions consumed by impoverished families in malarial districts is a commentary on the state of rural medical care in the South.[52]

The occurrence of malaria in depressed rural sections is associated not only with an abundance of anophelines breeding in undrained swamps, but also with a lack of proper screening on most Southern rural homes.[53] Even where screens are found, the country custom of sitting outside at dusk, when mosquitoes bite most heavily, is hard to change. The elimination of malaria becomes, therefore, not only a task of swamp drainage and the use of DDT, but one of housing and education in habits of living. With the return from overseas of thousands of infected soldiers and sailors, the epidemiology of malaria in the rural South and the whole nation takes on added importance.[54]

Another mosquito-borne disease, yellow fever, has disappeared from the United States, although the hazard of its revival through airplane importation of infected mosquitoes is ever-present. Outbreaks of dengue, however, occur from time to time, particularly in the Gulf states and in California.[55] Filariasis, once occurring indigenously in the area of Charleston, South Carolina[56] seems to be found

[51] ABRAMS, HERBERT K., *Epidemiological Malaria Survey, Phillips County, Arkansas.* U. S. Public Health Service, March, 1944. Unpublished.

[52] CRAMP, ARTHUR J., ed. *Nostrums and Quackery.* Chicago: American Medical Association, 1921.

[53] BISPHAM, W. N., *Malaria: Its Diagnosis, Treatment, and Prophylaxis.* Baltimore: The Williams & Wilkins Company, 1944, pp. 139-140.

[54] PARRAN, THOMAS, "Public Health Implications of Tropical and Imported Diseases," *American Journal of Public Health*, 34:1-6, January, 1944.

[55] JARCHO, SAUL, "Arthropod-borne Diseases, with Special Reference to Prevention and Control," *War Medicine*, 3:477-473, May, 1943.

[56] FRANCIS, EDWARD, *Filariasis in the Southern United States* (Hygienic Laboratory Bull. 117). Washington: Government Printing Office, 1919.

today only in servicemen returning from overseas.[57] Being carried
by the more ubiquitous Aedes mosquito, these diseases need not be
entirely rural in their occurrence. The equine encephalomyelitis
group carried from horses to man by mosquitoes, and the St. Louis
type of encephalitis, probably carried from man to man or from animal to man by mosquitoes, have been mentioned.

Occupational Diseases of Agriculture

All the diseases springing from contact with plants and animals
may, in a sense, be considered occupational hazards of farm life.
Beyond these are certain disorders related more specifically to the
nature and processes of agricultural work than to mere contact
with the animate rural environment.[58]

Long hours of work out in the sun naturally predispose the farmer
or farm laborer to sunstroke.[59] The farmer's wide-brimmed straw
hat is, indeed, more functional than symbolic. Repeated sunburn
or windburn causes "chronic actinic dermatitis" as almost a normal
condition of the farmer.[60] Whether lupus erythematosus and other
dermatoses related to actinic exposure are commoner in rural people
is not certain. Epitheliomas and other malignant growths of the
skin, however, have generally been regarded as liabilities of farmers
and other persons exposed to much sunlight.[61]

Related to the backbreaking toil of harvest labor, particularly
among seasonal farm workers, is the frequent occurrence of all
types of muscle strain and myositis. Early in the harvest season, when
field workers are still unaccustomed to the particular crop operation,
disabilities due to aches and pains of the lower back, legs, and
shoulders are common.[62] How much arthritis, on a traumatic or

[57] A few asymptomatic cases of filariasis have been discovered in West Indian
workers brought into the United States to meet wartime agricultural needs.

[58] LEGGE, R. T., "Occupational Hazards in the Agricultural Industries,"
American Journal of Public Health, 25:457-462, April, 1935.

[59] JOHNSTONE, RUTHERFORD T., *Occupational Diseases*. Philadelphia: W. B.
Saunders Company, 1941, p. 475.

[60] ANDREWS, GEORGE CLINTON, *Diseases of the Skin*. Philadelphia: W. B.
Saunders Company, 1938, pp. 83-84.

[61] *Ibid.*, p. 728.

[62] Unpublished reports of the U. S. Department of Agriculture, Office of
Labor, Health Services Branch, 1945.

"wear and tear" basis, is related to the stoop labor involved in cultivating or picking sugar beets or chopping cotton or the "walking on the knees" in the wet soil done in gathering potatoes, is a matter for investigation.[63]

Whether or not hernia is a more serious liability to the farmer than to the industrial worker is not clear. Certainly farmers generally lack the benefit of lifting cranes and it is known, as we shall see from studies by the Farm Security Administration, that hernias are frequent among them. That serious injuries due to accidents from farm machinery as well as livestock represent a definite occupational hazard in modern agriculture has already been made clear.

Poisonous insecticides or fungicides used as plant sprays create a chemical hazard to the farm worker either in the process of spraying or in harvesting.[64] Arsenate of lead, for example, has been known to cause virtual "epidemics" of lead poisoning in such places as the apple orchards of Washington State.[65] Chemical fertilizers may cause serious systemic poisonings.[66]

Dupuytren's contracture of the palmar fascia has been claimed to result from prolonged clasping of a tool handle, and bowlegs or knock-knees have been attributed to riding horseback (as by cowherders) in the early years of life.[67] Other diseases more definitely

[63] In 1902 Thomas Oliver regarded "rheumatic affections . . . foremost among the ills of field workers." OLIVER, THOMAS, *Dangerous Trades*. London: E. P. Dutton & Company, Inc., 1902, p. 232.

[64] SCHWARTZ and TULIPAN, *op. cit.*, pp. 304, 314.

[65] NEAL, PAUL A., and Others, *A Study of the Effect of Lead Arsenate Exposure on Orchardists and Consumers of Sprayed Fruit* (U. S. Public Health Service Bull. 267). Washington: Government Printing Office, 1941. Also, unpublished reports of the U. S. Department of Agriculture, Office of Labor, Health Services Branch, 1945.

[66] "Occupational Diseases Associated with Artificial Fertilizer," Queries and Minor Notes, *Journal of the American Medical Association*, 106:237, Jan. 18, 1936.

[67] OLIVER, *op. cit.*, pp. 233, 245. While bowlegs are undoubtedly caused by vitamin D deficiency above all, it is claimed that trauma to the joints, as in horseback riding, may play a contributory part. The etiology of Dupuytren's contracture is usually cited as "unknown," but it is pointed out that the preponderant occurrence of this condition in males suggests association with "injury or irritation of the palmar tissue, incident to certain occupations." See WHITMAN, ROYAL, *A Treatise on Orthopaedic Surgery*, 9th ed. Philadelphia: Lea & Febiger, 1930, pp. 549, 637.

associated with specialized agricultural occupations in certain sections of the country include cotton pickers' tenosynovitis in the South,
hop pickers' dermatitis in Oregon and Idaho, "muck sores" in the
Florida Everglades, carrot handlers' dermatitis, peat-dust conjunctivitis, and milkers' nodules.[68] The list of specific contact dermatitides
associated with harvesting certain crops is a long one.[69]

Aside from the liabilities of agriculture as such, the manifold
occupational diseases and accidents of mining must, in some degree,
be recognized as rural, in so far as most mining is done in truly
rural sections. Miners and their families often live in communities
which — while often quite different in culture pattern from the farming community — are rural in their size and civic development.

Rural Poverty

While, in a sense, many of the above diseases are related to poverty,
in that they could be prevented or eliminated by measures costing
money, there are a few "diseases of rural life" specifically related to
poverty rather than to agricultural life as such.

Most important are the nutritional deficiencies, among which
pellagra stands out in this country as a typically rural problem.
Although pellagra is seen occasionally in the cities, particularly
among chronic alcoholics, the disease is characteristically found
among poor white and Negro sharecroppers and tenants in the rural
South. It is part and parcel of the impoverishment which forces a
diet of corn bread and molasses and pork fat back for months on end.
It occurs most frequently in the spring and early summer following
the winter period of most inadequate diet.[70]

The actual reported death rate from pellagra is relatively low,
being about 5 to 6 per 100,000 in Alabama and Georgia, the states of

[68] Unpublished reports of the U. S. Department of Agriculture, Office of
Labor, Health Services Branch. Also, for further discussion, see KOBER, GEORGE
M., "Farmers, Gardeners, Planters, and Farm Laborers," Industrial Health,
George M. Kober and Emery R. Hayhurst, eds., Philadelphia: The Blakiston
Company, 1924, pp. 210-213.

[69] SHELMIRE, BEDFORD, "Contact Dermatitis from Vegetation," Southern
Medical Journal, 33:337-346, April, 1940.

[70] SMITH, D. T., The Story of Pellagra and Its Treatment with Nicotinic Acid.
Chicago: University of Chicago Press, 1942.

highest record.[71] With increasing knowledge and some small improvement in the economic level of the small Southern farmer, the prevalence of the disease has undoubtedly declined, but the extent of subclinical vitamin deficiencies probably remains high. The general debility, "shiftlessness," and laziness for which poverty-stricken Southern sharecroppers are often blamed are doubtless related to multiple vitamin deficiencies as well as inadequate intake of iron and protein.[72] The intimate relationship of nutritional status to economic circumstances is emphasized by the paradoxical fact that when the market for cotton has been poor the incidence of pellagra has actually declined, in that a little land is left free of cotton and devoted to a garden of vitamin-containing foods.

Related to uncleanliness of person and household associated with rural poverty is the occurrence of diseases like trachoma, follicular conjunctivitis, and impetigo contagiosum. While trachoma is not common in this country, it occurs in the rural sections of the Southwest, particularly among the Indian population[73] and in low-income rural sections of West Virginia, Kentucky, Tennessee, Missouri, southern Illinois, and Arkansas.[74] Impetigo and other diseases of the skin associated with poor personal hygiene are rife among infants and children in poverty-stricken rural homes in which indoor water and soap are lacking.

The lack of refrigeration facilities associated with rural poverty undoubtedly leads to a great deal of food spoilage and Staphylococcus toxin food poisoning.[75] Finally, though not particularly associated with poverty, the farm wife's practice of home preserving fruits and vegetables creates perhaps the greatest hazard of botulism in the nation.[76]

[71] U. S. Public Health Service, *The Notifiable Diseases: Prevalence of Certain Important Communicable Diseases, by States,* 1942.

[72] McLester, James S., *Nutrition and Diet in Health and Disease.* Philadelphia: W. B. Saunders Company, 1943, pp. 366-368.

[73] Forster, W. G., and J. R. McGibony, "Trachoma," *American Journal of Ophthalmology,* 27:1107-1117, October, 1944.

[74] Julianelle, Louis A., *The Etiology of Trachoma.* New York: The Commonwealth Fund, 1938, p. 27.

[75] For a general discussion, see Dack, *op. cit.,* pp. 71-72.

[76] *Ibid.,* p. 36.

Lack of Specific Medical Services

The numerous diseases that have acquired a higher prevalence in rural areas mainly because of the failure to apply known medical techniques have been considered in an earlier section. For the most part, these consist of the communicable diseases like diphtheria or smallpox, although they also include problems like those involved in pneumonia or puerperal and infant mortality.

Rural-urban differentials for these diseases have already been discussed. Suffice it to say here that the rural disadvantages are due not only to less effective public health programs, but also to less complete therapeutic management of cases. For diphtheria, for example, the higher rural case rate may reflect less effective active immunization programs on a mass basis than in the cities, but the higher rural death rate from diphtheria is probably partially due to the ineffective application even of passive immunization on an individual basis. Likewise, the rural resident bitten by a rabid dog is less likely to get the Pasteur treatment than a city dweller, and the farmer with an injury from a rusty nail is less likely to receive tetanus antitoxin than the industrial worker. For a few diseases, like typhoid fever or Rocky Mountain spotted fever, the country dweller may actually have a higher rate of immunization, in recognition of the greater hazards, than the urbanite. In the absence of more basic control measures, however, such immunizations are not entirely effective. As already suggested, higher rural occurrence of puerperal disease or serious respiratory tract infection is undoubtedly related to less adequate medical care.

This entire account of "diseases of rural life" is doubtless far from complete. It may give some reflection, however, of the ways that the contemporary rural environment and social structure influence the problems faced by rural medicine. Urban medicine obviously has its own characteristic problems by contrast: the manifold occupational diseases of modern industry, the chronic alcoholism or psychopathic personalities of the big city, the rheumatic fever of damp tenements, the hypertension of harassed businessmen, the rickets of children starved of sunlight by tall buildings and factory smoke. These more typically urban diseases have long had the attention of American medicine. With the war, however, certain of the parasitic or mycotic or insect-borne diseases that we have considered rural have taken on new importance, as urban physicians have seen cases at military stations in rural districts in this country and as American troops have returned from the tropics where these diseases are rampant.[77] It must be appreciated, nevertheless, that in relation to the total volume of sickness of all types the main problems in rural and urban medicine are more alike than they are different.

[77] GETTING, VLADO A., "Insect Vectors of Disease," *New England Journal of Medicine*, 232:315-321, 344-350, 373-378; Mar. 15, 22, and 29, 1945.

CHAPTER 7

PHYSICAL AND MENTAL IMPAIRMENTS

FREQUENT or recurring illness inadequately treated results often in a residue of chronic physical defects. The unattended middle ear infection leads to deafness, the improperly handled fracture of the leg leads to permanent crippling, the untreated rheumatic fever leads to chronic heart disease. Similarly, the behavior problem in a child without benefit of mental hygiene services may lead to a psychopathic condition in later life. Physical impairments going year after year without correction become the source of acute episodes of illness; the hernia may cause acute intestinal obstruction and the hyperactive thyroid may eventually cause heart disease and heart failure. The individual long retaining a physical defect or mental disorder may make an adjustment to it, but usually at a disadvantaged level.

Whatever may be the exact incidence of illness in rural areas, the deficiencies in medical and related services, to be investigated below, would lead one to expect a high prevalence of chronic physical impairments. Considerable evidence supports this expectation. In the nation as a whole it has been conservatively estimated that as many as 23,000,000 individuals are afflicted with handicapping physical impairments or chronic disease of some type.[1] What number of these persons are rural is impossible to say but, as we shall see, the number is probably higher than their proportionate share.

Physical Status of Military Registrants and Youth

The largest body of data on physical impairments in the population is that available from Selective Service System examinations of males for military service. On analysis, these data provide impressive evidence of a higher rural burden of physical defects and mental dis-

[1] HINDRICHS, F., Testimony before a Subcommittee of the Committee on Labor, U. S. House of Representatives, 78th Cong., 2d Sess., H. Res. 230, *Aid to the Physically Handicapped*. Washington: Government Printing Office, 1945, Part 7, pp. 1067-1074.

orders. While Selective Service data are obviously limited as to age and sex groups, they provide information on a segment of the population of the entire nation — from every geographic section and every walk of life. If these physical impairment rates characterize our presumably healthiest demographic group — males in the prime of life — it is fair to assume that findings for the rest of the population, if examined, would be even more startling.

The high over-all Selective Service rejection rate from physical and mental defects was appalling news to the nation. By June, 1944, 14,297,000 men 18 to 37 years of age had been examined and 4,217,-000, or 29.5 per cent, were disqualified for any military service whatsoever.[2] An additional number were qualified only for limited service because of physical impairments, so that 40 per cent were, in effect, rejected for general military duty. Beyond these, an additional number were admitted into the Army with defects which required correction before the soldier would be fit for duty.[3] A still further number were discharged shortly after induction for defects not detected or not considered disqualifying at the initial examination.

The significance of all Selective Service findings as a reflection of the health of the nation and the adequacy of medical care has been challenged by some who argue that a large share of the rejections could not have been prevented by the provision of medical care.[3a] Whether or not there is any partial validity to this claim, the fact remains that the data clearly point to a huge backlog of current needs for medical care and a continuing volume of need for care in the future. Even if the congenitally dislocated hip or the inguinal hernia cannot be attributed to deficient medical service as such, the prevalence of such cases calls for the provision of orthopedic or surgical services now and on a continuing basis.

[2] ROWNTREE, LEONARD G., Testimony before a Subcommittee of the Committee on Education and Labor, U. S. Senate, 78th Cong., 2d Sess., S. Res. 74, *Wartime Health and Education*. Washington: Government Printing Office, 1944, Part 5, p. 1624.

[3] Subcommittee of the Committee on Education and Labor, U. S. Senate, 78th Cong., 2d Sess., S. Res. 74, *Wartime Health and Education: Interim Report*. Washington: Government Printing Office, January, 1945, pp. 1-4.

[3a] GOIN, LOWELL S., Testimony before the Committee on Education and Labor, U.S. Senate, 79th Cong., 2d Sess., on S. 1606, *National Health Program*. Washington: Government Printing Office, Apr. 17, 1946, Part 2, pp. 624-625.

It is difficult to draw comparisons between rural and urban experience in the Selective Service program. In the first place, most of the
data have not been analyzed according to a rural-urban breakdown.
Secondly, the draft policies toward farm registrants changed in the
course of the war; the Tydings Amendment caused the deferment of
1,637,000 agricultural youth between November, 1942, and June,
1944, in the interest of preserving dwindling farm manpower.[4]
These deferred individuals, being on productive farms, have been
claimed to be a robust section of the rural sample, so that those remaining for draft examinations were allegedly below the average
in health status. The same effect, however, may well have been
exerted with regard to deferment of industrial workers, without
specific legislation. In fact, the Tydings Amendment actually operated to defer farmers chiefly in the older draft age groups[5] in which
physical defects are known to be more numerous. Thirdly, standards
for acceptance changed during the war and the general system of
examinations was modified. Up to January 1, 1942, examinations
were performed at local draft boards by some 35,000 local physicians,
so that results would naturally vary with local interpretation of military medical standards, diagnostic acumen, and attitudes. Only
after that date were examinations performed under reasonably
parallel conditions in all parts of the country, being the ultimate
responsibility of about 100 teams of Army physicians at induction
stations.

With these qualifications in mind, certain rural-urban comparisons
may be cautiously drawn. First of all, it is significant that examl-
nations during the First World War indicated that "a considerable
advantage accrues to the boy reared in the country."[6] The best available comparative data for the period of the recent military draft,
when examinations were standardized throughout the nation, are

[4] The Selective Training and Service Act of 1940, Sec. 5K was amended
November 13, 1942, as follows: "Every registrant found by a selective service
local board . . . to be necessary to and regularly engaged in an agricultural
occupation or endeavor essential to the war effort, shall be deferred from
training and service . . . so long as he remains so engaged and until such time
as a satisfactory replacement can be obtained."

[5] Based on unpublished data furnished by the Selective Service System.

[6] U. S. War Department, Provost Marshal General's Office, *Second Report of
Provost Marshal General on Operations of Selective Service System, to December
20, 1918.* Washington: Government Printing Office, 1919, p. 159.

for a two-month sample during November and December, 1943; these data show the opposite to be true. Urban men were rejected for all military service at a rate of 41.6 per cent, and an additional 4.9 per cent were qualified for only limited service. Rural men were

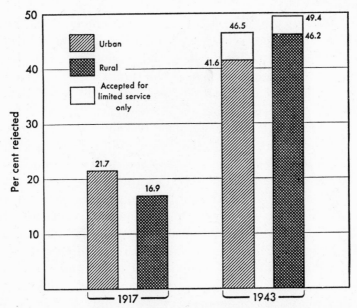

FIG. 10. Trend of Draft Rejections: Percentage of registrants rejected for military service on medical examination, by place of residence, 1917 and 1943. The 1917 study presents data for residents of selected large cities and for an all-state sample from places with Selective Service Boards having less than 1,200 registrants; the 1943 study is based on rural and urban place of residence as defined by the Census Bureau. Source: U.S. War Department, Provost Marshal General's Office. *Second Report of Provost Marshal General on Operations of Selective Service System, to Dec. 20, 1918,* p. 159. Also: Rowntree, Leonard G., Testimony before a Subcommittee of the Committee on Education and Labor, U.S. Senate, 78th Cong., 2d Sess., pursuant to S. Res. 74, *Wartime Health and Education,* Part 5, p. 1633.

rejected for all military service at a rate of 46.2 per cent, and an additional 3.2 per cent were qualified only for limited service. Thus the net rejection rate for general military duty was 46.5 per cent among urban males and 49.4 per cent among rural males (Figure 10). The presentation of state-by-state rejection rates in Figure 11 corroborates the finding of high rejection rates for rural youth, with the generally most highly rural states of the nation, in the Southeast and South

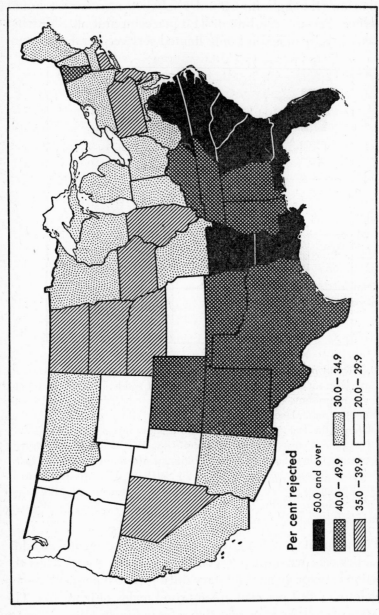

FIG. 11.   Draft Rejections: Percentage of registrants rejected for military service on medical examination, by states, February-August, 1943. Source: U.S. Selective Service System. *Physical Examinations of Selective Service Registrants during Wartime* (Medical Statistics Bull. 3), Nov. 1, 1944, Fig. 4.

Per cent rejected

50.0 and over
40.0 – 49.9
35.0 – 39.9
30.0 – 34.9
20.0 – 29.9

Central regions, having the highest rates. Even after induction it is reported that the inductees from rural states were discharged from military service because of disabilities at rates appreciably higher than inductees from more urban states. For example, one study showed that within a few months after entering service, 21 per cent of inductees from Alabama and 26 per cent of those from South Carolina were issued medical discharges, compared with 15 per cent of inductees from Pennsylvania and 11 per cent from Indiana.[7]

Analysis of rejection rates by occupational categories yields the same general conclusions. During the period April 1, 1942, to December 31, 1943, the rejection rate for all occupations was 42.6 per cent. "Farmers and farm managers," however, were rejected at a rate of 56.4 per cent, this being the third highest rejection rate among thirteen occupational groups classified. This rate was exceeded only by rejections among "emergency workers and unemployed" and "domestic service workers," the differentials being small (56.5 for emergency workers and 59.6 for domestic workers). The rejection rate for Negro farmers and farm managers was higher than for any other occupational group of either race, being 64.5 per cent. Another occupational group classified as "farm laborers and foremen" fell just below the rate for farmers, being 52.8 per cent.[8] Among 18 and 19 year olds, in fact, rejections for "farmers" were higher than for any other occupational group, exceeding even the rejection rate for "emergency workers and unemployed." The rate was 41.1 per cent, while the average for all occupations combined was 25.4 per cent.[9]

It has been asserted that Selective Service rejection rates give a false picture of the nation's health because they include rejections for mental and educational deficiency or, to use the official term, "failure to meet minimum intelligence standards." It is true that a substantial portion of all draft rejections were for "mental deficiency,"

[7] YOUNG, DUDLEY E., Farm Incomes in the Southeast in Relation to Cost of Medical Care. Atlanta: U. S. Bureau of Agricultural Economics, 1945, Processed.

[8] U. S. Selective Service System, National Headquarters, Physical Examinations of Selective Service Registrants during Wartime (Med. Stat. Bull. 3). Washington, Nov. 1, 1944, Processed.

[9] ROWNTREE, LEONARD G., KENNETH H. McGILL, and THOMAS L. EDWARDS, "Causes of Rejection and Incidence of Defects among 18 and 19 Year Old Selective Service Registrants," Journal of the American Medical Association, 123:181-185, Sept. 25, 1943.

including both educational deficiency and feeble-mindedness.[10] It is also true that a larger proportion of rural rejections was dependent on lack of schooling than urban. It is possible, however, to correct for these nonmedical causes for rejection, at least with respect to occupational categories that intimately reflect place of residence.

Of the over-all rejection rate of 42.6 per cent for all occupational groups, about one-sixth, or 15.7 per cent, were rejected for mental and educational deficiency. The comparable share of the rejections among the combined farmer and farm laborer occupational groups was 36.3 per cent.[11] It must be recognized, however, that a portion of these 15.7 per cent and 36.3 per cent nonmedical rejectees would have been disqualified for physical defects if they had come up for physical examination, instead of being eliminated at the outset because of illiteracy or "failure to meet minimum intelligence standards." Separate studies show that 38.2 per cent of those rejected for mental and educational deficiency actually had physical defects that would have disqualified them for military service anyway.[12]

When a correction, then, is made for rejections due to mental and educational deficiency, taking fully into account the untabulated physical defects in this group, the results presented in Table 9 are derived. It is seen that rejections of all persons engaged in farming for strict defects of health (not intelligence or education) were at a rate of 41.1 per cent compared with a rate of 38.1 per cent for all other occupations. The farm rejection rate was thus about 8 per cent higher than that for all others. This basic fact, derived from a study of 9,000,000 selectees, has great importance in our total evaluation of rural health needs.

This over-all differential in rejection rates is probably an understatement in that the data are not age-adjusted. Actually more farm than other selectees examined were in the younger age groups[13] bearing fewer defects in general, so that the farm figures are probably

[10] ROWNTREE, LEONARD G., Testimony before a Subcommittee of the Committee on Education and Labor, U. S. Senate, 78th Cong., 2d Sess., S. Res. 74, *Wartime Health and Education,* Part 5, pp. 1624-1626.

[11] Based on unpublished data furnished by the U. S. Selective Service System.

[12] ROWNTREE, LEONARD G., *op. cit.,* Part 6, p. 2034. When we consider the social and economic disadvantages that "educational deficiency" implies, its association with physical defects is not surprising. These rejectees were often denied even the limited health supervision of a school medical program.

[13] Based on unpublished data furnished by the U. S. Selective Service System.

unduly favorable. When data on the one age-specific group for which records are available are examined — the 18 and 19 year group — this point is borne out. For this group, when full correction is made for mental and educational deficiencies, the net rejection rate for farm youth was 32 per cent compared with 23 per cent for all other youth. Thus the farm rejection rate for strict defects of health for this known age group was 40 per cent higher than for all other youth. Similar differentials would probably be found for other age-specific

Table 9. Draft Rejections: *Percentage of registrants rejected for military service, in relation to mental deficiency, by occupation, 1942-1943*

Causes of rejection	All occupations except farming	Farming*
All causes	41.1	53.4
All causes except "mental and educational deficiency"—crude	36.2	34.0
All causes except "mental and educational deficiency"—adjusted†	38.1	41.1

Source: U. S. Selective Service System, *Physical Examinations of Selective Service Registrants during Wartime* (Medical Statistics Bull. 3). Washington, Nov. 1, 1944. Also, unpublished data furnished by the same office.

* Includes farmers, farm managers, farm laborers, and farm foremen.

† Includes medical defects that would have been disqualifying if registrant had not been rejected for "mental and educational deficiency."

comparisons. These net rejection rates, moreover, do not take account of the number of defects in an individual. These data are not available. It is altogether likely that if the rate of physical defects, per se, were classified for age-adjusted rural-urban groups, the differentials would be considerably more striking.

As of this writing rejection rates for rural and urban men, by specific cause of rejection, are not available. The causes of rejection throughout the nation as a whole are, of course, available in other publications.[14] For an inventory of specific physical impairments in

[14] U. S. Selective Service System, National Headquarters, *Analysis of Reports of Physical Examination* (Medical Statistics Bull. 1), Nov. 10, 1941, Processed; *Causes of Rejection and Incidence of Defects* (Medical Statistics Bull. 2), Aug. 1, 1943, Processed; *Physical Examinations of Selective Service Registrants during Wartime* (Medical Statistics Bull. 3); *Physical Examinations of Selective Service Registrants in the Final Months of the War* (Medical Statistics Bull. 4), June 1, 1946, Processed.

rural areas, we must turn to other studies. On the basis of Selective Service data we may simply conclude that rural disadvantages in health services have probably largely nullified any advantages that rural youth might have been assumed to enjoy by living in the "open country." The nation has paid the price in reduced military manpower.

Another set of examinations of a young age group give data on rural-urban comparisons with reference to specific defects as well as over-all fitness to work. These are the studies of 150,000 youths 16 to 24 years of age made by the National Youth Administration in 1941.

Considering youth with moderate defects, not disqualifying but only requiring some restriction in the type of NYA work to which they were assigned, white males from communities of under 2,500 population showed the best record. There were 25.5 per cent of rural youth in this group, compared with rising percentages in larger-sized communities up to 39.9 per cent of youth in cities of 500,000 and over. These comparisons, however, may not be valid because of varying physical standards demanded for industrial as against farm employment and because of varying diagnostic acumen between urban and rural practitioners performing the examinations.

For physical defects of such severity as to disqualify the youth entirely from NYA employment, the rejections of white males were highest in the rural areas. These disqualifying defects included communicable diseases, severe intestinal parasite infestation, severe heart lesions, active tuberculosis, marked orthopedic defects, and marked mental abnormalities.[15] This relationship was most striking for communities of different sizes in the South Atlantic, East South Central, and West South Central regions. In the East South Central region, for example, 12 per cent of the white males in the rural districts were rejected completely from NYA employment compared with only 2.5 per cent in the large cities of that region. Severe hookworm disease doubtless played a large part in this relationship.

In terms of the number of recommendations made for corrective measures, moreover, despite the fact that the rural examinations were

[15] National Youth Administration and U. S. Public Health Service, *The Health Status of NYA Youth: A Nation-Wide Survey of Youth of the National Youth Administration*. Federal Security Agency. Washington: Government Printing Office, 1942, p. 3.

probably less thorough, some correlation is found with rurality. Although for females no regular relationship to size of community is found, for total males the rate of recommended measures is highest in rural areas. For the largest sex-race group of the study,

Table 10. Physical Defects in Rural and Urban Youth: *Number of specific defects per 100 youth 16-24 years of age, by size of community, National Youth Administration, 1941*

Defects	500,000 and over	100,000– 500,000	25,000– 100,000	2,500– 25,000	Rural
Carious teeth	409.4	467.2	494.2	504.5	501.1
Eye refractions recommended	24.2	22.0	19.5	19.0	16.8
Diseased tonsils (white) . .	13.5	16.6	21.7	24.2	27.1
Underweight* (white males)	32.6	41.6	46.4	45.2	45.8
Underweight* (white females)	39.9	43.9	46.5	46.5	45.5
Overweight† (white males) .	35.2	24.6	21.9	21.9	20.5
Overweight† (white females)	33.6	29.2	27.8	27.3	26.9
Venereal disease (treatment recommended)	2.3	. . .	. . .	. . .	1.3
Hernia (recommended for herniotomy)	1.2	. . .	. . .	. . .	2.0
Phimosis (white males, recommended for circumcision)	1.7	. . .	. . .	. . .	5.9

Source: U. S. National Youth Administration and U. S. Public Health Service, *The Health Status of NYA Youth.*
* Five per cent or more below standard.
† Five per cent or more above standard.

white males, there were 163.9 recommendations per 100 youth examined in cities of 500,000 and over, 175.5 in cities of 100,000 to 500,000, 180.0 in cities of 25,000 to 100,000, 182.2 in cities of 2,500 to 25,000, and 187.9 in rural communities of under 2,500.

As for specific defects, some of the rural-urban differentials are revealing. Those for which comparative data are available are presented in Table 10. For visual defects calling for refraction, urban youth appear to be at a disadvantage, although the analysts of this study caution that these rates may partly reflect the use of eye specialists in the larger communities. Venereal disease cases likewise are more frequent in the more urban centers. For other recorded defects rural youth are at a disadvantage. The rate of carious teeth is significantly higher in rural areas than in the larger cities and the frequency of diseased tonsils is consistently greater in communities of smaller size. The frequency of hernia and phimosis, as reflected by recommendations for hernia repairs and circumcisions, is appreciably higher in rural youth than in big-city youth. Abnormalities of body weight are such as to suggest a lower caloric intake, relative to energy needs, by youth in rural areas and smaller communities than by those in large cities.

Physical findings with respect to rural youth take on added importance in view of the high percentage of the rural population we have observed to be in the younger age groups. These are the young men and women who migrate to our cities and provide manpower for our factories as well as our farms. Physical defects among them are a liability to the entire nation. That this is not mere rhetoric is demonstrated in one community studied where physical rejections for military service were dramatically related to school examination findings 15 years before of physical defects which had meanwhile gone uncorrected.[16]

Defects Revealed in Rural Surveys

Within rural population groups, medical examination studies have revealed the weighty burden of physical impairments in absolute terms. The most extensive study has been that made by the Farm Security Administration among low-income farm families in 21 representative rural counties of 17 states in 1940. Thorough examinations were performed by staffs of specialists, dentists, nurses, and technical assistants. A summary of some of the findings of this survey for adults (persons 15 years of age and over) is presented in Table 11 and for children (under 15 years) in Table 12.

[16] Ciocco, Antonio, Henry Klein, and Carroll E. Palmer, "Child Health and Selective Service Physical Standards," *Public Health Reports*, 56:2365-2375, Dec. 12, 1941.

Of the 9,776 white and 1,714 colored persons examined, only 4 per cent were found to be free of any significant physical impairments; 96 per cent had one or more impairments, with an average

Table 11. Physical Defects in Farm Adults: *Percentage of low-income farm persons 15 years of age and over with specified impairments, by race and sex,* 1940

Physical defects	White			Colored		
	All	Male	Female	All	Male	Female
Overweight	4.5	2.2	6.8	3.2	2.3	4.3
Underweight	2.5	2.2	2.8	1.2	1.1	1.2
Anemia*	8.1	7.6	8.6	39.6	38.5	40.9
Rickets†	0.7	1.3	0.2	. . .	. . .	. . .
Skin disease	5.9	7.5	4.3	3.0	4.6	1.6
Defective vision‡	33.9	29.3	38.9	33.6	33.6	33.6
Otitis media	3.8	3.5	4.1	2.1	2.3	1.9
Sinusitis	9.0	10.0	7.9	4.4	5.4	3.5
Tonsils slightly defective . .	33.6	30.7	36.6	27.4	21.7	33.1
Tonsils markedly defective .	11.3	11.0	11.5	8.8	10.2	7.4
Dental caries§	76.4	76.1	76.7	82.9	82.6	83.3
Heart defects	9.6	12.9	6.1	17.5	22.6	12.4
Hernia	4.7	7.2	1.9	4.0	4.8	3.3
Hemorrhoids	14.1	13.1	15.3	7.3	8.7	5.9
Varicose veins	10.5	8.1	13.2	4.6	4.0	5.3
Syphilis‖	1.1	1.2	1.0	10.6	10.1	11.2
Intestinal parasites¶	15.6	16.2	20.5	10.9	11.6	10.1

Source: Based on physical and laboratory examinations of 6,342 adults in 2,477 Farm Security Administration borrower families in 21 representative counties of 17 states. Rates for certain defects are derived from smaller samples.

* Based on photoelectric hemoglobinometer determinations, assuming 15.6 grams hemoglobin per 100 cc. as 100 per cent and considering 80 per cent as lower limit of normal for men, 70 per cent for women.

† Includes residual effects.

‡ Vision 20/25 or poorer in either eye.

§ One or more carious teeth.

‖ Based on serological tests.

¶ Southern states only.

of 3.5 defects for every man, woman, and child examined. The overall burden of defects was slightly higher among whites than among Negroes, 3.6 per white person and 3.3 per Negro. This is undoubtedly related to the fact, however, that the Negro sample was from a higher than average Negro agricultural income group, since all Farm Security borrowers had to be farm operators, while the white sample was probably from a lower than average white income group.

Among adults, the problem of deviation from normal weight was not great; it was most severe for white females and among them only 6.8 per cent were overweight according to standard weight tables.

Table 12. Physical Defects in Farm Children: *Percentage of persons under 15 years of age in low-income farm families with specified impairments, by race and sex,* 1940

Physical defects	White			Colored		
	All	Male	Female	All	Male	Female
Overweight	0.7	0.3	1.0	0.4	. . .	0.8
Underweight	8.8	6.5	11.2	5.7	3.4	7.8
Anemia*	8.2	7.4	9.0	4.8	3.8	5.8
Rickets†	6.4	6.7	6.0	9.9	12.9	7.1
Skin diseases	6.6	6.0	7.2	0.8	1.3	0.4
Defective vision‡	18.0	16.3	19.9	10.2	11.3	9.1
Otitis media	2.9	3.0	2.8	3.6	2.7	4.4
Sinusitis	9.3	6.9	11.8	0.2	0.4	. . .
Tonsils slightly defective . .	40.0	40.3	39.8	35.4	34.6	36.4
Tonsils markedly defective .	11.9	12.2	11.5	29.5	26.0	33.1
Dental caries§	56.8	56.3	57.3	51.0	50.6	51.3
Heart defects	5.9	6.0	5.8	3.8	4.5	3.3
Hernia	1.7	2.2	1.1	8.8	8.2	9.4
Intestinal parasites‖	25.4	26.9	23.8	12.0	12.8	11.2

Source: Based on physical and laboratory examinations among 5,148 children in 2,477 Farm Security Administration borrower families in 21 representative counties of 17 states. Rates for certain defects are derived from smaller samples.
* Clinical evaluation.
† Includes residual defects.
‡ Vision 20/25 or poorer in either eye.
§ One or more carious teeth.
‖ Southern states only.

Among children, weight deviations were more severe, with 8.8 per cent of the whites and 5.7 per cent of the Negroes being underweight. A higher percentage of underweight girls held for both races. There were sharp variations in different parts of the country; a physician performing examinations in Oklahoma reported, "The physical status of the children examined . . . was rather good, especially so considering the generally poor appearance of the adults," while another who did examinations in Arkansas, Louisiana, and Mississippi reported, "The general conclusion which I reached was that the children were all victims in some degree or other of malnutrition and malnourishment."[17] Other evidence of malnutrition was the 6.4 per cent of white children and 9.9 per cent of colored children with active or residual rickets. Anemia, as determined by photoelectric hemoglobinometer readings, was appalling among the Negro adults, affecting about 40 per cent of them and affecting 8.1 per cent of the white adults. The great majority of these cases were undoubtedly secondary anemias related to nutritional deficiencies. The smaller proportion of children reported to have anemia probably merely reflects the fact that the determination on them was made simply on clinical, rather than laboratory, study.

Skin diseases of some kind were found in 3.0 per cent of the Negro adults and about twice as many whites. While colored children seemed to be relatively free of skin disorders, 6.6 per cent of white children were affected.

Vision, as measured by Snellen chart performance, showed slight to severe abnormalities in about 34 per cent of both races. As in urban groups, impairments in vision rose sharply after about 30 years of age, reaching about 95 per cent for persons over 60 years.[18] Comparisons of visual deficiencies with certain urban groups suggest that rural vision has the advantage at practically all ages, as indicated by Snellen chart records. It should be borne in mind, however, that this test tends to be selective for myopia — just the defect most likely to develop in industrial employment which calls for close, refined work — while it may not discover a large percentage of hyperopic eye conditions — more likely to develop in the "wide open spaces." [18a] Yet farsightedness may be as great, if not a greater,

[17] Based on unpublished records of the U. S. Farm Security Administration, Office of the Chief Medical Officer.

[18] GOVER, MARY, and JESSE B. YAUKEY, "Physical Impairments of Members of Low-income Farm Families — 11,490 Persons in 2,477 Farm Security Administration Borrower Families 1940: II. Defective Vision as Determined by the Snellen Test and Other Chronic Eye Conditions," *Public Health Reports*, 59:1163-1184, Sept. 8, 1944.

[18a] While this point is controversial, there is much evidence that close, detailed work may contribute to myopia, perhaps by aggravating congenital tendencies. If this is so, prolonged vision at distant objects might possibly contribute to hyperopia, independent of the eye changes associated with aging. See: JACKSON, EDWARD, *The Eye and Its Diseases*, Conrad Berens, ed. Philadelphia: W. B. Saunders Company, 1936, p. 254.

handicap to reading than nearsightedness. More important, perhaps, is the fact that the great majority of farm people in this study requiring eyeglasses were not wearing them. Of white males over 40 years of age with defective vision, for example, only 12.8 per cent wore glasses compared with 45 to 65 per cent of comparable urban groups.[19] Cataracts were diagnosed at rates varying from 3.6 per cent of Negro males to 1.2 per cent of white females. Blindness in one eye was found in 1 out of 100 Negro males and 1 out of 200 white males. Trachoma was diagnosed or suspected in more than 1 out of 100 white persons of both sexes.

Diseases of the ear, sinuses, and throat were very common. Evidence of otitis media, acute or chronic, was found in 3 per cent, more or less, of white and Negro children and adults. Measured in terms of defective hearing, 10.7 per cent of Negroes (5 years of age and over) and 17.9 per cent of whites had some degree of impairment. In whites it varied from 6.2 per cent for the 5-14 year age group up to 82.6 per cent for persons 65 years and over. These rates of partial or complete deafness were appreciably higher than those found in hearing studies of representative urban groups.[20]

Deviated nasal septum was found in about 40 per cent of persons over 20 years of age, a rate lower than that found in metropolitan studies in New York and Baltimore but higher than found in other higher income groups throughout the nation. Bronchial asthma was found in 6.4 per 1,000 persons in low-income farm families, with a peak of 33.1 per 1,000 in males 35-44 years of age. Acute or chronic bronchitis was found in 6.9 per 1,000, with a peak of 25.2 per 1,000 in 45-54 year old males. The prevalence of pulmonary emphysema was 9.0 per 1,000, with a rate of about 80 per 1,000 being reached past 55 years of age. Sinusitis was found present in 54.9 per 1,000 persons, again showing a peak in the later years of life. For asthma, emphysema, and sinusitis — conditions on which comparative urban studies are available — rates among these low-income farm families appear to be higher than in most urban groups surveyed.[21]

[19] *Ibid.*

[20] GOVER and YAUKEY, "III. Impaired Hearing for Speech," *Public Health Reports,* 60:429-441, Apr. 20, 1945.

[21] GOVER AND YAUKEY, "V. Defects of the Nasal Septum; and Chronic Respiratory Affections, Exclusive of Diseased Tonsils," *Public Health Reports,* 60:1069-1085, Sept. 14, 1945.

Tonsils were found to be markedly defective in about 12 per cent of the white and 30 per cent of the colored children as well as in about 11 per cent of white adults and 9 per cent of colored adults. They were slightly defective in much larger proportions. Because of differences in medical criteria, it is difficult to make comparisons with findings among urban groups, but it appears that, by any criteria, these farm people are more likely to carry their defective tonsils along with them into adult life than comparable city people. The explanation manifestly is the very low rural rate of tonsillectomies.[22]

As in most urban studies, the physical defect of highest prevalence was dental caries. About 76 per cent of the white and 83 per cent of the Negro adults had one or more carious teeth and even children had rates of 57 per cent for the white and 51 per cent for the Negroes. Defects of the heart were diagnosed in 9.6 per cent of the white adults and 6.0 per cent of the white children as well as in 17.5 per cent of Negro adults and 3.8 per cent of Negro children. Among white heads of households and their wives, moreover, 13 per cent were found to have high blood pressure and 4 per cent presented clinical evidence of arteriosclerosis. Varicose veins were found in 10.5 per cent of white and 4.6 per cent of colored adults; hemorrhoids in 14.1 per cent of white and 7.3 per cent of colored adults. As many as 1 out of every 12 heads of white families had a hernia which had not been corrected. The high report on hernias in colored children is chiefly indicative of many umbilical hernias, reflecting improper infant hygiene. On the basis of a medical history and only the one examination, peptic ulcers were diagnosed in 6 out of every 1,000 white adults.[23]

Although only about 1 per cent of white adults were found to have syphilis, almost 11 per cent of colored adults were found afflicted with it. Intestinal parasites, on the other hand, were diagnosed in over 25 per cent of the white children and 12 per cent of the colored children from the South. Impressive evidence of poor obstetrical care was the fact that about 40 per cent of all married women in this study were found to have pelvic disrepair resulting from second- and third-degree perineal tears. In addition 21.5 per

[22] GOVER AND YAUKEY, "IV. Defective Tonsils and Adenoids," *Public Health Reports*, 60:693-710, June 22, 1945.
[23] Based on unpublished records of the U. S. Farm Security Administration, Office of the Chief Medical Officer.

cent of the white wives and 16.9 per cent of the colored wives showed some degree of uterine displacement.[24]

These findings all apply to low-income farm families. Among higher income farm and rural nonfarm families, the burden of physical impairments is probably lighter. In a relatively prosperous rural county of New York State, for example, dental caries was found in only 41 per cent of all persons, heart defects were found in only 1.8 per cent of persons, hernia was found in 3.0 per cent, varicose veins in 2.4 per cent, anemia in 0.5 per cent.[25] On the other hand, skin conditions were found in 9.0 per cent of persons examined. Among defects not analyzed in the Farm Security study, diffuse or nodular enlargement of the thyroid was found in 2.8 per cent of persons; varicocele in 8.8 per cent and hydrocele in 2.2 per cent; kyphosis and scoliosis in 4.4 per cent; flat foot and foot strain in 2.8 per cent; albuminuria in 3.8 per cent of urine specimens examined, glycosuria of some degree in 4.4 per cent of specimens; acute or chronic nephritis in 1.2 per cent and diabetes in 1.5 per cent of all subjects.

Other rural studies in selected areas have underscored the high prevalence of defects revealed in the nation-wide Farm Security Administration study. In southeast Missouri, for example, a special intensive study of 4,131 persons in Farm Security Administration borrower families revealed impairments such as hernias or enlarged inguinal rings in 14.6 per cent of the males; perineal disrepair in 74.7 per cent of the white women who had borne children; nasal defects (including deviated nasal septum) in 47 per cent of white males and 30 per cent of white females; defects of the eye other than poor vision (pterygia, cataracts, trachoma, strabismus) in 18 per cent of the males; heart abnormalities in 4.2 per cent of the males, 3.1 per cent of the white females, and 3.8 per cent of the Negro females; hemorrhoids in over 30 per cent of the females; diseases of the skin in 4.9 per cent of the males; and many others.[26]

[24] *Ibid.*

[25] WHEELER, RALPH E., "Impairments in a Rural Population: III. Physical Examination and Laboratory Data," *The Milbank Memorial Fund Quarterly,* 16:89-106, January, 1938.

[26] LIVELY, C. E., and HERBERT F. LIONBERGER, *The Physical Status and Health of Farm Tenants and Farm Laborers in Southeast Missouri* (Preliminary Rep. 2 and 3). Columbia: University of Missouri, July, 1942.

Farm laborer families bear a high prevalence of physical defects. Children of agricultural laborer families in a southern Texas county have been shown to be afflicted with a number of physical defects which, while mostly minor, could eventually cause serious handicaps. Only 3 out of 83 examined were not in need of some form of medical or dental care.[27] Examinations of Latin-American laborers and members of their families — largely seasonal agricultural workers — at San Antonio, Texas, have disclosed an extremely high prevalence of active tuberculosis and other conditions of the chest. Of over 18,000 individuals examined, 4.9 per cent showed x-ray evidence of reinfection tuberculosis and 3.8 per cent had other types of chest abnormalities.[28] Migratory farm-labor families, in general, are afflicted with particularly high rates of all communicable diseases, malnutrition, and most types of disabling illness.[29]

The most rural racial group in the United States, Indians, have an especially high burden of physical impairments. Their rate of rejection for any type of military service up to the end of 1941 was 37.5 per cent, compared with about 30 per cent for the nation as a whole in that period. The chief causes of rejection among them were relatively low on the list of the causes for the nation as a whole, consisting first of eye diseases (largely trachoma), second of tuberculosis, and third of venereal diseases.[30]

It is recognized that physical impairments seldom kill people. The major causes of death are quite distinct from the catalogue of defects. Physical impairments, on the contrary, cause debility and reduced efficiency. They constitute a ball and chain of which the bearer may lose consciousness through years of adjustment. Their human and their economic cost, however, is incalculable.

[27] WARBURTON, A. A., HELEN WOOD, and M. M. CRANE, *The Work and Welfare of Children of Agricultural Laborers in Hidalgo County, Texas* (U. S. Children's Bureau Pub. 298). Washington: Government Printing Office, 1943, pp. 57-61.

[28] GOULD, DAVID M., "Mass X-ray Survey in San Antonio," *Public Health Reports*, 60:117-126, Feb. 2, 1945.

[29] BLANKENSHIP, CHARLES F., and FRED SAFIER, *A Study of Medical Problems Associated with Transients* (U. S. Public Health Service Bull. 258). Washington: Government Printing Office, 1940.

[30] McGIBONY, J. R., "Indians and Selective Service," *Public Health Reports*, 57:1-7, Jan. 2, 1942.

Special comments should be made on a few major types of impairment which have been the subject of intensive study among rural and urban populations alike. Chief among these are the problems of malnutrition, dental defects, venereal disease, and mental disorder.

Nutritional Status

As for nutritional status, one might expect rural people to be far superior to urban. Whatever rural diets may lack in the tempting variety of foods available to the city family, it might be assumed that they are abundant in the natural wholesome products of the soil on which farm families live. Sunshine, an important factor in vitamin D and calcium metabolism, is certainly plentiful. Yet large numbers of farm families raise little in the way of vegetables, have neither a cow nor chickens, and have incomes too low to buy needed foods. Actual studies of rural nutritional status show it to be far poorer than life on the land might lead one to expect.

Farm families, nevertheless, appear to enjoy better diets than village or city families in the same income groups; they "eat larger quantities of protective foods."[31] The essential fact, however, is that farm families tend not to be of the same income groups as urban families, but, as we have noted, of considerably lower income levels. The net effect, therefore, is for farm families on the whole to have diets only moderately better than urban families. On the basis of a nation-wide study made in 1936-37, the United States Bureau of Human Nutrition and Home Economics has analyzed diets in relation to the optimum standards for nutrition established by the National Research Council. They determined, with respect to the seven essential nutrients recommended by the Council, that some 85 per cent of urban families fell short of the recommended levels and that as many as 75 per cent of farm families likewise fell short.[32] Recommended standards for calcium and vitamin A, for example, were not met by 25 per cent of farm families, and levels for thiamin,

[31] STIEBLING, HAZEL K., *Are We Well Fed? A Report on the Diets of Families in the United States* (U. S. Bureau of Home Economics. Misc. Pub. 430). Washington: Government Printing Office, 1941, p. 11.

[32] STIEBLING, HAZEL K., "Food Consumption Studies and Dietary Recommendations," *Federation Proceedings* (Federation of American Society for Experimental Biology), 1:327-330, September, 1942.

riboflavin (both in the vitamin B complex), and ascorbic acid (vitamin C) fell short in the diets of 50 per cent. Special studies such as those made on low-income farm families in Louisiana or rural adults in Chatham County, North Carolina, reveal an astonishingly high prevalence of inadequate diets.[33]

Perhaps more decisive than theoretical analyses of diets are evaluations of physical status reflecting the end results of nutrition. Such evaluations are by no means easy, since the ultimate anatomical or physiological effects of malnutrition are often difficult to determine. Taking underweight as a crude index of malnutrition, the National Youth Administration found that among older boys and girls there was "an increasing percentage below weight standard as the size of community decreased." Thus 46 per cent of rural boys and girls were found to be underweight compared with 33 per cent of boys and 40 per cent of girls in cities of 500,000 and over; with regard to overweight, the opposite relationship was found.[34] Height and weight measures made of some 14,000 urban children compared with 13,000 rural children in Utah showed the city children to be taller and heavier for their height and age, although both groups were from the same racial stock. Subsequent studies showed that, relative to their height, the rural children did not have any disturbing signs of undernutrition but that they had appeared to suffer distinct disadvantages in the early years, when body development was getting under way.[35] Studies in fairly prosperous rural sections like Pennsylvania may indicate opposite conclusions with respect to underweight, but for the nation as a whole the "lean and hungry" are found more often in rural than in city families. Even in Pennsylvania, however,

[33] GRIGSBY, NORA E., L. C. McBRYDE, and H. J. DAVIS, *A Study of the Adequacy of Diets of Farm Security Administration Families in Louisiana.* Baton Rouge: Louisiana State University College of Agriculture, Sept. 15, 1942, Processed. Also MILAM, D. F., "A Nutrition Survey of a Small North Carolina Community," *American Journal of Public Health,* 32:406-412, April, 1942.

[34] U. S. National Youth Administration and U. S. Public Health Service, *The Health Status of NYA Youth,* pp. 29-31.

[35] BROWN, ALMEDA P., *Comparative Size of Rural and Urban Utah School Children as Determined by the Weight-height-age Relationship.* Logan: Utah State Agricultural College Experiment Station (Bull. 266), April, 1936. Also BROWN, ALMEDA P., and FAYE Y. MOSER, "Nutritional Status Indices for Rural and Urban Utah School Children," *Child Development* (Society for Research in Child Development), 13:101-109, June, 1942.

lower values were found for visual adaptation to darkness, a reflection of vitamin A deficiency, among rural families than among urban.[36]

Clinical and laboratory studies of nutritional status within rural areas reveal varying degrees of nutritional failure. Detailed studies in a rural section of Tennessee, for example, showed serious deficiencies in caloric intake as manifested by body weight. There was clinical and laboratory evidence of a small degree of calcium and vitamin D deficiency although, according to National Research Council optimal dietary standards, the intake of calcium and vitamin D was highly deficient.[37] In Colorado, underprivileged rural families have been shown to present clinical and functional evidence of severe deficiencies of protein and vitamins.[38] As we have noted from Farm Security Administration studies, hemoglobin levels have been found below normal in a high percentage of low-income rural families. Special studies in southeast Missouri showed even more striking evidence of widespread anemia.[39]

The scourge of pellagra in the South has already been considered. Yet the subclinical consequences of a diet of fat back and hominy grits are undoubtedly greater than those made evident by pellagra or other out-and-out vitamin-deficiency diseases. The entire problem of rural malnutrition is tied up not only with rural poverty but with lack of education as well. Customs and habits play a large part. The problem is aggravated by economic pressures like those which, in the South, prevent the poor tenant or sharecropper from putting a half acre in vegetables, so that every square foot can be used for his cash crop — cotton. It is aggravated by poor soil practices that rob the soil of constituents contributing to the vitamin and mineral

[36] MACK, P. B., J. M. SMITH, C. H. LOGAN, A. T. O'BRIEN, and F. O. SMITH, *Human Nutrition Research and Improvement in Mass Nutritional Status*, Pennsylvania State College Bulletin, Vol. 36, Apr. 16, 1942.

[37] YOUMANS, JOHN B., E. WHITE PATTON, and RUTH KERN, "Surveys of the Nutrition of Populations, Vitamin D and Calcium Nutrition," *American Journal of Public Health*, 34:1049-1057, October, 1944.

[38] PIJOAN, MICHAEL, and R. W. ROSKELLY, *Nutrition and Certain Related Factors of Spanish-Americans in Northern Colorado*. Denver: Rocky Mountain Council on Inter-American Affairs, 1943.

[39] LIVELY, C. E., *The Physical Status and Health of Farm Security Clients in Southeast Missouri* (Preliminary Rep. 1). Columbia: University of Missouri, April, 1942.

content of the food raised and locally consumed. It is aggravated by the fact that, for foods other than those produced locally, the rural community is provided with a system of distribution inferior to that of the large city. All in all, the status of rural nutrition is far poorer than one would expect to find among the producers of the nation's food.

Dental Disease

The most prevalent of all physical impairments is probably dental disease. In the course of their lives practically 100 per cent of the population, both urban and rural, are afflicted with dental caries or with pyorrhea. Early in the Selective Service program, before physical standards were lowered, dental defects were the chief cause of rejection.[40] The special feature of carious teeth as a health problem is that, without treatment, the condition always persists and becomes worse; unlike many other common ailments, dental decay is neither self-limited nor self-healing. In general, the longer dental caries is neglected, the more expensive the task of correction becomes, unless one is satisfied with complete removal and nonreplacement of the tooth. Since the treatment of dental disease requires special skills and is time-consuming, its economic cost is enormous.

A determination of the relative rural-urban prevalence of dental disease is complicated by the factor of geographic location. For many years, caries prevalence appears to have followed a characteristic pattern in the United States, being highest in the Northeast and the Northwest and lowest throughout the entire South, particularly in the South Central states. That this is related to geographic location rather than urbanization is suggested by the fact that it has been observed in some degree in military selectees since at least 1865, when the northernmost states were still typically agricultural, and the fact that dental caries prevalence has been consistently lower in the more industralized Middle Atlantic states than the more agricultural New England states.[41] The causes of this geographic distri-

[40] "Dentistry and Selective Service," editorial, *Journal of the American College of Dentists*, 8:141, June, 1941.

[41] NIZEL, ABRAHAM E., and BASIL G. BIBBY, "Geographic Variations in Caries Prevalence of Soldiers," *Journal of the American Dental Association*, 31:1619-1626, December, 1944.

bution of dental caries have been a matter of much speculation, but whether it is related to exposure to sunshine, dietary habits, mineral content of the soil or water (including fluorides), or other factors, is not clear. The net effect of these regional differentials, nevertheless, is a higher occurrence of dental caries in the more urbanized regions of the country and a lower prevalence in the more rural regions.

Actual comparisons of the prevalence of dental disease by size of community have been drawn only sparingly. It must be recognized that the initial occurrence of dental caries is something quite different from its net prevalence, since the latter rate is obviously influenced by elimination, through fillings or extractions, of decay that has occurred in the past. Despite the probable lower initial occurrence of caries in the general rural population, therefore, we have noted that National Youth Administration examinations showed a higher residue of uncorrected caries in rural than in urban youth. More striking evidence of this effect is found in a study sponsored by the United States Public Health Service on children 6 to 14 years of age in several selected states.[42] The results of this study for the state providing the largest samples, totaling 959,500 children, are presented in Table 13.

It will be noted that, considering both present and past evidence of dental caries, the rural sections of three of the four states analyzed show lower rates. When the net prevalence of uncorrected caries is considered, however, the rate in rural sections is appreciably higher than in urban in the same three states and practically equal to urban in the fourth. The obvious explanation is that dental caries in rural children tends to go uncorrected, so that the residual burden of dental disease is greater in the country.

These studies probably all understate the true dimensions of the problem of rural dental disease, since they have been confined to children or young adults. As noted, dental disease if unchecked tends to increase cumulatively with the years and to grow more severe. This applies preeminently in rural sections where dental care is so often virtually unobtainable. Even the everyday instruments of oral

[42] MESSNER, C. P., W. M. GAFAFER, F. C. CADY, and H. T. DEAN, *Dental Survey of School Children Ages 6-14 Years Made in 1933-34 in 26 States* (U. S. Public Health Service Bull. 226). Washington: Government Printing Office, May, 1936.

hygiene — toothbrushes and dentifrices — are probably used less widely among rural families. The average rural adult, therefore, is undoubtedly prey to more extensive oral disease relative to the urban adult than holds for comparisons of rural and urban children or youth. An affected tooth in the farmer is likely to become more hopelessly carious than a decayed tooth in an industrial worker, and complete loss of the tooth is more frequently the end result.

Table 13. Dental Disease: *Prevalence rates of dental caries, past and present, among 6-14 year old children in four states* by place of residence, 1935*

State	Carious teeth, past and present† (number per 100 persons)		Present carious teeth (number per 100 persons)	
	Urban	Rural‡	Urban	Rural‡
Tennessee	200.8	171.9	71.7	82.5
Minnesota	304.9	258.3	48.3	60.6
Indiana	256.7	201.6	59.7	72.5
New Jersey . . .	235.7	303.0	70.8	70.2

Source: Derived from data presented in Messner, Gafafer, Cady, and Dean, *op. cit.*
* Sample of 959,500 children.
† Combined rates of decayed, missing, and filled teeth; often referred to as "DMF rate."
‡ Communities under 5,000 population.

Comparing the state of dental health in different parts of the country, the American Dental Association has recently pointed to the predominantly urban Northeastern states as enjoying dental health "on a considerably higher level . . . than in any other section of the country."[43] Despite the greater need for fillings, reflecting the high incidence of dental caries referred to above, it is in the Northeast that "the need for extractions, and for the treatment of pyorrhea, is in every instance less than in other sections, while the need for . . . partial dentures (indicative of the high percentage of natural teeth remaining in the mouth) is higher than in any other section."

In more rural regions, in other words, despite the lower initial occurrence of dental caries, loss of all or nearly all the teeth is more commonplace. Yet the scientific application of artificial dentures,

[43] American Dental Association, Committee on Economics, "A Comparative Study of the Dental Needs Found to Exist in Four Major Geographic Sections of the United States," *Journal of the American Dental Association*, 30:443, March, 1943.

partial or complete, is all too seldom achieved in hundreds of rural counties.

Venereal Disease

A word may be said about the problem of venereal diseases in rural areas. The prevalent notion has long been that venereal infection is associated with city life. While prostitution and high liquor consumption in the cities may mean that syphilis and gonorrhea are spread principally in urban places, the findings of Selective Service examinations indicate that the spirochetes by no means confine themselves to actual residents of the cities. Based upon Selective Service findings, it is estimated that the rate of prevalence for syphilis in 21-35 year old males for the nation as a whole is actually higher among rural than among urban residents. The relative rates for gonorrhea and the other venereal infections are not known, but they are usually assumed to be about parallel to those for syphilis. It may also be assumed that the rates among 21-35 year old males give a proportionate reflection of rates in the rest of the urban and rural populations, although the actual over-all rates are undoubtedly quite different.

Estimated prevalence rates of syphilis in the male population of 21-35 years of age residing in rural and urban areas are presented in Figure 12. It is noted that the prevalence rates for whites and Negroes taken separately are both higher in urban than in rural areas. The Negro rate is so much higher than the white rate, however, and the Negro population in the region of highest general prevalence (the South) is so predominantly rural, that the net effect is to produce a national rural prevalence rate for syphilis of 49.4 cases per 1,000 men of 21-35 years of age in rural areas compared with 46.5 cases per 1,000 in urban areas.[44]

This relationship obviously does not hold for many individual states, since even in the Southern states, where syphilis is most rampant, the small proportion of urban Negroes still have a higher prevalence rate than the large proportion of rural Negroes. In a few states, including Connecticut, Delaware, Florida, Maine, New Jersey, New York, and Pennsylvania, however, the prevalence of syph-

[44] VONDERLEHR, R. A., and LIDA J. USILTON, "Syphilis among Men of Draft Age in the United States," *Journal of the American Medical Association,* 120:1369-1372, Dec. 26, 1942.

ilis among whites alone is higher in the rural sections, and in Indiana and New York, prevalence among Negroes alone is higher in rural sections.[45] These few instances would suggest that, despite the manifestly greater hazard of contracting syphilis in urban centers, control measures in the cities have perhaps become so effective

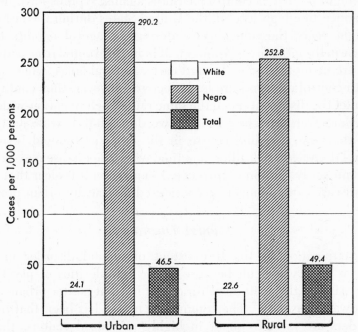

FIG. 12. Syphilis: Estimated prevalence rates in rural and urban areas, by race, in all 21-35 year old males, 1941. Source: Vonderlehr, R. A., and Lida J. Usilton, "Syphilis Among Men of Draft Age in the United States," *Journal of the American Medical Association*, 120:1369-1372, Dec. 26, 1942.

that the relative menace of the disease for rural residents, for whom control measures are probably less effective, is becoming greater.

An analysis of syphilis rates found in Selective Service registrants by age groups in rural and urban areas reveals some interesting features in the trend of venereal diseases. Keeping in mind that the syphilis prevalence rate represents a cumulative rate for untreated cases of previous years as well as recently contracted cases, it is found that the rate for rural men 31-35 years of age was 15 per cent lower than the urban rate; for rural men 26-30 years it was only

[45] *Ibid.*

5 per cent lower than the urban rate; and for rural men 21-25 years of age it was actually 12 per cent higher than the urban rate.[46] It might be that in early adult life, rural men are actually more liable to contract syphilis than city men, but as life continues the city resident becomes stricken at a much greater rate. Another explanation might be that as control measures against syphilis have become developed to a high level in the United States during the last seven or eight years, the young men entering the age of liability to the disease in the cities are to some extent being prevented from acquiring it or are being treated and cured early. In rural areas, where public health control measures are less effective, however, they continue to contract the disease at much the same rate as before nation-wide control efforts were launched. In other words, syphilis may be starting to take the same downhill course in the cities as typhoid fever did several decades ago, leading to a time when the disease may become predominantly rural in occurrence. In any case, it is clear that venereal disease can no longer be considered a typically urban problem.

Mental Disorder

Determination of the true extent of mental disorder in rural sections is very difficult because of the complexities of psychiatric diagnosis and the attitude of rural — or for that matter urban — people toward "insanity." The commonest notion has been that mental disorders are most frequent in highly urbanized centers; that, in fact, urbanization increases the likelihood of mental breakdown. Such conclusions, however, have been based almost entirely on studies of first admissions to mental institutions in relation to the residence of the patient. The invalidity of such reasoning is manifest. Not only are mental hospital beds considerably less available to rural people, but rural attitudes are such that even with mental institutions available, the rural family is more typically opposed to "committing" one of its members. The social milieu in rural areas, in fact, not only discourages institutionalization of mental cases but actually creates less urgent need for it.[47] Even when conclusions are drawn from mental hospital admissions within one state, therefore

[46] *Ibid.* Derived from data presented.

[47] LANDIS, C., and J. D. PAGE, *Modern Society and Mental Disease*. New York: Farrar & Rinehart, Inc., 1938, pp. 51 *ff.*

(with the same facilities supposedly being available for both rural and urban residents), one cannot be impressed with findings of lower rural mental disease rates.[48]

It has been demonstrated, as a matter of fact, that the generally reported increase in mental disease in recent years is due less to the increased urbanization of our society — a frequent explanation — than to factors such as the aging of the population and the increased availability of mental hospital beds.[49] There are even reasons for believing that the isolation of the individual from social contacts, occurring both in the rural areas and in certain sections of the big cities, is a major factor in causing mental breakdown.

When mental disorder rates are measured by psychological examinations of a general population group, other relationships are found. In Sweden, for example, the 1930 Census reported the total prevalence of insanity, hospitalized and nonhospitalized, to be 4.54 per 1,000 persons in rural areas (averaging 11 inhabitants per square kilometer) and 4.51 per 1,000 in urban areas (averaging 831 inhabitants per square kilometer).[50] Selective Service examinations in this country, in fact, have shown the highest rates for most mental disorders to occur in the most rural communities.[51] For all psychoses (schizophrenia, manic-depressive insanity, etc.), the communities of lowest population density (defined as "semirural") are reported with the highest rate of draft rejections, 4.5 per 1,000, compared with rates of 0.9, 3.3, 3.5, and 3.1 per 1,000 in communities of increasing size. For psychoneuroses also, the rejection rate is reported highest in the semirural communities, being 44 per 1,000 compared with 33, 37, 34, and 37 per 1,000 in towns and cities of increasing size. Among the psychiatric disorders, only chronic alcoholism and psychopathic personality were found more frequently in larger cities than in sparsely settled areas, and the latter was found with a rate

[48] MALZBERG, BENJAMIN, "The Prevalence of Mental Diseases among the Urban and Rural Populations of New York State," *Psychiatric Quarterly*, 9:55-87, 1935.

[49] DORN, HAROLD F., "The Incidence and Future Expectancy of Mental Disease," *Public Health Reports*, 53:1991-2004, Nov. 11, 1938.

[50] LANDIS and PAGE, *op. cit.*, p. 50.

[51] HYDE, ROBERT W., and LOWELL V. KINGSLEY, "Studies in Medical Sociology: II. The Relation of Mental Disorders to Population Density," *The New England Journal of Medicine*, 231:571-577, Oct. 26, 1944.

higher than the semirural only in the very largest cities (over 500,000). For mental deficiency, the semirural community is strikingly highest with 24 rejections per 1,000, compared with 13, 15, 16, and 18 in places of increasing size.[52]

Analysis of Selective Service data by occupational groups leads to the same conclusion. Rejections for all mental and personality disorders were higher for "farmers and farm managers" than for any other occupational group. Mental rejections among "farm laborers" were next in line, except only for "emergency workers, unemployed, and non-classifiable." A breakdown of the "farmer and farm manager" rejection rate of 143.4 per 1,000 registrants examined shows 80.9 to be due to psychoneurosis and 62.5 due to other mental and personality disorders; the "farm laborer" rejection rate of 118.7 per 1,000 registrants divides between 53.8 for psychoneurosis and 64.9 for other disorders. These component rates are higher in every instance than the comparable averages for all occupations.[53]

Whatever may be the need for institutional therapy in terms of environmental pressures in rural and urban communities, it appears that the over-all burden of mental disease is no less in rural than in urban America. The psychoneurotic or feeble-minded individual or even the psychotic may be able to "get along" more easily and cause less disturbance in a rural than in an urban community, but his personal need for help is probably as great and the burden he causes his family is probably greater — simply because it tends to be shared less through other social contacts. In an isolated rural county of Tennessee believed to be representative, intensive study revealed that twice as many cases of mental disease required institutionalization as were, in fact, hospitalized — 4.03 cases per 1,000 needing

[52] *Ibid.* In this study, based on the examinations at induction stations, urban rates of rejection may be lowered artificially because a higher proportion of urban mental cases may be in institutions and unable to appear for examination. This factor, however, could hardly account for more than a small part of the urban-rural differentials with respect to psychoses and would hardly apply at all for the psychoneuroses. The factor may be ignored entirely in analyses of over-all rejection rates, as in the discussion which follows, since even institutionalized mental cases were registered and recorded as rejected.

[53] ROWNTREE, LEONARD O., KENNETH H. McGILL, and LOUIS P. HELLMAN, "Mental and Personality Disorders in Selective Service Registrants," *Journal of the American Medical Association,* 128:1084-1087, Aug. 11, 1945.

hospital care and 2.10 cases per 1,000 actually getting it.[54] This study revealed rural rates of mental disorders, active and inactive, as follows: major psychoses, 6.3 per 1,000; psychoneuroses, 4.0 per 1,000; conduct and behavior disorder, 16.7 per 1,000; psychopathic traits, 7.5 per 1,000; special personality traits, 13.5 per 1,000; mental deficiency, 8.2 per 1,000; organic and miscellaneous mental conditions, 13.2 per 1,000. It has been estimated that a major mental disorder affects or has affected about 1 per cent of the general population and that over 6 per cent are suffering from some form of mental illness;[55] it seems most unlikely that the rural population is any more fortunate than the average.

Other major impairment problems warrant special consideration, but rural data on them are not available. What proportion of the approximately 2,600,000 persons in the nation with orthopedic impairments, for example, are rural cannot be stated.[56] High rural accident rates, in association with frequent lack of proper surgical care for the management of fractures and other injuries, would suggest that rural crippling is probably greater than urban. Some 230,000 persons in the United States are estimated to be totally blind, and there is suggestive evidence from the 1930 Census that blindness is less frequent in large cities than elsewhere. The rural sample of the National Health Survey, moreover, showed rates of 100 to 157 blind persons per 100,000 population, compared with 83 in the urban sample.[57] As with blindness, which often represents the end result of inadequately attended disease or injury, it seems prob-

[54] ROTH, WILLIAM F., and FRANK H. LUTON, "The Mental Health Program in Tennessee: II. Statistical Report of a Psychiatric Survey in a Rural County," *American Journal of Psychiatry*, 99:662-675, March, 1943.

[55] LEMKAU, PAUL, CHRISTOPHER TIETZE, and MARCIA COOPER, "A Survey of Statistical Studies on the Prevalence and Incidence of Mental Disorder in Sample Populations," *Public Health Reports*, 58:1909-1927, Dec. 31, 1943. Also PARRAN, THOMAS, Testimony before a Subcommittee of the Committee on Education and Labor, U. S. Senate, 79th Cong., 2d Sess., S. 1160, *National Neuropsychiatric Institute Act*. Washington: Government Printing Office, 1946, p. 7.

[56] KARPINOS, BERNARD D., "The Physically Handicapped," *Public Health Reports*, 58:1573-1592, Oct. 23, 1943.

[57] SANDERS, BARKEV V., "The Blind — Their Number and Characteristics," *Social Security Bulletin*, 6:17-26, October, 1943.

able that a disproportionate share of the nation's 60,000 to 100,000 persons with total deafness[58] are to be found in rural communities. There is much reason to believe, in effect, that the over-all burden of physical and mental impairments of almost every type is appreciably greater in rural areas than in cities.

[58] LEWIS, LAWRENCE Q., Testimony before a Subcommittee of the Committee on Labor, U. S. House of Representatives, 78th Cong., 2d Sess., H. Res. 230, *Aid to the Physically Handicapped*. Washington: Government Printing Office, 1945, Part 1, pp. 2-17. Also CRAMMATTEE, ALAN B., Testimony before a Subcommittee of the Committee on Labor, *Aid to the Physically Handicapped*. Part 3, pp. 241-254.

WHAT, THEN, IS THE STATUS of rural health? The answer must obviously be complex. As measured by reported death rates alone, it appears better than urban though certainly not so good as it could be. Accurate registration of deaths might even eliminate the dwindling differential. For infants and children and mothers in childbirth, in fact, rural death rates are today found to be generally higher than those in the big cities. As measured by the burden of illness and disability, rural health is probably somewhat poorer than urban health and to some extent different in kind. The very diseases that modern science is best able to prevent take a higher toll in rural areas. As measured by impairments and disorders, rural health is rather clearly poorer than urban.

Taking available records at their face value, one might conclude that rural people do not appear to be afflicted more than the average with the kinds of diseases or impairments that are fatal to the largest number of people today. At least, when rural people have these diseases, they seem to survive in the country longer than their city friends. As for the ailments causing discomfort, pain, inefficiency, and human wastage during life, country dwellers appear to bear more than their share. Of death and disability both, they suffer far more than the "natural benefits" of rural life would lead one to expect. The trend of rural in relation to urban health is such that we seem to be rapidly approaching the time when, for nearly all major indexes of health, the rural citizen will suffer a disadvantage.

PART III: RURAL DOCTORS AND
OTHER HEALTH PERSONNEL

IN THE FACE of a burden of illness, disability, and death that is on the whole as great or greater than that of the cities, rural America is supplied with fewer resources for medical service of every sort. The basic resources for medical care are, of course, personnel and facilities of specialized types. While they are functionally interdependent, the man is undoubtedly more fundamental than the building, so that first we shall consider the country doctor and all the other health personnel involved in rural medicine. In Part IV we shall consider health facilities.

Rural areas tend to have a smaller and less effective force of all types of medical and related personnel than the cities. Aside from comparisons, the rural supply of personnel of all categories is considerably below what competent professional judgment indicates to be desirable under modern conditions. The problem is not peculiarly American but has characterized the rural sections of all nations for many years.[1] Regardless of needs reflected, always inadequately, in vital statistics, if we consider the provision of medical services in the alleviation of suffering as an absolute good, then the serious inadequacies of rural health personnel give much cause for concern.

The economic and geographic features of rural life described earlier are the basis of the problem. Poverty creates difficulties which distance aggravates. From economic disadvantage springs a whole series of consequences affecting the quantity and quality of rural medical and related personnel. To the lack of hospital facilities, for example, or the sparsity of cultural and social attractions, or the failure of rural youth to get high-cost professional training, has been attributed the failure of rural areas to attract physicians and other personnel,[2] but these deficiencies themselves are for the most part economically generated. At rock bottom, therefore, the supply of health personnel appears to depend on purchasing power, and the trends leading up to the current crisis in rural medical manpower have this as their central thread.

[1] STAMPAR, ANDRIJA, "Observations of a Rural Health Worker," *New England Journal of Medicine*, 128:991-997, June 16, 1938.

[2] PUSEY, W. A.. "Medical Education and Medical Service," *Journal of the American Medical Association*, 84:281-285, 365-369, 437-441, 513-515, 592-595; 86:1501-1508, Jan. 24, and Feb. 7, 14, and 21, 1925; May 15, 1926.

The health personnel of the nation make up a vast army of over a million professional and technical workers, not including hundreds of thousands of lay workers engaged in the maintenance of hospitals, the manufacture of drugs and instruments, and related fields. The most numerous group is nurses, who in 1940 numbered about 370,000, including student nurses.[3] The next most numerous group consists of physicians, numbering about 175,000.[4] In addition there were in 1940 some 70,000 dentists, 85,000 pharmacists, and 75,000 laboratory technicians and assistants. There are thousands of optometrists and chiropodists, midwives, and practical nurses. There are groups of growing proportions, like medical social workers, and others of fortunately dwindling proportions, like chiropractors and similar cultists.[5]

Exactly how many battalions of this great medical army are available to serve the nation's 57 million rural people is very difficult to estimate. Much service to rural people is, of course, rendered by practitioners residing in urban communities; to some small extent physicians or other personnel practicing in the cities maintain their residence in rural or semirural suburban places. With these qualifications in mind it is, nevertheless, significant that among some 762,000 professional personnel classified by the Bureau of the Census according to place of residence in 1940 (including physicians, dentists, pharmacists, nurses, osteopaths, and midwives), only 18.6 per cent resided in the rural communities that include 43.5 per cent of the nation's population.[6] Such a measure of rural personnel inadequacies is, of course, very crude but we shall see that, even when the problem is considered in all its detailed ramifications, the net conclusion will reveal deficiencies of about the same order of magnitude.

[3] U. S. Bureau of the Census, Sixteenth Census of the United States, 1940. Population. Comparative Statistics for the United States, 1870-1940. Washington: Government Printing Office, 1943.

[4] American Medical Association, American Medical Directory 1940. Chicago, 1941.

[5] U. S. Census, op. cit.

[6] U. S. Census, Population. Vol. 3, The Labor Force.

CHAPTER 8

PHYSICIANS

THE BACKBONE of medical service is the physician. Where physicians are adequate in number, circumstances tend to be favorable for nurses and pharmacists and other personnel; where they are inadequate, as in rural areas, the over-all supply of medical personnel tends to be poor and the relative importance of the general medical practitioner is even enhanced, simply because auxiliary workers are not there to help carry the load. It will give us a reflection of the total problem of rural health personnel, therefore, to consider in some detail the supply of rural physicians, the trends that have brought about the current situation, and the characteristics of the present-day rural medical profession.

The Supply of Rural Physicians

The supply of physicians can be conveniently described in terms of the ratio of active and available practitioners to the population in the counties in which they practice.[1] Data on this basis summarizing the situation for the entire nation as of 1940 are presented in Table 14. The comparison between the ratios in the urban and rural counties is striking. As we proceed from the "metropolitan counties," through the counties bordering on them, over into the relatively isolated rural counties containing communities of under 10,000 population, and finally into the extremely rural counties containing not even a single place of 2,500 population, the number of persons who must be served by one physician consistently rises. It is to be noted that nearly 11 million people, in over 1,000 of the nation's most rural counties, were served in 1940 — before the war — by only one physician to about 1,700 persons.

At that time, when the nation as a whole could boast of an average ratio for available physicians of 1 to 831, the distribution of

[1] Such a description would omit physicians who have retired from practice and the personnel of federal health programs who are not primarily serving the population of the county in which they work.

Table 14. Supply of Physicians: *Number and percentage of available physicians,* * *and number of persons per physician, by rural-urban character of the counties in the United States, 1940*

Type of county	Number of counties	Population	Per cent of population	Number of physicians	Per cent of physicians	Persons per physician
All counties · · · · · · · ·	3,071	131,669,275	100.0	158,429	100.0	831
Metropolitan† · · · · · ·	289	70,193,236	53.3	107,510	67.9	653
Bordering‡ · · · · ·	720	21,071,996	16.0	18,873	11.9	1,117
Not bordering‡ · · · · ·	2,062	40,404,043	30.7	32,046	20.2	1,261
With largest urban place:						
10,000 or more · · · ·	277	12,598,620	9.5	12,850	8.1	980
5,000 to 9,999 · · · ·	330	8,761,964	6.7	7,022	4.4	1,247
2,500 to 4,999 · · · ·	441	8,277,154	6.3	5,839	3.7	1,417
Under 2,500 · · · ·	1,014	10,766,305	8.2	6,335	4.0	1,699

Source: Data furnished by the U. S. Public Health Service, based on 1940 *American Medical Directory* and U. S. Census, 1940. *Population.* Vol. 1, *Number of Inhabitants.*

* Excluding retired and federally employed physicians, and omitting 2,051 physicians for whom complete information is not available.

† A metropolitan county is one having within its boundaries all or any part of a city of 50,000 or more, or any of its suburbs included in the "metropolitan area" as defined by the Bureau of the Census.

‡ "Bordering" and "not bordering" designate counties that border or do not border on a metropolitan county.

practitioners was so unequal that for every physician in the most rural counties there were proportionately 2.6 physicians in metropolitan counties. Almost half the nation's population, moreover, residing outside of the 289 metropolitan counties with their 1 to 653 ratio, were served by a ratio of no better than one physician to 1,200 persons. This tally includes all types of locally available physicians — public health men, teachers, research workers, industrial physicians, and others — so that it actually overstates the supply of doctors engaged in clinical practice.

The relative rural deficiencies are not confined to any one section of the country. Figure 13 demonstrates that the rural sections of all but nine states, eight of them in the Northeast, have a ratio of fewer than one physician per 1,000 persons. Eighteen states spread through the Southern, Central, and Western regions have ratios poorer than 1 to 1,500. It should be recognized that the rural people involved in these state-wide ratios do not have easy access to physicians in the large cities since they reside in counties not even bordering on counties with cities of 50,000 persons or more. Yet, these ratios, poor as they are, include physicians in towns of up to 10,000 population.[1a]

While urban-rural comparisons may be striking, these ratios perhaps have little meaning without reference to an optimal standard of physician supply. Such an optimal standard is not easy to define, for it must depend on factors that vary from area to area and from year to year. During the Second World War, when the shortage of physicians became a nation-wide issue, it was customary to consider a ratio of one physician per 1,500 persons to represent the

[1a] There admittedly are limitations in any description of the supply of physicians based upon the confines of county lines, since doctors obviously serve patients across the political borders. It would be more fallacious, however, to define the area of coverage of physicians in terms of the mapped out locations of their individual patients, without regard for the number of people to be served by each physician. See: DICKINSON, FRANK G., "Medical Service Areas in the United States," *Journal of the American Medical Association,* 133:1014-1015, Apr. 5, 1947. Under any circumstances, a mathematical ratio between physicians and people is required to give a true picture of physician supply. The practice of considering the physician supply in "nonbordering" counties, used generally in this chapter, helps to take account of the tendency of rural people to travel to near-by metropolitan centers (places of over 50,000) for their medical service.

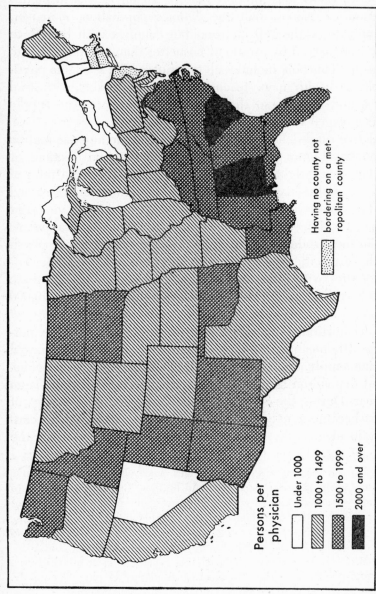

FIG. 13. Supply of Rural Physicians: Number of persons per available physician in counties having no place of 10,000 or more and not bordering on metropolitan counties, by States, 1940 (see Table 14). Source: Data furnished by the U.S. Public Health Service, based on 1940 *American Medical Directory* and U.S. Census, 1940. *Population. Vol. 1, Number of Inhabitants.*

upper limit of safety, beyond which physician resources might be considered seriously inadequate.[2] There is much to indicate, however, that while this wartime standard may have been a realistic adjustment to the national emergency, it is defeatist for normal times and is scarcely geared to a conception of good medical service.

A scientific definition of an optimal standard of physician supply should be based on an examination of the average incidence of illnesses of all types, including pregnancy, and a consideration of the professional time required for proper diagnosis and treatment, as well as for essential preventive services. This has been done by the Committee on the Costs of Medical Care. Based on a rather conservative estimate of the burden of illness, Roger I. Lee and Lewis Webster Jones estimated that on the average one practicing physician is required for every 742 persons.[3] Presumably in the belief that this approach may have been somewhat Utopian, a standard of adequacy of one physician per 1,000 persons has been proposed as a practical bench mark.[4]

If 1 to 1,000 is a realistic general standard for adequate physician supply, there are several reasons to suggest the need for a better ratio in rural areas. The volume of sickness and physical impairments we have found to be probably greater. The need for the individual practitioner to provide preventive services is probably greater, and the volume of maternity cases is larger. The long distances to be covered by the rural physician rob him of a large percentage of his time each day. Perhaps 10 to 20 per cent is spent in nonproductive travel. The lack of auxiliary personnel in rural practice increases the load of routine tasks for the harassed rural practitioner, and there is no specialist around the corner to whom a difficult case can readily be referred. As A. H. T. Robb-Smith has indicated in the perspective of British medical practice, it would

[2] LAPHAM, MAXWELL E., Testimony before a Subcommittee of the Committee on Education and Labor, U. S. Senate, 77th Cong., 2d Sess., S. Res. 291, *Investigation of Manpower Resources.* Washington: Government Printing Office, 1943, Part 2, p. 667.

[3] LEE, R. I., and L. W. JONES, *The Fundamentals of Good Medical Care* (Committee on the Costs of Medical Care Pub. 22). Chicago: University of Chicago Press, 1933.

[4] U. S. Public Health Service, Division of Public Health Methods, *Standards of Adequacy in the Supply of Medical and Public Health Personnel and Facilities.* Washington, February, 1942, Processed.

seem quite appropriate to expect a supply of physicians in general medical practice about 25 per cent better for rural areas than for urban.[5] If needs are to be properly met, one should accordingly expect rural people to be served by a ratio of one physician to about every 750 persons. Taking account of a certain proportion of rural cases, however, which should properly be referred relatively long distances to urban specialists and hospitals, it would be reasonable to expect rural counties to have within their borders an average of one physician to about every 800 persons.

Such a standard, of course, assumes fully active medical practitioners. It also obviously assumes the absence of any financial barriers to obtaining medical service; it is based totally on human needs. Naturally any standard is in some degree arbitrary and must change with advancing science which, on the one hand, may prevent illness or shorten the time required to treat it and, on the other hand, may advance the horizons of positive health and broaden the scope of the physician's duties.

With the optimal rural standard of 1 to 800 in mind, we may view with some perspective the available supply of rural practitioners. Since this standard assumes fully active or effective physicians, it is apparent that accurate evaluation requires correction for practitioners not capable of doing a normal full day's work. Experience has shown that as physicians, like other persons, get past the prime of life their "effectiveness," by this definition, declines. This effectiveness has been quantitatively measured and found to decline by 75 per cent, in terms of patients handled per week, from the period of peak effectiveness at 35-44 years of age to age 75.[6] On the basis of these findings, a formula has been devised by which the average effectiveness of the physicians in a community may be computed by considering each physician over 65 years of age as equivalent to "one-third of a doctor."[7] While all of us can think of exceptions to this somewhat callous generalization, it serves as a statistical device with a sound basis.

[5] ROBB-SMITH, A. H. T., "The Conjectures of Appendix E: With a Backward Glance to 1912," *Lancet*, 246:545-546, Apr. 22, 1944.

[6] CIOCCO, A., and ISADORE ALTMAN, "The Patient Load of Physicians in Private Practice: A Comparative Statistical Study of Three Areas," *Public Health Reports*, 58:1329-1351, Sept. 3, 1943.

[7] LAPHAM, *loc. cit.*

The fact is, as we shall see, that the average age of rural prac- titioners is considerably above that of urban. A computation of ratios of truly "effective" physicians, therefore, reveals over-all rural inadequacies and discrepancies between the rural and urban supply more striking than those found simply by "counting noses." This is demonstrated in Table 15, in which the effective physician-popula- tion ratios are presented for all the states according to the urban- rural character of their counties. For the nation as a whole, the correction for effectiveness reduces the reservoir of about 168,000 physicians of known age, not employed in federal programs (but including the retired), to about 150,000 effective practitioners. The greatest part of this "loss" of 18,000 doctors is felt in the rural areas. In the metropolitan counties, for example, the correction for effectiveness means a loss in medical manpower of about 3 per cent, but in the thousand-odd isolated "nonbordering" counties without a place of 2,500 population, the loss is 13 per cent. On this basis there is only one effective doctor in the most rural counties to 2.9 in metropolitan counties, rather than 1 to 2.6 by the crude computation previously noted.

With reference to the optimal standard of one effective practi- tioner for every 800 persons in rural counties, it may be observed that the nonmetropolitan counties in only a few states actually averaged this ratio. As we proceed either from the more urban to the more rural counties within a state or, within counties of a given urban-rural character, from states of low to states of high general rurality, the ratio of effective practitioners becomes less adequate. Even the metropolitan counties in the eight most rural states fail to average the 1 to 800 ratio. Although the supply of effective doctors becomes poorer in any given type of county as the general character of the state becomes more rural, even in the most urban states the rural counties are poorly supplied. The most constant ratio for a given type of county seems to be found in the non- bordering counties containing towns of 10,000 to 50,000, and even in these counties the most urbanized states have a ratio of 1 to 905 compared with 1 to 1,160 in the most rural states. It is difficult to explain these variations in personnel in counties of the same degree of rurality except, as we shall see, by virtue of differences in eco- nomic prosperity among the states of greater or lesser industrial- ization.

Table 15. Supply of Physicians: *Number of persons per effective physician* by rural-urban character of the counties, by states in order of rurality, 1940*

State	Population, per cent rural	Type of county†							
		All counties	Metropolitan	Bordering	Not bordering and largest urban place				
					All counties	10,000 or more	5,000 to 9,999	2,500 to 4,999	No urban place
All states	43.5	876	674	1,221	1,397	1,054	1,383	1,607	1,964
Population under 30 per cent rural .		637	596	948	981	905	1,022	978	1,409
District of Columbia . . .	0.0	431	431	. . .	. . .	. . .	. . .	. . .	. . .
Rhode Island	8.4	860	856	956	. . .	. . .	. . .	. . .	. . .
Massachusetts	10.6	626	621	732	. . .	. . .	. . .	. . .	. . .
New York	17.2	545	512	846	803	871	704	680	. . .
New Jersey	18.4	782	776	964	. . .	. . .	. . .	. . .	. . .
Illinois	26.4	746	552	1,041	1,127	1,015	1,181	1,141	1,730
California	29.0	693	639	1,103	905	643	1,070	1,004	1,144
Population 30 to 39 per cent rural .		848	771	1,112	1,227	1,111	1,171	1,472	1,576
Connecticut	32.2	731	711	965	. . .	. . .	1,158	1,436	1,686
Ohio	33.2	856	746	1,212	1,145	1,025	981	1,231	1,391
Pennsylvania	33.5	829	769	1,217	1,128	1,122	1,349	1,729	1,592
Michigan	34.3	922	850	938	1,445	1,311	1,343	. . .	. . .
Population 40 to 49 per cent rural .		915	692	1,207	1,306	1,093	1,343	1,480	1,795
Maryland	40.7	714	616	1,234	1,173	1,142	. . .	1,241	1,254
New Hampshire . . .	42.4	927	953	985	854	1,128	551	. . .	779
Utah	44.5	1,077	821	1,263	1,516	1,419	1,026	1,374	1,867

Florida	44.9	1,006	797	1,278	1,196	947	1,403	1,246	2,277
Indiana	44.9	993	805	1,237	1,146	1,055	1,237	1,351	1,370
Wisconsin	46.5	1,019	733	1,195	1,375	1,207	1,803	1,511	1,665
Washington	46.9	984	836	1,306	1,367	1,201	1,285	1,538	1,773
Colorado	47.4	721	521	907	1,118	912	986	1,128	1,311
Delaware	47.7	813	707	1,175	. . .	. . .	. . .	. . .	. . .
Missouri	48.2	885	595	1,545	1,607	1,097	1,477	1,941	2,163
Population 50 to 59 per cent rural		1,043	748	1,213	1,312	939	1,442	1,580	1,705
Minnesota	50.2	890	747	1,478	984	466	1,445	1,583	1,698
Oregon	51.2	878	662	1,001	1,212	1,068	1,267	1,648	1,143
Texas	54.6	1,144	788	1,601	1,474	1,208	1,397	1,714	1,906
Iowa	57.3	992	864	879	1,168	1,024	1,169	1,224	1,344
Kansas	58.1	1,086	832	1,089	1,263	948	1,261	1,226	1,617
Louisiana	58.5	1,107	604	2,092	1,744	1,156	1,957	2,259	2,386
Maine	59.5	1,081	753	1,122	1,222	958	1,612	1,333	1,188
Population 60 to 69 per cent rural		1,252	795	1,675	1,527	1,104	1,429	1,748	2,041
Nevada	60.7	817	. . .	. . .	769	550	. . .	970	976
Nebraska	60.9	951	602	1,255	1,223	870	989	1,267	1,539
Montana	62.2	1,254	. . .	. . .	1,254	981	1,178	1,519	1,690
Oklahoma	62.4	1,249	729	1,449	1,635	1,297	1,432	2,115	2,494
Wyoming	62.7	1,241	. . .	. . .	1,241	1,093	1,054	1,168	1,568
Virginia	64.7	1,138	826	1,439	1,368	883	1,356	1,435	1,886
Tennessee	64.8	1,201	713	1,985	1,786	1,331	1,771	1,802	2,200
Arizona	65.2	1,071	970	933	1,643	. . .	1,233	2,616	2,130
Georgia	65.6	1,332	818	2,014	1,767	1,219	1,376	2,024	2,297
Vermont	65.7	841	. . .	969	834	654	949	1,034	1,280
Idaho	66.3	1,458	. . .	1,643	1,435	1,164	. . .	1,792	1,748

Table 15. Supply of Physicians: *Number of persons per effective physician* by rural-urban character of the counties, by states in order of rurality, 1940—(Continued)*

State	Population, per cent rural	Type of county†			Not bordering and largest urban place				
		All counties	Metropolitan	Bordering	All counties	10,000 or more	5,000 to 9,999	2,500 to 4,999	No urban place
Population 60 to 69 per cent rural (cont.)									
New Mexico	66.8	1,636	....	2,047	1,609	1,151	1,553	1,553	3,738
Alabama	69.8	1,697	1,061	2,267	2,118	1,603	2,358	2,177	2,797
Population 70 per cent or more rural		1,428	834	1,655	1,632	1,160	1,538	1,808	2,256
Kentucky	70.2	1,280	772	1,656	1,579	885	1,348	1,547	2,380
West Virginia	71.9	1,186	938	1,338	1,283	1,011	1,277	1,648	1,746
North Carolina	72.7	1,462	806	1,629	1,842	1,595	1,697	1,951	2,284
South Dakota	75.4	1,624	2,335	1,802	1,604	1,149	1,246	1,454	2,256
South Carolina	75.5	1,581	934	2,054	1,741	1,281	2,169	2,618	2,647
Arkansas	77.8	1,382	727	1,719	1,490	911	1,566	1,593	1,944
North Dakota	79.4	1,483	....	....	1,483	776	1,344	1,587	2,446
Mississippi	80.2	1,758	901	1,840	1,851	1,328	1,553	2,000	2,392

Source: Data furnished by the U. S. Public Health Service, based on 1940 *American Medical Directory* and U. S. Census, 1940. *Population.* Vol. 1, *Number of Inhabitants.*

* Based on information covering 167,879 nonfederal physicians of known age, of whom 141,521 were under 65 years of age and 26,358 were 65 and over; totals of effective physicians were secured by adding the totals of those under 65 years of age and one-third of the totals of those 65 and over.

† For definitions, see Table 14.

Note: For number of counties in each general category and for population totals see Table 14.

The counties with which rural medicine is most deeply concerned are those not bordering on metropolitan counties and not having a town of 10,000 persons or more — counties with a total population of about 28 million. Among the 43 states containing such counties, only two, New York and New Hampshire, reach in these counties an average ratio equivalent to the optimal standard of 1 to 800. The average for nonbordering counties containing places of 2,500 to 5,000 population is only half this ratio, or 1 to 1,607. For the 11 million rural citizens in the nonbordering counties containing no urban center of even 2,500 persons, the ratio of effective physicians to population reaches the highly inadequate level of 1 to 1,964, ranging up to 1 to 3,738 in New Mexico. Considering all counties not bordering on a metropolitan county — counties with 40 million persons and containing towns or cities up to but not over 50,000 persons — the average ratio in even the most urban group of states falls below the standard, being 1 to 948, and it declines gradually to 1 to 1,655 in the most rural segment of states. If we compare the supply of effective doctors in the metropolitan counties of New York State with that in the most rural counties of New Mexico, we find that the doctor in the rural Southwest must serve more than seven times as many persons as his fellow practitioner in the Northeast. Consideration of the distribution of effective physicians by the geographic regions of the nation would, in effect, be found to be a reflection of the rurality of each region.

It should be realized that even a statement of the supply of "effective" physicians in rural areas fails to give a picture of the extent of inaccessibility of physicians to the rural population. For not only are effective rural practitioners too few, they are also too "far between." Distance obviously makes the smaller number that are to be found less accessible. In North Dakota, for example, each physician in active practice — including those in the cities — must cover an average area of 209 square miles.[8] Even this understates the problem of distances, however, for in a given county of 1,000 square miles with two physicians, for example, both might well be located in the same community so that each would cover, in effect, the entire area rather than half. Four counties in North Dakota, each

[8] North Dakota State Health Planning Committee, *Medical Care and Health Facilities in North Dakota*. Fargo: North Dakota Agricultural College, March, 1945, Processed, p. 10.

with over 1,000 square miles, in fact, were served in 1945 by only one physician each, and in one of these counties, with over 2,000 square miles, only 10 per cent of the population had telephones with which to reach the doctor.

It has frequently been pointed out that improved methods of transportation and communication have shortened distances for rural people. While the automobile and the telephone have had their effect, we have already observed how large a share of the rural population do without them. Even with better transportation, the farmer and the village dweller have been running a losing race to catch the doctor for, as we shall see, he has been moving entirely away from rural sections to the larger cities at an accelerated rate. In military parlance, one might say that the front lines of medical personnel have been moving to the cities faster than the "lines of communication" could be developed with the rural people in the rear. Detailed studies revealing the severity of the shortage of rural physicians have been made in North Carolina,[9] Virginia,[10] Ohio,[11] North Dakota,[12] Kentucky,[13] Alabama,[14] Missouri,[15] Nebraska,[16] and other states.

It should not be supposed that rural people are served only by rural physicians. Naturally there is considerable journeying to the

[9] North Carolina Agricultural Experiment Station, *Medical Care Services in North Carolina* (Reprint Prog. Rep. RS-4). Raleigh, February, 1945, Processed.

[10] TATE, LELAND B., *The Health and Medical-care Situation in Rural Virginia.* Blacksburg: Virginia Agricultural Experiment Station (Bull. 363), October, 1944.

[11] MANGUS, A. R., "Health and Human Resources in Rural Ohio," *Ohio State Medical Journal,* 40:880-886, 956-959, September and October, 1944.

[12] North Dakota State Health Planning Committee, *op. cit.*

[13] CRITTENDEN, C. B., and L. SKAGGS, "Influence on Public Health Progress of Inadequate Medical Services for the Rural Population," *Southern Medical Journal,* 33:1092-1097, October, 1940.

[14] NEWDORP, JOHN, "Planning for Medical Care in the Postwar Period, with Particular Reference to Alabama," *Journal of the Medical Association of the State of Alabama,* 14:183-189, 213-219, 239-247, February, March, and April, 1945.

[15] ALMACK, RONALD B., *The Rural Health Facilities of Lewis County, Missouri.* Columbia: University of Missouri Agricultural Experiment Station (Research Bull. 365), May, 1943.

[16] REINHARDT, JAMES M., and MARTIN H. SCHROEDER, "Physicians and Hospitals in Rural Nebraska," *Medical Care.* 1:332-343, October, 1941.

larger towns and cities, particularly by the small group of well-to-do farm people, in search of specialists or prominent physicians. The actual extent of this can only be guessed at, but that it tends to be done chiefly in the event of serious or alarming conditions is fairly certain — and for these, too, the more familiar home-county doctor is ordinarily seen first. By and large, for the vast majority of complaints and for all emergencies, the physicians considered here as "rural" are the sole source of medical service for rural families.

Background and Trends

The severe shortage of rural physicians has not always been a feature of American medicine, nor has it developed overnight. It has been a gradual process developing since the latter part of the nineteenth century.[17] The immediate cause of the growing maldistribution has been the accelerating settlement of physicians, particularly new graduates, in the cities. As early as 1906, when about 56 per cent of the nation's population was regarded as rural, there was a clear disproportion, for only 41 per cent of the available physicians were in rural practice.[18] By 1940 when the nation's rural population had declined relatively by less than one-fourth to 43.5 per cent, the physicians in rural practice fell to about 20 per cent of the nation's total, or half their former proportion. As early as 1914, the increasing settlement of new graduates in the large cities was beginning to be striking. In that year 47 per cent of medical graduates were settling in cities of over 100,000 population, while at the time less than 26 per cent of the national population were located in such cities.[19]

After the First World War there was already a marked discrepancy between the supply of physicians in rural and urban counties. In 1923, when there were 159.5 physicians per 100,000 persons in

[17] ROEMER, MILTON I., "Historic Development of the Current Crisis of Rural Medicine in the United States," *Victor Robinson Memorial Volume: Essays on History of Medicine.* New York: Froben Press, 1948.

[18] DAVIS, MICHAEL M., *Public Medical Services: A Survey of Tax-supported Medical Care in the United States.* Chicago: University of Chicago Press, 1937, p. 87.

[19] WEISKOTTEN, H. G., "A Study of Present Tendencies in Medical Practice," *Bulletin of the Association of American Medical Colleges,* 3:130-151, April, 1928.

metropolitan counties (containing a place of 50,000 population), there were only 91.9 per 100,000 in the rural counties that contained no urban place (2,500 or more).[20] By 1940, the proportionate supply in the metropolitan counties had actually increased, while that in

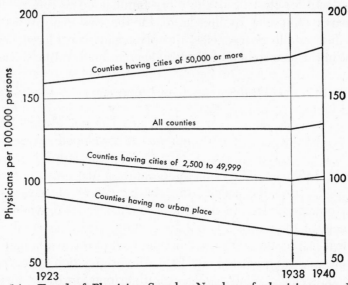

Fig. 14.   Trend of Physician Supply: Number of physicians per 100,000 persons by rural-urban character of counties, 1923-1940. Source: Mountin, J. W., E. H. Pennell, and V. Nicolay. "Location and Movement of Physicians, 1923 and 1938: Age Distribution in Relation to County Characteristics," *Public Health Reports,* 58:483-490, Mar. 19, 1943. Rates for 1940 from unpublished data furnished by the U.S. Public Health Service.

the rural counties and even in counties with places up to 50,000 persons had gone severely downhill.[21] The trend of affairs to the brink of the Second World War is portrayed in Figure 14. Considering settlement by whole states, in 1940-41 urbanized New York State, with about 10 per cent of the nation's population, was getting about 18 per cent of the new physicians, while rural Alabama with over 2 per cent of the national population was getting only 0.3 per cent

[20] The type of county for 1923 as well as 1940 is defined in accordance with Bureau of the Census findings in 1940. This applies, in general, to subsequent references to the "Location and Movement of Physicians" studies by the U. S. Public Health Service.

[21] MOUNTIN, J. W., E. H. PENNELL, and V. NICOLAY, "Location and Movement of Physicians, 1923 and 1938: Age Distribution of Physicians," *Public Health Reports,* 58:483-490, Mar. 19, 1943. Also, unpublished data furnished by the U. S. Public Health Service.

of them.[22] The wartime drainage of medical personnel to the armed forces, as we shall see, aggravated the situation even further.

An explanation of the accelerated settlement of physicians in the cities and the growing rural shortages is not far to seek. The growing industrialization of the nation has meant the increasing concentration of wealth in the cities. Physicians having a service to sell will naturally choose to sell it where purchasing power is greatest. While this may have always been true, it came to result in serious urban-rural discrepancies in personnel only as the cities became the concentrated centers of the nation's wealth. Other associated factors, of course, play a part, but economic pressures are at the root of most of them.

At the very time that the cities were beginning to exert a strong "pull" on the available supply of physicians, the total national supply of doctors began to fall. In 1900, counting all licensed physicians, we had a supply of one to every 580 persons in the nation. This was still the period of the "diploma mills" where degrees were virtually sold to any who could pay the price. After the movement to grade medical schools got under way, following Abraham Flexner's monumental report in 1910, the unqualified schools were forced to close down and the supply of new graduates fell off sharply. By 1920 the national physician-population ratio had declined to 1 to 730. After 1922 the output of medical graduates gradually rose again, but at a slower rate than the increase in the population.[23] By 1940, therefore, the total supply of licensed physicians[24] in the nation yielded a ratio of only 1 to 748. It is obvious, then, that the total reservoir from which rural physicians could be drawn was gradually getting lower.

Meanwhile, medical science was advancing rapidly and specialization had to develop.[25] From a mere scattering of specialists at

[22] PERROTT, G. ST. J., and BURNET M. DAVIS, "The War and the Distribution of Physicians," *Public Health Reports*, 58:1545-1554, Oct. 15, 1943.

[23] In view of recent experiences with personnel shortages, it is enlightening to recall the barrage of misguided talk during this period about the "overcrowded profession" and the aggressive policy pursued to keep down medical school enrollments.

[24] A distinction is to be drawn between this estimate of total "licensed" physicians and the more limited definitions of "available" or "effective" physicians used on earlier pages.

[25] ROSEN, GEORGE, *The Specialization of Medicine, with Particular Reference to Ophthalmology.* New York: Froben Press, 1944, p. 31.

the turn of the century, by 1928 about 26 per cent of the nation's physicians were partially or completely specialized and by 1940 over 50 per cent.[26] Since the specialist under present-day patterns requires a large and relatively prosperous population to provide a "market" for his more expensive services, he tends to settle in the cities. Meanwhile also an increasing proportion of physicians were going into full-time salaried positions — as medical school teachers, hospital administrators, public health officers, research workers —

Table 16. Physicians and County Wealth: *Changes in number of persons per physician by per capita income class of county, 1923-1938*

Per capita income class of county*	Number of persons per physician	
	1923	1938
Under $300	1,105	1,531
$300 to $599	839	959
$600 or more	639	585

Source: Mountin, Pennell, and Nicolay, *op. cit.*
* Based on 1940 income and population data.

chiefly in the cities. The number of physicians in such full-time positions rose from 13,000 in 1928 to 20,000 in 1942.[27] This clearly made still further drains on the reservoir of physicians from which the private practitioners for rural America could be drawn.

With the dwindling reserve of physicians for rural areas, the economic and other attractions of the cities exerted their effect at an accelerated tempo. This is demonstrated in Table 16. It may be noted that in 1923 the highest income counties were attracting not quite twice as high a proportion of physicians as the lowest income counties. Just 15 years later, however, the highest income counties were attracting more nearly three times the proportion of the poorest counties. This increasing "pursuit of wealth" and its associated technical facilities and cultural opportunities is found to apply particularly to the youngest physicians and new graduates.[28]

All the while the costs of a medical education were rising, both

[26] DAVIS, MICHAEL M., "The Supply of Doctors," *Medical Care*, 2:315-321, November, 1942.
[27] *Ibid.*
[28] MOUNTIN, PENNELL, and NICOLAY, *op. cit.*

in direct outlay and in the indirect withholding of earning power during increasingly long medical school years.[29] This has meant that young men and women from rural families have been less and less able to afford the cost of medical training. Yet it is among country families that one might expect to find the love or appreciation for rural life that is partially necessary to make a medical graduate choose a rural practice. Even for a youth from a rural home, however, modern medical training has become such as to induce him to settle in an urban center. Increasingly the young physician has naturally come to demand the institutions, equipment, and technical assistance in his practice that he has learned to depend on in medical school and internship — and these resources are sparse in rural sections.

The continuous settlement of young graduates in the cities has meant a residue in rural sections of physicians largely in the later years of life. In counties with no urban place, for example, 24.8 per cent of the physicians in 1923 were 58 years of age or over. By 1938 the proportion of these older men in the rural counties had risen to 45.1 per cent.[30] Older age levels, moreover, mean higher death rates, so that the over-all loss of rural practitioners through death tends to increase each year. Thus, in 1938 when the general annual death rate for large-city practitioners was 18 per 1,000, in the rural areas it was 29 per 1,000. Between 1923 and 1938, the number of rural physicians dying actually exceeded the number entering rural practice by over 3,400.[31] The rural profession, in other words, is almost acquiring the ominous earmarks of a dying civilization; its members are dying off at increasing rates and they are not being replenished by new blood.

Finally, among the trends leading up to the present crisis in the supply of rural physicians, is the influence of the migration of established practitioners. For even after initial settlement in a rural practice, there has been a growing tendency for physicians to move.

[29] ROEMER, MILTON I., "The Costs of Medical Education," *The Diplomate of the National Board of Medical Examiners,* 14:265-269, November, 1942.

[30] MOUNTIN, PENNELL, and NICOLAY, *op. cit.*

[31] MOUNTIN, J. W., E. H. PENNELL, and G. S. BROCKETT, "Location and Movement of Physicians, 1923 and 1938: Changes in Urban and Rural Totals for Established Physicians," *Public Health Reports,* 60:173:184, Feb. 16, 1945.

The pattern of migration appears to be chiefly to the smaller cities of 2,500 to 50,000 population from the rural districts and, to some very small extent, from metropolitan centers. Thus, between 1923 and 1938 the large cities of the nation lost 643 physicians by out-migration but gained 43,361 by new settlement. In the same period, however, rural areas acquired only 13,654 physicians by new settlement, but lost 4,361, or about one out of three new settlers, by out-migration.[32]

It is the net result of new settlements, deaths, and migration, as they have occurred in rural and urban counties, that has produced the divergent curves seen in Figure 14. Between 1923 and 1938 the net supply of physicians in the metropolitan counties increased by 29.2 per cent while the population increased by only 20 per cent. In the counties with small cities of 2,500 to 50,000, the net physician supply increased by 20 per cent while the population increased by 25 per cent. In the purely rural counties, however, while the population increased by 10 per cent, the net supply of physicians actually declined by 19.3 per cent.[33]

The Rural Medical Profession Today

With these trends in the number and distribution of physicians over the last several decades, the present picture of rural medical practice is almost self-evident. No sharp line, of course, can be drawn between the influence of past trends and the pressure of contemporary social forces. All the trends leading to the quantitative disparity between the rural and urban supplies of physicians continue today. The present picture of rural medicine, in effect, is only one "still" in the moving-picture film, stopped at about the prewar year 1940 and thrown on the screen for analysis. Wartime experience, as we shall see, has served only to aggravate the worst features of this prewar picture.

The acute lack of rural doctors at the outset of this decade has been described. The specific influence of economic forces in inducing the settlement of physicians in urban sections is demonstrated in Figure 15. It may be noted that when the states are arranged by groups in the order of increasing rurality, their per capita income

[32] *Ibid.*
[33] *Ibid.*

declines regularly and their supply of effective physicians, as
measured by physician-population ratios, declines with almost
identical regularity. The six most urban states and the District of
Columbia, having over twice the per capita wealth of the eight
most rural states, likewise have over twice the supply of physicians.
One cannot help but be impressed with the fact that the basic

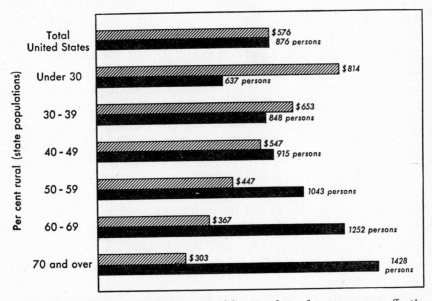

FIG. 15. Physicians and State Wealth: Number of persons per effective
physician in states grouped by rurality and relationship to per capita income,
1940 (see Table 15). Source: U.S. Department of Commerce, *Survey of Current Business*. August, 1944, p. 190. Also, data furnished by the U.S. Public
Health Service, based on 1940 *American Medical Directory* and U.S. Census,
1940, *Population*. Vol. 1, *Number of Inhabitants*.

factor accounting for the rural-urban distribution of physicians
is the economic level of the area in which they practice.

Even among rural counties, of course, per capita income exerts
its effect. Thus, in the relatively few rural counties with per capita
incomes of $600 or more, the physician-population ratio was 1 to
780 in 1938, while in the more typical rural counties with per capita
incomes of under $300, it was 1 to 1,670, or more than twice as poor.[34]

[34] MOUNTIN, J. W., E. H. PENNELL, and V. NICOLAY, "Location and Movement of Physicians, 1923 and 1938: Effect of Local Factors upon Location,"
Public Health Reports, 57: 1945-1953, Dec. 18, 1942.

Beyond state or county wealth as a determinant of physician supply, other relationships are found. All things being equal, the county with the greater supply of hospital beds tends to have the better supply of physicians. Which is causal is difficult to say, for while ordinarily one expects hospitals to attract physicians, in many rural communities it is the arrival of the physician that leads to the establishment of the hospital. In general, however, the urban concentration of hospital beds holds definite attractions for the new graduate.[35]

As we shall see, the supply of hospital beds itself tends to be directly related to state per capita wealth. As a result, there tends to be an amazingly constant relationship between physicians and hospital beds in states of all degrees of rurality, regardless of the supply of physicians. When states are grouped by rurality, as in Figure 15, there are exactly 3.2 general hospital beds per effective physician in five of the six groups of states, with 3.0 beds per doctor in the sixth (the most urban) group.[36]

Other factors, like the mere presence of other physicians with whom to exchange ideas, and the cultural and civic advantages of urban life for the doctor and his family, of course, play a real part in shaping the doctor's decision on where to settle. All these factors, in turn, like hospital beds, tend to be themselves related to local economic levels.

The past and present pressures inducing settlement of younger physicians in the cities, as already suggested, leave a supply of rural practitioners of very different age composition from urban. The net consequences are presented in Figure 16. Thus, in 1938 when 22.6 per cent of practitioners in metropolitan counties were 58 years of age or over, twice that proportion, or 45.1 per cent, of practitioners in the most rural counties were at this age level. Even within a generally rural state the differentials between the urban centers and country districts are striking. In Tennessee, for example, in 1936, 43 per cent of the physicians in the four main cities of the state were over 50 years of age, while in the villages of the state 77 per cent of the physicians were past 50.[37] These relationships tend

[35] *Ibid.*

[36] This is derived from data presented in Tables 15 and 24.

[37] HYMAN, O. W., "The Number and Distribution of Physicians in the Southern States as Bearing upon the Policies of Southern Medical Colleges," *Southern Medical Journal*, 30:85-88, January, 1937.

to be further aggravated in the poorer rural communities. In the few rural counties with per capita annual incomes of $600 or more in 1938, 52 per cent of the physicians were 45 years of age and over, while in the many rural counties with per capita incomes of under $300, as many as 86 per cent of the physicians were 45 years and over.[38]

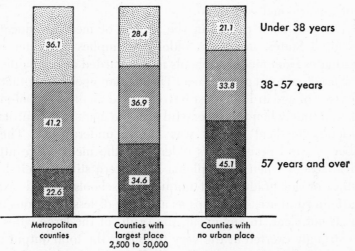

FIG. 16. Age of Physicians: Percentage of physicians in different age groups by rural-urban character of the counties in the United States, 1938. Source: Mountin, J. W., E. H. Pennell, and V. Nicolay. "Location and Movement of Physicians, 1923 and 1938: Age Distribution in Relation to County Characteristics," *Public Health Reports,* 58:483-490, Mar. 19, 1943.

In terms of median age levels, the large-city doctor in 1940 was 44 years of age, while the country doctor was 13 years older, 57 years.[39] Actually the median figures, however, overlook the rather numerous octogenarians who are carrying on in the country. In fact, the very survival of some of these venerable and often beloved old country doctors sometimes discourages the young medical graduate from even trying to stake his fortune in certain rural communities.

The age of rural practitioners has implications with reference not only to their "manpower" effectiveness, but also to their knowledge

[38] MOUNTIN, J. W., E. H. PENNELL, and V. NICOLAY, "Location and Movement of Physicians, 1923 and 1938: Age Distribution of Physicians," *Public Health Reports,* 58:483-490, Mar. 19, 1943.

[39] MOUNTIN, J. W., "Relocation of Physicians, a Prerequisite to Better Medical Care," *Journal of the American Medical Association,* 126:203-205, Sept. 23, 1944.

of current developments in medical science. With an obviously greater span of time since the completion of his formal medical training, the average rural practitioner tends naturally to be less responsive to changes in medicine than the younger city doctor. This is obviously aggravated by less exposure in the isolated rural districts to the new medical thinking associated with the urban centers of professional education.

At this particular period in the history of medical education in the United States, moreover, older age implies a greater residue of graduates from medical schools now regarded as unqualified and, for the most part, out of existence. The median-aged rural practitioner of 57 years of age in 1940 must have finished medical school in about 1908, at a time when the successful crusade against the substandard proprietary medical schools was hardly under way.[40] The large number of rural practitioners older than the median age attended medical school when the diploma mills were still in their heyday. Whether or not graduates of unqualified schools tended originally to settle in rural areas, perhaps as a sphere of less strenuous competition, is not clear. In any event, the "pull" of the large cities began to be strongly exerted at the very time that the total output of new doctors began to be practically all Class A school products. The residue of unqualified school graduates in the city, therefore, became rapidly neutralized by a fresh supply of qualified graduates, while the backlog of unqualified men in the rural sections remained relatively large.[41] National data on this point are not at hand but it has been found in Iowa, for example, that in rural communities of under 1,000 population, 1 out of every 5 physicians is a graduate of a school now out of existence, while in Des Moines (with a 1940 population of 160,000) only 1 out of 14 is a product of such a school.[42]

[40] This assumes 25 years of age as the average age of medical school graduation. Today 27 years is assumed to be the average age, but with fewer premedical requirements at the early part of the century, 25 years or even younger is probably a realistic estimate. LELAND, R. G., *Distribution of Physicians in the United States*. Chicago: American Medical Association, 1936, p. 5.

[41] The 200-odd graduates of unapproved American medical schools who in 1940 were still being licensed, chiefly in the relatively urban states of Massachusetts, Illinois, New Jersey, and New York, were by comparison only a drop in the bucket.

[42] MENGELBERG, KAETHE. "The Farmers' Physician," *Iowa Farm Economist*, 8:11, December, 1942.

The effect of this situation on the quality of rural medical practice is self-evident.

The rising cost of medical education over the years, already alluded to, has led to a situation in which medical students originate predominantly from urban centers and are naturally predisposed to a city practice. Despite efforts of many medical schools to select candidates from a broad representation of states, the tendency is for

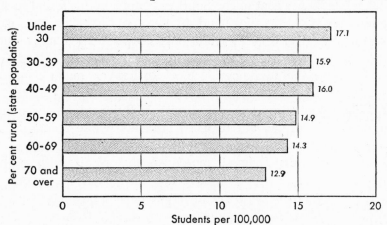

Fig. 17. Origin of Medical Students: Number of students per 100,000 population of their native states grouped by rurality, 1940. The number of students refers to those students in approved schools, with 2-year schools and those on probation included and Canadian schools excluded. Source: "Medical Education in the United States and Canada," *Journal of the American Medical Association*, 115:690-691, Aug. 31, 1940. Also U.S. Census, 1940, *Population*. Vol. 1, *Number of Inhabitants*.

students to originate predominantly from the more urban states. Thus, in 1940 the states with 70 per cent or more urban population contributed to the medical schools of the nation students at a rate of 17.1 per 100,000 population; over half of these students, moreover, went to schools in their home states. At the same time the states 70 per cent rural or more contributed medical students at a rate of only 12.9 per 100,000 population, and only about one-third of these went to schools in their native states.[43] The relationship between the origin of medical students and state rurality is illustrated in Figure 17.

[43] Derived from American Medical Association, Council on Medical Education and Hospitals, "Medical Education in the United States and Canada," *Journal of the American Medical Association*, 115: 690-691, Aug. 31, 1940.

State-wide data, however, fail to express the degree of urban selection, for in neither urban nor rural states do students tend to come from rural districts. An analysis of the place of origin of all the students enrolled in 1943-44 at one medical school located in a predominantly rural Southern state bears this out.[44] Although practically all the students enrolled in this school came from Southern states, only 17 per cent came from rural communities of under 2,500, while 63 per cent of the Southern population is found in such communities. On the other hand, 61 per cent of the students came from cities of over 10,000, while only 28 per cent of the South's population is in such cities.[45] C. Horace Hamilton has, in fact, recently shown that in the period 1938-40, first-year medical students came from urban centers throughout the nation at a rate of 66.4 per million population, compared with 18.6 per million from rural communities. Only 12 out of 6,000 students whose residence was studied gave an address on a rural mail route.[46]

It can hardly be claimed, moreover, that rural youth are not desirous of undertaking professional careers. A study of the occupational preferences of high school students in representative rural counties of Missouri has shown, for example, that medicine or dentistry was the sixth choice of all young men, with 6.2 out of every 100 making this their first choice. Among nonfarm young men in villages and towns up to 5,000 population, a medical or dental career ranked as third choice, with 10.6 per 100 giving this preference.[47] If only the best qualified of all these youth interested in medicine or dentistry were financially enabled to carry through their training, there can be little doubt that the professional schools

[44] Derived from data in *Bulletin of Vanderbilt University School of Medicine* (Register, 1943-44), Nashville, Tennessee, 1944.

[45] The operation at that time of the military "specialized training programs," which subsidized medical education, may in fact have had the effect of making the urban selection of students even less weighted than it would have been under ordinary laissez-faire circumstances.

[46] HAMILTON, C. HORACE, "Distribution of Medical College Students by Residence," *Journal of the Association of American Medical Colleges*, 21:33-37, January, 1946.

[47] MORGAN, E. L., and M. W. SNEED, *The Activities of Rural Young People in Missouri: A Survey of 2,297 Young People Attending High School*. Columbia: University of Missouri Agricultural Experiment Station (Research Bull. 269). November, 1937, p. 50.

would be turning out graduates more inclined to elect a rural practice.

The barriers preventing the average rural youth from undertaking a professional career are doubly high with respect to rural Negroes. Aside from financial handicaps, the medical school admission opportunities for Negroes are strictly limited. Despite the national population being about 9.8 per cent Negro in 1940 and proportionately higher in rural areas, there were only 372 Negro medical students enrolled in 1938, or less than 2 per cent of the total enrollment. In that year only 1.4 per cent of new graduates were colored.[48] Opportunities for postgraduate education for Negro physicians are, if anything, even more limited.[49]

With limited educational opportunities it is obvious that the supply of Negro physicians, needed so greatly in many rural sections, must be woefully inadequate. For the nation as a whole, there was only one non-white physician to every 3,570 non-white persons in 1940, compared with one white physician for every 735 white persons. To a considerable extent, of course, colored persons are served by white physicians and to some small extent the reverse is done, but by and large these ratios portray the real situation. In fact, in the Southern states where the Negro population is greatest and where racial lines are sharpest, the relative supply of Negro doctors for Negro patients is poorest of all, reaching levels of 1 to 10,000 in Alabama, for example, or 1 to 20,000 in Mississippi.[50] The situation, moreover, like that for rural physicians in general, is not improving. Between 1932 and 1942, while the Negro population of the nation increased by about 8 per cent, the number of Negro practitioners actually declined by about 5 per cent, and this decline was felt most intensely in the rural regions with the largest colored population.[51]

[48] American Medical Association, Council on Medical Education and Hospitals, "Medical Education in the United States and Canada," *Journal of the American Medical Association*, 113:771, Aug. 26, 1939.

[49] CORNELY, PAUL B., "Opportunities for Post-graduate Study for Negro Practicing Physicians in the South," *Journal of the American Medical Association*, 118:524-528, Feb. 14, 1942.

[50] North Carolina Experiment Station, *op. cit.*, p. 24.

[51] CORNELY, PAUL B., "Distribution of Negro Physicians in the United States in 1942," *Journal of the American Medical Association*, 124:826-830, Mar. 25, 1944.

With the small supply of rural physicians, one might suppose that the income per physician would be relatively high — higher than in the cities where competition is greater. Because of the wide urban-rural discrepancies in purchasing power, however, the financial advantages of reduced competition are quite lost and the opposite is true. The data on physicians' incomes, in effect, bear out the decision of most practitioners — so far as pecuniary objectives are concerned — to settle in urban communities.

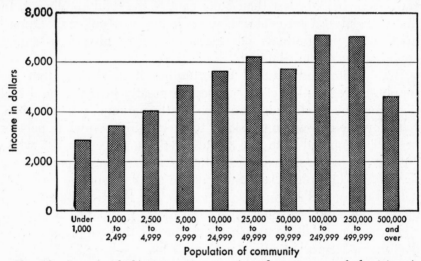

FIG. 18.   Income of Physicians: Average annual net income of physicians in private practice by size of community, 1941. Source: Denison, E. F., and A. Slater, "Incomes in Selected Professions: Part 4, Medical Service," *Survey of Current Business* (U. S. Department of Commerce), October, 1943.

The average annual net incomes of physicians in private practice in 1941, according to size of community, are presented in Figure 18. Whatever question may attach to the over-all accuracy of any income data, it may be seen that the private practitioner in rural communities of up to 2,500 population does less than half as well financially as the practitioner in large cities of between 100,000 and 500,000 population. In fact, the striking rise in average net income with size of community is significantly altered only in the few great metropolitan centers of over 500,000 population, where the forces of competition are so keen, new graduates with low incomes are so numerous, and professional expenses are so high. Regional variations in medical income tend to reflect the rurality of the region. The differentials between income in different-sized communities within a region, however, are much more striking than differentials between regions.[52]

The median net income of rural physicians in 1941, not shown in the figure, was $2,158 in communities of under 1,000 persons, $2,979 in communities of 1,000 to 2,500, and just $3,000 in communities of 2,500 to 5,000.[53] The country doctor of most typical income apparently has smaller annual earnings than many city taxi drivers or waiters in fashionable restaurants. These relatively low incomes may play some part in making the rural practitioner less opposed to social changes in the medical *status quo* than the general conservatism of rural people would lead one to expect.[54]

To some extent, the low incomes of rural physicians may be simply an expression of their higher age level, since after 50 years of age average earning power rapidly declines. How much average medical income in rural sections would rise if more physicians in the prime of life practiced there, it is impossible to say, but it seems that even in 1929, when the age differentials between rural and urban practitioners were not so great as they are now, the income differentials were just as striking.[55] Moreover, it must be recognized that the high proportion of new graduates in the cities, who have not yet built up a practice, would tend to reduce the average net income of urban physicians if age were the decisive consideration. The variations, therefore, are doubtless much less a reflection of age differences than of low "effective demand" for general medical services and particularly for the specialist services commanding high fees. Even when services are sought, payment for them tends to be lower because

[52] RICHARDSON, W. A., "Physicians' Incomes," *Medical Economics* (Rutherford, New Jersey), 17:47, September, 1940.

[53] DENISON, E. F., and A. SLATER, "Incomes in Selected Professions: Part 4, Medical Service," *Survey of Current Business*, 23:16-20, October, 1943.

[54] The wide cooperation by rural doctors in the prepayment medical care plans of the Farm Security Administration, to be discussed in a later chapter, demonstrates this. This program developed and grew at a time when more prosperous urban physicians were active in their opposition to nearly all forms of health insurance.

[55] LEVEN, MAURICE, *The Incomes of Physicians* (Committee on the Costs of Medical Care Pub. 24). Chicago: University of Chicago Press, 1932, p. 135.

of a generally lower scale of fees and a higher proportion of unpaid accounts.[56]

It may be, of course, that the *real* earnings of the rural physician are greater than would appear from income statements, since the over-all cost of living tends to be lower in rural communities. Furthermore, a good many medical bills incurred by farm families are paid in kind rather than in cash and such barter transactions are not readily reflected in accounts of earnings. These points, however, are easy to overemphasize. In the prewar South, for example, where rural living costs would be the lowest, the over-all cost of living, by a minimum standard, was barely 5 per cent lower than in the industrialized North. This refers to life in Southern towns, in which physicians serving rural people would usually be located.[57] Despite common notions, in fact, it is possible that the overhead expenses of rural practice are relatively higher than of urban. Office rentals may be lower, but with high transportation costs, the dispensing of drugs, numerous unpaid bills, and the relatively lower gross intake, rural practice overhead in the South, for example, has been claimed to be 50 per cent of gross income, compared with 40 per cent in urban practice.[58]

Physicians' incomes, of course, respond with particular sensitivity to changes in general economic conditions. When farm family income drops, the physician is usually the first creditor whose account is left unpaid and, in most cases, a lengthy postponement of payment means that the bill is virtually canceled.[59] On the other hand, with increases in farm income, the incomes of rural doctors will rise greatly and, during recent wartime prosperity, physicians in communities of up to 5,000 were reported to be averaging gross earnings of about $10,000 a year.[60] It is clear that the effective demand for professional services is a far more decisive influence on the income of physicians than the need for medical care at any particular time or place.

[56] GUILD, C. ST. C., *Surveys of the Medical Facilities in Three Representative Southern Counties* (Committee on the Costs of Medical Care Pub. 23). Chicago: University of Chicago Press, 1932, pp. 14-15.

[57] National Emergency Council, *Report on Economic Conditions of the South.* Washington: Government Printing Office, 1938, pp. 38-39.

[58] GUILD, *loc. cit.*

[59] LEVEN, *op. cit.*, pp. 81-82.

[60] Medical Economics, Inc., *Physicians' Income.* Rutherford, New Jersey, 1945, Reprint.

With incomes so unsatisfactory in ordinary times, it is no surprise that for years there has been a tendency for physicians to migrate out of rural districts, after a period of trial. Equally significant is the frequent migration within rural sections from one place to another. Turnover among rural physicians is so high that in six rural counties of Wisconsin, between 1912 and 1936, one out of every six or seven local practitioners was lost *each year* through migration, death, or retirement.[61] This turnover tends to be highest, judging by a Virginia study, among the youngest rural physicians.[62] Whatever may have once been true about the perennial family doctor in rural America is manifestly losing its validity.

Migration could hardly be considered objectionable, of course, if only it occurred in the direction of correcting the present maldistribution of doctors. But it is clear that, in general, the very opposite takes place. As a matter of fact, the restrictions of numerous state licensure laws (see Chapter 21) act to prevent the migration or relocation of many physicians into rural states in which they are desperately needed.

The Lack of Specialists

Especially serious among the deficiencies of rural medicine is the extreme lack of medical and surgical specialists to whom rural patients in need of their skills may be referred. The factors inducing physicians in general to settle in cities — a better "market" for their services, available facilities and equipment, opportunity to earn rewards commensurate with long and expensive training — hold doubly true for specialists. The result, as Figure 19 suggests, adds up to an over-all urban-rural discrepancy in scientific medical services, the cost of which in suffering and disability cannot be estimated.

For the 40 million people out beyond even the counties that border on metropolitan counties, it is evident that full-time specialists are available at less than a third the rate found in the metro-

[61] MASLOW, HAROLD, "The Characteristics and Mobility of Rural Physicians: A Study of Six Wisconsin Counties," *Rural Sociology*, 3:267-278, September, 1938.

[62] REED, LOUIS S., *Medical Needs in Virginia: Findings, Conclusions, and Recommendations of a Survey.* Unpublished study furnished by U. S. Public Health Service.

politan and surrounding areas. In 1941-42 there were only 3,826
full-time specialists in private practice in all the 2,062 nonmetropolitan and nonbordering counties throughout the entire nation, while
New York State alone had 5,815.[63] For more truly rural counties
that have, for example, no place of over 10,000, the supply of specialists undoubtedly comes closer to approaching the zero mark. In
North Carolina some 31 per cent of physicians in urban places were

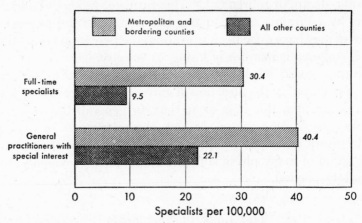

Fig. 19. Distribution of Specialists: Number of specialists in private practice
per 100,000 population by metropolitan and bordering counties (see Table 14)
and all other counties, 1941-1942. Source: Based on data furnished by the
U. S. Public Health Service.

full specialists in 1940 while only 3.9 per cent of rural practitioners
were so classified.[64] It cannot be supposed, moreover, that rural
residents in outlying counties need only go to the nearest good-sized
city in their state to find specialists, for rural states as a whole are
inadequately supplied. Thus, in the states over 60 per cent urban
in population there were 30.6 full specialists in private practice per
100,000 population in 1941-42, compared with 13.0 per 100,000 in
states over 60 per cent rural.[65]

It is difficult to define optimal ratios for specialists against which
to evaluate these ratios. It has been claimed that the "minimum population required to support" a specialist in diseases of the eye, ear, nose,

[63] Based on data furnished by U. S. Public Health Service.
[64] North Carolina Agricultural Experiment Station, *op. cit.*
[65] Based on data furnished by U. S. Public Health Service.

and throat, for example, is about 12,000, or that 100,000 population could "support" 8.5 such specialists.[66] The number really needed by a community, without respect to financial resources, would presumably be greater. Yet no state in the nation reached even this level, and the national supply as a whole was 4.54 per 100,000 in 1941-42.[67] Eye, ear, nose, and throat specialists in rural states were at ratios like 2.10 per 100,000 in Arkansas, 2.86 in Idaho, or 2.49 in South Dakota.[68] Despite some comments to the contrary, it would not seem that even urban states are oversupplied with specialists relative to true needs. A comparison of rural with urban supplies, therefore, undoubtedly reflects genuine rural deficiencies. If rural people were to have the benefit of specialist skills considered appropriate for the most affluent segments of the city population, the supply of specialists in rural states should come up to that in the best urban states.

All along the line, however, the availability of practitioners of specific medical or surgical specialties in rural states is far below that in urban states. Considering only specialists duly "certified" by the "Specialty Boards" maintained for the purpose, 71 per cent of the nation's 1,717 certified pediatricians, for example, were located in 1941 in cities of over 100,000 population, although 77 per cent of the nation's children under 10 years of age lived in the smaller cities and rural areas. While big-city pediatricians may care for some children in immediate surrounding areas, 2,762 out of the nation's 3,071 counties had no certified pediatricians in 1941.[68a] The rural supply of certified obstetricians is reflected by the fact that in 1941 Arkansas had only 3, Oklahoma had 7, Mississippi had 1, and Idaho,

[66] "Outlook for O.A.L.R.," *Medical Economics* (Rutherford, New Jersey), 19:40-44, October, 1941.

[67] Based on data furnished by U. S. Public Health Service.

[68] These figures include specialists in ear, nose, and throat as well as those in eye, ear, nose, and throat work; they include also specialists in full-time salaried positions as well as those in private practice.

[68a] The American Academy of Pediatrics, in cooperation with the Children's Bureau and the U. S. Public Health Service, is currently undertaking an extensive survey of pediatric personnel and facilities, for which only preliminary results are available at this writing. See BAIN, KATHERINE, JOHN P. HUBBARD, and CHARLES L. WILLIAMS, JR., "The American Academy of Pediatrics Study of Child Health Services: Results to Date," *American Journal of Public Health,* 37: 1297-1301, October, 1947.

New Hampshire, Nevada, and South Dakota had none.[69] This lack of specialists has an influence on the entire level of medical practice in an area. It comes to be expressed less in maternal or infant deaths than in high rates of birth palsies, pelvic tears, and a general burden of needless suffering and mental anguish associated with childbirth or the sick baby.

Half the nation's supply of certified ophthalmologists in 1941 were located in five urban states and 87 per cent of the total were in cities of over 25,000 population. Only 5 doctors certified even in general surgery were practicing in Vermont in 1941, all of them in Burlington, and only 4 certified surgeons were to be found in Mississippi.[70] Trained psychiatrists are almost unknown to rural people (outside of mental institutions); while New York State had 4.55 neuropsychiatrists per 100,000 in 1941-42 and Massachusetts had 5.28, Alabama had 0.53 per 100,000, Idaho had 0.19, and Montana had 0.18.[71]

In addition to specialists in private practice there are, of course, physicians in full-time salaried positions devoted to special fields like public health, research, medical education, or hospital administration. The scarcity of such specialists in rural areas will be considered in connection with the medical institutions and health agencies with which they are associated.

A Portrait of Country Practice

What then is the portrait of America's contemporary country doctor? Any generalized picture is difficult to draw, but out in the villages and farming communities one finds a rather characteristic type of rural doctor, presenting a quite different picture from that of the typical city physician. This is less the case in the enterprising small urban trade center, but out in the country districts, the physician — close to the soil and often a farmer himself — takes on his full share of local coloring. Generally overworked and underpaid, graying, he holds forth in an office in his home — or often in close association with the drugstore in which he may have a

[69] Advisory Board for Medical Specialties, *Directory of Medical Specialists Certified by American Boards.* New York: Columbia University Press, 1942.

[70] *Ibid.*

[71] Based on data furnished by U. S. Public Health Service.

financial interest. His office is meagerly equipped, commonly lacking all but the very simplest aids to diagnosis or treatment, and rarely tended by an office nurse or other aide. The roll-top desk may be piled high with largely unread medical journals, drug-house literature, and an assorted collection of pharmaceutical samples. All too often used and unsterilized instruments may be seen lying about and the examining table will reveal the telltale dust of disuse.

Those familiar with rural medical practice know that this picture is not overdrawn, and yet the aging country doctor is not to be blamed for his inadequacies. The environment of country practice is one of continuous frustration and continuous inability to do the things that the thoughtful physician realizes are indicated. Tied to his office to make even a moderate living, and with sick patients counting on his help, he rarely can find the opportunity to go away for a state medical association meeting, a refresher course, or postgraduate studies, and, after a while, he loses interest in the idea. As the years go by, he tends to become more firmly lodged in an intellectual rut, and soon the detail men from the various drug houses become his chief source of information on current therapeutics. Diagnostic methods stay pretty much as they were, with small use of such auxiliary refinements as the x-ray or the bacteriological laboratory. It is no surprise that after years of virtual isolation professionally some country doctors go completely to seed and lose all their effectiveness as providers of medical service.[72] Even local medical societies, which might tend to provide a certain amount of ethical and professional guidance to practitioners, are as a rule much weaker in every way in rural counties than in the cities.

The qualifications and services of rural physicians are by no means all of one type. There are many notable exceptions, many practitioners well past middle age who have kept up to the minute with modern medicine. There are many who have been responsible for

[72] Hospital admissions for drug addiction, for example, are found about 25 times more frequently among physicians than among the rest of the population and it is likely that rural doctors are found in at least proportionate numbers among the addicts. Rural people whose only doctor has become a drug addict or chronic alcoholic are obviously faced with a far greater problem than dwellers in the city, where other physicians are at hand to carry on. PESCOR, MICHAEL J., "A Statistical Analysis of the Clinical Records of Hospitalized Drug Addicts," *Public Health Reports,* Supp. 143, 1943.

the establishment of hospitals, who foster the adoption by their colleagues of the latest techniques of diagnosis or therapy, and who keep their lines of association with specialists and institutions in the nearest cities. Even in the case of less enterprising practitioners, there can be no doubt that, forced to get along without refined diagnostic aids, there is a tendency to develop a certain diagnostic sense and an ability to "see the patient as a whole," often quite lacking in the overspecialized city doctor.[73] Then, of course, some young alert physicians are, indeed, going into rural districts,[74] sometimes "buying out" the practice of a retiring practitioner. New patterns, such as the establishment of the doctor's office in the local hospital, are developing. It can hardly be denied, however, that by and large the rural doctor practices a brand of medicine many years behind the times. Thorough examinations are exceptional, and the dispensing of pills to strike at symptoms, rather than diseases, comes to be his major role.

If any picture has been overdrawn, surely it is that of the idyllic country doctor, who guards his flock of loyal families with a rough and ready skill through the years. While this picture may have had a certain poetic truth in the nineteenth century, it is a far cry from the realities of the present. The rural physician may make up with art what he lacks in science, and the heroism and resourcefulness of the "horse and buggy doctor" may win our admiration, but one cannot insist that, by modern standards, he renders a high quality of medical service.

The problem is intensified by the fact that the rural doctor actually carries greater responsibility than the city doctor. He is more completely the center of all health services, often owning and managing the hospital, leasing the drugstore, dispensing medicines and supplies at his office, doing all the surgery and obstetrics and general medicine as needs may arise, and even acting as local health officer. Since he is often one of the few college-trained men in the community and bears a sacred tradition, he is looked to for leadership

[73] HERTZLER, ARTHUR E., *The Horse and Buggy Doctor*. New York: Harper & Brothers, 1938.

[74] SINAI, NATHAN, "The New Country Doctor," *A Survey of the Medical Facilities of San Joaquin County, California:* 1929 (Committee on the Costs of Medical Care Pub. 12). Chicago: University of Chicago Press, 1931, pp. 198-207.

in all civic matters. For so broad a role, one would like to see rural physicians of Oslerian proportions.

While there are occasional signs of improvement in the quantitative and qualitative picture of rural medical practice, they are greatly outweighed by the generally downhill trend of affairs.[75] Sober evaluation gives little hope for a brighter future in rural medicine unless active steps are taken to strike at the fundamental causes of present problems.

[75] PERROTT and DAVIS, *op. cit.*

CHAPTER 9

DENTISTS

DESPITE the almost limitless need for dental care among country people, most of the deficiencies characteristic of the rural supply of physicians apply even in greater degree to rural dentists. The growing concentration of dentists in the cities where economic attractions are greater has left rural districts with a shortage of dentists relatively more critical than that of physicians. The rural dentists who are available tend to be in older age groups than the urban, less modern in their methods, and less inclined to engage in the specialties of dental practice.

The optimal number of dentists needed to serve a population group is difficult to estimate, since so much depends on the degree of organization of service, including the use of auxiliary personnel. The initial need for services in an over-all dental program, moreover, would be much greater than the continuing need after the great backlog of accumulated dental defects had been corrected. The Committee on the Costs of Medical Care estimated the optimal ratio to be between one dentist per 556 persons and one per 1,000 persons, depending on some of these factors.[1] Yet in 1941-42, before the serious personnel drainage of the war, even the nation's most urban counties did not enjoy the more conservative of these ratios. In the metropolitan counties the ratio in that year was 1,368 persons per dentist and in counties bordering on them it was 2,471 persons per dentist. It is among the more remote rural and semirural counties with communities under 10,000 population that the shortage of dentists is demonstrated most strikingly. In such nonbordering counties with places of 5,000 to 10,000 population, the ratio was one dentist to 2,847 persons; in counties with places of 2,500 to 5,000, it was one to 3,277; and in the most highly rural counties with no place of over 2,500 population, each dentist had to serve 4,235

[1] LEE and JONES, *op. cit.*

persons.[2] It will be recalled that the ratio of physicians in the 1,014 most isolated rural counties was about twice as poor as that in the metropolitan counties, but it may be noted that with dentists the corresponding rural ratio is three times as bad as the urban. In 1940, moreover, there were at least 177 counties without any dentist, and all of them were rural.[3]

As with physicians, these arithmetic ratios fail to take account of the reduced working ability of dentists in later life who are, in fact, found in disproportionate numbers in rural sections. A determination of the ratios of "effective" dentists to population may, therefore, be made comparable with that made for physicians. These ratios by states, in relation to their rurality, are shown in Table 17. It may be observed that in rural states like Arkansas or New Mexico there are three times as many persons per effective dentist as in urban states like California or Massachusetts. In the states over 70 per cent urban, we find one effective male dentist to 1,443 persons for 1940, compared with 1 to 4,256 in the states over 70 per cent rural. As one might expect, the scarcity of Negro dentists is really appalling. In the Southern states, where Negroes are predominantly rural, the Negro-dentist-to-Negro-population ratios in 1940 were as follows: for the South Atlantic region, 1 to 11,812; for the East South Central region, 1 to 18,057; and for the West South Central region, 1 to 14,156.[4]

Dentists set up practice in areas of high purchasing power, as do physicians.[5] In counties with per capita incomes of $600 a year or more, there was one dentist to 1,296 persons in 1942, with con-

[2] Based upon American Dental Association, Committee on Economics, *Distribution of Dentists in the United States*, Chicago, 1942; and U. S. Census, 1940. *Population*. Vol. 1, *Number of Inhabitants*. Analysis of data from 42 states omitting Illinois, Minnesota, Rhode Island, South Carolina, Washington, and West Virginia.

[3] *Ibid.*

[4] Data from U. S. Census presented in *Report of the Conference on Public Health Dentistry*. Ann Arbor, Michigan, July, 1944.

[5] O'ROURKE, JOHN T., "An Analysis of the Personnel Resources of the Dental Profession," *Journal of the American Dental Association*, 30:997-1006, July, 1943; "An Analysis of the Number and Distribution of Active Dentists in the United States," *Journal of the American Dental Association*, 30:1097-1110, Aug. 1, 1944.

Table 17. Supply of Dentists: *Number of male dentists and number of persons per effective male dentist* by states in urban-rural order, 1940*

State	Number of dentists	Number of effective dentists	Number of persons per effective dentist
All states	69,370	66,029	1,994
Population under 30 per cent rural . .	27,519	26,422	1,443
District of Columbia	491	463	1,432
Rhode Island	368	349	2,044
Massachusetts	2,777	2,613	1,652
New York	9,979	9,668	1,394
New Jersey	2,659	2,580	1,612
Illinois	5,907	5,632	1,402
California	5,338	5,117	1,350
Population 30 to 39 per cent rural . .	13,274	12,562	1,892
Connecticut	1,069	1,019	1,677
Ohio	3,716	3,497	1,975
Pennsylvania	5,872	5,561	1,061
Michigan	2,617	2,485	2,115
Population 40 to 49 per cent rural . .	10,269	9,690	1,882
Maryland	865	824	2,210
New Hampshire	219	196	2,508
Utah	304	288	1,911
Florida	713	686	2,766
Indiana	1,801	1,683	2,037
Wisconsin	2,094	1,987	1,579
Washington	1,234	1,181	1,470
Colorado	657	610	1,841
Delaware	105	97	2,747
Missouri	2,277	2,138	1,770
Population 50 to 59 per cent rural . .	8,626	8,196	2,178
Minnesota	2,060	1,991	1,402
Oregon	824	786	1,386
Texas	1,987	1,890	3,394
Iowa	1,606	1,507	1,684
Kansas	1,007	937	1,922
Louisiana	776	754	3,135
Maine	366	331	2,560
Population 60 to 69 per cent rural . .	5,808	5,485	3,289
Nevada	54	51	2,162
Nebraska	910	871	1,511

Table 17. Supply of Dentists: *Number of male dentists and number of persons per effective male dentist* by states in urban-rural order, 1940—(Continued)*

State	Number of dentists	Number of effective dentists	Number of persons per effective dentist
Population 60 to 69 per cent rural (cont.)			
Montana	275	264	2,119
Oklahoma	737	686	3,406
Wyoming	123	118	2,125
Virginia	837	797	3,360
Tennessee	832	785	3,714
Arizona	147	141	3,541
Georgia	819	764	4,089
Vermont	147	136	2,641
Idaho	212	197	2,664
New Mexico	113	106	5,017
Alabama	602	569	4,979
Population 70 per cent or more rural .	3,874	3,674	4,256
Kentucky	790	745	3,820
West Virginia	593	560	3,396
North Carolina	776	745	4,794
South Dakota	299	286	2,248
South Carolina	358	341	5,571
Arkansas	378	355	5,491
North Dakota	261	251	2,558
Mississippi	419	391	5,585

Source: U. S. Census, 1940. *Population.* Vol. 3, *The Labor Force.*

* Based on nonfederal male dentists, with those over 65 years of age counted as one-third effective; Census data unavailable for female dentists but the inclusion of such data would not materially affect these figures.

sistently poorer ratios in counties of decreasing wealth, down to a ratio of one dentist to 11,565 persons in counties with per capita incomes of under $100 a year.[6] The fact is that the relationship of the dentist-population ratio to rurality is actually a relationship to per capita income. As we might expect, therefore, the incomes of dentists in rural areas tend to be considerably below those in the

[6] PARRAN, THOMAS, Testimony before a Subcommittee of the Committee on Education and Labor, U. S. Senate, 79th Cong., 1st Sess., S. 190 and S. 1099, *Dental Research and Dental Care.* Washington: Government Printing Office, 1945, p. 22.

cities. In 1941, the average annual net income of dentists in rural communities of under 1,000 population was $2,470, compared with over $4,000 in the cities of over 25,000 population.[7] Despite much less competition and a much larger potential clientele, the rural dentist earns considerably less than the dentist in cities up to 100,000 population and even less than the dentist in cities of over 100,000, where competition and commercialized "mass production" dentistry reach their height.

Even rises in farm income levels do not have the effect of raising the effective demand for dental care in the same degree as do increases in industrial income levels. Between 1937 and 1940, while both rural and urban incomes rose markedly, the earnings of rural dentists increased much less than those of urban dentists.[8] Poor rural habits of dental care, developed over the years, are not readily improved even when family income rises.

The low incomes of dentists in rural communities reflect not only local purchasing power but also the lower number of dental specialists and the smaller proportion of practitioners in the middle-age years, both of which categories are associated with higher earning power. Full-time dental specialists such as orthodontists, specialists in dentures, or dental surgeons are almost entirely urban.

The total supply of rural dentists is obviously pitifully smaller than that necessary to handle rural dental needs, if the economic and educational barriers were eliminated. Assuming that the total output of dentists by dental schools were greatly increased, the problem of their distribution would, of course, remain. The necessity of training dentists who will practice in rural areas is complicated even more than for physicians by the highly uneven origin of dental students from the different states. In 1944, for example, the four urban states of New York, Pennsylvania, Illinois, and California, with 21 per cent of the nation's population, furnished 38 per cent of the nation's dental students while the four rural states of Alabama, Kentucky, Mississippi, and Tennessee, with 8.2 per cent of the national popu-

[7] DENISON, EDWARD F., "Income in Selected Professions: Part 5, Dentistry," *Survey of Current Business* (U. S. Department of Commerce), 24:17-20, April, 1944.

[8] O'ROURKE, *op. cit.*

lation, furnished only 3.9 per cent of the dental students.[9] Doubtless, data on the origin of dental students predominantly from the larger urban places within these states would be more striking. The relatively high cost of dental education naturally prevents many ambitious rural youth from ever undertaking the study of dentistry.

The typical rural dentist tends to be strong on extractions and full dentures and weak on protective services such as fillings and prophylaxes. This is due chiefly to the fact that his patients come to him so often with teeth and gums in an advanced state of disease. As the dentist constantly faces evidence of accumulated neglect, he is inclined even to lose interest in the more painstaking types of preventive or restorative work. He tends to surrender, so to speak, in despair, lacking the support of a broad program of dental health education in the community for early and regular dental care, and serving patients whose generally low incomes forbid costly restorative work.

Too often the rural dentist's office is located in some small commercial building not outstanding for its sanitary demeanor. Skilled office assistants or dental hygienists are rare indeed. The image of science and cleanliness that stays in the memory of the visitor to an up-to-date city dentist seldom emerges from a visit to the rural dentist. While there are exceptions, of course, the setting of rural dental practice seems fully as liable to allow a man to get into a "rut" as rural medical practice.

[9] American Dental Association, Council on Dental Education, *Dental Students' Register*, 1944. Chicago, 1945.

CHAPTER 10

NURSES

WITH FEWER and less effective physicians and dentists in rural areas, we might hope that nurses would be available to extend the doctor's arm and make up to some extent for the deficit. Unfortunately, this is not the case. In the areas where doctors are fewest, nurses are fewest as well.

Of the approximately 284,000 graduate trained nurses "employed or seeking employment" in the United States in 1940,[1] only 24.5 per cent were located in the 28 states with populations over half rural, which include 39 per cent of our national population. Only 18.3 per cent of them, in fact, were located in the nation's rural communities of under 2,500, which include 43.5 per cent of our population.[2] It is recognized, of course, that nurses tend to follow the distribution of hospitals and that many hospitals should reasonably be located in somewhat larger towns serving rural sections, but this striking disproportion in the distribution of nurses probably remains significant. The nurse-to-population ratios in states grouped by rurality are shown in Table 18. We see that the relative supply in the most rural group of states is less than one-third of that in the most urban group. The degree of the discrepancy is brought out by consideration of a ratio of trained nurses in Massachusetts of 1 to 248 persons or in New York State of 1 to 284, compared with a ratio of 1 to 753 in Louisiana or 1 to 1,273 in Alabama.[3] By 1946 there were estimated

[1] The Census reports 369,178 "trained nurses," including student nurses, "employed or seeking employment." The National League of Nursing Education records 85,156 student nurses for 1940. This leaves a net total of about 284,000 graduate trained nurses, although this figure includes many that may not be registered or active. Derived from U. S. Census, 1940. *Population.* Vol. 3, *The Labor Force;* also, unpublished data furnished by the National League of Nursing Education.

[2] *Ibid.*

[3] *Ibid.* Authorities are not prepared to suggest an optimal ratio of nurses to population at this time, pending the completion of studies involving a determination of total nursing needs and such considerations as the role of the practical nurse.

to be about 317,800 registered professional nurses available in the United States, with about 129,000 additional student nurses enrolled, but there was little to suggest any improved rural-urban distribution.[4]

As with physicians and dentists, these figures on nurses overstate the actual effective "manpower" available, since many of the nurses were not actively engaged in nursing when the Census was taken.

Table 18. Supply of Nurses: *Number of trained nurses* and number of persons per nurse in states grouped by rurality, 1940*

Per cent rural (state populations)	Number of trained nurses	Number of persons per trained nurse
Under 30	124,774	305.6
30—39	52,573	452.2
40—49	37,067	492.0
50—59	29,889	597.1
60—69	23,389	771.2
70 and over	16,330	957.6
U.S. total	284,022	453.6

Source: U. S. Census, 1940. *Population.* Vol. 3, *The Labor Force.* Also, data furnished by the National League of Nursing Education.

* Nurses "employed or seeking employment," exclusive of those employed in emergency work and exclusive of 85,156 student nurses enrolled in state-accredited schools of nursing on January 1, 1940.

Far more nurses than physicians or dentists drop out of their professional work, of course, to marry or take up other occupations. It was found, in fact, in the 1941 National Inventory of Registered Nurses that some 40 per cent of all reporting registered nurses[5] were inactive. As we might expect, recognizing the role of economic opportunity, there were over 10 per cent more inactive nurses in all states over 60 per cent rural than in the states over 60 per cent urban — despite the much lower over-all ratio of nurses to population in the more rural states.[6]

[4] American Nurses' Association, *Facts about Nursing* 1946. New York, 1946, pp. 9, 32.

[5] Questionnaires were returned by 286,697 registered nurses, estimated to represent about 75 or 80 per cent of all registered nurses in the United States, active and inactive (to be distinguished from Census data on trained nurses "employed or seeking employment").

[6] Derived from McIVER, PEARL, "Registered Nurses in the U.S.A.," *American Journal of Nursing,* 42:760-773, July, 1942.

With about two-thirds of all active nurses engaged full-time or in private duty in institutions, it is obvious that the serious shortage of hospital beds in country districts lies at the root of the rural shortage of nurses. Here again, and with respect to all active nurses, the same general relationship to per capita income holds as for physicians or dentists. The supply of Negro nurses is as desperately short as that of other Negro health personnel. With only about 7,200 colored nurses (including trained nurses and students) reported by the Census for the whole country in 1940, they represented about 2 per cent of the total supply of nurses, while the colored population was 9.8 per cent of the total.[7]

The shortage of rural nurses is due partially to the poor opportunities for nurses' training in rural districts. Nursing schools in the rural sections are of smaller total capacity (see Chapter 15) and the great majority of nurses are educated in urban institutions.[8] The young country girl going to the city for her training is naturally inclined to remain there, attracted by professional and social advantages. The relative infrequency of nursing schools in rural hospitals makes for further handicaps in rural nursing supply, simply because nursing service is not available from student nurses. The nurse who does obtain her training from a small rural hospital today is in general relatively poorly qualified in both the theory and practice of modern nursing. Yet, on graduation and employment in a rural hospital, she is saddled with greater responsibilities than the nurse in a city hospital, who is typically better trained and who has supervisors and resident physicians to fall back on for guidance.

In the 1920's and 1930's — before the eight-hour day became popular for nurses and helped to take up the lag — unemployment of nurses prevailed in the cities, but rural hospitals, despite their shortages, could not afford to offer them jobs. From about 1940 on, after rural hospitals became better able financially to support more nurses, they were not available and the hospitals remained understaffed. At nearly all times, the nurse attached to a rural hospital has been overworked, has been forced to assume numerous unprofessional hospital tasks because of insufficient maintenance per-

[7] American Nurses' Association, Nursing Information Bureau, *Facts about Nursing* 1944. New York, 1944, p. 12.

[8] These institutions rarely have affiliations even with modern rural hospitals in which the student nurse might get a taste of rural nursing and rural life.

sonnel, and all too often has been underpaid. According to a recent study, 22 per cent of hospitals with less than 50 beds (typically rural) required nurses to work 54 to 84 hours of day duty per week, whereas only 7 per cent of hospitals with more than 200 beds (typically urban) had similar work schedules.[9] In general, the more isolated the hospital, the longer the hours and the greater the burden of work.

To a greater relative extent than in the cities, no doubt, nurses actively practicing in rural areas are found to be in hospital work. Trained nurses available for services in the home, either on a private or on an agency basis, are rare indeed, and the number of public health nurses is likewise inadequate. In eight counties in Kentucky, for example, there were in 1940 no R.N.'s, while twenty additional counties had but one nurse each, thirteen of these doing public health work exclusively.[10]

To what extent "practical nurses," with little or no formal training but with certain skills acquired from experience, make up for the deficit of trained nurses in rural areas is hard to say. Like midwives, practical nurses have to a large extent come to the rescue in rural sections and provided some service where none would otherwise have been forthcoming.

It is significant that rural communities have a higher proportion of the nation's total supply of practical nurses and midwives than of the total supply of trained nurses — 28 per cent, compared with 18 per cent for trained nurses cited previously.[11] The practical-nurse-to-population ratio, nevertheless, is obviously lower in rural sections than in urban, since the rural 43.5 per cent of the national population is served by only 28 per cent of their total number, including midwives. The work of these practical nurses, moreover, is usually on a sporadic, part-time basis, little better than the friendly services of a neighboring housewife, and hardly comparable in quality or quantity to the output of a full-time professional nurse.

[9] American Nurses' Association, *Personnel Practices for General Staff Nurses.* New York, 1944, p. 26.

[10] CRITTENDEN, *op. cit.* The supply and the role of public health nurses are discussed in Chapter 19.

[11] U. S. Department of Labor, Women's Bureau, *The Outlook for Women in Occupations in the Medical Services: Nurses and Hospital Attendants* (Bull. 203, No. 5). Washington: Government Printing Office, 1945, p. 2.

A more substantial quality of service may be rendered by those practical nurses who are employed by hospitals on a regular basis. Counting these practical nurses and similar attendants on hospital staffs, there were 80,105 such personnel in the United States in 1945. In the 35 most rural states with about 50 per cent of the national population, however, only 34,000 of these were employed, compared with 46,000 in the more urban states with the other half of the population. As for licensed practical nurses, there were only 31,510 in the whole country in 1945; over 27,000 of these were in the three urban states of New York, Massachusetts, and Connecticut.[12]

While even in urban centers nurses tend to be underpaid, the average net income of rural nurses — at least those working on a private duty basis, for whom data are available — is below that for nurses in urban communities of all sizes. In 1941, nurses in communities up to even 10,000 population earned only slightly more than $1,000 per year, while in cities of 500,000 or more they earned about $1,400.[13] Doubtless the same general relationship holds for general-duty hospital nurses or office nurses employed by physicians. These lower earnings play a real part in discouraging nurses from practicing their profession in rural communities. It is true, of course, that when general duty nurses are provided living facilities by a hospital, their real earnings, in effect, tend to be higher. While this is often the case in rural hospitals, these emoluments are seldom adequate compensation for low salary checks.

[12] American Nurses' Association, *Facts about Nursing* 1946. New York, 1946, pp. 85, 96.

[13] DENISON, E. F., "Incomes in Selected Professions: Part 6, Comparison of Incomes of Nine Independent Professions," *Survey of Current Business,* 23:25-28, May, 1944.

CHAPTER 11

OTHER HEALTH PERSONNEL

IN ADDITION to physicians, dentists, and nurses, there are a number of other technical personnel involved in the provision of medical care. Some of these are essential members of the over-all medical team; they give effective service and are desirable. Others are more or less irregular, if not superfluous; they are offshoots that have usually grown up because of some inadequacy in conventional medical service. In general, we find that allied personnel of essential types follow the same pattern of rural inadequacy as physicians, dentists, and nurses. The nonessential or substandard types represent the one group of health personnel that fail — at least from the quantitative point of view — to follow this pattern.

All these personnel may be considered under three main functional headings — secondary practitioners, auxiliary workers, and cultists. Secondary practitioners who handle special categories of medical problems are not to be confused with cultists, who take virtually all disease problems as their province and follow single-track theories of treatment.

Secondary Practitioners

Practitioners available to handle special categories of medical problems include optometrists for visual refraction, chiropodists for the care of certain foot conditions, and midwives. The most abundant of the secondary practitioners in rural areas are the midwives — the category under least control through educational requirements or licensure. In fact, of all health personnel, midwives are the one type distinctly more plentiful in rural areas than in urban.

The exact number of midwives in the United States is not known, although their preponderance in rural sections is unquestionable. Lumped together with "practical nurses," as the Bureau of the Census considers them, there are about 91,000 in the nation.[1] While the distribution of the combined group among the states appears

[1] U. S. Department of Labor, Women's Bureau, *loc. cit.*

fairly even, the combined total in the urban states tends to be composed largely of practical nurses and in the rural states more largely of midwives. Much the largest concentration of midwives is found in the highly rural Southern states, where they attend births principally among the low-income Negro population. The extent of midwifery in this region is indicated by health department reports of over 25,000 practicing midwives in nine Southern states in 1938.[2] Obviously the midwife fills a gap where fully qualified medical personnel are not available and especially where the birth rate is high, as in rural areas.

Midwifery is not objectionable when, as in certain European nations, it is under strict supervision and is regarded as a field for formal training. In the United States, despite notable efforts at its control in recent years, midwifery has been mainly a custom of expediency developing among the most impoverished and poorly educated sections of our rural population. Facing the problem realistically, about half the state health departments make efforts to instruct midwives in the elementary principles of attending childbirth, and special licensure or registration is now theoretically required in three-fifths of the states.[3] The role of trained nurse-midwives, providing either supervision of untrained midwives or direct obstetrical service, has slowly been expanding. Even so, midwifery is as a rule simply a part-time avocation of elderly neighbor women who command a fee seldom exceeding $10 for their services and average for their work considerably less than $100 a year.[4] In the Spanish-American villages of our Southwest, midwifery is actually part and parcel of a persistent system of witchcraft, under which head lice are fed for the treatment of tuberculosis or knives are put under the delivery bed to "cut the pains" of labor.[5]

[2] U. S. Children's Bureau, *The Health Situation of Negro Mothers and Babies in the United States.* Washington, July 1, 1940, Processed.

[3] MOUNTIN, J. W., and EVELYN FLOOK, "Distribution of Health Services in the Structure of State Government," *Public Health Reports,* 57:1791-1821, Nov. 27, 1942.

[4] REED, LOUIS S., *Midwives, Chiropodists, and Optometrists* (Committee on the Costs of Medical Care Pub. 15). Chicago: University of Chicago Press, 1932.

[5] SANCHEZ, GEORGE I., *Forgotten People.* Albuquerque: University of New Mexico Press, 1940, pp. 34-35. The true proportions of the midwife problem are reflected better by the record of births attended by midwives than by their actual numbers; these childbirth services will be considered in Chap. 17.

The regional distribution of the 16,600 optometrists in the nation is almost opposite from that of midwives. While their relative supply appears to be fairly similar in the three most urban regions, it will be noted in Table 19 that their supply in the rural South is only about half of that in the rest of the country. An analysis by states discloses that of the 20 more urban states, only 2 have ratios poorer than one optometrist to 10,000 persons, but 17 of the 28 more rural states have ratios poorer than this.[6]

Table 19. Secondary Practitioners: *Number of active optometrists* (1940) *and chiropodists* (1941) *and number per* 100,000 *population, by regions in urban-rural order*

Region	Per cent rural	Optometrists		Chiropodists	
		Number	Number per 100,000	Number	Number per 100,000
Northeast	23.4	4,465	14.1	2,353	6.5
West	41.5	2,245	16.2	593	4.3
North Central	41.6	6,471	16.4	1,457	3.6
South	63.3	3,363	7.5	582	1.4

Source: American Optometric Association, *Professional Monograph: Optometry*. Minneapolis, 1943, p. 16; also National Association of Chiropodists, Council on Education, *Twenty-second Annual Report*. Washington, 1941, p. 15.

The relative supply of the nation's 5,000 chiropodists is more closely like that of physicians and dentists, corresponding markedly to regional urbanization. Only 2 of the 20 more urban states, moreover, are supplied with fewer than 4 "foot doctors" per 100,000 population, while 20 of the 28 rural states fail to reach this ratio.[7]

One might suppose that these secondary practitioners would tend to settle in rural districts where professional competition from physicians would be less. While this factor might account, for example, for the smaller supply of optometrists in the Northeast than in the less urban West, it is evident that general urbanization and purchasing power are more decisive. The settlement of optometrists and chiropodists in the larger cities has been augmented by recent tendencies — resisted by their professional organizations — for them

[6] American Optometric Association, *Professional Monograph: Optometry*. Minneapolis, 1943, p. 16.

[7] Derived from National Association of Chiropodists, Council on Education, *Twenty-second Annual Report*. Washington, 1941, p. 15.

to be employed by business establishments, such as jewelry stores for the former, shoe stores for the latter, and department stores for both. Yet there is little evidence that rural physicians are filling the gap by becoming more skilled at visual refractions or the treatment of local foot ailments.

Auxiliary Health Personnel

Health workers of continual assistance to the physician and dentist in the treatment or prevention of disease include — aside from nurses — pharmacists, laboratory technicians, and certain other personnel.

Despite the large part that drugs play in rural medical therapy, only 19 per cent of the nation's 79,000 active, male pharmacists were

Table 20. Auxiliary Personnel: *Number of active pharmacists and laboratory technicians and assistants, and number of persons per professional worker, by regions in urban-rural order, 1940*

Region†	Pharmacists*		Laboratory technicians and assistants*	
	Number	Number of persons per pharmacist	Number	Number of persons per laboratory worker
Northeast	25,233	1,426	23,905	1,505
West	11,255	1,234	7,985	1,738
North Central	24,127	1,664	18,981	2,115
South	18,732	2,224	12,127	3,436

Source: U. S. Census, 1940. *Population.* Vol. 3, *The Labor Force.*
* "Employed or seeking employment," exclusive of those employed in emergency work.
† For percentage rural of each region see Table 19.

located in 1940 in the rural communities comprising 43.5 per cent of our population. The distribution of active pharmacists among the four main geographic regions is presented in Table 20. While pharmacists in the most rural region must serve a considerably larger number of persons than those in the most urban region, it is significant that the rural-urban differential among the four regions is less striking than that for physicians or for other auxiliary personnel like laboratory technicians. This possibly reflects the disproportionately great use of drugs by rural people, both prescribed and unprescribed, to be studied in a later chapter. It is all the more significant since the rural doctor's rather common practice of doing his own dispensing of drugs, and to some extent even his own compounding, would lead one to expect an especially lean supply of pharmacists in rural communities.

The inability of many rural families to afford a physician gives especial importance to the local druggist. In rural communities, it is more than good sport that so often nicknames the pharmacist as "Doc." The medical advice he may give from time to time is less an indication of illegitimate conduct on his part than an unavoidable response to the demands of rural customers who cannot get all the physician's care they need. A great many across-the-counter drugs, furthermore, are sold in village general stores by untrained clerks, and not rarely one finds a "druggist" in an isolated community without benefit of training or licensure. The statutes in many rural states authorizing nonpharmacists to sell "nonpoisonous patent or proprietary medicines which do not contain narcotic, hypnotic or dangerous drugs, and commonly used household remedies" are laws that are loosely conceived and usually poorly enforced.[8] Such legislation merely reflects the compromises forced by the sparsity of registered pharmacists in rural communities.

The regional distribution of laboratory technicians and assistants is also given in Table 20. In the rather striking relationship between the relative supply of these personnel and the rurality of the region, one sees a reflection of the quality of rural medicine. As with specialists, the supply of laboratory technicians gives an index of the degree to which the medical practice of an area is scientifically developed. In the shortage of laboratory technicians in an area, one finds a measure of the inadequacy of laboratory facilities in hospitals, public health agencies, or private diagnostic units.

In the absence of qualified technicians, laboratory services in rural hospitals are often performed by hard-working nurses who have had a little extra training in doing blood counts or simple urinalyses. The scope of these services is clearly limited. The same applies to x-ray services which should properly be performed by trained technicians. A proportionately greater number of the lab-

[8] Personal communication from Dr. Robert P. Fischelis, American Pharmaceutical Association, Washington, 1945.

oratory technicians in rural areas are probably employed by public agencies, in view of the low effective demand for their services on a privately purchased basis in voluntary hospitals or independent laboratories. As for physiotherapists, now commonplace in large city hospitals, they are practically unknown in rural communities.

Auxiliary dental personnel are found in even fewer numbers in rural areas than are dentists. Dental hygienists and assistants, who can lighten the dentist's work load and free him for the more complex tasks, are seldom found. The dental specialists using the greatest number of these aides are, of course, concentrated in the cities.[9] Dental technicians, engaged chiefly in the preparation of artificial dentures, are found in the dental laboratories ordinarily located in the large cities. The rural dentist, as a result, must often spend hours at painstaking laboratory tasks.

Clerical and maintenance personnel in hospitals, clinics, and private professional offices are as limited in rural sections as the facilities with which they are associated. These personnel deficiencies obviously entail the loss of valuable professional time in the performance of relatively simple tasks. Associated with these deficiencies, also, is the poor system of medical records to be found in most rural hospitals or private offices, making difficult a careful follow-up of cases or analyses of clinical experience.

Any description of health personnel should mention the veterinarian as a type of trained person whose work indirectly affects the health of man. The elimination of cattle infected with bovine tuberculosis or Bang's disease obviously protects man from disease, both in the country and the city, though pasteurization of milk provides an additional protection for the urban consumer that rural people often lack. In some rural sections, as a matter of fact, the veterinarian assumes special importance because, in the absence of physicians, he may be called on for medical services. It is not unusual for the local veterinarian to serve as health officer, and many a farmer's baby has been delivered into the world by the doctor who ordinarily treats his livestock. Perhaps there is room for speculation in the fact that many rural sections that are amply supplied with their share of the nation's 11,000 veterinarians are inadequately served by doctors of medicine.

[9] LEVEN, MAURICE, *The Practice of Dentistry and the Incomes of Dentists in Twenty States: 1929.* Chicago: University of Chicago Press, 1932, pp. 14, 28.

Cultist Practitioners

For better or for worse, America must count among its health personnel many thousands of healing cultists, including mainly osteopaths, chiropractors, and faith healers. It is worth recognizing that, in large measure though not entirely, the various cults or sects have grown up because of the failures or inadequacies of "regular" medicine. Dr. Oliver Wendell Holmes pointed out in the last century that homeopathy, for example, with its infinitesimal dosages, had developed in reaction to the bold purgations and massive bloodlettings of the clinical medicine of the time.[10] By the same token, one might expect that medical sects would thrive in rural areas where qualified physicians, and especially resources for physical therapy, are sparse. This is probably the case to some extent, although the financial attraction of the cities is fully appreciated by the cultist and the sectarian.

While the national distribution of cultists is predominantly urban, it is significant that among male osteopaths, for example, 22.0 per cent are located in rural communities compared with 18.6 per cent of professional personnel as a whole.[11] More important, the partial dependence of cultism on inadequacies in scientific medicine evidently operates to produce a regional distribution of the nation's 10,600 chiropractors and 6,000 osteopaths quite at variance with that of physicians. In Table 21 it may be noted that the Northeast, with its lowest proportion of rural people and its highest supply of physicians, dentists, nurses, and other essential health personnel, has the lowest proportionate number of chiropractors and, except for the South, the lowest relative number of osteopaths. It is worth remembering that only with respect to midwives and chiropractors does the rural South exceed the urban Northeast in health personnel.

Of course, numerous other factors also contribute to the regional distribution of cultists. The West, particularly California, abounds with cultists partially because it is a haven for persons with chronic ailments that have not responded to conventional treatment; these discouraged souls will try anything, and the cultists, with their glib cure-all appeals, thrive on their misfortunes. The North Central

[10] HOLMES, OLIVER WENDELL, *Medical Essays* 1842-1882. Boston: Houghton Mifflin Company, 1892, pp. xiii-xv.

[11] U. S. Census, 1940. *Population.* Vol. 3, *The Labor Force.*

region, on the other hand, is the home of a number of formal cultist schools, largely because the founders of osteopathy (Still of Missouri) and of chiropractic (Palmer of Iowa) had their beginnings in this general section — at a time, in fact, when it was far more rural than today. Naturally the settlement of cultists is quite extensive around their centers of training, where their community standing is likely to be better than elsewhere. Furthermore, as we shall see, more urban than rural states have passed legislation in recent years which tends to keep out certain cultists, thus acting in some

Table 21. Cultist Practitioners: *Number of osteopaths and chiropractors and number per 100,000 population, by regions in urban-rural order*, 1940

Region†	Osteopaths*		Chiropractors*	
	Number	Number per 100,000	Number	Number per 100,000
Northeast	1,415	3.6	1,935	5.0
West	1,138	8.2	2,659	19.1
North Central	2,607	6.5	3,906	9.7
South	847	2.2	2,129	5.5

Source: U. S. Census, 1940. *Population.* Vol. 3, *The Labor Force.*
* "Employed or seeking employment," exclusive of those employed in emergency work.
† For percentage rural of each region see Table 19.

degree to concentrate them in more rural states, particularly in the North Central and Western regions.

Although their total number is not large, the cultists in rural districts have a special importance simply because of the relative shortage of qualified doctors of medicine. Cultist practice, moreover, is not static; it has changed markedly with the years. One illustration of this is the extent to which osteopathy has come to emulate the theories and practice of scientific medicine. By and large, nevertheless, the quality of most cultist performance today is poor, and it represents one more instance where rural people may have a choice of only second-class service.

Another small and variegated group of "drugless healers" includes the naturopaths and related faddists, who preach the cure-all blessings of sunshine or orange juice. Thriving on the city dweller's reaction against the mechanization of urban life, these marginal cultists seem to operate more in the cities, particularly on the West

Coast. Finally, there are the faith healers, including a number of non-orthodox religious sects, most important of which are the Christian Scientists. These, too, are most numerous in large urban centers, though many are found in small towns.[12] Most Christian Science practitioners perform their services only part-time and often they accept no fees; the chief danger in their activity is the inducement in the patient of a false sense of security, entailing a delay in obtaining needed medical services. Their significance in small towns, like that of other cultists, is that, in the absence of physicians, they may come to be depended on to a considerable degree.

Perhaps a final somewhat macabre commentary on the supply of rural health personnel is the fact that the distribution of funeral directors among the regions is considerably more equitable than the supply of physicians or dentists or nurses or technicians. In the Northeast there are about 30 undertakers per 100,000 population, in the West 23, in the North Central region 33, and in the South 25 per 100,000.[13] A visitor from Mars to rural America might get the impression that we are more concerned about conveying people toward the next world than keeping them in this one.

[12] REED, LOUIS S., *The Healing Cults* (Committee on the Costs of Medical Care Pub. 16). Chicago: University of Chicago Press, 1932.

[13] U. S. Census, 1940. *Population*. Vol. 3, *The Labor Force*.

CHAPTER 12

EFFECTS OF THE WAR ON RURAL HEALTH PERSONNEL

THE SECOND WORLD WAR naturally had profound effects on the adequacy of health personnel available to the rural population, as large numbers of physicians and others were withdrawn to serve the armed forces. Yet the manpower deficiencies might not have been so keenly felt if there had not been a coincident sharp rise in farm income, as in all national income, and accordingly heightened purchasing power for medical services. There was, in effect, an increased demand for medical care in the face of a decreased supply of its providers. The net effect of the war was to aggravate nearly all the deficiencies we have observed in rural medical manpower and to accelerate the long-time downhill trend in the supply of effective personnel.

The extent of the loss of effective physicians during the war is shown in Table 22. In relation to an acceptable state-wide ratio of one effective physician to 1,000 persons, it is seen that furnishing the armed forces with some 60,000 physicians of military age reduced the supply of all but three states below this standard. In recognition of wartime pressures, it became popular in official circles to consider a ratio of 1 to 1,500 as a minimal satisfactory level of physician supply. By this standard, we find that as of January, 1944, the populations of 22 states — all but four of them predominantly rural — were served by a supply of physicians below this wartime minimum. Of the 28 states with over half of their population rural, only 10 had ratios more favorable than 1 to 1,500 and all of these were poorer than about 1 to 1,200.

The situation in rural areas became acute very early in the war, as one rural state after another exceeded its designated quota of physicians for the armed forces. By September, 1942, 24 of the 28 rural states had exceeded their quotas, 11 of them by over 50 per cent.[1] As the war progressed, the actual percentage of decline in the supply of physicians came to be greater in urban areas than in rural, doubtless due merely to the fact that more physicians of

Table 22. Effect of the War on the Supply of Physicians: *Number of persons per effective physician, by states in urban-rural order,* 1940 *and* 1944*

State	1940	1944	State	1940	1944
United States . . .	935	1,284	Iowa	1,037	1,310
			Kansas	1,126	1,418
District of Columbia .	411	761	Louisiana	1,220	1,599
Rhode Island . . .	913	1,056	Maine.	1,136	1,250
Massachusetts . . .	696	740	Nevada	755	1,199
New York	597	860	Nebraska	922	1,217
New Jersey	842	1,272	Montana.	1,203	1,332
Illinois	789	991	Oklahoma	1,306	1,341
California.	747	1,224	Wyoming	1,076	1,637
Connecticut	780	1,023	Virginia	1,171	2,111
Ohio	927	1,340	Tennessee	1,257	1,653
Pennsylvania. . . .	891	1,156	Arizona	949	2,165
Michigan	1,017	1,413	Georgia	1,388	1,907
Maryland	801	1,278	Vermont	845	1,230
New Hampshire . .	975	1,168	Idaho	1,422	2,040
Utah	1,119	1,508	New Mexico . . .	1,422	1,885
Florida	1,012	2,185	Alabama	1,684	2,135
Indiana	1,039	1,443	Kentucky	1,324	1,800
Wisconsin	1,113	1,252	West Virginia . . .	1,226	1,543
Washington	1,017	1,601	North Carolina . .	1,504	1,973
Colorado	861	1,305	South Dakota . . .	1,657	1,925
Delaware	913	1,619	South Carolina. . .	1,565	2,257
Missouri	1,001	1,319	Arkansas.	1,392	1,565
Minnesota	903	1,405	North Dakota . . .	1,439	1,560
Oregon	927	1,396	Mississippi	1,784	2,113
Texas	1,245	1,836			

Source: Lahey, Frank F., and J. L. Kaukonen, "A Summary of the Activities of the Procurement and Assignment Service," *War Medicine,* 6:16, July, 1944.

* As a basis for the ratios, the number of "effective" physicians was calculated much as described in Table 15 except that interns and residents were excluded, this giving higher 1940 ratios than those in Table 15. The 1944 population base was the U. S. Bureau of the Census estimate as of November 1, 1943.

[1] MOTT, F. D., Testimony before a Subcommittee of the Committee on Education and Labor, U. S. Senate, 77th Cong., 2d Sess., S. Res. 291, *Investigation of Manpower Resources.* Washington: Government Printing Office, 1943, Part 2, p. 776.

military age were available for recruitment in the cities. The significant point, however, is that rural districts, which could ill afford to release any practitioners, lost so many that their supply was practically everywhere brought to critical levels, while urban centers, which might well have spared thousands more, retained enough doctors to keep their supply within relatively satisfactory limits.

The full effect of the war on the rural supply of physicians is seen more clearly when ratios are considered by counties. By 1944 there were 411 counties with a physician-population ratio of between 1 to 3,000 and 1 to 5,000; there were 122 additional counties with ratios between 1 to 5,000 and 1 to 10,000; there were 20 additional counties with ratios poorer than 1 to 10,000; and there were 81 additional counties with no active physician in them at all.[2] Thus, in 634 counties — over one-fifth of our total number, with a population of nearly 9 million persons — the physician-population ratio was worse than twice as poor as the wartime minimal level of 1 to 1,500, or there were no physicians in practice at all. The actual combined ratio in these counties, all but 18 of which are rural, was 1 to 4,219.[3] Considering counties with ratios poorer than 1 to 2,000 as critical, another 844 counties would have to be added, the vast majority of these, of course, also being rural. By this standard 1,478, or nearly half of the nation's counties, were in critical need of more doctors.

Viewed in terms of states with desperate shortages, we find that there were nine in 1944 that had ratios of 1 to 3,000 or poorer in over one-third of their counties. These were Alabama, Arizona, Florida, Georgia, Kentucky, North and South Carolina, South Dakota, and Virginia.[4] All of these but Florida have populations that are 65 per cent rural or more.

This drainage of younger physicians placed a severe strain upon

[2] "Distribution of Physicians in the United States 1940 and 1944" (prepared by the Subcommittee staff). Hearings before a Subcomittee of the Committee on Education and Labor, U. S. Senate, 78th Cong., 2d Sess., S. Res. 74, *Wartime Health and Education*. Washington: Government Printing Office, 1944, Part 6, pp. 2121-2123.

[3] Based on data furnished by the staff of the Subcommittee on Wartime Health and Education, Committee on Education and Labor, U. S. Senate, 1944.

[4] BARTON, PAUL C., Letter submitted to a Subcommittee of the Committee on Education and Labor, U. S. Senate, 78th Cong., 2d Sess., S. Res. 74, *Wartime Health and Education*, Part 6, p. 2176.

the generally older group of practitioners in rural communities.[5] A study in three representative states showed the average case load of physicians to increase from 84 patients per week in 1940 to 144 per week in 1944.[6] While this extra load may to some extent merely have filled some wasted-time lags in prewar practice, to a large extent it meant a greater wear and tear on the harassed practitioner and a more perfunctory type of medical service. Physicians' incomes in rural and urban practice alike soared to unprecedented levels. One of the special effects of the withdrawal of rural physicians for the armed forces was an enhancement of the importance of rural osteopaths and other cultists. In many rural communities only cultists were left behind to serve the population.

The effect of the war on the supply of dentists was like the effect on physicians. With the recruitment of 22,000 dental officers, the rural areas again were hit hardest. The reduction in the supply of graduate nurses to below 200,000 by the end of 1944[7] was likewise felt severely by rural districts. Some of the shortage of rural nurses was fortunately overcome by the return to duty of older nurses who had previously retired from active work. Rural shortages of laboratory technicians became particularly acute as the military demand for these workers almost outstripped the available supply. Many rural health departments were cut down to a skeleton staff. The very pressures created by these wartime manpower difficulties stimulated the organization of certain temporary governmental programs to make maximum use of, or to train, new personnel. These programs were significant in establishing the propriety of national concern for the supply of health personnel and may have long range value (see Chapter 21).

The aggravation by the war of rural shortages of medical personnel would be less distressing if it did not appear that the situation will continue to grow worse. We may be reminded that following the First World War, the same aggravation of previous inequities

[5] PICKENS, MARSHALL I., "The Effects of the War on the Medical Service in 38 North Carolina Counties with Limited Personnel," *North Carolina Medical Journal*, 3:570-571, October, 1942; also, "The Effects of the War on the Medical Service in 12 South Carolina Counties with Limited Medical Personnel," *Journal of South Carolina Medical Association*, 38:245-246, September, 1942.

[6] LAHEY, F. H., and J. L. KAUKONEN, "A Summary of the Activities of the Procurement and Assignment Service," *War Medicine*, 6:10-17, July, 1944.

[7] *Ibid.*

occurred, with one-time rural physicians returning from the front to settle in large cities.[8] Taking into account military requirements, the natural rate of deaths and retirements among physicians, the present rate of output of new medical graduates, and patterns of urban settlement established in recent years, George St. J. Perrott and Burnet M. Davis have ventured a prediction that the relative supply of physicians in all states will continue to decline and that in the most rural states it will decline at a greater rate. In Alabama, for example, it was estimated that by 1950 the state-wide ratio (including the urban sections within that state) will approach 1 to 4,000.[9] "Opinion polls" of physicians in the armed services concerning their future plans confirm these predictions. Among medical officers planning to settle in new communities or to set up practice for the first time, only 1 per cent designated a choice of communities of under 2,500 with their 43.5 per cent of the population, and only 20 per cent chose towns of 2,500 to 25,000.[10] Likewise, opinion polls among dental officers indicate that only 9.6 per cent of them intended settling in communities of under 5,000, comprising 47.3 per cent of the population, while 38.2 per cent intended practicing in cities of over 100,000, which include only 28.9 per cent of the national population.[11]

The pendulum of "medical manpower" has swung a long way from its place at the turn of the century. It is evident now that, in following policies restricting the number and the enrollments of approved medical schools over the last three decades or so, we may have cut too sharply into the total output of physicians. Mistaken notions of an "overcrowded profession" played a part in this.[12] There has probably never been a real surplus in the supply of quali-

[8] COLWELL, N. P., "Why There Is a Shortage of Country Doctors," *Hygeia*, 30:640, July, 1930.

[9] PERROTT and DAVIS, *op. cit.* Even discounting military requirements, the ratio would be between 1 to 3,500 and 1 to 3,800.

[10] LUETH, HAROLD C., "The Medical Officer Returns to Civilian Practice," *Journal of the American Medical Association*, 127:1039-1043, Apr. 21, 1945.

[11] CAMALIER, C. W., and I. ALTMAN, "Postwar Plans of Dentists in Service: I. General Findings," *Journal of the American Dental Association*, 32:568-580, May, 1945.

[12] BEVAN, ARTHUR DEAN, "The Over-crowding of the Medical Profession," *Journal of the Association of American Medical Colleges*, 11:377-384, November, 1937.

fied physicians relative to human needs in the United States. Even with respect to economic demand for services, the problem has always been more one of distribution than of excess numbers. We are now paying the price for our failure to recognize, or at least to act upon, this in the past. If we are to overcome past mistakes and counteract present unfavorable trends, it is clear that we must make the pendulum of medical personnel swing the other way.[13]

[13] For a general discussion of the trend of physician supply, see U. S. Bureau of Labor Statistics, *Postwar Outlook for Physicians* (Bull. No. 863). Washington: Government Printing Office, February, 1946.

WHEN ONE COMES TO VIEW the total picture of rural health and medical care, the shortage of essential health personnel stands out as probably the most striking deficiency. The lack of physicians, dentists, and nurses in rural communities is immediate and dramatic. Today's crisis — for it is hardly less — reflects the steady trend of urbanization which has left rural communities relatively disadvantaged economically and culturally. It is intensified by the constantly expanding technology of modern medical science, demanding for its application increasingly complex equipment and facilities. Clearly many factors are at play, but beneath all of them lies the handicap of rural poverty.

The dislocation of personnel due to the war has aggravated the situation immeasurably. Perhaps in this lies the chief hope, for — with thousands of farm families having money in their pockets to pay the doctor for the first time in years — the sheer unavailability of personnel has been brought home more forcibly than ever. While there are few if any signs of change in present regressive trends, rural people everywhere have been stimulated to tackle the problem, through both governmental and voluntary efforts.[14]

[14] See Chapters 21 and 24.

PART IV: RURAL HEALTH FACILITIES

THE PHYSICAL facilities in which rural health services are rendered are no more ample to meet needs than the supply of personnel. Much the same factors — largely economic — as those accounting for the deficiencies in the supply of rural physicians operate also to leave rural areas with inadequate hospitals and other essential facilities.

Health facilities are of many types, though we think most typically of hospitals for treating general illness. In addition to general hospitals, there are numerous other institutions for serving the sick. There are special or "allied" hospitals such as those for the isolation of communicable diseases, for orthopedic conditions, for children's diseases, for maternity cases, and for conditions of the eyes, ears, nose, and throat. There are also institutions for the care of major chronic diseases like mental disorder and tuberculosis. There are nursing homes and convalescent or rest homes, chiefly for persons in the later years of life. And there are infirmary units in institutions like schools or prisons.

In addition to institutions for the bed care of the sick, there are clinics and dispensaries for cases of ambulatory illness and there are facilities for the provision and the administration of public health or preventive services. There are laboratories for diagnosis and institutions for scientific research. There are drugstores, opticians' shops, and dental laboratories. Educational institutions for the professional training of physicians, dentists, nurses, and other personnel are an important part of the picture. Basic sanitation facilities for the disposal of sewage, provision of safe water, pasteurization of milk, and related environmental controls are an integral part of the nation's health plant. Finally, there are the front-line units, the thousands of private offices of physicians, dentists, and other practitioners rendering medical care.

Of practically all these facilities for conserving health, rural people are served by less than their proportionate share. Deficiencies in quantity are associated, all along the line, with deficiencies in quality as well.

Taking together all governmental and voluntary institutions for the bed care of the sick in the United States, there were 8,476 such units in 1939, not including educational and other institutions having

215

infirmaries.[1] Surprisingly, the majority of these institutions were actually located in communities of under 10,000 persons — 54 per cent, or about 4,600 units — and more than half of these, representing 32 per cent of all units in the nation, were even in communities of under 2,500 population. The decisive point, however, is not the number of institutional units but their aggregate number of beds and their general capacity to meet needs. The fact is that these rural and semirural institutions are characterized by small size, so that their aggregate bed capacity is considerably less than that of a smaller number of large institutions in the bigger urban centers. Moreover, a rural location for an institution may be deceptive in that certain types of facilities, like nursing homes or tuberculosis sanatoria, are typically set up in the country even though they may serve primarily or exclusively the residents of large cities.

The great majority of these 4,600 institutions for the bed care of the sick in communities of under 10,000 are general and allied hospitals. These 3,278 hospitals may be assumed for the most part to be serving rural people. The remaining units, consisting of 369 tuberculosis sanatoria, 394 mental institutions, and 568 nursing or rest homes, probably serve mostly urban people. In addition, there are 980 schools, prisons, and other nonmedical institutions in communities of under 10,000 that have some type of infirmary facilities.[2] The deceptiveness of these figures, however, in terms of actual bed capacity for handling rural illness, will be seen in the pages that follow.

[1] U. S. Bureau of the Census, "Hospital and Other Institutional Facilities and Services, 1939," *Vital Statistics — Special Reports*, 13:594, Mar. 2, 1942.
[2] *Ibid.*

CHAPTER 13

GENERAL AND ALLIED HOSPITALS

HISTORICALLY the rural hospital is a relatively recent phenomenon. Nearly all the general hospitals of the nineteenth century were located in urban centers of population and intended primarily for the indigent. The rural care of the sick was almost entirely in the home. It was not until well into the twentieth century, in fact, that the hospital became generally regarded as more than a haven for the sick poor and was recognized as a place of choice for the treatment of serious illness. The development of the rural hospital was actually quite different from that of the urban. Instead of being a function of government and charity, for the care of the poor, it grew as a function of private groups or individuals, mainly for the care of those who could afford to pay.[1]

The general hospital is the basic facility for the diagnosis and treatment of most serious illness and major injuries, and this holds doubly true in rural areas where other specialized or "allied" institutions are seldom at hand to serve special types of cases. Even cases of tuberculosis or mental disorder in widespread rural districts often get their initial and sometimes their only care in rural general hospitals. Increasingly the general hospital is coming to be recognized not only as a "temple of healing" but as a center for the highest development and expression of medical science in an area, a cultural center for physicians, and a base from which all types of community health services can be organized.[2] The elementary function of the hospital, nevertheless, remains the care of the sick, and the adequacy of rural general hospitals must first be measured in terms of their ability to perform this function.

[1] RANKIN, W. S., "The Small General Hospital," Hospitals, 10:48-52, October, 1936.

[2] BACHMEYER, ARTHUR C., and GERHARD HARTMAN, editors. The Hospital in Modern Society. New York: The Commonwealth Fund, 1943, pp. 15 ff.

The Supply of Hospital Beds

In 1940, counties with no urban place of 2,500 or more had beds in registered [3] general hospitals in a ratio of 0.97 beds per 1,000 people. By contrast, counties with towns of from 2,500 to 50,000 had an average ratio of 2.96 registered general beds per 1,000, and counties with larger cities had 5.38 registered general beds per 1,000 persons.[4]

A more detailed summary of the supply of general hospital beds for 1942, according to rurality of county, is presented in Table 23.

Table 23. General Hospital Beds: *Number and percentage of beds in registered general and allied hospitals* and number of beds per 1,000 persons, by rural-urban character of the counties in the United States, 1942*

Type of county†	Number of counties	Population	Per cent of popu- lation	Number of beds	Per cent of beds	Beds per 1,000
All counties	3,071	131,669,275	100.0	463,330	100.0	3.5
Metropolitan . . .	289	70,193,236	53.3	327,222	70.6	4.7
Bordering	720	21,071,996	16.0	49,630	10.7	2.4
Not bordering . .	2,062	40,404,043	30.7	86,478	18.7	2.1
With largest urban place:						
10,000 and over	277	12,598,620	9.6	45,996	9.9	3.7
Under 10,000 .	1,785	27,805,423	21.1	40,482	8.8	1.5

Source: Data furnished by the U. S. Public Health Service based on American Medical Association listing of registered hospitals.

* Including all general hospitals plus those rendering maternity, industrial, isolation, eye-ear-nose-throat, orthopedic, and children's care, and others offering similar specialized types of service. All federal hospitals, except those operated by the Office of Indian Affairs, are excluded, as are infirmary units of nonmedical institutions.

† For definitions, see Table 14.

[3] A "registered hospital" is one that meets minimum standards of recognition by the American Medical Association. This does not imply approval for internships or residencies or competence to handle every type of illness, but only minimum acceptance of the institution as having certain essential facilities and basic organization and as being free from definitely objectionable practices. American Medical Association, Council on Medical Education and Hospitals, "Essentials of a Registered Hospital," reprinted with modifications from *Journal of the American Medical Association,* 112:2166-2168, May 27, 1939.

[4] MOUNTIN, JOSEPH W., "Medical Care: A Private Enterprise or a Social Service," *Public Health Reports,* 59:1405-1411, Oct. 27, 1944.

It is evident that our most rural counties have less than one-third of the ratio of general hospital beds to population found in our most urban counties. It may be noted that almost 28 million people in these rural counties, served by only 1.5 general beds per 1,000, were located in counties not even bordering on "metropolitan" counties; the hospital facilities of these larger urban centers could hardly be considered readily accessible to them. Put in another way, these rural people constituted 21.1 per cent of our national population spread out through well over half the nation's counties, but they were in effect served by only 8.8 per cent of the total supply of general hospital beds. In fact, all nonbordering counties (including those counties with cities of up to 50,000), with over 40 million people, were as a whole served by only 2.1 beds per 1,000, or less than half the ratio found in the metropolitan counties.

A consideration of over-all hospital bed ratios by type of county fails to depict the serious extent of the rural hospital shortage. Marked differences are found among the states and in many sections the actual situation is much worse than the averages cited. Some of these differences are brought out in Figure 20, a map showing the ratio of hospital beds to population in 1940 for every county in the nation.[5] Analysis reveals that of our 3,071 counties only 326 enjoyed a ratio of 4.0 or more beds per 1,000 persons and only 273 counties had ratios of 3.0 to 3.9 beds per 1,000. In 1,219 counties having some hospital facilities, there were ratios of less than 3.0 beds per 1,000. Most important, in 1940 there were 1,253 counties entirely without any registered general hospitals, and the majority of these, 713 counties, had populations of over 10,000 people.[6] Of the counties with registered hospitals, moreover, 451 were served only by proprietary institutions, the significance of which will be considered later; these counties with over 9 million persons had a ratio of only 1.6 general beds per 1,000.[7]

[5] This map, prepared by the Bureau of Agricultural Economics, is based on the American Medical Association listing of registered general and allied hospitals exclusive of federal hospitals.

[6] MOTT, F. D., Testimony before the Committee on Education and Labor, U. S. Senate, 79th Cong., 1st Sess., S. 191, *Hospital Construction Act.* Washington: Government Printing Office, 1945, pp. 184-185.

[7] Data furnished by U. S. Public Health Service, based on American Medical Association listing of registered hospitals for 1942.

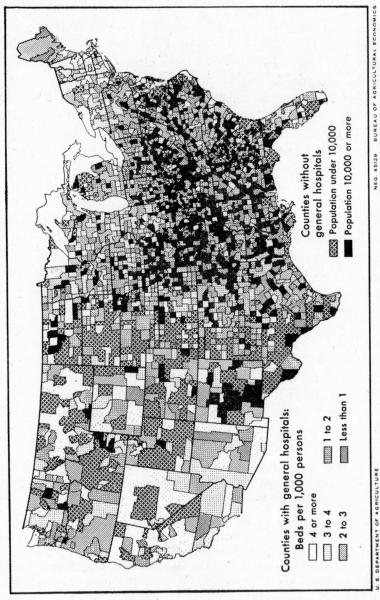

Fig. 20.   General Hospital Beds: Number of beds in registered general and allied hospitals per 1,000 population, by counties, 1940.

An evaluation of the meaning of these hospital bed ratios requires, of course, a determination of an optimal standard. Various standards have been proposed, some based on the average supply of beds in the nation as a whole (about 3.5 beds per 1,000) or in prosperous states, and some based on actual usage of hospitals by patients. The experience of Blue Cross group hospitalization plans, for example, has been suggested as a guide, on the assumption that in this experience the economic deterrent to using hospital service has been eliminated. Numerous considerations, however, cast doubt on these formulations.[8] A more reliable standard would seem to be that derived by the Committee on the Costs of Medical Care, based on the incidence of illness found to occur in a general population group and an estimate of the volume of hospitalization required to handle it. On this basis, the desirable supply of general hospital beds to meet average needs was shown to be 4.62 beds per 1,000 population.[9] This figure is often rounded off to the more conservative ratio of 4.5 beds per 1,000.

Quite often this "Lee-Jones standard" of 4.5 beds per 1,000 has been taken to apply to urban areas and a separate standard of 2.0 or 3.0 has been set for rural areas, in recognition of lower current rural usage of hospitals.[10] Is the defeatism implied in this double standard really justified? There is enough evidence to show (see Chapter 17) that the utilization of hospital care is dependent quite directly on local purchasing power. With economic and associated

[8] Accepting a national average as optimal is obviously unsound because it reflects the situation in admittedly inadequate areas. The Blue Cross experience, on the other hand, involves the hospitalization of a relatively middle-income, employed, and prime-of-life age group among whom hospital needs would be expected to be moderate. Various limitations in Blue Cross contracts, moreover, such as exclusion of care for pre-existing conditions or workmen's compensation cases, waiting periods for obstetrical care, or restriction to 21 or 30 days of coverage per year, necessarily lead to statistical data that understate the total need.

[9] LEE, ROGER I., and L. W. JONES, The Fundamentals of Good Medical Care (Committee on the Costs of Medical Care Pub. 22). Chicago: University of Chicago Press, 1933, p. 119.

[10] See, for example, MILLS, ALDEN B., and PATSY MILLS, "The Need for More Hospitals in Rural Areas," Hospital Facilities in Rural Areas. Chicago: Julius Rosenwald Fund, 1935, pp. 9-13. Also, U. S. Interdepartmental Committee to Coordinate Health and Welfare Activities, The Need for a National Health Program. Washington: Government Printing Office, 1939, p. 32.

psychological barriers removed, there is every reason to believe that rural hospital usage would approximate urban. The fulfillment of true needs, therefore, would seem to call for 4.5 beds to serve each 1,000 rural as well as urban people.

This does not mean to imply that every county in the nation should have within its borders a supply of 4.5 general hospital beds per 1,000, or even that every county should have a general hospital at all. Sometimes the population of a rural county can be served by the hospital in a neighboring county, so long as it is accessible in terms of time and transportation, and so long as it has enough beds.[11] More important, a certain proportion of rural cases should properly be sent relatively long distances to large urban centers, where special surgical or medical procedures can be effectively carried out.[12] If we were to estimate these cases as constituting about 10 per cent of the hospital burden, then the optimal ratio in a rural district would fall to about 4.0 general beds per 1,000, and the ratio in the urban center serving this district would have to be proportionately increased.[13] Any standard for an optimal supply of hospital beds within rural districts, therefore, depends on the effectuation of

[11] This principle can, however, be misused when applied loosely and can leave a quite false impression of hospital adequacy. It gives little assurance to know, for example, that "a hospital is to be found within 30 miles" of a rural community without considering the size of the hospital or the transportation facilities. There might, for example, be a hospital of 40 beds for a dispersed population of 40,000 people (1.0 beds per 1,000) and, at that, the roads to it might be impassable under the snows of winter or the mud of early spring. Even on this basis, however, it has been shown that between 2 and 3 million Americans were not "within 30 miles of a hospital" in 1938, even giving recognition to some 1,200 hospitals unacceptable to the American Medical Association for registration. It is clear that such calculations greatly understate the true extent of the deficiency of beds. See JOHNSON, VICTOR (Director of the Council on Medical Education and Hospitals of the American Medical Association), Testimony before a Subcommittee of the Committee on Education and Labor, U. S. Senate, 78th Cong., 2d Sess., S. Res. 74, *Wartime Health and Education*. Washington: Government Printing Office, 1944, Part 5, p. 1824.

[12] HOGE, VANE M., "Rural Hospital Needs," *Hospitals*, 12:27, November, 1938.

[13] For a general discussion of urban-rural distribution of hospital beds, see MOUNTIN, J. W., E. H. PENNELL, and VANE M. HOGE, *Health Service Areas: Requirements for General Hospitals and Health Centers* (U. S. Public Health Service Bull. 292). Washington: Government Printing Office, 1945.

regional patterns of hospital construction and operation (see Chapter 28).

The entire question of an adequate supply of hospital beds is complicated by day-to-day advances in medical and social sciences which, on the one hand, reduce the duration of illness (like the sulfa drugs or penicillin) or, on the other, expand our conceptions of a hospital's function (like the increased attention to the chronic diseases of later life or admissions for diagnostic study only).

Obviously, then, no absolute standard for general hospital beds can be rigidly defended. Taking the reasonable variations between rural and urban sections into account, nevertheless, it would seem sound to expect the supply of beds for the residents of, let us say, an entire state or a whole natural medical service area (including a large urban center and rural sections around it) to be served by a net average of 4.5 beds per 1,000. This standard has been advocated by Surgeon General Thomas Parran of the United States Public Health Service.[14] It has meaning, of course, only in terms of true needs and not in terms of "effective demand" for hospital services, conditioned as the latter is by cash income.

Lest it be thought that an optimal rural standard of about 4.0 beds per 1,000 is untenable, it should be recognized that the very conditions for which hospitalization is most frequently required have their highest natural occurrence among rural people. Thus, tonsil and adenoid operations[15] have been the most frequent cause for hospitalization (28.0 per cent of total cases) and rural areas have a higher proportion of young children, on whom this operation is usually performed. Maternity service is the second most frequent cause of hospitalization (16.3 per cent of cases) and rural areas have the highest birth rate. Accidents are the third major cause of hospitalization (9.0 per cent of cases) and accidental deaths have been noted to be more frequent among rural and small-town people.[16]

[14] PARRAN, THOMAS, Testimony before the Committee on Education and Labor, U. S. Senate, 79th Cong., 1st Sess., S. 191, *Hospital Construction Act.* Washington: Government Printing Office, 1945, p. 94.

[15] See footnote 23, Chap. 5.

[16] COLLINS, SELWYN D., "Frequency and Volume of Hospital Care for Specific Diseases in Relation to All Illnesses among 9,000 Families, Based on Nationwide Periodic Canvasses, 1928-31," *Public Health Reports,* 57:1399-1428, Sept. 18, 1942.

Traveling time in rural areas is so great, moreover, that the country doctor can find advantage in admitting his scattered patients to the hospital and keeping them there for longer periods to simplify the task of aftercare.[17] Likewise, longer hospital stays tend to be necessary because convalescence in a farmhouse without such conveniences as central heating and an indoor toilet can hardly be satisfactory; this factor alone would counterbalance any supposed advantage to the patient in a farm home compared with the patient in a city apartment.[18] If the standard of 4.5 general beds per 1,000 for the population as a whole is valid, it would seem that the ratio of 4.0 beds per 1,000 in rural sections is probably conservative.

Vast stretches of our nation fall miserably short of the optimal standard, as Figure 20 demonstrates. The striking feature is that shortages are not confined to any one section or group of states. They are found in practically every state. Exact data as of 1942 for each state by type of county are given in Table 24. It may be noted that even in a highly urban state like Illinois the counties with the largest town having less than 10,000 people and not bordering on a metropolitan county average only 1.4 beds in registered general and allied hospitals per 1,000 persons, and in Ohio such counties average only 0.9 beds per 1,000. In fact, in states of all degrees of rurality, the nonbordering counties with no place of 10,000 or more, on a state-wide basis, tend to have ratios hovering about 1.5 beds per 1,000. And in the counties bordering on metropolitan counties in every group of states except the most urban, the ratio of beds varies from 1.6 to only 2.6 per 1,000. Actually, the combined supply of all metropolitan and bordering counties — 4.1 beds per 1,000 —

[17] MILLS and MILLS, op. cit., p. 10.

[18] The requirement of facilities for convalescent care, as well as for the general care of chronic disease cases, has led some of the rural provinces in Canada, like Saskatchewan and Alberta, to plan for ratios of 6.0 or 7.0 hospital beds per 1,000 persons. This is in conjunction with tax-supported programs making hospitalization readily available to all who need it. In rural sections especially, facilities for the chronically ill belong chiefly with the general hospital, so that these high ratios should not be considered appreciably reducible by the construction of separate, specialized institutions for chronic cases. It is significant that the National Hospital Survey and Construction Act (see Chap. 28) authorizes state plans in the states of low population density to provide for ratios of 5.0 and 5.5 beds per 1,000 persons, compared with an over-all ratio of 4.5 per 1,000 in other states.

is not nearly great enough to handle any overflow of cases from nonbordering counties. Only in the nonbordering rural counties (with no place of 10,000 or more) of four states, New Hampshire, Montana, Nevada, and Arizona, does the ratio of beds reach the desirable rural standard of 4.0 beds per 1,000 and, in the latter three, distances are so great that accessibility of the institutions to the rural population is doubtless far from satisfactory.

In a word, it may be said that for counties of particular rural-urban character, the average ratio of general beds to population in most of the states is notably constant. Differences in state-wide averages, therefore, are not attributable simply to better or worse supplies within the state's rural counties, but rather to a greater or lesser number of such rural counties being located within the state. It is mainly because of the latter factor that we find state-wide differences as striking as those between 1.7 beds per 1,000 in rural states like Arkansas or 2.0 beds per 1,000 in Tennessee and 4.5 beds per 1,000 in urban states like California or 5.5 beds per 1,000 in Massachusetts. It should be kept in mind that the theory of 4.5 beds per 1,000 being adequate on a state-wide basis rests on the assumption of an integrated system of referrals between rural and urban areas throughout the state. Without such a system, even in states with ratios reaching 4.5 beds per 1,000, of which there are only nine, the population in many rural districts is still under-supplied with general hospital beds.

These calculations have not taken into account hospital units not registered with the American Medical Association. In 1943 a total of 523 such institutions, with an average of about 30 beds each, were rejected for registration because of failure to meet minimum standards.[19] In addition, there are a large, uncertain number of other substandard units hardly meriting the term "hospital." [20] A high proportion of these are actually in small towns and rural sections and they are widely distributed among the states. It would

[19] PARRAN, THOMAS, Testimony before a Subcommittee of the Committee on Education and Labor, U. S. Senate, 78th Cong., 2d Sess., S. Res. 74, *Wartime Health and Education.* Washington: Government Printing Office, 1944, Part 5, p. 1776.

[20] Many of these units, it should be stated, make no claim to be hospitals, are designed essentially as nursing homes, and will be considered as such in the next section.

Table 24. General Hospital Beds: *Number of beds in registered general and allied hospitals* per 1,000 population, by rural-urban character of the counties, by states in order of rurality, 1942*

State	Population, per cent rural	All counties	Type of county†			
			Metro-politan	Border-ing	Not bordering and largest urban place	
					10,000 or over	Under 10,000
All states	43.5	3.5	4.7	2.4	3.7	1.5
Population under 30 per cent rural . .		4.5	4.8	3.5	4.2	1.9
District of Columbia .	. . .	6.4	6.4	. . .	. . .	. . .
Rhode Island . . .	8.4	4.0	4.0	3.3	. . .	. . .
Massachusetts . . .	10.6	5.5	5.6	4.3	. . .	. . .
New York	17.2	4.9	5.1	3.2	3.9	3.1
New Jersey	18.4	3.9	3.9	3.0	. . .	. . .
Illinois	26.4	3.8	4.4	2.8	3.6	1.4
California	29.0	4.5	4.4	4.8	8.1	2.6
Population 30 to 39 per cent rural . .		3.8	4.4	2.3	3.1	1.5
Connecticut . . .	32.2	4.3	4.4	3.3	. .	. . .
Ohio	33.2	3.1	3.9	1.3	2.7	0.9
Pennsylvania . . .	33.5	4.0	4.3	2.4	3.2	2.3
Michigan	34.3	4.4	5.2	3.4	3.7	1.7
Population 40 to 49 per cent rural . .		3.5	4.8	2.6	3.5	1.4
Maryland	40.7	4.2	4.8	2.7	3.0	0.6
New Hampshire . .	42.4	4.5	5.0	3.8	4.0	6.3
Utah	44.5	3.0	4.7	2.8	4.0	1.6
Florida	44.9	2.9	4.1	2.2	3.0	1.4
Indiana	44.9	2.7	3.8	2.1	2.6	1.0
Wisconsin	46.5	3.9	5.1	2.4	4.5	2.1
Washington . . .	46.9	3.8	4.3	2.0	3.5	2.2
Colorado	47.4	4.6	6.1	4.8	2.1	2.3
Delaware	47.7	4.6	5.4	3.0	. . .	. . .
Missouri	48.2	3.4	5.7	0.2	4.3	0.7
Population 50 to 59 per cent rural . .		3.1	4.9	2.3	3.6	1.5
Minnesota	50.2	4.4	5.9	2.3	6.7	2.4
Oregon	51.2	4.3	5.6	3.9	3.5	2.9
Texas	54.6	2.3	3.7	1.6	2.2	1.3

Table 24. General Hospital Beds: *Number of beds in registered general and allied hospitals* per 1,000 population, by rural-urban character of the counties, by states in order of rurality, 1942.—(Continued)*

State	Popu-lation, per cent rural	All counties	Type of county†			
			Metro-politan	Border-ing	Not bordering and largest urban place	
					10,000 or over	Under 10,000
Population 50 to 59 per cent rural (*cont.*)						
Iowa	57.3	2.8	3.9	2.7	4.7	1.5
Kansas	58.1	3.0	5.3	2.6	3.6	1.8
Louisiana	58.5	3.0	6.9	0.7	3.7	0.4
Maine	59.5	3.3	6.0	3.0	3.3	2.4
Population 60 to 69 per cent rural . .		2.5	4.3	1.5	3.7	1.5
Nevada	60.7	6.9	. . .	3.7	9.2	6.5
Nebraska.	60.9	3.5	7.1	2.0	4.1	1.7
Montana	62.2	5.5	. . .	. . .	8.4	4.0
Oklahoma	62.4	2.1	3.9	1.6	2.4	1.3
Wyoming	62.7	3.6	. . .	. . .	4.4	3.2
Virginia	64.7	2.7	4.6	0.9	4.4	1.2
Tennessee	64.8	2.0	4.3	0.8	1.6	0.6
Arizona	65.2	5.0	2.9	6.1	. . .	6.6
Georgia	65.6	1.9	3.6	0.8	2.9	0.1
Vermont	65.7	3.6	. . .	4.6	5.1	2.5
Idaho	66.3	3.0	. . .	2.1	4.8	1.8
New Mexico . . .	66.8	3.8	. . .	0.8	5.2	3.4
Alabama	69.8	1.8	3.8	2.0	1.9	0.8
Population 70 per cent or more rural . .		2.2	4.5	1.6	3.7	1.3
Kentucky	70.2	1.9	3.9	0.7	3.7	0.9
West Virginia . . .	71.9	2.9	4.3	2.0	4.0	2.0
North Carolina . .	72.7	2.4	5.4	2.2	2.7	1.2
South Dakota . . .	75.4	3.5	. . .	. . .	6.7	2.6
South Carolina . .	75.5	2.0	3.4	1.5	3.2	0.9
Arkansas	77.8	1.7	6.2	0.9	3.5	0.8
North Dakota . . .	79.4	3.9	. . .	. . .	8.6	2.6
Mississippi	80.2	1.6	3.8	1.5	2.8	1.1

Source: Data furnished by the U. S. Public Health Service based on American Medical Association listing of registered hospitals.

* For types of hospitals included, see Table 23.

† For definitions, see Table 14.

seem no more appropriate, however, to include these units in an
inventory of hospitals than to include chiropractors in an inventory of acceptable medical practitioners. Aside from their generally
poor standards, these units are of negligible importance in the
volume of their service. It was estimated as of 1939 that all together
they maintained only 2.6 per cent of the bed accommodations in

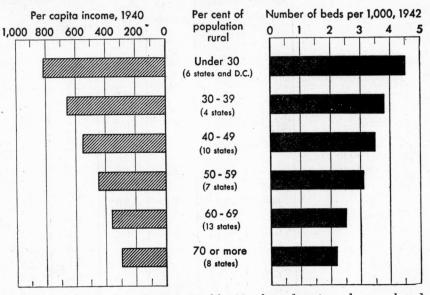

Fig. 21. Hospitals and State Wealth: Number of registered general and
allied hospital beds per 1,000 persons in 1942 in states grouped by rurality
and relationship to 1940 per capita income. Source: Hospital bed ratios derived
as in Table 24; per capita income data from U.S. Department of Commerce,
Survey of Current Business, August, 1944, p. 190.

the nation and rendered only 1.7 per cent of the total reported days
of care.[21] The existence of these inadequate facilities merely underscores the fact that thousands of rural people are forced to depend
on second-class hospital services.

The major explanation of rural shortages in general hospital beds
becomes evident on inspection of Figure 21. It is clear that the
supply of hospital beds varies with the per capita incomes of the
states as strikingly, if not more so, than was the case with physicians.
In the most urban group of states, with a per capita income more
than double that in the most rural group, we find an average bed

[21] U. S. Census, *op. cit.,* 13:11, Sept. 15, 1941.

ratio of 4.5 per 1,000, just over twice the 2.2 ratio in the most rural group of states. The construction and equipping of a hospital represent a large capital investment, calling for an ample supply of funds either from private philanthropy, public revenue, or the enjoyment of easy credit. Furthermore, maintenance and operation are dependent on adequate payment for hospital services. Financial resources of all these types are relatively lacking in rural areas with their generally low income levels. While other factors like the sparsity of the population or the lack of physicians and other personnel may play a part, community wealth is undoubtedly the governing factor in the establishment of hospitals.

Characteristics of Rural General Hospitals

The inadequate number of general hospital beds in rural districts fails to tell the whole story of rural hospital deficiency. Rural hospitals tend to be of much smaller capacity than urban and accordingly to suffer the handicaps associated with any small unit operation. While the average size of a metropolitan hospital is about 200 beds or more, the average rural hospital has considerably less than 100 beds and the most common units have less than 50 beds. Though 53 per cent of all general and allied hospitals are in communities of less than 10,000,[22] their small average size is responsible for the unfavorable ratios we have reviewed. Small size, of course, means that, for equivalent services, there is a relatively higher cost of operation per bed. Yet with rural income limited, the charges for care must be relatively low; hence it is difficult to set aside funds for the purchase and maintenance of modern technical equipment or the engagement of specialized personnel. Among other things, small size means little "clinical material" to attract interns or to justify the establishment of a school of nursing, and thus are lost the services these personnel render in the course of training.[23]

Small size is not entirely objectionable for a hospital, except in so far as it places economic handicaps on a high quality of performance. The necessarily small size of many rural hospitals, if they

[22] *Ibid.*, 13:594, Mar. 2, 1942.

[23] It should not be implied that nursing schools are desirable for the average small hospital. Moreover, the actual economies afforded through the low-cost nursing service made available by a school of nursing are currently under debate.

are to be within reach of people in thinly populated sections — even under the 50-bed capacity usually claimed to be essential for efficient hospital operation — simply means that their financial support must be relatively greater. In the face of low rural purchasing power, the horns of the dilemma can be broken only by economic support from outside the rural sections.

While the small size of rural hospitals is an inevitable response to the small population groups served and the low effective demand for hospital services, it is also partially due to the type of ownership and, accordingly, the mechanism of financing the construction. The very lack of financial resources of the general population as well as local government in rural areas has meant that relatively fewer hospitals could be financed either out of tax funds or by nonprofit voluntary associations. Thus a much larger proportion of rural hospitals have had to be financed by private individuals — ordinarily physicians — having a special professional or business interest in their establishment. The mere limitations on the financial resources of physicians acting singly or even as partners, in comparison with the resources of a whole community or an organized group, place restrictions on the size of proprietary institutions. As a result, we find that the average proprietary hospital throughout the nation has a capacity of only about 30 beds, while the average institution under voluntary nonprofit control has about 100 beds, and the average governmental unit for general illness (exclusive of the large tuberculosis or mental hospitals) has 180 beds.[24]

As may be seen in Table 25, more than twice as high a proportion of general hospital beds in rural states are under proprietary control as in urban states, while the proportion of beds under governmental auspices in the most rural states is less than half that in the most urban states. Since this data is state-wide, it doubtless understates the disparity that comparison of hospital beds in rural and urban counties would reveal. Expressed in number of hospitals rather than number of beds, the relative disproportions would be

[24] MOUNTIN, J. W., E. H. PENNELL, and K. PEARSON, "Hospitals in the South," *Southern Medical Journal*, 33:402-411, April, 1940. Also, for a general discussion of different types of hospital control, see MOUNTIN, JOSEPH W., ELLIOTT H. PENNELL, and EVELYN FLOOK, *Hospital Facilities in the United States: I. Selected Characteristics of Hospital Facilities in 1936* (U. S. Public Health Service Bull. 243). Washington: Government Printing Office, 1938.

further exaggerated. In the South, for example, although as many as 20 per cent of the beds are under proprietary management, about 50 per cent of all the hospital units are so controlled.[25] Put in another way, 49 per cent of all the general hospitals in towns under 10,000 in the United States were proprietary in 1939, compared to 19 per cent in cities of over 100,000. These small towns, in fact, had some 72 per cent of all proprietary general hospitals in the nation, or more than 1,600 such units.[26]

Table 25. Control of Hospital Beds: *Percentage of beds in registered general hospitals* under different types of control in states grouped by rurality, 1942*

Per cent rural (state populations)	Type of control		
	Governmental	Nonprofit association	Proprietary
Under 30	38	55	7
30–49	28	69	3
50-69	29	53	18
70 and over	18	64	18

Source: Derived from Parran, Thomas, Testimony before a Subcommittee of the Committee on Education and Labor, U. S. Senate, 78th Cong., 2d sess., S. Res. 74, *Wartime Health and Education.* Washington, 1944, Part 5, p. 1776.

* For types of hospitals included, see Table 23.

It should be appreciated that the proprietary hospital in a rural community, despite representing a private enterprise, performs a genuine public service. The rural surgeons who have frequently built these units have done so usually because other facilities were simply not at hand. Quite often financial support for building a hospital was nowhere available except in the doctor's own bank account and in the credit he could muster.

Yet the introduction of the profit motive into hospital management entails certain distinct disadvantages, so far as general public welfare is concerned.[27] Most important, the proprietary institution tends necessarily to allot few if any beds for "free" or low-cost care. Since it has little or no community financial support, it cannot afford

[25] *Ibid.*

[26] Derived from U. S. Census, *op. cit.*, 13:594, Mar. 2, 1942.

[27] For a general discussion, see SOUTHMAYO, H. J., and GEDDES SMITH, *Small Community Hospitals.* New York: The Commonwealth Fund, 1944.

to. Then, the medical staff tends to be strictly "closed," not open to many well-qualified physicians in the community and often confined to the single surgeon owning the institution. Only by referring their patients to the proprietor-physician can these other doctors arrange for local hospitalization of their patients; this is acutely true in the case of Negro physicians. The problem of cash payment from patients becomes so critical in the maintenance of a proprietary institution that, if it is not forthcoming fairly promptly, needed hospitalization is often postponed or entirely withheld. The small proprietary hospital is deprived of economies enjoyed by most non-profit or governmental institutions, such as the large-scale purchase of commodities or exemption from taxes. Finally, the day-to-day policies of the proprietary institution are not subject to public control, except in the most indirect way, and the personal interests of the owner are almost bound to receive first consideration in the management of affairs.

Of course, these disadvantages apply to some extent to any voluntary nonprofit institution operated on a narrow financial margin. The point, however, is that the financial operation of the privately owned unit is particularly unstable, since it tends to be cushioned least with tax funds or voluntary philanthropy to withstand the stresses of bad times. Quite often the proprietary hospital can be kept going only because the owning surgeon sinks a considerable part of his professional fees into the costs of hospital operation. He may not mind taking money from his surgical pocket and putting it into his hospital pocket, but this hardly makes for ample funds to maintain a good quality of hospital service. Quite often, also, proprietary hospitals are forced to close down entirely or undergo reorganization and, as we will see, their total number has actually been declining since 1928. Beyond these factors, it must be recognized that the general hospital in a low-income rural section, under any type of control, has its recurrent financial problems.

The meager supply of rural hospital beds might lead one to expect that those available would be kept occupied with patients all the time. Yet the very economic factors that account for the lean supply of rural beds and the wide extent of private control make also for low occupancy. The paradox brought out in Figure 22 can only be explained by the low effective demand, through private purchasing power or public or voluntary subsidy, for use of the rural facilities that are available. That there is no relationship between this effective demand and true medical need can hardly be repeated too often.

Further evidence of the dependence of hospital occupancy on purchasing power is found in the fact that occupancy is lowest in institutions depending most for their support on private, as against public, resources. Thus, where only 10 per cent or less of

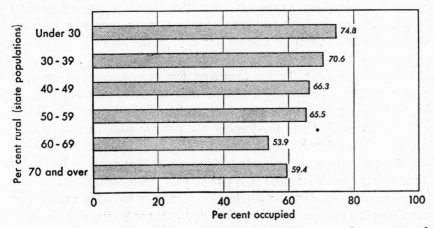

FIG. 22. Hospital Occupancy: Percentage of beds occupied in registered general hospitals in states grouped by rurality, 1940. (Hospitals offering specialized services and all federal hospitals not included.) Source: Derived from American Medical Association, Council on Education and Hospitals, "Hospital Service in the United States," *Journal of the American Medical Association,* 116:1059, Mar. 15, 1941.

hospital income is derived from private patients, occupancy has been found to exceed 70 per cent, but where 90 per cent or more of hospital income must come from private sources, occupancy has been shown to fall below 50 per cent.[28] Another reflection of this relationship is the fact that the occupancy of general hospital facilities operated by units of government in 1942 was 84.5 per cent, for voluntary nonprofit institutions it was 74.7 per cent, and for proprietary institutions only 60.4 per cent.[29] It is significant, for example, that in Louisiana, despite the rurality of the state, hospital occupancy is high — exceeding 75 per cent in 1940 — associated with

[28] MOUNTIN, PENNELL, and PEARSON, *op. cit.*

[29] American Medical Association, Council on Medical Education and Hospitals, "Hospital Service in the United States," *Journal of the American Medical Association,* 121:1010, Mar. 27, 1943.

a unique state-wide system of governmentally owned general hospitals.[30] In terms of hospital size, likewise, occupancy declines as capacity becomes less. One study showed that, taking nongovernmental units alone, those with 25 beds or fewer reported only 46 per cent occupancy while those with more than 300 beds reported 68 per cent.[31] It is no surprise that in all nonregistered general hospitals, as a group, occupancy is lower than in all registered general hospitals, being in 1939 (by coincidence with the previous figures) 46 per cent in the former and 68 per cent in the latter.[32]

It goes without saying that the optimal occupancy of a hospital is not 100 per cent. To be prepared for emergencies or unusual peak loads, it is ordinarily assumed that an average occupancy of about 80 per cent is quite satisfactory for general hospitals. Rural institutions, with their predominantly private and usually scanty support, their extensive proprietary management, and their relatively low-income patients, clearly fall far short of this optimal level. To some extent, small hospital size per se may theoretically contribute to low occupancy, but the predominant factors in today's record of rural hospital occupancy are undoubtedly the low effective demand for care by rural people and the relatively high cost of services in small units.

The geographic inaccessibility of rural hospitals is another reason for their low occupancy; yet ambulance service to overcome the handicap is scant. The typical form of rural ambulance service is that conducted by the local taxi driver or undertaker, as a private enterprise. The service must be paid for and it is usually beyond the means of the average farmer, except in so far as he may "beg, borrow, or steal" to foot the bill when an emergency arises. Of course, for the patient who is not too critically ill, the farmer's car or that of a neighbor may be used for transportation to the hospital. Partly because of ambulance costs, however, patients at a greater distance from the hospital tend to get less care.

Ambulance service by airplane is still rare in the United States, despite our remarkable advances in aviation and our wartime med-

[30] *Ibid.*, 116:1059, Mar. 15, 1941.

[31] FALK, I. S., C. RUFUS ROREM, and MARTHA D. RING, *The Costs of Medical Care* (Committee on the Costs of Medical Care Pub. 27). Chicago: University of Chicago Press, 1933, p. 321.

[32] U. S. Census, *op. cit.*, 13:13, Sept. 15, 1941.

ical experience. Air transportation of desperately sick persons is done occasionally at public expense — as in the helicopter service for the isolated residents of Hatteras Island off the coast of North Carolina, operated by the U. S. Coast Guard — but no systematic public service has been developed. Private airplane ambulance services, like those recently inaugurated in Virginia, North Carolina, and Montana by commercial airlines, are obviously inaccessible to low-income rural families located long distances from a modern hospital.[32a]

Low occupancy only aggravates the other forces for inefficiency in the operation of the small rural hospital. With overhead expenses continuing while beds remain empty, the cost per patient-day must rise so that the margin, small at best, between operating expenses and hospital income is reduced further.

That all these forces tend to leave rural hospitals with scanty and outworn equipment is manifest to all who have observed them at first hand. While a few rural institutions are outstandingly well equipped, many are without such essential accoutrements of modern medicine as an electrocardiograph or basal metabolism apparatus.[33] Substantial numbers of rural hospitals, in fact, lack even diagnostic x-ray apparatus, while many more get along with inadequate out-dated equipment, often usable only for limited types of work. As for such items as dark-field microscopes, special instruments like cystoscopes and bronchoscopes, equipment for chemical analyses of the blood, and effectual physiotherapy apparatus, they are rare, indeed, in typical rural hospitals.

But the equipment in the rural institution is less important than its staff. Operation and maintenance are hardly facilitated by the generally low wages and salaries, which fail to attract competent

[32a] Elizabeth City (North Carolina) *Daily Advance*, Apr. 4, 1947; Richmond (Virginia) *News Leader*, Jan. 3, 1947; Great Falls (Montana) *Tribune*, Dec. 23, 1946; "New Air Ambulance Service," *The Journal Lancet*, 67:40, Jan., 1947.

[33] Even in a survey by questionnaire in 1944 which admittedly under-represented small hospitals, metabolism apparatus was reported by only 72.2 per cent of civilian hospitals in states with populations 70 per cent or more rural, compared with 80 per cent for hospitals in states 70 per cent or more urban; electrocardiographs were reported by only 40.5 per cent of the institutions in the most rural states, compared with 56.7 per cent in the most urban. Derived from American Hospital Association, "Survey of Civilian Hospitals," *American Hospital Directory*, 1945, Chicago, 1945, pp. 585-600.

personnel. The professional staff is typically shorthanded and opportunities for self-improvement through training are meager. Many rural hospitals are actually without benefit of a single registered nurse. Few, indeed, have nursing staffs that even approach adequacy. There are many examples of rural hospitals where the competence of one lone and valiant professional nurse in keeping "her" hospital under control is exceeded only by her self-effacing devotion to duty. It is noteworthy, in fact, that the rural hospital is typically under the regular administration of a nurse. A 1940 study of hospitals in small towns, predominantly units of less than 50 beds, disclosed 80 per cent of them to be under the direction of a nurse superintendent. In addition to performing her administrative role, she often supervises the operating room, gives anaesthesia, and assumes numerous other functions.[34] This rural pattern of the veteran institutional nurse acting as hospital superintendent, however, is more a tribute to the nurse's versatility than proof that she has had the background and training necessary to administer a hospital effectively.

Bearing in mind the general deficiencies in medical and related personnel in most rural communities, we may agree that Bertram M. Bernheim has not greatly exaggerated the realities of the situation when he states "However diligently one may search the rural districts for master surgeons, skilled diagnosticians, bacteriologists, pathologists, x-ray men, laboratory technicians, nurses, and all other adjuncts necessary and of the proper calibre to man the modern hospital, they will not be found." [35]

With inadequate equipment and personnel, the average rural hospital necessarily provides services of limited scope. It rarely assumes the function of a community health center for the people or of a scientific medical center for the medical and allied professions in the area. It seldom extends its arm through outpatient facilities for diagnosis or therapy, and the role of the urban medical social worker is almost unknown. By and large, the rural hospital is geared to handle medical and surgical emergencies, maternity

[34] American Nurses Association, "Nursing in Small Hospitals, in Small Towns," *American Journal of Nursing*, 40:1370-1371, December, 1940. Also, "She Administers a Small Rural Hospital," *American Journal of Nursing*, 41:167-173, February, 1941.

[35] BERNHEIM, BERTRAM M., "Hospital Beds: Sociological Problem," *The American Scholar*, 10:145-155, Spring, 1941.

cases, and the more commonplace types of elective surgery. It is poorly prepared to handle the increasingly important group of chronic diseases. Patients with advanced heart disease, chronic nephritis, diabetes or arthritis get little more than custodial care in most rural hospitals. Aged country people with such conditions are usually kept at home. The rocking chair by the stove is about as close to geriatric facilities as most rural sections have come.

Other factors often contribute to keeping the quality of scientific service below par in the average rural hospital. The frequent use of the same room for both surgical operations and deliveries, for example, creates an obvious hazard of infection for the woman in childbirth. Other hazards for the spread of disease are associated with reliance on auxiliary workers lacking professional training. The sparsity of laboratory services, furthermore, often reduces medical service virtually to a rule-of-thumb empirical level. If we recognize, with Graham L. Davis, the performance of autopsies as ". . . perhaps the best index of the quality of professional service rendered by a given hospital, and of the medical service generally that is available in the community," [36] then by this measure, too, rural hospital performance falls significantly below urban. In 1942, for example, the percentage of hospital deaths that came to autopsy in the 20 predominantly urban states and the District of Columbia was 40 per cent higher than the experience of the 28 rural states, with a rate of 25.2 per cent compared with 18.0 per cent in the rural states.[37]

Perhaps the most comprehensive measure of hospital performance is found in the system of approval by the American College of Surgeons. While data on the proportions of hospitals approved in rural and urban areas are not at hand, ratings by size of hospital reflect the relationship. Mindful of the small capacities of rural hospitals, we may note that 93 per cent of registered hospitals of 100 or more beds were approved in 1942 while only 40 per cent of 25-50 bed units received approval. For units with a capacity of less than 25 beds, the proportion meeting the standards of the

[36] DAVIS, GRAHAM L., A Survey of El Dorado, Kansas, as a Postwar Medical Center. Chicago: American Hospital Association, 1945, p. 18.

[37] Derived from data in American Medical Association, Council on Medical Education and Hospitals, "Hospital Service in the United States," Journal of the American Medical Association, 121:1019, Mar. 27, 1943.

American College of Surgeons has tended to be so low that approval at present is not even considered.[38] Yet, other than possible approval by this professional body or the rather perfunctory process of registration by the American Medical Association, there are few inducements toward elevation of standards in the small rural hospital. Until the recent flurry of state laws stimulated by the requirements of the Hospital Survey and Construction Act of 1946, only a handful of states had legislation requiring even the licensure of establishments providing care for the sick.

There are, of course, a few advantages to rural hospitals over big-city institutions. Their small size tends to give them a certain personal touch and often a quality of "belonging" to the community that is lacking in the large metropolitan hospital. The rural hospital is free from large, impersonal wards, for their biggest rooms usually contain no more than about four beds. These small rooms tend to lend flexibility to hospital usage (for women, for men, for surgical cases, for medical cases, as the needs may vary). Deep loyalties may be developed in the staff and there is less of the professional chauvinism that sometimes mars relationships in the large urban institution.

A special word should be said about hospital facilities for that large segment of the nation's rural population that is Negro. The quantitative and qualitative deficiencies of rural hospitals are aggravated many times over for this group. In the South, where rural Negroes are most numerous, colored patients are customarily not admitted to the same facilities as are white. Either they are not admitted to certain hospitals at all or else they are assigned to special Negro wards which almost invariably suffer some disadvantage in design or operation. The private control of hospitals, typical of rural areas, appears to predispose to such discriminatory practices. Even on a nation-wide basis in 1940, 48 per cent of proprietary institutions declined to accept Negro patients entirely, in comparison with 22 per cent of nonprofit voluntary units and 16 per cent of governmentally operated units.[39]

[38] American College of Surgeons, "Twenty-sixth Annual Hospital Standardization Survey," *Bulletin of the American College of Surgeons,* 28:303, December, 1943.

[39] Derived from American Medical Association, Council on Medical Education and Hospitals, "Hospital Service in the United States," *Journal of the American Medical Association,* 116:1066, Mar. 15, 1941.

Yet, to compensate, the number of hospitals devoted entirely to Negroes is pitifully small, being only 124 for the whole country in 1944. Most of them are regarded by hospital experts as inadequate with respect to physical plant, equipment, and personnel. Even in the South, where about three-fifths of these hospitals are located, they are found principally in the larger cities, although almost two-thirds of the Negroes in the South live in rural places.[40]

Among the states of the deep South the very best supply of beds for Negroes in general nonfederal hospitals in 1940 was found in Florida, where the ratio was as low as 1.5 beds per 1,000 Negroes, compared with 3.2 beds per 1,000 whites. Most Southern Negroes are served by even fewer beds, and in the state with the greatest proportion of Negroes, Mississippi, there was only 1 bed for about 2,000 colored people (0.5 per 1,000) compared with 1 bed for every 435 white persons (2.3 per 1,000).[41] Frequently, even in governmentally sponsored units, only a gesture toward "equal accommodations" is made, with the provision, for example, of an identical number of ward beds for white and colored under circumstances where the need for such beds by Negroes is manifestly greater. In hospitals of any type of control, the maintenance of segregated facilities tends to depress over-all occupancy rates and accordingly to raise per diem costs [42] — an extravagance that most rural communities can ill afford.

There is a corresponding or even greater discrimination against the professional use of rural hospitals by Negro doctors. Even where separate Negro bed facilities are maintained, Negro physicians are seldom admitted to the hospital staff. This means that the Negro doctor referring a colored patient to the hospital loses the manage-

[40] BRADLEY, EUGENE H., "Health, Hospitals and the Negro," *The Modern Hospital*, 65:43-44, August, 1945.

[41] American Medical Association, Council on Medical Education and Hospitals, "Hospital Service in the United States," *Journal of the American Medical Association*, 116:1071-1082, Mar. 15, 1941. Also PONTON, T. R., "Hospital Service for Negroes," *Hospital Management*, 51:14, March, 1941. For a detailed discussion of the situation in one Southern state, see MAYO, SELZ C., *Negro Hospital and Medical Care Facilities in North Carolina.* Raleigh: North Carolina Agricultural Experiment Station, 1945, Processed, pp. 8-12.

[42] Commission on Hospital Care, "The Bed Occupancy Rate in General Hospitals," *Hospital Survey News Letter.* June, 1946, p. 4.

ment of his case, not to mention his loss of the general professional stimulation associated with hospital connections. It is small wonder that young Negro physicians are especially reluctant to set up practice in rural districts.

Unlike the long-time trend of physician supply, the rural hospital situation is showing some signs of improvement. After the First World War there was expansion of hospital facilities of all kinds. Since the greater part of this, however, consisted of the enlargement of existing institutions rather than the establishment of new units,[43] the increment was doubtless primarily in the cities. During the 1930's, under the stimulus of a federal public works program, more construction took place although this too was predominantly in urban regions (see Chapter 21). In the meantime, after 1928 there was a gradual decrease in the number of proprietary institutions as business failure overtook them or as they were supplanted by, or reorganized into, nonprofit or governmental institutions.[44] After 1938, the trend of total construction apparently began to be reversed and, somewhat in compensation for past retardation, the relative supply of general and allied hospital beds in the rural states increased at a somewhat greater rate than in the urban.[45]

With the Second World War and its associated economic prosperity, the hospitals of the nation felt greater demands for their services than ever before. Rural hospitals began to enjoy greatly increased occupancy and higher incomes. Because of wartime production priorities, however, they were often unable to purchase the equipment necessary to improve their services, and personnel were hard to find. Some large institutions serving rural people, including state hospitals, were forced to close down whole sections because of insufficient personnel to staff them and some small rural units had

[43] FALK, ROREM, and RING, *op. cit.*, p. 325.

[44] American Medical Association, Council on Medical Education and Hospitals, "Hospital Service in the United States," *Journal of the American Medical Association*, 112:917, Mar. 1, 1939.

[45] Thus, the ratio of general and allied hospital beds to population in the states over 70 per cent urban rose between 1938 and 1942 by less than 2 per cent, while in the states over 70 per cent rural the ratio improved by about 13 per cent (federal hospitals excluded except those operated by the Office of Indian Affairs). Derived from *Ibid.*, 112:918-919 and 933-993, and corresponding data for 1942 from 121:1015-1016 and 1027-1084, Mar. 27, 1943.

to close down completely. As early as December, 1941, a canvass of hospitals showed that voluntary nonfederal institutions were in need of 40,000 additional employees, mostly nurses.[46] Although there was actually an increase in civilian, not to mention military, hospital facilities during the war, it was practically all confined to so-called congested war areas, in which the in-migration of war workers put a heavy strain on existing facilities. Most of these areas were, of course, urban but some were in relatively rural sections or in trade centers serving farm people, among others. Outside of these areas new construction or replacement of hospital or other health facilities came virtually to a standstill.

All in all, the net supply of hospital beds for rural people has improved in the last few decades, though undoubtedly less than the supply for city dwellers. The increased provision of hospitals throughout the nation has gone hand in hand with increased recognition of the hospital as a community medical center. Not only does it play an important part in attracting physicians and other health workers to rural areas, but it can present a symbol of medical science to awaken the health consciousness of the entire community. To the extent that rural hospital facilities are too few or too meanly maintained, these functions as well as the elementary task of serving the sick are not fulfilled.

Special or Allied Hospitals

Among the hospitals meeting general community needs that we have considered are several types of specialized or "allied" institutions designed to handle special groups of conditions other than tuberculosis and mental disorder. Most important among these are hospitals for maternity cases, for diseases of children, for orthopedic cases, for conditions of the eye, ear, nose, and throat, and for contagious diseases. With respect to all types of special hospitals, rural people are less well supplied than residents of large cities, either in their own communities or even in larger near-by towns.

It would not be reasonable to expect these specialized institutions to be located directly in rural communities, but at the present stage

[46] PERROTT, G. ST. J., and HAROLD F. DORN, "Current Needs for Health Personnel," *Public Health Reports*, 57:997-1000, July 3, 1943.

of hospital development, one might well expect that the large cities in every state, serving rural people around them, would provide such facilities. Yet considering entire states, it is clear from Table 26 that the 50 per cent of our national population residing in the 13 most urban states is served by about double or more the number of beds in each type of special facility, compared with the number available to the other 50 per cent living in the 35 more

Table 26. Special Hospitals: *Number of beds in special hospitals by urban-rural population halves,* 1942

	Number of beds		
Type of hospital	United States, total	Population halves	
		More urban states	More rural states
Isolation	6,279	5,138	1,141
Maternity	5,903	4,168	1,735
Eye, ear, nose, throat	2,546	1,800	746
Children's	4,314	2,974	1,340
Orthopedic	7,313	4,864	2,449

Source: American Medical Association, Council on Medical Education and Hospitals, "Hospital Service in the United States," *Journal of the American Medical Association* 121:1015–1016, Mar. 27, 1943.

* Population halves are derived by listing the 48 states in urban-rural order and dividing them in two groups of 13 and 35 states, having approximately equal combined populations.

rural states. But even in the more urban states, it is questionable whether many specialized units are actually accessible to people living in the country. Barriers of cost and distance, and lack of professional relationships between city specialists and country doctors, considerably reduce the use of these specialized facilities by people from the farms and villages.

The most typically urban of the special or allied hospitals is the institution for contagious diseases, established and operated nearly always by units of government. Growing out of the old "pest house" on the outskirts of the big city, "isolation hospitals" are practically unknown to rural people. This type of facility may well be unnecessary in rural sections compared to the need in the congested cities. The maintenance of isolation rooms in the rural general hospital might well be more practical and have certain positive advantages,[47] but even this provision is seldom made. The average case of acute communicable disease in the rural family, therefore, is kept at home without benefit of scientific hospital care and is free to infect others in the household. We have noted that death rates from most of the infectious diseases of childhood are higher in the rural states, due not only to generally higher morbidity rates but very likely to higher case fatality rates for several of them, reflecting inadequate medical care.

A handful of specialized institutions are available in the United States for the management of relatively uncommon problems like trachoma and drug addiction, and a number have been recently developed for the rapid treatment of the venereal infections. These institutions, sponsored by government, are theoretically as available to rural people as to urban, but the limitations of case finding and referrals in rural sections probably make a difference in their utilization.

Another type of special health facility, but one not included in the inventory of general and allied hospitals, is the nursing or rest home. It has been observed that a majority of these quasi-medical institutions are located in the small towns and open country, but since they are predominantly operated for private profit (87 per cent of the 1,233 units in the nation were proprietary in 1939),[48] they are beyond the means of most rural people. These units are typically used by the chronically ill or convalescent patient — often well along in years — from the well-to-do urban family, although some are specifically for children's diseases, tuberculosis, orthopedic conditions, or maternity cases. To some extent, of course, they serve rural people as well, particularly the maternity homes. In fact, the utilization of a nursing home for an acute medical condition is an occasional expedient for the country-dweller to whom a full-fledged hospital is not accessible.

The counterpart of the nursing home for persons of limited means is the "old-age home," maintained usually by the county or municipal

[47] Today it is possible to carry out sound isolation measures without resort to a separate building, thus rendering the benefits of general medicine and surgery more accessible for the infectious disease case. The same principle applies as well to the handling of other special conditions in general hospitals.

[48] U. S. Census, *op. cit.,* 13:578, Mar. 2, 1942.

government or by a religious group. Of 2,168 old-age homes in 1939, 966 maintained infirmaries of some kind for the sick.[49] In urban and rural sections alike, these institutions are often little more than a carry-over of the nineteenth century poorhouse and their medical facilities tend to be far from ample, especially for an age group in such continual need of medical care. Many so-called general hospitals operated by county governments, likewise, eventually deteriorate into little more than places for domiciliary care of the aged, with a more or less defeatist attitude toward the diseases of old age and with little medical service rendered except for intercurrent emergencies.[50]

It may be thought that the country resident has little need for these facilities for the chronic diseases of later life, on the assumption that the farm or village home provides the appropriate peaceful atmosphere. While this may hold for the prosperous rural family, one can hardly expect the elements of good nutrition, physiotherapy, nursing care, and other aspects of sound geriatric medicine to be forthcoming in the home of the average small farmer, tenant, or sharecropper. On the other hand, organized home care programs for the chronically sick, such as those operated by a few of the large urban hospitals in New York state, are unknown in rural districts.

Other institutions such as schools, orphanages, schools for the deaf or blind, and prisons often provide infirmary facilities for their residents or inmates. Typically the medical facilities in these institutions in the rural states are unimpressive, reflecting generally limited financial resources, both public and private.

Finally, among the general and allied hospitals are facilities maintained by the Federal Government for especially dependent groups like veterans, Indians, and a few other categories. Inasmuch as these are related to special governmental programs modifying the general pattern of American medicine, they will be considered, with their rural implications, in Chapter 21.

[49] *Ibid.*, p. 579.
[50] For a general discussion of chronic disease facilities, see BOAS, ERNST P., *The Unseen Plague — Chronic Disease*. New York: J. J. Augustin, Inc., 1940.

CHAPTER 14

MENTAL AND TUBERCULOSIS HOSPITALS

THE CARE OF mental disorder and tuberculosis among rural and urban people alike has long been rendered in special institutions. The high cost of the management of these long-term illnesses puts them beyond the financial resources of all but the wealthiest individuals, while at the same time the unhospitalized case creates a problem for the whole community. As a result, the management of mental disease and tuberculosis was early assumed as a responsibility of government. Many of the shortcomings we have found associated with the private control of hospitals, therefore, are not found. Despite this, the rural population is served by a far smaller share of beds than it needs for these chronic, incapacitating disorders.

The economies of large-scale construction and operation have led to the establishment by government of mental and tuberculosis institutions usually of several hundred beds, in marked contrast to the typically small-capacity rural general hospital. The per bed cost of construction of these facilities is appreciably less than that of general hospitals, not only because of the size but also because of relatively less need for technical equipment. These large installations are ordinarily designed to serve the needs of many counties or even entire rural states. For this reason, it is especially appropriate to judge the adequacy of such facilities by whole states.

The most widely accepted standard for mental hospital facilities is 5.0 beds per 1,000 population. This would include beds for the psychoses and psychoneuroses, epilepsy, and feeble-mindedness. Our consideration of the volume of mental disorder among rural people shows that it is certainly no less and possibly more than among urban people. The differentials in the supply of mental beds among rural and urban states shown in Figure 23, therefore, represent actual differences in the meeting of needs. It is clear that none except the most highly urbanized segment of states reaches the minimum standard. Taking individual states and even including federal institutions (notably those for veterans), we find that of the 28 states that are over 50 per cent rural, only 4 reach the standard of 5.0 beds per 1,000 — Minnesota, Oregon, Vermont, and Wyoming. On the other hand, 11 of the 20 predominantly urban states reach the standard. New York State with its 17 per cent rural population is served by 7.47 mental beds per 1,000 while Arizona with its 65 per cent rural population has only 1.86 beds per 1,000.[1]

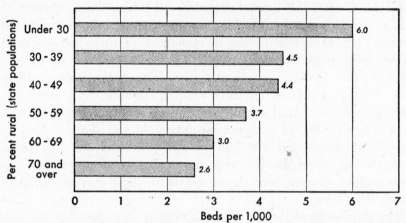

FIG. 23.   Mental Hospitals: Number of beds in mental hospitals per 1,000 population, in states grouped by rurality, 1940. (Beds in federal hospitals not included.) Source: Derived from American Medical Association, Council on Medical Education and Hospitals. "Hospital Service in the United States," *Journal of the American Medical Association,* 116:1071-1082, Mar. 15, 1941.

It might be claimed that despite the prevalence of mental disorder in the rural population, the less complex rural environment creates less need for institutionalization. Fallacies in this notion have already been considered but beyond these, of course, the function of the modern mental institution is not merely to remove the individual from circulation so that he can do no harm. New methods of organic and psychological therapy used today in our leading mental institutions give hope for the complete recovery of a large proportion of mental cases. It would seem no more proper to deprive rural mental patients of these benefits merely because they can "get along" in their home communities than it would be to deprive them of medical care merely because they can "get along" with their rheumatism or their hernias.

[1] U. S. Census, *op. cit.,* p. 543.

As with general hospitals, the mental institutions serving the people of the most rural states tend to be substandard in operation. State per capita income tends to determine the per bed disbursements for mental hospitals, and these expenditures are lowest in the rural states (see Chapter 18). The mental hospital in the rural state is often understaffed, maintained with a pinchpenny frugality, and it all too often continues to use outworn methods of handling the "insane." It is actually little wonder that rural people, and many city people, are apprehensive of "insane asylums" and will often tolerate any inconvenience to keep their loved ones out of them. Waiting lists for commitment of cases, nevertheless, are common and often a rural community is forced to incarcerate a mental patient in the local jailhouse, for want of any better place.

Beds for the care of tuberculosis, still the chief killer of the prime-of-life years in rural and urban areas alike, fall as far short of meeting rural needs as those for mental disease. While the rural death rate for tuberculosis, as we have seen, is still slightly lower than the urban, the supply of rural beds is far smaller than this slight differential would warrant.

The need for tuberculosis beds has been defined by authorities as equivalent to about 2.5 beds for each annual death from the disease reported in the area.[2] By relating the number of deaths from tuberculosis reported in each state to the available beds and comparing the ratio with the minimum standard, it is possible to evaluate the adequacy of tuberculosis facilities in proportion to the need of each individual state.

It is clear from Figure 24 that only the most highly urban group of states comes close to the present-day standard of 2.5 beds per annual death. The 21 states with 60 per cent or more rural population have less than half the supply of beds found in the most urban states, falling considerably below the national average of 1.4 beds per annual death.

Institutionalization of cases of pulmonary tuberculosis serves two main functions: it greatly facilitates medical or surgical treatment of the patient and it isolates the infectious individual so he cannot spread the disease to others. It may be claimed that, so far as the

[2] In view of new case-finding methods by mass x-ray studies, this standard may have to be revised upward, and 3.0 beds per annual death is being proposed as desirable.

treatment of the case is concerned, it is easier for the rural patient
to get rest — the basic element in therapy — in his home than the
city case. This view would lose sight of all the other features of
institutional care already suggested, but whether or not it is true,
the need for preventive isolation of the rural case is as great or
greater than for the urban case.[3] We know that the hazard of tubercu-

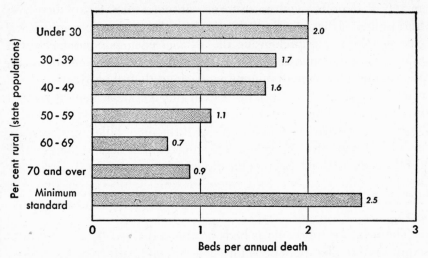

FIG. 24.   Tuberculosis Beds: Number of beds in tuberculosis sanatoria per
annual death from tuberculosis (average for 1939-41) in states grouped by
rurality, 1942. (Beds in federal institutions and in preventoria not included.
Minimum standard citation from report of the Committee on Sanatorium
Standards of the American Trudeau Society, 1944.) Source: National Tuberculosis Association. *Tuberculosis Hospital and Sanatorium Directory*, 1942. Also,
U.S. Bureau of the Census. *Vital Statistics of the United States.* Supplement
1939-1940, Part III, pp. 314-475; 1941, Part II, pp. 240-273.

losis is by far the greatest for family contacts of infectious cases.
Not only does the rural family have more members to be exposed
than the urban but, as we have observed, the housing of the individual rural family tends actually to be more congested.

Beds for the hospitalization of tuberculosis are so limited in many
rural sections that some institutions have adopted a policy of accepting only the early cases having a good chance of therapeutic benefit
and recovery. Obviously such a practice leaves the most advanced
cases in their homes, free to pass on the infection before they die.

[3] DOWNES, JEAN, "How Tuberculosis Spreads in a Rural Community,"
American Journal of Public Health, 26:30-36, January, 1936.

Limited facilities for tuberculosis, moreover, have led most institutions to adopt fairly strict admission policies, demanding not only state residence but often residence in designated political subdivisions within the state. This has worked particular hardships on that large segment of the farm population consisting of migratory farm workers. Tuberculosis has been found to be especially high in this underprivileged group. Yet without facilities for their care and isolation, they are free to spread the disease from state to state.[4] Special needs attach also to the rural Negro population, among whom the tuberculosis death rate is considerably higher than among whites and for whom bed facilities are considerably less.[5]

[4] BLANKENSHIP, C. F., and FRED SAFIER, *A Study of Medical Problems Associated with Transients* (U. S. Public Health Service Bull. 258). Washington: Government Printing Office, 1940, pp. 59-62, 97-109.

[5] National Tuberculosis Association, *Tuberculosis Hospital and Sanatorium Directory*, 1942. New York, 1942.

CHAPTER 15

AUXILIARY HEALTH FACILITIES

B EYOND facilities for the bed care of the sick are a number of auxiliary medical facilities which, in the development of modern medicine, have become increasingly complex and numerous. Most important among them are clinics and health centers, drugstores, laboratories, professional schools, and research institutions.

It should be mentioned, of course, that the most elementary facility for serving the patient not sick enough to be hospitalized or put in bed is the office of the private physician. In this sense there were some 140,000 privately managed medical facilities for the diagnosis and treatment of ambulatory patients throughout the country in 1940. The urban-rural distribution of these units was naturally almost identical to that of their medical proprietors inventoried as a whole in Chapter 8, although some allowance must be made, of course, for physicians in salaried positions. To some small extent one physician may maintain two or even more separate offices and several physicians may share one office, although on the whole the distribution of offices parallels that of physicians. The same applies, of course, to the offices of dentists and other practitioners.

Clinics and Health Centers

Since about 1900 there has been an accelerated establishment of organized clinics or dispensaries, typically under the sponsorship of a public or voluntary nonprofit body. Characteristically, patients of certain types come at stated times to these facilities, where auxiliary personnel and equipment are available, and where, in general, a greater efficiency with respect to time and cost is achieved. Starting mainly as an expedient way of providing medical care to the "worthy poor" in the large cities, the public clinic has remained preponderantly urban, serving particularly those unable to afford private medical services.

The prototype of the public clinic is the "outpatient department" of the general hospital, often known significantly as a "dispensary" because of its beginnings as a place where, above all, drugs were dispensed. As we have observed, however, most rural hospitals have no outpatient departments. Even when small fees are charged for clinic attendance, the outpatient department is not a profit-making operation and the average small rural hospital, even when not under proprietary control, cannot afford to render the service.

The Committee on the Costs of Medical Care found that hospital outpatient departments in 1931 were largely concentrated in the New England and Middle Atlantic states. They were typically associated with the large, long-established institutions in the metropolitan centers.[1] While there has been a steady growth in the number and capacity of clinics, it has been less marked in the rural sections. Accurate current data on the distribution of hospital clinics throughout the nation are not available, but a 1946 study indicated that only about 44 per cent of general hospitals had outpatient departments.[2] The deficiencies undoubtedly remain greatest in the rural states. Analysis of recent data on outpatient department visits compiled by the American Hospital Association reveals an almost constant decline in the rate of visits in states of increasing rurality. In states over 70 per cent urban there were hospital clinics sustaining a case load of 348 visits per 1,000 population in 1944, compared with 153 visits per 1,000 in states over 70 per cent rural.[3]

It is quite evident that few if any of the 1,253 counties without registered general hospitals are served by hospital clinics; even where there is a nonregistered general hospital in any of these counties, it can seldom be expected to maintain a public clinic. The same would tend to hold true of the additional 451 counties having only proprietary institutions. It may probably be stated that the great majority of the medically needy in the nation's rural population do not have access to a hospital outpatient facility of any type. Even in rural hospitals in which clinics are maintained, they are likely to be of small capacity and operated at relatively infrequent

[1] FALK, ROREM, and RING, op. cit., pp. 347-348.

[2] Commission on Hospital Care, Hospital Care in the United States. New York: The Commonwealth Fund, 1947, pp. 316-320.

[3] Derived from American Hospital Association, "Survey of Civilian Hospitals," loc. cit.

intervals. The rural hospital has nothing comparable to the large, diversified polyclinic of the cities in which the various medical and surgical specialties are practiced at designated sessions. Difficulties in transportation, moreover, and the application of a means test usually more rigid than in the cities, reduce the usefulness of the few rural hospital clinics available.

In recent years there has been a growing development of public clinics unassociated with hospitals, chiefly under the auspices and in the quarters of public health agencies. While hospital clinics, for the most part, provide therapeutic medical services of more or less general scope, independent clinics tend to furnish preventive services of specific types such as infant hygiene, tuberculosis control, venereal disease management, school hygiene, and the like. The development of these preventive clinic facilities has been much greater in rural areas than that of therapeutic facilities typically associated with hospitals but is still considerably less than the extension of independent clinics in the cities. By and large, the establishment of such clinics parallels the organization of public health and related voluntary agencies in rural areas, to be considered in detail in later chapters.

Some reflection of the adequacy of preventive clinic facilities may be given by considering the number of clinic sessions for handling a specific problem in each state in relation to the extent of the particular problem. Clinics for handling venereal disease, for example, representing one of the most numerous types of preventive clinic, may be compared with the prevalence of venereal disease in a state to derive a measure of clinic adequacy (Table 27).[4] In general it may be assumed that a lower potential case load per clinic session represents greater adequacy in the same sense that a lower number of persons per physician represents a more adequate supply of professional personnel. Although the relationship is not exact, it is evident that the adequacy of clinic facilities for venereal disease control tends to be less in the more rural states. The index of adequacy in the most rural group of states is only half that in the most urban group.

[4] The prevalence of syphilis as revealed by Selective Service examinations has been used as an index of the potential venereal disease case load among all 21-35 year old males in each state. The number of VD clinic sessions held per week, rather than merely the number of clinic facilities, has been used to give an idea of total clinic capacity.

That this is probably an understatement, moreover, seems evident from the fact that in the wealthier, more urban states a higher proportion of syphilitics is handled by private practitioners, lessen-

Table 27. Clinic Facilities for Venereal Disease: *Theoretical syphilis case loads (21–35 year males) per clinic session available,* in states grouped by rurality, 1943*

Per cent rural (state populations)	Clinic sessions per week	Estimated syphilis cases, 21–35 year males†	Theoretical syphilis case load per clinic session
Under 30	1,953	130,980	67
30–39	764	73,409	96
40–49	811	103,367	128
50–59	778	126,361	162
60–69	1,218	170,752	140
70 and over	1,123	152,669	136

Source: U. S. Public Health Service, *Directory of Clinics for the Diagnosis and Treatment of Venereal Diseases*, Supp. 4 to Venereal Disease Information, rev. 1943. Washington, 1943. Also: Vonderlehr, R. A. and Lida J. Usilton, "Syphilis among Men of Draft Age in the United States," *Journal of the American Medical Association*, 120:1369–1372, Dec. 26, 1942.

* See footnote 4 in this chapter.

† Estimated number of cases of syphilis among all 21–35 year old males in each state, based on Selective Service findings.

ing the actual load to be borne by the clinics. Among individual states, the highest adequacy is found in urban Connecticut with a potential case load of only 30 per clinic session and the lowest in rural Texas with an index of 305.[5] While the absolute number of clinic sessions in the rural states of the South is greater, it is evident that in relation to the size of their syphilis problem their facilities are less adequate. The same general relationship is found with regard to prenatal or infant hygiene clinic facilities, despite the greater rural needs reflected in higher rural birth rates.[6]

The operation of a clinic does not necessarily imply the existence of a special or appropriate physical facility for health service. The lack of proper physical structures for the purpose has forced rural health agencies to use ingenuity in holding clinics in places designed for every other purpose: schoolrooms, fire stations, courthouses,

[5] Derived as in Table 27.

[6] U. S. Children's Bureau, *Building the Future for Children and Youth: Next Steps Proposed by the National Commission on Children in Wartime.* Washington: U. S. Department of Labor (Pub. 310), April, 1945, pp. 6-7.

churches, abandoned stores, or whatnot. As a result, the average rural clinic is typically bleak and far from having the sanitary and health-educational aspect suitable for a medical facility and necessary to make attendance attractive and worth while to patients.

Particular mention should be made of a scattering of "mobile clinics" especially designed to reach isolated rural communities. They may consist of fully equipped trailers or self-propelled units in which the clinic is held, or vehicles with movable equipment which may be set up at points along the route of travel.[7] These mobile health facilities had their principal origin in the "round-up" health projects for attacking hookworm disease in the South a generation ago.[8] They are still confined chiefly to specialized programs of dental care for children, tuberculosis case finding, immunizations, or other preventive services provided by health departments. A number of mobile clinics, serving both for preventive and therapeutic medical and dental service, have been operated as part of the special federal health program for migratory farm workers (see Chapter 22). These come-and-go units have, in a sense, been developed as a measure of expediency where permanent facilities were lacking.

The number of mobile clinic facilities serving special sections of the rural population was estimated to be about 100 in 1931.[9] Today the number is doubtless substantially larger, though far smaller than the need warrants. The perfection of the photofluorographic x-ray unit to detect tuberculosis has provided probably the greatest extension of mobile health facilities. As adequate permanent facilities are established, the need for these mobile clinics may be expected to diminish.

Although the development of public clinics, either attached to or separate from hospitals, has been retarded in rural areas, there has been a somewhat compensatory development of another type of clinic. This is the private clinic which, while operated by private

[7] Mobile clinics sometimes involve a pattern in which technical personnel travel from place to place, using fixed facilities at each location. In adjustment to recent wartime shortages of physicians, in fact, private practitioners have sometimes made periodic visits to outlying villages, to render general medical care at "clinics" set up for the purpose.

[8] ROSENAU, MILTON J., *Preventive Medicine and Hygiene*. New York: D. Appleton-Century Company, Inc., 6th ed., 1935, p. 186.

[9] FALK, ROREM, and RING, *op. cit.*, p. 351.

physicians, shares the essential features of a clinic in that equipment and personnel are pooled to achieve greater efficiency with a reduction in operating costs. The private clinic ordinarily consists of a group of physicians, practicing in a suite of offices with space, equipment, and technical aides considerably more plentiful than found in the average private physician's office in the same area. This forward-looking pattern of group practice is of tremendous significance to rural people, for it is a way to bring specialists within their reach and, through medical teamwork, to make services of high quality available far from large urban centers. The private group clinic, in fact, like the proprietary hospital, has in a sense developed to meet a need in the rural regions where large medical centers under public or university auspices were not to be found.

Private clinics are of many types and may vary from a partnership between a surgeon and a general practitioner to a complex team of specialists of many kinds, but in smaller communities they tend to be least complex. Their services, of course, are customarily purchased on a private basis by individual patients, though quite a few enter into contracts with mining companies, for example, or industrial concerns, serving the employees on a prepayment basis. The private clinic generally bears the name of its senior staff member and director, and rural people for miles around will be heard referring to the "Smith Clinic" or the "Jones Clinic" as the medical court of last appeal in the handling of serious disease problems.

While private clinics today are seldom found in small towns, they are actually most plentiful in generally rural regions, located usually in their more or less urban centers. In 1930, C. Rufus Rorem found the greatest concentration of private group clinics in Minnesota, Wisconsin, Iowa, South Dakota, North Dakota, and Texas.[10] Undoubtedly the Mayo Clinic, founded in 1887 in the small town of Rochester, Minnesota, exerted considerable influence in the establishment of these clinics in the Midwestern states. In 1945, a sample of 675 private group clinics in the files of the Medical Administration Service still showed the greatest numbers to be located in the generally more rural regions.[11] Thus the urban Northeast was recorded

[10] ROREM, C. RUFUS, *Private Group Clinics* (Committee on the Costs of Medical Care Pub. 8). Chicago: University of Chicago Press, 1931, pp. 15-17.

[11] The definition of a private group clinic used was "three or more physicians, practicing together, pooling professional skills, office space, etc."

with 35 group clinics while the West had 136, the North Central region had 304, and the South had 200. Texas was credited with the largest number, 77, and Wisconsin with the second largest number, 69.[12]

Several other nations have made substantial progress in developing "rural health centers" — health facilities from which all the preventive services for a rural district are administered and at which diagnostic and treatment services for all ambulatory illness and even for emergency bed illness may be obtained.[13] This concept has reached the discussion stage in the United States and figures prominently in many long-term plans for improved rural health services. In the public clinics and the private group clinics of rural sections lies the germ of the health center pattern, although each of the present types of unit taken by itself is incomplete. Another intermediate tendency toward the rational organization of rural health services is the growing custom of having the physician's or surgeon's office located in the local hospital. This significant departure from tradition, while to some extent an incident of proprietary ownership of hospitals by physicians, puts much more equipment and personnel at the disposal of the doctor. The custom seems to be more prevalent in rural sections than in urban. Another slight approach to the health center idea is found in the "medical arts building," containing offices of physicians, dentists, optometrists, and so on, and also laboratories and pharmacies. This pattern has developed widely but it has been most extensive in the larger urban centers of the generally agricultural stretches of the Midwest and West.[14] All these patterns represent steps away from the individualized office of the country doctor, often attached to his home, and toward a centralized facility for the provision of medical services.

[12] Based on unpublished data furnished in 1945 by Dr. Kingsley Roberts, Medical Administration Service, New York City. For more detailed information on about 400 group practice clinics, see HUNT, G. HALSEY, *Medical Groups in the United States*, 1946. Washington: U. S. Public Health Service, Processed, February, 1947.

[13] For a discussion of the conception of the rural health center throughout the world, see League of Nations Health Organization, *European Conference on Rural Hygiene: Vol. 2, Minutes.* Geneva, 1931, pp. 94-99.

[14] SIGERIST, HENRY E., *American Medicine.* New York: W. W. Norton & Company, Inc., 1934, pp. 175-176.

Hardly an instance is known in the United States, nevertheless, where a rural community is fully served by the broadly conceived type of health center that provides all preventive and therapeutic services. A number of rural communities have cooperative or similar hospitals, with the offices of staff physicians attached, and — while not including quarters for community public health administration — these provide reasonably broad preventive and therapeutic care. Others have what should be called "public health centers," facilities from which the preventive activities of the local department of health and sometimes of voluntary health agencies are administered or provided. For certain limited rural groups under special governmentally sponsored medical care programs, like Indians, low-income farmers, or migratory farm workers, the comprehensive pattern has been at least partially achieved. So far as the main body of the rural population is concerned, strict separation is maintained between the physical facilities of the individual physician, the hospital, the department of health, and other personnel or agencies concerned with health.

Drugstores and Laboratories

Perhaps the most characteristic local health facility in rural areas today is the small-town drugstore or the village general store with its patent medicine counter. It is not that rural sections are served by more pharmacies than urban but simply that where hospitals and clinics are missing, or where physicians and dentists are too few, a place can usually be found near by where the farmer or village dweller can buy drugs. Actually the relative supply of drugstores is considerably greater for city dwellers. In 1930, when the over-all national supply of drugstores was estimated to be about 1 for every 2,000 persons, the ratio in urban sections was estimated to be about 1 to 1,525 and in rural sections about 1 to 3,155, or only half as large a supply.[15] A ratio of 1 drug store to about 2,000 persons has been suggested as a standard, though much obviously depends on the general organization of medical services.

The supply of drugstores in 1939 in groups of states of different rurality is shown in Table 28. While no consistent trend appears for

[15] ROREM, C. RUFUS, *The Costs of Medicines* (Committee on the Costs of Medical Care Pub. 14). Chicago: University of Chicago Press, 1932, p. 56.

the relative supply of drugstores in states that are over 50 per cent
urban, for states that are over 50 per cent rural the relative supply
goes sharply downhill. In the most rural group of states the supply
of pharmacies is more than 50 per cent poorer than in the most urban
group; rural West Virginia reaches a national low, with each unit

Table 28. Drugstores: *Number of licensed drugstores and number of persons per
drugstore in states grouped by rurality, 1939*

Per cent rural (state populations)	Number of drugstores	Persons per drugstore
United States	57,925	2,273
Under 30	18,254	2,089
30–39	10,581	2,247
40–49	8,845	2,062
50–59	8,711	2,049
60–69	6,807	2,650
70 and over	4,727	3,308

Source: U. S. Census, 1940. *Census of Business. Retail Trade*, 1939.

having to serve 4,000 persons.[16] Yet these ratios certainly understate
the differentials, because the country drugstore tends to be much
smaller than the city unit and probably less well stocked. In 1930
the gross annual sales of drugstores in rural communities averaged
$18,000 compared with $33,000 for drugstores in places of over
10,000.[17]

The figures cited apply only to facilities maintained by registered
pharmacists. But just as the rural community must depend to some
extent on nonregistered institutions for hospital care, it must often
depend for its drugs on a medicine counter not under the guidance
of a registered pharmacist. Actually the number of general merchan-
dise stores selling drugs and patent medicines in rural communities
seems to be larger than the number of properly staffed pharmacies.
A typical Southern rural county studied in 1930, for example, in
which there were seven drugstores, all in two towns, had 25 more
or less remotely located general country stores selling patent medi-

[16] U. S. Census, 1940. *Census of Business. Retail Trade*, 1939. Washington:
Government Printing Office, 1943. The dispensing of drugs by mine doctors,
serving a large share of West Virginia's population, may account partially for
the low supply of drugstores in this state.

[17] ROREM, *op. cit.*, p. 53.

cines and home remedies.[18] In addition, country towns are still occasionally visited by itinerant medicine wagons and "medicine shows," selling cure-all herb remedies of all sorts, although these are rapidly dying out. We might learn something, incidentally, even from the itinerant quack about "selling" health on wheels to remotely situated rural people.

The rural drugstore is less often associated with a chain system[19] although, like the urban store, it tends to be replete with a selection of commodities ranging from ice-cream sodas to pulp magazines. It is likely to have a far more variegated selection of patent medicines on its shelves than its neon-lighted counterpart in the city and yet a poorer supply of relatively expensive items like endocrine or tissue extract preparations. Many rural drugstores are owned by physicians who often keep their own offices in back of the store or on the floor above. Under such circumstances, the physician naturally stands to profit from the sale of prescribed medicines. On the other hand, the complexities of distance in rural districts have led to the quite common practice of physicians dispensing their own drugs, to eliminate the necessity of a long trip from the patient's home to the village drugstore. This practice has probably contributed somewhat to the less extensive establishment of pharmacies in rural areas.

Diagnostic laboratories, essential to modern medicine, are as limited in rural sections as the restricted rural development of medical science would lead one to expect. In widespread areas even the most highly trained rural physician must practice under the frustrating handicap of inability to submit clinical specimens to a readily accessible laboratory for chemical, bacteriological, or morphological examination.

As in the case of x-ray equipment and other types of diagnostic apparatus discussed previously, the average rural hospital tends to be seriously deficient in clinical laboratory facilities. Thus it can ordinarily offer little more than the most elementary diagnostic service either to the bed patient or, for that matter, to the ambulatory case so frequently served by the city hospital laboratory. Although

[18] GUILD, C. ST. C., *Surveys of the Medical Facilities in Three Representative Southern Counties* (Committee on the Costs of Medical Care Pub. 23). Chicago: University of Chicago Press, 1932, p. 63.

[19] ROREM, *op. cit.*, p. 53.

the situation has undoubtedly improved, as many as 3,000 of the nation's 7,000 hospitals in 1930 were without clinical laboratories[20] and these were presumably concentrated in rural areas.

To some small extent, laboratories operated independently by private physicians or technicians make up the gap, but these still represent a characteristically urban development. To a greater extent, deficiencies in some areas may be partially overcome by laboratories operated under departments of public health. The pattern that is emerging is that of the district public health laboratory, often under state auspices, set up to serve several rural counties. Public health laboratories typically perform only tests required for the detection of communicable diseases although, where other facilities are lacking, they may handle a few other procedures in clinical pathology as an accommodation to the practitioner. Nevertheless, even public health laboratories are more plentiful and more highly developed in urban sections, particularly in large municipalities, where they are set up to carry a heavier and more complex load of work.

A good over-all measure of clinical laboratory facilities of all kinds in an area is the number of qualified clinical pathologists.[21] As one might expect, analysis of the roster of membership of the American Society of Clinical Pathologists shows a disproportionate concentration of pathologists in the more urban states. In the 13 most urban states and the District of Columbia which include about half of our national population, there were 504 members of the Society in 1944, while in the 35 most rural states with the other half of our population there were only 352 members.[22] It is evident that laboratories under the direction of specially qualified physicians must be relatively deficient in the rural states. It will be recalled that another reflection of

[20] FALK, ROREM, and RING, op cit., p. 303.

[21] Since 1933 the American Medical Association's Council on Medical Education and Hospitals has considered this a more accurate reflection of the availability of satisfactory laboratory services than a listing of laboratories as such. Personal communication from Dr. M. G. Westmoreland, Council on Medical Education and Hospitals, Nov. 19, 1945.

[22] Derived from "Roster, the American Society of Clinical Pathologists, 1943," American Journal of Clinical Pathology, 13:644-665, December, 1943; also "New Members Elected at the 1944 Meeting," American Journal of Clinical Pathology, 14:454-455, August, 1944. (The data presented apply to all members of the Society, including those in military service listed by residence.)

over-all discrepancies in the rural-urban distribution of laboratories was seen in the concentration of technicians and assistants in urban regions.

Under these circumstances, one would like to assume that the rural physician, in compensation for the lack of laboratory facilities, does considerable laboratory work of his own. Beyond such routine procedures as simple urinalyses, however, little is done. Observation of itemized bills rendered by rural doctors shows them to be singularly free from reference to the numerous laboratory procedures almost taken for granted by the up-to-date clinician. The fact that certain types of laboratory specimens may be sent by mail or common carrier to a city laboratory may help but it obviously fails to meet the need adequately.

Medical Schools and Related Institutions

Schools for training physicians, dentists, nurses, technicians, pharmacists, and other health workers must also be counted among the facilities related to rural health. For many reasons these technical schools generally are and should be located in the larger cities. There is a point, however, beyond which concentration of professional schools in large cities, and certainly in particular highly urban states, gives no special technical advantages. More important, their urban concentration tends to add further handicaps to the task of providing adequate and good quality medical services to rural areas — handicaps over and above the fundamental economic ones already considered.

We have noted the disproportionate selection of medical and dental students from urban centers and urban states and the influence of their origin on their final place of settlement. While the chief determinant of this selective process is doubtless higher urban family income levels, it is more than likely that the mere location of the professional school plays a part. In 1944, more than two-fifths of the nation's 69 four-year medical schools were located in 5 urban states and the District of Columbia, and 14 of these were located in three cities, New York, Philadelphia, and Chicago.[23] Yet there were

[23] American Medical Association, Council on Medical Education and Hospitals, "Medical Education in the United States and Canada," *Journal of the American Medical Association*, 125:1110, Aug. 19, 1944.

18 states, all but 6 of them predominantly rural, without any four-year medical schools at all.[24] Of the 6 urban states without schools, 4 are in the Northeast within a short distance of the great metropolitan centers having several schools. It is certainly not mere coincidence that 11 of the 12 rural states without full-term medical schools lacked a state-wide ratio of one effective physician per 1,000 persons in 1940, although 23 states throughout the nation reached this ratio.

The location of a medical school in an area would seem to favor the "production" of graduate physicians for that area in several ways. The mere presence of the school may provide some inducement to the youth of the area to study medicine, particularly if the school is attached to a university attended in large measure by local youth. Applicants from the state in which a medical school is located, moreover, tend to enjoy admission preferences. Finally, numerous professional influences play on the graduates of a particular school encouraging them to seek a career in the general region of the school. A demonstration of some of these influences is the fact that the medical schools of the rural Southeast, for example, actually contribute 70 per cent of the physicians practicing in that region.[25] Nevertheless, medical schools in the South were recently graduating one new physician each year for every 41,000 persons in the region, while the ratio for the rest of the nation was 1 to 22,000.[26] The location of schools opening their doors for the training of Negro physicians is much more inequitable, with all but a handful of graduates each year coming from two schools, one in Washington, D. C., and the other in Nashville, Tennessee.

The location of a medical school in an area exerts important influences beyond the training of physicians likely to go into practice locally. A medical school functions as a general center of higher

[24] Of these 18 states, 6 have schools teaching basic sciences or the first two years of conventional medical education. *Ibid.*, p. 1118. They do not, however, turn out graduate physicians, and many students starting out in these preliminary schools never complete their training.

[25] LASSEK, A. M., "Role of Southeastern Schools of Medicine in the National Distribution of Physicians," *Journal of the Association of American Medical Colleges*, 19:217-223, July, 1944.

[26] HYMAN, O. W., "The Number and Distribution of Physicians in the Southern States as Bearing upon the Policies of Southern Medical Colleges," *Southern Medical Journal*, 30:85-88, January, 1937.

learning for its whole area, an academy for postgraduate studies, a sort of Aesculapian temple at which help may be sought in difficult cases. Most of the continuation courses for practicing physicians (lasting five days or more) given throughout the nation are sponsored by medical schools.[27] It is evident that the physician in a state lacking a medical school tends to be deprived of equal opportunity for self-improvement in medical science.

It must be recognized that most medical school training today fails to equip the graduate for practice in a rural district. The general emphasis of modern medical training is geared to urban practice. The student is taught to depend extensively on specialized techniques and professional consultations quite inaccessible in most country districts. Disproportionate emphasis is put upon the rarities seldom encountered in rural — or for that matter urban — practice, and the everyday medical problems confronting the rural practitioner are given scant attention. It is especially unfortunate that so little interest is shown by the medical schools in training the young physician in the social aspects of medicine with which he is so intimately faced in rural America.[28]

The formal training of the physician today includes a period of hospital internship virtually as an essential, and a subsequent period of residency as a desirable phase of training. Yet the hospitals in rural sections, because of their size and quality, tend to be considerably less attractive to candidates for internship or residency than hospitals in the larger cities. In 1941, 66 per cent of all hospitals approved by the American Medical Association for intern or resident training were in the 13 most urban states and the District of Columbia, which together have 50 per cent of the national population. More important, 72 per cent of all interns and 73 per cent of all residents (including assistant residents) were in these hospitals.[29] The most rural state, Mississippi, lacked even a single general hos-

[27] American Medical Association, Council on Medical Education and Hospitals, "Medical Education in the United States and Canada," *Journal of the American Medical Association*, 117:727, Aug. 30, 1941.

[28] SIGERIST, HENRY E., "The Medical Student and the Social Problems Confronting Medicine Today," *Bulletin of the Institute of the History of Medicine*, 4:411-422, May, 1936.

[29] Derived from American Medical Association, Council on Medical Education and Hospitals, "Hospitals in the United States and Canada," *Journal of the American Medical Association*, 118:1070, Mar. 22, 1942.

pital offering an approved residency. Yet the professional connections built up during the period of hospital training exert a strong influence on the young physician to settle in the vicinity of his training institution. Rural communities and whole rural sections lose not only the benefit of this influence, but they lose the direct medical services rendered by the intern or resident in the course of his training.

Table 29. Schools for Training Professional Personnel: *Number and enrollments of approved schools of medicine and related fields by groups of states in urban-rural order having equal quartiles of the population, 1943-44*

Population quartile	Number of states	Medicine		Dentistry		Nursing		Laboratory work (number)
		Number	Enrollment	Number	Enrollment	Number	Enrollment	
Most urban .	6*	19	6,238	9	2,479	326	27,981	48
Second . .	8	19	5,616	11	2,947	318	27,431	75
Third . . .	14	15	4,790	10	2,463	317	24,852	76
Most rural .	21	16	4,105	6	1,125	336	17,709	41

Source: American Medical Association, "Medical Education in the United States and Canada," *Journal of the American Medical Association*, 125:1116–1117, Aug. 19. 1944; American Dental Association, Council on Dental Education, "Accrediting of U, S. Dental Schools," *Journal of the American Dental Association*, 32:663–668, June, 1945; National League of Nursing Education, *A List of Schools of Nursing Meeting Minimum Requirements Set by Law and Board Rules.* New York, 1943; American Medical Association, Council on Medical Education and Hospitals, "Hospital Service in the United States," *Journal of the American Medical Association*, 124:919–922, Mar. 25, 1944.
    * Includes the District of Columbia.

The location of other professional schools follows the same general inequitable pattern as the medical schools. Training schools for dentists, pharmacists, and nurses, and those for technicians in several fields like clinical laboratory work, x-ray work, or dental hygiene, all tend to be concentrated in large cities. The dental schools in particular follow the pattern of distribution of the medical schools closely. Some of the difficulties involved in operating nursing schools in rural hospitals have been mentioned.

The distribution of schools in 1943-44 for training members of the principal health professions is shown in Table 29. It is to be noted that each population quartile contains an approximately equal number of people, but the geographic area is obviously much greater for the more rural quartiles. Yet in all instances, except for nursing schools, the most rural quartile in the vast area of 21 states, containing one-fourth of our national population, has fewer schools than the smaller areas containing any other quarter of the population. The situation is more accurately reflected by school enrollments. It is evident that the schools in rural states tend to have smaller capacities so that their aggregate enrollments are consistently lower in the states with the two most rural quartiles, despite the fact that these states contain an equal population in a vastly greater geographic area. While this is not a regional analysis, it reflects rural-urban discrepancies in facilities that must eventually be tackled primarily on a regional basis.

It would be reasonable, of course, to have a certain concentration of these training facilities in urban states if at the same time there were positive measures in effect to counteract the inequities in the distribution of health personnel to which the location of schools contributes. In the absence of such measures, the uneven distribution of facilities for training physicians and others creates substantial difficulties for rural medicine.

While the medical and dental schools of the nation all operate on a fairly high level, the professional school in a rural region is to some extent a victim of the same economic handicaps as other medical facilities in rural states. Its income from students, endowments, and government tends to be less ample than that of the longer established institutions in the wealthier, industrialized states.[30] As a result, it is usually unable to build up the kind of staff and facilities characterizing the schools in the large metropolitan centers or to reach quite the same level of scientific development.

Schools of nursing have not reached the generally high level of performance of the medical and dental schools, and many of the nursing schools attached to smaller hospitals in rural districts suffer particular deficiencies. While they may meet state requirements for registration of their graduates, many rural schools fall short of widely accepted standards. The training they provide, for example, often fails to fulfill requirements for federal civil service appointment or for admission to graduate schools in public health nursing, not to mention qualifications for service in the armed forces. Special schools

[30] For a discussion of variations in medical school budgets, see Commission on Medical Education, *Final Report of the Commission on Medical Education.* New York: Columbia University Press, 1932, pp. 283-287.

for training nurse-midwives who might serve in rural districts — either directly or as supervisors — are to be found only at a few places in the United States: New York City, Santa Fe, New Mexico, and Hyden, Kentucky.[31]

Finally, mention should be made of institutions and facilities for medical research. It is obvious that the principal centers for research are, and should be, in the largest cities where technical personnel as well as clinical material is most accessible. Nevertheless, some facilities and opportunities for research should be available in all sections, not only to advance our knowledge but also to provide stimulation for keeping up the day-to-day level of medical performance. Yet facilities for research in rural hospitals, laboratories, or public health agencies tend to be at a minimum. Of more importance, doubtless, is the fact that the benefits of research conducted in our great metropolitan centers tend to reach rural areas only after a considerable lag. This is due not only to the usual psychological and sociological barriers to the diffusion of new knowledge,[32] but especially to the sheer lack of personnel, facilities, equipment, and effective organization through which to apply known advances in the medical sciences.

[31] Unpublished data of the United States Public Health Service, Division of Nursing.

[32] STERN, BERNHARD J., *Social Factors in Medical Progress*. New York: Columbia University Press, 1927.

CHAPTER 16

FACILITIES FOR ENVIRONMENTAL SANITATION

BEFORE disease strikes and has to be treated, it should obviously be prevented. Yet facilities for environmental sanitation
designed to prevent filth-borne disease are more desperately deficient in rural areas and small towns than facilities for medical care.

Family Sanitation Units

Geographic isolation naturally makes difficult the construction
and maintenance of all types of sanitary facilities. Water conduits or
sewer lines are economically out of the question for scattered farm
families in the open country. As a result, individual unit types of
water supply and excreta disposal are necessary. At their very best,
such units can be maintained properly only with constant attention
and effort. Without expenditures that are prohibitive for the great
majority of farm families, it is impossible for them to enjoy the
safety and convenience of sanitary facilities that have come to be
taken for granted by city families.

The typical facility for excreta disposal in rural sections, even in
the more prosperous farm areas, is the outdoor pit privy. Indoor
toilets with septic tanks and various drainage systems are still the
exception rather than the rule. Likewise, the outdoor well is the
typical facility for water supply, and indoor running water is an
uncommon luxury. Even in relation to the modest standards required
of these relatively primitive facilities, the great majority of rural
sanitary units are in need of replacement or improvement if rural
people are to be protected from filth-borne disease.

Of the 13,000,000 rural dwellings in unincorporated territory, the
1940 Census reported that about 8,500,000 were provided only with
outdoor toilets and an additional 850,000 had no toilet facilities
whatsoever. Yes, the approximately 4,000,000 rural people in these
latter homes had to dispose of human waste on the surface of the

ground. About 6,550,000 rural homes, farm and nonfarm, in unincorporated territory lacked indoor running water, and over 1,500,000 of these did not have a supply within even 50 feet of the house.[1] Taking farmhouses alone, running water was found in less than 18 per cent of them and indoor toilets in only 11 per cent. In urban

Table 30. Rural Sanitation Deficiencies: *Percentage of rural dwellings in open country and unincorporated places with specified sanitation deficiencies, by geographic divisions, 1940*

Geographic division	Number of dwellings	Sanitation deficiencies			
		No running water in house	No water supply at all within 50 feet	No indoor toilet	No toilet or privy at all
United States . .	12,971,360	50.5	11.8	72.1	6.5
New England . .	656,851	12.7	3.2	32.4	1.4
Middle Atlantic . .	1,518,092	18.7	3.1	47.2	1.3
East North Central .	2,033,798	45.5	5.3	73.3	2.0
West North Central	1,495,835	61.6	14.4	84.7	3.9
South Atlantic . .	2,285,741	60.7	15.2	79.8	10.4
East South Central .	1,668,543	79.8	20.9	90.3	16.4
West South Central	1,770,380	69.0	16.1	86.6	8.5
Mountain	558,164	47.0	20.8	74.2	6.6
Pacific	983,956	13.5	4.3	39.3	1.8

Source: Atkins, C. H., "National Inventory of Needs for Sanitation Facilities: IV. Rural Sanitation," *Public Health Reports*, 59:969-984, July 28, 1944.

dwellings, by contrast, 94 per cent had running water and 83 per cent had flush toilets.[2]

The extent of the major deficiencies in rural farm and nonfarm houses alike in the open country and unincorporated places is shown in Table 30, according to the geographic regions of the nation. It is evident that the greatest problems are found in the more underprivileged sections of the South, but it is just as significant that even in the more industrialized and prosperous sections rural dwellings have serious deficiencies. In the industrially developed Middle At-

[1] ATKINS, C. H., "National Inventory of Needs for Sanitation Facilities: IV. Rural Sanitation," *Public Health Reports*, 59:969-984, July 28, 1944.

[2] U. S. Census, 1940. Housing. Vol. 2, *General Characteristics*.

lantic states, for example, 18.7 per cent of the rural dwellings have no indoor running water and 47.2 per cent have no indoor toilets. Taking farmhouses alone, moreover, other data indicate that 61 per cent of the units in relatively prosperous New England have no indoor flush toilet and 43 per cent have no running water. In the large commercial farming section of the West North Central region, 86 per cent of the farmhouses have no running water and 91 per cent have no indoor toilets.[3]

Of the existing outdoor privies in the nation, 50 per cent are estimated by the United States Public Health Service to be insanitary and a menace to health, requiring replacement, in addition to the new units needed for families totally without any toilets. Of the water supplies within 50 feet of the house, 75 per cent are estimated to require improvement, and most of the sources over 50 feet from the dwelling require complete replacement.[4]

The determining factor in the adequacy of sanitation facilities within rural districts is clearly general income level. In the eight states with the highest per capita income, only 2 per cent of the farm dwellings were completely without any toilet or privy in 1940, while in the eight states with the lowest income, 16 per cent of the farm dwellings lacked such facilities. Likewise, only 3 per cent of the farm dwellings in the upper income states had no water supply within 50 feet of the house, compared with 19 per cent of the farm dwellings in the lower income states.[5]

Community Sanitation Facilities

Even in small, well-knit rural communities, free from the engineering difficulties of the open country, public sanitation systems are highly inadequate. Sanitary deficiencies are far greater in incorporated rural communities of under 2,500 population than in urban communities of over 2,500.

It may be seen in Table 31 that the greater deficiencies in villages and very small towns are evident not only in terms of the number of communities involved and their proportion in the total number of such communities in the nation, but also in terms of the number of

[3] *Ibid.*
[4] ATKINS, *op. cit.*
[5] Derived from ATKINS, *op. cit.*

persons affected. The rural-urban contrast is understated in the table, in that a large share of the communities of over 1,000 lacking sanitary facilities are, of course, under 2,500 in population and are accordingly rural. The relative disadvantage of the smallest communities, compared with the larger places, is greater with regard to water supply than sewer systems — although the absolute number of persons unprotected by sewer systems is greater in both types of communities. Furthermore, in addition to those indicated in the table,

Table 31.Community Sanitation Deficiencies: *Number and population of incorporated communities* needing new waterworks and sewer systems with sewage treatment plants, by size of community,* 1940

Community sanitation deficiency	Size of community	
	Under 1,000	1,000 and over
Waterworks needed:		
Communities	4,709	154
Percentage of all such communities	47	3
Population	1,589,063	222,366
Sewer system needed:		
Communities	6,723†	995
Percentage of all such communities	67†	15
Population	2,919,844	1,916,003

Source: U. S. Public Health Service, Sanitary Engineering Division "National Inventory of Need for Sanitation Facilities: III. Sewerage and Water Pollution Abatement," *Public Health Reports*, 59:857–882, July 7, 1944. Also Streeter, H. W. and Ray Raneri, "National Inventory of Needs for Sanitation Facilities: I. Public Water Supply," *Public Health Reports*, 59:1–20, Jan. 7, 1944.

* Data for certain states are incomplete; for details, see original source.

† Includes only communities of 201 to 1,000 population, omitting 1,537 incorporated places of 200 persons or less.

there are 686 communities of under 1,000 population, with an aggregate population of 450,000, that require new sewage treatment plants to supplement existing sewer systems.[6]

It must not be supposed that these villages in need of new sewer systems or waterworks are confined to the low income states of the South. Analysis of the deficiencies in the ten most urban and the ten most rural states for which data are available reveals the extensive

[6] U. S. Public Health Service, Sanitary Engineering Division, "National Inventory of Needs for Sanitation Facilities: III. Sewerage and Water Pollution Abatement," *Public Health Reports*, 59:857-882, July 7, 1944.

lacks in rural communities of urban and rural states alike. While the proportion of the state populations involved is greater for the rural states, the actual number of rural people in villages lacking sanitary facilities is greater in the urban states. Thus sewer systems are needed in 1,939 communities of 201 to 1,000, with a total population of 920,517 persons, in the ten most urban states, compared to 1,271 communities with 523,401 persons in the ten most rural states. Similarly, there is need for new waterworks in 1,065 towns of under 1,000 with 425,048 residents, in the most urban states, whereas there are 380,935 persons in 1,085 such towns in the most rural states.[7]

Deficiencies in other facilities for environmental sanitation, like the screening of houses or refrigeration for foods, have been touched on in Chap. 3. In the very sections where inadequate outdoor privies provide a breeding place for flies, the rural dwellings are least well screened. In a survey in the 1930's covering typical counties in 46 states, no screens at all were reported for 26.8 per cent of all farmhouses; and they were reported as poor for an additional 20.0 per cent, and as just fair in the case of 21.8 per cent more.[8] In the South only about 20 per cent of all the farmhouses surveyed had screens in good condition.[9] The price is paid in the occurrence of sporadic cases of fly-borne typhoid fever or mosquito-borne malaria in widespread rural districts.

Improper facilities for the collection and disposal of garbage, moreover, help keep alive the cycle of trichinosis between man and swine. Lack of proper facilities for the pasteurization of milk in rural regions is responsible for thousands of cases of milk-borne disease every year. In open country areas, the greater part of the milk supply is consumed unpasteurized. Even in communities of

[7] Derived from *Ibid.;* also STREETER, H. W., and RAY RANERI, "National Inventory of Needs for Sanitation Facilities: I. Public Water Supply," *Public Health Reports,* 59:1-20, Jan. 7, 1944.

[8] Some of the cases where screens were not reported may have been caused by failure on the part of the enumerator to report on the item rather than by lack of screens. There is strong evidence in the survey, however, that in the great majority of cases screens were lacking when not reported. Thus, screens were not reported for 4.3 per cent of farmhouses in New England, whereas the corresponding figure was 50.6 per cent for the South Atlantic region.

[9] U. S. Bureau of Home Economics, *The Farm-housing Survey* (U. S. Department of Agriculture Misc. Pub. 323). Washington: Government Printing Office, 1939, pp. 20-27.

between 1,000 and 2,500 population, only 25 per cent of the total milk supply marketed is pasteurized, compared with 98 per cent in cities of over 500,000.[10]

The inadequacies of rural sanitation, as well as rural housing, have an influence on rural life that far surpasses the effect of a few thousand cases of typhoid fever, dysentery, or undulant fever. Haphazard and slipshod sanitation has its effect in slovenly living. A child brought up without even the most elementary idea of acceptable personal habits is gravely handicapped in his development as an individual and as a member of society. The ultimate effects of poor sanitation on the health, morale, and social usefulness of many thousands of disadvantaged rural people are beyond measurement.

[10] ANDREWS, J., and A. W. FUCHS, "National Inventory of Needs for Sanitation Facilities: II. Milk Pasteurization Facilities," *Public Health Reports*, 59:189-204, Feb. 11, 1944.

THE TOTAL PICTURE of medical and sanitary facilities in rural areas is characterized by deficiencies both in quantity and quality, and above all, by lack of plan. In no way does the disparity in technical development between rural medicine and urban medicine become more evident than by comparing a typical small, proprietary rural hospital with a large, modern city institution. The disadvantages in supply and type of rural health facilities would be less distressing if full advantage could be taken of the potentialities of modern transportation. But to do this, more than combustion engines and gasoline are needed. Organization is required. Not only are new hospitals, health centers, clinics, laboratories, pharmacies, ambulances, and other units desperately needed, but — along with those already available — they must be tied together in a dynamic network to serve people wherever they live. With adequate organization, the loneliest farm family would be served by the specialized equipment in the teaching medical center of the metropolis. Without such organization, the liabilities of rural poverty and distance will serve to perpetuate present inequities.

PART V: MEDICAL SERVICES AND EXPENDITURES

WITH THE INADEQUACIES of medical personnel and facilities in rural areas, it is clear that rural people must receive a volume of medical services far below their true needs. The fact is that for practically every category of service, with the exception perhaps of the dubious benefits of midwives and patent medicines, the rural population receives services smaller in quantity and lower in quality than the urban and far less adequate than would be warranted by the burden of illness and impairment that it bears.

As with personnel and facilities, the chief determinant of the volume of services received appears to be income. The former Director of the Bureau of Medical Economics of the American Medical Association has stated

"Even if good medical service is desired, it cannot usually come into a community unless the demand for it is supported by adequate purchasing power. The most important factor in determining the character and extent of medical service in a community is the economic one."[1]

Not only does the income level of a family determine the volume of medical and related services that this family will receive, but the average income level of the entire community tends to put limits on the volume of services available to all its residents. The very lacks in personnel and facilities in rural areas obviously influence the amount of medical care received, and we have observed these conditions, themselves, to have economic origins. Geographic inaccessibility of existing facilities further aggravates the situation. Scarcity of physicians and hospitals in an area limits the availability of services even to the prosperous families in the area. Money, of course, allows a family in a community of meager resources to travel long distances for medical services; to some extent, nevertheless, the wealthy landowner or the village banker must share the deficiencies in services suffered by the poorest farmer in the county. Even for the same income groups, rural people tend to receive fewer medical and related services than city dwellers. Negative attitudes of mind toward medical care often ascribed to rural people are essentially a result rather than a cause of rural deficiencies.

[1] LELAND, R. G., "Medical Care for Rural America," *Rural Medicine* (Proceedings of the Conference Held at Cooperstown, New York, Oct. 7 and 8, 1938). Springfield, Illinois: Charles C. Thomas, Publisher, 1939, p. 228.

Less service is predominantly the result of low medical expenditures by rural families. Yet the percentage of income they spend for medical care actually exceeds the percentage spent by urban families. The sparsity of high-quality services in country districts even suggests that, for the same money spent, the rural family tends to get less real value. Proportionately more is spent on self-prescribed drugs, for example, proportionately less on specialists. Finally, the unevenness with which medical costs fall on rural families, depriving them often of other essentials of living or impeding farm production, is quite as distressing as among urban families.

CHAPTER 17

MEDICAL SERVICES RECEIVED

THE MEDICAL and allied services received by a family or a community naturally bear some relation to the volume and kinds of sickness experienced. It cannot be stressed too much, however, that purchasing power is a far more decisive determinant of services received than health needs. When a country dweller gets sick he is less likely to get medical services of almost any kind than a city dweller. Considering just illness disabling for a week or more, for example, 83 per cent of the cases in cities of over 100,000 population received some type of physicians' care and 30 per cent were hospitalized, according to the National Health Survey of 1935-36. In cities and towns of under 25,000, 75 per cent of disabling cases were attended by a physician and only 19 per cent were hospitalized. In representative rural counties of Missouri, investigated as part of the same survey, only about 57 per cent of the patients disabled for a week or more received medical attention.[1]

For all illnesses, including those which may not drive the patient to bed but which may be quite as serious in the long run, the discrepancy between medical services received by rural and urban populations is undoubtedly greater. In one rural community of Arkansas, for example, 85 per cent of all reported illnesses in the lowest income group were unattended by a physician, and even among the highest income families ($2,000 a year and over) 61 per cent of illnesses went unattended.[2] In communities of all sizes, the proportion of unattended illnesses is higher in the lower income groups. Because of the lack of publicly supported community facilities for medical care in rural sections, the discrepancy in services received by rural families of different income is especially striking. Thus in five representative rural counties of Missouri studied during

[1] BRITTEN, ROLLO H., "Receipt of Medical Services in Different Urban Population Groups," *Public Health Reports*, 55:2199-2224, Nov. 29, 1940.

[2] WILSON, ISABELLA C., *Sickness and Medical Care among the Rural Population in a Petroleum-producing Area of Arkansas*, 1938. Fayetteville: University of Arkansas Agricultural Experiment Station (Bull. 413), June, 1941.

1939-42, families with annual incomes of $2,000 and over had more than twice as many calls by medical practitioners, were twice as likely to use a dentist, and had 13 times as many days in a general hospital as those with incomes of under $250.[3] In the course of a year, regardless of the illness rate, at least 20 per cent more rural persons receive no medical care at all than persons of comparable income in the large cities.[4]

The Services of Physicians

Of all health services, the services of physicians are probably most fundamental. In a sense, an adequate amount of good care by physicians will reduce the need for other types of service like hospitalization, drugs, nursing care, or appliances; the early diagnosis and effective treatment of illness can prevent advanced disease requiring more extensive care. In rural districts the services of the "family doctor" take on added importance because they represent to so great an extent the sum total of available medical care. A crude reflection of the desperate lack of medical services in some rural sections is seen in the high proportion of deaths in rural states not attended by a physician. In Mississippi, for example, 18.5 per cent of the persons dying in 1933 were not seen by a physician even in their final illness. In Georgia in that year 16.9 per cent of the deaths were completely without medical attendance, and in Arkansas 15.3 per cent of the deaths.[5] What then must the medical attendance be for illness of less serious character?

Some idea of the specific deficiencies of medical attendance in rural areas is conveyed by a 1937 study in two Southern counties.[5a]

[3] KAUFMAN, HAROLD F., *Use of Medical Services in Rural Missouri.* Columbia: University of Missouri, Agricultural Experiment Station (Research Bull. 400), April, 1946, p. 4.

[4] Data of the Committee on the Costs of Medical Care in HOLLINGSWORTH, HELEN, and MARGARET C. KLEM, *Medical Care and Costs in Relation to Family Income* (U. S. Social Security Board, Bureau of Research and Statistics Mem. 51). Washington, March, 1943, Processed, p. 105.

[5] UNDERWOOD, FELIX J., Testimony before the Committee on Finance, U. S. Senate, 74th Cong., 1st Sess., on *Economic Security Act.* Washington: Government Printing Office, 1935, pp. 411-416.

[5a] MOUNTIN, JOSEPH W., ELLIOTT H. PENNELL, and HAZEL O'HARA, "Relationship of a Rural Health Program to the Needs in the Area," *Public Health Reports,* 52:1264-1284, Sept. 10, 1937.

Considering only illnesses confining the individual to bed for at least one day, it was found that about 40 per cent were not attended by a physician. The lowest rate of attendance was for epidemic, endemic, and infectious diseases — affecting predominantly children — of which 59 per cent were not seen by a doctor. Respiratory diseases, the most frequent cause of disability, were unattended in 45 per cent of the cases. Diseases of the eyes, the ears, the skin, and the teeth were not attended in about 53 per cent of the cases. Disabling illnesses of the kidneys and the circulatory system and accidents were not medically attended in 10 to 15 per cent of the cases; rheumatism and certain general diseases in over 20 per cent of the cases; digestive and nervous disorders and nonvenereal diseases of the genitalia in over 30 per cent of the cases; and diseases of the bones, congenital malformations, and ill-defined conditions in over 40 per cent of the cases. That these deficiencies in medical care did not simply reflect trivial disorders is indicated by the fact that 72 per cent of the cases were confined to bed for three days or longer. As might be expected, nonattendance was higher among the poorer families.

The best over-all index of physicians' services is probably the number of medical calls in the home or office per 1,000 persons per year.[6] In 1928-31, it was found that while in cities of 100,000 and over this ratio was 3,000 calls per 1,000 persons per year, and in cities of 5,000 to 100,000 it was 2,680 calls, in towns of under 5,000 and rural areas it was only 2,240 calls per 1,000 persons per year.[7] With the accelerated concentration of physicians in the cities since the time of this study and the aging of country doctors, it is likely that the differentials today are more striking.

The additional fee charged by the country physician for travel to a patient's home tends to induce the rural patient either to visit the

[6] Some 90 to 92 per cent of all physicians' calls have customarily been for the management of illness, the remainder being for such services as immunizations or examinations of the presumably healthy individual. FALK, I. S., MARGARET C. KLEM, and NATHAN SINAI, *The Incidence of Illness and the Receipt and Costs of Medical Care among Representative Families* (Committee on the Costs of Medical Care Pub. 26). Chicago: University of Chicago Press, 1933, p. 283.

[7] COLLINS, SELWYN D., "The Frequency and Volume of Doctors' Calls among Males and Females in 9,000 Families, Based on Nation-wide Periodic Canvasses 1928-31," *Public Health Reports*, 55:1977-2020, Nov. 1, 1940.

doctor's office or to go without needed care. If we consider home calls alone, in large and medium-sized cities the respective rates were 1,190 and 1,170 calls per 1,000 persons per year, while in small towns and rural areas the rate was only 830.[8] It is not surprising that the lowest rate of physicians' calls is for those made to the homes of families living farthest out in the open country.[9] In any one illness, moreover, the services to rural families are fewer. In large cities there has been an average of 3.8 office and home calls per case, in medium-sized cities 3.2 calls, and in small towns and rural areas only 2.6 calls for each case of illness.[10]

Table 32. Physicians' Services: *Number of home and office calls per 1,000 persons per year, by size of community and annual family income, 1928–31*

Size of community	Family income group			
	Under $1,200	$1,200–$1,999	$2,000–$2,999	$3,000–$4,999
New York City and Chicago	2,710	2,080	1,880	2,380
Other cities over 100,000	2,060	1,740	2,320	3,000
5,000–100,000	1,950	2,180	2,480	2,640
Under 5,000	1,970	2,090	2,360	2,470
Open country	1,150	1,570	1,780	2,280

Source: Data of the Committee on the Costs of Medical Care, 1928–31, in Hollingsworth, Helen, and Margaret C. Klem, *Medical Care and Costs in Relation to Family Income* (U. S. Social Security Board, Bureau of Research and Statistics Mem. 51). Washington, March, 1943, Processed, p. 137.

The relationship of these medical services to family income in rural communities is even more striking. It is evident from Table 32 that for each income level the physicians' home and office calls received by families in the open country are considerably fewer than for the same income level in urban communities of any size. The volume of care for the lowest rural income group, moreover, is only half of that for the highest. An analysis of this experience by age groups shows that the greatest rural-urban discrepancies in volume

[8] *Ibid.*

[9] ALMACK, R. B., *The Rural Health Facilities of Lewis County, Missouri.* Columbia: University of Missouri College of Agriculture (Research Bull. 365), May, 1943, p. 6.

[10] COLLINS, *op. cit.*

of services received are in the care of babies under 1 year of age and in the 45-64 year age bracket.[11]

Among the most distressing medical deficiencies in rural areas is the inadequacy of maternity services. The rural baby is brought into the world by unskilled hands far more often than the city baby. In the rural state of Mississippi, as many as 46.2 per cent of live births were not attended by a physician in 1942 compared with less than 1/10 of 1 per cent of the births in urbanized Massachusetts.[12] Rural-urban discrepancies in obstetrical services are more striking than for physicians' care in general. Since maternity care is related closely to hospitalization, general rural-urban comparisons will be presented in the next section, which deals with hospital care.

Concerning the services of specialists, other than surgeons, there are few comparative data, but it may be inferred that with the meager supply of specialists accessible to rural people, services received from them must be few indeed. Regarding surgical care, specific data are at hand. It is no surprise that, of all illnesses, fewer receive surgical intervention in the rural areas than in the cities. In communities of over 100,000, 9.0 per cent of all illnesses have been found to be treated surgically; in cities of 5,000 to 100,000, the percentage was 7.8; in towns of under 5,000, it was 6.4; and in open country districts 6.0 per cent.[13] Some might claim that this withholding of the knife is a good thing and that the cities are all too "surgically minded." The rural community and small town, however, have their own share of unnecessary surgical interference, especially where the local doctor is "physician and surgeon," as his shingle often displays, and the tempering influence of the consulting internist is not at hand. That real surgical needs, nevertheless, are simply not being met is cogently demonstrated by the heavy burden of uncorrected physical impairments that we have found revealed on medical examination of rural groups.

The Committee on the Costs of Medical Care found surgical oper-

[11] HOLLINGSWORTH and KLEM, *op. cit.*, p. 139.

[12] U. S. Bureau of the Census, *Vital Statistics of the United States*, 1942. Part 2, *Natality and Mortality Data for the United States Tabulated by Place of Residence*. Washington: Government Printing Office, 1944.

[13] COLLINS, SELWYN D., "Percentage of Illnesses Treated Surgically among 9,000 Families, Based on Nation-wide Periodic Canvasses 1928-31," *Public Health Reports*, 53:1593-1616, Sept. 9, 1938.

ations performed at a rate of 72.8 per 1,000 persons per year in cities of 100,000 and over, 69.0 per 1,000 in cities of 5,000 to 100,000, 60.4 in towns of under 5,000, and 47.7 in open country districts. It is evident that residents of cities of over 100,000 have 53 per cent more surgical operations than country dwellers. An analysis of these figures by age groups demonstrates that the differentials hold for all ages. Analysis by income levels discloses that for the lowest annual income group, under $1,200 per family, rural sections lag behind the big cities by an even greater amount — by 73 per cent.[14]

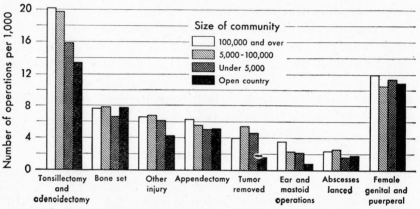

Fig. 25. Types of Surgical Procedure: Number of specified types of operation per 1,000 persons per year, by size of community, 1928-31. Source: Collins, Selwyn D., "Frequency of Surgical Procedures among 9,000 Families, 1928-31" (Committee on the Costs of Medical Care data), *Public Health Reports*, 53:587-628, Apr. 22, 1938.

Consideration of the precise types of surgical operations performed discloses more clearly the nature of rural surgical services. It may be observed in Figure 25 that for the period under study, the performance of operations of a more or less emergency nature differed little in rural and urban sections. Thus the rate of fracture reductions is about the same in all places and the rate of appendectomies appears to be only slightly lower in rural communities.[15] When medical

[14] COLLINS, SELWYN D., "Frequency of Surgical Procedures among 9,000 Families, Based on Nation-wide Periodic Canvasses, 1928-31," *Public Health Reports*, 53:587-628, Apr. 22, 1938.

[15] It is possible that some operations recorded, particularly in rural practice, under "appendectomy" as a catch-all are due actually to conditions other than appendicitis.

service appears to be a matter of life and death, handicaps of distance and money can often be overcome. For elective conditions, however, where well-being and working efficiency are at stake, the country dweller gets much less surgical care than the urbanite. The frequency of ear surgery, removal of tumors, miscellaneous abdominal operations, and care of general injuries, not to mention tonsillectomies,[16] is considerably lower in small towns and open country. The close comparability of surgical rates for female genital and puerperal conditions probably understates the real relationship, for, in view of higher rural fecundity, rural needs for this type of surgery are doubtless greater.

An evaluation of the quality of medical service rendered by most rural physicians and surgeons is almost self-evident from our earlier consideration of the characteristics and current professional setting of rural medicine. If the quality of medical service were to be expressed quantitatively, most of the rural-urban differentials reviewed would doubtless be widened.

Hospitalization

Being more costly than physicians' care in the home or office, hospital services in rural areas might be expected to fall farther below urban experience than the rate of physicians' services. Such is the case. By whatever index we judge, rural people get considerably less hospital service than urban and this holds for all age groups and income levels. Hospital experience has become rather commonplace in American cities, but in rural districts it remains a relatively unusual event.

Around 1930, the Committee on the Costs of Medical Care found 7.1 per cent of large-city residents to have some hospital experience in an average year, compared with 4.6 per cent in small towns and rural sections.[17] Today urban experience has risen closer to 10 per cent, judging somewhat by Blue Cross hospitalization plan experience, and the occupancy of rural hospitals has likewise risen with relative prosperity, as previously noted. The discrepancy, however, between country and city experience undoubtedly remains.

Of all known cases of illness, the Committee on the Costs of Medi-

[16] See footnote 23, Chap. 5.
[17] FALK, KLEM, and SINAI, *op. cit.*, p. 280.

cal Care found 8.5 per cent hospitalized in the cities of over 100,000 population, compared with 5.2 per cent among open country residents.[18] This meant that 67.5 cases of illness were being hospitalized per 1,000 persons per year in the large cities for a total of 858 hospital days; as communities declined in size, these rates consistently fell, and among open country residents the experience was only 42.0 cases per 1,000 persons per year and a total of 505 hospital days. These figures describe experience in general and allied hospitals (not tuberculosis or mental institutions) at any location, not necessarily in the local community. More recent data on hospitalization experience by groups of whole states are presented in Table 33. It

Table 33. Hospitalization Experience: *Rates of admission to general hospitals, duration of stay, and number of days hospitalized per 1,000 persons per year in states grouped by rurality, 1940*

Per cent rural (state populations)	Hospital admissions per 1,000 persons	Average hospital days per case	Hospital days per 1,000 persons
Under 30	84	13.4	1,126
30–39	69	13.3	921
40–49	71	12.4	883
50–59	71	10.1	768
60–69	56	12.0	673
70 and over	50	10.3	517

Source: Derived from American Medical Association, Council on Medical Education and Hospitals, "Hospital Service in the United States," *Journal of the American Medical Association*, 116:1083–1142, Mar. 15, 1941.

may be noted that the most rural segment of states shows 68 per cent fewer hospital admissions than the most urban segment. Once hospitalized, the rural case tends to stay a somewhat shorter period of time, so that the aggregate of hospital days per 1,000 persons per year in the most rural states is less than half that in the most urban states.

Analysis of hospitalization experience by economic levels reveals a much more striking dependence of hospital care on income in rural areas than in urban. Figure 26 indicates this relationship. It

[18] COLLINS, SELWYN D., "Variation in Hospitalization with Size of City, Family Income, and other Environmental Factors," *Public Health Reports*, 57:1635-1659, Oct. 30, 1942. (Based on data of the Committee on the Costs of Medical Care.)

is clear that for all income levels rural experience is much less than urban but in the lowest bracket, in which most rural people are actually found, the differential is greatest. In fact, it may be seen that in the large cities persons of lowest income actually have more hospital admissions than persons of highest income — a fact related not only to higher illness rates among the poor but also to a relative

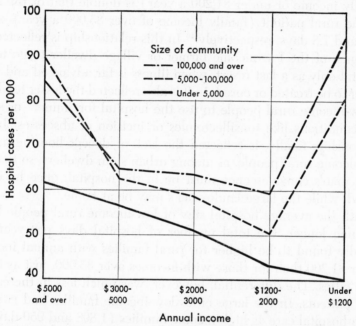

Fig. 26. Hospitalization and Income: Number of hospital admissions per 1,000 persons per year by annual family income and size of community, 1928-31. Source: Collins, Selwyn D., "Variation in Hospitalization with Size of City, Family Income, and other Environmental Factors 1928-31" (Committee on the Costs of Medical Care data), *Public Health Reports*, 57:1635-1659, Oct. 30, 1942.

abundance of "free" or so-called charity beds in the big cities. Even in medium-sized cities this tendency is found, with the lowest income persons having more admissions than those with incomes up to $5,000 a year. In rural sections, however, where community-sponsored beds are few, we find the most prosperous groups having the most admissions and the poorest groups having the fewest. Whatever is true in the cities about the "great middle-income group" suffering the most inadequate medical care is certainly not

true in the country, where hospital admissions quite directly follow
the dollar sign.

The average lengths of hospital stay of different income groups
reflect the influence of the cash barrier to medical care on the entire
problem of sickness. For, although admission rates are lower, the
average hospital stay of the relatively low-income rural patient
(family income of under $1,200 a year) is double that of the high-
income rural patient (family income of over $5,000 a year) — 16.3
days and 7.8 days, respectively.[19] In this relationship is reflected the
tendency of the low-income farmer or village dweller to go to the
hospital only as a last resort, when illness is far advanced and takes
longer to be treated or cured. In it is also reflected the lesser tendency
of low-income rural people to use the hospital for "minor" or short-
stay conditions like tonsillectomies or incision of abscesses. In the
relationship, finally, is reflected the lack of decent housing among
low-income rural people, as among urban slum dwellers, so that the
hired man's convalescence must be in the hospital, once he is admitted, while the large landowner's may be at home.

With the average hospital stay of low-income rural people being
so much longer, the total number of hospital days per year was
actually found to be higher for rural families with annual incomes
under $1,200 than for those with incomes over $5,000, just as in the
large cities. The differential, however, was much less in the case of
rural patients. In the large cities low-income families had twice as
much hospital care as high-income families (1,808 and 950 days per
1,000 persons per year, respectively), while in rural areas the low-
income exceeded the high-income experience by only 40 per cent
(695 and 499 days per 1,000 persons, respectively).[20] This rural
differential may even be overdrawn, inasmuch as the top limit of the
lowest income bracket, $1,200, actually represents a moderately good
income in most rural sections. If rural income brackets were to be
more realistically defined, it might be found that aggregate hospital care experience in the lowest income group (for example, under
$600 a year family income) would, in fact, be less than that in the
highest income group.

Analysis of hospitalization by type of case gives further insight
into the characteristics of rural hospital service. In 1930, just about

19 *Ibid.*
20 *Ibid.*

half the days of hospitalization of open country residents were for surgical cases and the other half for nonsurgical, while in large cities the surgical days exceeded the nonsurgical by 21 per cent. The differential was mainly referable to the 20-44 year age bracket,[21] the group among whom perhaps most elective surgery — such as for hernias, gall bladders, deviated nasal septums, and so forth — is performed. Since that time the introduction of new forms of chemo- therapy may have altered the picture somewhat, but a consideration of the matter by rural-urban groups of states shows the same essen- tial relationship. Thus, in 1942 about 46 per cent of hospitalized cases in states over 70 per cent urban were operated on, while in states over 70 per cent rural the comparable percentage was 41.[22] For better or for worse, rural medicine appears to be less surgically minded.

One of the most characteristic benefits of modern medicine is the hospitalization of women in childbirth. Yet at present only a minority of rural babies are born in hospitals. Among residents of urban com- munities in 1942, 84.4 per cent of all maternity cases were hos- pitalized, whereas the rural rate was only 44.8 per cent. Of rural white births alone, 50.9 per cent were hospitalized and of rural non-white births, only 10.5 per cent. Only 2.6 per cent of urban births were without either hospital care or medical attendance in 1942, but such backward conditions characterized 14.2 per cent of all rural births.[23] The relative maternity care experience in rural and urban areas is presented in Figure 27. The degree of disparity is further illustrated by a maternity hospitalization rate of 10.2 per cent in rural sections of Kentucky, compared with 96.9 per cent in the urban parts of Oregon — or even in comparison with 62.6 per cent in the urban centers of Kentucky. It is significant that even in prosperous New York State some 21 per cent of the rural babies were born in 1942 without benefit of hospital surroundings.[24]

The relation of this disparity in hospital care for childbirth to the high maternal and infant mortality rates in rural areas need hardly

[21] *Ibid.*

[22] Derived from American Medical Association, Council on Medical Educa- tion and Hospitals, "Hospital Service in the United States," *Journal of the American Medical Association*, 121:1018, Mar. 27, 1943.

[23] U. S. Census, "Live Births by Person in Attendance, United States, 1942," *Vital Statistics — Special Reports*, 19: 93-106, Mar. 24, 1944.

[24] *Ibid.*

be mentioned. The general reduction in infant and maternal deaths in recent years[25] bears a striking relationship to the over-all increase in the percentage of births hospitalized. The lesson to be drawn, if rural rates of maternal and neonatal death are to be reduced, is self-evident.

It is sometimes claimed that hospital usage in rural areas is low because, on the one hand, rural people may consider it a sign of

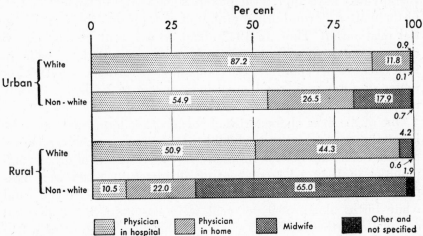

FIG. 27. Hospital and Medical Care at Childbirth: Percentage of live births occurring in hospitals and births otherwise attended, by urban and rural character of place of residence and by race, 1942. Source: Derived from U. S. Bureau of the Census, *Vital Statistics of the United States, 1942. Part 2, Natality and Mortality Data for the United States Tabulated by Place of Residence.* Washington, 1944, p. 142.

weakness to yield to hospitalization or, on the other, they may be afraid of doctors and scalpels and fear that hospitalization means they risk their lives. The real effect of attitudes and fears of this kind cannot be denied, but that they develop as psychological adjustments to customary lacks is reflected by the relation of hospital usage to the mere physical accessibility of the institution. Selwyn D. Collins found, for example, that hospital care experience in small towns and

[25] This trend has been associated not only with a rise in purchasing power, but also with special programs to be discussed later like the expanding maternal hygiene services under the Social Security Act, the Emergency Maternity and Infant Care program for the wives of servicemen, and the spread of group hospitalization insurance.

open country where facilities were deemed to be reasonably accessible amounted to 47.9 cases and 603 hospital days per 1,000 persons per year, while in such places without accessible facilities the experience was 40.5 cases and 483 hospital days per 1,000.[26] When rural families lived within 5 miles of the hospital, 6.0 per cent of all cases of illness were hospitalized, while in families living over 15 miles from the hospital, this was true of only 4.8 per cent of cases. The same relationship held for both surgical and nonsurgical cases. Even the character of the roads appeared to have an effect, with somewhat more of the disabling cases becoming hospitalized if the roads to the hospital were good than if they were poor. The educational and suggestive influence of having a hospital close at hand, as well as its physical accessibility, must be partly accountable for these influences. Distance means unfamiliarity, so that there would be less inclination for the country dweller to leave home for some rather strange, far-off institution.

Long distances, of course, are less of a handicap to hospitalization if funds are ample. Antonio Ciocco has shown, with respect to hospitalized births, that when local facilities are lacking, income is the decisive factor in out-of-county movement.[27] Thus, in poor counties, with per capita effective buying income of $300 or less, and despite having no hospital beds at all, only 12 per cent of births were hospitalized outside the county. In prosperous counties, on the other hand, with $900 or more per capita income, as many as 53 per cent of births were hospitalized out of the county when local beds were lacking.

The attitudes of many rural people toward hospitalization are undoubtedly conditioned by their seldom having enjoyed the experience of service in a modern, well-operated institution, with a thoroughly competent and well-rounded staff of professional personnel. As measures are taken to make such resources available, and as economic barriers are broken down, attitudes built up over the years may confidently be expected to change. Meanwhile there is little in actual experience to warrant the extreme attitude ascribed

[26] COLLINS, SELWYN D., "Variation in Hospitalization with Size of City, Family Income, and other Environmental Factors 1928-31," op. cit.

[27] CIOCCO, ANTONIO, "Birth Statistics as an Index of Interdependence of Counties with Regard to Medical Services," Public Health Reports, 60: 973-985, Aug. 24, 1945.

to many rural people that "hospitals are places to die in." It is possible that a higher proportion of admissions of rural people eventuate in death than among city dwellers, simply because relatively more country dwellers use the hospital only as a last resort when sickness is advanced. A much smaller share of total rural deaths, however, is associated with hospitalization than of total urban deaths. In 1942, almost 40 per cent of the deaths in the seven most urban states occurred in general hospitals, whereas only 24 per cent of the deaths in the seven most rural states were in such institutions.[28] If the alleged fear of hospitals were based upon actual mortality experience, rather than defense mechanisms in adjustment to handicaps stemming from economic and geographic roots, one might expect it to be more characteristic of persons in the big cities.

The general quality of service provided by most hospitals serving rural people may be surmised from the earlier consideration of their deficiencies in equipment and staff. A "day of hospitalization" in the average rural hospital clearly implies less in diagnostic and therapeutic services than a comparable day in the average urban institution. Resources for highly specialized types of care are meager, indeed, in local general hospitals, and special or allied institutions are seldom within reach. Country dwellers of high income, it is true, can sometimes afford to travel long distances in their search for specialized care. The Texas ranch owner with a cataract may be satisfied with nothing less than service at an eye hospital in Philadelphia. Yet, between the barriers of cost and the frequent disinclination of the local doctor to refer the patient to a specialist at a distance, the great majority of rural patients simply fail to get the benefit of special skills in first-rate institutions.

Hospital services available to rural people either in tuberculosis sanatoria or in mental disease hospitals run parallel to the general sparsity of facilities of these types in the more rural states. The tuberculosis sanatorium in a rural state, unlike the general hospital, is usually filled to capacity, and the length of its waiting list is a partial reflection of serious unmet needs. So far as the care of mental disorders is concerned, the rates of hospitalization for the principal types of disorder are shown in Table 34. Despite the general simi-

[28] U. S. Census, "Deaths in Institutions by Type of Service and Control, United States, 1942," *Vital Statistics — Special Reports*, 19:127-130, Apr. 3, 1944.

larity of the problem in rural and urban areas, it is evident that for the three principal categories of mental disorder — mental disease, mental deficiency, and epilepsy — the most rural regions tend to have the lowest admission rates. The poorer quality of service provided in the mental institutions serving relatively more rural than

Table 34. Mental Hospital Care: *Number of admissions to mental hospitals for specified conditions per* 100,000 *population aged* 15 *and over, by regions in order of rurality,* 1938

Region	Per cent rural	Admissions per 100,000				
		Mental disease	Mental deficiency	Epilepsy	Other	Total
Middle Atlantic . . .	23.2	619.2	135.4	25.0	2.5	782.1
New England	23.9	677.8	159.1	27.5	6.9	871.3
East North Central . .	34.5	472.5	125.6	25.2	12.5	635.8
Pacific	34.7	470.6	84.0	11.4	10.1	576.1
West North Central . .	55.7	455.9	120.2	30.6	8.0	614.7
Mountain	57.3	375.8	87.2	15.5	6.1	484.6
West South Central . .	60.2	333.6	37.7	17.8	8.8	397.9
South Atlantic . . .	61.2	383.2	48.0	12.7	5.2	449.1
East South Central . .	70.6	328.9	33.4	4.7	3.7	369.7

Source: Hamilton, S. W., G. A. Kempf, G. C. Scholz, and E. G. Caswell, *A Study of the Public Mental Hospitals of the United States*, 1937–39 (Supp. 164 to the Public Health Reports). Washington: Government Printing Office, 1941, pp. 25–26.

urban people is reflected by the average number of patients handled by each hospital employee in the more rural states. Ratios of 4.0 or 4.2 patients per employee in urban states like Massachusetts or New York may be compared with ratios of 10.2 or 11.4 patients per employee in rural states like Kentucky or Montana.[29]

Nursing Services

Associated naturally with the low volume of rural hospital services and the inadequate supply of rural nurses is a low volume of nursing services for rural people. Less hospitalization in rural communities

[29] HAMILTON, S. W., G. A. KEMPF, G. C. SCHOLZ, and E. G. CASWELL, *A Study of the Public Mental Hospitals of the United States*, 1937-39 (Supp. 164 to the Public Health Reports). Washington: Government Printing Office, 1941, pp. 47-48.

obviously implies less service from general duty nurses in hospitals. As for individual nursing services, the Committee on the Costs of Medical Care found rural experience likewise to be lower, with about 15 per cent of small-town and rural families getting such services in a year, compared with about 20 per cent of families in urban places of over 5,000 population.[30] These figures include the services

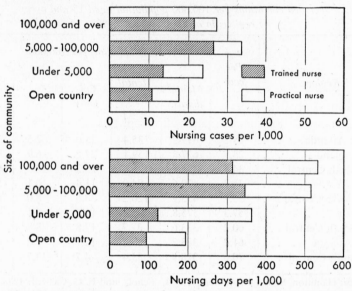

FIG. 28. Nursing Services: Number of cases and days per 1,000 persons per year with private duty service from trained and practical nurses, by size of community, 1928-31. Source: Collins, Selwyn D., "Variation in Nursing Service with Family Income and Size of City" (Committee on the Costs of Medical Care data), *The Milbank Memorial Fund Quarterly*, 21:188-213, April, 1943.

of visiting or public health nurses. When private duty nursing services alone are considered, the differentials are more striking. As shown in Figure 28, in cities of 100,000 and over there have been 21.5 cases with private trained nurses (in or outside the hospital) per 1,000 persons per year, compared with 10.8 cases per 1,000 persons in the open country.[31]

Rural-urban differentials in the private services of practical as

[30] FALK, KLEM, and SINAI, *op. cit.*, p. 92.

[31] COLLINS, SELWYN D., "Variation in Nursing Service with Family Income and Size of City," *The Milbank Memorial Fund Quarterly*, 21:188-213, April, 1943. (Based on data of the Committee on the Costs of Medical Care.)

well as trained nurses are illustrated in Figure 28. The total rate of nursing service in days per year in the large cities is much more than twice that in the open country. It is evident that rural and small-town residents receive private nursing care not only in fewer cases and for a shorter aggregate period of time, but their nursing tends to consist more largely of the work of practical rather than professional nurses. Thus while about 32 per cent of all days of nursing service in urban places of over 5,000 were rendered by nongraduate nurses, about 58 per cent of all such days in small towns and rural areas were so rendered.[32] The chief source of these over-all urban-rural discrepancies is found in the care of surgical cases. The practical nurse, so important in the rural pattern, is utilized chiefly for nonsurgical cases. It seems particularly unfortunate that the services of visiting nurses, who could save the doctor many hours of travel, are found least in rural sections. This differential, again, is mainly referable to surgical cases.

Among open country residents there are marked differences in the receipt of nursing services depending on family income. Families with annual incomes under $1,200 had a total of 101 days of nursing service per 1,000 persons per year in 1928-31, compared with a rate five times as high for families with annual incomes of over $5,000. Only for visiting nurses' services, provided largely out of tax or philanthropic funds, was the volume of services higher in lower income groups.[33]

There is naturally a vast degree of variation among rural counties in nursing services received. In rural counties like Crawford, Otsego, or Roscommon in Michigan, 10.3 per cent of disabling illnesses were found to be getting private duty and 9.1 per cent getting visiting nurse care, while Livingstone and Linn Counties in Missouri showed comparable service to only 1.5 and 1.4 per cent of disabling illnesses, respectively.[34] These findings apply only to residents of towns and villages under 2,500; families in the open country receive less service all along the line.

The nurse in the rural hospital, working with few auxiliary employees, has less time to devote strictly to the nursing care of her patients than the city hospital nurse. Without the student nurses

[32] *Ibid.*
[33] *Ibid.*
[34] BRITTEN, *op. cit.*

provided by a nursing school, moreover, the net hours of general duty nursing time available to each hospital patient in a small rural hospital tend to be fewer than in the average city institution. A nation-wide study recently showed that in hospitals without nursing schools 2.8 hours of nursing time were provided per patient per day, compared with 3.7 hours in hospitals with schools of nursing, or 3.1 hours when the lesser effectiveness of student nurses is taken into account.[35] The general quality of performance of the average rural nurse may be gathered from her frequent training handicaps and the technical qualifications of the physicians under whose supervision she works. However, the rural public health nurse often excels her urban associate in training and professional performance.

Dental Services

To an even greater extent than other health services, dental care represents a serious deficiency in rural life. To the extent that dental services are received, their net results are slightly mindful of those produced by the old-time country-fair artisan who would yank out the farmer's painful tooth, rather than of the modern preventive and prosthetic dentistry practiced widely in our larger cities.

According to the Committee on the Costs of Medical Care, only 17.1 per cent of persons in small towns and open country received any dental service in a year, compared with 22.7 per cent in medium-sized communities and 26.7 per cent in the big cities. Among rural families with incomes under $1,200 a year, the comparable experience was 9.1 per cent.[36] It is easy to evaluate these figures, for we know that good dental care would call for virtually 100 per cent of the population receiving services at least once yearly. The vast accumulation of untreated dental defects in our population shows how far we are from this goal, and the evidence of neglect is greater among rural people.[37] As for dental cases treated, 313 received care

[35] ALTENDERFER, M. E., "Wartime Nursing Care in Representative General Hospitals," *Public Health Reports*, 60:90-99, Jan. 26, 1945.

[36] FALK, KLEM, and SINAI, *op. cit.*, p. 280.

[37] PARRAN, THOMAS, Testimony before a Subcommittee of the Committee on Education and Labor, U. S. Senate, 79th Cong., 1st Sess., S. 190 and S. 1099, *Dental Research and Dental Care*. Washington: Government Printing Office, 1945, pp. 18-19. See also the section "Dental Disease" in Chap. 7.

per 1,000 persons per year in large cities, during 1928-31, compared with 159 cases among open country people, or only about half as many. This relationship held for all ages, but the greatest differential applied to the youth group (15-19 years) and to the years past 45.[38]

The relationship of dental services to income in rural areas is more striking than for almost any other type of medical care, indicating

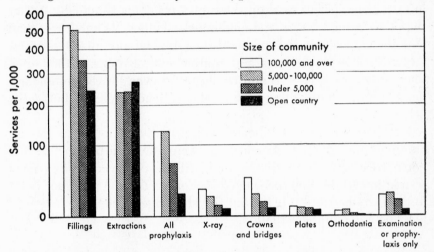

FIG. 29. Dental Care: Number of specified dental services per 1,000 persons per year, by size of community, 1928-31. Source: Collins, Selwyn D., "Frequency of Dental Services among 9,000 Families" (Committee on the Costs of Medical Care data), *Public Health Reports*, 54:629-657, Apr. 21, 1939.

perhaps the minor extent to which dental care has been made a public or a "charitable" function. The frequency of dental cases receiving services in small towns and rural areas in the family income bracket under $1,200 has been reported as 107 per 1,000 persons per year. This may be compared with 320 cases for the $3,000-$5,000 bracket or 459 cases for the $5,000-and-over bracket. Although the same relationship holds in big cities, it is less striking there; due perhaps to free public facilities, the poorest persons in big cities get 37 per cent of the rate of services received by the wealthiest, while

[38] COLLINS, SELWYN D., "Frequency of Dental Services among 9,000 Families, Based on Nation-wide Periodic Canvasses, 1928-31," *Public Health Reports*, 54:629-657, Apr. 21, 1939.

in rural sections the poorest get only 23 per cent of the services obtained at the highest income levels.[39]

The true nature of rural dental care is better revealed by a consideration of the specific services rendered. These are illustrated in Figure 29. It is evident that for extractions or the fitting of dental plates — services representing the end result of failure to preserve teeth — rural services are only slightly below urban. For extractions, in fact, the experience of open country residents is actually higher than that in small towns and medium-sized cities, though lower than that in large cities. For preventive or highly specialized services, however, like prophylaxes and routine examinations, orthodontia, diagnostic x rays, crowns and bridges, and even for the commonest dental service of all, fillings, the rural experience is greatly below the urban.[40]

For sheer want of dental care, such primitive practices as the use of almost any common chemical, like kerosene or turpentine, for the home treatment of toothache may still be observed among farm people in certain underprivileged sections.[41] Yet one need not point to the extreme case to bring out the challenge to effective action in meeting a deplorable situation.

Drugs and Appliances

Although drugs probably play a proportionately larger part in rural medical care than in urban, because of the inadequacies of professional services, the actual consumption of drugs in rural areas is less than in the cities. Drug consumption is best expressed by expenditures, to be considered later, but the general nature of drugs used in rural areas is shown in Table 35. The impressive fact is that a much smaller proportion of rural cases of illness get drugs prescribed by a physician but a higher proportion get self-prescribed or patent medicines, widely condemned by the medical profession.

[39] *Ibid.*

[40] *Ibid.*

[41] LANTIS, MARGARET, M. R. HANGER, and PHILIP W. WOODS, "The Farm Security Administration Dental Program of Randolph County, Georgia," in Hearings before a Subcommittee of the Committee on Education and Labor, U. S. Senate, 79th Cong., 1st Sess., S. 190 and S. 1099, *Dental Research and Dental Care.* Washington: Government Printing Office, 1945, p. 220.

The smaller proportion of sick persons getting prescribed drugs in rural communities is obviously related to the smaller share of such cases ever reaching medical attention. It also appears related to a tendency of the rural physician, at least as of 1928-31 findings, to prescribe drugs somewhat less frequently.[42] This may be somewhat offset, however, by the rural doctor's informal practice of recommending simple remedies that may be purchased across the

Table 35. Drugs: *Percentage of all cases of illness getting prescribed and unprescribed drugs, by size of community, 1928–31*

Size of community	Source of drug		
	Prescribed*	On druggist's recommendation only	Completely unprescribed
100,000 and over	51.2	4.6	11.4
5,000–100,000	44.8	2.5	9.5
Under 5,000	37.2	2.1	13.5
Open country	32.0	2.5	13.8

Source: Collins, Selwyn D., "The Frequency of Doctors' Prescriptions and of Laboratory and Related Services in the Treatment of Illness" (Committee on the Costs of Medical Care data), *The Milbank Memorial Fund Quarterly*, 21:376, October, 1943.

* Includes new and refilled prescriptions and all medicines furnished directly by the doctor.

counter without a prescription. Everyday observation at present would indicate, as a matter of fact, that the rural doctor relies more exclusively on drug therapy than the city doctor. The prescribing of "shotgun" compounds with half a dozen or more constituents, each with its hypothetical action, is rapidly disappearing from modern urban practice but is still quite characteristic of rural medicine. The extensive promotion of proprietary brands, well advertised to the medical profession, is clearly making inroads into this practice in rural and urban medicine alike, and the simplicity of these ready-made preparations has probably fortified the rural doctor's custom of dispensing drugs himself.

The wide use of patent medicines and home remedies in rural sections may have its historic roots in the ancient use of wild herbs

[42] COLLINS, SELWYN D., "The Frequency of Doctors' Prescriptions and of Laboratory and Related Services in the Treatment of Illness," *The Milbank Memorial Fund Quarterly*, 21:344-388, October, 1943. (Based on data of the Committee on the Costs of Medical Care.)

of all kinds. Undoubtedly an element of magic remains in the selection of home remedies, seasoned by a bit of empiricism and fortified by many an old wives' tale.[43] There is almost a characteristic train of events in the low-income farm family stricken with illness: first home remedies and patent medicines are tried, then advice is sought — perhaps from a neighbor, perhaps from the druggist — and only as a last resort is the more expensive care of the physician obtained. The underlying basis for patent medicine consumption is the lack of adequate and effective medical services. It has been well stated that patent medicines are the "poor man's medical care."

The harmful effects of patent medicines, in alleviating symptoms without striking at their cause, need not be reviewed here. It may be pointed out, however, that the "big sellers" of today are no longer the cure-alls with secret formulas but rather the well-known commercial preparations widely advertised in drugstores, on billboards, on the radio, in rural newspapers, and even in small-town movie houses. Aside from these not so harmful but vastly overused preparations, a great variety of less popular preparations is still used in rural households. One recent study of a single Missouri county disclosed the use of 182 different patent medicines — ranging from old stand-bys like Lydia Pinkham's Vegetable Compound to confidence-inspiring potions like Dr. Pierce's Golden Medical Discovery. Some 71 different ailments were occasionally or habitually treated, furthermore, by a selection of 258 home remedies ranging from simple substances like turpentine for the treatment of colds, appendicitis, tonsillitis, bites, toothache, scratches, sore throat, bruises, tumors, and snake bites to complicated compounds of catnip, horehound, scaly bark hickory, witch hazel, wintergreen, and dogwood for the treatment of coughs.[44] In another Missouri county, out of 317 households investigated, only 27 purchased prescribed drugs (though additional drugs had been dispensed directly by the doctor), but 310 of them had purchased unprescribed medicines.[45]

The utilization of special appliances by rural people may be

[43] See, for example, HAGGARD, HOWARD W., *Mystery, Magic, and Medicine.* New York: Doubleday, Doran & Company, Inc., 1933, p. 192.

[44] MEIER, I., and C. E. LIVELY, *Family Health Practices in Dallas County, Missouri.* Columbia: University of Missouri College of Agriculture (Research Bull. 369), 1943.

[45] ALMACK, *op. cit.*

judged by the volume of the specialized professional services with which these appliances are ordinarily associated. Thus, orthopedic appliances like leg braces, sacroiliac belts, or corrective shoes are undoubtedly used less than among urban people, as are some other devices like abdominal supports or elastic stockings. Mechanical hearing devices are seldom seen on rural people, mainly because they have been prohibitive in price, although the less exacting demands of rural life for good hearing may play a part. Yet the hard-of-hearing farmer with the loud voice has almost become a prototype in American folklore.

Appliances that can substitute for surgical correction, like hernial trusses, may actually be more widely used in rural sections. In any event, appliances that may be purchased across the counter, without strict medical specifications, are doubtless used more frequently in rural sections than those requiring medical orders. Eyeglasses are still frequently obtained in the village general store or the "five-and ten-cent store" in rural trade centers, although the over-all use of eyeglasses is much less than in the cities.

Other Services

Among other services that should be considered to complete the picture are those rendered by auxiliary medical personnel, by secondary practitioners, and by healing cultists.

The general lack of good laboratory, x-ray, or physiotherapy facilities and technical personnel to operate them in rural areas does not mean that those available are worked overtime to meet the needs that continually arise. It is evident from Table 36 that the proportion of attended illnesses receiving each of these technical services is consistently least in the most rural territory. Recalling that the proportion of all illnesses that are attended is lower in rural areas, it is clear that the rural deficiencies, as applied to *all* illnesses, must be even greater.

Of each of these services, rural people tend to get only the most elementary type. The more rural the community or the smaller the hospital, the greater the deficiency in technical services tends to be. Clinical laboratory services in a small town, for example, seldom involve more than ordinary blood counts and urinalyses. X-ray services cited in the table include both diagnostic and treatment functions but, by and large, roentgen-ray or radium therapy in rural sections is a rarity; the tragedy lies perhaps not so much in the lack of this specialized equipment in rural places as in the infrequency with which the rural patient is referred by his doctor to an urban center with complete facilities.

Among the services of secondary practitioners, those rendered by midwives are the most important in rural areas. Their extent is reflected by the distribution of midwives and the details of mater-

Table 36. Laboratory, X-ray, and Physiotherapy Services: *Percentage of attended cases of illness getting specified service, by size of community, 1928–31*

Size of community	Laboratory service	X-ray service	Physio- therapy
100,000 and over	10.0	4.9	2.2
5,000–100,000	7.4	3.6	1.5
Under 5,000	5.7	3.3	1.6
Open country	5.2	2.9	1.3

Source: Collins, Selwyn D., "The Frequency of Doctors' Prescriptions and of Laboratory and Related Services in the Treatment of Illness" (Committee on the Costs of Medical Care data), *The Milbank Memorial Fund Quarterly*, 21:379, October, 1943.

nity service already considered. Although the general character of midwifery is substandard, it is manifest that, in the absence of physicians' services, midwife services are almost indispensable in certain rural districts. Under the influence of the supervisory programs of many of the state public health agencies, the quality of midwife services has doubtless improved and a smaller number of more or. less "trained" midwives are becoming established in the work. In Macon County, Alabama, for example, a county of 26,000 people of whom 81 per cent are Negro, the number of "granny midwives" declined from 129 in 1930 to 50 in 1938. The smaller number of midwives, however, still delivered 75 per cent of the babies, and the maternal mortality rate was still at the disgracefully high level of 90.2 per 10,000 live births.[46] There can be little doubt that midwifery thrives under the same conditions of inaccessible medical care as the resort to patent medicines.

The smaller rural supply of optometrists undoubtedly implies a lower volume of services provided by them. Yet, with the scarcity

[46] THOMAS, M. W., "Social Priority No. 1: Mothers and Babies," *Public Health Nursing*, 34:442-445, August, 1942.

of physicians trained in eye work in rural sections, it is likely that the proportion of all visual refractions that must be done by optometrists is actually greater than in the cities. (In the nation as a whole, it has been estimated that over 50 per cent of refractions and prescriptions of eyeglasses are handled by optometrists.)[47] More important, the total volume of refractions — by optometrists or by physi-

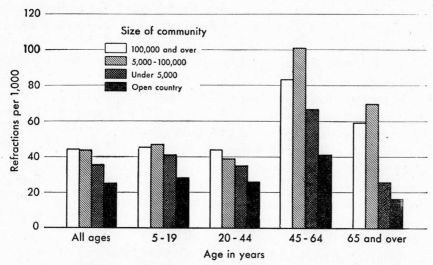

FIG. 30. Eye Refractions: Number per 1,000 persons per year in different age groups, by size of community, 1928-31. Source: Collins, Selwyn D., "Frequency of Eye Refractions in 9,000 Families" (Committee on the Costs of Medical Care data), *Public Health Reports*, 49:649-666, June 1, 1943.

cians — is considerably less in rural sections. In 1930, 32 out of every 1,000 persons had an eye examination or preparation of eyeglasses in small towns and open country, compared with 46 per 1,000 in the large cities.[48] In Figure 30 we observe that rural experience in refractions is lower for all age groups but that the differential is greatest after 45 years of age, when the need for visual correction is actually greatest. The lower proportion of rural people wearing eyeglasses cannot be attributed simply to less demand upon them for fine vision.

[47] FALK, I. S., C. RUFUS ROREM, and MARTHA D. RING, *The Costs of Medical Care* (Committee on the Costs of Medical Care Pub. 27). Chicago: University of Chicago Press, 1933, p. 284.

[48] COLLINS, SELWYN D., "Frequency of Eye Refractions in 9,000 Families, Based on Nation-wide Periodic Canvasses, 1928-31," *Public Health Reports*, 49:649-666, June 1, 1934.

Their need of good vision for reading, as well as for the housewife's sewing or the farmer's work with farm machinery, is as essential, if for fewer hours per day, as that among industrial and white-collar workers.

The services of chiropodists for rural people are of almost negligible proportions. The rural physician, however, more than the urban, does not hesitate to put his hand to the trimming of a corn, so that some of the basis for the special development of chiropody is lacking. The discarded razor blade, nevertheless, is probably the hazardous substitute for chiropody as frequently among rural persons as it is among urban.

As for the services of rural cultists — including osteopaths, chiropractors, naturopaths, and faith healers — the Committee on the Costs of Medical Care found that in large cities they provided all together 221 calls per 1,000 persons per year and in small towns and open country 165 calls per 1,000.[49] It may be noted that this rural-urban differential of about 34 per cent is almost identical with that found for physicians' services in the 1928-31 study. As previously noted, however, the differential for physicians today is probably greater while that for cultists may well be less.

It should be realized that large numbers of farm and village people do not clearly distinguish between different kinds of "doctors" and the services of a "doctor of osteopathy" are considered about like those of a "medical doctor." This is partly an inevitable result of limited experience with qualified medicine in many rural districts. It is also undoubtedly related to the fact that many rural cultists, especially osteopaths, prescribe drugs, set fractures, or deliver babies in about the same way as other physicians. Without pausing to evaluate the merits or deficiencies of the "drugless arts," however, it should be evident that cultism is generally inferior to scientific medicine, often positively harmful, and more objectionable to the extent that it attempts to handle all types of illness. Yet the special feature of osteopathy and chiropractic in rural practice is that their scope tends to be quite broad, in contrast to their relative confinement to rheumatic, neuritic, and related conditions in the cities.

[49] COLLINS, SELWYN D., "Frequency and Volume of Doctors' Calls among Males and Females in 9,000 Families, Based on Nation-wide Periodic Canvasses, 1928-31," *op. cit.*

Services to Rural Negroes

A special word should be said about the medical services available to the important and underprivileged Negro section of the rural population. Of all categories of medical care, the rural Negro receives less than the rural white. Much of the unfavorable experience of rural people in general, particularly in the Southern states, is referable to the extremely low volume of service received by the colored population.

That a seriously ill person from a Negro family in the country is far less likely to get essential medical service is seen in Figure 31. The

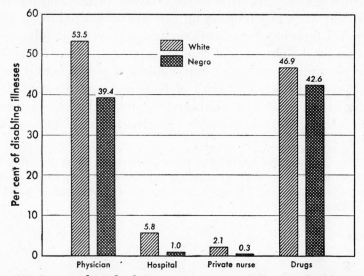

FIG. 31. Race and Medical Care: Percentage of illnesses disabling for one week or more receiving specified services, in rural counties of Georgia, by race, 1935-36. Source: Unpublished data furnished by the U. S. Public Health Service based on the Georgia Health Survey, a section of the National Health Survey, 1935-1936.

differential is greatest for the more expensive types of service, like hospitalization or nursing care, with white patients getting from five to seven times as much service, while for an elementary type of service, like drugs, it is least. The racial contrasts with respect to childbirth attendance were brought out in Figure 27. It is evident that for every five rural white babies delivered in a hospital by a physician, only one rural Negro baby was so delivered, and for every rural white baby that had to be delivered in the home by a midwife, fifteen Negro babies had to be so delivered. This is not only a problem of the deep South, for in a border state like Maryland, 39.5 per cent of the rural Negro live births went without medical attendance in 1942, compared with only 3.4 per cent of the rural white births.[50]

It cannot be stressed too much that the inequitable share of available rural health services received by Negroes is an expression of their greater poverty rather than their smaller need or desire for these services. In general, the health needs of Negroes are much greater than those of whites. That the smaller amount of care they receive is almost entirely a result of lower purchasing power will be evident when expenditures for care are considered in the coming pages. Yet their lower medical purchasing power is hardly compensated for by the provision of services supported by tax funds. While many preventive services of departments of public health are provided predominantly on behalf of Negroes, in recognition of their greater needs, general medical services provided by welfare departments have been made available even less to rural Negroes than to rural whites.[51]

[50] U. S. Census, *Vital Statistics of the United States*, 1942. Part 2, *Natality and Mortality Data for the United States Tabulated by Place of Residence.*

[51] STERNER, RICHARD, *The Negro's Share.* New York: Harper & Brothers, 1943, p. 389.

CHAPTER 18

RURAL EXPENDITURES FOR
MEDICAL CARE

A T THE VERY heart of all the inadequacies in rural health
resources and in the services received by rural people is the
smaller purchasing power for medical care in rural areas. For all types
of essential medical services, rural families spend less money than urban. Of the total national expenditure for all health services of about
5 billion dollars, coming from private as well as public sources, far
less is spent on behalf of rural people than their proportionate numbers and their needs would justify.

Average Expenditures

Rural families spend less for medical care, not essentially because
they value it or feel the need for it any less, but simply because they
have less money to spend. In relation to their total income, rural
people actually appear to spend greater proportionate amounts for
medical care than urban people. Thus, in 1935-36, a nation-wide
study found urban people to be spending 3.9 per cent of their net
income for medical care, while rural farm people were spending the
identical percentage and rural nonfarm people (composing nearly
half the total rural population) were spending 4.2 per cent.[1] In 1941,
another study showed this relationship to be even more marked
(Table 37), with rural farm and nonfarm people both spending
generally higher proportions of income for medical care than urban
people at income levels below $3,000 (where the vast majority of rural
people are found). The 5.3 per cent of generally low farm cash incomes spent for medical care in 1941, moreover, represents a greater
sacrifice than the same percentage would be out of higher urban

[1] U. S. National Resources Planning Board, *Family Expenditures in the
United States: Statistical Tables and Appendixes.* Washington: U. S. Government Printing Office, 1941. (Based on U. S. Bureau of Home Economics, U. S.
Bureau of Labor Statistics, and U. S. Work Projects Administration, Consumer Purchases Study, 1935-36.)

incomes.[2] In fact, considering the actual average percentage of income spent by farm families for medical care — rather than the proportion of aggregate farm income — one finds that the average farm family spent 8.7 per cent of its net cash income for medical care in 1941. It is significant that with farm income elevated in the later period, the percentage of total income allotted for medical care was considerably increased, although such alteration was less marked among urban families. With more ample funds, farmers seem to seize the chance to obtain medical services put off in bad times.

The average money expenditure of rural families for medical care is difficult to estimate, since the outlay fluctuates so markedly with changing economic circumstances. In 1928-31, the average annual charges for medical care per person (that is, charges incurred by the family rather than money spent by government, through philanthropy, and so forth) were $32.39 in cities of 100,000 and over, $23.89 in cities of 5,000 to 100,000, and $15.80 in towns of under 5,000 and open country.[3] Strictly comparable data are not available for later periods, but in 1935-36 the average expenditure of all urban nonrelief families for medical care was $72, compared with $59 for rural nonfarm families and $47 for farm families. These expenditures on a per capita basis were roughly $19 for the cities and $15 and $10, respectively, for the rural nonfarm and farm sections.[4] By 1941, under more prosperous conditions, families all over the nation were spending larger sums for medical care, but the rural-urban differentials were just as striking. As illustrated in Figure 32, the median-income farm and rural nonfarm families were still spending much less per capita for health services than median-income urban families. At this time, however, when the median annual net cash income of farm operators was much less than half the median urban income ($760 and $1,857, respectively), the farm family was spending per member somewhat more than half of what the city family was spending for medical services.[5]

[2] Data of the U. S. Bureau of Home Economics and U. S. Bureau of Labor Statistics, Study of Family Spending and Saving in Wartime, 1941-42, in HOLLINGSWORTH and KLEM, op. cit. p. 46.

[3] FALK, ROREM, and RING, op. cit., p. 93.

[4] U. S. National Resources Planning Board, op. cit.

[5] U. S. Bureau of Human Nutrition and Home Economics, What Families Spend for Medical Care. Washington, April, 1944, Processed. (Based on Study of Family Spending and Saving in Wartime, 1941-42.)

Average expenditures for medical care, among rural families as well as urban, vary markedly with family income. The striking variations are demonstrated in Table 37. It is evident that among rural nonfarm families, for example, the income class under $500 a year spends less than one-fourth as much for medical care as the income class over $3,000 a year, although their respective medical needs

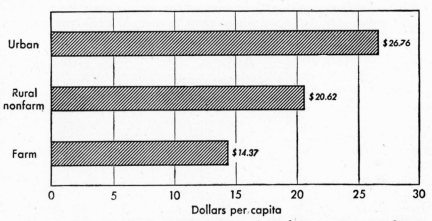

Fig. 32. Expenditures for Medical Care: Annual per capita expenditures by median income families in rural and urban areas, 1941. Source: U. S. Bureau of Human Nutrition and Home Economics, *What Families Spend for Medical Care.* Washington, April, 1944, Processed. (Based on U. S. Bureau of Home Economics and U. S. Bureau of Labor Statistics, Study of Family Spending and Saving in Wartime, 1941-42.)

are doubtless in reverse. Even with these smaller total outlays in the lower income brackets, however, the financial sacrifice involved is greater. As shown in the table, the percentage of available income spent for medical care actually rises as family income falls, and this regressive relationship is more striking in rural communities than urban.

Within the same money income groups, it may be noted that actual cash expenditures for medical care are closely parallel in rural and urban areas, even a little higher for low-income rural families. The large size of rural families, however, affects their actual per capita expenditures for medical care. Without respect to income, as the size of family increases there tends to be some increase in the total family outlay, but at a much slower rate than is warranted by the increase in family size; when family size reaches seven or more, the increase tends to stop. As a result, in larger families the per person expenditure for medical care actually declines. Thus in 1935-1936, among farm families of only two persons in the $750-$999 income bracket, the average annual medical expenditure per family was $36, while in families of three to six persons

Table 37. Medical Expenditures and Income: *Estimated annual medical care expenditures of families and single consumers and percentage of annual income spent for medical care, by annual income group in rural and urban areas,* 1941

Income group	Average medical care expenditure (dollars per year)			Per cent of income spent for medical care		
	Urban	Rural nonfarm	Rural farm	Urban	Rural nonfarm	Rural farm
Less than $250 . . .	}26	}24	29	}8.3	}8.2	21.2
$250–$499			34			9.0
$500–$749	}32	}51	40	}4.3	}6.9	6.4
$750–$999			58			6.7
$1,000–$1,499 . . .	58	70	65	4.7	5.7	5.3
$1,500–$1,999 . . .	77	85	94	4.4	5.0	5.5
$2,000–$2,499 . . .	96	}102	}114	4.3	}4.3	}4.7
$2,500–$2,999 . . .	115			4.4		
$3,000–$4,999 . . .	153	}162*	}124*	4.1	}3.5*	}2.2*
$5,000–$9,999 . . .	236			3.8		

Source: Based on data of U. S. Bureau of Home Economics and U. S. Bureau of Labor Statistics, Study of Family Spending and Saving in Wartime, 1941–42, in Hollingsworth, Helen, and Margaret C. Klem, *Medical Care and Costs in Relation to Family Income* (U. S. Social Security Board, Bureau of Research and Statistics Mem. 51). Washington, March, 1943, p. 46.

* Relates to income group of $3,000 a year or more.

of that income, the expenditure rose to only $42, and in large families of seven or more persons it was $37 — even less.[6]

It is evident that rural children are the chief sufferers from this relationship. Other studies have indicated that medical care expenditures for rural children under 10 years of age are less than half the average expenditure for all ages, while the expenditures for these children in large cities average about 60 per cent of the average for all ages. For every age group, of course, the expenditures in rural areas are considerably below those in the

[6] U. S. National Resources Planning Board, *op. cit.*

cities. The most striking differentials have been found for 5-9 year old children, for whom big-city expenditures are three times those in rural areas, and for persons 65 years and over, for whom urban expenditures are almost four times the rural.[7]

In farm life, more than city life, the total income and hence the funds to spend on medical care depend largely on factors beyond the individual's control. The general movements of the business cycle, the level of employment or international trade, of course, affect the farmer, the villager, and the city dweller alike But, in addition, the farmer is a victim of the vicissitudes of the weather; a drought or a cloudburst may mean the difference between medical care or no medical care. The rainfall will determine whether Johnny's badly infected tonsils will be removed or will remain to cause recurrent tonsillitis through the winter.

It may be recalled, moreover, that the nature of a great deal of farm production means that available cash comes only about once a year, at harvest time. Family income tends to be at its lowest ebb at the end of the winter when, in general, the need for medical service, because of respiratory tract infections, tends to be high. Undoubtedly, therefore, farm family expenditures for medical care have sharp seasonal variations, probably bearing only a partial relation to any periodicity of health needs. The off-season needs payable by "I.O.U.'s" or barter are hardly as well met as when cash can be put on the line.

Distribution of Expenditures

A consideration of *average* rural expenditures for medical care naturally overlooks the unevenness with which medical costs fall upon individual families in any one year. This uneven incidence of medical costs is one of the most significant single facts emerging from all major studies of the economics of medical care.

In rural and urban areas alike, a great share of the total costs of medical care in any one year falls heavily upon a small share of all the families, while a large proportion of them have only light expenses. Although practically 100 per cent of families in rural and urban areas alike have some expenses for one or another item of medical care — be it only for drugs — in the course of a

[7] FALK, KLEM, and SINAI, *op. cit.*, p. 293.

year, the proportionate distribution of the costs is highly irregular. The details of this inequitable distribution are illustrated in Table 38, according to the actual size of the charges incurred. It may be noted that, in any one year, while about 58 per cent of the families throughout the nation bear only 18 per cent of total medical costs, an unfortunate 10 per cent sustain 41 per cent of the costs. In rural areas, this inequitable distribution of costs is even somewhat exaggerated, with 68 per cent of the families.

Table 38. Distribution of Medical Charges: *Percentage of families bearing specified shares of total annual medical charges to all families, by type of community, 1928–31*

Total annual charges per family	Communities of all sizes		Towns under 5,000 and open country	
	Per cent of families	Per cent of charges	Per cent of families	Per cent of charges
Under $60	57.8	17.9	68.0	22.6
$60–$99	13.7	12.5	11.8	12.8
$100–$249	18.2	28.4	13.4	26.8
$250–$499	6.6	21.1	4.9	21.0
$500 and over	3.7	20.1	1.9	16.8
All charges	100.0	100.0	100.0	100.0

Source: Falk, I. S., Margaret C. Klem, and Nathan Sinai, *The Incidence of Illness and the Receipt and Costs of Medical Care among Representative Families* (Committee on the Costs of Medical Care, Pub. 26). Chicago: University of Chicago Press, 1933, p. 305.

bearing 23 per cent of the costs, while 7 per cent of the families are weighted down by 38 per cent of the total costs.

Analysis of this distribution of expenditures by rural income groups shows that the unevenness of incidence applies to all income levels. In the rural income group under $1,200 a year, for example, half of the families bear only one-tenth of the costs while one-fourth must bear a staggering three-fourths of the costs. Likewise, in the rural income group between $5,000 and $10,000 a year, 67 per cent of the families bear only 13 per cent of the costs, while an unfortunate 24 per cent bear 82 per cent of the burden.[8] This uneven distribution of costs holds true for all items

[8] Data of the Committee on the Costs of Medical Care in HOLLINGSWORTH and KLEM, *op. cit.,* pp. 91-92.

of medical service in rural and urban areas alike. It tends to be most extreme for high-cost items like hospitalization or surgical care and relatively less extreme for lower cost items like general practitioner services or drugs.

Expenditures for Specified Items of Medical Care

Just as the story on *average* expenditures obscures the individual economic burdens, the story on *total* expenditures obscures the relative amounts spent for each item of medical service. How much of the rural medical care dollar is spent in paying physicians' bills, how much is spent for hospitalization, for drugs, and so forth?

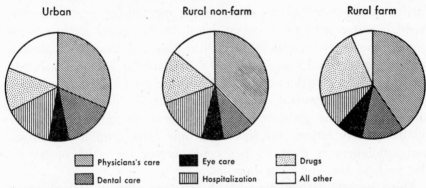

FIG. 33. Composition of the Medical Dollar: Proportionate expenditures for specified health services by median income families in rural and urban areas, 1941. Source: U. S. Bureau of Human Nutrition and Home Economics, *What Farm Families Spend for Medical Care* (U. S. Department of Agriculture Misc. Pub. 561). Washington, April, 1945. (Based on U. S. Bureau of Home Economics and U. S. Bureau of Labor Statistics, *Study of Family Spending and Saving in Wartime*, 1941-42).

The allotment of the fractions of the medical dollar to the several components of medical service, as they are purchased in rural and urban areas, is illustrated in Figure 33. In all sections the physician is found to get the lion's share of the medical dollar. Although there are other general similarities in the rural and urban patterns, certain differences are significant. Of their smaller total expenditures, farm and rural nonfarm families both appear to spend a larger share on drugs. The farm family spends a much smaller share of its medical dollar on hospitalization and the village family spends a smaller share on dental service. Services regarded as "all other" would tend to include laboratory, physiotherapy, and similar technical items, and it is significant that farm families spend a much smaller share in this category. As a result of this cost distribution, the rural families on the farm and in the village tend to spend a larger part of their total on physicians than the city families. It is evident that the pattern of rural medical spending is characterized by larger proportionate amounts for more elementary services and smaller proportionate amounts for more specialized services.

Within rural areas, the pattern of expenditures varies strikingly for different income levels. In general, it may be stated that the characteristics of the over-all rural pattern of spending are further exaggerated as we descend the income ladder. While the trend is not consistent in every detail, in the lower income farm groups the relative expenditures for hospitalization, for private nursing, for dental care, and for miscellaneous medical services tend to be less. But the relative expenditures for physicians' services (predominantly general practitioners) and for drugs and appliances tend to be greater with lower farm income. In fact, the relative outlay among the lowest income farm families for drugs and appliances is over 60 per cent greater than the outlay of the highest income farm families.[9]

More important than the variable patterns of spending, absolute expenditures for practically all items of medical care decline with family income. The consistency of these graduations is evident in Table 39. Farm income groups below $500 a year spend for physicians' services only about one-third of the amount spent by income groups over $2,000 a year. For hospital care the ratio is about 1 to 5 or 6 and for dental care it is about the same. For eye care (including examinations and eyeglasses), for private nurses, and for the services of "other practitioners" (including cultists as well as secondary practitioners like chiropodists), there is a fairly steady rise in expenditures from the lowest to the highest income levels. Even for drugs and appliances there is a definite relationship of the absolute expenditures to income although it is less striking than for other components of medical service, being about twice as high in the income group over $2,000

[9] Derived from data of the U. S. Bureau of Home Economics, Study of Family Spending and Saving in Wartime, in HOLLINGSWORTH and KLEM, *op. cit.*, p. 57.

Table 39. Medical Expenditures and Farm Income: *Average annual expenditures in dollars of farm families* for specified items of medical care, by annual income group,* 1941

Income group	All medical care	Physicians' care	Dental care	Eye care	Other practitioner	Hospital and private clinic care	Private nursing	Drugs and appliances	X-ray examination or treatment	Health and medical insurance	Other medical care
Less than $250	$29.02	$10.90	$3.87	$2.64	$0.14	$3.00	...	$6.21	...	$2.08	$0.18
$250–$499	33.61	12.47	4.35	3.28	0.90	2.56	$0.48	7.03	$1.06	1.47	0.05
$500–$749	40.16	14.60	5.10	3.56	0.40	5.35	0.40	9.89	0.05	0.76	0.05
$750–$999	58.36	23.56	7.65	4.69	0.39	6.00	0.36	13.18	0.62	1.78	0.13
$1,000–$1,499	65.49	22.70	11.06	6.66	1.91	8.35	0.30	11.10	0.45	2.30	0.66
$1,500–$1,999	94.49	35.62	13.44	6.76	0.91	15.27	2.30	13.75	1.17	4.49	0.78
$2,000–$2,999	114.32	38.29	15.23	5.17	6.09	18.81	3.34	13.99	0.62	12.27	0.51
$3,000 or more	123.51	34.67	25.29	11.26	5.37	15.34	7.22	16.37	0.98	4.16	2.85

Source: Derived from data of the U. S. Bureau of Home Economics, Study of Family Spending and Saving in Wartime, in Hollingsworth, Helen, and Margaret C. Klem, *Medical Care and Costs in Relation to Family Income* (U. S. Social Security Board, Bureau of Research and Statistics Mem. 51). Washington, March, 1943, p. 57.

* Includes farm operator families only; excludes families of farm managers and farm laborers.

a year as in the group under $500. The very irregular trend found in x-ray services is probably due to sampling irregularities which reflect, in a sense, the extremely low volume of such services at all income levels among farm people. Expenditures for health insurance of different types appear to follow an irregular course in relation to income, though they are significantly somewhat higher in the upper brackets.

Special Economic Problems in Rural Medical Costs

Certain economic problems are bound up with the provision and purchase of each of the major items of medical service in rural areas. They spring fundamentally from the prevailing pattern in the United States of purchasing medical and related services on a private fee-for-service basis.

The purchase of physicians' services on an individual fee-for-service basis is poorly adapted to the agricultural economy in which, as we have seen, income tends to be sporadic. Payment in kind for medical services is actually infrequent, and the more usual consequence of the "cash nexus" in rural medical care is failure of the rural family to seek service at all or else simply unpaid medical bills. In one typical rural county of Georgia, for example, of twelve practicing physicians, six reported to the Committee on the Costs of Medical Care that they wrote off 50 per cent or more of their accounts as uncollectible and all but two considered at least 30 per cent uncollectible.[10] The problem of unpaid bills is greater in rural medical practice than in urban not only because of rural poverty but also because of the sparsity of public clinics to absorb indigent patients and because of social compulsions on the country doctor to be the beneficent "keeper of his flock." To avoid the nuisance of bill collections, nevertheless, some rural physicians have come to the policy of virtually restricting their practice to patients who have the cash to pay.

The sliding scale of fees, often heralded as a way to equalize the financial burden of medical care among different income groups, rarely operates in rural practice. Not one of eight physicians

[10] GUILD, C. ST. C., *Surveys of the Medical Facilities in Three Representative Southern Counties* (Committee on the Costs of Medical Care Pub. 23). Chicago: University of Chicago Press, 1932, p. 51.

questioned in a typical rural county of Tennessee, for example, varied his charges according to the patient's income.[11] This is probably because, unlike the situation in large cities, the range of incomes in given rural districts tends to be small; it is also claimed that news of varied fees would "get around" in rural sections and cause discontent.

The undesirable urban practice of fee-splitting, on the other hand, is less common in rural communities by virtue of their lack of specialists. Nevertheless, competition among rural doctors, frequently intense in the face of limited purchasing power among their patients, does induce other undesirable practices. Consultations between physicians are notably infrequent partially because of fear that patients may be "stolen." The rural physician may refrain from ordering supplementary technical services that might deplete family funds for his remuneration. Obstetrical deliveries may be done at home, simply so that the doctor's bill will not have to compete for payment with a hospital bill.

Rural medical fees differ in several ways from those in cities. Fees for office calls tend to be lower — frequently $1 or $1.50, rarely the $2 to $5 urban fee — with remarkable uniformity in any one section. Obstetrical fees tend to be lower than in the cities because practically every country doctor does maternity work and competition more or less keeps the price down. The midwife with her $5 or $10 fee, moreover, enters the competitive arena. As for surgical fees, the rural doctor, like the city surgeon, tends to charge what the traffic will bear, but again the charges are on the average somewhat lower. Published fee schedules are still known in rural communities, issued by the local medical societies, though in the cities they are now practically obsolete.

On the other hand, the great distances to be covered in rural medical practice render fees for home calls considerably higher than in urban practice. The time and transportation costs of travel to a distant farmhouse compel the rural doctor to charge a mileage fee — typically $1 per mile, one way — in addition to the regular service fee. The service fee for a day call is typically about $3, for a night call about $5. A farmer 10 miles from the doctor, therefore, whose child gets sick at midnight must pay $15 to get the doctor to his home. A frequent unfortunate practice

[11] *Ibid.*, p. 12.

is for the rural physician to charge a full mileage fee to each of two or more neighboring farm families whom he may visit in the course of one trip. The deterring effects of such charges on the demand for medical service are obvious, and despite such charges as these, rural physicians' incomes are not high. Even when the members of a farm family go to the doctor's office, the costs of their travel constitute an additional medical expense. With respect to this whole phase of medical service, it is obvious that rural families get less for their money than city families.

For most of the heroic tales of country doctors and their valiant devotion to their patients, there are others disclosing the seamy side of rural medicine caused by some of these economic difficulties. An astute physician working in a public medical program in the mountain section of one of our rural states writes:

> One night there came a most urgent call. "Some doctor should come quick. Mrs. A — is dying; her baby can't be born. No doctor in town will come because we have no money in hand. We will get it up as soon as we can." I started out with all necessary equipment but on the road about three miles from the place was met by a man on horseback. He was coming to tell me I needn't come as the mother had died in convulsions. . . . It is of course the large price for calls that keeps people from calling a doctor till the last hope is gone. I could multiply cases like this indefinitely. . . . I have known doctors to take the kitchen stove from the home (in payment of their bill) or the only cow from the barn as well as the hogs that were to furnish food for the family in the winter.[12]

Grim episodes of this type can be recounted by any serious observer of rural medicine with its inherent economic dilemmas.

The cash barriers to rural hospital service are even greater than those to physicians' care. While the payment of the doctor's bill may be postponed or charges whittled down, hospitals must meet pay rolls and buy food and their collection policies must be more stern. Yet, because of their small capacities and low occupancy, charges in rural hospitals tend to be high relative to the quality of service rendered. Despite their less specialized services, the cost per patient-day of rural hospitals tends to be only slightly less than that of large-city institutions.[13]

[12] Personal communication, 1945.

[13] Unpublished data of U. S. Children's Bureau in connection with the administration of the Emergency Maternity and Infant Care Program, 1945.

A much larger share of rural hospital costs, moreover, must be borne by private patients. In 1935, hospitals in metropolitan and bordering counties were supported only 57 per cent by private payments, 15 per cent by organized voluntary sources, and 28 per cent by tax funds. On the other hand, hospitals in all other counties throughout the nation received 77 per cent of their support from private payments, 9 per cent from other voluntary sources, and only 14 per cent from tax funds.[14]

Only for the hospitalization of cases of mental disorder or tuberculosis does the rural family, along with the urban, find the financial burden borne chiefly by government. The actual expenditures for maintenance of these institutions, nevertheless, are still much less in the rural states. Thus in the rural Mountain and East South Central states, the annual per patient maintenance expenditures for mental hospitals in 1938 were $242 and $146, while in the urban New England and Middle Atlantic states they were $379 and $390.[15]

The critical feature of hospitalization expenses for the farm family is that, while they come seldom, they strike hard when they come. Among rural farm and nonfarm families in 1941, expenditures for hospitalization were incurred by only 4 to 20 per cent of families — the higher percentages being at the higher income levels — while the costs of physicians' services were spread over 55 to 80 per cent of the families.[16]

Taking into account the physician's or surgeon's fee, auxiliary medical costs, and associated economic losses due to absence from farm work, hospitalization often represents a financial catastrophe to the farm family. The unlucky 14 per cent of the families with median farm income who in any one year use the hospital spend three times as much for medical care as families without need for hospitalization, and all together they bear 36 per cent of the total costs of medical care.[17]

[14] Derived from PENNELL, E. H., J. W. MOUNTIN, and K. PEARSON, *Business Census of Hospitals*, 1935 (Supp. 154 to the Public Health Reports). Washington: Government Printing Office, 1939, p. 25.

[15] HAMILTON, KEMPF, SCHOLZ, and CASWELL, *op. cit.*, p. 82.

[16] Data of the U. S. Bureau of Home Economics, Study of Family Spending and Saving in Wartime, 1941-42, in HOLLINGSWORTH and KLEM, *op. cit.*, p. 51.

[17] U. S. Bureau of Human Nutrition and Home Economics, *op. cit.*, pp. 11-12.

The economic aspects of dental practice are similar to those described for medical practice. Rural dental fees are usually lower than urban, and competition for the limited number of persons exerting effective demand is probably as keen. Payments for dental care are more exclusively on a private basis, unaided by subsidy from government or philanthropy, than payments for physicians' services or hospitalization. Dental expenditures in rural areas are made in a pattern akin to that for hospitalization; that is, the service is relatively seldom obtained, but when it must be sought, the costs — because of past neglect — are often relatively high. Thus, analysis of data of the Committee on the Costs of Medical Care on the $1,200-and-under income class, for example, shows that in cities of over 100,000 the average dental charge for persons seeing dentists was 53 per cent of the average total cost for medical care among persons incurring charges; in towns under 5,000 and rural areas, the average dental charge was 63 per cent of the average total.[18]

Expenditures for nursing care, for eye services, for appliances, for secondary practitioners, and for cultists all tend to follow the pattern of being sustained by a small fraction of the total rural population. All these expenditures usually fall on much fewer than half the families in a single year — and for most of the items, fewer than 10 per cent of the families. Only for drugs are costs spread so evenly that in any one year as many as two-thirds of the families in every income class make some purchases. For every income group the spread of the expenditures among different families is broader for drugs than for physicians' services or any other medical item.[19]

"Free" and Prepaid Medical Services

The medical and related services considered in the last chapter have included services from any source, whether privately purchased, tax-supported, charitable, or obtained through insurance. The expenditures for medical care so far reviewed, however, have

[18] Data of the Committee on the Costs of Medical Care, in HOLLINGSWORTH and KLEM, op. cit., pp. 72, 78.

[19] Data of the U. S. Bureau of Home Economics, Study of Family Spending and Saving in Wartime, 1941-42, in HOLLINGSWORTH and KLEM, op. cit., p. 51.

been almost exclusively from private sources. The gap between these two definitions is actually not great, since almost the entire volume of therapeutic service for the care of general illness is, in fact, financed privately. Before discussing in detail the variety of programs under which medical services are obtained on an organized basis, it will give perspective to summarize the over-all part played by services secured through other than customary private resources.

While the volume of "free" services received by the general population, relative to the total volume of medical care, is quite small, that received by farm families is particularly slight. Considering tax-supported care sponsored by government agencies, services financed by philanthropy, the charitable work of physicians, and even the care financed by relatives and friends, only 6 per cent of farm families and 11 per cent of rural nonfarm families were found to have received some such "free" care in 1941. This compares with 12.5 per cent of urban families getting such care in the same year.[20] It is likely that these figures greatly understate the true differential, since they do not consider volume of services but only the receipt of *any* services. Despite frequent claims made for the practice, free care was reported to be rendered by physicians on a private basis to only 4 per cent of rural nonfarm families and less than 2 per cent of farm families.[21] The greater part of free care is in the form of hospitalization, supported typically by departments of public welfare.

The striking feature of "free" care in rural sections is that, unlike that in the cities, it does not increase as we descend the income ladder. In Table 40 it appears that the middle-income farm families are the chief beneficiaries of free care. It is possible that this may reflect chiefly regional variations, since farm families in the income groups under $500 a year tend to be largely from the South, while higher levels are commoner in other regions.

[20] Unpublished data furnished by U. S. Bureau of Human Nutrition and Home Economics and U. S. Bureau of Labor Statistics, from the Study of Family Spending and Saving in Wartime, 1941-42.

[21] The governmental study on which these conclusions are based was made on a small sample of families and further investigation is needed. To some extent the definition of "free" care differed between rural and urban communities, in line with different cultural settings, so that the data here should be taken only as an approximation.

The fact remains that it is lack of resources for tax-supported medical care in the South, or for that matter in other low-income farming sections, that yields a low volume of free care among the lowest income groups that need it most.

On the whole, the expenditure of funds for medical services through organized group prepayment of some type is likewise

Table 40. Group-supported and "Free" Medical Services: *Percentage of farm families receiving some tax-supported or charitable medical care during the year and annual expenditures on health insurance, by annual income group*, 1941

Income group	Per cent receiving "free care"	Health insurance expenditures (dollars per year)	
		Group prepayment plans	Commercial sickness or accident indemnity
Less than $250	5	$1.84	$0.24
$250–$499	7	0.46	1.01
$500–$749	8	0.45	0.31
$750–$999	10	0.31	1.47
$1,000–$1,499	4	0.25	2.05
$1,500–$1,999	5	0.51	3.98
$2,000–$2,999	6	1.03	11.33
$3,000 or more	5	0.07	4.09

Source: Unpublished data furnished by U. S. Bureau of Human Nutrition and Home Economics, based on U. S. Bureau of Home Economics Study of Family Spending and Saving in Wartime, 1941–42.

small and again especially so for rural families. In 1941, an average of only $0.66 a year was spent by farm families for services through a prepayment medical plan, compared with $2.52 by rural nonfarm families and $3.59 by urban families. Likewise the average farm family spent $2.35 a year for commercial sickness or accident insurance in 1941, compared with $3.75 spent by rural nonfarm families and $5.45 by urban families.[22] Expenditures of these kinds by farm families do not appear to show any regular trend related to family income. With respect to membership in prepayment medical plans, the peak level in the lowest income farm

[22] Data furnished by U. S. Bureau of Human Nutrition and Home Economics and U. S. Bureau of Labor Statistics, from the Study of Family Spending and Saving in Wartime, 1941-42.

group seen in Table 40 is doubtless due to the medical care program of the Farm Security Administration. As for expenditures by farm families on commercial sickness and accident insurance, however, it is evident that they are greater at upper income levels, as one might expect.

THAT EXPENDITURES for medical care bear little relation to health needs must be concluded from all available evidence. The central fact of medical economics in rural and urban areas alike is that expenditures, and hence services, tend to vary with family income and to be borne disproportionately by the minority of families that in any year are afflicted with serious illness. That habit patterns or incidence of illness exert much less influence on expenditures than income level is demonstrated by the fact, for example, that medical expenditures of white and colored families of the same income in Southern villages are practically identical.[23] The small volume of services we have found to be received by Negroes, therefore, or by other population groups for that matter, is related to nothing else so intimately as it is to their general income level. When the cash barrier to medical care is eliminated, as is done in certain organized programs, the volume of medical services is found to rise tremendously.

As organized social services in the United States have come of age, the proportionate distribution of medical costs among private individuals, philanthropy, and government has gradually altered. In 1929 about 79 per cent of the total national medical bill was borne by private individuals, 7 per cent by philanthropy or business enterprise, and 14 per cent by government.[24] By 1942 the proportions had changed so that the share borne by private individuals declined to 75 per cent, the share borne by philanthropy fell to 5 per cent, and the share borne by government rose to 20 per cent.[25] This trend will doubtless continue, although in

[23] HOLLINGSWORTH, HELEN, and others, *Family Expenditures for Medical Care: Five Regions* (U. S. Bureau of Home Economics in cooperation with the U. S. Work Projects Administration). Washington: U. S. Department of Agriculture (Misc. Pub. 402), 1941, pp. 89-90.

[24] FALK, ROREM, and RING, *op. cit.*, p. 10.

[25] U. S. Social Security Board, *Need for Medical-care Insurance* (Bureau of Research and Statistics Mem. 57). Washington, 1944, Processed, p. 25.

rural areas it lags behind the situation in the cities. As the trend proceeds, the distribution of medical expenditures and the provision of medical services become gradually more equitable, more closely approximating the varying levels of health needs. The forces responsible for this decisive trend will be reviewed in the coming chapters.

PART VI: GOVERNMENTAL EFFORTS TO IMPROVE RURAL HEALTH

TO OVERCOME the inequities we have found in rural health personnel, facilities, and services, many positive steps have been taken. So far we have considered the resources of rural medicine available along more or less traditional lines. Country doctors and rural hospitals throughout the years have, of course, used all sorts of resourcefulness to overcome their handicaps on an individual basis. The general approach to problems in medical care, however, as in other social services, has been to seek improvement through increased organization and rationalization of services and this has, indeed, been the trend in American medicine for the last hundred years.[1]

It seems fitting, therefore, to discuss in some detail the main efforts promoting a heightened organization of rural health services. These organized efforts range from firmly established and now traditional services to the sick poor through welfare departments to such recent measures as the Emergency Maternity and Infant Care program for the wives and babies of servicemen. They range from such strictly governmental functions as the programs of rural health departments to such typically voluntary efforts as the education of farm youth about physical fitness and good nutrition through the activities of 4-H clubs.

The American pattern of remedial social action appears to be one in which initial responsibility is often assumed by voluntary groups and gradually passed over to government as particular needs become firmly recognized.[2] This has been the case, for example, with respect to organized activities for the control of tuberculosis or the services of visiting nurses. Today, in fact, we are still at a transitional stage with regard to many functions that are carried on by both governmental and voluntary agencies. In general it may be said that the governmental health programs of today represent the voluntary programs of yesterday. It seems proper, therefore, to discuss governmental health programs in rural areas first and to follow with a discussion of voluntary efforts that tend to give us a view to the future. Between the two there has been an extensive set of government-

[1] STERN, BERNHARD J., *American Medical Practice in the Perspectives of a Century*. New York: The Commonwealth Fund, 1945.

[2] ROEMER, MILTON I., "Government's Role in American Medicine: A Brief Historical Survey," *Bulletin of the History of Medicine*, 18:146-168, July, 1945.

sponsored activities in medical care launched chiefly by the Department of Agriculture, the main effect of which has been to stimulate voluntary action in rural areas.

Almost all the various activities of government in health have some direct or indirect bearing on the lives of rural people. Among these we may consider public health services, medical services for the needy, programs for special beneficiaries of the national government such as veterans, and the more indirect though in no way less important governmental activities that affect the provision or qualification of health personnel, the construction of physical facilities, and the promotion of scientific research. Special attention will then be directed to the programs sponsored by the Department of Agriculture on behalf of farm families and seasonal farm workers.

The importance of governmental health activity is somewhat reflected by the financial outlay. Prewar expenditures by Federal, state, and local governments for all kinds of health and medical services, exclusive of those for the armed forces, amounted to nearly 850 million dollars a year. This sum represents about a fifth of the total health bill of the nation. Most of these government expenditures are made from state and local funds; for every dollar of federal money spent, states and local communities spend three. The largest share of government expenditures for health goes for hospital care and hospital construction. Thus, approximately 75 cents of the total government health dollar goes for this purpose, while about 17 cents is spent for public health work (including maternal and child health services and services for crippled children), and about 8 cents for other services, chiefly medical care for the indigent.[3]

It would be of considerable interest to know what proportion of total governmental health expenditures finds its way to rural areas and what proportion remains in urban communities whence the bulk of tax funds originates. Although an over-all breakdown of this type is impossible, the general trend of expenditures by local units of government for most categories of health services gives some indication of rural-urban differences. Figure 34 shows the per capita health expenditures of municipalities of varying size for all kinds of public health and hospitalization services. It may be seen that health expenditures decline with size of community almost in geometric

[3] U. S. Social Security Board, Social Security Yearbook, 1942. Washington: Government Printing Office, 1943, p. 84.

ratio. Although this finding must at once be qualified by the reminder that these figures do not take account of the health expenditures of county governments nor of direct state health expenditures, they do include local municipal expenditures of funds from federal or state sources as well as local. Definite conclusions cannot be drawn from these data, of course, concerning the actual volume

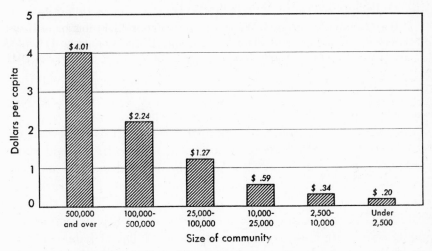

FIG. 34. Governmental Health Expenditures: Per capita municipal expenditures for all public health and hospitalization services, by size of community, 1942. (Municipal expenditures include funds derived from all sources — local, state, and federal — but omit consideration of direct expenditures by state or county governments for services within municipal borders.) Source: U. S. Bureau of the Census. *City Finances, 1942, Cities Having Populations over 25,000*, Vol. 3, *Statistical Compendium* (Census of Governments, 1942); also, *Finances of Cities Having Populations Less Than 25,000, 1942.*

of governmentally supported health services reaching all rural people. The trend illustrated, however, is consistent with other data reflecting real differences between over-all rural and urban rates of governmental expenditures for health purposes.

Another clue to rural-urban differences in general health expenditures is found in the United States Public Health Service estimates of 1940 expenditures by all official state agencies for health activities of every type. The greatest part of state health expenditures are for institutional care, especially for mental disorder, but scores of other functions are involved. The rate of expenditure for all health services sponsored by state governments tends to be substantially higher in the more urban states. In all states with populations over 60 per cent urban the estimated average annual per capita expenditure of funds from all sources for these state services was $2.70, whereas in all states over 60 per cent rural the average per capita expenditure was only half as much, or $1.34.[4] For all specific types of governmentally sponsored health services on which data are available, we shall find that the same general relationship holds.

[4] Derived from MOUNTIN, J. W., and EVELYN FLOOK, "Distribution of Health Services in the Structure of State Government: I. The Composite Pattern of State Health Services," *Public Health Reports*, 56:1673-1698, Aug. 22, 1941.

CHAPTER 19

PUBLIC HEALTH SERVICES

A MONG THE earliest health functions recognized by government was the assumption of community responsibility for the control of the environment necessary to prevent the spread of epidemics.[1] The necessity for rigid sanitation of the environment was naturally greatest in the cities and there the first organized departments of public health developed. It was not until about 1911, in fact, that the first health departments were organized on a county basis in this country, thus offering environmental protection to rural people — those in Jefferson County, Kentucky, in Guilford County, North Carolina, and in Yakima County, Washington.[2] Even in these counties the organization of public health agencies was largely influenced by the need of urban centers within their borders, and not until the following year, 1912, was the first full-time health department established in a county having no incorporated place of 2,500 or more. This was in Robeson County, South Carolina.[3]

Preventive services of different categories are actually carried out by a variety of boards, departments, and commissions in the arena of government. School hygiene, for example, is often supervised by boards of education and milk sanitation by state departments of agriculture. Typically, however, the agency having principal jurisdiction over preventive health services is the department of health.

Public Health Functions — Local, State, and Federal

The most fundamental role of the health department has been the organization and provision of preventive measures to protect people

[1] WINSLOW, C.-E. A., *The Conquest of Epidemic Disease*. Princeton: Princeton University Press, 1944.

[2] MUSTARD, HARRY S., *Rural Health Practice*. New York: The Commonwealth Fund, 1936, p. 4.

[3] FREEMAN, ALLEN W., "Rural Health Organization in the United States: Past, Present, and Future," *Southern Medical Journal*, 27: 518, June, 1934.

from environmental hazards.[4] In the last few decades, however, there has been a rapid expansion in the scope of official health activities into the field of personal health services. The task of supervising environmental sanitation still remains basic, but even in the traditional field of communicable disease control the functions of health agencies have inevitably broadened into individual disease therapy. The control and prevention of venereal diseases, for example, requires the treatment of infectious cases; since the management of the most important venereal infection, syphilis, is seldom effective on a private basis — for economic and other reasons — it has had to be assumed by public health agencies. The same situation has long been recognized with regard to tuberculosis. The protection of expectant mothers and of infants has likewise come to be assumed as a public health responsibility because they represent a part of our population toward which society has historically assumed a protective attitude. School children and, in recent years, factory workers have been provided special public health protection. Dental hygiene programs, particularly for children, have been extended widely in recognition of the practically universal need. Pneumonia, cancer, and rheumatic heart disease have lately come to be of public health concern as serious problems affecting great numbers of people.

By and large, the effort is still made to separate prevention of disease from treatment and to assign the latter to private auspices, but increasingly the concern of public health agencies has turned from the impersonal control of the environment to concern for the health needs of individuals.[5] This progressive expansion in the role of health departments tends to be considerably more advanced in urban communities, however, than in rural areas.

Much the greater part of public health functions is carried on by local units of government, although in recent years increasing responsibilities, including financial assistance, have been assumed by the Federal and state governments. While urban people are served generally by health departments maintained as a branch of municipal government, rural people — if served at all by health depart-

[4] For a general discussion of health department functions, see SMILLIE, WILSON G., *Public Health Administration in the United States*. New York: The Macmillan Company, 1940, pp. 3-10.

[5] ROEMER, MILTON I., "A Program of Preventive Medicine for the Individual," *The Milbank Memorial Fund Quarterly*, 23:209-226, July, 1945.

ments.— find them organized usually under county government. Too often, however, an incorporated community in a rural county will have one public health agency, while the county exclusive of the town will have another. Sometimes the county health department will function in effect only in the county seat in which it is located. In the nation as a whole there are some 18,000 independent health jurisdictions in villages, towns, cities, counties, city-county units, or multicounty units ranging in population from 8 persons to over 7 million persons.[6] The lines of authority are so confused and the coverage so irregular, however, that a great share of rural counties remain without any public health protection.

Local health departments in rural areas are set up usually under authorities granted by the state government, in exercise of "police powers" granted by the state constitution.[7] Practically all states have permissive legislation empowering local units of government to take such action, usually by way of organizing a local board of health in which executive powers are vested. These local boards can promulgate local regulations and may delegate a health officer as their agent to promote their enforcement. Unfortunately many state governments, in empowering county governments to raise revenue for the support of public health activities, fix maximum taxing limits above which revenue may not be collected for health purposes.

All sorts of "sanitary codes" and laws on special health problems are passed by state governments to enhance the authority of health departments. The wealthier urbanized states, however, have been in the forefront in such legislation and the more rural states have lagged behind. Laws requiring premarital examinations for the detection of venereal disease or prenatal tests for syphilis are an example. Of the 13 states that in 1945 had no law requiring premarital examinations, 10 were predominantly rural; likewise, of 13 states lacking a legal requirement of prenatal tests for syphilis, 10 were again predominantly rural.[8]

[6] EMERSON, HAVEN, and MARTHA LUGINBUHL, *Local Health Units for the Nation* (American Public Health Association). New York: The Commonwealth Fund, 1945, pp. 10-14.

[7] TOBEY, JAMES H., *Public Health Law*. New York: The Commonwealth Fund, 1939.

[8] Derived from "New Social Hygiene Laws in 1945," *Social Hygiene News*, Vol. 20, No. 9, September, 1945.

State health departments usually exercise only a general advisory or consultative function in relation to local health units, although in a few of our most rural states direct supervisory control emanates from the state agency. Many of our strongest state health departments, in terms of personnel and budgets, are in our most rural states, but it is unrealistic to evaluate total public health functions by operations at the state level. A strong state health department program may simply be compensating for weaknesses in local health administration, while conversely strong local units may call for only a skeleton state staff organization. In Mississippi, for example, with nearly all the counties organized under full-time public health units, the state health department in 1940 employed only 10 physicians, while in Virginia, with relatively meager local organization, 63 physicians were employed by the state health agency.[9] In general it may be said that the state health departments of the rural states of the Southeast are relatively strong, while in most of the other rural states public health agencies at both state and local levels tend to be relatively weak.[10]

By and large, there is no direct line of authority from the Federal to the state governments with regard to public health, except in so far as standards have been set, in recent years, in relation to the use of federal grant-in-aid funds. While the grant-in-aid mechanism had its beginnings in Civil War times, when Abraham Lincoln established the land-grant colleges, it came into wide use in public health work with the passage of the Social Security Act in 1935. It is noteworthy that the size of grants to states is determined in some degree by the relative financial needs of the various states. This policy obviously benefits the rural states, tending to raise their public health expenditures toward the level found in the wealthier urban states. In 1941, for example, grants by the United States Public Health Service to the states with 70 per cent or more urban population averaged 6 cents per capita while grants to the states with 70 per cent or more

[9] MOUNTIN and FLOOK, op. cit.

[10] As already noted, other agencies of state government, such as boards of education or state departments of agriculture, are concerned sometimes with special aspects of public health. In two states, Massachusetts and New York, industrial hygiene functions are under state departments of labor. The decisive agency in preventive services at the state, as at the local, level, however, remains the health department.

rural population averaged 12 cents per capita.[11] The Service requires that the states in some degree match the federal grant with state or local appropriations, but enforcement of this requirement is liberal and it is rare that a state is denied any funds because of inability to match. Encouraging as is this program, it is a long way from meeting true needs. There is a natural tendency for funds to go to the states and ultimately to the local units already having some public health organization that can absorb the money. Hundreds of rural counties, therefore, have never enjoyed the benefits of this federal aid except in so far as state-sponsored programs have reached local residents.

The agencies allotting these federal grants to the states, under the Public Health Service Act and the Social Security Act, are the United States Public Health Service and the Children's Bureau in the Federal Security Agency. The funds allotted by the Public Health Service provide resources for expanded activities in such fields as sanitation, vital statistics, public health nursing, laboratory work, communicable disease control (including tuberculosis and venereal diseases), industrial hygiene, training of personnel, and general administration. Funds allotted by the Children's Bureau are devoted to the promotion of programs for maternal and child health and for crippled children. In the fiscal year ending June 30, 1944, federal grants to the states for public health work were as follows: $11,000,000 for general public health functions, $10,276,200 for venereal disease control, and $9,690,000 for maternal and child health services.[12] A major part of these funds, in turn, are allotted by the state agencies to local units of public health administration.

The Public Health Service and the Children's Bureau, furthermore, engage in numerous other activities which benefit rural people either directly or indirectly. Consultative services are available in virtually all fields of public health, and urban and rural groups alike benefit from federal activities in scientific research, in health education, and in foreign and interstate quarantine. Growing out of wartime

[11] Derived from data in U. S. Public Health Service, *Annual Report*, 1941. Washington: Government Printing Office, 1942.

[12] "Federal Health Aid to the States," *Medical Care*, 4:181, May, 1944. In addition, in that year $11,179,000 was appropriated by the Federal Government for direct federal wartime measures for emergency health and sanitation in extra-cantonment or war production areas, for malaria control, and for industrial hygiene.

malaria control activities, a special field training and consultation program in communicable disease control, of particular value for rural public health agencies, was organized by the United States Public Health Service in 1946, operating from the Communicable Disease Center at Atlanta, Georgia.[13]

Several other federal agencies play direct or indirect roles in the general field of public health. The nation as a whole has benefited from programs such as the control of drugs by the Food and Drug Administration, the handling of vital statistics by the Bureau of the Census,[13a] the health education activities of the Office of Education, and the wartime social hygiene program of the Office of Community War Services. This brief listing of federal activities in the public health field is by no means complete; federal programs in medical care, rather than conventional public health, including the special rural activities of the Department of Agriculture, will be considered in Chapters 20, 21, and 22.

Coverage of Public Health Agencies

The critical agency in the provision of public health services to rural people is beyond doubt the local department of health. Nearly all functions of numerous agencies, federal and state, must reach their point of delivery at this level, and the most elaborate programs of federal and state agencies do little good if an effective local public health organization is not at hand to do the ultimate job. Yet the fact is that, compared with the cities, rural sections are very inadequately served by local health agencies.

Experience has shown that even an approach to adequate public health services requires the employment of a full-time health officer, assisted by a staff of public health nurses, sanitarians, clerks, and others. Recent reports have set the minimum standards of supply

[13] ANDREWS, JUSTIN M., "The United States Public Health Service Communicable Disease Center," *Public Health Reports*. 61:1203-1210, Aug. 16, 1946.

[13a] In 1946 the Division of Vital Statistics of the Bureau of the Census, Department of Commerce, was transferred to the U. S. Public Health Service, as the National Office of Vital Statistics. Other statistical functions, however, relating to population, housing, education, and related fields useful in public health administration, remain in the Census Bureau.

at about one public health nurse per 5,000 population,[14] two sanitary officers per 50,000 (one preferably a sanitary or public health engineer), and one clerk per 15,000 population, in addition to the medical officer of health for every jurisdiction of at least 50,000 population.[15] Measured even by these conservative standards, only a small fraction of our rural counties are adequately served with public health personnel. This omits consideration, furthermore, of needs for additional specialized personnel such as public health dentists and dental hygienists, health educators, laboratory technicians, vital statisticians, and others that should be available in units serving large numbers of rural people.

There has, indeed, been a steady growth in the number of counties covered by full-time public health units — that is, units headed by a full-time health officer as distinguished from a part-time official. In 1915 there were 14 counties so covered; in 1920 there were 109 counties; in 1925, 280 counties; in 1930, 505 counties;[16] and in 1935 there were 762 counties.[17] The early development of these health departments was concentrated chiefly in the rural states of the Southeast, due largely to the sanitation programs launched by the Rockefeller Foundation and the United States Public Health Service in the effort to control hookworm infestation. By 1942, through the strong stimulus of federal grants under the Social Security Act, health departments had been established on a full-time basis covering 1,828 counties.[18] These units covered either individual counties or small groups of counties and were under the jurisdiction of either local or state governments. There still remained, therefore, 1,242

[14] As public health nursing broadens into a community nursing service and comes to include home care of the sick, a trend already in evidence, the ratio will have to be one public health nurse to about 2,500 population or better. National Organization for Public Health Nursing, Committee on Nursing Administration, "Administration of Home Nursing Care of the Sick by Health Departments," *Public Health Nursing*, 37:399-342, July, 1945.

[15] American Public Health Association, Committee on Local Health Units, "Units of Local Health Service for All the States," *American Journal of Public Health*, 33:404-409, April, 1943.

[16] LUMSDEN, L. L., "Extent of Rural Health Service in the U. S., 1926-1930," *Public Health Reports*, 45:1065-1081, May 9, 1930.

[17] KRATZ, F. W., "Status of Full-time Local Health Organization at the End of the Fiscal Year 1941-42," *Public Health Reports*, 58:345-351, Feb. 26, 1943.

[18] *Ibid.*

counties — 40 per cent of all the counties in the nation — in which no full-time county or district health departments were functioning. Nearly all of them were entirely rural or contained large rural sections. Although some communities in these counties were served by municipal health agencies, nevertheless, there still remained 33 million people — one-fourth of our national population — lacking the protection of a full-time health department.[19] The distribution of county and district health units as of 1941 is illustrated in Figure 35.

The striking feature of Figure 35 is that some of our lowest income rural states of the South have the broadest county public health coverage. In response to the challenge presented by widespread hookworm disease, typhoid fever, malaria, pellagra, high infant mortality, and the relative meagerness of private medical facilities, these county units have become extended through the years. Within rural America, the South is doubtless in the forefront of public health coverage.

This fact gives no ground for confidence, however, in comparing public health coverage in rural and industrialized sections. Figure 35, in a sense, presents the picture of public health only within rural confines, since it considers only county or district units. The great sections of our urban population covered by well-organized municipal health agencies are not reflected on the map at all. Many areas served by so-called district units, moreover — New Mexico, for example, or southern Indiana — have barely more than token service, with several counties coming under the jurisdiction of a staff hardly ample to handle one county.[20] Health officials in these states will be the first to admit the inadequacies. The existence of a county unit, for that matter, gives no real information on the scope or volume of public health services available in that county. Most important, of course, we see vast stretches of territory in practically all regions of the nation without any full-time public health coverage whatever. Unlike the situation for private medical resources, furthermore, the population of a county without a public health agency cannot depend on the health department in a neighboring county for services.

[19] *Ibid.*

[20] This should not discredit the idea of a district unit, when adequately staffed and financed. As we shall see later, the organization of strong district units is particularly applicable to the problem of providing public health coverage to thinly settled and relatively low-income rural areas.

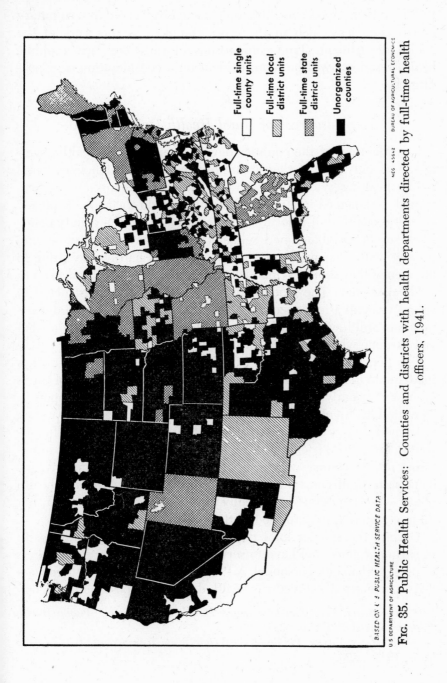

BASED ON U. S. PUBLIC HEALTH SERVICE DATA

U. S. DEPARTMENT OF AGRICULTURE   NEG. 43642   BUREAU OF AGRICULTURAL ECONOMICS

FIG. 35. Public Health Services: Counties and districts with health departments directed by full-time health officers, 1941.

Rural sections, moreover, are only meagerly served by voluntary health agencies which in the cities complement the work of the health department. True comparisons of rural and urban public health resources will be more evident on a consideration of expenditures.

The Resources of Rural Health Departments

Consideration of the counties devoid of any official health coverage gives only part of the picture of the gross deficiencies in rural public health services. Few rural health departments are housed, staffed, or financed in a manner adequate to do their job. Typically the rural health unit is located in the basement of the county courthouse or in an abandoned schoolhouse.[21] Interior furnishings are usually of the meanest sort and the setting is hardly one fitting to an agency that should symbolize sanitary maintenance and modern medical science. The modern public health centers constructed in recent years in a few dozen rural places to house the health department are still few and far between, although they demonstrate what can be done when funds and leadership are provided.[22]

The personnel of the rural health department are nearly always inadequate in numbers and type of training because of lack of funds or, more recently, because of sheer lack of available manpower. The rural health officer has often been some venerable old physician, untrained in the techniques or attitudes of public health administration but a loyal friend of the community, whom the county supervisors or the county court wish to reward in his declining years. This pattern, of course, applies more often to the part-time health officer who is appointed nominally to fulfill a legal requirement, but all too often it applies to the full-time official as well.

Despite the smaller total populations to be served, rural health department personnel have to serve proportionately larger numbers of persons than city personnel. A 1945 study revealed that there were 4,200 persons to be served per health department position in the city

[21] MOUNTIN, J. W., "The Housing of Health Departments," *Public Health Reports*, 57:781-789, May 22, 1942.

[22] GOLDMANN, FRANZ, *Public Medical Care*. New York: Columbia University Press, 1945, p. 57.

units and 5,800 persons per position in the county units.[22a] The actual ratios of personnel to population are less favorable than this in most county health units, since many of the positions are vacant.

One of the best indexes of public health resources in any area is the ratio of public health nurses to the population. When this is computed, we find that the apparent superiority of public health coverage in the rural South suggested in Figure 35 disappears. In 1940, considering public health nurses employed by voluntary as well as official agencies, the urbanized Northeast had a ratio of one public health nurse to 4,267 persons while the South had less than half that supply, or one to 9,307 persons. Even the North Central region, with its very poor coverage of county health departments, had a ratio of 1 to 7,913 and the West had a ratio of 1 to 5,701.[23] These data do not even include public health nurses working in industrial establishments, so that they actually understate the supply in urban regions. It will be recalled that the minimum desirable ratio of public health nurses to population is between 1 to 5,000 and 1 to 2,500.

In 1941 there were 20,441 public health nurses employed in the United States, and the vast majority of these, 19,461, were working in local agencies. Of these only 34.7 per cent were in rural communities with their 43.5 per cent of the national population.[24] State health agencies, moreover, do not make up the gaps in local supply. In 1940, over half the states each employed fewer than 30 public health nurses and among the predominantly rural states only Virginia had a staff of over 100.[25] The relative supply of Negro public health nurses, as with Negro physicians, is far below the resources necessary to meet the especially great public health needs of the rural Negro population.[26] In certain counties not served by full-time units, the

[22a] ALTENDERFER, MARIAN E., "Full-time Public Health Positions in Local Health Departments," *Public Health Reports*, 61:866-874, June 14, 1946.

[23] Derived from data in U. S. Public Health Service, *Annual Report*, 1940, pp. 29-30.

[24] American Nurses Association, Nursing Information Bureau, *Facts about Nursing*, 1944. New York, 1944, p. 62.

[25] MOUNTIN, J. W., and EVELYN FLOOK, "Distribution of Health Services in the Structure of State Government: X. State Health Department Organization," *op. cit.*, 58:541-577, Apr. 2, 1943.

[26] CORNELY, PAUL B., "A Study of Negro Nursing," *Public Health Nursing*, 34:449-451, August, 1942.

rural population is served by public health nurses affiliated with neighboring health jurisdictions or with voluntary agencies. In 1940, however, the rural population of 857 counties was not receiving even this limited type of health supervision; yet only 20 cities were equally devoid of service.[27]

Beyond these inadequacies, the rural public health nurse is faced with a heavier load of responsibilities than the nurse in the city public health program. With the shortage of rural physicians she must perform many functions of health instruction to families or even carry out certain services done usually by the medical practitioner in the cities. In the absence of sufficient clerical assistance on the health department's staff, on the other hand, she must perform numerous clerical duties that rob her time. Long distances to be traveled, bad roads, and lack of telephones make further inroads on her busy day. Because of these pressures, most rural health departments have found it impossible to furnish bedside care as a function of the public health nurse or they have had to reduce it to merely a minimum demonstration basis.

It is encouraging to find that a new generation of well-trained personnel is developing to carry on the many essential tasks of the rural public health nurse. While most public health nurses in rural communities have not had formal academic training in their field, the percentage with such training is higher in rural health departments than in urban, 32 per cent in the former and 19 per cent in the latter having had one or more years of formal study.[28] It is ironic that, despite this, the public health nurses employed by county health departments are paid salaries 16 to 26 per cent below those employed by municipal health departments for the same grade of responsibility — a differential hardly warranted by differences in cost of living.[29]

In view of her training, one of the most distressing problems met by many a rural public health nurse is the recurrent conflict of newly indoctrinated knowledge with the outdated ideas of some well-meaning country doctor. While not exclusively rural, this problem

[27] PERROTT, G. ST. J., and DOROTHY F. HOLLAND, "The Nation's Health Resources," *Survey Graphic*, 31:139-141, March, 1942.

[28] McIVER, PEARL, "The 1944 Census of Public Health Nurses," *Public Health Nursing*, 36:498-501, October, 1944.

[29] American Nurses Association, Nursing Information Bureau, *op. cit.*, p. 75.

is intensified by the limited choice of physicians in country districts. Many are the heartaches of the newly trained public health nurse who sees one of her patients having syphilis treated with mercury and iodides when she is well aware that he should be getting an arsenical and bismuth — or penicillin. At the same time, the rural public health nurse is often largely responsible for acquainting local physicians as well as community groups with the objectives and methods of the entire public health program.[29a]

The most decisive reflection of public health resources is the ratio of the health department's budget to the population it must serve, or its per capita outlay. Competent authorities agree that $2 per capita is required to provide satisfactory public health services to a community.[30] Most rural counties, however, spend for public health work hardly $0.50 annually for every person under their jurisdiction, counting funds from all sources. In 1936, before federal grant-in-aid funds were having a major effect, Joseph W. Mountin showed that, among 94 typical counties studied, the more populous urban counties had considerably higher per capita expenditures than the thinly populated rural counties. In counties with a population of 500,000 persons or more the per capita expenditure of funds from all sources for public health service was $0.93, while it fell gradually to $0.40 in counties with a population of 20,000 to 60,000 persons.[31] Mountin concluded that "generally speaking, public health organization reaches its highest development in cities of large size."[32] This relationship was found for expenditures coming from all official sources, and the contributions of funds from voluntary sources serve to aggravate the disparity.

The provision of federal grants-in-aid to the states and separate state or private grant funds has done more to elevate expenditures in rural counties than in urban. Thus, evaluation studies of the American

[29a] BUCK, FRANCES S., "The Rural Public Health Nurse in Venereal Disease Control," *The Journal of Venereal Disease Information*, 28:60-64, April, 1947.

[30] HISCOCK, IRA V., *Community Health Organization*. New York: The Commonwealth Fund, 1939, pp. 295-307.

[31] There was a rise to $0.54 per capita expenditures for counties with populations of under 20,000 but this was attributed to "unusual expenditures by a few contained counties that receive large grants-in-aid from an endowment."

[32] MOUNTIN, J. W., "How Expenditures for Selected Public Health Services Are Apportioned," *Public Health Reports*, 52:1384-1389, Oct. 1, 1937.

Public Health Association for 243 selected communities in 1943-44 showed that outside funds raised the budgets of health departments in "larger areas" (over 100,000 population) from a median per capita expenditure of 55 cents in local funds to a total of 82 cents per capita — an increase of about 50 per cent. In "smaller areas" outside subsidy raised the median per capita expenditure of 27 cents in local funds to a total of 64 cents per capita — an increase of over 135 per cent.[32a]

It is evident that even with the partially equalizing effects of the federal grant-in-aid program, rural-urban differentials in expenditures for public health remain. Data are available on all expenditures by local health agencies of funds from all sources, according to states. The principal relationship is illustrated in Table 41. It is clear that expenditures in the most rural segment of the states are at only about half the rate of those in the most urban states. Of the 20 states with populations over 50 per cent urban, the component local jurisdictions of only 3 spent less than $0.50 per capita for public health services, while in the 28 states with predominantly rural populations, the component jurisdictions of 16 spent less than this. Nevertheless, certain exceptions to the general rule give significant reflections of the influence of governmental subsidies on the health services available to rural people. Mississippi, for example, with the greatest proportionate rurality, the lowest per capita income of all the states, the lowest ratio of physicians, and the smallest supply of hospital beds, reports a per capita expenditure for local public health services of $0.57, exceeding that of 26 other states. Illinois, on the other hand, the fifth most urban state, with a high ratio of medical care resources and ninth among the states in per capita wealth, reports a corresponding expenditure of only $0.53, falling below that of 10 states that are predominantly rural.[33]

The absolute expenditures for public health services in all rural states, however, remain considerably below optimal standards. The range of expenditures for local services in the predominantly rural states, between $0.24 per capita in North Dakota and $0.72 in Louisiana, is given perspective when compared with the per capita expendi-

[32a] American Public Health Association, *Health Practice Indices*, 1943-44 (Subcommittee on State and Local Health Administration), New York, 1945, p. 76.

[33] EMERSON and LUGINBUHL, *op. cit.*, pp. 17-18.

Table 41. Public Health Expenditures: *Annual per capita expenditures for all local public health services, by states in order of rurality,* 1942

State	Per capita expenditures	State	Per capita expenditures
United States	$0.61	Population 50 to 59 per cent rural (*cont.*) . .	
Population under 30 per cent rural	0.90	Texas	$0.40
District of Columbia .	1.59	Iowa	0.25
Rhode Island . . .	0.58	Kansas	0.27
Massachusetts . . .	. . .	Louisiana	0.72
New York	0.99	Maine	0.33
New Jersey	1.10	Population 60 to 69 per cent rural	0.49
Illinois	0.53	
California	0.94	Nevada	0.60
Population 30 to 39 per cent rural	0.57	Nebraska	0.33
		Montana	0.41
Connecticut	0.75	Oklahoma	0.32
Ohio	0.58	Wyoming	0.41
Pennsylvania	0.49	Virginia	0.51
Michigan	0.68	Tennessee	0.64
Population 40 to 49 per cent rural	0.52	Arizona	0.54
		Georgia	0.52
Maryland	0.71	Vermont	0.58
New Hampshire . .	0.56	Idaho	0.30
Utah	0.67	New Mexico	0.68
Florida	0.63	Alabama	0.49
Indiana	0.30	Population 70 to 79 per cent rural	0.47
Wisconsin	0.54	
Washington	0.65	Kentucky	0.54
Colorado	0.58	West Virginia . . .	0.33
Delaware	0.54	North Carolina . . .	0.57
Missouri	0.46	South Dakota . . .	0.28
Population 50 to 59 per cent rural	0.42	South Carolina . . .	0.43
		Arkansas	0.38
Minnesota	0.42	North Dakota . . .	0.24
Oregon	0.65	Mississippi	0.57

Source: Emerson, Haven, and Martha Luginbuhl, *Local Health Units for the Nation* (Report of the Subcommittee on Local Health Units of the Committee on Administrative Practice, American Public Health Association). New York: The Commonwealth Fund, 1945, pp. 17–18.

ture of farm people for drugs alone, amounting in 1941 to well over $2 per capita. Within rural states, of course, there are marked differences in public health expenditures between urban and rural counties. In North Carolina, for example, the per capita expenditure of the five largest cities in 1943-44 ranged from $0.89 to $1.67, while in five typical rural counties it averaged $0.41. These expenditures include contributions from local, state, and Federal governments and they omit consideration of some of the most rural counties in the state that lack health departments entirely.[34]

Preventive Health Services Rendered

With inadequate physical facilities, personnel, and financial resources, it is obvious that the volume of public health services rendered by rural health departments must be far below the needs. Accurate data on this are unfortunately difficult to obtain. The volume of preventive services of different types received by families, either at public health clinics or from private practitioners, is some reflection, however, of a health department's effectiveness, and some data on this are available.

In 1930, the Committee on the Costs of Medical Care found that in rural areas only 34.2 per cent of persons of all ages had been vaccinated against smallpox compared with 71.5 per cent in cities of 100,000 and over.[35] A decade later, despite great advances in rural public health work, the differential still held. A study of low-income farm families in 1940 showed that only 37 per cent of children up to 8 years of age, had received smallpox vaccination,[36] whereas 89 per cent of such children had been vaccinated among

[34] Derived from data in North Carolina Agricultural Experiment Station, *Medical Care Services in North Carolina* (Reprint Prog. Rep. RS-4). Raleigh, February, 1945, Processed, pp. 64-66.

[35] COLLINS, SELWYN D., "History and Frequency of Smallpox Vaccinations and Cases in 9,000 Families," *Public Health Reports*, 51:443-479, Apr. 17, 1936.

[36] GOVER, MARY, and JESSE B. YAUKEY, "Physical Impairments of Members of Low-income Farm Families — 11,490 Persons in 2,477 Farm Security Administration Borrower Families, 1940: VI. Extent of Immunization against Smallpox, Diphtheria, and Typhoid Fever," *Public Health Reports*, 61:97-114, Jan. 25, 1946.

families in 28 large cities surveyed as part of the 1935-36 National Health Survey.[37]

In 1930 the record of diphtheria immunizations was somewhat higher in rural communities than in large cities,[38] although this may have been due to certain special immunological considerations.[39] By 1940, in fact, the relationship was apparently reversed, for among low-income farm families 52 per cent of children had been immunized against diphtheria by their eighth year,[40] while in the large cities the National Health Survey showed that 60 per cent of such children had been protected.[41]

Another index of the effectiveness of public health work is the performance of routine examinations of infants and children either under health department or private auspices. In 1930, such preventive services were performed on 235.4 children per 1,000 in cities of 100,000 and over, compared with 135.1 per 1,000 in rural areas.[42] Yet in 1945 it was pointed out that some two out of three rural counties provide no regular "well baby" or "child health conferences" or clinics under health department auspices. Likewise three out of four rural counties provide no regular monthly prenatal clinics for expectant mothers despite the higher rural birth rate.[43]

[37] COLLINS, SELWYN D., and CLARA COUNCELL, "Extent of Immunization and Case Histories for Diphtheria, Smallpox, Scarlet Fever, and Typhoid Fever in 200,000 Surveyed Families in 28 Large Cities," Public Health Reports, 58:1121-1151, July 23, 1943.

[38] COLLINS, SELWYN D., "History and Frequency of Diphtheria Immunizations and Cases in 9,000 Families," Public Health Reports, 51:1736-1773, Dec. 18, 1936.

[39] In this period the routine practice was to Schick test children and to immunize only the positive reactors. Since greater epidemiological contacts in the cities would tend to give a greater proportion of urban children natural immunity, the proportionate number of positive reactors for whom immunization was considered indicated was probably greater in the country. Today the usual practice is to immunize all infants without preliminary testing.

[40] GOVER and YAUKEY, op. cit.

[41] COLLINS and COUNCELL, op. cit.

[42] COLLINS, SELWYN D., "Frequency of Health Examinations in 9,000 Families," Public Health Reports, 49:321-346, Mar. 9, 1934.

[43] U. S. Children's Bureau, Building the Future for Children and Youth: Next Steps Proposed by the National Commission in Wartime (U. S. Department of Labor Pub. 310). Washington, April, 1945, pp. 6-7.

The higher infant and maternal mortality rates in rural sections are doubtless related to these deficiencies in public health services.

Other categories of public health service show corresponding rural-urban differentials. School health services are well known to be especially deficient in rural areas and small towns,[44] due as much to weaknesses in rural boards of education as in rural health agencies. The comparison between venereal disease clinic services in rural and urban states, in relation to the size of the disease problem, has been considered in Chapter 15. The same story could doubtless be told with respect to tuberculosis control, health education, or other accepted functions of health departments. The weakness of much rural public health work is reflected by the finding in two southern rural counties in 1937 that members of only about 6 per cent of local families had attended a public health clinic during the year.[44a]

The War and Current Trends

With the Second World War, public health agencies in rural areas suffered serious losses in personnel at a time when their financial appropriations were greater than ever. For the first time, manpower became a more critical problem than money. As early as January, 1942, state and local health departments estimated needs for over 6,000 new workers, or an increase of their supply by about 30 per cent.[45] The supply of public health nurses in rural health departments rose somewhat between 1940 and 1943, but in the face of the vastly increased burdens imposed by the shortage of physicians, health agencies were more shorthanded than ever. The number of counties lacking public health nursing services entirely actually rose during the war from 679 in 1941 to 845 in 1944, although the number of cities lacking such service declined from 31 to 13 during the same period.[46] Moreover, there was an associated decline in the number of nurses employed by local voluntary agencies and by school boards. Even after the war improvement was not evident, and in 1946 the number of counties having no nurses engaged in full-time rural

[44] Ibid.

[44a] MOUNTAIN, JOSEPH W., ELLIOTT H. PENNELL, and HAZEL O'HARA, "Relationship of a Rural Health Program to the Needs in the Area," Public Health Reports, 52:1264-1284, Sept. 10, 1937.

[45] PERROTT, G. ST. J., and H. F. DORN, "Needs for Health Personnel," Public Health Reports, 57:997-1000, July 3, 1942.

[46] U. S. Public Health Service, Annual Report, 1944.

public health work had risen to 1,133.[47] The supply of trained sanitarians and sanitary engineers declined, as these personnel were absorbed by the armed forces and, most critical of all, the number of full-time health officers fell. Between 1941 and 1945 there was a 13 per cent decline in the number of full-time local health officers, mostly in the South.[48] Many health departments had to be carried on under the direction of hard-working public health nurses.

Despite the handicaps, new responsibilities were placed on many rural health departments by the war. Among these were revitalized programs of malaria control (especially to protect the armed forces from infection), an enormously increased task of venereal disease control, the administration of the program of Emergency Maternity and Infant Care for the wives and infants of servicemen, and other war-connected jobs. To ease the burden of war-affected areas, the United States Public Health Service developed a program of "lend-leasing" public health personnel to local areas of need. Scores of rural sections affected by war mobilization benefited from this federal assistance.

Another adjustment to wartime shortages in personnel was the increased tendency for adjacent counties to combine into public health districts, making joint use of available personnel. By June, 1942, 32.3 per cent of counties with full-time public health services were in local or state-sponsored district units, when in 1935 the comparable percentage had been 13.4.[49] Under the pressure of events, therefore, long-standing inertia or notions of county sovereignty were somewhat overcome and the framework of more effective patterns of local health administration for rural areas was built, although serious understaffing was the usual situation.

All in all, we must recognize that while rural public health resources and services are still considerably below urban, the situation, unlike that regarding physicians and related personnel, is gradually improving. Numerous remedial measures have already been set under way, chiefly through programs of grant-in-aid financing from the Federal Government, tending to raise the level of performance

[47] HEISLER, ANNA, "The 1946 Census of Public Health Nurses," *Public Health Nursing*, 28:519-522, October, 1946.

[48] DAVIS, BURNET M., and MARION E. ALTENDERFER, "Effect of the War on the Distribution of Full-time Local Health Officers," *American Journal of Public Health*, 35:1047-1052, October, 1945.

[49] KRATZ, *op. cit.*

in the more underprivileged rural areas. Despite federal financial aid, however, the main burden of public health support falls on the states and local communities. In a relatively heavily subsidized rural state like North Carolina, for example, 41.6 per cent of all public health funds expended were from the Federal Government in 1943-44 while the remainder came from state and local sources. Considering expenditures at the local level alone, more than 65 per cent depended on state and local sources.[50] For the country as a whole, less than 15 per cent of funds used to support all local public health work in 1943-44 came from federal grants made by both the Public Health Service and the Children's Bureau.[51]

The trend, nevertheless, is clearly toward increased federal support of public health functions, particularly in rural sections. With this, the absolute per capita amounts being used for public health work are increasing, although we have seen that in rural areas as well as urban they still fall far below true needs. As the general organization of health services increases, therapeutic as well as preventive, the health department is looked to more and more for leadership and its scope is inevitably broadening. Divisions of geriatrics and adult hygiene are being established in state health departments;[52] federal funds are being made available to the states specifically for a public health attack on cancer;[53] a great variety of special responsibilities in medical care administration is almost daily being assigned to public health agencies at state and local levels.[54] One of the key questions of the day is the extent to which the health department should and will become concerned with the actual administration of expanding medical care programs for the general population.

[50] North Carolina Agricultural Experiment Station, *op. cit.*, p. 66A; also, personal communication from Dr. Selz C. Mayo of the University of North Carolina, 1945.

[51] U. S. Public Health Service, *Annual Report*, 1944, p. 117; also, unpublished data furnished by U. S. Children's Bureau.

[52] Indiana State Board of Health, *Adult Hygiene and Geriatrics*. Indianapolis, 1946.

[53] For the fiscal year 1946-47, over $2,000,000 of Public Health Service grants to the states was earmarked by Congress for cancer control.

[54] MOUNTIN, JOSEPH W., "Participation by State and Local Health Departments in Current Medical Care Programs," *American Journal of Public Health*, 36:1387-1393, December, 1946.

CHAPTER 20

PUBLIC WELFARE MEDICAL SERVICES

W HILE preventive services for everyone have long been regarded as the province of government, general medical care has by and large been a public responsibility in the United States only for certain dependent or pauperized sections of the population. For the poor, various systems of medical relief have been provided since Colonial times, and a great variety of programs of medical assistance of different coverage, benefits, and administration has developed.[1]

Public medical services include not only the medical care of the indigent and the "medically indigent" but, properly speaking, the public care of persons with special high-cost illnesses like tuberculosis, mental disorders, or leprosy, and the public care of specially protected groups in the population like veterans, Indians, or merchant seamen.[2] As these specialized categories of services will be considered later, we may examine here the welfare medical services available to the indigent members of the rural population.

The General Structure of Welfare Medical Programs

The number of the "indigent" in the population for whom welfare medical care is available naturally varies in different economic periods. Considering all persons receiving public assistance from federal, state, or local governments, this group numbered about 4.7 million even in relatively prosperous 1940. If to these are added the approximately 2.9 million persons who were employed in federal work relief programs at the time, we see that 7.6 million persons, or 5.8 per cent of the total population, were in some degree eligible for welfare medical services, as a publicly recognized

---

[1] For a general discussion, see ALTMEYER, A. J., "Medical Care for Persons in Need," *Social Security Bulletin*, May, 1945, Reprint.

[2] GOLDMANN, FRANZ, "Medical Care," *Social Work Year Book*, 1943. New York: Russell Sage Foundation, Reprint.

right.[3] Beyond these there is in any period a far larger though less definite group of the "medically indigent" whose characteristics will be discussed below.

Until recent years the medical care of the indigent has been provided almost entirely as a feature of local poor relief systems having their origin in Elizabethan times. The local Overseer of the Poor had authority to pay for desperately needed medical services to a local pauper, based usually on his own judgment of need.[4] In the nineteenth century the poorhouse developed as an institution to care for the local poor, sick and well alike. A physician was sometimes engaged to visit the place at intervals or when called. In the larger cities hospitals were developed for the bed care of the indigent, and gradually special physicians came to be appointed as "physicians for the poor," paid for their services out of local government revenue. In the main, the development of these medical relief services in rural areas was rudimentary and today, relative to provisions in urban areas, the same holds true.

With the onset of the economic depression of the 1930's, a fundamental change took place in the manner of provision and the financial support of welfare medical services. In 1933, with the collapse of local relief services associated with the huge burden of unemployment, financial responsibilities were very substantially assumed by the Federal Government. Under the Federal Emergency Relief Administration (FERA), federal funds were allotted to all the states for relief purposes; state and local support continued in varying degrees, particularly in the more prosperous states. Out of these funds medical expenses could be paid for ambulatory or home medical services; hospitalization remained a local or a local-and-state responsibility. The predominant pattern followed in the use of these funds was the provision of services by local private practitioners, freely chosen by the welfare recipient, with remuneration being made upon a fee-for-service basis.[5] While services usually required authorization by welfare officials,

[3] U. S. Social Security Board, op. cit., p. 70.

[4] DEUTSCH, ALBERT, "Historical Interrelations between Medicine and Social Welfare," Bulletin of the History of Medicine, 11:485-502, May, 1942.

[5] FALK, I. S., and ANNE E. GEDDES, "Medical Care in Public Welfare Programs," Medical Care, 1:64-77, Winter, 1941.

bills were customarily reviewed and approved by local committees of physicians. In some rural sections, however, the salaried "poor doctor" system persisted even under FERA subsidy, simply because in some areas it was FERA policy to foster continuation of well-established local systems and to use federal funds merely to augment these.

After a few years the system of federally assisted home relief was in large measure supplanted by federally supported work relief, through the Work Projects Administration (WPA), the Civilian Conservation Corps (CCC), and the National Youth Administration (NYA). While state and local relief expenditures — which had never disappeared completely — continued, this change represented a fundamental revision in the philosophy of federal public aid to those persons whom the normal economic market could not absorb. The income provided through work relief to employable but indigent persons was assumed, then, to cover the costs of medical services along with other expenses of living. All direct medical care responsibilities for the remaining indigent, on home relief, were left with the states and local communities; since state plans were few, this meant preponderantly with local units.[6] In rural communities, where local revenues were scanty, this usually meant a sharp decline in welfare medical services. Accordingly the relatively expensive free-choice and fee-for-service patterns of service usually provided under FERA lapsed back in many places into the antiquated county "poor doctor" pattern — or services were almost entirely discontinued. In many other communities the patterns induced under FERA subsidy were continued.

In 1935, with the passage of the Social Security Act, a federal program was established to assist states in providing public assistance to certain specified needy groups. This program was limited to indigent persons past 65 years of age, dependent children, and the needy blind.[7] Under the public assistance

[6] DAVIS, MICHAEL M., *Public Medical Services.* Chicago: University of Chicago Press, 1937, pp. 26-28.

[7] This is not to be confused with the old-age and survivors' *insurance* provisions of the Social Security Act, which provide for insurance benefits to covered workers and their dependents or survivors when they reach 65 years and retire or after the insured dies.

program, the Federal Government makes grants to the states on a 50-50 matching basis up to specified maximums for the relief of these three categories of indigents.[7a] In order to avoid "pauperizing" the individual, however, a special provision was made in the Social Security Act that federal matching would be available only for cash grants, not for benefits in kind or in service. In other words, federal funds cannot be used for the direct payment of physicians or others for the provision of medical services to welfare clients; the closest approach to this is the policy in most states of including in the cash allowances the estimated costs of needed medical care, except when the maximum does not permit this. The client then may choose to purchase medical services on a private basis.[8]

State and local funds, however, may be used to supplement these grants with direct medical services to these "categorical" assistance cases. Thus, in 1940 the old-age assistance cases received some type of direct medical care out of state or local funds in 34 states, dependent children cases received such service in 29 states, and the needy blind in 32 states. The largest share of these expenditures has been for hospitalization.[9] It may be significant, however, that 11 states did not report any such supplemental medical service provided to federal-state assistance cases, and these were practically all rural states.

The policy of matching federal public assistance grants on an approximately 50-50 basis, without respect to the financial need of the state, has placed the less prosperous rural states at a distinct disadvantage. Thus with regard to the old-age grants, which represent much the largest category of public assistance payments, the average total monthly grant in Alabama, for example, in 1942 was $9.84, and in Kentucky was $10.20, compared with an average of $34.23 in Massachusetts and $36.91 in California. These grants

[7a] In August, 1946, the Social Security Act was amended to provide federal matching in a 2-to-1 ratio for the first $15 per month granted to public assistance recipients, retaining the 50-50 ratio for amounts above this. This minor change will mean slightly more favorable federal matching ratios for the rural states, since their over-all grants tend to be lower. The amendment is to be effective until 1950 and whether it will be continued beyond this remains to be seen.

[8] FALK and GEDDES, op. cit.

[9] Ibid.

are, of course, in addition to the private financial resources of the individual, but these are seldom great. Obviously with such pittances, even in urban sections, few funds are left for the procurement of medical services after the elementary needs of food, clothing, and shelter are met.[10] It is encouraging that during the recent wartime prosperity, 29 states eliminated statutory maximums on the cash grants made to the categorical relief cases. This means that, when state funds are adequate, the client may be more amply enabled to secure medical services.

As noted, the provision of welfare assistance for persons on general relief (all except the three federally shared categories) remains a state and local responsibility; under these programs medical services of a kind are provided directly to welfare aid recipients. These services are most often but not always administered by welfare departments. In many states they are administered by special boards or commissions. In Louisiana, for example, a highly developed hospital and clinic program is provided for the indigent through special hospitals in the larger population centers, administered by the State Hospital Board. For the most part, the development of special programs of medical assistance for the indigent, whether for general relief clients exclusively or for categorical relief clients as well, has taken place in the wealthier urbanized states, through state administrative machinery. The populations of rural states have been left chiefly to their own meager resources at the county level.

The important point is that much the greater part of welfare money used for medical services, in rural and urban states alike, comes from state and local funds. While federal assistance has been forthcoming for the cash relief of special categories of the indigent and while federal works programs have provided jobs and incomes for others, direct medical services remain mainly a state and local responsibility. This, in effect, means that welfare

[10] U. S. Social Security Board, *op. cit.*, p. 76. Federal legislation has recently been under consideration which would modify the cash-grant rule for recipients of federal-state relief, and which would allow direct medical services to be provided and paid for by federal funds. It would also remove the federal grant maximums, provide for variable matching in relation to state needs, and include funds for general, as well as categorical, relief. None of this has been enacted, as of this writing, except for the minor change indicated in footnote 7a on p. 356.

recipients in the rural areas tend to receive less service, simply because the financial resources of those areas are less. Whatever the source of funds, moreover, administrative responsibilities for medical services in rural areas remain chiefly on a county basis. Despite contentions of certain political protagonists to the contrary, we may generalize that the more the financial responsibilities for a service are vested predominantly with local authorities, the more rural sections tend to suffer — simply because of their relative poverty.

Volume of Services and Expenditures

Accurate data on the actual volume of welfare medical services provided in rural areas are not available. Even allotments, reflecting medical services, are seldom figured separately in local welfare budgets. Some indication of the relative expenditures of urban and rural states, however, is given by a consideration of per capita expenditures for all public assistance among the states. While, as shown in the 1942 data presented in Table 42, there are considerable variations among individual states in the same urban-rural groups, certain trends become evident on consideration of the weighted averages. It may be noted that with respect to work relief programs, in which financial support is almost entirely federal, the per capita expenditures are variable but to some extent they tend to be higher in the more rural states. Yet these funds, it will be recalled, are not available for direct medical services. With respect to special categories of public assistance, in which financial support is generally half federal and half state and local, there is a more or less gradual reduction of per capita expenditures with increasing rurality of the states. These funds, it will also be recalled, are not available for medical services. For general assistance, however, in which funds are entirely state or local in origin, there is the most consistent and impressive decline in per capita expenditures, with increasing rurality of state, from $2.92 in the most urban group of states to $0.25 in the most rural group.[11] As with other health resources, it is evident that these deficiencies are associated chiefly

[11] It might be supposed that these differentials in over-all state per capita welfare expenditures reflect solely a smaller proportionate welfare case load in the rural states. It should be noted, however, that the trend of per capita expenditures for federal work relief would not support this claim; it might,

with the states of the South. The significant fact is that from these state and local funds the greatest part of direct medical care expenditures must come.

The actual per capita amounts available from state and local funds, furthermore, are considerably lower than the amounts available from federal or matched federal-state sources. For the nation as a whole the amount is $1.38 from the state and local funds for general assistance, compared with $6.00 from federal-state funds for categorical assistance and $4.44 from federal funds for work relief.[12] Despite the somewhat equalizing effects of federal funds, the combined per capita amounts from all sources shows a downward trend with increased rurality. It would seem reasonable to infer that where over-all per capita allowances are low, the proportion available for medical services is probably even lower, since nearly every penny is needed for the elementals of food and shelter. In 1940, outlays for medical care and hospitalization were estimated to have been about 7 per cent of all expenditures by general relief agencies at the state and local levels,[13] although, as suggested, the percentage in rural sections was undoubtedly lower. In contrast to general medical care experience, the greater part of the welfare medical bill for direct services is for hospitalization, a fact probably reflecting the philosophy of much welfare administration that, by and large, care should be confined to emergency conditions. Yet even for hospitalization, public expenditures tend to decline rapidly with decreasing size of community.[14] The disadvantages of the rural welfare client in need of medical care are reflected by the expenditure pattern in North Carolina, for example, where per capita expenditures for physicians' care and hospitalization are sometimes twenty times as great in urban counties as in rural.[15]

---

in fact, suggest that the proportion of state populations in rural states "on relief" according to federal criteria of indigency is even higher than in urban states.

[12] Derived from U. S. Social Security Board, *op. cit.*

[13] FALK and GEDDES, *op. cit.*, p. 73.

[14] U. S. Bureau of the Census, *City Finances,* 1942, *Cities Having Populations over* 25,000, Vol. 3. *Statistical Compendium* (Census of Governments, 1942). Washington: Government Printing Office, 1944.

[15] North Carolina Agricultural Experiment Station, *op. cit.*, p. 68.

Table 42. Public Welfare Expenditures: *Annual expenditures* per state resident for different types of welfare assistance, by states in urban-rural order*, 1942

State	Total expenditures (in thousands)	Expenditure per state resident			
		Total	Work relief (federally financed)	Special public assistance (federal-state financed)	General assistance (state and locally financed)
All states	$1,547,073	$11.81	$4.44	$6.00	$1.38
Population under 30 per cent rural	538,660	14.15	4.51	6.72	2.92
Dist. of Columbia . . .	4,744	5.78	3.09	2.10	0.59
Rhode Island	6,920	9.60	3.37	4.04	2.19
Massachusetts	76,514	17.91	6.04	9.81	2.06
New York	180,452	14.01	4.55	4.41	5.06
New Jersey	35,130	8.31	4.40	2.72	1.19
Illinois	122,333	15.34	4.96	7.45	3.93
California	112,567	15.67	3.35	11.34	0.97
Population 30 to 39 per cent rural	268,763	11.22	3.93	6.02	1.27
Connecticut	12,028	6.81	1.56	4.20	1.06
Ohio	82,840	11.95	3.95	6.87	1.14
Pennsylvania	111,455	11.47	4.34	5.82	1.31
Michigan	62,440	11.37	3.94	5.91	1.42
Population 40 to 49 per cent rural	239,919	13.08	4.22	7.85	1.01
Maryland	11,161	5.89	1.80	3.18	0.90
New Hampshire . . .	5,283	11.06	3.86	5.38	1.81
Utah	10,705	19.33	5.62	11.92	1.80
Florida	22,990	11.84	6.70	4.83	0.31
Indiana	38,598	11.09	3.62	6.53	0.95
Wisconsin	36,926	11.75	3.56	6.76	1.43
Washington	36,281	20.73	3.30	16.44	0.99
Colorado	28,369	26.04	5.29	18.85	1.90
Delaware	1,462	5.31	2.82	1.98	0.50
Missouri	48,144	12.89	5.31	6.86	0.72
Population 50 to 59 per cent rural	208,773	11.87	4.56	6.70	0.77
Minnesota	40,700	15.21	5.71	7.88	1.62
Oregon	11,378	10.69	2.74	6.92	1.03
Texas	76,254	11.84	4.69	7.02	0.13

Table 42. Public Welfare Expenditures: *Annual expenditures* per state resident for different types of welfare assistance, by states in urban-rural order, 1942.—(Continued)*

Population 50 to 59 per cent rural (*cont.*)				
Iowa	26,380	10.79	3.21	6.47	1.11
Kansas	21,258	15.28	4.44	6.83	1.10
Louisiana	24,399	10.06	5.98	4.71	0.58
Maine	8,404	10.22	2.29	6.40	1.53
Population 60 to 69 per cent rural	166,797	9.38	4.65	4.46	0.27
Nevada	1,489	11.62	4.35	6.67	0.59
Nebraska	16,231	13.06	5.19	7.29	0.57
Montana	9,226	17.69	8.29	8.53	0.86
Oklahoma	38,579	17.77	6.30	11.23	0.23
Wyoming	2,484	10.71	3.82	6.13	0.76
Virginia	11,141	3.99	2.40	1.38	0.21
Tennessee	20,709	7.10	3.96	3.08	0.61
Arizona	8,754	17.68	5.86	10.51	1.31
Georgia	23,586	7.71	4.50	3.06	0.15
Vermont	2,749	7.99	2.92	4.18	0.89
Idaho	7,275	15.25	6.18	8.65	0.43
New Mexico	7,391	14.19	9.88	3.99	0.32
Alabama	17,183	5.95	4.44	1.42	0.09
Population 70 per cent or more rural	125,991	8.27	5.11	2.90	0.25
Kentucky	22,018	8.00	5.27	2.57	0.18
West Virginia	24,039	12.96	6.88	5.20	0.87
North Carolina	19,691	5.70	3.45	2.15	0.10
South Dakota	8,038	13.68	5.90	7.02	0.77
South Carolina	15,914	8.39	6.02	2.25	0.12
Arkansas	15,121	7.70	5.25	2.30	0.15
North Dakota	6,636	11.19	5.31	5.22	0.65
Mississippi	14,534	6.82	4.91	1.90	0.02

Source: Derived from data in U. S. Social Security Board, *Social Security Yearbook,* 1942, p. 72.

* For explanation of methods by which these were determined, see original source.

Characteristics of Rural Welfare Medical Services

The entire level of welfare medical services in rural areas is conditioned by a narrower definition of eligibility for care than is usually followed in the cities. As the costs of scientific medical services have risen with expanding knowledge and technology,

an increasingly large section of the population has become unable
to meet the special financial burdens of medical service, though
still able to meet the costs of ordinary family living. These are
the so-called medically needy or medically indigent, and their
number obviously increases when general economic conditions
are poor.[16] Depending on one's definition of adequate medical
services, the medically indigent along with the fully indigent may
compose anywhere up to perhaps 90 per cent of the population,
the figure undoubtedly being higher in rural areas. In large cities
this concept of public responsibility for the medically indigent
has developed to a relatively high point and persons who can
demonstrate financial inability to purchase private medical services
are often able to obtain them, in some degree, through a public
agency without personal cost or at very low rates.[17] In the rural
areas, however, eligibility for services "on the county" depends
by and large on the applicant's being actually on the relief rolls;
anyone able to buy his own food and clothing is usually assumed
to be able to pay for his own medical care.

The public clinics for ambulatory care of public assistance
recipients and the medically indigent, found so generally in the
cities, are rare in rural districts. Municipal or county hospitals
for the bed care of the indigent, as we have noted, are less
numerous in rural sections, and the cost of hospitalization in
voluntary institutions is probably less often assumed out of public
funds than in the cities. The numerous voluntary agencies usually
supplementing the public medical provisions of welfare departments in the cities are seldom found in rural districts. Because
of limited funds for medical relief, relatively severe restrictions
are imposed in the authorization of hospitalization, when it is
provided, or of physicians' care beyond the limit of a call or
two. As a rule, the rural welfare client must have some serious
condition before care is authorized, and authorizing officials in

[16] GOLDMAN, FRANZ, *Public Medical Care*. New York: Columbia University
Press, 1945, pp. 74-83.

[17] There has, indeed, been much controversy in the cities about the "abuse"
of these free services by persons able to afford private care, though investigation usually reveals that upward of 90 per cent of such beneficiaries qualify
for "charity" care by a means test. Ross, MARY, "Why Not Do Without
Clinics?" *Survey Graphic*, 25:81-85, February, 1936.

the county government tend to be over-vigilant for possible evidence of abuse by patient or physician.[18]

The actual operating consequences of these policies in terms of services received is indicated by a few recent investigations. A welfare study in Montgomery County, Alabama — a relatively urbanized county of a highly rural state — disclosed that out of 1,459 individuals in families receiving A.D.C. (aid to dependent children) assistance, 1,053 showed no record of a medical examination during a 2-year period under study. Illnesses were known to have occurred in 677 individuals, undoubtedly an understatement, but 301 of these went without benefit of any medical attendance. Among those ill and medically attended, there were 439 illnesses, and it is illuminating to observe the source of support for these services; they were provided either without charge by private physicians, or by the local department of public welfare, by "clinics," by the "town physician," by relatives, by the Junior League, by the Lions Club, by the Kiwanis Club, or by the Hospital Committee of the Charity and Welfare Council.[19] The standard of quality of the services can perhaps be inferred from this dispersion of responsibility.

A similar study in New Mexico showed that, while about seven out of ten families receiving public assistance were in need of medical care, only four of them were examined or treated by a physician.[20] More than 50 agencies and organizations were involved in the provision of this care. Of the funds administered by the Department of Public Welfare for this service, 40 per cent was more or less budgeted in cash grants to the clients and 60 per cent was paid directly to physicians, hospitals, or others for the services rendered. The average medical expenditure from all sources per person eligible for welfare assistance was under $13 a year at a time (1943) when the national average was probably

[18] American Public Welfare Association, *Report of the Committee on Medical Care.* Annual Meeting, Seattle, Washington, June, 1938, Processed, p. 17.

[19] Alabama State Department of Public Welfare, "Health Problems in A.D.C. Families," *Alabama Social Welfare*, 9:13-14, December, 1944.

[20] New Mexico Department of Public Welfare, *Survey of Medical Care and Health Status of Recipients of Public Assistance.* Santa Fe, January, 1944, Processed, pp. 5-6.

between $30 and $40, and this for a group with considerably higher than average medical needs. Similar inadequacies have been shown in a study of medical care in Maryland.[21]

Because of the rising proportion of aged persons on the public assistance rolls, welfare agencies have become increasingly faced with the general problem of chronic disease. As cash grants for recipients of federal-state old-age assistance have had the effect of reducing the occupancy of outdated almshouses, there has been a movement to convert these structures into institutions for the custodial care of the chronic sick and even into chronic disease hospitals with competent medical staffs.[22] Broad-scale programs for the care of the chronically ill have been developed in a few states like New York, Illinois, Massachusetts, Connecticut, Indiana, Maryland, and New Jersey,[23] but again these steps have been virtually confined to the prosperous, urbanized states.

The characteristic pattern of administration of "free" medical services is a potpourri of mixed responsibilities, with chaotic overlapping in some fields and serious gaps in others. Responsibilities are divided between agencies for public health, public welfare, hospitalization, crippled children, tuberculosis, mental disorder, not to mention voluntary agencies of a dozen descriptions, medical societies, and whatnot. In a typical Southern county studied recently six agencies (three state and three county) were involved in providing public medical services, and in a typical New England town some 11 agencies were involved.[24] At the state level, the lack of uniformity and system is equally appalling; in the nation as a whole, some 11 different types of state agencies are concerned with the general medical care of the needy. What is worse, in

[21] Report of the Committee on Medical Care of the Maryland State Planning Commission, *Medical Care in the Counties of Maryland* (Pub. 40). Baltimore: Johns Hopkins University, 1944.

[22] American Public Welfare Association, *Institutional Care of the Chronically Ill*. A report of the Joint Committee on Hospital Care of the American Hospital Association and the American Public Welfare Association, Chicago, January, 1940.

[23] New York State Health Preparedness Commission, *Official Planning for the Care of the Chronically Ill in Other States*. Albany, May, 1946, Processed.

[24] STURGES, GERTRUDE, "Public Medical Care at the Grass Roots," *Medical Care*, 1:229-245, July, 1941.

14 states, all but four of which are over 60 per cent rural, no state agency is set up to handle the general administration of welfare medicine.[25] The abundant literature in this field is all insistent in pointing out these problems.

Welfare departments in most rural areas are inadequately staffed with trained personnel and lacking in medical supervision. In recent years some significant steps have been taken to unify, coordinate, and improve welfare medical services and to provide them with technical supervision — for example, in New York, Massachusetts, Connecticut, Illinois, Indiana, Minnesota, Oregon, Pennsylvania, Rhode Island, West Virginia, and Washington.[26] It may be noted, however, that nearly all these are predominantly urban states and all are in the North. Particular efforts have been made in New York State to improve the quality of welfare medicine through promotion of active interest by local medical societies.[27] In the state of Washington a special program of state-supported welfare medical services for "senior citizens" (recipients of old-age assistance) has naturally benefited the aged persons in rural and urban areas alike.[27a] In Kansas a special prepayment program for providing services to welfare clients has been developed in about 30 counties — highly significant in terms of possible future integration of welfare medicine with a more generalized health insurance program.[28]

[25] MOUNTIN, JOSEPH W., and EVELYN FLOOK, "Distribution of Health Services in the Structure of State Government: I. The Composite Pattern of State Health Services," op. cit.

[26] STURGES, GERTRUDE, "Medical Services under Public Welfare Departments," Medical Care, 4:206-211, August, 1944.

[27] DOWLING, L. C., "New York State's Public Medical Program," New York State Journal of Medicine, 42:904-914, May, 1942.

[27a] ANDERSON, ODIN W., Administration of Medical Care: Problems and Issues. Ann Arbor, Michigan: University of Michigan, School of Public Health, 1947. (Based on an Analysis of the Medical-Dental Care Program for the Recipients of Old-Age Assistance in the State of Washington, 1941-1945.)

In 1945 this outstanding program was extended to all recipients of public assistance in Washington. In 1947, however, the state legislature eliminated all state funds for the program, returning responsibility to the counties; this will undoubtedly mean curtailment of medical services in the rural sections far more than in the cities.

[28] BENNER, P. V., "Medical Insurance Plans for Federal Assistance Cases in Kansas," Medical Care, 3:145-148, May, 1943.

It is difficult to state which particular pattern of paying the physician for welfare medical services is commonest today in rural areas. Some authorities believe that the county doctor system is still perhaps most typical, with a flat salary being given the designated practitioner for all services to the poor.[29] A survey of Wisconsin in 1930 showed how prevalent this pattern was a few years ago; in every jurisdiction but one, medical care for the indigent was in the hands of a "county physician" or "city physician" who was appointed "not always on the basis of qualification."[30] This was before the far-reaching influence of the FERA program, however, and in the late 1930's, surveys in Minnesota showed that in rural communities in particular there was a tendency to "spread the business" of welfare medicine on a fee-for-service basis among all the physicians; all were interested in supplementing their relatively low incomes with this public subsidy.[31] The frequency of one pattern or another depends to some extent on general economic circumstances. In bad times, when the sources of private medical fees are lean, physicians tend to prefer panel systems with "free choice of doctor" and fee-for-service payment.[32] When times are good, the average practitioner has less time for welfare clients and the salaried "poor doctor" may be welcomed back on the scene. On the other hand, with welfare funds more ample in good times, more expensive free choice patterns can be financed, and this probably represents the general trend of the day.

There can certainly be no inherent objection to a system of providing services through part-time or full-time salaried practitioners, as distinguished from fee-for-service arrangements with different private physicians, except that as executed in the American setting the "poor doctor" system has become associated with numerous below-par practices. Because of the usually low remuneration for care to the poor, only the least competent practitioners, eager

---

[29] Personal communication from Dr. Gertrude Sturges, Consultant on Public Medical Services to the American Public Welfare Association, 1945.

[30] Wisconsin Public Welfare Department, *Medical Relief in Three Wisconsin Counties.* Madison, June, 1937, Processed.

[31] CLARK, DEAN A., Unpublished surveys conducted for the U. S. Public Health Service, Division of Public Health Methods, 1940.

[32] American Medical Association, Bureau of Medical Economics, *Care of the Indigent Sick.* Chicago, c. 1935.

for a few extra dollars from the government, have in the past tended to be attracted to this type of work. Being out of the main stream of professional practice and relationships in a community, this work offers little incentive to maintain a high quality of performance. The practitioner chosen for the job is often a political favorite and commonly superannuated, especially in rural districts. The territory he must cover is generally beyond his physical capacity and frequently matters are aggravated by his lack of devotion to the job.

Nevertheless, as was demonstrated during FERA experience, the fee-for-service pattern of care to the indigent, with free choice of physician from a panel of participating practitioners, has its abuses and its qualitative deficiencies. In general it is more expensive and, being spread out among numerous practitioners, is less amenable to medical supervision, even if such supervision is conscientiously attempted. There is an unfortunate tendency for a double standard of medicine to develop, with the physician giving only cursory attention to his welfare patients.[33] A determination of the best possible method of paying for welfare medical services certainly requires an objective re-evaluation, in the light of changing patterns in the whole structure of medical economic relationships.

The provision of special services, like dental care or nursing, to the indigent in rural counties is probably even less satisfactory than physicians' care or hospitalization. The criteria of need for dental service from public funds have usually been extremely narrow, with few services given except for the immediate relief of acute pain.[34] Through departments of public health, additional dental services may be provided, but these are usually confined to children of low-income families. While conventional public health nursing services are, of course, available to welfare families, bedside nursing is seldom provided in rural sections.[35] The provi-

[33] STURGES, GERTRUDE, "Public Medical Care at the Grass Roots," *op. cit.* For a general discussion of the quality of welfare medical services, see REED, LOUIS S., and DEAN A. CLARK, "Appraising Public Medical Services," *American Journal of Public Health*, 31:421-430, May, 1941.

[34] American Public Welfare Association, *Report of the Committee on Medical Care.*

[35] *Ibid.*

sion of drugs to rural welfare clients, on the other hand, is often more ample than necessary, as a cheap substitute for medical service. In one Southern state, for example, up to $4.00 a month may be allowed a welfare recipient for "medicines,"[36] a sum which, if planned through the year on a group basis, could sustain a good quality of complete medical services.

Whether welfare medical and related services are rendered through practitioners on part-time salary, through full-time personnel, through private practitioners on a fee-for-service or a capitation basis, through public clinics or private offices, through public or voluntary institutions, the care in rural areas tends to be poor in quality and volume. Whatever the pattern, it must be admitted that, by and large, the notion is still prevalent in rural communities that the man "on the county" is fortunate to be getting any service at all. The controls set up in the way of reviewing committees, authorizations, and so forth, are all with the somewhat negative purpose of eliminating abuses rather than enforcing a positive high quality of service. Perhaps little may be expected in improving the quality of public medical care for the indigent in rural areas until the double standard of private and public services is broken down and the same pattern of medical practice, and remuneration for it, is followed, whatever may be the source of financial support. Nevertheless, despite all its deficiencies, it must be recognized that public welfare medicine represents the elementary stages of an effort to provide organized medical care to a section of the population that cannot obtain it through private resources.

With recent economic prosperity, many of the less satisfactory aspects of welfare medical service have brightened. With unemployment relatively low, welfare funds have accumulated and more money has been available per case. Pinchpenny economies have been eliminated and restrictions have been removed in many state laws. Certain long-run benefits are bound to result from these developments, even with a down-swing in the business cycle.

[36] Personal observation, 1945.

CHAPTER 21

SPECIAL GOVERNMENT PROGRAMS AFFECTING MEDICAL CARE

BEYOND THE benefits of public health services and welfare medical care that theoretically if not actually have a place in every rural community, there are a great many special governmental programs that represent positive steps toward better organization of rural health services. These include the provision of services for certain types of illness or injury, the provision of general medical care for particular categories of the population (other than the indigent), the licensure of professional personnel and efforts to improve their distribution, the construction of health facilities, and the promotion of research and scientific standards. Few of these special efforts are devoted specifically to solving rural problems, but all of them, in one way or other, directly or indirectly benefit rural people.

Services for Certain Types of Illness or Injury

The provision of care by units of government for tuberculosis, mental disorder, venereal disease, or hookworm infestation — along with rural-urban disparities — has already been discussed. In addition, the management of certain uncommon but serious conditions, like leprosy or drug addiction, has to some extent been assumed by government; despite equal rural-urban opportunities for treatment, less complete rural case finding probably means less care for these conditions.

Protection of workers against the medical costs of occupational accidents has long been afforded by state legislation. Since the first state workmen's compensation legislation was passed by New York State in 1910, the area covered and the medical benefits of these laws have been steadily extended.[1] With regard to rural health services, however, the significant fact is that in practically all

[1] MILLIS, HARRY A., and ROYAL E. MONTGOMERY, *Labor's Rights and Social Insurance*. New York: McGraw-Hill Book Company, Inc., 1938, p. 194.

jurisdictions agricultural employment is excluded from obligatory coverage. The one state, moreover, which lacks legislation for its agricultural and industrial employees alike is Mississippi, the nation's most rural state.[2]

Agricultural employment has been excluded from workmen's compensation coverage and its associated medical benefits for a number of political and administrative reasons, despite the fact that farm work, as we have seen, is quite as hazardous as most industrial employment. In 24 states, while agricultural employment is excluded from the general legal requirements, voluntary coverage of his farm workers by an agricultural employer is allowed.[3] Experience has shown, however, that in practice this voluntary prerogative is seldom acted on. One of the main reasons is that commercial insurance rates for agriculture's poor risks are prohibitively high. Eleven states specifically disallow workmen's compensation for farm workers, even on a voluntary basis, and seven states allow certain limited coverage of farm workers with numerous qualifications and reservations. Only in five states, California, Connecticut, New Jersey, Ohio, and Vermont, is the farm worker specifically covered by legislation. Even in these states there are numerous limitations and escape clauses, and investigation in Ohio, for example, showed that only 2 per cent of the farmers employing labor were actually assuming their legal responsibilities.[4] As a matter of fact, the great majority of American farm people are not laborers, of course, but are self-employed and covered by no protective legislation whatever. Probably only the small number of agricultural or forestry employees working for the Federal Government are really adequately protected with the medical benefits of workmen's compensation legislation.

A special federal grant-in-aid program of vocational rehabilitation has been operating since 1920. Originally confined largely to the correction of orthopedic defects among industrial workers, in 1944 the medical aspects and financial resources of the program were

[2] U. S. Department of Labor, Division of Labor Standards, *Workmen's Compensation: An Outline of Legislation in the United States and Territories as of January, 1, 1943* (Bull. 56). Washington, August, 1943.

[3] ZIMMER, VERNE A., "New Developments in Workmen's Compensation," *Social Security Bulletin*, 7:8, October, 1944.

[4] LISS, SAMUEL, *Status of Farm Labor under State Workmen's Compensation Laws* (Farm Security Administration, U. S. Department of Agriculture). Washington, 1939, Processed.

greatly broadened. Under the current law medical and hospital services for the correction of physical or mental disabilities may be provided to any person engaged in agriculture, as well as industry, if working efficiency will thereby be improved and if the services cannot be purchased privately.[5] Except in a few states like Wisconsin and Minnesota, however, the program still tends to be geared preponderantly to the needs of industrial workers. While the potentialities of this program for rural people are great, much organized effort will be required before the practice is brought up to the broad intent of the federal law.[6]

The wartime Emergency Maternity and Infant Care (EMIC) program, providing maternity care and infant care for the first year, including hospitalization, to the wives and babies of servicemen in the lowest four pay grades, has been of great benefit to rural and urban people alike. Financed entirely by the Federal Government through the Children's Bureau, the $40,000,000 annual outlay has been administered by state departments of health, with payments being made to the individual physicians and hospitals performing the service.[7] The organized medical profession raised numerous objections to the program, claiming it was "regimentation" and "socialized medicine" and demanding cash grants to the patient instead of direct payment by the government. Congress retained the stated policy, however, in the interests of assuring actual services to the military dependents, protecting government funds, allowing the enforcement of high professional standards, and preventing any element of cash bargaining between doctor and patient.[8]

In rural sections in particular, where lack of funds so often keeps births from being attended by physicians and in hospitals, this program has been a special boon. In 1944, 99.9 per cent of EMIC deliveries were attended by a physician and this percentage was as high in

[5] Office of Vocational Rehabilitation, Federal Security Agency, *Charting the Way in Vocational Rehabilitation*. Washington: Government Printing Office, August, 1944.

[6] CLARK, DEAN A. "The Vocational Rehabilitation Program," *Medical Care and Health Services for Rural People*. Chicago: The Farm Foundation, 1944, pp. 149-151.

[7] ELIOT, MARTHA M., "Emergency Maternity and Infant Care Program," *Journal of the American Medical Association*, 124:833-838, March, 1944.

[8] BUTLER, ALLAN M., "The Emergency Program for the Wives and Babies of Our Enlisted Men," *Medical Care*, 4:212-217, August, 1944.

the rural states as in the urban. Deliveries were hospitalized in 90 per cent of EMIC cases during 1944, compared with 76 per cent of maternity cases with live births for the general population in the same year. In the states 60 per cent rural or more, about 80 per cent of EMIC deliveries were hospitalized, compared with the general rate in those states of 46 per cent; in the states 60 per cent urban or more, EMIC hospitalization experience was 95 per cent compared with 92 per cent generally in those states.[9] While EMIC experience in hospitalization exceeded the general experience in both urban and rural states, it is evident that the poorer showing in rural states is referable to deficiencies in facilities, even with payment for services guaranteed by the government.

Rural doctors under the EMIC program have been paid much more adequately for their services than formerly, and it is significant that the professional objections to the program have come predominantly from urban sections. Extremely valuable experience in the economics and administration of medical care has been provided for public health agencies, particularly in rural areas. Valuable policies of uniform hospital cost accounting have been encouraged by a public agency for the first time, inducing many rural hospitals to improve their administrative practices and laying the basis for sound financing of other programs of hospitalization.[10] It is unfortunate that this program is gradually coming to an end, but the patterns it has set up will have lasting value.

Medical Care for Special Groups

General medical care is provided by governmental agencies for certain population groups which historically, for one reason or another, have been considered proper subjects of public support. Some of these groups, like Indians, happen to be mainly rural in character; others, like veterans of the nation's wars, are found in more or less natural urban-rural proportions; still others, like merchant seamen, are hardly rural at all. In so far as any of these pro-

[9] Based on unpublished data furnished by the U. S. Children's Bureau, August, 1945.

[10] BECKER, H. J., "E. M. I. C. — Much Has Been Learned So Far," *Hospitals*, 18:38, 41-42, October, 1944.

grams encompass rural people, they represent organized measures advancing the health services of rural America.

Of widest significance in recent years among these programs have been the medical services given to members of the nation's armed forces. During their period of military duty, millions of rural young men and women have enjoyed a level of comprehensive medical care far superior to anything that most of them knew before. The services readily available without economic deterrents, the emphasis on preventive measures, the thorough attention to even minor complaints are bound to have had an effect on the thinking and the expectations of the rural veteran returning to the farm or village. The veteran physician returning to a country practice, moreover, has doubtless found his concepts of professional work altered; it is no surprise that among 20,000 military physicians surveyed in 1944, a majority of those choosing private practice expressed preference for postwar practice on a group rather than a solo basis.[11]

Special medical services have for some years been provided for war veterans. Since the end of the First World War, an extensive program of hospitalization has been in operation under which bed care and outpatient service are offered for all service-connected disabilities and bed care is offered for non-service-connected conditions if there is room and if there is financial need. The distribution of the hospital facilities administered by the Veterans Administration is fairly equitable and the rural states appear to be served about as well as the urban. In 1944 there were some 88,000 beds in 94 units located in all states except New Hempshire, Rhode Island, and Delaware. Tremendous expansion has been planned to accommodate the veterans of the Second World War.[12]

The quality of medical and hospital service rendered in the veterans' program has lately come in for some severe criticism that has stimulated important corrective measures. Whatever may be their defects, it must be recognized that, relative to the hospital resources available to the general rural population, these facilities constitute a real benefit for rural veterans. The distance and strangeness of veterans' facilities undoubtedly discourage their utilization for the

[11] Lueth, H. C., "Economic Aspects of Future Medical Practice," *Journal of the American Medical Association*, 128:528-529, June 16, 1945.

[12] Office of War Information, Advance Release 3361, "Veterans Administration," prepared for July 5, 1945.

care of acute conditions among rural and urban veterans alike. To
the extent that rural veterans are unable to obtain hospitalization
for chronic conditions like tuberculosis or mental disorder, however, it may be that they rely on veterans' facilities even more than
their urban comrades. The recently developed program for medical
care of service-connected conditions by local physicians and hospitals in the veteran's home town should do much to extend the
general availability of these services.[13] While there are certain
objectionable features in the administration of this new plan from
the point of view of over-all national health planning, it represents
an important step toward decentralized medical care for government beneficiaries. The special services available for veterans will
doubtless play a larger role in the whole picture of rural medical
care during the coming period than ever before.[14]

The 377,000 Indians in our country, nearly all of whom are rural,
have for some years been eligible for governmentally sponsored
medical care through the Department of the Interior. Some 4,500
beds are maintained in 94 relatively small hospitals, averaging 50
beds each, located in association with the Indian reservations.[15] An
extensive preventive program is promoted, directed particularly
against tuberculosis, infant mortality, and trachoma, all of which are
excessive in the Indian population. Numerous periodic clinics are
held and ambulance service is provided to bring patients from isolated places into the hospitals. In normal times some 200 full-time
and 125 part-time physicians are engaged in this work, along with
800 hospital and public health nurses and 1,200 other employees.[16]

In the Southwest, where Indians represent the highest proportion
of the local population, the Indian Service medical care program —
despite its avowed inadequacies — makes an appreciable contribution to rural health services. Some of the benefits of this special

[13] "Medicine and the War," *Journal of the American Medical Association*,
130:86, Jan. 12, 1946.

[14] Subcommittee on Wartime Health and Education, Interim Report to
the Committee on Education and Labor, U. S. Senate, 79th Cong., 1st Sess.,
S. Res. 62, *Health Needs of Veterans*. Washington: Government Printing
Office, 1945.

[15] U. S. Department of the Interior, *Statistical Supplement to the Annual
Report of the Commissioner of Indian Affairs*. Washington, 1943, p. 4.

[16] McGIBONY, J. R., "The Indian Service Hospital Program," address given
at the Annual Convention of the American Hospital Association, Cleveland,
Oct. 3, 1944. Processed.

program are reflected in the fact, for example, that 75 per cent of Indian babies are now born in hospitals, compared with under 20 per cent for other rural groups of the same low income.[17] The cost of this entire program to the Federal Government is about $17 to $20 per capita. Without it, it is likely that medical services for Indians would be largely confined to the imbibition of herb extracts and the ministrations of the still persistent medicine men. As Indians have lost their ties to the reservations, however, the utilization of many of their medical facilities has declined so that in some sections we find the anomaly of half-empty Indian facilities in the face of unmet hospital needs for the general rural population. The Indian Service medical care program, nevertheless, serves as a demonstration of organized health services for a culturally as well as geographically isolated rural group.

Another essentially rural group served by a governmentally sponsored medical care program has been represented by the employees of the Tennessee Valley Authority and their families during the construction phase of that power project. While the payment for most therapeutic services in this program was assumed by the families themselves, through prepayment plans, the provision of medical personnel and facilities, the organization of preventive services, and the care of illness or accidents resulting from employment have been financed directly by government. Proper protection of the health of the thousands of employees of this public utility project required the organization of health services in several isolated communities lacking in local resources, usually at the sites of the dams on the Tennessee River and its tributaries. At the peak of construction, ten small but well-equipped "medical centers" were set up, staffed with full-time medical and related personnel and averaging about 18 beds each.

These units rendered service both in the preventive and industrial programs financed by government, and in the general medical care of the families. For the latter, families paid $2 per month in 1941, with certain extra charges for special procedures. Membership was voluntary; at the Kentucky Dam in 1941, for example, 1,167 out of 2,000 local families were members of the plan.[18]

[17] Personal communication from Dr. J. R. McGibony, Director of Health, Office of Indian Affairs, December, 1944.

[18] BISHOP, EUGENE L., and H. L. CASE, "Medical Care at a T. V. A. Project," *Medical Care*, 2:247-253, July, 1942.

In addition to the services organized for employees and their families, the TVA has promoted a broad program of health education for all of the rural residents of the Valley. Other government-sponsored power projects are being contemplated along the Missouri and Columbia rivers, but whether or not the TVA health service pattern will be appropriate under the circumstances is not at all clear at this time.

Agencies of the Federal and state governments have for some time provided preventive and emergency health and safety services for many of their employees. For the tens of thousands of agricultural agency employees dispersed throughout the rural counties of the nation, this "industrial hygiene" type of service does not exist to any great extent, but where special field operations create a concentration of government workers, services are often organized. Thus employees of the Forest Service, for example, or of the National Park System, working in rural sections, are served by special health and safety programs, including in some places voluntary prepayment plans for general medical care. The enactment in 1946 of the Federal Employees Health Service Act will encourage the better development of preventive and first-aid services for Uncle Sam's 2 million or more employees in rural and urban places from coast to coast.[19]

Providing and Qualifying Medical Personnel

Government has been concerned with the scientific qualifications of medical personnel far longer than with their total numbers or distribution. The legal enforcement of certain standards of medical practice has long been a responsibility of government, and educational standards for engagement in the healing arts are embodied in the medical practice acts of all the states.[20]

So far as rural medical practice is concerned, there is some evidence that the more rural states are less demanding of qualifications in their licensees than the more urban states. Qualifications in formal schooling do not appear to be significantly different between the

[19] CRONIN, JOHN W., "Plans for Federal Employees Health Service," *Medical Annals of the District of Columbia,* 14:199-202, May, 1945.

[20] For a background discussion, see SIGERIST, HENRY E., "The History of Medical Licensure," *Journal of the American Medical Association,* 104:1057-1060, Mar. 30, 1935.

rural and urban states;[21] in recent years, however, a number of states have gone beyond academic requirements and demanded a hospital internship as a prerequisite to licensure. Of the 20 states that in 1941 had such a requirement, 12 were among the urban half of the states and 8 among the rural half. The percentage of failures in state board examinations for licensure may be taken perhaps as an index of the strictness of application of the licensure standards prescribed by law. For the two-year period 1940-41, the percentage of candidates from medical schools in the United States and Canada failed by the state boards of medical licensure in the 24 most urban states was 10.4, while in the 24 most rural states it was only 1.3. In fact, 16 rural states did not fail a single candidate.[22]

Cultist practitioners, moreover, have a somewhat easier time in getting licensure in the rural states than in the urban. While every state licenses osteopaths in some capacity and all but a few states license chiropractors, the enactment of "basic science examination" statutes has to some degree weeded out the poorest of the sectarians. Of the 17 states with such laws, 10 are among the urban half of states and 7 among the rural half.[23] Of the cultist candidates taking these examinations in the two-year period 1941-42, in the more urban states 55.2 per cent were failed, while only 28.6 per cent were failed in the more rural states.

It might be supposed that more lenient standards for medical licensure in the rural states are a realistic adjustment to their need for acquiring a greater supply of doctors. Yet an analysis of reciprocal licensure relationships among the states hardly bears this out. The rural half of the states do not appear to be characterized by any more liberal reciprocity laws than the urban half.[24] Chinese Wall barriers to the entrance of out-of-state practitioners appear about as high in the more rural states as in the more urban, although the policy of many states to grant licenses to out-of-state practitioners

[21] Based upon an analysis of statutes as presented in American Medical Association, *American Medical Directory* 1942. Chicago, 1943.

[22] Derived from American Medical Association, Council on Medical Education and Hospitals, "Medical Licensure Statistics for 1941," *Journal of the American Medical Association*, 119:141-182, May 9, 1942.

[23] HEILMAN, S. E., "Legal Control of Medical Charlatanism," *North Carolina Law Review*, 22:23-43, December, 1943.

[24] Based upon data presented in American Medical Association, Council on Medical Education and Hospitals, *op. cit.*

"at the discretion of the Medical Examining Board" makes evaluation of actual practices difficult. The latter practice, indeed, allows too often for arbitrary decisions by which qualified physicians are barred from a state simply in the interest of limiting professional competition.

Even with no greater restrictions against the immigration of practitioners licensed in other states, it is evident that the rural states, with their personnel shortages, must suffer most. During the war, even under the pressure of the emergency shortages and the pleading of numerous groups for a relaxation of licensure barriers, only five states amended their laws to allow temporary licensure, without examination, to any qualified physician — and three of these were predominantly urban states.[25]

The problem of reciprocity among the states in dental licensure is even greater; 35 states grant no reciprocal licenses whatever, and of the 13 states that have some reciprocity with others, 5 reciprocate with fewer than 4 other states.[26] After the war, a bill was introduced in Congress which would have granted every veteran dentist a certificate to practice in any state, but every state dental association and state board of dental examiners, without exception, opposed it ". . . because it is in conflict with state dental laws and constitutes an infringement on state rights."[27] Only licensure for nursing appears to be relatively free from serious restrictions among the states.[28]

The pressure of physician shortages in numerous rural communities, nevertheless, has on occasion induced rural state legislatures to throw all professional requirements to the winds — even while barriers to out-of-state entrants were maintained. The legislature in Tennessee, for example, has repeatedly authorized licensure, by special act, to persons not meeting regular legal requirements. In some rural communities men have practiced who had no license

[25] STUCKE, ADELA, "Notes on State Legislative Provisions for the Temporary Licensing of Physicians," *Public Health Reports*, 59:1609-1614, Dec. 15, 1944.

[26] American Dental Association, Committee on Legislation, *Requirements of Dental Licensure as Stated in State Dental Laws: Reciprocity Information 1942*, Chicago, 1942.

[27] American Dental Association, "Reports of Councils and Committees," *Journal of the American Dental Association*, 32:1307, October, 1945.

[28] American Nurses Association, "The Question of National Registration for Nurses," *American Journal of Nursing*, 44:238-239, March, 1944.

whatever, many of them without any formal training, protected by local sentiment from legal prosecution by the state.[29]

Even at best, licensure controls over the quality of medical practice are rather flimsy. A license granted 20 to 30 years ago is little proof of medical competence today. The periodic re-registration of physicians required by many states is associated with no new determination of qualifications, and the rare instances when a state revokes a medical license are nearly always due to a criminal conviction of some kind rather than to professional incompetence.

Aside from licensure requirements, little is done by government to maintain or improve standards in the practice of medicine. State governments do, indeed, often play some role in medical education, both undergraduate and postgraduate. The very poverty of privately endowed institutions in the more rural states is such that state-sponsored universities probably play a larger part in medical education in these states. Postgraduate courses on subjects of public health importance are sometimes given for physicians by departments of health, but these are more a feature of city than of rural agencies.

Although licensure requirements have been set up by government in the United States since the very birth of our country, government has been very slow to recognize the more basic problem of the entire supply of medical and related practitioners for all sections of the population. Legal and official attitudes toward medical practice have been dictated more by a conception of medicine as a professional business enterprise than as a social service necessary for the public welfare. Most organized efforts to bring physicians and other health personnel to isolated areas have been on a voluntary basis.

A few scattered but significant steps to provide physicians for rural districts have, however, been taken by units of government. As early as 1923, provision was made by law in New Hampshire, Vermont, and New York whereby citizens could be taxed to raise a fund toward the support of a resident physician. The New Hampshire act reads in part as follows:

Towns may at any annual meeting vote to raise such sum of money as they may deem necessary towards the support of a resident physician

[29] HYMAN, O. W., "The Number and Distribution of Physicians in the Southern States as Bearing upon the Policies of Southern Medical Colleges," *Southern Medical Journal*, 30:85-88, January, 1937.

in such towns which in the absence of such appropriation would be without the services of such physician.

Advantage of this authority was taken, however, by only a few semi-rural communities in these states.[30] In this period certain small towns in Massachusetts obtained physicians by offering them official subsidies under the legal guise of salaries for school health work. In some communities rent-free houses were provided for the doctor and his family. In still other communities a minimum income from private practice was more or less guaranteed by the town fathers, with the difference between the actual and the guaranteed earnings being made up by a bonus out of local tax assessments. As recently as December, 1946, Plainfield and Cornish townships in New Hampshire voted to hire a physician to serve them on a predetermined schedule of fees, with the townships guaranteeing on a quarterly basis any difference between his gross earnings and minimum annual income of $5,000.[30a]

Similar sporadic efforts to attract physicians through the use of local tax subsidies have been made in isolated Washington Island, Wisconsin, and in a few other places. At Indian Lake, New York, the school board paid a dentist $1,500 a year plus expenses for providing dental care to 300 local school children as a special inducement to his settling there.[31] In 1944, Andover, Maine, paid a physician a direct subsidy to retain his services.[32] Records on these special programs are not complete but it is clear that their extent has never been great and they have been confined largely to the relatively prosperous communities of the Northeastern states. The distinction in these efforts between voluntary action by local groups of civic-minded people and action by local units of government is often hazy, and nothing has been done in this country comparable to the well-organized plans for rural "municipal physicians" in the Canadian provinces of Manitoba and Saskatchewan.[33]

[30] MOORE, HARRY H., American Medicine and the People's Health. New York: D. Appleton-Century Company, Inc., 1927, pp. 194-195.

[30a] Manchester Union (Manchester, New Hampshire), Dec. 23, 1947.

[31] DAVIS, op. cit., p. 91.

[32] Personal communication from Dr. Frederick R. Carter, Secretary-Treasurer of the Maine Medical Association, February, 1945.

[33] ROREM, C. RUFUS, The "Municipal Doctor" System in Rural Saskatchewan (Committee on the Costs of Medical Care Pub. 11). Chicago: University of Chicago Press, 1931.

Systematic governmental action, on other than a local community basis, toward effecting a better distribution of medical personnel does not seem to have been undertaken until the Second World War pointed up acutely the problem of rural shortages. Official federal recognition of the problem came, even then, only as a by-product to the task of recruiting medical and related personnel for the military forces. To do this the national Procurement and Assignment Service for Physicians, Dentists, Nurses, and Veterinarians was set up and later put under the War Manpower Commission. Although its first job was military recruitment, this agency, which operated largely through the state and county professional societies, was intended also to maintain, so far as possible, satisfactory supplies of physicians and dentists for the civilian population, rural and urban. Total war required the protection of civilian as well as military health. It was also intended to facilitate relocations of practitioners from areas of relative surplus, like the large cities, to areas of shortage, like rapidly developed war industry centers or rural districts. Accordingly, between 1942 and 1944 some 3,000 relocations of physicians from one area to another were recorded by the Procurement and Assignment Service,[34] although unpublished analyses cast serious doubt on the effectiveness of these movements. Evidence has not been presented to prove that these movements were appreciably beyond the normal year-to-year migration or that they were in a direction to correct rather than to aggravate existing rural-urban inequities. Although there was widespread opinion that the performance of this program fell considerably below its potentialities, the principle of official governmental concern about the distribution of the nation's health personnel was at least established.

Other evidence of this concern was shown in the passage by Congress in late 1943 of Public Law 216, providing direct federal subsidy for the relocation of medical and dental personnel to communities of need if the local community was willing to contribute partially to the cost of resettlement. Travel and moving expenses, as well as $250 a month for the first three months of practice in the new location, were financed out of government funds. This legislation was short-lived and under it only nine medical and dental relocations

[34] LAHEY, F. H. and J. L. KAUKONEN, "A Summary of the Activities of the Procurement and Assignment Service," *War Medicine*, 6:10-17, July, 1944.

were effected, most of them to more or less urban communities.[35] The significant point, again, was that government funds had been appropriated — though too little and too late — to face a problem of mounting importance in the entire field of rural medical care.

The problem of an adequate supply of medical and related personnel, under the stimulus of war, was even tackled at its source: in schools of professional training. Medical, dental, and other technical students were included in the specialized training programs of the Army and Navy, so that they were in effect sent through school at government expense. To maintain the necessary supply of military and civilian nurses the Cadet Nurse Corps was set up under the Public Health Service in 1943. Under this program, federal grants were given to schools of nursing to provide scholarships and stipends for nursing students. While these several training programs did not benefit rural sections directly, they enabled many young men and women from rural areas to get a professional education which, with their own financial resources, might have been impossible. Moreover, they helped to maintain, to some extent, the total reservoir of health personnel from which the future rural supply must be drawn.

On the state level, a few minor but significant steps to reverse the regressive trend of rural physician supply were taken in the same period. In 1942 the state of Virginia enacted a law providing scholarships for prospective rural physicians. This statute set up a fund providing scholarships for eight medical students a year on the condition that, among other things, on completion of their training they engage continuously in general medical practice in a rural community for a period of time equal to that during which they received the scholarship.[36] The community is chosen by the State Health Commissioner, with the approval of the State Board of Health. In 1945 North Carolina enacted a law with similar objectives, although the state subsidy is on a loan basis. Under this statute the student receiving a loan must agree to practice medicine in some rural area in North Carolina for at least four years.[37] Similar bills were sub-

[35] PARRAN, THOMAS, Testimony before a Subcommittee of the Committee on Education and Labor, U. S. Senate, 78th Cong., 2d Sess., S. Res. 74, *Wartime Health and Education.* Washington: Government Printing Office, 1944, Part 5, p. 1784.

[36] Acts of the General Assembly of Virginia 1942, Chap. 354, p. 531.

[37] North Carolina Session Laws, 1945, Chap. 1,096, p. 1425.

sequently passed by Mississippi, Alabama, and Georgia. In Kentucky, when such a bill, passed by the state legislature, was vetoed by the Governor, its purposes were set under way through a fellowship loan fund raised by voluntary contributions.[38] In the first year of its program, Mississippi subsidized the medical training of 60 native sons, 7 of them Negro, at 11 medical schools.[38a]

Mississippi has initiated a further program which may have indirect effects in attracting physicians to its rural areas, especially for public health work. In 1946, the State Board of Health provided opportunities for junior medical students to work in a county health department program, under the health officer's supervision, over the summer months between the third and fourth years. In 1947, the program was extended to provide field experience for medical school graduates, pending the beginning of their internships. Whether or not this field training will later attract these doctors back to a rural county, it is felt that the experience will encourage their future cooperation with public health activities.[38b]

Another approach by the states has been through subsidy of educational institutions. In 1943, the Alabama state legislature appropriated $1,000,000 for the establishment of a full four-year medical school at Birmingham, in the effort to meet the "acute need for more physicians throughout the state of Alabama, particularly in the rural areas."[39] It is the policy of the new school to encourage graduates to practice in small Alabama communities; one measure in this direction will be a system of rotation of interns and residents from the Birmingham center among a number of small but carefully chosen hospitals throughout the state. Relative to the size of the problem, all these measures may be feeble, but at least they signify official recognition of the difficulties and may presage bolder steps in the future.

[38] ROEMER, MILTON I., "The Nation's Health: A Survey of Major Plans to Meet the Health Needs of the Nation," *American Journal of Nursing*, 47:12-15, January, 1947.

[38a] Mississippi State Medical Education Board, *Doctors to Come*. Jackson, April, 1947.

[38b] Mississippi State Board of Health, *Summer Internships in a Public Health Program for Medical Students*. Jackson, 1946, Processed. Also personal communication from Dr. Felix J. Underwood, Executive Officer, Mississippi State Board of Health, May 17, 1947.

[39] KRACKE, ROY R., and J. W. MACQUEEN, "Developments in the Medical College of Alabama," *Southern Medical Journal*, 39:8-12, January, 1946.

Improvement of Health Facilities

Governmental action to improve health facilities in rural as well as urban areas has been more forthright than action involving health personnel. As we have noted, the proportion of hospital beds being maintained by government has gradually increased over the last few decades and this has held in rural areas as well as urban, although in lesser degree. As for standards of quality, legislation has recently been passed by a number of states requiring licensure of hospitals and nursing homes.[40] Hospitals and other health facilities have been constructed by units of government at all levels, but the most deliberate and systematic programs have been financed with federal funds.

Construction programs have, in the main, been more a phase of work relief efforts than of plans to correct deficiencies in facilities where they are most serious. Since the primary objective of these federal public works programs has been to relieve unemployment, their major concentration has been in the larger cities where unemployment has been most critical. In the 1930's under the Federal Emergency Relief Administration (FERA), about 2,000 projects to improve or construct hospitals were sponsored, and under the Public Works Administration (PWA), almost 1,000 health facility units were constructed or enlarged.[41] About 100 million dollars was put out by the Federal Government in these programs in the form of grants or loans to units of state or local government or to nonprofit institutions. Other public works providing certain rural health benefits were launched under the National Youth Administration (NYA) and the Work Projects Administration (WPA).

Despite greater rural hospital needs, the relative urban concentration of construction projects under these federal works programs is reflected in an analysis of the PWA record. Of the 50,428 additional hospital beds provided in the 48 states under this program,

[40] GUERIN, MARY M., "Legislation on Hospital Surveys, Construction, and Licensing Considered by State Legislatures in 1945," *Public Health Reports,* 60:1519-1539, Dec. 21, 1945.

[41] Federal Emergency Relief Administration, *Final Statistical Report.* Washington: Government Printing Office, 1942. Also Federal Emergency Administration of Public Works, *PWA Provides Modern Hospitals.* Washington: Government Printing Office, 1937, p. 7.

73 per cent, or 36,925, were located in the 20 states with more than half urban population, containing 61 per cent of the national population. The 39 per cent of the total population in the 28 predominantly rural states meanwhile were provided with 13,503, or only 27 per cent, of the new beds.[42] This disparity between whole states, of course, fails to reflect rural-urban discrepancies within the states, which were probably even greater. In 1939, when a special bill was introduced in Congress for appropriating 10 million dollars to construct rural hospitals, it failed to pass.

Specifically beneficial to the rural population was the extensive construction of family unit sanitary facilities launched by a number of federal agencies. Under the successive sponsorship of the Civil Works Administration (CWA), the FERA, and the WPA (in cooperation with state health departments and the United States Public Health Service), nearly 3 million sanitary privies were constructed in 38 states and Puerto Rico between 1933 and 1942.[43] In this work, the significant principle was developed that government funds could properly be used for the improvement of private property when community health is involved. The WPA and the Civilian Conservation Corps (CCC), in addition, sponsored drainage, sewerage, or water-supply projects directly affecting health in many small towns and villages. By bringing electricity to isolated rural sections, the Tennessee Valley Authority (TVA) made possible better refrigeration of milk and foods in thousands of farm households. The role of agricultural agencies in the construction of health facilities and in rural electrification will be cited later.

With the onset of the Second World War, health facility construction passed from a work relief program to a wartime emergency measure.[44] Here again, the rural areas were on the short end. The Community Facilities (Lanham) Act provided federal funds to subsidize the construction of hospitals, health centers, or sanitation facilities in congested areas springing up incident to war production or military mobilization. As of April 30, 1944, 100 hospitals or hos-

[42] Derived from Federal Emergency Administration of Public Works, *loc. cit.*

[43] ATKINS, C. H., "National Inventory of Needs for Sanitation Facilities," *Public Health Reports*, 59:969-978, July 28, 1944.

[44] PLUMLEY, M. L., "Federal Aid to Hospitals," *Medical Care*, 3:6-14, February, 1943.

pital additions had been built, as well as 88 health centers, 43 centers for the rapid treatment of venereal diseases, and 175 nurses' homes and schools.[45] In addition, 362 community water supply systems, 354 sewage disposal systems, and 30 garbage disposal plants were built or extended.[46] In so far as the facilities in many of these "congested war areas" served a surrounding rural population or in so far as many of these centers will undergo a postwar de-urbanization, this wartime contribution may render certain long-run benefits to the rural population.

After the war, in 1946, the first federal hospital construction program specifically designed to tackle rural needs was launched. This was through the national Hospital Survey and Construction Act, a bill providing federal grants-in-aid to the states for subsidizing the construction of health facilities in areas of greatest bed deficiency. Based on the concept of state-wide regional planning, this measure made all kinds of special provisions for meeting the needs of scattered rural people. As of this writing, the program is still largely in the preconstruction planning phase; its details and implications for the future will be considered in Chapter 28.

Promotion of Research and Scientific Standards

Finally, advancement of rural health services is fostered by the activities of government in scientific research and the promulgation of scientific standards. Problems of disease and health are so broad that research is generally designed to give information of use in all areas — seldom for rural areas alone. The application of knowledge, however, derived from governmentally promoted research, or, for that matter, any research, is usually less complete in rural than in urban areas.

Research in medicine and related fields is conducted by several agencies of government at the federal level. To name only the major programs, there are the National Institute of Health of the United States Public Health Service, the National Bureau of Standards of the United States Department of Commerce, the medical divisions of the Army, the Navy, and the Veterans Administration, and several bureaus of the United States Department of Agriculture to be dis-

[45] PARRAN, THOMAS, op. cit., pp. 1781-1782.
[46] U. S. Public Health Service, Annual Report 1944, p. viii.

cussed below.[47] Of special relevance to the problems of rural health has been the research of the Public Health Service on pellagra and Rocky Mountain spotted fever, for example, and the work of the Department of Agriculture on insecticides used in malaria control and on the diseases of animals afflicting man.

Studies on the social aspects of health service, on the basis of which better organized programs of rural as well as urban medical care may be planned, have been made by numerous federal agencies. These have included the Social Security Board (now the Social Security Administration), the Work Projects Administration, the Public Health Service, the Children's Bureau, and — particularly in the rural field — the Department of Agriculture.

Research is, of course, carried on also by government agencies at the state level, bringing benefits to rural health. Among such are state health departments, state university medical schools, state departments of agriculture, and state agricultural colleges.

The promulgation by government of high standards of medical or public health practice has been of particular assistance in rural districts. Proper standards for immunizations, milk sanitation, rodent control, and other matters developed by the Public Health Service are widely followed by rural health agencies. Children's Bureau standards for maternal and child hygiene are followed by rural practitioners as well as urban. Flagrant abuses in the labeling and, more recently, the advertising of patent medicines have been controlled by the federal Food and Drug Administration,[48] although little reduction in rural consumption of nostrums and cure-alls seems to have been achieved.

Despite the variety of government research projects and activities in the promulgation of standards, the significant fact is the relative meagerness of official support for this phase of medicine in the United States. Much the greater part of the nation's medical research is conducted by privately endowed institutions or commercial interests. Even less has been done by government in the coordination of research activities throughout the country, although scientists have again and again deplored the vast waste

[47] U. S. Office of War Information, *United States Government Manual.* Washington: Government Printing Office, Winter, 1943-44.

[48] KALLET, A., and F. SCHLINK, 100,000,000 *Guinea Pigs: Dangers in Everyday Foods, Drugs, and Cosmetics.* New York: The Vanguard Press, 1933.

of money, time, and effort in needless duplications of work, while major medical problems go untackled.[49] This want of coordination has its ultimate effects in retarding progress in rural medicine. It has been encouraging, nevertheless, to see demonstrations during the war of the productiveness of federal coordination of specific research projects, through agencies like the Office of Scientific Research and Development.[50] And in 1946, the United States Public Health Service, doubtless under the stimulus of wartime experience, inaugurated a program of federal grants for approved medical research projects, to be conducted by public or private institutions or by individuals throughout the nation. Along with this is a new program of research fellowships, designed to train and encourage scientific workers.[51] In so far as institutions and individuals in rural regions tend to have greatest financial need, it is possible that this subsidy program may render special benefits for rural medicine.

This bird's-eye view of government programs promoting an increased organization of rural health services is doubtless incomplete, but it may give some idea of the general scope of such activities and their variety.[52] It omits consideration of a whole segment of government activity which, because of its special orientation toward the needs of farm families, will be considered separately in the following pages. This is the health work of the United States Department of Agriculture, which to some extent cuts across the lines of the categories described so far, although in a larger sense it has attempted to meet needs that were not being faced by any other organized programs.

[49] See, for example, COWDRY, E. V., Testimony before a Subcommittee of the Committee on Education and Labor, U. S. Senate, 78th Cong., 2d Sess., S. Res. 74, *Wartime Health and Education, Medical Research*: 1. Washington: Government Printing Office, 1945, Part 7, pp. 2220-2229.

[50] BUSH, VANNEVAR, "Science: The Endless Frontier," in Hearings before the Subcommittee on War Mobilization of the Committee on Military Affairs, U. S. Senate, S. Res. 107, 78th Cong., and S. Res. 146, 79th Cong., *Legislative Proposals for the Promotion of Science*. Washington: Government Printing Office, 1945, pp. 47-76.

[51] U. S. Public Health Service, National Institute of Health, *Research Assistance*. Washington, 1946, Processed.

[52] For a general discussion, see DAVIS, MICHAEL M., *America Organizes Medicine*. New York: Harper & Brothers, 1941.

CHAPTER 22

RURAL HEALTH ACTIVITIES OF THE DEPARTMENT OF AGRICULTURE

THE UNITED STATES Department of Agriculture, the largest department in the Federal Government before the Second World War, has long been interested in rural health. With its numerous direct channels to farm people and rural communities, and through its cooperative endeavors with the state agricultural extension services, it has gradually come to engage in a whole range of health activities — from its basic efforts to improve farm income and its fundamental work in human nutrition to such enterprising developments as the sponsorship of hundreds of health insurance plans. It may seem a far cry, in fact, from the days when the Bureau of Animal Industry first undertook its crusade to stamp out disease among domestic animals over 60 years ago to the day when prepayment medical plans were organized among low-income farmers all over the United States, or when tax-supported preventive and therapeutic medical services were administered for migratory farm workers.

It seems appropriate to discuss the manifold rural health activities of the Department of Agriculture in connection with governmental efforts to improve rural health, even though the prepayment plans have simply been sponsored, rather than directly administered, by the Department or one of its bureaus. Although these plans are voluntary, they represent the result of governmental activities, and it is safe to say that very few of them would have been launched if it were not for the initiative taken by the Department and the continued stimulation exerted through governmental channels.

Nutrition, Sanitation, and General Health Promotion

The functions of the Department of Agriculture relating to rural health that have been longest established are certain activities concerned with the farmer's means of livelihood rather than with his personal welfare. Among these, for example, are the functions of the Bureau of Animal Industry and to an extent of the Bureau of Dairy Industry relating to the control of diseases among animals, many of which may affect man. Meat inspection by agricultural officials, of course, protects urban health as well as — or even more than — rural. Another program with a direct bearing on farm production is that of the Bureau of Entomology and Plant Quarantine, which has done outstanding work in the development of DDT, the insecticide that did so much to control diseases like malaria and typhus fever during the war and is now expected to help wipe out malaria in the United States. Other farm programs, moreover, have their indirect influence in improving rural health through measures taken to support farm prices and to ensure a generally higher level of farm income.

Over the years the Department has made one of its greatest contributions to the nation's health through its nutrition work. The Bureau of Human Nutrition and Home Economics has done notable work on the essentials of a balanced diet. The nation-wide wartime nutrition education program, of benefit to rural and urban people alike, was developed under the leadership of the Department, and the universally popular school lunch program is administered by the same branch of the Production and Marketing Administration. The latter program, calling for federal aid to schools and child care centers in the amount of 50 million dollars annually, has had dramatic results in improved nutritional status among school children and has been credited with better attendance records and better work as measured by higher grades.[1]

In the general field of health education the Department of Agriculture has played a steadily expanding role not only through the federal and state extension services, the Department's principal education channel, but also through such bureaus as the Farm Security Administration,[1a] which works directly with low-income farmers. Commendable work on the fundamentals of sound health and hygiene, particularly nutrition, is being carried out through

[1] For an illustration of what hot lunches meant to the children of 20 mountain schools in Kentucky, Tennessee, and Virginia, see TAYLOR, ALVA W., "What Hot Lunches Do for Mountain Children," *Mountain Life and Work*, Vol. 20, No. 2, Spring, 1944.

[1a] This agency was recently reconstituted as the Farmers Home Administration; see footnote 3 on p. 392.

4-H clubs, with their 1,800,000 members, and through many hundreds of Home Demonstration clubs. Several state extension services (such as those in Ohio, Nebraska, and North Dakota), in fact, have engaged full-time "health specialists" not only to promote general health education, but also to help rural people work out ways of improving the medical services available to them. Health education and planning hold promise of being an expanding phase of extension service work in the coming years. The Farm Security Administration has laid stress on home gardens and better housing and, on behalf of the many thousands of farm families in its program, is emphasizing the fullest possible use of community health resources of all kinds. Several bureaus in the Department as well as the cooperative state extension services are stressing farm safety and reduction of the tremendous loss in human resources due to accidents and fires.

In addition to extensive scientific research undertaken by various bureaus of the Agricultural Research Administration and by the related state agricultural experiment stations, frequently having a bearing on the health of both rural and urban people, the Department has also engaged in highly useful studies in the field of organized health services. Thus the Bureau of Agricultural Economics has undertaken a number of field studies of operating medical care programs, has gauged the attitudes of farm people toward health facilities and services, and has studied the application of social security, including health insurance, to the farm population. Related studies have been carried out from time to time by various state experiment stations, and the Bureau of Human Nutrition and Home Economics has made a contribution through its studies of consumer expenditures for medical care.

The Department's role with respect to rural sanitation is an extensive one and yet one with potentialities far exceeding achievements so far. Bureaus such as the Extension Service and the Bureau of Dairy Industry are stimulating, through education and example, substantial accomplishments in general farm and home sanitation. Moreover, decent sanitation for certain special groups has been promoted by the Forest Service, for example, in its camps, by the Labor Branch of the Production and Marketing Administration in its several score camps for migratory and imported farm workers, and by the Farm Security Administration on behalf of its borrowers. Through direct grants over a period of years covering the cost of materials, and more recently through loans, Farm Security by 1944 had helped its borrowers in over 1,000 counties obtain 73,400 sanitary privies, 37,500 new or improved water supplies, and screening for 49,600 dwelling units.[2] This program, carried out very largely by self-help groups under technical direction, has not only been of tremendous benefit to the families concerned but it has served in many areas as a stimulus to other farm families to improve their sanitary facilities. The Soil Conservation Service has helped to bring good water supplies to thousands of farms. The Rural Electrification Administration has made modern refrigeration facilities possible on farms and has furnished the basis for indoor running water and flush toilets. A number of other vital effects of electrification on rural health have been discussed previously.

Farm Security Administration Medical Care Plans

Perhaps the most important step taken to meet the need for medical and dental services among farm people in an organized way has been the program sponsored by the Farm Security Administration.[3] This agency, which has worked with well over 1 million farm families during the past 10 years, met the urgent problem of medical services head-on and developed one of the most extensive programs of voluntary health insurance in the United States. This program at its peak, at about the time of Pearl Harbor,

[2] Data furnished by U. S. Farm Security Administration.

[3] In August, 1946, the Farm Security Administration was abolished by act of Congress and its functions were substantially taken over by a new federal agency, the Farmers Home Administration. Among the administrative modifications that this change implies are the elimination of all direct grants, the reduction of agency supervision over farm and home loans, and the abolition of regional offices. Exactly what effect these changes will have on the health program is not clear as of this writing. It appears likely that the elimination of agency supervision over farm and home loans, including loans made for membership in prepayment health plans, will lead to the collapse of many of these plans. In the pages that follow, the program will be described in terms of the Farm Security Administration, by which it is generally known.

covered 117,000 farm families, or over 600,000 persons, and extended into over one-third of the counties in the nation. It has been the most widespread program of its kind among farm people, furnishing such services as general practitioner care and dental services as well as the more customary hospitalization and surgical services slowly becoming available through other programs.[4]

Starting in 1935 under the auspices of Farm Security's predecessor agency, the Resettlement Administration, the program was developed with the assistance of the United States Public Health Service and in cooperation with state and local professional societies from coast to coast. This pioneering effort in the field of voluntary health insurance for low-income farm families grew out of recognition of the fact that health often contributes to success or failure in operating a farm.[5] The program was thus based on the thesis that good health is vital to successful farm operation and that applying the insurance principle to health serves not only to make existing medical services more readily available but also to level the unpredictable costs of sickness. Mass health studies by questionnaire, like those made by the FSA in Texas and Oklahoma early in the program, were convincing evidence that most serious illness was going unattended and that a large share of farm failures were ultimately traceable to poor health.[6]

The group medical care program was almost an inevitable development in a rural rehabilitation program based on long-range planning with farm families; the lesson was driven home very early that it was impossible for an individual family to budget for medical care expenditures on any sound basis. Only on a

[4] When data are presented in this section without supporting references, they represent information furnished by the United States Farm Security Administration.

[5] BALDWIN, C. B., "The Medical Program of the Farm Security Administration," *Social Security in the United States* 1941 (A Record of the Fourteenth National Conference on Social Security, April 4-5, 1941). New York: American Association for Social Security, Inc., 1941, pp. 137-144.

[6] U. S. Farm Security Administration, *Farm Security Administration — Health Services Program* (Report to the Select Committee of the House Committee on Agriculture to Investigate the Activities of the Farm Security Administration). Washington: Government Printing Office, 1944, p. 4, Reprint.

group basis could costs be predicted.[7] From the viewpoint of a credit agency extending farm-operating and farm-purchase loans, moreover, the insurance feature of the program has played a part in protecting government funds totaling several hundred million dollars.

The general plan of operation of Farm Security medical care plans is actually very simple. The insurance principle is applied by giving borrower families in a county or district an opportunity to establish a special health insurance fund from which payments are made for medical services throughout the year. The annual membership fees are geared to the average ability to pay of the farm families involved. These fees are paid out of family resources or, when necessary, loans are made to help the families meet the expense. Such loans, as a rule, are simply part of the loans made for other phases of farm and home management such as for purchasing seed or fertilizer, or a tractor or livestock, or a new stove for the kitchen. The record made by the borrowers in repaying these loans is excellent. No Farm Security borrower has been obliged to join a medical care group or association; membership is entirely voluntary.[8]

In the great majority of these plans, the families are entitled to general practitioner care, that is, the services of the family physician in the office, home, or hospital. This alone sets off this program as rather unusual in a day when the provision of day-to-day physicians' care has been carefully avoided by most medical service organizations. For such care and for the drugs that the family doctor may dispense himself, the families pay about $15 or $20 a year. Many plans provide for additional services, such as surgical care, hospitalization, prescribed drugs, or dental services. These additional services, of course, call for higher annual membership fees, with an upper range in relatively prosperous farming areas of about $50 to $60 per family. To give an idea of the type of services received by families participating in this program, we find that as of June, 1944, 77 per cent were eligible for physicians'

[7] For a general discussion of the objectives of the Farm Security Administration, see U. S. Department of Agriculture, *Toward Farm Security*. Washington: Government Printing Office, 1941.

[8] WILLIAMS, R. C., "Development of Medical Care Plans for Low-income Farm Families," *American Journal of Public Health*, 30:725-735, July, 1940.

services, 61 per cent were receiving additional surgical services, 65 per cent hospital care, 33 per cent dental services, and 27 per cent were entitled to prescribed drugs. Since membership fees are necessarily set rather low, being related to the general level of incomes of the membership, it is usually necessary to restrict services to some extent. Thus care is often limited to relatively acute cases and to surgical emergencies, for example, although in actual practice the concept of emergency is quite broadly interpreted.

Before a plan is organized in a county, an over-all agreement or understanding is ordinarily reached with the state medical or dental association and then the full approval of the local medical or dental society is obtained. The doctors wishing to participate often sign an informal agreement. The participation of physicians or dentists, as in the case of the borrowers, is voluntary. There is complete free choice of participating doctor by the patient and likewise freedom among the doctors to accept or reject a patient for care. Strictly professional matters, like fee schedules, the relations among professional groups or individuals, and the entire control over the quality of services, are left in the hands of the local professional societies or the participating physicians or dentists.

The funds collected from participating families are deposited in a special health insurance account handled by a "trustee" or by the treasurer of a board of directors chosen by the membership. Ordinarily the total annual fund is apportioned into monthly allotments and the bills are paid each month on the basis of the funds available for that month. When bills can be paid in full, this is done; when a monthly allotment is insufficient to pay that month's bills in full, the allotment is distributed on a pro rata basis. As a rule any funds which are surplus at the end of a month are carried over to the end of the plan's fiscal year, when accumulated surplus funds are applied against any balances still due from previous months. If a surplus still remains after the settlement at the end of the fiscal year, it is usually carried over to supplement the next year's funds. If, on the other hand, there remain certain bills not paid in full, the accounts are generally written off in accordance with the agreements with the professional groups.

In actual practice there was an average payment of 61 per cent of all physicians' bills throughout the country in 1941, 81 per cent of dentists' bills, and 74 per cent of hospital bills.[9] The device of proration customarily employed in the program is a common device that must be used in one form or another by any medical service organization paying bills on a fee-for-service basis and depending on limited funds.

This rather brief account of the way typical Farm Security plans operate fails to reveal the tremendous variety of plans in the program as a whole.[10] Actually, a wealth of experience has been gained through the operation of prepayment plans of almost every conceivable pattern. Any developments, of course, were necessarily within the framework of an over-all agricultural program in which there has been concentration on the problems of low-income farmers, in which extensive use of subsidy was out of the question, and in which the voluntary approach was the only one feasible. Even within these limitations, however, the various plans have differed widely in membership and geographic scope of operation, in type of organization, in services provided, in annual costs to the members, and in the method of paying bills.

The size of membership in the various plans varies from just a handful of families in some plans to several thousand families in others; the geographic scope varies from the county, or even just a portion of a county, to programs covering Farm Security borrowers throughout whole states. The great majority of plans are confined to single counties, in accordance with both the Farm Security field organization and the typical organization of local medical and dental societies. Thus in 1944, of 592 plans offering physicians' services, 504 were single-county plans, whereas 57 covered two counties, 15 covered three counties, 5 extended into four counties, and 11 covered districts of five or more counties

[9] Since early in the war, the volume of services under the plans has tended to decline and membership fees have tended to rise, so that the percentage of payment of bills has been higher. The schedules of fees and charges adopted by professional groups for these plans are ordinarily in line with those customary for persons in like circumstances, though occasionally somewhat lower.

[10] WILLIAMS, R. C., "The Medical Care Program for Farm Security Administration Borrowers," *Law and Contemporary Problems* (Duke University School of Law), 6:583-594, Autumn, 1939.

or whole states. In geographic scope these 592 plans averaged 1.3 counties.

There is a tendency for the plans offering hospital services, which are often set up as separate plans, to be organized in larger geographic areas, and the same applies to a considerable extent to plans providing surgical care. This development is natural, since the relatively large bills involved in hospitalization or surgical operations may result in unreasonable fluctuations in payment unless the risk is spread over a relatively large group of participating families. As of June, 1944, only about half of the separate hospital care plans were confined to one county each, whereas almost one-fourth of them extended into five or more counties. There was an average of 5.6 counties among these plans.

So far as the various types of organization are concerned, the great majority of Farm Security plans have their own administrative structure, but in a few cases the opportunity is afforded the borrower simply to participate in the programs of existing medical or hospital service organizations. In roughly half the local plans the administrative structure is represented simply by a trustee to hold and administer the health insurance fund, possibly a committee representing the borrowers, and ordinarily one or more committees representing the professional groups. In the other areas the borrowers are organized in "health associations" with their own elected boards of directors, though usually unincorporated. In several instances incorporated associations have been organized. In Virginia, for example, the Farmers' Health Association, Inc., with a board of directors composed of Farm Security borrowers, has operated on a state-wide basis, securing hospital and surgical care for the families participating.

In several places groups of borrowers, either informally or acting through their own organizations, have tied in with existing health service programs, particularly the Blue Cross group hospitalization plans. The general policy has been to promote such participation when advantageous to the families concerned. As a rule, this has meant some concession in the form of special rates for low-income farm families or, on occasion, more liberal benefits than customary. In North Carolina, for example, several thousand borrower families have participated in two state-wide Blue Cross plans, receiving liberal benefits at an annual cost of $12 a family, with the additional incentive of a "cost-plus" arrangement which credits the families with any unused portion of each year's contributions.[11] Borrowers have joined other Blue Cross plans in states including New York, Pennsylvania, Delaware, Minnesota, Oklahoma, and Colorado.

So far as existing medical service plans are concerned, special cooperative programs have been launched in several states. Thus the Medical Service Administration of New Jersey, for example, has for several years conducted a special program of home, office, and obstetrical care for Farm Security borrowers.[12] More complete programs have been administered by the Western New York Medical Plan, Inc., which operates in several counties in the Buffalo area, and by the California Physicians' Service.[12a] The latter program, though negotiated by Farm Security, was extended to any farm family with a net income of under $2,000. It is noteworthy that virtually the only medical service organizations sponsored by the medical profession that in recent years have offered rather complete service, including general practitioner care, are the few that have been induced to do so by the Farm Security Administration on behalf of its borrower families.

It is the care provided by the family doctor, of course, that is of the most direct significance to the farm family, and it is here that the Farm Security Administration has placed its chief emphasis in developing the medical care program. Since no insurmountable difficulties have been encountered in operating a program providing office visits and home calls, it seems surprising to those familiar with the Farm Security program that there is so much hesitation, on the part of medical service plans generally, to include this fundamental phase of medical care. There has been, for example, surprisingly little evidence of abuse of privileges by participating families. Evidence of this is seen in the over-all national ratio of 4.7 office calls to one home call during the year ending June 30, 1943. The ratio reported by the Committee on the Costs of Medical

[11] "FSA and Health Insurance," editorial, *The Progressive Farmer,* 59:24, 51, November, 1944.

[12] Medical Service Administration of New Jersey, "Report to House of Delegates of the Medical Society of New Jersey 1943," *Journal of the Medical Society of New Jersey,* 40:192-193, May, 1943.

[12a] By 1947, relationships with both of these programs were terminated.

Care for families in towns under 5,000 population and rural areas was 2.0 office calls to one home call. In other words, despite removal of the financial barrier between patient and physician, the members of these plans have rarely abused the privilege of calling a physician out to the farm.

Almost every possible combination of other services has been offered in the various plans. Hospitalization has been popular, as in the case of our urban population, and at least partial surgical and other specialists' care has frequently been included among the benefits. Because of the limited ability of the families to pay, only a few plans have found it possible to include elective surgery, and the great majority of the plans have been weak with respect to provision for consultations, referrals to specialists at a distance, and the more unusual laboratory procedures. Perhaps the most limited services of all have been those offered in dental care plans which have either been organized as separate entities or have been developed in combination with other services. In such plans services have often been confined very largely to extractions, with both protective and restorative dentistry being neglected.[13] Here again, sheer lack of purchasing power on the part of Farm Security borrowers has been largely responsible for the limited service, even with funds pooled.

In general the services in these plans reflect rather closely the services customarily available in the rural communities concerned. Thus when a plan offers little more than general practitioner care, hospitalization, and emergency surgery, it is entirely likely that it represents a scope of services seldom exceeded within the particular area, regardless of the income level of a local family in need of service.

There is great variation, too, in the annual costs of these plans, since membership fees depend not only on the services provided and often on the size of family but also on the average ability to pay of the borrowers in that area or state. The amount paid for hospitalization, for example, may vary everywhere from about

[13] LANTIS, MARGARET, M. R. HANGER, and PHILIP W. WOODS, "The Farm Security Administration Dental Program of Randolph County, Ga.," in Hearings before a Subcommittee of the Committee on Education and Labor, U. S. Senate, 79th Cong., 1st Sess., S. 190 and S. 1099, *Dental Research and Dental Care*. Washington: Government Printing Office, 1945, pp. 215-217.

$4 a family for limited emergency care in a Southern state to about $15 a family among borrowers in much better circumstances. Similar variations are found with respect to all the other services, though the range in costs is seldom this extreme.

Although typical, the fee-for-service basis of payment for professional services is by no means universal in the Farm Security program. Well over 100 plans, in fact, have been operated on a capitation basis, whereby the physician receives a flat sum monthly for each family selecting him as their regular doctor, regardless of the amount of service he is called upon to provide. These capitation plans, all of which have been adopted by choice of the medical societies concerned, appear to have their historic origin in rural America in provisions made on some of the big plantations in the South for a neighboring physician to look after the plantation hands. Payment on a full-time or part-time salary basis has also been effectively employed from time to time in the Farm Security program, particularly in several of the earlier resettlement communities and in certain special plans, to be discussed. Another method of payment, which has been called the "time-fee" basis — the per hour system of payment — has been used to some extent in certain dental care plans. The dentist is paid an hourly fee for providing service to members regardless of the amount or type of service rendered within the hour. There is reason to feel that this pattern results in more services received for the funds at hand, is less subject to abuse, and when associated with some supervision is more conducive to the provision of protective services. It would be an oversight not to mention still another payment method, again an outgrowth of rural custom — payment in kind. A hospitalization program has been in operation in Oklahoma in which the families pay $5 annually in cash and are responsible for delivering an additional $5 worth of farm produce to supply the larder of the community hospital.

Special FSA Health Programs

Aside from the wide variety of medical care plans developed for scattered Farm Security borrowers, the agency has sponsored a number of unique health programs designed to meet special situations. Thus a somewhat different approach was followed in the early resettlement projects, where it was often not feasible to enroll families in a program for borrowers on the rehabilitation rolls. In about forty of these community projects, in each of which about 100 to 200 families had been given the opportunity to relocate on more productive land, small health centers were set up and public health nurses were engaged.[14] At the same time the families organized local health associations to provide themselves with medical, hospital, and sometimes dental services. In a number of the communities full-time or part-time physicians — and in three or four cases, dentists — were employed by the associations. In a few instances the government paid part of the salary of the community physician, although as a rule the medical service plan was self-supporting.

The experience gained in some of these homestead projects offers lessons of value to many rural communities, particularly those isolated from medical resources. It has shown how broad programs of both preventive and therapeutic services can be built around the framework of a community health center attended by a physician and nurse.[15] This pattern has provided a generally higher volume of medical service and has made possible greater emphasis on preventive activities of all kinds than has been possible in typical Farm Security prepayment plans. It is noteworthy that these resettlement community programs have been among the very few in the United States financed through a combination of tax support for facilities and nursing services, together with the insurance mechanism for the payment of ordinary medical services.[16] In several plans, in fact, a method of financing has been followed that may hold the key to the problem of attracting physicians to isolated rural districts. In these plans, the government paid part of the physician's salary, thus making it possible for him to earn a higher total income than the resources of the community could have provided.[17] The subsidy was extended either as a direct stipend, for which the physician per-

[14] WADE, MATILDA ANN, "Community Nursing — FSA Style," *Public Health Nursing*, 34:82-88, February, 1942.

[15] Experience has also shown the feasibility of having part-time physicians serve isolated communities, visiting the local health center on a regular schedule.

[16] GOLDMAN, FRANZ, *Public Medical Care*. New York: Columbia University Press, 1945, pp. 51-52.

[17] U. S. Department of Agriculture, "Health Security for the Economically Insecure," *Consumers' Guide*, 6:3-5, 14, June, 1939.

formed certain general preventive services for the whole community, or as a grant of funds to the local health association to help it balance its budget.

A special demonstration program, analogous in many ways to those in the resettlement communities, has been developed to meet the acute health needs of the predominantly Spanish-American rural population in a section of northern New Mexico. Taos County, the site of the program, is representative of a large area in the Southwest in which a generally impoverished farming population lives largely in small villages, carrying over the traditions of centuries and comparatively little influenced by the main stream of American rural life.[18]

Largely because of the marginal character of this area, it was possible to promote a program of organized medical services quite different from the conventional pattern of private practice. The Taos County Cooperative Health Association, embarking on its program in the summer of 1942 with a membership of about 1,000 families, was helped by the Farm Security Administration to set up health centers and to engage the services of physicians, nurses, and a dentist on a salary basis. The three principal health centers and two subcenters are located at strategic points throughout the county, bringing the services of doctors and nurses close to this scattered population for the first time. Attached to each principal health center is a full-time public health nurse, who organizes services in both preventive and therapeutic clinics and visits the homes, teaching the simple principles of healthful living. The whole professional staff works under the direction of a full-time medical director. The staff includes two other full-time physicians, two part-time surgeons, one full-time dentist, and a supervising nurse.[19]

For rather complete preventive and therapeutic services, including referrals to specialists at a distance when necessary, the mem-

[18] LOOMIS, CHARLES P., *Putting a Cooperative Health Association over to Spanish Speaking Villagers.* Washington: U. S. Extension Service, War Food Administration, 1944, Processed.

[19] It is of interest that, because of the wartime shortage of physicians and because of the barriers to licensure in New Mexico, it was necessary during the war to "import" two young Mexican physicians to practice under the supervision of the medical director. Their work during the first few months represented the period of "social service" required of all medical graduates in Mexico.

bers of the Taos County Cooperative Health Association make annual payments in accordance with a formula representing approximately 4 per cent of their meager cash income; the remainder of the cost of the program has been met by annual grants to the association by the Farm Security Administration. The annual per family cost of the program has averaged about $50, roughly the same amount as in the "experimental" programs to be described, but more emphasis on health education and preventive services has been possible. It is significant that this program could be financed only through governmental subsidy amounting to 78 per cent of its total cost, as of 1945.

Taos County holds lessons not only for vast areas of the Southwest but for many rural areas throughout the nation characterized by grossly inadequate health resources and deplorable health conditions.[20] The program could, of course, be even more far-reaching if it were community-wide rather than confined to the low-income rural population. Even as it is, however, we see an organization with its own elected board of directors, with a full-time lay executive, with an organized professional staff assisted by clinic aides and maintenance personnel, with its health centers and station-wagon "ambulances." We see a steadily developing program that supplements the activities of what has been a weak district health department and provides its members not only with preventive services but with practically all the diagnostic and therapeutic services required by any population group. In this bypath of America, where once nearly all maternity cases were handled by superstitious midwives, today we see every maternity case in the association hospitalized and a full-scale attack being made on what was one of the worst infant mortality rates in the nation — over 100 infant deaths for every 1,000 live births.[21] In 1947, plans were under way for launching a

[20] MEYER, AGNES E., *Health for Taos,* derived from a series of articles in *The Washington Post,* April 25, 26, 27, and 29, 1946. Washington: U. S. Department of Agriculture, 1946, Processed.

[21] For a detailed report on the Taos County program by the U. S. Bureau of Agricultural Economics, see *The Experimental Health Program of the United States Department of Agriculture,* a study made for the Subcommittee on Wartime Health and Education of the Committee on Education and Labor, U. S. Senate, S. Res. 74, 78th Cong., and S. Res. 62, 79th Cong. (Subcommittee Monograph 1). Washington: Government Printing Office, 1946, pp. 116-146. See also HARDING, T. SWANN, "Better Health for Country Folks: II. In the Mountains of New Mexico," *Survey Graphic,* 34:374-375, September, 1945.

similar program just north of Taos County, in Costilla County, Colorado. In this sparsely settled, low-income county a health center is to be constructed with FSA funds, public health nursing services are to be furnished through the state department of health, and medical care is to be provided by a physician on a full-time salary supported by a prepayment plan.

Another special program that deserves attention was launched by the Farm Security Administration in six counties in the "boot heel" of southeastern Missouri on January 1, 1943. The Southeast Missouri Health Service, an incorporated association, reported a membership in 1945 of about 750 families from among Farm Security borrowers in the area. The association employed a full-time business manager and several public health nurses. Here too, grants have been made by Farm Security to supplement the payments of members who have contributed a percentage of their incomes — in this case 6 per cent of net cash income annually. Grant assistance has also been extended to cover the cost of certain supplemental services beyond those within the ability of even the higher income borrowers to afford. Thus the families have contributed toward basic medical services, including both general and surgical care, hospitalization, and prescribed drugs. Direct subsidy, on the other hand, has been used to provide for the care of chronic diseases or preexisting conditions, for special diagnostic work including x rays, for eye care, and for a program of protective dental services for children. The latter have been furnished by a salaried dentist who conducts clinics in a dental trailer moved from place to place throughout the area.[22]

The only departure from the ordinary pattern of private services in this program has been in connection with the nursing and children's dental care programs, since other services have been obtained through private practitioners in their own offices and through existing hospitals. In 1946, steps were taken toward expanding the membership of the Southeast Missouri Health Service to include any farm family in the area with a net cash income up to $1,500. At the same time, the geographic scope of the program was reduced so that,

[22] Missouri State Medical Association, Committee on Medical Economics, "Southeast Missouri Health Service from January 1 to December 31, 1943," *Journal of the Missouri State Medical Association*, 41:138-141, July, 1944.

with subsidy funds limited, it might be possible to do a more concentrated and effective job of demonstration.[22a]

Before taking inventory of the lessons of Farm Security experience in prepayment plans, a brief review of the trend of population coverage will be helpful.

Trends in Coverage and Benefits

Getting off to a slow and exploratory start in 1935 and 1936, the Farm Security medical care program was characterized by steady expansion until it encountered special stresses incident to the war. The number of counties in which plans were in operation increased from 8 counties in 3 states in 1936 to 514 counties in 25 states in 1939, and to 1,074 counties in 41 states in 1942, when the membership in these plans was at its peak. After another 3 years during the war period, there were plans in June, 1945, in 1,048 counties in 38 states and Puerto Rico. After the end of hostilities, in June, 1946, there were plans in 951 counties in 36 states and Puerto Rico.[23]

The period of expansion was associated with strong administrative emphasis on the importance of health services in "farm and home planning." There were negotiations of an increasing number of agreements with state and local medical societies and related professional groups. Membership of the numerous medical, hospital, and dental care plans was marked by a steady climb from a few hundred families in 1936 to a peak of 613,854 persons in 117,460 families in June, 1942. There was then a sharp drop during the war years to a total of 528,094 persons participating in the program in 1943, 363,443 persons in 1944, 284,100 persons in June, 1945, and 236,780 persons at the end of June, 1946. The trends of total membership in

[22a] With the termination of federal grant funds in 1947, both these programs suffered setbacks. The Taos County program, as of this writing, is getting a temporary lease on life through the financial assistance of the New Mexico Foundation and it is expected that relative local prosperity may yield for a time a larger number of members requiring no subsidy. The program in southeastern Missouri is reported to be continuing on a modest basis in Butler County alone, without benefit of any subsidy.

[23] For further details, one may consult processed annual, quarterly statistical, and other reports issued by the U. S. Farm Security Administration, Office of the Chief Medical Officer.

the plans and of coverage for major categories of service, together with the number of counties involved each year, are shown in Figure 36.

As reflected in the figures, the Farm Security Administration medical care program was subjected to a severe trial by the manpower and economic consequences of the war. Perhaps the most serious effect was the wholesale withdrawal of rural physicians and dentists into the armed forces. The practitioners who remained were, as a rule, under a tremendous burden, they were earning higher incomes then ever before, and they were often unwilling to serve under an agreement in which they were obliged to render services to any particular group. At the same time, there was a substantial increase in farm income, so that a much smaller percentage of farm families fell into the lower income brackets. Thus, the effective demand for medical services purchased on a private basis increased while simultaneously the supply of practitioners able to meet the demand decreased. Aggravating this, there was a depletion of the field staff of the Farm Security Administration, so that in this period of stress local supervision was meager and often in the hands of inexperienced personnel.

The general effect of all these pressures was to cause a steady decline in the membership of FSA plans. The operation of these forces has been manifested by the fact that the decline in membership has been most extreme in the relatively prosperous farm sections of the North and West. Almost two-thirds of the total decline can be accounted for by the decrease in the number of FSA borrowers during the war years from about 500,000 to a little over 200,000. Local physicians have usually been reluctant to retain "paid-up borrowers" (that is, FSA borrowers who have paid back their entire government loan) in health associations, on the ground that they are no longer in need and can afford to purchase medical services privately. In a few places the strong bargaining power of the local board of directors has been effective in stipulating that paid-up borrowers may retain membership, but in general such efforts have failed.

More significant has been the fact that a steadily decreasing proportion of borrowers have actually chosen to participate. Thus, even in the counties in which plans have been in active operation, there was a drop in the percentage of eligible FSA borrowers who joined

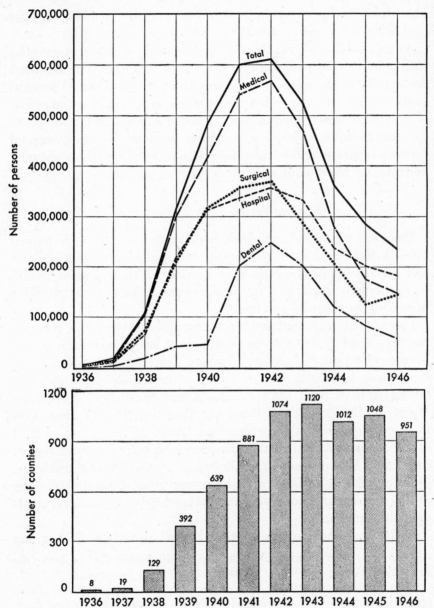

Fig. 36. Farm Security Administration Medical Care Plans: Trends of membership by type of service offered and number of counties with plans, 1936-46. (Membership data prior to 1940 represent estimates based on slightly incomplete reports; temporary emergency programs in the Dakotas during this period are omitted.) Source: based on data furnished by U. S. Farm Security Administration.

plans from 60.5 per cent in 1941 to 55.3 per cent in 1942, 49.0 per cent in 1943, 41.0 per cent in 1944, and 30.8 per cent in 1945.

As indicated in Figure 36, the decline in the number of counties with plans has been less than the drop in membership. This has been due mainly to the relative expansion of hospitalization and surgical care plans covering large districts or whole states. During the period of general decline in membership, in fact, there has been an absolute increase in the number of participants in plans providing hospital care as a separate service. Hospitalization protection in the aggregate, however, declined along with other types of benefits.[24]

Evaluation of FSA Experience

From the extensive and varied background of experience gained through the Farm Security medical care program, certain positive and certain negative lessons may be drawn. These lessons should be particularly applicable to the development of over-all plans for improving rural health services.[25]

Foremost among the positive accomplishments of the program has been the fact that tens of thousands of low-income farm people have received needed medical services. Lowering the financial barrier to care has made possible the provision of services that might otherwise have been foregone. An American Medical Association report on the program pointed out that through the plans low-income farm families have received "more or better, or at least earlier medical care than they had received before introduction of the plan."[26] The prevention or alleviation of suffering and disability, the actual saving of lives, and the preservation of farm manpower during a period of serious wartime shortages have been achievements difficult to measure.

Aside from the benefits in actual medical service, FSA group

[24] See U. S. Farm Security Administration, *Health Service Groups during the Fiscal Year Ending June* 30, 1945, Washington, 1946, Processed.

[25] For a critical evaluation of the Farm Security Administration medical care program, see GOLDMANN, FRANZ, "Medical Care for Farmers," *Medical Care,* 3:19-35, February, 1943.

[26] SIMONS, A. M., "Medical Service Plans of the Farm Security Administration" (Report of the Bureau of Medical Economics of the American Medical Association), *Journal of the American Medical Association,* 120:1315-1316, Dec. 19, 1942.

health plans have offered real financial protection to participating families. Farm families repeatedly testify, moreover, that they value highly the sense of security that membership gives them. The assurance that they are free to call on their doctor for help is a benefit felt to be well worth the cost, even though no actual services may be required for months on end. Government rehabilitation and farm-purchase loans have been safeguarded both through the promotion of better health among the borrowers and the prevention of financial losses incident to serious illness.

Through the Farm Security program, professional groups, despite initial reluctance, have cooperated with the government in extending health insurance. Even through these limited voluntary plans, physicians found that they were receiving more payment for their services than before and the majority opinion became definitely favorable toward the program.[27] It was the country practitioner more than the town doctor who displayed a liberal attitude; he had long been in intimate touch with the medical needs of farm people and had experienced the economic pinch of serving many without compensation.[28] The establishment of these plans out in country districts has, incidentally, often served to revive an inactive county medical society or even to stimulate rural practitioners to organize locally for the first time.

One could hardly expect a plan covering only a small segment of the rural population to be effective in attracting practitioners to an area. Physicians and dentists have been induced to locate in only a few places such as Taos County, New Mexico, San Juan County, Utah, and at the sites of several resettlement projects. In each case there has been the inducement of a guaranteed income or of facilities and auxiliary personnel, or both. Yet there is some evidence that the program has served to hold physicians in certain areas and to keep them from withdrawing to urban centers. This was doubtless true in the Dakotas during the drought and grasshopper period in the 1930's when the Farm Security Administration financed state-wide emergency programs of medical care largely with outright grants.[29]

[27] *Ibid.*

[28] HELLMAN, RICHARD, "The Farmers Try Group Medicine," *Harper's Magazine*, 182:72-80, December, 1940.

[29] LUBELL, SAMUEL, and WALTER EVERETT, "Rehearsal for State Medicine," *The Saturday Evening Post*, Dec. 17, 1938.

To some extent, likewise, rural hospitals have benefited financially through the mobilization of more effective purchasing power for their services.

One of the most worth-while effects of the FSA program has been the stimulation of a great many farm people as well as farm organizations and agencies, voluntary and governmental, concerning the importance of positive action on the problem of health services. While the percentage of all rural people covered by FSA plans has been small, some experience in health insurance has been provided in practically every state and in over one-third of the counties in the nation. The fact that the pooling of funds on an insurance basis works, and levels the costs of sickness, has been demonstrated a thousand times over. Farm groups in widely scattered places have been stirred into action. There is evidence that they will not long be satisfied with limited coverage plans but will simply use them as steppingstones to more comprehensive services. Farm Security's experience with plans of every variety — with differing services, costs, and organization — will hold its lessons for the future. And the far-flung local experience provided should prove useful in the detailed local administration of any broad program of health security for the general population.

Despite the direct health benefits and the positive organizational lessons growing out of the Farm Security experience, certain negative lessons have been driven home that demand careful attention. Before reviewing these, however, it must be remembered that the primary objective of the FSA medical program was to get a job done rapidly and effectively in a difficult economic period. To do this, many compromises with sound principles of medical administration were necessary. In general, medical practice in rural sections was taken for what it was and improvement was attempted in little but the method of payment for services. The agency has had neither the authority nor the tools at its command to do much more than this in the field of medical care.

One of the most serious weaknesses in these plans has been that far too few potential members actually join them. We have seen how — despite general FSA supervision, persuasion, ready credit, even direct grants of funds for participation in the early years — the percentage of active plan members among eligible borrower families has fallen steadily to the discouraging figure of 30.8 per cent.

Moreover, the plans have been "subject to a highly selective turn-over resulting in a situation where participants consist of dispropor-tionately large numbers of people who require an excessive amount of medical care."[30] A study of several FSA plans in Ohio showed that over a period of 3 years only 24 per cent of the original members retained membership throughout. These families represented only 8 per cent of the total number of families who were in the plans at one time or other during the 3-year span. There was a marked tend-ency for the "good risks" to withdraw and the "poor risks" to stay in. Among families who dropped out after 1 year there had been 2,031 physicians' calls per 1,000 persons annually, while families holding membership for two years had required 2,764 calls, and 3-year members had received 3,055 calls per 1,000 persons annually.[31] This adverse selection of risks has added further handicaps to a pro-gram confined in the first place to a low-income, and thus high-illness, population group.

The usual patterning of plans in accordance with FSA's organiza-tional structure on a single-county basis has aggravated the inherent actuarial unsoundness of the plans. Even in heavy case-load areas, there have seldom been more than 200 or 300 families from which to draw a county plan's membership. With dwindling participation and a coincidental drop in the agency's case load, many plans came to have absurdly low memberships. As of June, 1944, in fact, there was an average enrollment of just 92 families in the plans offering physicians' services, with an average geographic scope of 1.3 counties covered by a plan. It is small wonder that many of these plans have had to be discontinued.

Confining Farm Security plans to low-income farmers has meant meager financial contributions. There has been no high-income group to pay larger annual fees and thus raise the average contribution. The result has been that benefits have had to be limited. Although few plans are strictly confined to emergency care, most of them are weak with respect to such essential aspects of good medical care as the care of chronic illness, elective surgery, consultations, periodic health examinations, diagnostic laboratory service, physiotherapy,

[30] McNamara, Robert L., and A. R. Mangus, *Prepayment Medical-care Plans for Low-income Farmers in Ohio*. Wooster: Ohio Agricultural Experiment Station (Bull. 653), October, 1944, p. 26.

[31] *Ibid.*

or referrals to specialists at a distance. Dental care plans, similarly, are woefully weak on both protective and restorative services. An unfortunate consequence of these limitations has been that many families have had to spend as much or more for services not provided through the plans as for membership dues — and yet an increase in contributions to cover more services is seldom feasible. Moreover, little has been possible in the way of improving the quality of the medical services available. Any system of medical administration that limits itself to county lines tends, to some extent, to provincialize medical technology. Free and complete interchange of thinking and practice between rural counties and urban centers is necessary if rural people are to receive the full benefits of medical science.

Necessarily low family contributions have meant a relatively low volume of services. While there can be no doubt that the volume of care in most plans tends to be greater than before for the particular families involved, it does not compare too favorably with the experience of the general rural population. When the services received by farm and rural families of generally comparable income groups, as revealed in studies by the Committee on the Costs of Medical Care and the Consumer Purchases Study, are compared with the services received by members of Farm Security prepayment plans, no consistent relationship is found. There is perhaps a tendency for FSA borrowers in most of the states to receive a slightly higher volume of services than these "control" families. On the other hand the FSA experience compares rather poorly with the experience of the general population throughout the United States. The conclusion must be that FSA plans have succeeded in increasing the volume of medical services for part of the low-income segment of the farm population but such services have probably failed to reach the average for the nation as a whole.

A particular difficulty has arisen from the customary fee-for-service method of paying physicians' bills. The necessary proration of charges, since funds are limited, has introduced a dilemma between good service and adequate payment. The more services provided, the lower the percentage of payment for each service. Out of this has come an almost inevitable tendency to hold down the volume of services, a result satisfactory neither to the patient nor the physician. Sharp variations in the percentage of payment of bills from month to month has often put stresses on relationships with professional groups, sometimes to the breaking point. Actuarial soundness and general stability can hardly be achieved when the fee-for-service system is used in connection with an insurance fund built from minimal membership payments of small groups of voluntary participants.

One of the most widely recognized inadequacies of the FSA group health program has been the relative lack of membership participation in the formulation and management of the plans, despite the fact that each plan theoretically represents an agreement between local families and local professional groups. It must be recognized that FSA borrowers, being among the more underprivileged members of any rural community, have had little opportunity to develop qualities of leadership, initiative, and responsibility; while many attempts are made to promote such qualities, the task is a difficult one requiring several years to accomplish. As a result, many of the plans fall into the natural error of being considered the responsibility chiefly of the FSA county supervisor, with little concern forthcoming from the member families. As of 1944, only 30 per cent of the local health associations could be considered to be active functioning groups, gauged by the definition of having at least one meeting of their board of directors during the year. It may be stated that where membership participation has been good, as evidenced by actively functioning boards of directors, the ability of health plans to survive the stress and strain of changing times has been greater.

Despite the assumption of responsibility for plans by FSA county personnel, associated with poor membership participation, it is clear that the average plan has suffered from too little positive supervision even from a business management point of view. By and large, the management of plans has been confined to provision for expeditious payment of submitted bills. More important, perhaps, little direction has been given by cooperating medical societies or their committees to improve the quality or quantity of services, despite the implications of formal professional agreements.

With the wartime stresses cited above, most of these deficiencies of Farm Security prepayment plans became plainly exposed to view. To overcome them, several steps have been taken that may hold significance for the future. They are measures aimed at overcoming to some extent the instability of plans typically organized on a single-county basis, among an exclusively low-income group, and with voluntary participation.

In the first place, membership rates were increased in many plans to be more in line with higher farm incomes and to foster the continued cooperation of the professional groups. The necessity for providing more inclusive services along with increased membership fees was stressed but in practice was seldom accomplished. A second measure was to develop plans covering wider areas, even whole states, so as to broaden the membership base. As we have seen, hospitalization and surgical care were services more easily organized on this basis than general practitioner care.[32]

A third measure to broaden the actuarial base of plans has been to extend membership to farm families other than FSA borrowers, generally other low-income farm families. The percentage of all participants in the Farm Security program representing these other families has increased slowly from 1.1 per cent in 1941 to 1.6 per cent in 1942, 2.1 per cent in 1943, 4.5 per cent in 1944, and 7.9 per cent in 1945. While this participation is small, the idea has been incorporated in about one-fourth of all FSA plans. The objection of professional groups has been largely responsible for the relatively slight progress in extending membership in this way. The dilemma faced is that physicians and others will seldom agree to the inclusion of higher-income members unless membership fees are increased substantially, and such a course is obviously impracticable from the viewpoint of lower income farmers.

Other measures taken by the Farm Security Administration to reverse the downhill trends in the program have included emphasis on the utilization of all community health resources by borrower families. These have included the services available through health departments, the Vocational Rehabilitation program, and local voluntary agencies. There has also been emphasis on drawing the membership into more active participation in the planning and administration of their own programs.

These various measures taken to broaden the membership, to widen the area of operation, to expand the services, to promote participation in planning and management, and to emphasize preventive

---

[32] Local general practitioners as a rule have resisted the amalgamation of local county plans with plans in near-by counties; they tend to prefer the establishment of an independent fund which will not be drawn on by doctors beyond the county border.

services and coordination of the program with that of available local health agencies give some indication of the kind of developments needed on a nation-wide basis if rural as well as urban medical needs are to be met.[32a]

Experimental Rural Health Program

The prepayment medical care program of the Farm Security Administration won such general approval among agricultural groups that interest developed in extending the pattern to all rural families. The idea was given life in the launching by the Department of Agriculture of a special demonstration or experimental program of voluntary health insurance for all farm families in a half dozen selected, representative rural counties. The program was sponsored by the Department's Interbureau Committee on Postwar Programs, representing all of Agriculture's agencies, but it was financed by Farm Security Administration funds and supervised by FSA health services personnel.[33]

The objective of this program was to learn what was involved in the task of helping farm families to provide themselves with comprehensive medical services. Two assumptions, representing partly an underlying philosophy and partly the limitations of law and of finances, were taken over from the Farm Security experience. These were that membership should be voluntary and that the plans should be set up on a single-county basis. The new elements, however, were the eligibility for membership of any farm family (and later, in some counties, any local family at all), the variation of membership fees in direct proportion to family income, and provision of financial subsidy in order to make available a relatively comprehensive scope of services. This program has given us what is probably an unmatched body of experience in the possible achievements and deficiencies of tax-assisted voluntary health insurance plans in rural areas.

[32a] For a general discussion of the current issues involved in the survival of the entire Farmers Home Administration prepayment medical care program, see ZEIGLER, MARK, E. RICHARD WEINERMAN, and MILTON I. ROEMER, "Rural Prepayment Medical Care Plans and Public Health Agencies," *American Journal of Public Health*, 37:1578-1585, December, 1947.

[33] U. S. Bureau of Agricultural Economics, *The Experimental Health Program of the United States Department of Agriculture*.

With the assistance of state agricultural planning committees, suitable counties were selected[34] and the program got under way in the latter half of 1942. The counties chosen were Cass County and Wheeler County in Texas, Hamilton County in Nebraska, Nevada County in Arkansas, Newton County in Mississippi, and Walton County in Georgia.[35] In each county a health association of local farm families was organized and incorporated. Membership enrollment drives were launched, agreements were signed with professional groups, funds were granted from the Federal Government, and the plans were ready for operation.

Details differed in each of the six counties, but a standard pattern of operation was generally followed. Families desiring to join paid 6 per cent of their annual net cash income as a yearly membership fee;[36] there was usually a minimum and maximum as well. For the great majority of farm families, however, the amount paid was much less than the average cost of the services per family per year. Family contributions varied in the first year from an average of about $6 per year in Newton County, Mississippi, to $25 in Hamilton County, Nebraska — although, with higher incomes and more careful accounting, they rose in all counties in subsequent years. The actual average cost of the complete program, on the other hand, was about $50 per family per year, varying a little between associations and from year to year. The balance was made up out of govern-

[34] Choice of county was guided by these conditions: an active local agricultural planning committee or similar organization, local interest in medical care needs, a rural county representative of the general region, farm income close to the state-wide average, medical and related physical facilities reasonably adequate and accessible, receptive attitude among the professional groups, and a full-time public health unit as a desideratum but not an essential. U. S. Department of Agriculture, Interbureau Coordinating Committee on Postwar Programs, *Experimental Rural Health Program*. Washington, March, 1942, Processed.

[35] U. S. Bureau of Agricultural Economics, *op. cit.* Additional detailed information on the programs in each of these counties is available in processed reports of the Bureau.

[36] Since a farmer's *net cash* income is less than his over-all net income (including home-produced foods, and so forth), this 6 per cent was assumed to be equivalent to about 4 per cent of net income. This was the amount estimated to be spent by the average American family for medical care at the time.

ment grant funds.[37] Thus, in the first year of operation the proportion of total expenditures derived from tax support was about 80 per cent; it fell gradually as farm prosperity increased and local families assumed greater financial burdens, but in the last year of record the government was still paying about half the cost.[37a]

For these funds, member families were initially provided with broad health services including care by the general practitioner in home or office, surgical and specialist care, hospitalization, certain dental services, prescribed drugs, and home nursing. Patients had free choice of doctor, and doctors had freedom to accept or reject individual patients. As the program developed, it became necessary to limit the scope of services to some extent because of restricted subsidy funds. Drugs were eliminated in every program but one and in that one they were offered only when the member paid part of the cost personally; nursing services were eliminated everywhere, but the fundamental medical services were continued substantially.

In this program, separate financial accounts were maintained for each type of service throughout the year; only at the end of the year, if there was a surplus of funds in one account and a deficit in another, was reshuffling done. Payment for service was typically along traditional fee-for-service lines, with proration of charges when necessary. In one county, however, services were financed on a capitation basis. A full-time business manager was attached to each plan; administrative costs accounted for less than 10 per cent of total expenditures.

The membership in all six plans aggregated about 35,000 persons in the first year of operation. In the second year, there was a decline to about 27,000 persons, due partly to the discontinuation of the Nebraska program but mainly to a lowered membership in the operating plans. In the third year of operation, the aggregate membership was about 23,700 persons, ranging from about 9,200 in the Mississippi plan to about 1,700 in Wheeler County, Texas.

While the final story of this program remains to be told, an evaluation of the first three years of experience gives much insight into the

[37] YAUKEY, JESSE B., *Activities of an Experimental Rural Health Program in Six Counties during Its First Fiscal Year, 1942-43.* Washington: U. S. Farm Security Administration, 1945, Processed.

[37a] The termination of all federal grant funds in 1947 brought this program to an end as an experimental project of the Department of Agriculture. Its partial continuation, in other forms, is indicated on p. 421.

major economic and professional problems faced by rural medicine. On the positive side, the increase in services provided by the elimination of the cash barrier to medical care, through insurance and federal subsidy, has been impressive.[38] Comparison of the record of serv-

Table 43. Services under Health Insurance: *Number of specified health services per 1,000 persons per year in experimental prepayment plans of the Department of Agriculture and among the general rural population.*

Service	General rural population*	Prepayment plans†
Physicians' care:		
All cases	526	1,409
Calls, home and office	1,570	2,821
Calls at office	1,040	2,613
Calls at home	530	208
Surgical care:		
All cases	47.7	70.4
Tonsillectomies	13.5	34.3
Appendectomies	5.2	8.4
Gynecological cases	5.5	9.0
Hospitalization:		
Admissions	42	110
Days hospitalized	505	424
Dental care:		
All cases	159	294
Extractions	275	571
Fillings	249	368

Source: Yaukey, Jesse B., *Activities of an Experimental Rural Health Program in Six Counties During Its First Fiscal Year*, 1942–43. Washington: U. S. Department of Agriculture, Farm Security Administration, 1945, Processed.

* Data of the Committee on the Costs of Medical Care (1928–31). For details, see the source cited.

† Weighted average of experience in all six experimental prepayment plans of Department of Agriculture: Wheeler and Cass Counties, Texas; Hamilton County, Nebraska; Walton County, Georgia; Newton County, Mississippi; and Nevada County, Arkansas, in 1942–43.

ices in the program's first year of operation with general rural experience is shown in Table 43. It may be observed that, for practically every index of medical care, the record of services received

[38] This may be compared with the relatively unimpressive record of services in the regular FSA prepayment program, in which financial support from outside the rural counties was not available.

under the plans is better than in the general rural experience. The volume of physicians' calls in the experimental program was almost twice as great, and of hospital admissions more than twice as great. In fact, the only exceptions may actually be a reflection of the adequacy of care in the insurance program. Thus, the rate of home calls by physicians, as distinguished from office calls, was lower under the plans, indicating perhaps less need to call the doctor to the house for advanced illness when it has been freely possible to see him at the office at an incipient stage of an illness. Likewise, the smaller number of days of hospital care under the plans, combined with higher admission rates, perhaps reflects hospitalization earlier in illness when recovery can be more rapid, as well as hospitalization for less serious conditions. As the program developed, moreover, there tended to be a gradual increase in the rate of all services, especially in hospital admissions. This over-all improvement in volume of care has been the experience under health insurance generally.[39]

Much of the benefit in the way of increased services is not even included in these figures. Because of the insurance protection, many families had more ample funds to spend on supplemental services outside the program — services not covered in the plan like eyeglasses, drugs, prosthetic dental care, or extended periods of hospitalization. As for the quality of service, the vast majority of families questioned in three of the counties stated that they thought it was the same as or better than it had been before the plan; less than 2 per cent thought it was poorer.[40]

Public opinion in the experimental counties has been found to be overwhelmingly favorable toward the plans. There has been full acceptance of the principle of prepayment and variation of membership fees with family income; there has been practically no objection to the role of the Federal Government in providing funds and in furnishing some supervision over the program. Professional attitudes have been variable, but that they have been generally favorable is attested to by the continued operation of the plans in five of the six counties throughout the experimental period of federal subsidy.

On the negative side, many of the same conclusions emanating

[39] See, for example, RICHTER, L., "The Effect of Health Insurance on the Demand for Health Services," *Canadian Journal of Economics and Political Science*, 10:179-205, May, 1944.

[40] U. S. Bureau of Agricultural Economics, *op. cit.*, p. 31.

from the general Farm Security Administration experience apply also to the experimental health program. Only about half the farm population in the counties elected to join the plans the first year. This proportion declined in all counties the second year and in three out of five counties it declined still further during the third year. A high turnover of membership occurred, many families discontinuing membership and being replaced by a smaller number. In Cass County, for example, there were about 2,400 families in the plan the first year; in the second year about 1,100 of these families failed to re-enroll and they were replaced by only about 500 new families. Families not joining gave as their reasons chiefly that they lacked the money or that they simply didn't want to bother to join up. Those remaining were presumably the higher risk families.

The high proportion of direct government subsidy required to support the entire experimental health program must be taken as a negative value. With the plans confined to typical rural counties, average contributions have obviously been low, too meager to finance anything like complete services without outside support from general revenues. Even within the counties, there has been a tendency for membership to be confined largely to the lower income families so that the financial spread of their membership fees has been slight. The extension of this pattern to any considerable number of rural counties would involve federal expenditures that could not reasonably be expected to be authorized. In so far as subsidy funds have been limited, moreover, there has had to be some restriction of services. Only a broad distribution of costs over families of all levels of income, rural and urban, could eliminate the need for all or most of this subsidy, with its attendant limitations.[41]

The type and volume of services have varied considerably among the test counties. It is significant that the volume of services obtained in each county has been roughly proportional to the general rural level-of-living index of the county, as measured in 1940; in other words, the volume of services has been limited largely by local circumstances and past customs.[42] There is little reason to believe that the scientific quality of rural medicine in these counties has been appreciably improved. Although cases could be referred out-

[41] See MONTGOMERY, JAMES E., "Experimenting in Rural Health Organization," *Rural Sociology*, 10:296-308, September, 1945.

[42] U. S. Bureau of Agricultural Economics, *op. cit.*, pp. 25-33.

side the county, this has been done only rarely and the content of medical service has, by and large, been confined to the narrow limits of a rural county's boundaries. While the program has induced some expansion of hospital facilities,[43] little has been achieved in way of attracting new personnel or in setting up new patterns like group practice clinics. Solo medical practice in private offices has been preserved.

Within the operations of the plans, many lessons have been learned about administrative and fiscal problems of prepaid medical care. Data have been gathered on the relative proportions of funds to be allocated to accounts for different classes of service. Lessons have been learned on the difficulties involved in the provision of drugs in prepayment plans. The necessity for local variations with respect to benefits, payments, and operating policies — even under a federally sponsored program — has been recognized, as well as the need for changes from year to year.

With the elimination of grant authorities in the successor agency to the Farm Security Administration, the Farmers Home Administration (see footnote 3 in this chapter), the experimental phase of this program came to an end. As of this writing, the health associations in Newton County, Mississippi, and Nevada County, Arkansas, have discontinued operations entirely. In Walton County, Georgia, and Wheeler County, Texas, efforts are being made to continue without subsidies; benefits are reduced, membership charges are relatively higher, and enrollments are lower. Only in Cass County, Texas, have steps been taken to modify the conventional pattern of rendering services, in adjustment to the reduction of funds. Here plans are under way for establishment of a health center with a full-time salaried medical staff, to be financed by the voluntary prepayment contributions.[44]

Thus, while the experimental health program of the Department of Agriculture has demonstrated the advantages of health insurance over private laissez-faire rural medicine, it has likewise underscored the deficiences of plans built within county lines on a voluntary basis, even with financial subsidy. During its entire course, almost

[43] GLOVER, KATHERINE, "Better Health for Country Folks: I. In a Georgia Cotton County," Survey Graphic, 34:372-374, September, 1945.

[44] Information furnished by the Chief Medical Officer, Farmers Home Administration, November, 1947.

1 million dollars of federal funds has been spent on this program. There can be no doubt that, for both its positive and its negative lessons, not to mention the health services provided for thousands of rural people, the money has been well spent. Perhaps the most compelling conclusion must be that the difficulties of voluntary health insurance plans among rural people dictate the need for a nation-wide program for financing medical care for the entire population.

Health Services for Migratory Farm Workers

Just as the prepayment medical care program developed out of the effort to rehabilitate low-income farm families, another special health program was developed by the Department of Agriculture in the effort to alleviate the plight of migratory agricultural workers and their families. This was the tax-supported program of general medical care and preventive services launched by the Farm Security Administration in 1937, transferred to the Office of Labor of the War Food Administration during the war, and administered lately by the Labor Branch of the Production and Marketing Administration of the Department of Agriculture.[45] This activity is significant not only for the services provided to the most marginal section of the rural population, but also for the mechanisms of health administration developed and the patterns of rendering care that have been organized.

The migratory farm family, immortalized in John Steinbeck's *The Grapes of Wrath*, was too poor to be expected to make prepayment contributions, even if it could have had loan assistance, to finance medical care. Outright public assistance was necessary if these families were to receive any medical services. The individual states reasonably felt that this problem was not all theirs. While certain public funds were available for medical assistance to indigent families, the migrants were not state residents and were therefore often barred from welfare assistance by state or

[45] As of this writing, it appears that the over-all federal farm-labor program will have been liquidated by Congress at the end of 1947. Some of the activities will be turned over to the state employment services, but no special measures have been authorized for the continuation of the direct health service functions.

local settlement laws tracing back to feudal England.[46] Clearly the national government had to help.[47]

A complex problem was faced. How could federal financial assistance for medical services be provided within the framework of current legislative authorization and contemporary professional attitudes toward the role of government in medical service? The solution was one utilized by other programs in agriculture, such as the extension of credit for production or marketing operations: nonprofit corporations were established, subsidized by the Federal Government, for a specific purpose. In this instance the purpose was to provide health services to the farm worker families for whom the Federal Government assumed responsibility. The first of these corporations was the Agricultural Workers Health and Medical Association organized in the spring of 1938 to operate in California and Arizona, chief area of concentration of out-of-state seasonal farm labor in the United States.[48] The program has, in answer to the needs, gradually extended so that one or another of six "agricultural workers health associations" has come to cover every state in the nation.

The corporation charters of these associations grant them the right to engage the services of physicians and dentists, purchase drugs and equipment, negotiate with hospitals, employ nurses and clerical personnel, and carry on other activities necessary to provide health services to eligible farm workers.[49]

The definitions of eligibility for medical services under this program have been modified with changing federal legislation. Early definitions required, in addition to employment in agriculture,

[46] BLANKENSHIP, CHARLES F., and FRED SAFIER, *A Study of Medical Problems Associated with Transients* (U. S. Public Health Service Bull. 258). Washington: Government Printing Office, 1940.

[47] A few states have given some attention to the problem. For example, California's Commission on Immigration and Housing has attempted to set standards for sanitation on premises furnished for farm workers. More recently New York and New Jersey have given special attention to the public health aspects of the problem. General medical care provisions, however, have been lacking at the state level.

[48] SCHAUPP, KARL L., "Medical Care of Migratory Agricultural Workers," *California and Western Medicine*, May, 1944, Reprint.

[49] LELAND, R. G., "Medical Care for Migratory Workers," *Journal of the American Medical Association*, 114:45-55, Jan. 6, 1940.

low-income status and also nonresidency and hence ineligibility for local welfare medical assistance. With the Second World War, the concept changed, and some relationship to the federal farm labor recruitment, transportation, and housing program became the principal governing factor. As the domestic labor supply dwindled, the chief beneficiaries came to be farm workers brought in under contract from other countries.

Throughout the course of a year, the total number of persons served by this health program has probably been over 150,000. The number varies with the season, the peak for the country as a whole coming in the summer months. The general movement of the seasonal farm-labor force is a continuous flow of groups of workers following the crops, supplemented in recent years by the dispatch of "shock troops" of the "agricultural army" by rail and bus to save the harvest in areas of acute labor shortage.[50]

With the agricultural workers health association mechanism, great latitude was possible in the engagement of part-time local physicians and dentists or payment of local hospital bills or purchase of drugs. Physicians' bills could be paid promptly and practitioners were dealing with a local association in their own region — important factors in winning professional cooperation.

To ensure representation of local interests, the board of directors of each association is composed generally of seven members, of whom only three represent government, while the remainder are representatives of professional groups, public health authorities, and agricultural interests, or simply public-spirited individuals. A full-time business manager and auxiliary clerical personnel are engaged to operate the business affairs of the association, and the field medical officer of the Department of Agriculture's Labor Branch acts as medical advisor or medical director.

Professional and institutional services are rendered almost entirely through local resources. Early in the program, practically all physicians' and dentists' services were rendered through referral of patients to private offices, with payment being made on a fee-for-service basis. Fee schedules were developed by the board

[50] MOTT, F. D., and M. I. ROEMER, "A Federal Program of Public Health and Medical Services for Migratory Farm Workers," *Public Health Reports*, 60:229-249, Mar. 2, 1945. Also MOTT, F. D., "Health Services for Migrant Farm Families," *American Journal of Public Health*, 35:308-313, April, 1945.

of directors in cooperation with the professional societies. The efficiency and economy of a clinic form of operation, however, with physicians and dentists paid on a per hour basis, gradually became recognized.

In order to make the most judicious use of physicians' services and to provide a continuous program of preventive services, the characteristic pattern evolved has been the establishment of clinics or health centers in the charge of a registered nurse, usually full-time. Local physicians serving on a panel rotate in attending the clinic two or three or more times a week at designated hours.

In the course of a year such health centers or clinics have been set up in about 250 key areas of seasonal labor concentration throughout the country. Most of them have been associated with farm-labor supply centers or camps developed by the Department of Agriculture to house and provide community life to the Joads of America.[51] Some clinics have been organized, however, not associated with such centers but located on the property of large growers, in local health departments, or at some point easily reached by a large number of scattered workers.

Since agricultural work is highly seasonal and the stream of migration moves on from month to month, many of the clinics, too, must be mobile. Accordingly, use has been made of specially constructed medical trailers furnished with equipment, supplies, and drugs, which could be towed on to the next location on an hour's notice. Health personnel, particularly nurses, also must be "mobile" and may be transferred from area to area along with the workers. Furthermore, in the off season for a health association in the North, an entire group of health personnel may be transferred to an association in the South, where the harvest is at its height. Medical records follow the worker in his travels.

The nurse is the keystone of the preventive as well as the therapeutic medical care program.[52] When an eligible farm worker

[51] "Farm Labor: After Shelter Comes Health," New Pencil Points, December, 1942, pp. 32-41, Reprint. See also U. S. Department of Labor, Division of Labor Standards, Harvest Nomads (Bull. 73). Washington: Government Printing Office, 1945.

[52] WILLIAMS, R. C., "Nursing Care for Migrant Families," American Journal of Nursing, 41:1028-1032, September, 1941. Also, WADE, MATILDA ANN, and LLOYD W. JONES, "The Land Army Nurse," American Journal of Nursing, 44:849-852, September, 1944.

or his dependent comes to the health center with a complaint, the nurse decides whether or not he needs immediate medical attention. If he does, she refers him at once to a local physician on the panel of practitioners who have agreed to participate. Otherwise, the nurse gives palliative treatment, based upon standing orders approved by the local clinic physician, and usually advises the patient to return at the next regular clinic hour. On this basis, it has been found that about 50 per cent of all initial applicants for care can be screened out by the nurse, obviating the need for referral.

For special services, such as surgical care, visual refractions, or the application of orthopedic appliances, patients may be referred to outside resources. The same applies to consultant services for any case presenting complex diagnostic or therapeutic problems.

In some areas, particularly in the Midwest and the Great Plains, seasonal farm labor is so thinly dispersed that it is generally impracticable to establish fixed clinics. Here "roving" nurses have been engaged to visit the small groups of workers on scattered farms and render such preventive and educational services as they can. All medical and dental services are then rendered on a referral basis, with the nurse, the farm-labor supervisor, the local health officer, or the employer acting as the authorizing agent.

With the wartime shortage of practitioners, the panel system of rotating physicians for clinic service was not feasible in a number of areas and sometimes it was even necessary to engage the only available physician to serve several clinics. In some areas, local health officers serve as medical clinic physicians. In sections of Idaho, Washington, and Florida where the shortage of local physicians has been especially critical, it has been found necessary to detail full-time medical officers from the United States Public Health Service to handle a group of medical clinics. This has been done with the full approval of local professional groups.

Cases requiring hospitalization are referred to local hospitals, with which prior arrangements have been made by the agricultural workers health association. Because of the generally meager living conditions of the farm workers, an unusually high proportion of cases require hospitalization. This is particularly true of single male workers for whom even simple bed rest at home is impractical because there is no one at hand to care for them. To cope with some of these problems, infirmaries have been established in a few sections, chiefly for the bed care of convalescents or cases with minor ailments. Other small infirmaries have been set up for the isolation of cases of communicable disease.

At two points in the country, where seasonal labor concentration was great and where local hospital facilities were inadequate, hospitals were constructed especially for eligible farm workers and their families. These are at Belle Glade, Florida, and at Eleven Mile Corner, Arizona. Each hospital has about 60 beds and is well provided with modern medical equipment, far better than in the average rural hospital. In the Florida institution, all medical and surgical services have been rendered by a resident staff of Public Health Service officers, while in Arizona services have been rendered by attending private practitioners.[53]

In order to assure even partially adequate dental services, the assignment of full-time personnel has quite often been necessary. Thus, while local private dentists are generally utilized for dental care on a clinic or referral basis, full-time dentists have been engaged in several sections, including California, the Pacific Northwest, Texas, Florida, and Connecticut. These men have worked in dental trailers or with portable equipment, moving from camp to camp at intervals through the year or sometimes serving several camps in one area in rotation.

In areas where families rather than single workers predominate, there is emphasis on preventive dental care for children. The dental services rendered adults are necessarily limited, being confined largely to extractions, fillings, and prophylaxes, although artificial dentures may be supplied when essential to the general health of the individual.

With regard to preventive services, the policy has been to seek advice and assistance of state and local departments of health.[54] Clinics for maternal and child hygiene or venereal disease control

[53] During the war, the once full stream of migration in southern Arizona was largely dried up, and use of the Eleven Mile Corner hopsital had to be discontinued.

[54] DICKIE, WALTER M., "Health of the Migrant," *Weekly Bulletin* (California State Department of Public Health), 17:81-83, June 18, 1938.

are organized at the farm-labor camps when they are not available through a local health department. Mass case-finding programs through serologic testing for syphilis and photofluorographic chest studies for tuberculosis have been conducted. General health education of all kinds is carried out.

All adults are generally immunized against the typhoid-paratyphoid group of diseases and vaccinated against smallpox if this has not been done during recruitment. In addition to these immunizations, children receive diphtheria toxoid. In the Northwest, Rocky Mountain spotted fever immunization is given in the tick regions. In parts of California, protection has been given against equine encephalomyelitis.

In farm-labor camps where only males are housed, a program of mass feeding has usually been conducted. This has provided an opportunity for education on nutrition and for the provision of a balanced diet. Food handlers are routinely examined, particularly for enteric diseases, and kitchen sanitation receives considerable attention.

Constant promotion of environmental sanitation is an essential phase of the preventive program. In "permanent" type farm-labor camps the sanitary facilities are reasonably modern and well maintained but in the "mobile" camps problems are numerous. The most difficult task of environmental sanitation is associated with the protection of workers housed on hundreds of scattered private growers' premises. Finally, an active program of safety education is conducted to keep down the toll of farm injuries.[55]

A few words should be said about the volume of services rendered in this program and their costs.[56] Because of a general poverty of medical attention in the past, the farm worker family carries a high complement of uncorrected physical defects such as infected tonsils, chronic bronchitis, middle ear infections, recurrent appendicitis, orthopedic defects, varicose veins, hemorrhoids, and pelvic disorders in women. Malnutrition and secondary anemia are common.

[55] CROZER, WALLACE C., "Saving Farm Labor," Farm Safety Review, 3:6-7, 13-14, November-December, 1945.

[56] U. S. Department of Agriculture, War Food Administration, Office of Labor, Activities of the Agricultural Workers Health Associations, quarterly reports, 1943-45, Processed.

As a result, and because of the conditions of migrant living, there is a high rate of applications for medical service compared to the experience of the general rural population. While the computation of specific rates is difficult without an accurate population base,[57] it is estimated that of those eligible at least 1 out of 10 seeks medical service for a case of illness each month. There have been about 3.5 visits to a physician or nurse per case of illness, of which about 40 per cent have been services of physicians and 60 per cent services of nurses. This represents an annual incidence of about 4,200 physicians' or nurses' services per 1,000 persons, of which about 1,700 are physicians' services. The volume of service naturally varies markedly with the accessibility of a clinic to the workers, the presence of women and children, and other factors. The removal of the economic barrier to the receipt of services undoubtedly increases to a large extent the utilization of the services offered.

The effectiveness of the volume of services delivered may be partially reflected by data available on sickness absenteeism among these farm workers. In the country as a whole, an average of only 1.5 per cent of total available man-days of labor was lost due to sickness in 1944. While comparative data for other farm workers are not available, the national average for industrial workers has been about 3.7 per cent.[58] The difference may be partially explained by the fact that seasonal farm work is chiefly a warm-weather operation, when illness rates are lower, by the relatively smaller proportion of women workers, among whom sickness rates tend to be higher, and by the medical selection of many of these workers before they start work. To the early and continuous provision of medical services, however, and the entire preventive program, may be attributed part of the credit for the good record. It is significant that in 1946 one-third of all cases handled involved the provision of preventive services.[58a]

[57] Because migrants in the area surrounding a farm-labor supply center may at any time apply for service, it is quite difficult to estimate accurately the total number of persons eligible for the service of a particular clinic.

[58] Derived from GAFAFER, W. M., "Absenteeism," *Manual of Industrial Hygiene* (U. S. National Institute of Health, Division of Industrial Hygiene). Philadelphia: W. B. Saunders Company, 1943, pp. 420-466.

[58a] U.S. Department of Agriculture, Production and Marketing Administration, Labor Branch, *Agricultural Workers Health Associations: Report of Activities, January-December,* 1946, Washington, October, 1947, Processed.

The total operating medical cost of the program has approximated 2 million dollars a year. This does not include the initial costs of most of the physical facilities. Since the actual population served cannot be accurately determined and since the composition of this population changes from month to month (continuously introducing new individuals with a backlog of untreated illness or defects), it is difficult to estimate the over-all cost per person served. In 1945 the services were estimated, however, to cost between $18 and $24 a year per person, or, more accurately, in terms of the seasonality of farm work, between $1.50 and $2 per person per month. By 1946, with the rising general price level, costs had risen to an estimated $2.25 per person per month.

The vast bulk of this expenditure has gone for the payment of direct medical, surgical, specialist, nursing, dental, hospital, or related services. Only a small percentage is referable to the cost of administration or of the supervision rendered by medical, sanitary engineering, or other technical personnel. Nearly all the funds have been granted by the Federal Government to the agricultural workers health associations, in accordance with the volume of services rendered, and are spent directly by these associations. In regions where services are rendered predominantly on a clinic rather than a referral basis, it is not surprising that the cost per service or the cost per person served has been somewhat lower.

Starting as a welfare program in the depression period, the farm-labor health activities had their greatest expansion in the war years. As American agriculture moved from an economy of vast farm-labor surplus to one of relative farm-labor shortage, the Federal Government had to supplement local manpower mobilization with an extensive program of farm-labor transportation at government expense, including the importation of tens of thousands of farm workers from foreign countries.[59] It became necessary, therefore, to conduct mass physical examinations of workers at far-flung points to assure the transportation of persons free from communicable disease and without illness or physical defects that might make farm work hazardous to themselves or render them incompetent as workers.[60] Once workers were located in

[59] These included workers from Mexico, Jamaica, the Bahamas, Barbados, Canada, and Newfoundland.

[60] MOTT and ROEMER, op. cit.

an area of employment, however, the provision of medical care was along the lines already described.

After the end of the war, the beneficiaries of this program increasingly consisted of domestic migratory farm workers. Heightened interest in organized medical services for domestic migrants came to be expressed by state agencies of agriculture, labor, and public health. In a number of states, these agencies contracted with the agricultural workers health associations to provide services for migrants not under the jurisdiction of the federal farm-labor agency. Recognition of the recurring problem of migrant labor throughout the nation led to the establishment in 1946 of a federal Interagency Committee on Migrant Labor to develop a long-term health and welfare program. The final report of this committee recommended, among other things, that a federal program of grants-in-aid to the states be instituted to finance complete preventive and therapeutic health services for migrant labor families. For use of these funds, states would have to waive residence restrictions. Standards similar to those followed in the federal program were suggested.[61] A small step in this direction was the appointment in the Public Health Service, Division of States Relations, of a medical officer to be concerned exclusively with the health problems of migrants.

Viewed against the perspective of total farm-labor health needs, only the surface of the problem has been scratched by this special federal program. Nevertheless, a great volume of needed health services has been provided for migratory farm workers. Important demonstration purposes have been served that may prove useful in developing patterns of medical service not only for the migratory farm population but for any isolated agricultural community. The pattern of small health centers attended by full-time public health nurses, making efficient use of physicians' limited time through organized planning of both preventive and treatment services, is one that should be helpful, in fact, for most rural sections.

[61] Federal Interagency Committee on Migrant Labor, *Migrant Labor — A Human Problem* (Report and Recommendations), Washington: U. S. Department of Labor, Retraining and Re-employment Administration, 1947, pp. 28-30.

THE ROLE OF THE DEPARTMENT of Agriculture in organizing rural health services has, in a sense, been to fill in the gaps left by other public or voluntary agencies. Since the greatest deficiencies were in the provision of general day-to-day medical care to the rural population, it is in this province that Agriculture's actions have been broadest. Taken all together, the activities of government — in public health, in welfare medical services, in the medical care of certain illnesses or groups of persons, in the improvement of resources in facilities and personnel, in research, and along the manifold paths taken by the Department of Agriculture — represent an attack on health problems along a broad front, although often with insufficient ammunition and forces.

While we must recognize and acknowledge the piecemeal character of government programs, the trend toward a gradually expanded government role in all organized medical services in rural and urban sections alike is, nevertheless, unmistakable.[62] As the essentiality of health to individual and community welfare, social and economic, becomes more firmly established, the responsibilities of government will inevitably broaden and its armamentarium will be strengthened. In the varied efforts and approaches of the past, we find the clues to the pathways that will mark the future.

[62] For a general discussion of the government in medical care, see STERN, BERNHARD J., *Medical Services by Government.* New York: The Commonwealth Fund, 1946.

PART VII: VOLUNTARY HEALTH PROGRAMS

THE VARIED types of government programs for improving health services that we have reviewed have usually been preceded by voluntary efforts. An account of organized voluntary programs grappling with the problems of rural health services, therefore, will not only complete the picture of what is being done to improve rural health but will give us a preview of the probable official programs of the future.

It is not laboring the obvious to state that the most basic voluntary effort of all in rural health improvement has been the unmeasured toil and sacrifice of the thousands of individual country doctors, dentists, nurses, and others who through the years have done all they could to bring to rural people the best kind of medical care within their ability. The handicaps under which they have operated and the resulting deficiencies, relative to urban experience, have been considered in earlier chapters. Here our attention must be turned to the efforts of organized voluntary groups.

Voluntary action typically originates from the recognition of a specific need and naturally is directed toward the satisfaction of that particular need. While single-minded crusades may gain their ends, the result, from the over-all health point of view, is often patchwork. A score of zealous groups set out to attack a score of problems, each in its own special way. Prerogatives tend to become jealously guarded, efforts are duplicated, emphasis is often given in accordance with pressures rather than needs, and coordination among the many separate voluntary and governmental programs becomes a special task in itself.

Despite these commonly recognized difficulties, no one would deny that great benefits are rendered by the variegated health programs of the nation's voluntary agencies. The benefits may be measured not only in the services provided in specific areas but in the demonstrations created for other areas.[1]

As in most other phases of health work, however, rural areas enjoy less than their due share. Voluntary organized action requires both a high level of group consciousness and an adequate reservoir of philanthropy. Neither of these is as plentiful in rural

[1] GUNN, SELSKAR M., and PHILIP S. PLATT, *Voluntary Health Agencies: An Interpretative Study*. New York: The Ronald Press Company, 1945.

435

areas as in the cities. As a result, the most significant type of voluntary action benefiting rural people has been that originating outside rural communities. In so far as the acute needs of rural people have been recognized by national or state groups, some positive programs of improvement have been brought in from without. Despite this assistance, the whole structure of voluntary action to improve health is less mature in rural districts than in cities.

The most important voluntary measures can be categorized in terms of the main aspects of the rural health problem. There have been efforts to ease the payment of medical and related bills, chiefly through health insurance plans. There have been steps to attract medical personnel to rural communities. There have been organized efforts to expand and improve hospitals and health centers in rural areas. There have been programs to improve the quality of rural medical service in a technical sense. Finally and perhaps most important, there has been a great variety of organized efforts to expand preventive or public health services for rural people and to educate them about sound personal and environmental hygiene. In practice, these five main lines of action have, of course, been closely interrelated, but they may be conveniently described under these several headings.

CHAPTER 23

TACKLING THE PAYMENT PROBLEM

PROBABLY the most widespread method of easing the payment of medical bills in rural areas has been the extension of "credit" for professional services rendered to farm families or, to some extent, the acceptance of barter payment. The most significant measure in an organized way, however, has undoubtedly been the development of voluntary health insurance plans. Beyond the extensive prepayment health program developed under the sponsorship of the Farm Security Administration, a variety of prepayment programs unrelated to any government agency have taken root in a number of rural communities.

As with most organized health programs, general rural development of voluntary prepayment plans has been much less than urban. By and large, prepayment health plans have grown up under circumstances where periodic contributions could be conveniently collected from large groups of people. To be actuarially sound and within the ability to pay of the average person, it is desirable for any plan to reduce individual voluntary enrollment to a minimum and to spread risks over a large unselected group of people — like the workers in a factory or the members of a fraternal lodge. Such organic groups are obviously found more often in cities. Not only are such administrative short cuts as payroll deductions unfeasible in rural areas, but the low level and variability of rural incomes put further handicaps in the way of organization of rural prepayment plans.

Prepayment Plans with Rural Roots

The principle of paying for medical care through a prearranged contract has been part of agricultural life in the United States as far back as Colonial times. George Washington engaged a physician to take care of the people on his estate for a fixed amount of money, £15 a year.[1] The plantation doctor, moreover, paid by the landlord

[1] *The Diaries of George Washington* 1784-1799 (John C. Fitzpatrick, ed.). Boston and New York: Houghton Mifflin Company, 1925, Vol. 1, p. 108.

to provide some modicum of care to the resident slaves was an occasional feature of the antebellum South.[2] The pattern is still found in some Southern farm enterprises, with the sums paid to the physician usually derived from a sort of rough deduction out of the funds due to the tenants, sharecroppers, or farm laborers.

Some of the earliest prepayment medical care plans, even as we know them today, had their origin in rural sections. These were the medical plans set up in the late nineteenth century in lumbering, mining, and railroad establishments, where relatively concentrated groups of workers were located in isolated spots not accessible to ordinary community health facilities.[3] Only by assuring physicians guaranteed incomes, such as could be done through building a fund from prepayment contributions, and by providing certain facilities, could medical services be obtained for these isolated groups. This pattern has gradually become extended to industrial enterprises of all types.[4]

While these plans have not covered farmers as such, they have made available to certain rural nonfarm groups services that would otherwise have been lacking. Despite the growth of numerous voluntary medical care plans of all kinds, in 1943 the largest aggregate membership was found in these "industrial" plans, which included nearly 43 per cent of all members of prepayment plans for general medical care.[5] The great bulk of these plans, however, have today lost their "isolated area" character and are found in large metropolitan centers like Birmingham or Chicago. In smaller industrial communities, like Gadsden, Alabama, or Camden, Arkansas, where farmers from the surrounding country work part of the year in a factory, rural people are to some extent benefited by these plans today. In a good many small metal mining or lumbering centers, the groups served are still essentially rural. In some of these places, private

[2] Shryock, Richard H., "Medical Practice in the Old South," *South Atlantic Quarterly*, 29:160-178, April, 1930.

[3] Williams, Pierce, *The Purchase of Medical Care through Fixed Periodic Payment*. New York: National Bureau of Economic Research, 1932.

[4] Avnet, Helen Hershfield, *Voluntary Medical Insurance in the United States: Major Trends and Current Problems*. New York: Medical Administration Service, Inc., 1944.

[5] Klem, Margaret C., *Prepayment Medical Care Organizations*. (Social Security Board, Bureau of Research and Statistics, Mem. 55). Washington: Federal Security Agency, June, 1944, p. 112.

physicians have themselves organized prepayment plans for the workers, such as the District Clinic Medical and Hospital Plan at Cripple Creek, Colorado.[6] In Southampton County, Virginia, a group practice clinic and hospital, organized by Dr. Rufus L. Raiford and serving mainly rural people in the area on a fee basis, provides care to about 1,000 employees of a local industrial plant on a prepayment basis.[7] Such arrangements, with a strong emphasis on industrial medicine and workmen's compensation cases and without coverage of the employee's dependents, are not uncommon in the South or Southwest, where rural stretches are occasionally interrupted by a textile plant or a milling operation.

Special mention should be made of the prepayment medical care plans for coal miners and sometimes for their families. Most mining communities peppered through the coal fields of the United States are essentially rural, and in a major share of them special arrangements have been made for prepayment of medical or hospital costs or both, through wage deductions. Numerous abuses have become associated with these plans, especially in relation to the handling of compensable injuries.[7a] In recent years, however, the entire question of medical services for workers has entered into the sphere of collective bargaining, as a result of which major plans are under way to reorganize health services in the mine fields.[7b] The recent establishment of an industry-wide Health and Welfare Fund, through negotiations between the United Mine Workers of America and the bituminous coal mine operators, may have far-reaching effects in bringing better prepaid medical care to several hundred thousand mining families in rural communities of some twenty states.

Except for the government-stimulated program of the Farm Security Administration, the prepayment health plans organized in rural

[6] *Ibid.*, p. 24.

[7] Extension Division, University of Virginia, *Medical Care in the Country: A Country Doctor Shows His Community the Way to Health,* Charlottesville (New Dominion Series, No. 77), Feb. 1, 1946.

[7a] ROBERTS, KINGSLEY, DEAN A. CLARK, and KATHERINE G. CLARK, Medical *Care in the Appalachian Coal Fields.* New York: Bureau of Cooperative Medicine, 1939, Processed.

[7b] U. S. Department of Interior, Coal Mines Administration, *A Medical Survey of the Bituminous Coal Industry.* Washington: Government Printing Office, 1947, pp. 115-164. See also BAKER, HELEN, and DOROTHY DAHL, *Group Health Insurance and Sickness Benefit Plans in Collective Bargaining.* Princeton: Princeton University, Industrial Relations Section, 1945.

areas primarily for farm people have been few and far between. Despite the organizational difficulties, however, a handful of small but significant plans have been launched.

Best known, perhaps, is the cooperative health association for farmers at Elk City, Oklahoma, sponsored by the local chapter of the National Farmers Union.[8] The Farmers Union Hospital Association, as it is called, served about 10,000 farm people in 1943 with a staff of full-time physicians, dentists, and nurses. A subscriber, spouse, and two or more children paid $25 a year for family membership in addition to an initial $50 share of stock in the cooperative association. Office and hospital calls, laboratory examinations, and surgical services are covered without further cost to the patient, but additional charges are made for home calls, dental care, and hospitalization. Despite attacks from many sources, the Farmers Union health plan has thrived through the loyal support of its members and the pioneering efforts of its medical director, Dr. Michael A. Shadid. At Mooreland, Oklahoma, a similar cooperative hospital and medical care plan has been developed in recent years.

Comparable prepayment plans for farm people have been launched in Texas and Nebraska. At Amherst, Texas, the South Plains Cooperative Hospital Association served a membership of about 4,600 farm people in 1943.[9] In the thinly settled cattle country of Nebraska, the Sandhills Regional Health Association has served farm families in an area of some 2,000 square miles. Families contribute $30 a year toward the support of a full-time salaried physician and the public health nurse. Regular weekly clinics are held at the main villages in the region and a new hospital is currently being planned. This program has been stimulated, on a demonstration basis, by the Farm Foundation; it has been supported by the three principal national farm organizations and the University of Nebraska; and it has received financial assistance from the Nebraska State Department of Health.[10] In connection with the Cooperstown hospital demonstra-

[8] SHADID, MICHAEL A., A Doctor for the People. New York: The Vanguard Press, 1939.

[9] JOHNSTON, HELEN, "Texans Team up for Health." in Cooperative Health Articles, reprinted from News for Farmer Cooperatives (U. S. Farm Credit Administration), May, 1946, pp. 9-11.

[10] ANDERSON, ELIN L., "Adequate Medical Care for Rural Families," Journal of Home Economics, 36:397-400, September, 1944; "Nebraska Pioneers in Rural Medical Care," Medical Care, 2:303-313, November, 1942.

tion in rural Otsego County, New York, a small prepayment plan was organized, but with opposition from several sources, including restrictive state legislation, it came to an end in 1940 after 9 years of operation.[11]

Interesting possibilities for comprehensive prepayment protection of rural people living near college communities are developing at Hamilton, New York (Colgate University), and Tuskegee, Alabama (Tuskegee Institute). To support a competent and complete medical staff for these relatively small student bodies, it has been considered advisable to enroll surrounding residents in a joint college-community health service.[12] New rural prepayment plans are likewise contemplated in connection with a number of cooperative hospital construction projects being planned in Texas and the Pacific Northwest (see Chapter 24).

Limited as has been the development of voluntary prepayment medical care plans with rural roots, the few plans in operation are a tribute to the resourcefulness of rural leaders who have attempted to build projects for rural betterment even on the shifting sands of rural poverty. The few plans functioning are all different in the details of their scope of services, method of administration, coverage, and costs. There are various restrictions in benefits or supplemental charges for special services, and hardly a plan provides truly complete medical care. Aside from the Farm Security Administration program, rural areas have had an indigenous development of voluntary health insurance that, in the total picture of rural health needs, is of minor proportions.

Prepayment Plans with Urban Origins

Outside of rural areas certain voluntary prepayment plans have been developed that, to a relatively small extent, have included rural members. Chief among these have been the plans of state and county medical societies, policies offered by commercial or cooperative insurance companies to indemnify for sickness, and the group hospitalization insurance program, supported chiefly by the

[11] MacKenzie, G. M., "The Social Orientation of a Rural Hospital," an address delivered at the Institute of Public Health Economics, University of Michigan, Ann Arbor, June, 1943.

[12] Unpublished reports of the U. S. Public Health Service.

hospital associations, known as the Blue Cross program. Practically all these voluntary programs have confined their main activities to the cities and have reached rural people only incidentally.

In recent years, medical societies in more than half the states have undertaken the organization of voluntary prepayment plans. Protection offered by these plans is largely limited to surgical and obstetrical benefits during hospitalization. Income ceilings on eligibility for membership are generally imposed and some plans authorize the collection of supplemental private fees, over and above the payment to the physician by the plan.[13] By 1947 about 6 million persons were enrolled in these professionally generated plans, and a major share of these represented industrial groups in Michigan and the three Pacific states.[14] The very requirement of organic groups for membership in nearly all these programs necessarily discriminates against the relatively unorganized and scattered farm population. Their rural connections, as a matter of fact, have been chiefly through the organized program of the Farm Security Administration. In 1945, the American Medical Association gave recognition to the problem and set up a Committee on Rural Medical Service, with comparable committees in the state medical societies.[15] One of the functions of these committees is to explore methods of enrolling rural people in medical society prepayment plans. By 1947, after much effort had been applied to the problem, the American Medical Association stated that about 7 per cent of the subscribers to medical society plans were from rural communities.[15a] This represents less than 1 per cent of the rural population.

Commercial insurance companies have for many years sold individual policies providing either insurance for income loss during disability due to illness or accident, indemnification (not necessarily complete) for high-cost surgical or hospital bills, or both. Unlike the prepayment plans so far discussed, it is important to recognize that these policies provide cash and not service; the cash may or

[13] DAVIS, MICHAEL M., "Health Insurance Plans under Medical Societies: II. Accomplishments and Outlook," *Medical Care*, 4:17-36, February, 1944.

[14] American Medical Association, Council on Medical Service, "Six Million Plus," *Newsletter*, 4:1, Aug. 20, 1947.

[15] American Medical Association, *Rural Health Service*. Chicago, undated (c. 1945).

[15a] American Medical Association, Council on Medical Service, "Rural Community Enrolment in Medical Society Plans," *Newsletter*, 4:7, May 28, 1947.

may not be sufficient to cover the actual medical costs incurred. Typically the policy covers only one individual and no dependents. Analyses have shown that relative to the benefits received, the cost of these policies, which are sold by a great many small companies, is inordinately high. Many companies have for years paid out in benefits only 50 cents for every premium dollar collected.[16] The extent of such policies among rural people is considerably less than among urban. In 1941, studies of the Department of Agriculture and the Department of Labor found 24.2 per cent of urban families to have members with some form of "health and accident insurance," compared with 17.0 per cent of rural nonfarm families and 10.8 per cent of rural farm families.[17] A Virginia study found that, considering all types of health insurance, a higher proportion of rural Negroes than of rural whites were covered — a significant fact in view of the meager financial returns of individual commercial policies and greater Negro poverty.[18]

Commercial sickness and disability indemnity policies sold on a group basis are considerably more economical. In compensation for wartime wage restrictions, employer-subsidized group insurance programs have increased rapidly in recent years, and the Life Insurance Association of America estimates that as of December 31, 1945, nearly 6 million persons were covered by commercial group policies for disability indemnification.[19] There were also about 8 million persons covered in group hospital expense indemnification policies, about 4,600,000 in group surgical expense indemnification policies, and about 450,000 in group medical expense indemnification policies — there being, of course, considerable overlapping of the same indi-

[16] OTEY, ELIZABETH L., *Cash Benefits under Voluntary Disability Insurance in the United States.* Bureau of Research and Statistics, U. S. Social Security Board (Bur. Rep. 6). Washington: Government Printing Office, June, 1940.

[17] Data furnished by U. S. Bureau of Human Nutrition and Home Economics and U. S. Bureau of Labor Statistics, from the Study of Family Spending and Saving in Wartime, 1941-42.

[18] GARNETT, W. E., *Virginia Rural Health and Medical Care Study and Related Questions,* Preliminary Report (Rural Sociology Mimeograph Rep. 27). Blacksburg: Virginia Agricultural Experiment Station, October, 1943, Processed, p. 6.

[19] Life Insurance Association of America, "Group Insurance and Group Annuity Coverage — United States Business 1945: All Life and Casualty Insurance Companies," Special Report. New York, 1946.

viduals with more than one type of policy. Like other forms of group insurance, however, these policies are largely confined to factory workers, from whom premiums can be conveniently collected on a payroll deduction basis.

In recent years, some farm organizations, as a membership boosting device, have enrolled their members in these group insurance plans. Most active in this have been the state and county Farm Bureaus,[20] some of which have offered policies through their own mutual insurance companies. Farmers Union locals likewise offer their members surgical and hospital expense indemnification policies, carried by their own insurance organization, which, in conjunction with life and burial insurance, they promote as their Triangle Family Service program.[21] Other organic groups like milk producers' associations have enrolled their memberships in group indemnity plans that often give death benefits as well as indemnification for hospital or medical costs.[22] The deficiencies of indemnity, as distinguished from service, health plans apply in general to group as well as individual policies offered by commercial insurance companies. Despite their greater economies, studies have shown that even these group insurance policies under commercial auspices yield average returns to subscribers of only 62 to 75 cents on the premium dollar.[22a]

The most extensive pattern of voluntary prepayment for health services in the United States has been in the field of hospitalization insurance. While commercial policies to indemnify for hospital costs on an individual or group basis are hold by the thousand, the vast majority of persons covered are protected by membership in service plans sponsored by nonprofit groups, under the leadership of the hospitals themselves or the hospital associations. From an inauspicious beginning in Dallas, Texas, in 1929, this "Blue Cross" group

[20] SEWELL, MRS. CHARLES W., "Better Health for Rural America," *The Nation's Agriculture* (American Farm Bureau Federation), 19:7, April, 1944.

[21] National Farmers Union Education Service, *Rural Health Tomorrow.* Denver, Colorado, 1946.

[22] LARSON, GUS, "Farmers Can Get Better Health Services," *The Country Gentleman*, 115:14, 70, 72, 73, October, 1945.

[22a] BLANCHARD, RALPH H., *Survey of Accident and Health Insurance* (U.S. Social Security Board, Bureau of Research and Statistics, Mem. 62). Washington: Government Printing Office, August, 1946.

hospitalization movement has grown to a national coverage of 24 million in 1947.[23] This expanding program has acquired nation-wide significance not only because of the protection afforded against high-cost hospital services and the increased hospital usage made possible, but also because of the general demonstration of the feasibility of the insurance principle as applied to sickness.[24]

Within the sphere of hospital administration, the Blue Cross move-ment has had tremendous influence. Since the plans have preferred to pay hospitals for services rendered to members on an all-inclusive per diem basis — the fee including all items of service but often vary-ing among hospitals — uniform cost-accounting and record systems have been encouraged. As enrollments have increased and risks have become more broadly spread, many of the limitations and exclusions have been abandoned and the tendency has been toward more com-prehensive benefits. Coincidentally, however, there has been a tend-ency for membership charges to rise. In the postwar period, more-over, hospital service costs spiraled so high that some of the plans simply could not pay the bills, even though membership charges had been elevated; there was even some tendency for plans to shift from a service to an indemnity basis, leaving it to the subscriber to pay the difference between his cash allowance and the cost of room accom-modations.

The group hospitalization movement is seen in true perspective, when it is realized that the expenses insured against actually rep-resent only about 15 per cent of the average family's total medical bill per year[25] and that the total membership represented in January, 1947, only 17 per cent of the national population.[26] It is true that some Blue Cross plans are combined with medical or surgical care

[23] For an excellent analysis of the entire Blue Cross program, see REED, LOUIS S., *Blue Cross and Medical Service Plans.* Washington: U.S. Public Health Service, October, 1947, Processed. See also Richardson, J. T., *The Origin and Development of Group Hospitalization in the United States.* Columbia: Uni-versity of Missouri (University of Missouri Series, Vol. 20, No. 3), 1945.

[24] ROREM, C. RUFUS, "Blue Cross Hospital Service Plans," *The U. S. Senate Hears about Hospitals and Hospital Service.* Chicago: American Hospital Association, 1944.

[25] FALK, I. S., C. RUFUS ROREM, and MARTHA D. RING, *The Costs of Medical Care* (Committee on the Costs of Medical Care Pub. 27). Chicago: University of Chicago Press, 1933, p. 89.

[26] REED, *op. cit.,* p. 22.

plans sponsored by medical societies, but these include only about 10 per cent of all Blue Cross members and ordinarily encompass only services for certain types of hospitalized illness.[27]

With respect to rural medical care, the important fact is that Blue Cross plan membership is concentrated in the larger cities and the industrialized states. Of the 18 states which in 1947 had a Blue Cross membership of more than 15 per cent of the state population, all but 4 were predominantly urban.[28] Of the approximately 25 million Blue Cross members in November, 1946, only about 1,638,000 were rural people, according to a Blue Cross survey. A few of the plans, like those at Providence, Rockford (Illinois), Boston, Kingsport (Tennessee), and Buffalo, reported rural people to constitute in excess of 20 per cent of their membership. Despite a gradual increase in rural enrollment, however, by the end of 1946 "only 2.65 per cent of the rural population was Blue Cross protected."[29] A certain proportion of rural Blue Cross members, moreover, have been members of Farm Security Administration medical care plans that subcontracted for hospital services with a Blue Cross association.

The striking concentration of this hospital insurance program in urbanized states is demonstrated in Figure 37. This urban concentration is, of course, not surprising. Not only do the usual organizational handicaps to rural enrollment in prepayment plans play their part, but membership fees are simply beyond the means of most farm families. Except through the special arrangements made with the Farm Security Administration, membership fees have not been geared to the rural situation with its meager hospital facilties and their currently lower utilization.

Farm people, nevertheless, have been eager to have hospital insurance protection and rural enrollment has been increasing. Spirited community campaigns by the Blue Cross staff have enrolled the largest number. Organized farm groups often provide the mechanism for enrollment and periodic collections. Rural banks, farm cooperatives, creameries, farm organizations, and well-organized

[27] REED, LOUIS S., and HENRY F. VAUGHAN, JR., "The Coordination of Medical and Blue Cross Plans," Journal of the American Medical Association, 128:22-25, May 5, 1945.

[28] REED, op. cit., p. 24.

[29] "Rural Membership up 200 Percent Since 1944 Survey," Blue Cross Bulletin, 9:4, December, 1946.

agricultural business organizations have been utilized.[30] Farm Bureau groups in 20 states were reported in 1944 to be enrolling their members in Blue Cross plans.[31] From its beginning in Hennepin County, Minnesota, in April, 1938, this pattern has spread, chiefly among the Midwestern states.[32] Blue Cross participation has figured prominently in the membership programs of many of these Farm

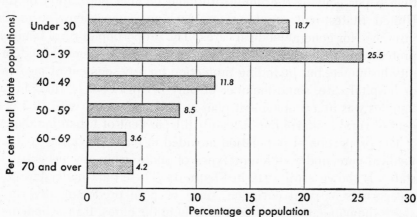

Fig. 37. Blue Cross Plan Membership: Proportion of populations of states grouped by rurality enrolled in the Blue Cross group hospitalization plans, July 1, 1945 (state populations as of November, 1943). Source: Based on data of the Hospital Service Plan Commission, American Hospital Association; furnished by the U. S. Public Health Service. (Figures on enrollments in Nevada, South Dakota, and Vermont are approximate.)

Bureaus[33] and some Granges as well. In a few rural or semirural communities such as Tupelo, Mississippi, individual hospitals have

[30] MONTGOMERY, GEORGE A., "Group Hospital Service," *Capper's Farmer*, 56:12-13, June, 1945.

[31] LIEBELER, VIRGINIA M., "How the Blue Cross Came to Rural America," *The Modern Hospital*, 62:53-56, February, 1944.

[32] SMITH, JOYCE, "Blue Cross for Rural America," *The Nation's Agriculture*, 19:8, 12, 13, October, 1944.

[33] Group hospitalization protection, in effect, requires payment of additional Farm Bureau membership fees in many rural sections. In at least one Midwestern state the Farm Bureau Federation has concluded an exclusive contract with a Blue Cross association under which no farmer may obtain Blue Cross protection except by also joining the local Farm Bureau. Another organization of farmers in this state, to obtain hospitalization protection for its members, has been forced to contract with a commercial insurance company for a less favorable policy.

organized their own independent prepayment plans for hospital care to serve the families in the area who wish to join.[34]

The variety of programs for prepaid medical care in the United States should not lead to any rosy optimism that the payment problem is being conquered along voluntary lines, leaving no need for over-all social security protection. In 1943, it was estimated that less than 5 per cent of the noninstitutional civilian population of the United States had anything approaching comprehensive health insurance for general medical care.[35] The proportion of rural families protected is, of course, much lower. Aside from commercial indemnity insurance, but including protection for any segment of medical or hospital care, some member of only 3.0 per cent of rural farm families was in a prepayment plan in 1941, compared with 10.5 per cent of rural nonfarm families and 18.1 per cent of urban families.[36]

The proportion of population included in plans providing general medical care under different types of sponsorship, by urban-rural states, is shown as of 1945 in Figure 38. These data understate the meagerness of rural coverage, since even in predominantly rural states the population covered is chiefly in the cities. It may be noted that the greatest urban-rural disparity is found with respect to medical care insurance sponsored by medical societies. Except for the special influence of the governmentally sponsored prepayment plans for low-income farm families under the Farm Security Administration, there is a direct relationship, as we have seen, between investment in this type of health protection and family income.

Under any circumstances, voluntary health insurance plans suffer from numerous inherent defects. The lowest income groups needing the protection most are least able to join. Even the group enrollment mechanism does not eliminate the inevitable tendency to get a selection of the poorest risks. As a result, average costs are kept high and services tend to be restricted.[37] Turnover in membership

[34] GOLDMANN, FRANZ, "A Hospital Service Plan in a Small Community," *Hospitals*, 16:56-59, January, 1942.

[35] KLEM, *op. cit.*, p. 112.

[36] Data furnished by U. S. Bureau of Human Nutrition and Home Economics and U. S. Bureau of Labor Statistics, *op. cit.*

[37] U. S. Social Security Board, *Need for Medical-care Insurance* (Bureau of Research and Statistics Mem. 57). Washington: Federal Security Agency, 1944, Processed, pp. 31-32.

tends to be high and plan solvency varies with changes in general economic circumstances. There tend, in practice, to be few controls over standards of quality and little emphasis on preventive services. The defects of voluntary health insurance plans in general are particularly applicable to the rural population with its lower income and the numerous handicaps to large-scale enrollment.

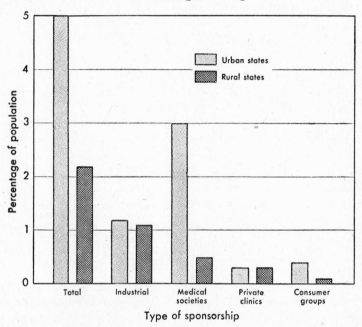

FIG. 38. Voluntary Medical Care Insurance Plans: Proportion of populations of urban states (less than 50 per cent rural) and rural states (50 per cent rural or more) with membership in voluntary prepayment plans providing general medical care, by type of sponsorship, 1945. (Government-sponsored plans of the Department of Agriculture are excluded.) Source: Based on Klem, Margaret C., *Prepayment Medical Care Organizations,* 3d ed. (U. S. Social Security Board, Bureau of Research and Statistics, Mem. 55). Washington: Government Printing Office, June, 1945.

An unfortunate by-product of the voluntary health insurance movement has been the passage of legislation in a number of states which precludes the organization of plans not under the control of professional societies.[38] By 1946 there were at least 13 states with

[38] See LAUFER, JOSEPH, "Ethical and Legal Restrictions on Contract and Corporate Practice of Medicine," *Law and Contemporary Problems* (Duke University School of Law), 6:516-527, Autumn, 1939.

such legislation, which, in one way or another, tends to foster monopolistic control of voluntary prepayment medical service plans by professional bodies.[39] Such restrictive legislation has forced the discontinuation of certain medical service plans for low-income farmers, for example, and has prevented community and consumer groups from initiating their own plans. There is, of course, nothing inherently wrong in the idea of enabling legislation providing a legal base for the growth of plans without conventional insurance restrictions, and the acts passed under Blue Cross stimulation have in general had good effects.[40] As it happens, the handful of states lacking hospitalization insurance acts are predominantly rural.

The positive benefits for rural people of the voluntary prepayment movement, nevertheless, cannot be gainsaid. Better medical care has doubtless been available to the families enrolled in plans than would otherwise have been the case. Experience in the field of health insurance has been gained. Mechanisms of administration have been developed and patients as well as doctors have been educated to the insurance idea. One can hardly miss the analogy of the experience of some thirty-five other nations in which the growth of voluntary plans was invariably the preliminary step to the organization of national systems of "compulsory" or universal health insurance.

[39] KLEM, MARGARET C., "Recent State Legislation Concerning Prepayment Medical Care," *Social Security Bulletin,* January, 1947.

[40] ANDERSON, ODIN W., *State Enabling Legislation for Non-profit Hospital and Medical Plans,* 1944. Ann Arbor: University of Michigan, January, 1944.

CHAPTER 24

IMPROVING RURAL HEALTH RESOURCES

A VARIETY of voluntary efforts, originating both within and outside rural areas, have been made to improve rural health resources. These activities may be considered with respect to the supply of medical and related personnel, the extension of physical facilities, and the improvement of the quality of rural medicine.

Attracting Medical Personnel to Rural Areas

With regard to improving the supply of medical personnel in rural areas, organized voluntary action has been only of the most sporadic type. Some steps have been taken by the medical schools, by certain philanthropic foundations, and here and there by local community groups.

In some of the more rural states the medical schools have for some years attempted to influence the settlement of physicians by attracting students from rural communities and by spreading information on the opportunities in rural practice. The University of Tennessee School of Medicine, for example, conducted a publicity campaign in every county in the state during 1925-30, calling attention to the immediate and prospective need for rural physicians and encouraging applications to the medical school. O. W. Hyman reports some improvement in Tennessee's distribution of physicians due to these efforts because of the increased proportion of rural students and the fact that "70 per cent of (medical school) graduates entering private practice return to their home communties."[1] The Commission on Medical Education reported in 1932, however, that general experience at the time did not support this policy in that there seemed to be no greater tendency of rural youth to set up rural practices on graduation than of youth originating in large

[1] Hyman, O. W., "The Number and Distribution of Physicians in the Southern States as Bearing upon the Policies of Southern Medical Colleges," *Southern Medical Journal*, 30:85-88, January, 1937.

cities.[2] Scholarships have here and there been offered to medical students from rural districts and information is provided to physicians seeking new locations, but little in the way of a systematic program has been conducted by the schools.

Among the foundations, the Commonwealth Fund has made the greatest efforts to effect the settlement of young physicians in rural areas. Fellowships have been given to medical students on the condition that they undertake a rural practice for a specified period. Several years' experience with this policy, however, gave discouraging results in that, after their period of obligation, the fellowship recipients usually left the rural setting for an urban practice.[3] Programs of settling young physicians in rural areas, upon completion of their training, have evidently been more successful in other nations like Mexico, the Soviet Union, and Sweden.

In addition to the official efforts of units of local government to attract physicians to rural communities, discussed earlier, independent community groups in Kansas, Indiana, Texas, Nebraska, Maryland, and other states have made similar efforts.[4] Most often a minimum income is guaranteed the prospective practitioner by a citizens' group. In Economy, Indiana, for example, a $3,000 annual income was guaranteed the practitioner through the support of a prepayment plan.[5] Residents of Smith Island, Maryland, attracted and held a physician for 25 years by paying him a "capitation salary" of 75 cents a month for each inhabitant.[6]

In the last few years the organized medical profession has shown increased responsiveness to the problem of the rural shortage of doctors. While county medical societies in rural sections have more often discouraged than welcomed the settlement of new practitioners, the state and national organizations have taken some steps to induce choice of a rural practice. In Indiana, for example, the state

[2] *Final Report of the Commission on Medical Education* (Willard C. Rappleye, Director of Study). New York, 1932, pp. 111-112.

[3] Personal communication from Dr. Lester J. Evans, Medical Associate, The Commonwealth Fund, 1945.

[4] MOORE, HARRY H., *American Medicine and the People's Health*. New York: The Macmillan Company, 1927, pp. 281-282.

[5] American Medical Association, Bureau of Medical Economics, *Organized Payment for Medical Services*. Chicago, 1939, pp. 138-139.

[6] HENRY, FRANK, "Islets of Crabbing and Independence," *The Baltimore Sun*, July 22, 1945, p. A-2

medical association has set up a scholarship fund for assisting six young men and women each year in getting a medical education, on condition that they agree to practice in those counties of Indiana in which the association believes "medical service is most urgently needed."[6a]

The organization of special prepayment plans by rural industries or farm groups, like those discussed earlier, has of course also served to attract and hold physicians and dentists in isolated sections. The establishment of modern community hospitals in rural areas by foundations and other groups has served the same purpose. The Mary Imogene Bassett Hospital at Cooperstown, New York, or the Mary Hitchcock Memorial Hospital at Hanover, New Hampshire, for example, have attracted staffs of well-trained specialists to serve surrounding rural sections. Institutions of this type have provided other outlying rural hospitals with the part-time services of pathologists or radiologists. The rather negligible effect of all of these voluntary efforts, direct and indirect, is manifest from the steadily downhill trend that we have found to characterize the supply of rural medical and related personnel.

Providing Better Rural Health Facilities

The construction of America's voluntary hospitals by local nonprofit community associations, churches, fraternal orders, and other groups is a saga of its own. The greater part of our nation's general hospitals have been established by such voluntary groups setting out to serve public needs in their home communities. Suffice it to say that this type of local initiative has been much less effective in founding hospitals in rural areas than in the cities.

A few cooperative hospital projects in rural areas stand out because they represent healthy, "grass roots" action to fulfill a need that had not been met by conventional methods. In connection with the prepayment plan at Elk City, Oklahoma, referred to above, a hospital of 100 beds has been constructed and maintained by the local Farmers Union cooperative. The cooperative at Amherst, Texas, likewise has brought to some 4,500 farm people in Lamb

[6a] "Indiana Tackles Rural Doctor Shortage," *American Journal of Public Health*, 37:487, April, 1947.

County a hospital accommodating 50 or 60 patients.[7] Another type of cooperative action has been taken in Mooreland, Oklahoma, where the Northwest Community Hospital Association has leased and operated a hospital built largely from public funds, and — as in other cooperative units — has staffed it with full-time medical personnel.[8] Recently, about 1,500 families in Two Harbors, Minnesota, formed a cooperative to purchase a 35-bed hospital from a local physician. The institution is said to be used as a "health center" providing care to outpatients as well as bed patients and it is claimed to be the first cooperative health center established in the Northern half of the nation.[9] Another cooperative hospital, aided by the bequest of a wealthy farmer, has been established at Hardtner, Kansas.[10]

Considering the high initial cost of constructing a hospital, it is no surprise that the cooperative pattern has not spread more widely in rural areas. Not many rural communities can furnish 1,000 or more families who can afford shares of $50 or $100 toward a building fund — the approximate cost of a small rural hospital in ordinary times. With the end of the Second World War and unprecedented farm prosperity, however, a flurry of plans for rural cooperative hospitals seemed to be getting under way. In Texas, under the impetus of a special enabling act,[11] active plans were being developed for cooperative hospitals, associated with prepayment plans, in some 25 or 30 communities as of late 1946.[12] Likewise in Washington, Oregon, and Idaho, a half dozen or more "cooperative hospital asso-

[7] BUTLER, EUGENE, "They Helped Each Other Pay the Doctor," *The Progressive Farmer* (Texas ed.), 60:20-21, February, 1945.

[8] REID, E. B., "Mooreland — Where Town and Country Cooperate," *News for Farmer Cooperatives* (U. S. Farm Credit Administration), November, 1945, pp. 4-5, 17-18.

[9] "Complete Health Center Is Opened in Minnesota," *Washtenaw Post-Tribune*, Ann Arbor, Michigan, Jan. 12, 1945.

[10] Cooperative League of the U. S. A., "Intensive Drive on for Organization of Cooperative Hospitals," *Cooperative League News Service*. New York, Jan. 24, 1946.

[11] This 1945 Texas statute allowed the organization of voluntary hospitals under nonprofessional consumer control in communities of less than 2,500 population; an earlier statute had required all such units to be under the direction of boards with physicians or hospital administrators in the majority.

[12] Unpublished report of Texas Rural Health Committee, furnished by Eugene Butler, editor of *The Progressive Farmer*, Dallas, September, 1946.

ciations" were organized in 1946, united into the Northwest Hospital Federation.[13] How many of these spirited plans for constructing hospitals in Texas, the Northwest, or elsewhere will be carried through to completion — a prospect depending on general economic circumstances — remains to be seen.

Private financial resources from outside of rural areas have assisted certain selected rural communities in establishing hospitals. The model hospital at Cooperstown, New York, is a classic example of such a project and there are many others. The home missions of several church denominations have set up hospitals in needy and isolated rural districts, such as at Embudo, New Mexico, or Cordele, Georgia.[14]

Perhaps the most outstanding work of this type has been done by the philanthropic foundations. Some 14 hospitals have been built in rural communities, for example, through the efforts of the Commonwealth Fund.[15] The Fund ordinarily contributes two-thirds of the cost of the building and equipment while the community is expected to pay the remainder and to furnish the site, the management, and the maintenance. Conditional to the issuance of such grants are requirements for the maintenance of certain high standards, such as nondiscrimination in admissions, open-staff policy, provision of outpatient service, and regular clinical staff conferences. In addition, the Commonwealth Fund has subsidized the construction of rural health centers in connection with public health programs in Tennessee and Mississippi. The Kellogg Foundation has subsidized the construction and modernization of hospitals and health centers in seven counties of Michigan.[16] Strengthening of the rural hospitals in North and South Carolina has been made possible through the donations of the Duke Endowment.

In 1945, the Commonwealth Fund undertook a significant demonstration in the operation of a regional hospital plan, in an

[13] SHADID, M., *Co-op Hospital Catechism*. Walla Walla, Washington: Pacific Supply Cooperative, new rev. ed., 1946, p. 6.

[14] Personal communication from Mark A. Dawber, Executive Secretary, Home Missions Council of North America, July, 1945.

[15] SOUTHMAYD, HENRY J., and GEDDES SMITH, *Small Community Hospitals*. New York: The Commonwealth Fund, 1944.

[16] Trustees of the W. K. Kellogg Foundation, *W. K. Kellogg Foundation: The First Eleven Years*. Chicago: Lakeside Press, 1942.

effort "to show how the existing resources of rural medicine — good, bad, or indifferent — can profitably be supplemented by those of a regional center." The locale chosen was a seven-county area around and including Rochester, New York, with a total population of 714,-000, more than half of which is outside the metropolitan center.[17] The program has included the promotion of improved administrative practices in the cooperating rural hospitals, periodic visits of consultants from the regional center to the rural hospitals, assignment of interns and residents to the rural units, provision of special laboratory and x-ray services, and various other measures to improve the performance of rural institutions. The greater part of the funds, however, have been planned to go as grants to the cooperating hospitals for construction of needed extensions or the purchase of new equipment.[17a] A parallel regional project on a smaller scale has been launched by the Commonwealth Fund around Richmond, Virginia.

It is evident that organized voluntary actions have improved rural health facilities only in a spotty way. Their significance, however, has been in the demonstration of how leadership and outside financial aid can render benefits to low-income rural communities. These lessons have an important influence on the formulation of governmental policies regarding public works programs.

Improving the Quality of Rural Medicine

Organized efforts to improve the quality of rural medical service have stemmed principally from over-all programs influencing the quality of medicine throughout the nation. Only to a minor extent have voluntary programs been developed that are directed specifically toward elevating the scientific quality of rural medicine.

The national professional associations have for many years endeavored to maintain the quality of scientific performance and of "professional conduct" in medicine and allied fields. The American Medical Association has done much to elevate the standards of medical education and hospital service, to standardize the use of high-

[17] The Commonwealth Fund, *Twenty-seventh Annual Report of the General Director for the Year Ending September 30, 1945.* New York, January, 1946, pp. 21-23.

[17a] Council of Rochester Regional Hospitals, *The Regional Hospital Plan: The First Year's Experience, Summary.* Rochester: 1946.

quality drugs and appliances, and to set high levels of professional scientific literature.[18] The development of the several national "specialty boards" has promoted standards in medical specialization. The American Dental Association, the American Nurses Association, and the American Hospital Association have done comparable work in their fields. The American College of Surgeons has done much to elevate the standard of performance of hospitals, and the several academies or colleges in specialized fields like pediatrics or psychiatry have made their contributions. The Association of American Medical Colleges has helped maintain high levels of medical education. The National Medical Association, the National Dental Association, and the National Association of Colored Graduate Nurses have done valuable work among colored personnel.

The impact of these national professional societies on rural medicine, nevertheless, has undoubtedly been much less than on urban. With the smaller numbers of professional people and their thin dispersal, moreover, the local chapters of professional societies have been smaller and weaker — less likely to bear direct influence on professional performance or conduct. Many rural medical societies hold hardly a meeting a year, and there are few instances of a professional society taking disciplinary action against one of its ranks strictly because of scientific incompetence. In recent years, the rural public has become familiar with the local medical societies more through their opposition to modifications in the economic relationships of medical practice than through any championship of an improved quality of rural medicine.[19]

Perhaps the most promising trend toward an improved quality of service in rural sections has been the organization of a certain number of group practice clinics. This type of professional organization has made available the services of specialists and the use of technical equipment ordinarily beyond the reach of rural patients. These units have been typically organized by physicians themselves and, as discussed earlier, they are found predominantly in more or less urban centers of rural regions. In the Mary Imogene Bassett Hospital

[18] "American Medical Association," *Fortune*, 18:88-92, 150, 152, 156, 158, 160, 162, 164, 166, 168, November, 1938.

[19] The voices of young liberal groups like the Committee of Physicians for the Improvement of Medical Care, the Physicians Forum, or the Association of Internes and Medical Students have hardly been heard in the rural districts.

at Cooperstown, New York, we find a rare example of a rural hospital organized on integrated group practice lines. In this institution it has been demonstrated that a professionally up-to-the-minute staff of competent physicians and auxiliary personnel can be organized to render first-rate preventive, diagnostic, and therapeutic services to a rural community — with time and opportunity for research and study. The decisive factor has been outside financial aid.

Courses of postgraduate medical education for rural physicians have occasionally been given by the medical schools, often in cooperation with the medical societies.[20] In Michigan, for example, postgraduate courses are offered at several centers throughout the state, under the direction of the University of Michigan and the State Medical Society, and formal recognition is awarded the practitioner who completes courses over at least 4 years. The New York University College of Medicine has recently launched an interesting course of postgraduate instruction for doctors in semirural communities around New York City, in connection with a regional hospital plan.[20a] Postgraduate courses in general, however, are attended least by the older rural physicians needing such courses most. Some postgraduate courses have also been sponsored for rural dentists and nurses by their professional schools.

Some of the most significant efforts at postgraduate training for rural practitioners have been made by the philanthropic foundations. Oustanding has been the program of the Commonwealth Fund, which has financed courses of instruction to hundreds of physicians, nurses, and public health workers in the rural sections of Mississippi, Tennessee, New Hampshire, Oklahoma, Alabama, Massachusetts, and other states.[21] Courses have ranged from 6 days to 4 months and stipends have been given to the enrollees. In addition to "refresher" courses, itinerant medical and surgical consultants have been sent out into rural communities to advise local practitioners. The establishment of community hospitals and regional programs has stimu-

[20] LONG, T. W. M., "Extension (Postgraduate) Courses of State Medical Associations," *Journal of the American Medical Association*, 110:53-54B, Jan. 29, 1938.

[20a] DE LA CHAPELLE, CLARENCE E., "The New Regional Hospital Plan," *New York University Medical Quarterly*, Vol. 3, No. 3, pp. 2-3, October, 1947.

[21] EVANS, LESTER J., "Activities of the Commonwealth Fund in Postgraduate Medical Education," March, 1944, Processed.

lated self-education among rural doctors. The Kellogg Foundation has likewise supported a wide range of postgraduate courses for rural physicians and dentists in Michigan.

Perhaps the most effective demonstration of an improved organization of rural medicine has been that supported by the Bingham Associates Fund in cooperation with Tufts College Medical School. This program has set out squarely to improve the scientific quality of medical service in the rural sections of Maine.[22] To do this, it has organized a functional relationship among 24 small community hospitals, three larger district hospitals in Maine, and the New England Medical Center in Boston. Cases may be referred from the community hospital to the district or central facilities and detailed reports of findings with recommendations are sent back to the local physicians. Consultants visit the community hospitals from the central or district units periodically. The more complex laboratory services are routinely done for the local units by the district units. Technical personnel as well as physicians receive postgraduate courses of study at the Boston center. Medical literature is systematically sent to the community hospitals. All in all, a comprehensive program is conducted designed to keep the rural physician on his toes by providing him, on the one hand, with information and advice and, on the other, with facilities and specialized services available only in larger urban centers. Happily the Bingham Associates Fund program is being extended to New Hampshire, Vermont, and western Massachusetts.

As other measures become effective in attracting new medical graduates to rural sections, the quality of rural medicine will undoubtedly improve. The construction of adequate facilities and the extension of purchasing power for medical care will probably have more far-reaching effects on the quality of rural practice than the direct educational measures discussed here. As rural people read about the remarkable advances of modern medicine and as they get a taste of it now and then, their demand for a generally higher level of service becomes more insistent.

[22] PROGER, SAMUEL H., "The Bingham Associates Fund, the New England Medical Center, and Rural Medicine," *Anniversary Volume, Scientific Contributions in Honor of Joseph Hersey Pratt.* Boston, 1937.

CHAPTER 25

PROMOTING PREVENTIVE HEALTH SERVICES

W HILE THE improvement of medical care has won increasing attention, the principal objective of organized voluntary health efforts in rural areas has been to extend special projects of a preventive or educational nature. The great majority of these programs have been launched by voluntary groups originating outside rural areas. The variety of programs has been so great that it is convenient to summarize them according to the sponsoring group.

Health and Welfare Organizations

Best known among the broad voluntary programs of health education and preventive services have been those of the national health organizations.[1] General public health work in rural areas has, for example, been stimulated and advanced through the varied activities of the American Public Health Association.[2] Rural public health workers from all over the nation have profited from the carefully formulated standards of public health practice issued by this professional body and the contacts afforded with other public health personnel. Similar benefits have come from specialized professional public health organizations like the National Organization for Public Health Nursing, the American Association of Public Health Dentists, or a number of others.

The American Red Cross has sponsored health education, home nursing, first aid, and related activities in communities throughout the nation for years, in addition to direct visiting nurse services. In the 10 years ending June 30, 1946, some 1,873,000 homemakers

[1] CAVINS, H. M., *National Health Agencies*. Washington: Public Affairs Press, 1945.

[2] In the last few years, the Association has significantly broadened its educational program to extend into the general field of medical care.

460

were trained in home nursing and a substantial share of these were in rural communities, where the Red Cross put special stress on this program.[3] The emergency medical relief activities of the Red Cross during catastrophes like floods and hurricanes have, of course, provided concrete benefits to farm families in regions like the Mississippi Valley.

National associations have been active in public crusades against particular diseases or health problems in rural, as well as urban, sections. The National Tuberculosis Association has led the attack on the great white plague since 1905 and local chapters promote health education and case finding in all parts of the country.[4] The American Social Hygiene Association has organized communities for the control of the venereal diseases and the National Cancer Society has spread the word that cancer can be cured. The National Association for Mental Hygiene has promoted programs for the prevention and early care of mental disorders, and the National Safety Council has done much educational work to prevent accidents on the farm as well as in the factory. The Planned Parenthood Federation of America has promoted the control of conception, for health as well as general social purposes, in many rural sections, particularly in the South.[5] One of the youngest of the health associations, the National Foundation for Infantile Paralysis, has made great strides in promoting research on this dreaded disease and the actual care of cases.[6]

Numerous professional organizations not primarily in health work, like the American Public Welfare Association, the American Association for Social Security, and the American Association of Social Workers, have made contributions by promoting, among other things, understanding of some of the fundamental economic and social

[3] Data furnished by Office of Public Information, American National Red Cross. Also, American National Red Cross, *Annual Report for the Year Ending June* 30, 1946. Washington, 1946, p. 89.

[4] National Tuberculosis Association, *Annual Report, April* 1, 1943, *to March* 31, 1944. New York, 1944.

[5] EASTMAN, NICHOLAS J., "The Aims of Birth Control and Their Place in Preventive Medicine," *New International Clinics*, Vol. 1, Ser. 5. New York: J. B. Lippincott Company, 1942, pp. 271-306.

[6] The National Foundation for Infantile Paralysis, Inc., *Annual Report for Year Ended May* 31, 1945. New York, 1945.

problems at the root of health needs.[7] Several national groups devoted
to the general social betterment of rural life, like the Country Life
Association, the Catholic Rural Life Conference, or the Southern
Conference for Human Welfare,[8] include improved rural health
services among the objectives for which they strive. Commercial
entities, like the large life insurance companies or the manufac-
turers of drugs and biologicals, have, for their own interest,
sponsored much health education to encourage sound living
habits and greater use of physicians' and dentists' services. The
United States Chamber of Commerce has supported "Health
Conservation Contests" to stimulate improved public health programs in rural counties as well as cities.

A recitation of the state and local voluntary agencies dealing with
all kinds of special health problems in rural sections would fill
volumes. Nearly every community at some time or other has undertaken the organization of a local group to meet some particular
health problem. The Visiting Nurses Associations, providing bedside nursing services in the home, are perhaps the most extensive
type of such local association.[9] Special mention should be made
of such particularly rural programs as the Frontier Nursing Services
of Kentucky or North Carolina, supported by private donations
to bring health services to isolated families in the backwoods
and the hills.[10] Their training and utilization of personnel have
been particularly effective, and the rugged public health nurses
in these agencies make up to a considerable extent for the
unavailability of physicians to these mountain families. In some of
the rural counties of Mississippi a series of health projects for
Negroes has been sponsored since 1934 by the national Negro
sorority, Alpha Kappa Alpha.[11] Utilizing volunteer services of

[7] More than 80 such organizations engage in activities having some relation
to health promotion. CAVINS, op. cit.

[8] The Southern Patriot (Southern Conference for Human Welfare), 3:1-8,
May, 1945, "Good Health Issue."

[9] COOK, BEATRICE G., "The Visiting Nurse," Hygeia, 23:30-31, 42, January,
1945.

[10] BRECKINRIDGE, MARY, The Frontier Nursing Service, Inc. Wendover, Kentucky, 1946 (leaflet). See also The Quarterly Bulletin of the Frontier Nursing
Service.

[11] Alpha Kappa Alpha Sorority, Health Project (Mound Bayou, Mississippi),
Annual Reports 1938-1941.

physicians, dentists, and nurses, clinics are held to provide immunizations, prenatal care, venereal disease case finding, general medical and dental examinations, and education on nutrition. An interesting "movable school" project for rural Negroes, including a health education program, has been sponsored for some years by the Tuskegee Institute in Alabama.[12]

A great many voluntary organizations serving general civic or social purposes in local communities make some contributions to rural health as one phase of their activity. Among these may be mentioned such organizations as the Parent-Teachers Association, the National Education Association, and the League of Women Voters, which have promoted, in particular, improved preventive health services for children. Health objectives rank high in the programs of youth-serving agencies like the Campfire Girls, the Boy Scouts, and the Girl Scouts, as well as in the programs of organizations like the Y.M.C.A. or Y.W.C.A. Service groups like the Masons, Kiwanis, Lions, Rotary, Optimists, Civitan, Shriners, and others have launched community health projects, usually for crippled children, premature babies, or similar objects of general concern. Church groups have often stimulated public health efforts, and veterans' organizations have lent their aid on specific projects. In nearly every locality with a Community Chest program, financial support for certain voluntary health agencies is included, although several of the national voluntary health agencies are, surprisingly enough, independent.[13]

In many rural communities the preventive health programs of these voluntary agencies have gone hand in hand with the official programs of the local health department. Occasionally the voluntary agency has appropriated funds directly to the health department for its use in various special programs. In some communities, on the other hand, there are jealousies and overlapping functions, with each agency fearful that the other one will "steal the show." This type of friction, however, probably occurs less in rural localities than in large cities where voluntary agencies abound. By the same token, voluntary health agencies of all types in rural sections tend to be fewer in number and those operating tend to be weaker than the

[12] CAMPBELL, THOMAS M., *Movable School Goes to the Negro Farmer*. Tuskegee: Tuskegee Institute Press, 1936.

[13] GUNN and PLATT, *op. cit.*, p. 211.

urban chapters.[14] Even among the national organizations which
can use funds raised throughout the nation, the customary practice
of retaining 50 per cent of funds raised at their source acts to favor
the wealthier urban centers. All in all, the well-meaning but scattered
efforts of these myriad voluntary agencies have made only small
inroads into the enormous problem of sickness and disability that we
find in rural America.

Philanthropic Foundations

New pathways in public health services have been blazed by a
number of philanthropic foundations. The most varied and extensive
health work of the foundations, in fact, has been in the field of preventive services, rather than with respect to medical personnel, facilities, or the quality of practice, discussed previously. The total
of all grants of American foundations for health purposes in 1940
was $12,275,000, representing the work of some 70 foundations and
constituting 30.4 per cent of grants for all purposes.[15] The exact
amount of these funds that reaches rural areas cannot be stated, but
in so far as the usual practice has been to apply funds where local
resources are lacking, the proportion used for meeting rural needs
is probably large.

The Rockefeller Foundation has sponsored some of the most significant rural public health work ever launched in this nation. Demonstrations in sanitation, designed to control hookworm infestation
in certain Southern counties, sponsored by the earlier Rockefeller
Sanitary Commission (1909), were instrumental in stimulating the
entire public health movement in the rural South.[16] Research and
field studies have been carried on in malaria, tuberculosis, syphilis,
influenza, nutrition, mental hygiene, and other public health problems. Much of this work has been conducted in predominantly rural
areas and many full-time rural health departments have received
their initial support from Rockefeller funds. Special rural projects
have been conducted by the Foundation's International Health Division in North Carolina, Arkansas, Colorado, South Dakota, Tennes-

[14] *Ibid.*, p. 285.

[15] SEYBOLD, GENEVA (compiler), *American Foundations and Their Fields.*
New York: Raymond Rich Associates, 1942.

[16] The Rockefeller Foundation, *Annual Report* 1939. New York, 1940.

see, California, and Florida. As government funds for public health work and training have increased, however, the Foundation's grants for rural public health work have declined rapidly. Other divisions of the Rockefeller Foundation have, of course, made an ultimate contribution to rural health through their generous support of medical research, in addition to the direct activities in this field of the Rockefeller Institute for Medical Research.

Much important work in rural public health has been accomplished by the Commonwealth Fund in the past quarter-century.[17] Full-time and amply staffed rural health units have been sponsored, as demonstrations, in cooperation with the state departments of health in Tennessee, Mississippi, Oklahoma, Massachusetts, Alabama, and New Mexico. Earlier projects were concerned chiefly with child health but later work has encompassed the full range of public health services.

The Milbank Memorial Fund has done a variety of work in public health and medical care, but its chief contribution has been its demonstration project in rural public health services sponsored in Cattaraugus County, New York, from 1923 to 1931.[18] This program, which pioneered in new methods of maternal and child health work, health education, and tuberculosis control, has become a classic in the annals of rural public health.[19] Similar demonstration public health projects, including the construction of health centers for housing the health department and other community health agencies, have been sponsored in seven largely rural counties of Michigan by the Kellogg Foundation.[20] Particular emphasis has been given in this program to dental hygiene among children. Until it terminated its health activities recently, the Julius Rosenwald Fund sponsored numerous special health projects for Negroes, particularly in the control of tuberculosis, syphilis, and maternal and infant deaths.[21]

[17] The Commonwealth Fund, *Twenty-fifth Annual Report* 1943. New York, 1944.

[18] *Milbank Memorial Fund*, 1905-1940, *Thirty-five Years in Review*. New York, 1941.

[19] WINSLOW, C.-E. A., *Health on the Farm and in the Village*. New York: The Macmillan Company, 1931.

[20] Trustees of the W. K. Kellogg Foundation, *op. cit.*

[21] Julius Rosenwald Fund, *Review for the Two-year Period*, 1942-44. Chicago, 1944.

A foundation coming to the fore in promoting health work exclusively among rural people is the Farm Foundation.[22] In addition to the special medical care program sponsored in Nebraska discussed above, this foundation has promoted the expansion of rural public health work, particularly in the Great Plains states, through efforts to educate farm people about health problems. Much is being done to promote the organization of rural medical care as well, through stimulating local action by farm organizations, official agricultural agencies, and all sorts of state and local groups. The Farm Foundation operates under the policy that the best solutions to rural health problems will come from farm people themselves, once they are given the facts.[23]

Various other foundations have played some part in promoting one or another phase of rural public health, either through direct operations, grants for research purposes, or support for the training of rural public health personnel.[24] Finally, among the contributions of the foundations to improved rural health should be mentioned the special subsidized social research organizations in the field of medical economics and medical care, such as the Committee on Research in Medical Economics or the Medical Administration Service. By exploring the fundamental social and economic factors involved in the provision of medical care, these organizations have contributed much to the ultimate solutions of the problems of rural medicine.

Despite their great variety, taking the nation as a whole, the health activities of the philanthropic foundations have been spotty. While the value of their programs as demonstrations is largely beyond measurement, the foundations will be the first to admit that the surface of the actual needs has hardly been scratched. More important, the reservoir of private philanthropy is gradually drying up; each year the role of government in preventive health services is expand-

[22] *The Farm Foundation — Its First Ten Years,* 1933-43. Chicago, 1944; *Looking Ahead with the Farm Foundation.* Chicago, 1946.

[23] See, for example, ANDERSON, ELIN L., *Do We Want Health?* Lincoln: University of Nebraska (Ext. Circ. 1021), September, 1940.

[24] Among these have been the Children's Fund of Michigan (James Couzens), the E. O. Robinson Mountain Fund (Kentucky), the Josiah Macy Jr. Foundation, the Spelman Fund of New York, the John and Mary R. Markle Foundation, the Zachary Smith Reynolds Foundation, the Charles H. Hood Educational Trust, the Buhl Foundation, and others. See SEYBOLD, *op. cit.*

ing while the role of philanthropy contracts. So long as areas of rural health remain uncharted, nevertheless, we may expect the foundations to offer constructive approaches to the solution of the problems faced by the nation and not yet entirely solved by official action.

National Farm Organizations

Finally, and highly important among voluntary health efforts, there are the activities of organized farm groups themselves. Beyond the direct medical care programs of these groups, organized farmers have played an important role as "pressure groups" in the promotion of improved public health and related services for rural areas.

As early as 1911 the Farmers Educational and Cooperative Union (National Farmers Union) recognized the relation between medical care and economic circumstances. Mr. Campbell Russell, a former president, addressing the annual convention that year, said, "The doctors know how much easier it is to collect bills from the proceeds of 12-15 cent cotton than it used to be from 5-8 cent cotton. . . . They bid you welcome, they respond to your call day or night." This convention recommended federal and state legislation to protect the health of children, through "bureaus of child and animal protection."[25] Support of this kind doubtless contributed to the establishment in 1912 of the Children's Bureau in the Department of Labor. The Farmers Union in 1917 pointed to the 38 per cent of farm boys found physically unfit for military duty as justification for an improved child health program in rural areas, an action mindful of current discussion.[26]

The oldest of the major farm organizations, the National Grange, did not appear to show special concern for rural health until 1915. In that year several of the state Granges participated in the current anti-tuberculosis campaign, and rural health and sanitation came under discussion.[27] The American Farm Bureau Federation began to show an active interest in rural health in 1930 by representation

[25] National Farmers Educational and Cooperative Union, *Minutes of Seventh Annual Session,* held at Shawnee, Oklahoma, September, 1911.

[26] National Farmers Educational and Cooperative Union, *Minutes of Thirteenth Annual Session,* held at Jonesboro, Arkansas, November, 1917.

[27] National Grange, *Journal of Proceedings of the Forty-ninth Annual Session,* held at Oakland, California, 1915, pp. 60, 69, 70.

at the White House Conference on Child Welfare.[28] Maternal and infant care legislation was promoted during the 1930's by the organization, chiefly through the Associated Women of the Farm Bureau.

After 1938 the primary concern of the farm organizations shifted from the promotion of preventive services to an exploration of systems to improve the provision of medical care. Through the political adventures in health represented by the National Health Conference in 1938 and the principal federal health bills — the Wagner bill of 1939 and the Wagner-Murray-Dingell bills of 1943, 1945, and 1947 — a set of policies has gradually been formulated by each of the major farm organizations.[29] The Grange in 1938 emphasized its opposition to "any form of socialized medicine which would be administered by any branch of Government"[30] but in recent years has given increasing attention to the entire problem of rural medical facilities and personnel. The Farm Bureau has typically fostered improved organization of payment for health services, so long as action remains on a voluntary basis under local administration. The Farmers Union has been significant in backing up the principle of including health insurance for farm people in national social security legislation.[31]

In the last three or four years all three organizations have come to promote voluntary prepayment medical and hospital plans, albeit on the basis of different ideologies. In April, 1944, a national rural health conference was held, under the auspices of the Farm Foundation, at which common fundamental objectives were agreed upon.[32] Further study of the problem in every state was called for, a continuing national committee to study rural health needs was estab-

[28] "Public Health Organization: II. Public Health Service and Administration, Report of the Committee on Public Health Organization," *White House Conference on Child Health and Protection*. New York: D. Appleton-Century Company, Inc., 1932.

[29] For a discussion of the background of these national health insurance bills, see KINGSBURY, JOHN A., *Health in Handcuffs*. New York: Modern Age Books, 1939.

[30] National Grange, *Journal of Proceedings Seventy-third Annual Session*, held at Peoria, Illinois, 1939, p. 166.

[31] National Farmers Union, 1945 *Program Adopted by the Delegates of the National Farmers Union*. Denver, 1944.

[32] Farm Foundation, *Health Services and Medical Care for Rural People*. Chicago, 1945.

lished, and fellowships for the medical education of rural youth were to be promoted.

The ultimate influence of these organizational policies among farm groups may not be measurable for many years. One effect, as we note, is the organization of a number of voluntary medical care programs. Of greater ultimate importance will doubtless be the influence exerted on the formulation of state and national health legislation. It is evident that the national spokesmen of the nation's farmers, in expressing demands for improvements in rural health services, are helping to formulate issues and pave the way for future actions.

FINALLY, among the voluntary efforts being made to improve the organization of rural health services, mention must be made of the plans being proposed by groups in all parts of the country. With the Second World War, occasion has been presented for the formulation of ambitious "postwar plans" to correct the deficiencies in rural medical care. All sorts of voluntary committees have been organized, many even stimulated by government, to propose steps for increasing rural hospital facilities, attracting physicians and dentists to rural communities, extending public health services, easing the payment of medical bills, and related tasks. These voluntary movements have served as a continuous goad to action by government.

The important fact is that the needs for improvement in rural medical care have been increasingly recognized by both rural and urban leaders. In general, rural needs have been acknowledged as most severe of all and the aid of government has been more earnestly invited for rural sections than for urban. Hardly a proposal can be made for an ideal program of rural health services that has not already been under active consideration by voluntary groups in some community or even presented in the form of specific legislation. As we look toward an ideal program in the following chapters, we shall find how these seeds of future action are already being sown at many points along the way.

PART VIII: THE ROAD AHEAD

IT IS MUCH easier to define the problems of rural health and medical care than to propose their solutions with assurance. Yet out of an analysis of these problems, their underlying causes, and the measures taken so far to meet them, several steps toward overcoming today's deficiencies become almost self-evident.

Charting a course of action is less complicated if we first recognize clearly our major objectives. In view of the deficiencies we have observed, these objectives can be defined rather simply:

Purchasing power for medical services must be so mobilized that rural people will have access to care according to their medical need.

Hospitals, health centers, and sanitation facilities must be constructed, and an integrated system of health facilities developed on a regional basis.

Physicians and other health personnel must be attracted to rural areas in numbers sufficient to provide adequate service.

The scientific quality of rural medical services must be enhanced.

Preventive and educational public health services of broad scope must be extended throughout every rural section and all preventive and treatment services must be coordinated.

All five objectives are obviously interrelated; all are part of a single goal and must be approached simultaneously. New hospitals are of little use without physicians, while physicians cannot function properly without hospitals. Neither physicians nor hospitals can be expected to serve people without satisfactory economic support. Treatment of disease is foolish without preventive services and the case finding of public health programs is wasted if cases cannot be treated. Science and research are sterile if they cannot be applied in everyday practice. The delivery of a high quality of service to the rural patient is a product of interlocking endeavors all along the line.[1]

There are, naturally, certain obstacles in the path toward these objectives. There are geographic handicaps associated with a dispersed population. There are psychological handicaps growing out of educational and experiential disadvantages of the rural popula-

[1] For an informal and popular discussion of a program for improving rural health services, see U. S. Department of Agriculture, Interbureau Committee on Post-war Programs, *Better Health for Rural America: Plans of Action for Farm Communities*. Washington: Government Printing Office, 1945.

tion. Certain vested interests must be faced, interests that cling to the old-fashioned way of doing things. But fundamentally most of the problems can be defined in economic terms. Ours is a wealthy nation and, with proper organization and wise leadership, these economic barriers can be hurdled.

CHAPTER 26

GENERAL SOCIAL MEASURES

REVIEW OF THE sociological and economic features of rural life makes clear that in a sense rural health deficiencies are only one aspect of a far broader problem — the maladjustments of American agriculture. As fundamental to health as medical care are adequate family income and the food, housing, clothing, and other essentials of life that it must buy. Since the core of rural prosperity is the economy of agriculture, a well-ordered farming economy is essential to the assurance of adequate income for most of the rural population. It need hardly be added that the physical as well as the economic well-being of the nation depends largely on its agricultural productivity.[1]

Only passing mention can be made of the fundamental conditions for a prosperous rural economy. Most important is full employment and high wages in the nation as a whole; the farmer gets the best prices for his products and earns the highest income when industrial activity is greatest.[2] Closely related is the need for a high level of international trade without restrictive trade barriers.[3] The unhampered commerce promoted by the United Nations, the Bretton Woods monetary plan, and the Food and Agriculture Organization would be of direct benefit to the American farmer. Programs to increase the domestic demand for farm products, such as an expanded school lunch program, should be developed, and improved nutrition throughout the world should be a constant goal — through financial subsidies to the extent necessary.[4]

[1] CHEW, ARTHUR P., "The City Man's Stake in the Land," *Farmers in a Changing World* (*Yearbook of Agriculture*, 1940). Washington: Government Printing Office, p. 366.

[2] Association of Land-grant Colleges and Universities, *Postwar Agricultural Policy* (Report of Committee on Postwar Agricultural Policy), October, 1944, pp. 8-9.

[3] U. S. Department of Agriculture, Interbureau and Regional Committees on Post-war Programs, *What Post-war Policies for Agriculture?* Washington: Government Printing Office, January, 1944, pp. 12-13.

[4] *Ibid.*, p. 2.

Within this basic framework, several corollary measures are called for in the field of agriculture itself. The promotion, through educational and financial incentives, of improved farming techniques is important. Economic measures to curb land prices from inflation and to improve farm tenure conditions are necessary. Programs to extend agricultural credit, such as those of the Farmers Home Administration (formerly the Farm Security Administration) or the Farm Credit Administration, should be expanded. Balanced farming operations, not dependent solely on a single cash crop, like cotton, must be encouraged. The entire economic base of the "cotton poor" South should be steadily broadened. Marketing methods should be modernized and farmers' cooperatives further developed. Nationally organized programs to conserve our soil, forest, and water resources are essential to continuing agricultural prosperity.[5] As agricultural technology improves, a relatively smaller share of the population will be required to produce the food and fiber needed by the nation; the "surplus" population must be absorbed in industry if agriculture is not to suffer from chronic underemployment.[6] The development of local industries in many agricultural sections would help take up the slack through the off-farm employment opportunities created.

Beyond these fundamental economic measures to ensure adequate income, other social improvements are necessary. Rural educational standards must be vastly improved, an objective attainable only through federal financial assistance. Teachers should be better trained and better paid, schools further consolidated, and school terms lengthened — for the benefit of both colored and white children. A poorly educated population cannot maintain sound health practices.[7] Country roads must be greatly improved, to give farm people an easy outlet to markets, services, and social life, and in turn to make farms more accessible to the physician, the ambulance, or the school bus. Telephones must be brought to millions of rural

[5] For an excellent succinct discussion of over-all conditions for agricultural prosperity, see U. S. Department of Agriculture, *Report of the Interbureau Committee on Post-war Programs at the War's End.* Washington, Sept. 27, 1945, Processed.

[6] U. S. Department of Agriculture, Land Settlement Work Group of the Interbureau Committee on Post-war Programs, *Farm Opportunities? Prospects, Problems, Policies.* Washington, May, 1945, Processed.

[7] National Education Association of the United States, *The White House Conference on Rural Education.* Washington, 1944.

homes.— a goal attainable through federal loans to cooperative associations, as in the Rural Electrification Administration program. What electricity on the farm can mean in terms of health, sanitation, and safety is sufficient reason alone for extension of rural electrification to every farming district. Farm housing must be greatly improved, through appropriate credit facilities and subsidies such as those used to wipe out comparable urban slums. Families living on substandard and uneconomic farming units must at least have temporary housing improvements essential to health until they can build up or obtain an economic unit or be absorbed in the nonagricultural economy. A special housing and general welfare program should be developed for migratory farm worker families. Rural nutrition should be improved through economic measures as well as through education about balanced farming practices and good dietary habits.[8]

Social security against the hazards of old age or loss of the breadwinner should be extended to all farmers and farm laborers. Social insurance protection should be broadened for both agricultural and industrial workers to assure continuity of income when earnings are interrupted by temporary or permanent disability.[9]

Unemployment compensation should be extended to hired farm laborers, and state workmen's compensation laws should be broadened to cover all agricultural employees.[10] Child labor laws should be made to apply to all children doing farm work and they should be enforced. There are administrative handicaps in the way of effectuating all these social welfare programs but they are not insurmountable. It is no longer defensible to deny the farm population the protection of social security legislation merely because the

[8] National Planning Association, A Food and Nutrition Program for the Nation (Planning Pamphlet 46). Washington, 1945.

[9] Rhode Island and California recently enacted state disability insurance laws, but agricultural workers are not covered. Similar legislation is contemplated in several other states. For a general discussion, see FALK, I. S., BARKEV S. SANDERS, and DAVID FEDERMAN, Disability among Gainfully Occupied Persons. Bureau of Research and Statistics, Social Security Board (Bur. Mem. 61). Washington, June, 1945. See also ROEMER, MILTON I., "Opportunities for Public Health Agencies in Disability Insurance Programs," Public Health Reports, 62:1657-1667, Nov. 21, 1947.

[10] FALK, I. S., and WILBUR J. COHEN, "Social Security for Farm People," Journal of Farm Economics, 28:84-96, February, 1946. Also, U.S. Social Security Board, Social Security for Farm People (Fact Sheet 5). Washington, May, 1945, Processed.

task of collecting their insurance contributions is somewhat difficult.[11]

All these economic and social measures are part of a rural health program in its broadest sense.[12] Any improvements in the economic base of rural life or the level of rural family living mean improvements in health. Yet no one can seriously counsel that we sit by and await the solution of these problems in the hope that medical care needs will then be automatically met. On the contrary, many specific steps toward better rural health and medical care can be taken now, without delay. Many of the general economic problems, in fact, will be partially eliminated by helping farm families become healthier and by reducing the financial burdens of medical care itself. Keeping in mind the unity of a health program with all efforts for improving rural life, we may consider the five main paths that converge toward the common goal of better health for rural people.

[11] In August, 1946, Congress enacted a number of amendments to the Social Security Act, but extension of coverage to farm people was not among them, although it was under discussion in the hearings. The only amendment that will indirectly benefit rural people is a revision of the grant formula for federal public assistance funds, which will have the effect of giving relatively larger federal contributions to the states of lower per capita income. *Social Security Act Amendments of* 1946, Public Law 719, 79th Cong., 2d Sess., August, 1946.

[12] For a recent presentation of a general program for rural improvement, see FRYER, LEE, *The American Farmer: His Problems and Prospects.* New York: Harper & Brothers, 1947.

CHAPTER 27

PAYMENT FOR MEDICAL CARE

THE CHIEF deterrent to modern medical care in rural areas is low purchasing power and the consequent economic barrier between patient and physician. Rural deficiencies in health resources and in medical services stem almost entirely from economic roots. If the farmer and the villager could pay for all the care they need, the physician and the dentist and the hospital would probably be there to serve, the patient would be cared for, and rural medicine would not be an issue today. We must look for the solution in a system that will provide payment for medical services in rural sections on the most equitable and effective basis that the resources of a wealthy nation make possible.

There is general agreement that organized measures must be taken to mobilize the financial resources of the population in order that medical care may be purchased on an easier basis. Before exploring any specific approaches, let us remind ourselves of a few facts regarding rural income and the medical purchasing power of farm families.

Passing over the strikingly low prewar farm income figures revealed by the 1939 Census of Agriculture and coming up to the period when the war was having a marked influence on farm incomes, we may recall that in 1941 half of all farm operators had annual net cash incomes of less than $760 per family, including income from all nonagricultural sources. As the war went on, farm income soared to unprecedented heights, but the disparity between farm and city income levels was still far from eliminated. In 1943, when farm income was approaching its peak, the total net income from all sources of persons on farms was only 12 per cent of the national income, although farm people made up 20.5 per cent of the population that year. The serious disadvantage of the families looking to the soil for their main livelihood, moreover, is seen in the remarkable fact that the per capita net income in 1943 of all persons in the United States not living on farms was twice as high as the per capita income of persons on farms.

As for rural medical purchasing power, as contrasted to general purchasing power, it is revealed perhaps most readily in the annual expenditures per person for medical care by median income families. In 1941 median income urban families spent $26.76 per person for medical care while median income rural nonfarm families spent $20.62 and corresponding farm operator families spent $14.37 per person, or barely half as much as city families. And within rural areas, medical expenditures vary directly with family income although illness and death strike with rates in the opposite direction. Under present circumstances, in other words, medical services bear very little if any relation to health needs.[1]

Prepayment of Medical Costs

The highly uneven incidence of medical costs in any one year, the variable costs to one family from year to year, and yet the close predictability of annual costs for a large population group long ago suggested the application of the insurance principle to the costs of medical care. It has been more than sixty years since other nations began to handle medical care as a feature of social insurance protection,[2] and, as we have seen, prepayment plans have operated in the United States on a local basis for many decades.[3] Although the recommendation of the Committee on the Costs of Medical Care in 1932 for extensive development of voluntary health insurance plans was greeted by some as "socialistic and communistic," we have at last come to a time when the health insurance principle per se is no longer in dispute. The issue today is whether health insurance should be voluntary or compulsory, whether it should be sponsored entirely by independent private groups or by the Federal Government on a nation-wide basis.[4]

There is no question about the practical and the ideological contributions of the variety of voluntary health insurance plans developed here and there throughout the United States. Their estab-

[1] See Chaps. 17 and 18.

[2] FALK, I. S., *Security against Sickness*. New York: Doubleday, Doran & Company, Inc., 1936.

[3] AVNET, HELEN HERSHFIELD, *Voluntary Medical Insurance in the United States*. New York: Medical Administration Service, 1944.

[4] MOTT, F. D., "Rural Health Parity: Federal-State Cooperation," *Land Policy Review* (U. S. Department of Agriculture), 8:9-14, Spring, 1945.

lishment has represented a natural response to a widely felt problem that was not being met by government. Yet to claim that voluntary health insurance plans can solve the overwhelming problem of medi- • cal costs, as is done by certain articulate groups, is simply not to face economic facts or the lessons of world-wide as well as American experience. In assessing this claim, we must not only face the cold facts regarding the highly uneven levels of income in different parts of the nation, but we must examine, in particular, how many farm families could afford to join comprehensive voluntary medical service plans.

The benefits of modern medical science are great but, relative to agricultural earnings, they are extremely expensive.[4a] There is general agreement that a prepayment plan offering physicians' and specialists' care, hospitalization, prescribed drugs, and limited dental services would cost at least $100 a year and probably more, for a family of average size.[5] We have observed that farmers had to have net cash incomes averaging well above $2,000 in 1941 before they made average expenditures of $100 or more for medical care, and we have seen that not more than 20 per cent of all farm operators (not even considering farm laborers) had such incomes in 1941, counting income from all sources.[6] Although the proportion of farmers able to afford an adequate plan has doubtless increased since 1941, there is no question that the great majority of farm families

[4a] Mott, F. D., "A Public Health Program for Rural Areas," *Public Health Reports*, 61:589-598, Apr. 26, 1946.

[5] This estimate is quite conservative. To illustrate, one can interpolate for the cost of complete medical care, through a voluntary prepayment plan, on the basis of Blue Cross plan charges for hospitalization insurance. The most frequent charge for family protection has been about $24 a year. Expenditures for hospital care represent on the average about 15 per cent of a family's annual outlay for all medical care. Accordingly the total cost of membership in a voluntary plan providing comprehensive services would, at this rate, amount to $160 a year. To carry the point further, if one assumes that the average family should budget about 4 per cent of its income for medical care, an annual family income of $4,000 would be required to sustain the cost of comprehensive health protection through a voluntary prepayment plan. It is evident that this would rule out the great majority of American families, urban as well as rural. With Blue Cross membership fees recently up to about $36 per family per year, comprehensive protection at this rate would cost $240 annually and call for family incomes of about $6,000 a year.

[6] See Chap. 18.

throughout the nation simply could not afford to purchase comprehensive health protection on a voluntary prepayment basis.

Actual experience offers little basis for confidence in the future of voluntary prepayment plans. Despite the widespread efforts we have reviewed, fewer than 5 per cent of the whole population now receive general medical services on a prepayment basis. Less than 3 per cent of all rural people are covered even for Blue Cross hospitalization. And taking whole states, we have seen that the states that are over 70 per cent rural had just 4.2 per cent of their population in Blue Cross plans in 1945 as against 18.7 per cent in the states over 70 per cent urban. Furthermore, in voluntary plans offering physicians' care — aside from those sponsored by the Department of Agriculture — the greatest urban-rural disparity is found with respect to medical care insurance sponsored by medical societies. Despite the extravagant claims being made for this type of voluntary insurance, in 1945 medical society plans covered just 3 per cent of the population in the 20 predominantly urban states and only ½ of 1 per cent of the population in the 28 predominantly rural states.[7]

One might be more hopeful about the future of voluntary prepayment plans if their growth were not inevitably hampered by numerous inherent weaknesses. These have already been reviewed in some detail, particularly in the light of the experience of the Department of Agriculture in this field. We may simply remind ourselves of the generally low participation, the high turnover, the adverse selection of risks, and the resulting high cost for the services offered.[8] The restriction of benefits in most plans to narrow segments of medical care, like hospitalization alone or surgical operations in the hospital, has been a subtle adjustment to the fact that plans providing comprehensive services — with voluntary enrollment and private fee-for-service remuneration — would simply have to charge too high a membership fee to "sell."[9] More important in the long run, we have seen that voluntary health insurance has failed to improve rural health resources, since it simply lacks the power of maintaining better physical facilities, of attracting more competent or specialized per-

[7] See Chap. 23.

[8] KLEM, MARGARET C. "Voluntary Medical Insurance Plans: Their Extent and Limitations," *Medical Care*, 4:263-270, November, 1944.

[9] ROEMER, MILTON I., "The Rural Health Problem," *American Cooperation* 1946. Washington: American Institute of Cooperation, 1947, pp. 397-403.

sonnel, or stimulating a more effective organization of medical services. In 1937, the American Medical Association correctly pointed out, "Whatever may be its merits or demerits, it (voluntary health insurance) does not seem to offer any prospects of providing medical services to districts where the supply of physicians and medical facilities appear to be inadequate."[10]

One of the special deficiencies of voluntary insurance is the practical necessity to charge flat-rate membership fees regardless of family income. Fees proportionate to income have, indeed, been charged in the Department of Agriculture's experimental program, but this has been only in the presence of heavy subsidy and in a few selected areas. On the whole, the well-to-do country dweller or urbanite will hesitate to pay a higher than average charge for membership in a voluntary prepayment plan in order to sustain membership for a lower income family. If voluntary plans should develop on a wide scale, moreover, flat-rate plans would rapidly outcompete plans with graduated fees, drawing off their upper income members and eliminating the entire basis of equitable financing.

Experience throughout the world has confirmed these deficiencies of voluntary insurance plans. In practically every nation where they have developed, they have sooner or later led to compulsory plans — not because voluntary plans were not rendering a service, but because they were not doing it well enough.[11] On the other hand, none of the 30 or more nations that have established programs of compulsory health insurance has ever withdrawn such a program; the general trend has rather been in the direction of expansion of coverage and benefits.[11a]

Those who, in a spirit of eighteenth century liberalism, have a philosophical aversion to any program depending on governmental compulsion will propose other alternatives. It is advocated, for example, that federal grants-in-aid be made to the states to subsidize the development of voluntary prepayment plans, as well as to pro-

[10] American Medical Association, Bureau of Medical Economics, *Rural Medical Service*. Chicago, 1937.

[11] SIMONS, A. M., and NATHAN SINAI, *The Way of Health Insurance*. Chicago: University of Chicago Press, 1932.

[11a] MOUNTIN, JOSEPH W., and GEORGE ST. J. PERROTT, "Health Insurance Programs and Plans in Western Europe: A Summary of Observations," *Public Health Reports*, 62:369-399, Mar. 14, 1947.

vide medical care to the indigent.[12] This was substantially the intent of legislation introduced in Congress in 1946 and 1947, in frank opposition to proposals for nation-wide health insurance.[13] The ineffectiveness of this approach as a long-range solution should have been adequately demonstrated by the Department of Agriculture's experimental program. Even under this mechanism, only a portion of the persons needing care elect to join and all the other adverse features of voluntary participation continue to operate, leading to relatively higher average costs and restricted services. The support in funds from general revenues that would be required to approach satisfactory benefits and coverage would be far greater than it is politically realistic to expect. A multiplicity of independent plans, furthermore, would mean a great variety of standards, and there is every reason to believe the poorest of them would be found in low-income rural areas. Administrative problems such as those associated with the negotiation by various plans of overlapping professional contracts, or with movements of people from area to area to seek medical care or to change residence, would be endless.

It is clear that a choice must be made today. The way of voluntary health insurance is an improvement over the past, but its toll is one which must be calculated honestly. It has its cost in almost certain failure to bring anything approaching maximum health opportunity to the majority of our 57 million rural citizens. There is a hidden cost in terms of delay that must be faced, a cost that can be measured in daily suffering and deaths that need not occur. The plain people on the farms and in the villages of America want competent physicians near by; they want a modern hospital within reach; they want certain specialists closer than the metropolis 200 miles away; and they want a simple and sure method of paying their share for the support of these essential resources. Such objectives are not Utopian. On the contrary, they are attainable within a relatively short space of time, but it will take more than voluntary health insurance to reverse the trends dictated by economic law.

[12] KELLY, T. HENSHAW (Secretary, California Physicians' Service), Testimony before a Subcommittee of the Committee on Education and Labor, U. S. Senate, 78th Cong., 2d Sess., S. Res. 74, *Wartime Health and Education*. Washington: Government Printing Office, 1944, Part 6, pp. 2093-2095.

[13] Proposed "National Health Act of 1946," 79th Cong., 2d Sess., S. 2143, July, 1946. Introduced by Senators Taft, Smith, and Ball. Also, proposed "National Health Act of 1947," 80th Cong., 1st Sess., S. 545, February, 1947.

The way of voluntary health insurance may be followed — for 3 years, for 5 years, or for 10 years — but if we choose this way let us count the cost along with any gain.

Nation-wide Compulsory Health Insurance

Fortunately, another way lies before us, the course charted by President Truman in his message to the Congress on a National Health Program in November, 1945.[14] The keystone of his proposal, which would have been implemented by the National Health Bill of 1945 [15] introduced in Congress the day of his message, is the establishment of a national system of compulsory health insurance.[16] The general plan is to extend the federal social security system to cover approximately 85 per cent of the whole population, including self-employed farmers and hired farm workers, and at the same time to broaden the benefits of the system to include comprehensive medical services.[17]

This course of action, which lies within our grasp, would effectively cut through the economic barrier, bridge the uncertainties of individual medical costs, and build a solid economic foundation for all the other challenging measures necessary to build good health services for everyone. The costs of medical care would be borne in proportion to family income, the only effective way to apply the

[14] U. S. Senate Committee on Education and Labor, 79th Cong., 1st Sess. *National Health Act of* 1945 (Committee Print No. 1). Washington: Government Printing Office, 1946.

[15] Proposed "National Health Act of 1945," 79th Cong., 1st Sess., S. 1606, November, 1945. Introduced by Senators Wagner and Murray and Representative Dingell.

[16] U. S. Senate, Committee on Education and Labor, *Medical Care Insurance: A Social Insurance Program for Personal Health Services.* Report from the Bureau of Research and Statistics, Social Security Board (Senate Committee Print 5), 79th Cong., 2d Sess., Washington: Government Printing Office, 1946.

[17] The administrative handicaps to collecting insurance contributions from farm beneficiaries are not insurmountable; a number of devices, including supplementary income-tax payments, separate income estimates, regular wage deductions in the larger agricultural enterprises, and the European "stamp plan" offer practical solutions to the problem. FALK, I. S., and WILBUR J. COHEN, *op. cit.* Also, ALTMEYER, ARTHUR J., "Social Security for Farm People," *Social Security Bulletin,* 7:3-4, April, 1944.

time-honored sliding scale principle.[18] Services would be received in proportion to need. The system would obviate delays in seeking care and hesitations as to referring a case to a specialist or to a hospital because of the costs involved. As childhood and filth-borne diseases have been largely conquered, our major health problems by far have become the chronic and degenerative diseases of later life. Since we lack effective measures for preventing these afflictions, the soundest mode of attack on them is through early diagnosis and adequate treatment. In this sense, universal health insurance is the best preventive medicine for the future.[19]

There are those who view the contributory insurance mechanism as too conservative. They contend that the development of a public medical care system financed through general revenues would cover the entire population and would permit a more rational organization of medical services. A contributory system, however, represents an evolutionary change that appeals today to far more people, for it would be built around the framework of the social security program in which we have already had more than ten years' experience, and it would operate through the existing patterns of professional practice and of health institutions and agencies. From the viewpoint of practical politics in the United States today, a program of complete tax-supported medical care would be out of the question. The dependence of medical services on year-by-year appropriations from general revenues, moreover, would tend to mean subjection to the vicissitudes of political and economic events. If pressures increased, a means test might well come to be applied. In generally industrialized economies, history has proved social insurance to be a stable source of support that establishes benefits as a right of those who have contributed.[20]

It should not be inferred that the contributory principle of social insurance is inconsistent with universal coverage of the population.

[18] FALK, I. S., "Proposed Extension of the Social Security Program, with Special Reference to Health and Medical Aspects," New England Journal of Medicine, 230:243-249, Mar. 2, 1944.

[19] BOAS, ERNST P., Testimony before a Subcommittee of the Committee on Education and Labor, U. S. Senate, 78th Cong., 2d Sess., S. Res. 74, Wartime Health and Education. Washington: Government Printing Office, 1944, Part 6, pp. 2058-2068.

[20] EPSTEIN, ABRAHAM, Insecurity, a Challenge to America. New York: Random House, Inc., 1936.

Exclusion of certain sections of the population has been a feature of health insurance in most other nations, but it is not strictly necessary. Even under orthodox social insurance, supplementation in greater or lesser degree from general revenues is desirable, and there is no sound reason why such supplementary funds could not be used to finance services for all who have not earned insurance eligibility. With relatively few exceptions, such excluded persons would in any case be individuals of low income who would ordinarily be eligible for public assistance (financed out of general revenues). For the rural population, a health insurance system providing universal coverage would be especially desirable — since a strictly applied rule of limited eligibility for insurance protection would tend to exclude larger proportions of farm than of city people. All in all, if universal coverage can be attained within a framework of insurance financing, administration would be far simpler and benefits obviously more equitably available.

There are other critics of national health insurance who have less objection to the development of compulsory programs by individual states.[20a] It would naturally be within the capacity of states like California or New York to establish their own systems of compulsory health insurance and, indeed, an increasing number of bills to this effect are being introduced in state legislatures.[21] But who can ignore the fact that many states simply lack the resources to develop adequate programs? We may recall that the average per capita income of the states over 70 per cent urban was about $800 in 1940, whereas for the states over 70 per cent rural it was only about $300. There were, of course, more striking variations between some of the individual urban and rural states. The implications of these income figures are obvious in terms of the fruitfulness of efforts within individual rural states to make comprehensive medical services available.

There are other reasons, moreover, why compulsory health insurance should be national rather than on a state-by-state basis. Our population is perhaps the most mobile of that of any nation in the world and the interstate migration of seasonal farm workers is a

[20a] See, for example, New York Academy of Medicine (Final Report of the Committee on Medicine and the Changing Order), *Medicine and the Changing Order*. New York: The Commonwealth Fund, 1947.

[21] The California legislature, for example, considered two state-wide compulsory health insurance bills in 1945.

definite feature of our agricultural economy. Chaotic conditions will occur unless a system is developed with common obligations and uniform benefits the country over.[22] It is important for the rural population in particular, as well as for minority groups, that standards be determined by the Federal Government and be maintained on a uniformly high level in all parts of the nation. Finally, the Federal Government is already equipped to administer social security on an efficient basis, not subject to local political pressures, and this could be extended to health insurance with the least possible overhead cost.

With the adoption of national compulsory health insurance, medical purchasing power would be spread equitably over the entire country. While funds would be collected in proportion to local wealth, they could be allocated from a central fund to states and localities in proportion to their population and needs.[23] Hospital planning would at last have real meaning for rural people, for hospitals could be placed where needed, once their maintenance was assured. The urban-rural double standard could be wiped out; rural people could be assured the medical personnel and facilities they need and not just those they can support today.

It is estimated that proposed national health insurance legislation would eventually make available approximately $10 per person to pay physicians' bills each year — $10,000 for every 1,000 people, $20,000 for every 2,000 people.[23a] One can visualize the opportunities this would create in hundreds of under-served rural counties with their present-day ratios of one physician to 2,000, 3,000, 5,000, and even 10,000 people. One can picture the flow of new graduates into rural districts with this economic guarantee of a good

[22] Committee on Research in Medical Economics, *Principles of a Nation-wide Health Program* (Report of the Health Program Conference). New York, 1944.

[23] ALTMEYER, ARTHUR J., Testimony before the Committee on Education and Labor, U. S. Senate, 79th Cong., 2d Sess., S. 1606, *National Health Program*. Washington: Government Printing Office, 1946, Part 1, pp. 169-208.

[23a] This is perhaps an oversimplification, since per capita allotments for medical services in different parts of the country would not necessarily be uniform at the outset of a national health insurance program. At first, adjustments would have to be made to take some account of existing disparities in the supply of personnel and the fees charged in different areas. Gradually it would be hoped that a nationally uniform allowance for medical services would be instituted, so that the funds reaching an area, whether urban or rural, would depend solely on the number of people to be served.

income and the corresponding assurance of economic support for hospital or health center facilities. Still, no physician or dentist would be compelled to participate unless he wished to, and the method of payment — whether fee-for-service, capitation, or salary — would depend on the majority choice of local practitioners. Rates of payment for service would not be uniform but would depend on the physician's specialty status, skill, and experience, and his total earnings would depend largely on his ability to attract patients, as is the case today.[24]

From the point of view of the conscientious physician interested in a high quality of medical service, much is to be gained. Referral of his patient to a specialist, the performance of x-ray examinations or laboratory tests, or arrangements for hospitalization need not depend on the patient's pocketbook. The frustrations of the doctor trying to practice good medicine, particularly in rural communities, would be largely eliminated.[25]

The establishment of compulsory health insurance would not alone solve the major problems of rural medical service, but it would provide the solid economic base without which efforts of other kinds can never be fully effective. It is vitally important that this be recognized by rural leaders. There is much wishful thinking today about attracting doctors to rural communities solely through building hospitals, and there are notions that establishing a new medical school or providing a few medical fellowships for rural youth will solve the main problems of rural medical care. These measures are all frankly marginal to the central need for universal health insurance.

It is essential that farm people know all the facts when they choose the road they hope will lead to health security. They should know all the strong and weak points about voluntary prepayment plans. They should know the facts about the national health program proposed by the President. They should know that compulsion attaches only to financial support and that no one would be "compelled" to get medical care in any particular manner or to seek

[24] MOUNTIN, JOSEPH W., Testimony before the Committee on Education and Labor. U. S. Senate, 79th Cong., 2d Sess., S. 1606, *National Health Program.* Washington: Government Printing Office, 1946, Part 1, pp. 134-168.

[25] CABOT, HUGH, *The Patient's Dilemma.* New York: Reynal & Hitchcock, Inc., 1940.

it at all. They should know that the day-to-day administration of a national health insurance program would be essentially local, and that there would be representation of local people and local professional groups on advisory committees that would help to adapt national standards to local circumstances. They should know that they would be free to choose their own doctors and dentists and hospitals — that, in fact, their free choice would be enhanced and personal doctor-patient relationships improved by the elimination of the cash barrier to service.

Finally, farm people should know the cost of either the voluntary or the compulsory insurance course in dollars. Under the public program, costs would be borne chiefly by social insurance contributions, supplemented to some extent by general revenues. The farm operator family would pay an estimated 3 per cent of net income for medical services, which would amount to perhaps 4 or 4.5 per cent of net cash income. The farm laborer would pay only half this amount, the remainder being paid by his employer. The average percentage of net cash income spent by farm operator families in 1941 — for inadequate medical service — was actually 8.7 and the percentage spent by low-income farmers was higher yet.[26] It seems unlikely that farmers will miss the point or will fail to recognize the clear advantage to farm people and entire rural states of pooling the resources of the whole nation to tackle this problem.

Not only will insurance mean a lower financial burden for the farm family, but it will mean that the money spent will bring greater returns. Much of the money now spent, as we know, is spent in a hit-or-miss fashion, much is spent on the expensive care of advanced illness that might have been prevented if there had not been deterrents to prompt care of early illness, and much is wasted on cultists and patent medicines. Ready availability of proper services would obviate much of this wastage.

Nation-wide compulsory health insurance would not, of course, create adequate medical care for all rural persons overnight. It would, however, make all existing medical personnel and facilities economically accessible and it would rapidly set into motion forces to bring new resources into areas previously lacking them. A complete scope of services, likewise, could not be included in the program at the very outset, largely because the nation lacks the personnel

[26] See Chap. 18.

to provide them. This applies, for example, to home nursing care and particularly to dental service; these services could be introduced only gradually as technical manpower is brought up to the level necessary to serve the needs. Limitations of some kind might have to be placed on drugs for a time because of the liabilities of over-usage. On the other hand, families could be expected to obtain a greater volume of even non-included services on a private basis — simply because the cost of most fundamental medical services would have been borne by the insurance fund.

Aside from the obvious benefits that farm people along with city people stand to gain from national health insurance, it is interesting to note certain special benefits that would accrue to country dwellers. The larger size of the rural family means that, for the same contribution of the breadwinner, more benefits would be received. Children would be the chief benefactors, for under private medical arrangements—since their health is economically less essential to the family—their illnesses often are least attended.[27] Furthermore, veterans living in rural areas would derive special advantages. Although efforts are being made to arrange for medical care for service-connected disabilities in the veteran's own community, such care will remain all too frequently an illusion unless the economic base is provided, through national health insurance, to assure the kind of health facilities and medical services to which the veteran has become accustomed in the armed forces. It is clear, moreover, that the present scope of government-supported medical care for the veteran will leave perhaps 90 per cent of the medical needs of himself and his family unmet unless a national health program is established. Yet it has been pointed out that 10 years hence, 50 per cent of the nation's children will be the children of veterans.

The proposed National Health Bill of 1945, which formulated a basic structure for national health insurance, was not perfect. On the basis of criticisms offered during extensive Congressional hearings, another bill was introduced by the supporters of the President's program in the 80th Congress in 1947.[28] While substantially like the

[27] RICHTER, L., "The Effect of Health Insurance on the Demand for Health Services," *Canadian Journal of Economic and Political Science*, 10:179-205, May, 1944.

[28] Proposed "National Health Insurance and Public Health Act of 1947," 80th Cong., 1st Sess., S. 1320, May, 1947. Introduced by Senators Murray, Wagner, Pepper, Chavez, Taylor, and McGrath.

earlier bill, it put greater stress on state and local administration, was more specific about contractual arrangements with voluntary health organizations, indicated the basis for allocating funds from the federal treasury to the states, and offered a number of other changes. Of particular interest was a new section on "Rural Areas" which, among other things, provided for a guaranteed minimum annual income to practitioners settling in rural areas of personnel shortage, for certain transportation expenses incurred by rural people in traveling to distant facilities, and for special postgraduate educational programs for rural practitioners. Likewise a new bill was introduced in the 80th Congress by the opponents of nation-wide insurance — a bill resting its main hopes on the development of voluntary prepayment plans, subsidized by federal grants to the states; the emphasis was on government assistance for the lower-income groups rather than insurance for all self-supporting persons.[29] As of this writing, the outcome of the battle between the different philosophies represented by these two bills is not clear, but unless world experience can teach no lessons some form of national health insurance will ultimately be developed.

Care for the Needy and Other Measures

With or without nation-wide health insurance, special provisions must be made for the needy, for those too low in income to be covered under contributory requirements. Support for their medical services must be derived from general revenues. So long as such revenues are solely from state and local sources, however, needy persons in rural states and rural counties will receive lower levels of care.

The provision of federal assistance to the states is essential if needy persons in rural areas are to receive anything like adequate medical services. Under a program of national health insurance, the Federal Government might make grants to the states, to be matched in proportion to state wealth, out of which contributions into the insurance

[29] See footnote 13 in this chapter. Some believed that the most objectionable feature of this bill was the administrative powers over the expenditure of public funds that would be conferred upon private agencies, especially prepayment medical service plans under professional sponsorship. See, for example, Physicians Forum, "Double Standard Medicine," *The Physicians Forum Bulletin*, March-April, 1947, pp. 8-14, 23.

fund would be made on behalf of needy persons; this should entitle them to the same benefits as other insured persons.

Even without national insurance, federal grants might be made to the states, on a variable matching basis, to pay directly for medical services rendered to needy persons. It will be recalled that present federal public assistance allotments cannot be used for this purpose. Statutory maxima on cash benefits to needy persons, moreover, should be eliminated and residence requirements should be dropped or made more lenient. Even without federal legislation of any type, it is obvious that welfare medical services everywhere need increased financial support from state and local authorities as well as stream- lined administration.

Such broadened provision for medical care to the needy through official agencies is not to be confused with the proposal of grants to voluntary prepayment plans for "persons of low income." The latter would place public funds at the disposal of private agencies and fortify vested interests. It is put forward as a substitute for, not a sup- plement to, universal health insurance. Until insurance is launched on a broad, social basis, it would be wisest to expand medical care for the needy within the framework of present official health and welfare agencies.

Pending the establishment of a national health insurance pro- gram, certain further steps should be taken to strengthen existing measures to help solve the problem of payment for medical services in rural areas. The federal program of health services for migratory farm workers administered by the Department of Agriculture, for example, should be fully revived and expanded so that it can come closer to meeting the medical care needs of all migratory seasonal workers and their families. Even with the development of national health insurance and the inclusion of most migratory farm workers in the system, there will be continuing necessity for special facili- ties and appropriate patterns of service especially designed to meet their needs. Local communities can hardly be expected to provide adequate medical, hospital, and dental services when a sudden influx of migrants at harvest time may more than double the local popula- tion. There will be continuing need, therefore, for such special facilities as mobile or other types of temporary clinics and for the assignment of supplementary health personnel to accompany large groups of migrants as they follow the crops.

Another governmental health activity that should be strengthened is the federal-state vocational rehabilitation program. The physical and mental restoration services available through this program could benefit many thousands of handicapped rural people now unable to purchase such care on an individual basis. Fortunately, progress is being made toward orienting this program to the needs of all segments of the population rather than to industrial workers alone. Other specialized programs providing medical care to sections of the rural population should be strengthened and improved, such as the Indian Service and the Veterans Administration home-town medical care programs.

Voluntary health insurance can do only part of the job, but this interim period, pending the establishment of a national program, offers the opportunity to experiment and to perfect administrative techniques. The prepayment health program of the Farmers Home Administration (formerly the Farm Security Administration) should certainly be continued and strengthened. Farm people should throw their support behind prepayment health plans in their local communities, such as the "medical cooperatives" being organized in Texas and the Pacific Northwest. Such plans, built around group practice units of salaried general practitioners and specialists, offer real hope of bringing high-quality service to certain sections of the rural population. These consumer-controlled plans, in contrast to the professionally controlled plans, appear to offer most promise of providing comprehensive benefits at prices that at least a substantial minority of rural people can afford.

It is important to recognize that a national health insurance program would not and should not sweep aside all voluntary prepayment plans. On the contrary, voluntary plans of many types could play an essential role as agents of various providers of health service. They could continue to operate for the purpose of providing supplemental benefits beyond those assured in a national program. Within any public program, moreover, there will always be need for enlightened local leadership to press for imaginative patterns of service that will assure the scattered rural population the best of care. Today's leaders will be found on tomorrow's local advisory committees helping to administer a national program.

Rural people should insist on representation in Blue Cross or similar medical service organizations. They should seek liberal state enabling legislation that will permit the establishment of consumer-sponsored prepayment plans, as well as assure democratic consumer participation in plans sponsored by professional groups. Membership of rural families in existing voluntary prepayment plans should be extended as much as possible. Every step in this direction will have its beneficial influence on the development of a national health program that will place the needs of rural people on a par with those of city dwellers.

CHAPTER 28

RURAL HEALTH FACILITIES

IF THE PROBLEM of payment for medical services were solved, if the financial resources of the nation were mobilized and applied so as to spread medical purchasing power evenly the country over, forces would be put into play that would lead ultimately to the establishment of all the hospitals needed by rural people. Nevertheless, there is little point in waiting years for these forces to exert their full effect, when steps can be taken without delay. Provision of resources in both physical facilities and professional personnel is in fact essential to the most effective functioning of a system of national health insurance.

Rural people are becoming increasingly aware of the serious deficiencies in health facilities in rural sections and in whole rural states. Their goal can be expressed simply. The rural population must have access to all the modern facilities they need for preventive, diagnostic, and therapeutic services, including facilities for the convalescent or chronically ill patient, for the care of acute communicable disease, and for the mentally ill and those afflicted with tuberculosis. Facilities for emergencies and for maternity care must be close at hand, and those for the common run of diseases and disabilities must be reasonably accessible in distance and time. The realization is growing that facilities are needed not simply for bed care. They are needed almost as urgently as a foundation for elevating the quality of everyday professional practice in an area, and as a concrete means of coordinating community-wide and personal health services.

Subsidized Hospital Construction

Fortunately, there is some prospect today that the goal of extended rural health facilities may be attained in the years ahead. This nation has seldom seen such concentration of interest on any phase of health services as that in evidence today with respect to hospital and health center planning. Stimulated by the United States Public

Health Service and the American Hospital Association's Commission on Hospital Care and urged on by hundreds of local organizations, agencies, and whole communities, a dynamic hospital construction movement is under way.

In August, 1946, after extended discussion, Congress enacted the National Hospital Survey and Construction Act. This will aid the states in developing over-all "master plans" and will furnish federal grants-in-aid to facilitate the construction or improvement of both public and nonprofit hospitals and related institutions, including health centers.[1] There is gratifying emphasis in this legislation on meeting health needs rather than on simply providing employment relief, even to the extent of authorizing state plans to provide for a higher ratio of hospital beds in the more thinly settled rural states. Such provisions, however, may represent little more than good intentions in the face of the grant arrangements of the bill. Instead of authorizing federal grants on a variable matching basis, every state is required to put up $2 for each dollar received from the Federal Government.[2] It would hardly seem that the effects of this formula will be counterbalanced by the provision that the allotments of funds to which the states are each entitled are proportionately greater for the states of lower income. Congress authorized the appropriation of 75 million dollars a year for this program for five years, but how much will actually be appropriated remains to be seen.[3]

The passage of this act, despite its weaknesses, gives strong impetus to a movement that will have effects far beyond the brick and mortar value of 375 million dollars of federal funds. Because of the stimulus of state-wide planning, scores of new institutions will doubtless be built even without benefit of government subsidy. Employment opportunities will be offered to thousands of hospital mainte-

[1] U. S. Senate Committee on Education and Labor, 79th Cong., 2d Sess., Report relating to Senate Bills 1606 and 191, *National Health Act of 1945 and Hospital Survey and Construction Bill* (Committee Print 3). Washington: Government Printing Office, pp. 15-87.

[2] "National Hospital Survey and Construction Act," Public Law 725, 79th Cong., 2d Sess., August, 1946.

[3] HOGE, V. M., "The Hospital Survey and Construction Act," *Public Health Reports,* 62:49-54, Jan. 10, 1947. Fortunately five states, as of November, 1947, had enacted legislation providing state funds to match local expenditures, so that local, state, and federal bodies would each be putting up one-third of total construction costs.

nance workers in rural districts, in addition to nurses, technicians, and other personnel. Strong inducements will be provided for the organization of prepayment plans to assure utilization of the new units, especially since "reasonable assurance that adequate financial support will be available . . . for maintenance and operation" is a condition for receiving grant funds. At the same time, rural leaders must be vigilant lest this clause have the effect of disqualifying grants to low-income rural communities in greatest need.

Even before the passage of this federal legislation, 38 states had taken some action toward surveying their existing health facilities and analyzing the deficiencies. Surveys were actually under way in 22 states at the end of 1945.[4] Moreover, the legislatures of 18 states enacted formal legislation during 1945 providing either for hospital surveys or for the administration of health facility construction programs or both.[5] Following the passage of the National Hospital Survey and Construction Act, surveys were undertaken in the remaining states and, as of this writing, they have been completed in all but three states (Delaware, Wyoming, and Arizona). State plans indicating the specific needs for new construction have been completed in 27 states.[5a]

It need hardly be reiterated that rural hospital planning can never be fully implemented unless the economic support of rural hospitals is assured through national health insurance. It has been conceded by Dr. Morris Fishbein, in fact, that such a measure as the National Hospital Survey and Construction Act "in itself will not . . . meet the rural need; many a community most in need of medical facilities and medical care would not be able either to staff or maintain an institution even if the Government provided it."[6] With this economic relationship firmly in mind, we may consider the principal features of a program of expanded rural health facilities.

[4] Commission on Hospital Care (Chicago), *Hospital Survey News Letter,* November, 1945, p. 8.

[5] GUERIN, MARY M., "Legislation on Hospital Surveys, Construction, and Licensing Considered by State Legislatures in 1945," *Public Health Reports,* 60:1519-1539, Dec. 21, 1945.

[5a] U.S. Public Health Service, Division of Hospital Facilities, *State Plan Report,* Nov. 14, 1947, Processed.

[6] FISHBEIN, MORRIS, "Farm Health Tomorrow," *Successful Farming,* 43:19 and 28-31, July, 1945.

Regionalized Hospital Planning

Happily for the rural population, today's planning for improved health facilities is based largely on the concept of regionalization.[7] The concept of a health region is that of a logical medical care area falling within the direct sphere of influence of the sort of center typified at its best by a medical school and its teaching hospitals. The Commonwealth Fund, which is promoting active experiments in this field, has defined a hospital region as "an area large enough to absorb fully the consultant, technical, and educational services which a full-fledged medical center can offer to practicing physicians and hospitals; small enough to permit the convenient and continuous distribution of such services through all its parts."[8] Occasionally such a region will coincide closely with the area comprising one state. In certain states, such as New York, several regions could be defined. On the other hand, the region centering about Memphis, for example, would include large portions of adjacent states.

The importance to long under-served rural communities of this concept of regionalization can hardly be overemphasized. It calls for the coordination of hospital and medical services within the whole region, from the most outlying rural hospital or health center to the hub of scientific knowledge around which the region takes its form. Medical science reaches its highest point of development in the university medical center or the large, well-staffed metropolitan institution. Such a center represents medical knowledge, medical skills, scholarship, research, and the inquiring mind. It offers the most highly specialized medical and surgical services and can extend its influence to the farthest reaches of the medical service area.

While serving as a facility for the immediate urban population and as a source of medical standards throughout the whole area, the center should naturally have a moderate number of beds available to receive from a distance perplexing or complicated cases. A Public Health Service study estimates the number of beds that should be

[7] U. S. Senate Subcommittee on Wartime Health and Education, 78th Cong., 2d Sess., Interim Report to the Committee on Education and Labor pursuant to S. Res. 74, *Wartime Health and Education* (Subcommittee Report 3). Washington: Government Printing Office, 1944, pp. 14-17.

[8] The Commonwealth Fund, *Twenty-seventh Annual Report,* 1945. New York, 1946, p. 21.

available in such a center as 0.5 beds per 1,000 of the entire surrounding population, in addition to 4.5 beds per 1,000 people in the immediate area.[9]

No hard and fast pattern can be applied to the development of hospital facilities in other parts of a hospital region. To a large extent, the pattern would take its shape from those general hospitals already in existence in cities and towns throughout the area.[10] A construction program would make it possible to consolidate certain hospitals into larger units or to replace old structures with new. These general hospitals would often fit into the organizational pattern as secondary centers with direct channels of association to and from the principal teaching center. As a rule these district hospitals would have available not only the services of general practitioners and general surgeons, but often the services of specialists such as internists, pediatricians, radiologists, psychiatrists, obstetricians, ophthalmologists, otolaryngologists, and sometimes others. The district hospital of this type should ordinarily have a moderate number of beds for difficult cases referred from outlying rural hospitals.

In peripheral and intermediary zones of a health region, the pattern for the development of rural hospital facilities would depend on transportation facilities and the population density. There are some areas in which virtually all the needs of rural people could be met in near-by urban institutions. There are many more areas, however, in which hospitals are needed directly in rural communities. Such hospitals should ordinarily serve the needs of at least 12,000 to 15,000 people, so that they might have capacities of about 50 beds, a minimum size for efficient operation in the opinion of some authorities. Hospitals of this kind may serve only one county or occasionally two or three counties or more. As observed in Chapter 13, rural people should be served by at least 4.5 general hospital beds per 1,000, although some of the beds serving them would not, of course, be located in their immediate area.[11] As the services of the general hos-

[9] MOUNTIN, JOSEPH W., ELLIOTT H. PENNELL, and VANE M. HOGE, *Health Service Areas: Requirements for General Hospitals and Health Centers* (U. S. Public Health Service Bull. 292). Washington: Government Printing Office, 1945, p. 7.

[10] For example, see *Hospital Resources and Needs: Report of the Michigan Hospital Survey*. Battle Creek: W. K. Kellogg Foundation, 1946.

[11] In very sparsely settled territory, ratios of 5.0 or 5.5 beds per 1,000 may be required if adjustment is to be made to the occupancy limitations of small

pital expand for the care of convalescent and chronic cases, even this over-all ratio will probably prove to be inadequate, and a ratio of as much as 6.0 or 7.0 beds per 1,000 may come to be required.

It is important that rural hospital planners put human needs above theory in their calculations. The small and perhaps "uneconomic" rural hospital has a definite place. It is easy to talk in terms of better roads, ambulance service, and the simplicity of getting a patient to a good-sized hospital 40 or 50 miles away. There are factors, however, other than miles and miles per hour. A family cannot be fully at ease if it lives more than 20 or 25 miles from hospital facilities. And distance creates psychological, as well as geographic, handicaps to hospitalization.

The comparatively small rural general hospital, occasionally with as few as 25 to 35 beds, is amply justified on other grounds.[12] Unless such facilities are made available, widespread sections will remain under-served with respect not only to hospital care but to physicians' care as well. The carefully planned provision of hospital facilities, with open-staff policies and close relationships with a larger district hospital, can do much to reverse the downhill trend in the supply of rural doctors. As Graham L. Davis has pointed out, moreover, we must not forget about the "90 per cent of illnesses that do not need hospital care and the influence that the local hospital should have on the quality of service these patients get."[13]

As functional networks of hospitals are developed and as new institutions are built, the public interest will be served best if rural hospitals are operated by and for the entire community. Under local governmental sponsorship they can enjoy the greatest financial stability and can render the broadest type of public service. Rural communities should be encouraged and financially assisted to take over existing proprietary hospitals. Even without such steps, rural hospitals under proprietary — or, for that matter, nonprofit — control might extend their usefulness through the addition of outpatient

---

and independent hospital units, without proper arrangements for transportation of patients among the facilities of a region. See MOUNTIN, PENNELL, and HOGE, op. cit.

[12] MOTT, F. D., "Planning the Postwar Rural Hospital," The Hospital Yearbook, 1943. Chicago: Modern Hospital Publishing Co., pp. 954-957.

[13] DAVIS, GRAHAM L., "Those Horse-and-buggy Hospitals Must Go," The Modern Hospital, 62:50-53, March, 1944.

departments, expansion of laboratory facilities for general use by practicing physicians, and other such measures. With occupancy raised through a health insurance program, such improvement should be financially feasible.[14]

Health Centers and Mobile Units

Even with the regionalized pattern of rural and urban general hospitals built around a focal medical center, there is still the problem of sparsely settled rural areas typified by regions like the Great Plains but found in outlying sections the country over. The need in such areas is not just for hospitals as we usually think of them but for community health centers. It makes for both economy and efficiency to combine public and private health services in one facility in such areas.

In all sections, indeed, urban and rural alike, the health center can serve a key purpose. The health center can house the local health department or serve as a subcenter in the public health program; it can include laboratory, x-ray, and other diagnostic facilities to be used both in the public health program and by local physicians and dentists; it can provide office space for local practitioners; and in sparsely settled sections it can maintain infirmary or auxiliary hospital beds for maternity cases, emergencies, and perhaps isolation cases. The center should not be considered a hospital; it should be used for inpatient care only in association with a more completely equipped institution to which cases can be readily referred.[15]

Merging public health and private practice under one roof is not Utopian. The day has passed when preventive and therapeutic services can operate in completely separate worlds.[16] If the standards of rural medical practice are to be elevated, moreover, rural physicians must have access to the use of diagnostic facilities that they could hardly maintain individually. When medical care facilities are

[14] For a comprehensive discussion, see Commission on Hospital Care, *Hospital Care in the United States*. New York: The Commonwealth Fund, 1947.

[15] U. S. Public Health Service, Hospital Facilities Section, "Planning for Integrated Service: A Health Center Unit," *Hospitals*, 19:52-53, May, 1945. Also, U.S. Public Health Service, Hospital Facilities Section, "Building Types Study No. 67 — Public Health Centers," *Architectural Record*, 92:63-78, July, 1942.

[16] MOUNTIN, PENNELL, and HOGE, *op. cit.*, p. 1.

combined in the same center with public health facilities, there is economy in investment and operation and an opportunity to integrate all phases of health work impinging on the same individual. Rural practitioners should welcome the location of their offices in health centers, affording an opportunity to share secretarial, nursing, and laboratory assistance.

Wherever practicable the educational, laboratory, and other facilities needed by a local health department should be combined with the rural general hospital, either in the same physical structure or very close to it.[17] A true community health center has a contribution to make to rural living. It goes beyond the provision of specific medical and public health services. It serves to focus interest on health and, along with the rural church and school, it can do much to build a more complete and meaningful rural community life.

In some sparsely settled areas, which can support neither a general hospital nor a full-fledged health center, there is need today for a wide variety of even smaller local facilities. Hundreds of small communities and isolated sections would welcome the imaginative thinking of health facility architects and planners in devising flexible plans to meet a multitude of differing situations. One community may wish, for example, to build a facility for three physicians, two dentists, a public health nurse, a laboratory, and the local welfare agency. Another community may wish to house its two physicians and its dentist and to provide common facilities for its local voluntary organizations. Still another may simply wish to provide modern office facilities for a single physician whom they hope to attract to the community.

The concept of the health center is not new. It has been advocated in nations throughout the world for years.[18] Hermann Biggs drew elaborate health center plans for the rural sections of New York State after the First World War, plans that never came to life.[19] The Medi-

[17] U. S. Public Health Service, Hospital Facilities Section, "Planning for Integrated Service: A 50-bed Rural Hospital and Health Center," *Hospitals,* 19:40-43, July, 1945. Also MOUNTIN, JOSEPH W., and AUGUST HOENACK, "The Health Center: Adaptation of Physical Plant to Service Concepts," *Public Health Reports,* 61:1369-1379, Sept. 20, 1946.

[18] League of Nations Health Organization, *European Conference on Rural Hygiene.* Vol. 2, *Minutes.* Geneva, 1931, pp. 94-99.

[19] TERRIS, MILTON, "Hermann Biggs' Contribution to the Modern Concept of the Health Center," *Bulletin of the History of Medicine,* 20:387-412, October, 1946.

cal Planning Commission established by the British Medical Association has given powerful backing to the idea of health centers having staffs combining preventive and educational work with group or cooperative medical practice.[20] Emphasis is being placed on the rural health center or "doctor's workshop" in current planning in Canada, particularly in Manitoba [21] and Saskatchewan.[22] In the United States, however, there is still much to be done to translate our plans into brick and mortar.

Distance and transportation factors in some rural sections point up the additional need for mobile clinic facilities. The worth of the medical or dental trailer or self-contained mobile unit has been amply proved in the Department of Agriculture's program of health services for migratory seasonal farm workers. These units can stop at the country school or the crossroads church to handle mass immunization work, chest x-raying, or case finding of other conditions such as malaria, hookworm infestation, or syphilis. There are manifold opportunities for the effective use of dental trailers in attacking the almost insurmountable problem of bringing dental service to isolated rural people. Dental care, in fact, lends itself particularly well to this device, for the backlog of dental disease is such that there is always work to be done when the clinic trailer makes its visit. Still, mobility must not be an end in itself, despite its rural appeal; a fixed facility, where it can be maintained, is always preferable.

Another facility on wheels, which is as important as it is scarce today in rural sections, is the ambulance. A special need for ambulance service is created by the lack of automobiles among many low-income farm families or the lack of anything more suitable for the transportation of an acutely ill patient than a pickup truck. The ambulance assumes new importance, too, in relation to the concept of a network of hospital facilities providing ready referral of the pa-

[20] British Medical Association, Medical Planning Commission, "Interim Report," *British Medical Journal*, 1:749-750, June 20, 1942.

[21] Manitoba Pool Elevators and Provincial Department of Health and Welfare, *The Rural Health Centre: A Living Memorial*. Winnipeg, Manitoba, June, 1945.

[22] SIGERIST, HENRY E., *Report of Saskatchewan Health Services Survey Commission*. Regina: Thos. H. McConica, King's Printer, 1944. Also SHEPS, MINDEL C., "Saskatchewan Plans Health Services," *Canadian Journal of Public Health*, 36:175-180, May, 1945.

tient from outlying to central institutions. In the great stretches of the West we may anticipate the use of airplane ambulances — perhaps helicopters, which could land and take off right from the farm. A governmental airplane ambulance service has already been established on this continent in the province of Saskatchewan, where it is handled by the Department of Public Health.[23] Rural ambulance service should, indeed, be provided by an agency of government, since a private ambulance by land or air is usually beyond the means of the farm families needing the service most.

It is important to recognize that fine maps depicting a network of large and small hospitals, health centers, or clinics in a region do not guarantee the operation of the regional system for sick people. To assure medical care in any facility, financial support is necessary, whether it comes from private pocketbooks, insurance funds, or public revenues. Patients will probably not be readily referred from an outlying unit to a central institution unless payment of the bill is assured and unless standards are maintained determining the level of service for which each type of hospital may be paid. It is difficult to see how such objectives can be attained without a nation-wide program of health insurance.

Special Facilities

In many states the need for beds for tuberculosis and mental cases is even greater than for general hospital beds. We have seen that the deficiencies become greater as the states increase in degree of rurality. To some extent, the National Hospital Survey and Construction Act offers hope of remedying the situation. In addition, federal aid for the continued maintenance of this type of institution may be needed in the more rural states, since these long-term illnesses would not be financed by a prepayment fund such as proposed under national health insurance legislation.

While the problem of sufficient modern facilities for the tuberculous or the mentally ill is not one facing the rural community as such but is a problem for the state as a whole, it is still important

[23] "Saskatchewan's Air Ambulance Service Sets New Health Style for North America," *Saskatchewan News*, (Bulletin issued by the Provincial Bureau of Publications, Regina), Vol. 1, No. 19, Feb. 11, 1946, p. 1.

that the location of these institutions should take into account accessibility to every rural section. Tuberculosis hospitals, moreover, should be so planned that they can be used for other purposes as the disease is brought under control. Most important in the long run, the rural general hospital must be equipped to provide at least temporary care for virtually every type of case, including tuberculosis and mental disorder. The same holds, in fact, with respect to infectious cases that should be isolated, cases requiring temporary convalescent care, or some long-term cases of chronic degenerative disease. In other words, the rural hospital must be prepared to render quite comprehensive services, a policy which may ultimately apply to all hospitals, replacing present practices with respect to tuberculosis, mental disorder, and other high-cost chronic illnesses.[24]

In connection with the prospective program of health facility construction, many have hoped that costs would be cut and progress facilitated by the availability of huge stores of surplus hospital and medical equipment and supplies from the armed forces. The Surplus Property Act of 1944 gave recognition to the special importance of disposing of medical property on liberal terms, to promote the public welfare.[25] After long delays, in 1946 official procedures were finally set under way, offering surplus property for sale to health agencies of state and local government and to nonprofit institutions at a flat discount of 40 per cent below "fair value."[26] It could hardly be said, however, that hopes have been realized in the administrative practices of a succession of business-minded agencies responsible for this program.[27]

[24] BLUESTONE, E. M., "The Chronics: They Belong in General Hospitals," *The Trained Nurse and Hospital Review*, 114:17-20, January, 1945.

[25] *Surplus Property Act of 1944* (Public Law 457, 78th Cong., Chap. 479, 2d Sess.).

[26] Surplus Property Administration, Information Branch, *Non-profit Institutions and Surplus War Property*. Washington, 1946, Processed. Later, as this policy proved ineffective, further discounts were offered.

[27] Among the policies tending to prevent rural communities from equipping their hospitals and health centers and from purchasing mobile clinic equipment, for example, have been policies that required the sale of items in large commercial lots, that resulted in warehousing certain classes of property in specific regions and yet prohibited the sale of materials across regional lines, that failed to reserve hospital and medical equipment until arrangements could be completed for their purchase, and that displayed an over-all tendency to dispose of equipment precipitantly through ordinary commercial channels.

If suitable surplus property were actually made available at low cost, it might well serve as an inducement for rural communities to take action toward establishing hospitals or health centers. At the same time rural communities could use modern medical or dental equipment as concrete inducements to attract new practitioners. The equipment could be offered free to the prospective physician or dentist or made available for his use with free or low-cost office space.

Before leaving the subject of rural health institutions, consideration should be given to the question of hospital facilities for veterans. The Servicemen's Readjustment Act of 1944, better known as the "GI Bill of Rights," provides for the vast expansion of hospital facilities for veterans.[28] It has been estimated by the Veterans Administration that there will ultimately be need for a total of 300,000 hospital beds in special facilities for veterans, a peak which is expected to be reached about 1975.[29] If such a vast system of hospitals for one special but widely distributed segment of the population is to be built up and administered as an independent direct-service program, it is evident that the whole character of hospitalization in the United States will be altered. The approximately 10 per cent of our population consisting of veterans would be served by hospital beds amounting to some 20 or 30 per cent of the total, and only for a portion of their hospital needs. The remaining 90 per cent of the population, along with the nonindigent veterans who will seek hospital care for nonservice-connected disabilities elsewhere, would have to be served by just 70 or 80 per cent of the total beds throughout the nation. The inequity resulting from such a development would affect rural areas most seriously, for a larger proportion of the rural than the urban population would be ineligible for veterans' benefits.[30]

No one will deny the need for special veterans' facilities, where there can be concentration on all the therapeutic and rehabilitation services needed in the aftermath of war. Few would discourage any expansion that is clearly indicated for the care of service-connected

[28] *Servicemen's Readjustment Act of* 1944 (Public Law 346, 78th Cong., Chap. 268, 2d Sess.).

[29] "Veterans Will Get 183 New Hospitals," *New York Times*, Feb. 17, 1946, pp. I-1, 34.

[30] We may remind ourselves that in the rural population there are proportionately more children and, because of wartime deferment policies and higher rejection rates, there are proportionately fewer veterans than in urban communities.

disabilities. It would seem, however, that every possible emphasis should be put on providing care for the veteran in his home community, not through an isolated and independent program, but as part of a nation-wide system of medical care. Medical benefits due the veteran, in fact, might be provided in the form of partial insurance contributions paid on his behalf by the Veterans Administration. Through such broader arrangements, the economic support for rural hospitals would be strengthened, the quality of their services would be improved, and the veteran would receive needed care near his home and family.

Brief reference may be made to a number of other types of health facilities related closely to the provision of good rural medical care. There is definite need, for example, for setting and maintaining higher standards for various kinds of nursing homes. This will ordinarily require state legislation, including provision for inspection and periodic licensure, such as some states have already enacted. As the prevalence of chronic illness in the population increases, the entire provision and operation of nursing homes takes on added importance. The proper utilization of such facilities will conserve beds in general hospitals for acute cases. Organized programs of home care for many of the chronically sick, operating through general hospital out-patient departments, will conserve additional beds and give recognition to the psychosomatic needs of many aged persons.[30a]

Another facility which should be provided more amply than in the past, as a full-scale hospital and health center construction program develops, is the diagnostic laboratory. The trend toward district laboratories administered by state health departments may be expected to continue, and in the blueprints of rural hospitals and health centers should be found provision for adequate laboratory facilities for the use of private practitioners and local public health agencies as well. Two other kinds of facilities might be expected to be expanded with any trend toward the settlement of more medical and dental practitioners in rural communities — drugstores and dental laboratories. On the other hand, there may be a counter tendency in the case of drugstores for, as physicians come to establish

[30a] American Hospital Association, American Public Welfare Association, American Public Health Association, American Medical Association (Joint Statement of Recommendations), "Planning for the Chronically Ill," *Journal of the American Medical Association*, 135:343-347, Oct. 11, 1947.

their individual or joint offices in hospitals and health centers, it will be entirely appropriate for pharmacists employed in such institutions to handle dispensing and prescription work.

The United States Public Health Service estimated in 1945 that throughout the nation there was a deficiency of 231,000 modern general hospital beds, 75,550 tuberculosis beds, and 212,560 nervous and mental disease hospital beds. Of these 519,110 beds, 340,110 would be new and 179,000 would be replacements. These estimates do not include chronic disease or Veterans Administration hospital bed needs. The costs for construction and equipment, at 1943 prices, would be $2,613,974,000. There is also need for approximately 14,000 health centers of various types, costing an estimated $679,765,000. The total comes to $3,293,739,000.[31] Just what proportion of all these facilities could be defined as rural would be difficult to say, but certainly a very substantial portion of the general hospitals and health centers would be devoted to rural needs, and the tuberculosis and mental disease beds would be largely required to meet deficiencies in the rural states. Assuming that the entire $375,000,000 authorized by the National Hospital Survey and Construction Act is appropriated and matched by the states and localities in the 2 to 1 ratio required, a total of $1,125,000,000 would become available. Add to this the fact that construction prices have risen considerably since 1943 and it will be recognized that far more funds than are authorized in current legislation will be required to meet our needs. In any case, there is a challenge in the realization that the total cost of these modern health facilities would represent only a tiny fraction of the amount the nation spent during the war. Taking price rises into account, this entire construction program of such inestimable value to the nation could be financed in about 16 days of spending at the rate of wartime expenditures reached during the second quarter of 1945.[32]

[31] MOUNTIN, PENNELL, and HOGE, op. cit. Also PARRAN, THOMAS, Testimony before the Committee on Education and Labor, U. S. Senate, 79th Cong., 1st Sess., S. 191, Hospital Construction Act. Washington: Government Printing Office, 1945, pp. 53-101; and FICHTER, JOSEPH W. (for National Planning Association), Testimony before the Committee on Education and Labor, U. S. Senate, 79th Cong., 2d Sess., S. 1606, National Health Program. Washington: Government Printing Office, 1946, Part 1, pp. 309-319.

[32] Derived from "Economy in War and Transition: A Review of 1945," Survey of Current Business, 26:8, February, 1946.

Rural Sanitation

Finally, among the health facilities needed by rural people, we must count the facilities for better environmental sanitation. We may remind ourselves of the extreme deficiencies both in rural communities and on individual farms, deficiencies found in urban and rural states alike.[33]

Literally thousands of small rural communities need new water supply or sewerage systems or the extension of existing systems. The answer to the needs of such communities would seem to lie in a federal grant-in-aid program through which the states, in turn, would supplement the funds of the localities on a variable matching basis in accordance with financial need. It is estimated, moreover, that milk pasteurization plants are needed in more than 400 small communities, a conservative figure; here again the grant-in-aid mechanism, or at least the availability of low-interest federal loans would seem to be the answer.[34] The same might well apply to community refrigeration lockers needed in scores of small towns. The availability of war surplus sanitation equipment and materials could give impetus to all these community sanitation projects.

The problem of replacing over half the outdoor privies in the United States, improving or replacing over three-fourths of all the family-unit rural water supplies, and screening millions of rural dwellings is a more complicated one. Education and demonstration efforts can play a large part, but the deficiencies typically spring from the basic difficulty of financing. One of the chief barriers to the improvement of sanitation in the open country has been the lack of a suitable organization for farm families, through which a sanitary program could be promoted and financed on a group basis. A practical solution has been proposed in the organization of "sanitary districts," a measure frequently used in well-to-do suburban sections.[35]

Through this legal device, any sanitary improvements agreed upon could be submitted to a vote of the taxpayers in the area. Loans

[33] See Chap. 16.

[34] U. S. Senate Subcommittee on Wartime Health and Education, *op. cit.*, pp. 7, 21.

[35] Personal communication from Mr. Ivan F. Shull, formerly Chief Sanitary Engineer for the U. S. Farm Security Administration, 1945.

could be secured to finance the improvements, with repayment handled by assessments against the farm owners whose property had benefited. The sanitary district would also be in a position to obtain grants-in-aid from the state or Federal Government, if such financial assistance were forthcoming through legislative action. The effect would be to acquire funds for the improvement of individual farms that would not be available to the farm owners as private individuals. Following a construction program, moreover, the sanitary district would provide an effective mechanism through which maintenance and repair services might be furnished.

Although first emphasis must be placed on basic sanitation facilities essential to the prevention of disease, there is no reason why farm families should not come to have the same household conveniences as city families. Ample hot and cold running water and indoor toilets spell more healthful living as well as comfort and convenience. Rising economic levels and the extension of rural electrification will play primary roles in progress along these lines. Improved sanitation, like better housing, can play a part in providing a general enrichment of rural life.

CHAPTER 29

MEDICAL AND ALLIED PERSONNEL

THE MOST fundamental way to assure a sufficient number of physicians, dentists, and other health personnel to meet the needs of the rural population is to assure them good incomes and modern facilities through nation-wide health insurance and hospital construction programs. Nevertheless, immediate steps toward the training and equitable distribution of health personnel will accelerate the whole process of bringing greater health opportunities to rural America. Unless vigorous efforts are made to supply rural communities with medical personnel, in fact, there is a real danger that the people and their state governments will, in virtual desperation, take undesirable steps such as lowering licensure standards or in other ways surrendering the field to substandard or "irregular" practitioners.

Professional Training

It is clear that if rural needs are to be met, along with all the nation-wide needs that would be heightened under national health legislation, there must be a vast training program. It is not simply a question of redistribution of presently available personnel. Absolute increases are needed in the number of physicians, dentists, nurses, and other professional, subprofessional, and auxiliary health workers.

The number of additional physicians required can be estimated with some degree of accuracy only after consideration is given to the size of our postwar armed forces, the ultimate needs of the Veterans Administration, and the needs associated with other organized programs of medical service, education, and public health. The American Medical Association has estimated that in 1948 the number of physicians available to civilians will actually be reduced by 15,000 because of such factors as those mentioned, and this calculation took no account of general population growth or any increased demands of the civilian population for improved medical care.[1] This deficit is anticipated in spite of the accelerated professional training program during the war. Maintenance of the general level of economic prosperity known during and since the war, even without a national health insurance program, will elevate the need for physicians considerably beyond prewar numbers.[2] Considering only the needs of underprivileged rural areas, the Public Health Service has estimated a requirement of about 25,000 more physicians to bring about a reasonable measure of equalization in the distribution of medical personnel.[3]

As the population grows, of course, the need for additional physicians will increase. Assuming as an objective that the nation as a whole should be supplied with doctors at the ratio to population now found in the 12 best supplied states, it has been computed that by 1960 a total of 270,000 physicians will be required. Taking into account deaths among physicians and population growth, it has been estimated that current medical school enrollments must be increased by about 1,500 to 3,000 students a year if future needs are to be met.[3a]

The need for additional dentists is even more acute. Entirely aside from the staggering task of clearing up the accumulated dental defects in the population,[4] it is conservatively estimated that the dental disease arising each year in the American population would require for its care about twice the number of dentists available before the

[1] American Medical Association, Council on Medical Education and Hospitals, "Deferment of Premedical and Medical Students," *Journal of the American Medical Association*, 125:1045-1046, Aug. 12, 1944.

[2] U. S. Bureau of Labor Statistics, *Postwar Outlook for Physicians* (Bull. 863). Washington: Government Printing Office, 1946.

[3] MOUNTIN, JOSEPH W., "Relocation of Physicians: A Prerequisite to Better Medical Care," *Journal of the American Medical Association*, 126:203-205, Sept. 23, 1944.

[3a] Preliminary data from forthcoming report: MOUNTIN, JOSEPH W., ELLIOT H. PENNELL, and ANNE BERGER, *Health Service Areas: II. Physician Requirements* (U. S. Public Health Service).

[4] The Public Health Service has estimated that the correction of all accumulated dental defects in the population would require a force of over 443,000 dentists — or more than six times the present number — if the task were to be done in 1 year. PERROTT, GEORGE ST. J., Remarks in *Report of Conference on Dental Care for Children*. Washington: U. S. Children's Bureau, February, 1945, Processed, p. 16.

war.[5] Many thousands of these additional dentists are, of course, urgently needed in rural communities. The shortage of dentists is such that only very limited dental care could be included at the outset of a national medical care program, aside from the tremendous costs that would be involved in complete dental rehabilitation.[6] To make optimal use of available dental manpower, it is all the more necessary to promote such techniques as group practice among dentists, the full use of auxiliary personnel, and the addition of extra dental chairs in dentists' offices.[7]

Paralleling the need for many more physicians and dentists to meet rural requirements, there is almost equally urgent need for training more professional nurses, practical or vocational nurses, secondary practitioners such as optometrists and chiropodists, and auxiliary personnel like laboratory technicians and pharmacists. The need for nursing personnel is especially urgent and it is generally . recognized that at least two levels are required: the well-trained professional nurse and the more briefly trained nurse's aide or practical nurse. So long as needs remain in excess of the number of young women naturally attracted into the nursing schools, a system of publicly subsidized nursing education, as in the wartime Cadet Nurse Corps, may be the only answer. Subsidy would make possible emphasis on the education of the student nurse in welcome contrast to today's emphasis on the service she renders in the wards of the training-school hospital. An orientation of this kind might step up the whole output of nurses by allowing the training period to be reduced from three years possibly to two and by heightening the appeal of a nursing career as against the attraction of industrial or other employment.

[5] DOLLAR, MELVIN, "The Present and Probable Future Role of Dentistry in American Society," *Journal of the American Dental Association*, 30:1454-1463, September, 1943. Also KLEIN, HENRY, "Civilian Dentistry in Wartime," *Journal of the American Dental Association*, 31:648, May, 1944.

[6] Competent authorities estimate that for the average adult it would cost $50 to bring the teeth into a healthful condition, while the subsequent maintenance expense would be about $12 a year. American Dental Association, Committee on Economics, *Study of Dental Needs of Adults in the United States,* Chicago, 1940.

[7] McCALL, JOHN OPPIE, "Dental Practice and Dental Education in the Future, with Consideration of Social and Health Aspects," *Journal of the American Dental Association*, 31:16-30, January, 1944.

There are likewise needs for other specialized personnel such as medical care and public health administrators, hospital administrators, psychiatric and mental hygiene personnel, health education specialists, and medical social workers. The most pervading need of all is perhaps that of training Negro health personnel of all kinds by making better provision for their basic education and by eliminating the bars that have kept them from institutions of higher learning.

Aside from the necessity for training health personnel in considerably larger numbers than in the past, there is need for a whole variety of positive measures in the field of training to induce their more equitable distribution throughout the country. These measures would be secondary to the powerful forces exerted on distribution by a national health insurance program and the provision of up-to-date health facilities. But action should not be withheld pending such larger accomplishments. Current efforts should be directed mainly toward the initial location of professional personnel, rather than toward their relocation from former places of settlement. The one notable exception is found in the thousands of veteran physicians, dentists, and related personnel who have been uprooted for a period of years, have become engaged in prolonged postgraduate training, and are frequently open to relocation.

Starting at the beginning, the place of origin of medical and dental students must be given full weight when the distribution problem is faced. We have seen that one of the underlying causes of rural personnel shortages is the fact that prospective practitioners tend to come from the cities and from the more urban states. There seems to be some justification for facilitating the professional education of rural youth on the ground that they will often go into practice in their home communities or at least in communities similar to those from which they came. That home ties can be quite strong is seen in the experience of the University of Tennessee, where about 70 per cent of the medical graduates who entered private practice were found to be returning to their home communities.[8] Although this experience may be exceptional, it seems quite clear that the social and cultural characteristics of rural life will have more appeal to the

[8] HYMAN, O. W. "The Number and Distribution of Physicians in the Southern States as Bearing upon Policies of Southern Medical Colleges," *Southern Medical Journal*, 30:85-88, January, 1937.

rural graduate than to the young physician or dentist who grew up in a city.

Since the principal barrier keeping rural youth from gaining a medical education has been its high cost, it is important that generous fellowships be made available. Financial assistance should not be confined to rural youth, of course, but in the face of the nation's needs, there can be no criticism of giving some preference to well-qualified rural candidates.[9] A number of state legislatures, as we have seen, have already taken some action toward establishing fellowships of this kind, but federal aid, such as would be available under the National Health Insurance and Public Health Bill of 1947, is needed to give real effect to this idea. Making loans to rural students is not enough, for this simply results in saddling the young physician or dentist with a burdensome debt at a time when he is struggling to get a start. A combination of direct aid and loan funds would be more justifiable, particularly if national health insurance were at hand to assure a more rapid start for the young practitioner.

Associated with fellowships might be the obligation of the graduate to practice in a rural community for a given number of years — a stipulation of all of the recent state laws and legislative proposals on this matter.[10] On the other hand, rural states might simply require that a fellowship recipient educated in his own state or elsewhere practice in his home state for a given period of time. While the experience of the Commonwealth Fund with fellowships carrying the obligation to engage in rural practice was not very favorable, this seems to have been mainly due to the lack of assurance of good incomes and the meager facilities in the rural communities selected by the graduates.[11] This experience underscores the necessity for underpinning any personnel distribution program with more fundamental measures.

In planning for a greatly expanded training program for medical and other personnel, it must be borne in mind that the location of the training school seems to have some bearing on the ultimate place

[9] Care must be exerted, of course, to avoid using a policy of selecting rural candidates for professional schools as a subterfuge for discrimination against qualified urban youth on the basis of religion or national origin.

[10] See Chap. 21.

[11] EVANS, LESTER J., Personal communication to the U. S. Senate Subcommittee on Wartime Health and Education, Jan. 30, 1945.

of practice of the graduate. We have seen how the more rural states have less adequate training facilities and a lower output of professional graduates of various kinds. Although a comprehensive health insurance program would make it less necessary to take into account the location of training facilities, there is reason to consider the matter when new schools of training are to be established or when decisions are made regarding expansion of present schools or the extension of partial courses to full length. Schools in rural regions will not only tend to attract more students from the surrounding territory but, more than the schools concentrated in our highly urban states, they are likely to make positive efforts to slant the thinking of their graduates toward meeting needs throughout the general area. This has, indeed, been the emphasis of a few of the medical schools now located in the more rural states. Perhaps more important, a professional training school becomes a center of learning and scientific work for its entire area.

The place where a medical graduate takes his internship or residency is probably more significant in determining where he will practice than either his community of origin or the location of his medical school. It is evident, therefore, that the distribution of physicians to rural sections will be furthered to the extent that approved internships and residencies are available in new or improved hospitals in rural districts. The kind of hospital construction envisioned today will have positive benefits along these lines.

Hospital training for general practice might well include 6 months in a rural hospital during the second year of internship or 6 months with a preceptor practicing in a rural community. The other half of the second year could be spent in the parent hospital with emphasis on the common medical, surgical, and obstetrical problems met in rural practice. This type of arrangement would not only encourage men to get into general practice and prepare rural physicians better for their task, but it would provide intern service for many rural general hospitals and they would be accordingly induced to maintain high standards.[12] A variation of this proposal is followed in Mexico, where medical graduates are required to spend from 6 to 12 months in rural practice following a period of internship. They do not receive their medical degrees until this

[12] LAW, JOHN H., "Making Rural Practice Attractive to the Young Physician," *Hospitals*, 19:56-58, May, 1945.

rural externship, or so-called period of social service, has been completed. It is said that as a result of this policy many externs decide to remain in practice in the rural areas to which they have been assigned.[13]

Effective Distribution

Beyond these training measures which would influence new graduates to practice in rural sections, there is clear need today for an agency to carry out the kind of functions in peacetime that were the responsibility in wartime of the National Procurement and Assignment Service for Physicians, Dentists, Veterinarians, and Nurses. Such an agency would encourage the location of medical and dental veterans and new graduates in areas needing such personnel. It would not have to conduct a compulsory program but could provide a clearing house of information to medical personnel on the one hand and rural communities on the other.

The armed services have been offering a host of candidates for rural health work during the demobilization period, but certainly no reliance can be placed on natural forces to draw these physicians, dentists, nurses, technicians, and others to the spots where they are most needed. The American Medical Association has, indeed, set up a Bureau of Information that provides economic and social data on individual counties about which a physician may specifically inquire. This kind of service shows the veteran where he can make a good living today, but the Association has declared that "The Bureau is not a placement agency and does not in any way influence a physician in his choice of a location." The applicant is referred to the county medical society "to provide accurate information on the needs of communities for physicians and to safeguard the practice of doctors now in service."[14] It is likely that little can be expected from such an approach. It is also obvious why so little has been accomplished by "organized medicine" toward solving this entire problem, when one contemplates the philosophy underlying such counsel to the young doctor as the following:

[13] MOLL, A. A., *Aesculapius in Latin America*. Philadelphia: W. B. Saunders Company, 1944.

[14] American Medical Association, Bureau of Information, *Information Bulletin for Medical Officers*. Chicago, 1945, p. 13. Also, *Location of Physicians in the United States*. Chicago, 1947.

Whether a rural or an urban location is selected, it is advisable to avoid the proximity of a large hospital or free clinic. The average physician, especially the young one, cannot possibly survive this type of competition. For obvious reasons, neighborhoods unable to support a physician should also be avoided, as should locations with inadequate transportation facilities, as inaccessibility is a serious handicap.[15]

It would be logical for an effective clearing house of information for physicians and rural communities to be set up as an integral part of the United States Public Health Service. Its functions could then be coordinated with the hospital and health center planning in which the Public Health Service is engaged, and also with the administration of any general medical care program for which the Public Health Service may be assigned responsibility.

Such a program would be more effective, of course, if there were legislative authority and appropriated funds to cover the moving expenses of a practitioner, the cost of transporting his dependents, and possibly special subsidy of some kind for practice in a community needing personnel. Continuing financial aid would hardly appear to be required if medical purchasing power were spread evenly through national health insurance, since ample support — in the form of salaries where indicated — could be available from the insurance fund for doctors who would practice in isolated areas. In the meantime, subsidy would seem to have its place at the outset of a newly established practice in a sparsely settled or low-income section.[16]

Another current possibility, applicable without or even with national health insurance, would be the long-term payment of a moderate basic salary, for which the rural practitioner would perform preventive services in his ordinary practice and in the community. This could be done in association with the local department of health — a step that backs the logic of having the Public Health Service administer the whole personnel location program. If federal or federal-state subsidies of this kind were made available to physi-

---

[15] WOLF, GEORGE D., *The Physician's Business*. Philadelphia: J. B. Lippincott Company, 1938, p. 31.

[16] It is interesting to observe that the Soviet Union rewards its doctors practicing at outposts in the great stretches of rural territory by paying them salaries 10 to 50 per cent higher than those paid to doctors of comparable training in the cities. SIGERIST, HENRY E., *Socialized Medicine in the Soviet Union*. New York: W. W. Norton & Company, Inc., 1937, p. 137.

cians entering practice in rural communities, similar benefits might have to be offered the physicians already practicing in such places.

Certain practical steps may be taken by rural communities themselves to attract physicians and dentists. The provision of health center or hospital facilities, of course, would exert powerful appeals that rural communities might publicize through advertisements in medical journals. Free or low-cost office space and equipment could be offered in the health center or elsewhere. A resourceful approach would be to offer the practitioner an attractive house rent-free for a year or two. Pending health insurance legislation, the local government or a voluntary prepayment plan might pay the doctor's moving expenses and guarantee a minimum income for the first year, such as $6,000 or $7,000.[17] For a quarter of a century "rural municipalities" in western Canada have been employing physicians on full-time salary; over one-fourth of Saskatchewan's rural population gets care on this tax-supported basis and both patients and doctors appear to like it.[18] Cooperative hospital or health center organizations in rural communities in Texas are successfully attracting physicians today by guaranteeing "drawing accounts" of several hundred dollars a month, plus a share in any surplus at the year's end. Aside from the other practical benefits of these schemes, it is gratifying to see salaried rural practice replacing the conventional private fee-for-service pattern, with all its limitations. Rural communities everywhere are becoming increasingly conscious of their personnel shortage and are eagerly seeking help.[19]

[17] As they formulated their postwar plans, the great majority of veteran medical officers formerly in practice were apparently thinking in terms of returning to their home communities. In response to a questionnaire, however, 11 per cent indicated they would go to a new community in need of physicians if they were subsidized for several months, 13 per cent would go if an office were established for them, 15 per cent would go if diagnostic facilities were at hand, and nearly 29 per cent would settle in such a community if hospital facilities were available. The medical officers answering questions on full-time salaried practice suggested a wide range of acceptable monthly salaries, with a median figure of $583. LUETH, HAROLD C., "Economic Aspects of Future Medical Practice," *Journal of the American Medical Association,* 128:528-529, June 16, 1945.

[18] SIGERIST, HENRY E., *Report of Saskatchewan Health Services Survey Commission.* Regina: Thom. H. McConica, King's Printer, 1944.

[19] See, for example, "33 Counties Seek Doctors for 46 Towns," *The Montgomery Advertiser.* Montgomery, Alabama, Sept. 22, 1946.

A basic requirement for the free movement of physicians and dentists from any part of the nation into rural states or the rural sections of any state is the elimination of licensure barriers. If federal licensing is out of the question in our present constitutional framework, the remedy might lie in adoption by the states of nationally uniform and high-standard licensure laws, with full reciprocity among the states having such legislation. This might well be promoted by the Council of State Governments, which has been backing model hospital licensure and hospital planning legislation, for hospitals must have competent personnel to man them. The entire relationship between licensing boards and the medical schools requires re-examination, with a view to assigning the well-qualified schools a share of the responsibility for licensure. In the meantime, state governments should learn to use boards of medical licensure as social instruments to serve state health needs, rather than permitting them — as is too often the case — to be tools in the hands of those who would simply limit professional competition.

There are naturally problems surrounding the equitable distribution of other types of health personnel beside physicians and dentists. Yet if conditions are established under which physicians and dentists will enter practice in rural communities, there need be little doubt that health workers of other kinds will follow. The distribution of nurses, for example, is known to follow that of hospitals and physicians. Secondary practitioners like optometrists and auxiliary personnel such as pharmacists, physiotherapists, laboratory technicians, and dental hygienists will follow the establishment of hospitals, the settlement of physicians and dentists, and organizational developments such as group practice. Public health workers of all kinds involved in medical, sanitary engineering, or educational activities will follow the establishment of full-time local health departments. In tackling this whole problem, therefore, the goal of good distribution of health personnel of every kind can be achieved through concentration on measures that will bring physicians and dentists to rural districts and will extend public health organization.

When the problem of financing medical care is solved and when planned and up-to-date physical facilities are available, there need not be as much concern as some have expressed that the lack of social and cultural advantages in rural sections will remain a barrier to the settlement of medical personnel. There are already many psychological and social values in rural life that need only be experienced to be appreciated. There is real prospect, moreover, of steady cultural improvement in such fields as child and adult education, library service, recreational activities, and rural church programs. The lines of transportation and communication are constantly shortening, with better roads, the growth of air travel, continuing developments in radio transmission, and the prospect of television. Social and recreational facilities may be on a simpler plane than in the metropolis, but there are human satisfactions in community gatherings and in knowing your neighbor as an individual. Life in the open country still has a fundamental appeal and rare is the physician who would not enjoy fishing or hunting close at hand without undertaking an expensive expedition. More important, there are unique satisfactions in doing a needed job and in being a respected leader in the life of a community — indefinable values found less often in the turmoil and competition of the city.

CHAPTER 30

MEDICAL SERVICE OF HIGH QUALITY

IN THE LAST analysis, what matters most in medical care is that the patient will receive truly scientific medical service. Making service of high quality available throughout rural America is as challenging a cause as has ever faced the medical profession. Legislatures, universities, and health and welfare agencies may blueprint and budget, but when the doctor meets the patient, it is his skill in restoring soundness to mind and body that counts. Major responsibility for the quality of care belongs to the medical profession; it is a responsibility that should not be neglected on account of preoccupation with matters belonging more properly to economists and health administrators.

Solving the problem of the doctor's bill and providing modern health facilities will substantially improve the quality of rural medicine, if nothing else is done. Young, well-trained physicians will no longer shun rural practice. More doctors, and doctors of higher average caliber, will mean better medical care. Both quantitative and qualitative improvements in care may be anticipated under national health insurance. Accessible service, with cash barriers down, ordinarily means earlier care in an illness and preventive services that may forestall illness entirely. The proposed national program of prepaid personal health services, moreover, would place at the disposal of the family physician special means of facilitating diagnosis and therapy, which spell service of higher quality. Thus the program would provide specialist services and consultations, x rays and laboratory procedures, physiotherapy, refractions and eyeglasses, expensive drugs, and related items involved in good medical care. Furthermore, standards would be set for the designation of specialists and the certification of hospitals for general or special services. Professional specialty boards and hospital appraisal bodies, representing current efforts of the medical profession to foster service of high quality, would doubtless be called on by government to guide the determination of standards.

Beyond these forces toward improving the quality of care that a combined health insurance and hospital construction program would set in motion, there is need for a series of positive measures aimed rather specifically at elevating the general level of rural medicine. These measures would be directed toward training better rural physicians and helping them to keep abreast of current scientific developments. They involve also the improvement of organizational patterns of rural practice and the fostering of opportunities for active research.

Graduate and Postgraduate Education

Medical education must be broadened and opportunities for postgraduate education must be increased if the rural physician is to give top-notch medical care. This will require the cooperative efforts of government, including health departments, and of medical schools and professional societies. The financing of improved levels of medical education would be facilitated by federal grants-in-aid to medical and allied schools, as proposed in the President's health program. The educational benefit features of the G.I. Bill of Rights are of current value in this connection. In addition, financial backing from state governments or voluntary sources could be of further assistance.

Despite remarkable advances in medical education, medical schools today still fall short of training physicians who can actually apply twentieth century knowledge and skill to keeping their patients well and building positive health. The schools have a much broader job to do than in the past.[1] Several areas of training need further development, including as a rule psychiatry, the field of occupational diseases, public health, and the preventive aspects of all fields of clinical medicine. Perhaps most important from the point of view of rural welfare is the need for diligent analysis of the social and economic aspects of illness.[2] There is an all too familiar tendency today for the medical graduate to look on the patient as a disease entity rather than as an individual whose deviation from good health may be profoundly affected by his relationships to his family, his

[1] ALLEN, RAYMOND B., *Medical Education*. New York: The Commonwealth Fund, 1946.

[2] BROWN, ESTHER LUCILE, "Comparative Developments in Social Work, Medicine, and Law," *The Family*, November, 1943, Reprint.

job, and his community. Analysis of the social and economic circumstances of the patient is no less essential to an understanding of his case than the medical history, the physical examination, and all the galaxy of technical procedures in which the medical student is quite soundly trained today.[3] If the student is to get this broader conception of his responsibility as a physician, he must have training in the sociology as well as the technology of medicine. As Dr. Henry E. Sigerist has emphasized, the physician of the future must be scientist and social worker combined.[4]

Besides learning to know the patient in his total setting, the medical student must be taught more about community health resources in general and the organization and administration of medical care in particular. Such training would prepare the physician for playing a substantial part in planning and administering newly organized health activities of all kinds. This broadened training in psychosomatic medicine, in medical economics, and in community health organization is of particular importance to the prospective rural physician, who must depend largely on his own resources and to whom the rural community looks for special leadership.

With the increasing complexity of medical science and the concentration of interest in the specialties, the medical schools and teaching hospitals have largely lost sight of the continued necessity for training general practitioners. The general practice of medicine is fully as complex and demanding of high skill as practice in most of the specialties. The medical school, by giving the student more opportunity to become familiar with the variety of common conditions met in everyday practice, could contribute greatly toward turning out a new generation of well equipped general practitioners. An internship, as discussed earlier, spent partly in an affiliated rural hospital under qualified supervision, would provide further grounding for a competent rural general practitioner.

There is much to be said for actually making general practice a

[3] ROBINSON, G. CANBY, *The Patient as a Person: A Study of the Social Aspects of Illness.* New York: The Commonwealth Fund, 1945. Also RICHARDSON, HENRY B., *Patients Have Families.* New York: The Commonwealth Fund, 1945.

[4] SIGERIST, HENRY E., "Trends in Medical Education: A Program for a New Medical School," *Bulletin of the History of Medicine,* 9:177-198, February, 1941.

"specialty," with all the status which the term implies.[5] It should not be difficult to set up criteria covering the qualifications in training and experience that the establishment of this new specialty would require. Certification could be made possible through periodic postgraduate study, rather than necessarily requiring an internship or residency exceeding two years in length. Giving this recognition to the enormous complexity of really well-conducted general practice would undoubtedly help to raise the standards of rural medicine.

Medical training should be modernized in such a way that the costs for the individual student will not be increased. Any further increase in the personal cost of medical education would enhance the forces that tend to keep financially disadvantaged students, including most rural candidates, from taking professional training. A national health insurance program could lessen this danger, not only by providing direct financial aid for teaching institutions, but by ensuring payment for the care of patients in teaching hospitals and thus removing a financial burden ordinarily falling on medical schools today. The money saved could be used for employing more full-time staff members for teaching and investigative work.[6]

No matter how well trained he may be when he starts in practice, the country doctor runs the constant danger of falling steadily behind current developments in medical science. One of the principal points of attack on this problem is through the enlargement of opportunities for postgraduate training. One cannot overemphasize the importance of developing means whereby the rural practitioner can take periodic "refresher" courses at a university medical center. Such courses might take 3 to 4 weeks every other year or perhaps 2 months or so every third or fourth year.[7] If the small-town doctor

[5] "Speed-up Teaching of Medicine Scored," (Report of symposium on "Medicine's Tomorrow" sponsored by New York University), *New York Times,* Jan. 23, 1946, p. C-29.

[6] Committee of Physicians for the Improvement of Medical Care, *Public Medical Care Programs and Medical Education: Effects on the Quality of Medical Practice* (Committee Statement 15). New Haven, July 13, 1945.

[7] The experience of the Commonwealth Fund seems to indicate that a period of 2 months of study at any one time is the practical maximum to be expected of the rural practitioner. The Commonwealth Fund, *Activities of the Commonwealth Fund in Postgraduate Medical Education.* New York, March, 1944, Processed.

In the Soviet Union, on the other hand, a law has been in effect for several years granting 3 months' special leave every 3 years to all rural physicians —

is to obtain such postgraduate training, it is advisable that he receive a generous stipend and, where it is indicated, that he be helped to leave his practice in the hands of a temporary substitute, or locum tenens. The teaching institution might also need subsidy to offer these courses. The source of financial support for such a training program should probably be a combination of federal and state funds. The best source of physicians for locum tenens arrangements might be the interns and residents of teaching hospitals, particularly those wishing practical field experience in rural practice.

The experience of the Commonwealth Fund in providing fellowships for postgraduate study to rural physicians has shown the special difficulties encountered in the effort to reorient general practitioners who have been out of school for many years. A period of study for such practitioners was found to be more productive, however, when the physician had some special stimulation such as the opening of a community hospital — another beneficial effect to be expected of the hospital and health center construction program. Despite the difficulties, the Commonwealth Fund experience in Tennessee, for example, showed definite improvement in the performance of about three-fourths of the physicians who engaged in postgraduate studies. Improvements were noted in such points as the medical equipment maintained, methods of diagnosis, knowledge of therapy, record keeping, interest in preventive medicine, and reading of medical literature.[8] Attaining such ends is fully worth the cost and effort involved.

---

leave during which the physician receives his full salary, all expenses, and an additional stipend of 300 rubles. LEBDEVA, VERA, "Refresher Courses for Doctors," *Information Bulletin of the Embassy of the Union of Socialist Soviet Republics*, 4:5, Nov. 18, 1944.

In the new model contract for salaried rural practitioners in Saskatchewan, there is provision for 3 weeks' study leave on salary every second year, with the leave cumulative so that longer periods of study may be elected. (Communication addressed to all physicians in Saskatchewan by Provincial Health Services Planning Commission, June 27, 1945.) A more recent model contract used in Manitoba calls for two weeks' study leave with pay every year. (Manitoba Department of Health and Public Welfare, "Agreement for a Municipality to Employ a Municipal Physician," Winnipeg, 1947).

[8] YOUMANS, JOHN B., "Experience with a Postgraduate Course for Practitioners: Evaluation of Results," *Journal of the Association of American Medical Colleges*, 10:154-173, May, 1935.

An imaginatively planned program of extension teaching, bringing the latest in medical science to rural physicians at their home bases, is another approach to the problem of keeping rural medicine up to par. Aside from series of lectures on special topics, which will always have their place, outstanding "guest teachers" might visit rural hospitals and work with medical staffs for periods of a week or more. Outside of ward rounds and perhaps private consultations, the basic teaching service would be the discussion in clinical conferences of cases presented by the local doctors. Of almost equal value, according to the Commonwealth Fund, which has supported such programs, is the opportunity afforded for informal discussions throughout the day, at meals, in the laboratory or x-ray department, and over the autopsy table.[9]

Extension teaching can be most effective if it is jointly sponsored by medical schools and health departments, with possible representation of the state medical association. Such an arrangement helps to assure emphasis on preventive medicine and furnishes a channel for instruction in every field from modern obstetrical care or infant feeding to the latest laboratory technique, or recent approaches in psychosomatic or geriatric medicine. Through this channel, too, useful extension courses may be arranged in medical economics, community health organization, and medical administration. Finally, there is a place for carefully planned instruction by correspondence that would bring special bulletins or even entire outlined courses in certain fields to rural physicians — a technique that has been applied successfully, for example, to instruction in up-to-date prescription writing.

Virtually all the methods of graduate and postgraduate training suggested for physicians apply as well to the training of dentists, nurses, laboratory technicians, public health and medical care or hospital administrators, and other types of health workers. There is need for broadening and strengthening educational facilities for all these groups and for developing techniques that will enable them to keep fully abreast of the scientific advances in their respective fields.

[9] EVANS, LESTER J., "The Place of the Small Community Hospital in Postwar Medical Education," *Journal of the Association of American Medical Colleges*, 19:97-104, March, 1944.

Special problems are associated with the training of nurses. It is important that good nursing schools be found in the relatively large urban centers of rural states, but it would unquestionably be desirable to close down a great many of the inadequate schools of nursing established in the past in conjunction with small rural hospitals.[10] While most of these schools meet state standards for the registration of their graduates, many of them do not meet the requirements for federal civil service appointment or for admittance to graduate studies in public health nursing. The well-operated rural hospital of about 100 beds, on the other hand, can give a nurse first-rate training, especially if affiliations for some of the specialties are maintained with larger urban institutions. Another field of nursing education that demands careful consideration and planning today is that of the training of practical or vocational nurses. There is increasing agreement that the services of professional nurses can be effectively supplemented with those of well-trained practical nurses who would be subject to corresponding registration or licensure and would be utilized under professional supervision.

The importance of physicians and other health workers keeping up with medical science is such that consideration might even be given to mandatory provisions for postgraduate training. A professional journal recently suggested, "Perhaps we should all voluntarily or otherwise submit to re-examination at regular intervals for continual qualification for licensure, or at least be obliged or compelled regularly to attend postgraduate courses of instruction and receive certificates for permission to continue to practice."[11] It would seem perfectly legitimate for a state to require attendance at postgraduate courses for continued licensure, provided that the state, through stipends or fellowships, made it possible for the practitioner to get training without undue financial loss. As medical science has advanced, moreover, good reason has developed for establishing licensure requirements for practicing the various specialties, along the lines of the private certifying boards. The public is entitled to this protection, which is now enjoyed only by those well enough informed to know about the "American Board" ratings.

[10] GELINAS, AGNES, *Nursing and Nursing Education.* New York: The Commonwealth Fund, 1946, p. 47.

[11] "Better Medical Care," editorial, *Pennsylvania Medical Journal,* 48:815-816, May, 1945.

In some states there is the basic necessity for raising licensure requirements with respect to all the "healing arts." Such steps might lead to a situation in which osteopaths, for example, would simply be absorbed into the medical profession and certain schools of osteopathy might be converted into approved schools of medicine. Through such a course, one of the knottiest problems of rural medicine — the problem of the sectarian — could ultimately be solved.

New Patterns of Practice and Medical Research

The development of effective organizational patterns of rural medical care is just as important in elevating its quality as improvements in professional training. Even if the country doctor were to be kept constantly abreast of the times, the field of medical science has become so complex that he could not possibly be expected to master it all. Specialization is obviously essential for the provision of modern scientific medical services. Yet, as we have noted, specialists are rarely to be found in rural areas today. They can hardly be expected to practice under conditions in which rural people cannot afford to pay for their higher cost services or in an area where there are too few people who will use the services of a specialist to fill his time, even with purchasing power being ample. Moreover, specialists will not settle in rural districts so long as local general practitioners have such meager incomes that they hesitate to refer patients to others because of the financial loss. Equally important, specialists will have little place in rural medicine so long as rural family doctors simply do not appreciate their own limitations and the medical value of specialist care.

It is evident that nation-wide health insurance would provide an economic base for bringing specialists to rural areas. The expansion of hospitals and health centers will provide the facilities on which specialists depend for much of their work. But more immediate than these programs, there are organizational steps that can be taken to make the services of specialists more readily available to rural people. Essentially they boil down to the promotion of group practice clinics. The functional combination of general practitioners, specialists, and auxiliary personnel in medical groups overcomes many of the handicaps to rural specialization. By effecting economies, it puts specialist care more within the reach of low-income rural people. By setting up several specialists in one place, it helps overcome some of the travel difficulties which are so great in sparsely settled districts. By uniting the general practitioner and the specialist in the same organization, it eliminates the financial rivalry which retards referrals to specialists in ordinary rural practice. Most important, the group practice unit can become a kind of medical center, widely known through an area by patients and physicians alike and hence able to attract a larger patient load than could the several specialists independently. Aside from the practical and psychological advantages of group practice, the inherent coordination of techniques achieved assures a higher quality of medical service than would be possible even if the same specialists were at hand, but as independent practitioners.[12]

Group practice units would obviously be impracticable for many small towns, but their establishment in connection with modern rural hospitals or health centers to serve areas of about 10,000 to 50,000 population would be entirely feasible. In a group of moderate size there might be, for example, three or four general practitioners, a surgeon, a pediatrician, an obstetrician-gynecologist, an eye, ear, nose, and throat specialist, and a neuropsychiatrist. Two or three dentists might also be part of the group. Indeed, separate group dental clinics are becoming equally advisable, as specialization is developing in the treatment of diseases of the teeth and supporting structures. The services of the physicians and dentists of a group would, of course, be supplemented by professional aides of all kinds, such as nurses, medical social workers, oral hygienists, technicians, and often a pharmacist.

Lest all this seem unrealistic, we may remind ourselves that a population of as few as 12,000 people can support an eye, ear, nose, and throat specialist, and fewer would be required, for example, to support a specialist in the diseases of children or of women.[13] It is even possible to have the services of a radiologist and a pathologist readily available to rural people, as the Kellogg Foundation has shown, by arranging for such specialists to serve several centers. A radiolo-

[12] CLARK, DEAN A., and KATHERINE G. CLARK, *Organization and Administration of Group Medical Practice.* New York: Joint Committee of the Twentieth Century Fund and the Good Will Fund, and Medical Administration Service, Inc., October, 1941.

[13] See Chap. 8.

gist, for example, can serve about 50,000 people and could thus be on the staffs of two or three group clinics in the same general rural section.[14]

The importance of fostering the development of rural group practice units can hardly be exaggerated. It is virtually the only way to bring specialists reasonably close to the rural population; furthermore, it is a step without which a community may have no physician at all. A sample of the 60,000 physicians with the armed forces during the war showed that 16 per cent of them were certified specialists and that an additional 63 per cent wanted to acquire this status.[15] Even if many fall short of this goal, it is clear that specialization is the trend of the day and that specialists will concentrate in the cities unless rural areas develop a pattern of practice into which they can fit. The accelerated medical training of the war years and the atypical medical experience of military service have given us a generation of young doctors in special need of the professional support and stimulation that come from a closely knit group practice unit. Happily, among medical officers polled on the question, 58 per cent of those planning to enter private practice indicated a preference for group practice.[16] The limited opportunities for postgraduate training, falling short of current veterans' demands, underscore the benefits to be derived from the widespread development of group clinics. Fortunately the tradition of group clinics, already found in several rural regions, lays a groundwork for the extension of the pattern to all sizable rural trade centers.

A desirable feature of group practice is that it lends itself readily to the salary method of paying physicians for their services. For many reasons a salary basis of payment is preferable to any other known method.[17] It can take training, experience, responsibility, and general competence into account as no other method can. Prospects for advancement in income, position, and prestige furnish incentives for thorough and diligent work. Unlike the fee-for-service doctor,

[14] DAVIS, GRAHAM L., *A Survey of El Dorado, Kansas, as a Postwar Medical Center*. Chicago: American Hospital Association (Official Bull. 223), 1945.

[15] LUETH, HAROLD C., "Postgraduate Wishes of Medical Officers: Final Report on 21,029 Questionnaires," *Journal of the American Medical Association*, 127:759-770, Mar. 31, 1945.

[16] LUETH, HAROLD C., "Economic Aspects of Future Medical Practice," *Journal of the American Medical Association*, 128:528-529, June 16, 1945.

[17] Committee of Physicians for the Improvement of Medical Care, *op. cit.*

the salaried doctor will not have the same tendency to handle cases that might preferably be referred to another physician or to give unnecessary services to collect a fee. From the point of view of a health insurance program, moreover, there are both administrative and professional objections to the red tape of forms and records required in any fee-for-service arrangement. It is widely known that abuses tend to creep in when every item of service is related to dollars and cents and that the orientation is toward treatment rather than prevention. Fees may, of course, be offered for items of preventive care, but the organized attention to preventive services possible in salaried medical programs is simply not achieved.

While the point is debatable, payment by the capitation method in an insurance program appears to be hardly less objectionable than payment by fee-for-service in that there is real danger of perfunctory medical care and neglect of the patient. Although financial incentives to give an unnecessarily high volume of service are removed under capitation arrangements, they are not replaced with the administrative organization associated with salaried practice. Salaries, unassociated with a rational organization of medical services — as in group practice clinics — may entail hazards of their own, but all things considered, they probably represent the most sensible way to pay for medical services. It is surprising that medicine should be so far behind the rest of our economic society in recognizing this. The usual objections to medical salaries, as destructive of initiative and leading to a deterioration of the quality of medical service, are simply not borne out by the experience of our greatest teaching medical centers or the achievements of the medical departments of our armed forces.

Notwithstanding any of these facts, no realist anticipates salaries as the dominant pattern of professional payment in the United States, even under health insurance, for many years. Fee-for-service will undoubtedly remain the prevailing method for some time and administrative adjustments can and will be made to it under any national insurance program. The value of providing incentives toward salaries, nevertheless, in the interest of promoting high-quality service, should be recognized by all who are not emotionally chained to tradition.

Aside from the extension of group practice, the development of an integrated and regionalized system of hospitals and health centers, such as we have reviewed, gives further basis for an improved quality of rural medicine. Any system of facilities must have its counterpart in functional relationships among physicians and their coworkers. Starting at the periphery, it should be possible, for example, for virtually every physician to be affiliated with a hospital. This can be done without endangering the quality of service, if physicians are permitted privileges in strict accordance with their abilities. The association with his colleagues that a hospital staff appointment provides, and the stimulus of having laboratory and related facilities readily at hand, will tend to make almost any physician a better doctor.[18] Each rural health center or hospital in an integrated system will derive professional nourishment from its parent facility. When the rural patient referred to a district or central hospital returns to his home community, with a complete report of the findings and therapy made available to his physician, an educational process has taken place. There would be occasions, moreover, when the rural physician would spend some profitable hours in the associated district or big-city hospital, aside from periods of formal postgraduate study. If a medical school is at the center of the health region, it can be a constant source of inspiration, guidance, and service to all practitioners in the region.

Under circumstances such as these, which are not visionary, there can be rapid diffusion of advances in medical science to the most distant rural hospital and the most outlying rural practitioner. Through such a functional pattern, the continuous education of physicians becomes practicable for the first time and in a sense every hospital, with its organized staff, becomes a teaching center. As Dr. Lester J. Evans has said, the rural hospital then becomes an institution

. . . from which the public expects good work; one where the board and the interested public are cognizant of their obligation to provide adequate facilities for the care of patients; one where the doctor must show his qualifications before receiving the privilege of working there; one where the staff maps out plans of procedure for the complete study and treatment of all patients; one where the physicians as individuals and as a group give critical study to their experience; and one which assures itself of continuous help and advice from outside medical and educational

[18] EVANS, LESTER J., "The Place of the Small Community Hospital in Postwar Medical Education," *op. cit.*

centers. Such a hospital makes its contribution to education simply by being the kind of hospital it is. In it the doctor finds opportunity for professional growth by learning from what he does and by hearing about what others do.[19]

In all aspects of improving the quality of rural medicine through training and organization of services, the special problems of Negro health personnel must be kept in mind. The Negro physician today is all too often barred from hospital affiliation and overlooked when opportunities for advanced or postgraduate training are at hand — not to mention opportunities for professional training at all. The answer lies not in the development of new segregated facilities but in following the simple Christian rule of eliminating from all centers of learning or medical care every taint of discrimination based on race, creed, or national origin.[19a]

Local professional societies have an opportunity to make a real contribution in the years ahead. They should be encouraged to play a more direct role in promoting high-quality medical or dental service. While efforts of the organized professional groups at the national level have been noteworthy, the efforts of rural county societies along these lines have certainly been piecemeal. The application of self-discipline or the positive promotion of generally higher standards has been infrequent indeed. In a total program for improving rural health, the unique and indispensable contribution that can be made by the organized professional groups lies in the challenging field of promoting a better quality of technical performance.

A constantly improving quality of medical service in rural and urban areas alike will depend in the last analysis on advances in our knowledge about disease and health, possible only through energetic and imaginative research. Even though in the present state of rural medical practice there are many benefits of medical science not being generally applied, there are unquestionably many more facts about disease and disability that have not yet been discovered. The major centers of medical research will naturally remain in the cities, but opportunities for research must be open to rural practitioners as well as urban. The ideas born in a village should have the same

[19] EVANS, LESTER J., "The Rural Hospital an Educational Center," *Journal of the American Medical Association*, 110:945-948, Mar. 26, 1938.

[19a] COBB, W. MONTAGUE, *Medical Care and the Plight of the Negro*. New York: National Association for the Advancement of Colored People, 1947.

chance for development through detailed experiments as ideas born in a great city laboratory.

Research activities throughout the nation should be coordinated and extended through government financial assistance, as provided in the proposed National Science Foundation Bill of 1946.[20] The war has shown the value of organized research efforts such as those which yielded the mass production of plasma, DDT, and penicillin. Research is needed in fields like cardiovascular disease, cancer, arthritis, mental disorder, dental caries, and the common cold, with efforts commensurate with the magnitude of these problems. Special legislation has been proposed federally to expand research in the cause and treatment of cancer[21] and, while as of this writing none of this has been enacted, enlarged appropriations have been authorized for the National Cancer Institute of the Public Health Service.

Our university medical centers will doubtless lead the way in such major research undertakings. Nevertheless, there is a place for a wide variety of relatively small research projects along these and other lines in every hospital, health center, or health department. The kind of organization of medical services that we have reviewed should give the active rural practitioner occasion to let his mind go beyond the task at hand and to draw lessons from the volume of his day-to-day experience. Clinical and laboratory investigation by the rural physician not only advances medical knowledge but it provides stimulation for keeping up the day-to-day level of medical performance.

Research is needed also in the whole field of organized provision of medical services. There could be local studies, for example, on

[20] U. S. Senate Subcommittee on War Mobilization, 79th Cong., 2d Sess., Report to the Committee on Military Affairs pursuant to S. Res. 107 (78th Cong.) and S. Res. 146 (79th Cong.), *National Science Foundation* (Subcommittee Rep. 8). Washington: Government Printing Office, 1946. A 1947 version of this bill, with numerous fundamental amendments, was passed by Congress but vetoed by the President because of objectionable administrative provisions. For an over-all report on the need for an organized national research program, see STEELMAN, JOHN R., *Science and Public Policy: V. The Nation's Medical Research.* Washington: Government Printing Office, 1947.

[21] U. S. House of Representatives, Committee on Foreign Affairs, *Mobilization of World's Cancer Experts in Supreme Endeavor to Discover Means of Curing and Preventing Cancer.* Report to accompany H.R. 4502, 79th Cong., 2d Sess., Washington, 1946.

the effect of preventive measures on a population group, on the optimal make-up of a group practice unit, on the most effective use of auxiliary personnel, or on the serving of rural hospitals by part-time radiologists or pathologists. Rural medicine and rural medical organization are faced with special problems of their own and the best laboratory in which the solutions can be investigated is found right in the rural community.

CHAPTER 31

PUBLIC HEALTH ORGANIZATION

THE VITAL importance of extending organized preventive services as widely as possible in rural areas needs no argument. The generally higher rural mortality and morbidity rates from preventable causes, coupled with the deficiencies in rural public health services, are a challenge to action. No program for improving rural health conditions would be complete or sensible without constant attention to the field of preventive health services.

Clearly the most fundamental preventive approach would be the assurance to all rural people of certain basic elements of good living. An adequate family income with which to sustain decent housing, a well-balanced diet, and sufficient rest and recreation is the most substantial kind of preventive medicine. Education in the elements of well-rounded and healthful living is also fundamental. As indicated in Chapter 26, progress along these economic and social lines should be promoted vigorously.

In medicine today, it is becoming increasingly unrealistic to draw a sharp line between prevention and treatment. The treatment of a communicable disease in one individual may be preventive of its occurrence in another. Likewise, the early treatment of an illness may be preventive of its advancement to an incurable stage. Nevertheless, certain mass measures to prevent disease have come to be the responsibility of government and to constitute the field of public health services. Public health has had a long and upward development in the United States, but it is still far from its goal, especially in rural areas.

Extension of Public Health Agencies

The most elementary requirement for the improvement of rural public health services is the extension of health departments to serve every rural community in the nation. We have noted that the most fundamental reason for the lack of public health organization in hundreds of rural counties is the limited financial resources of rural county governments, a problem often aggravated by the small numbers and sparse settlement of the population.

To overcome this problem, the American Public Health Association has proposed that the entire nation be reorganized into units of local health service with populations of not less than about 50,000 people, a minimum number to support a qualified staff and an effective program. This would ordinarily require the amalgamation of from two to four rural counties into unified public health districts. On this basis, the 3,071 counties in the nation would be grouped into fewer than 1,200 units of local health administration.[1] Most of the state health departments have already agreed to this proposal in principle. In certain states there has been district organization of public health units for some time, although the district units have often been under state control, lacking local support and participation, and they have generally been meagerly financed. The development of effective district health departments requires some sacrifice of local county autonomy, which in the arena of rural county politics always presents difficulties. No state has a law specifically forbidding such consolidation of counties, however, and a few states have already authorized it by law.[2] If rural people throw their support behind the idea, there is no question that it can be effectuated.

The district plan must do more than merely amalgamate the populations of two or more counties to acquire a total of at least 50,000 people. The district must constitute as logical a geographic trade area as possible, taking channels of communication and transportation into account. The accessibility of every section is important and districts should be mapped out in such a way that the distance from the principal center to the periphery seldom exceeds 25 to 40 miles. There must, of course, be exceptions to this in such thinly settled sections as the Great Plains and the West. From the point of view of public health services alone, it might be desirable to design districts with outlines having little relation to county boundaries; as a matter of practical administration, however, it

---

[1] EMERSON, HAVEN, and MARTHA LUGINBUHL, *Local Health Units for the Nation* (American Public Health Association'. New York: The Commonwealth Fund, 1945.

[2] *Ibid.*

seems wise for the district to take account of political realities and be composed ordinarily of established county jurisdictions.

Even the energetic organization of districts would not alone assure public health coverage for all rural communities. Financial assistance from outside rural areas would still be necessary to sustain a satisfactory level of local public health organization. The pattern of federal grants-in-aid to states for public health work, already well established, furnishes a mechanism for extending both federal and state financial aid on a more liberal basis. This mechanism would be greatly strengthened by removal of present statutory limits on federal grants by the Public Health Service and the Children's Bureau and introduction of a variable matching formula. A condition for receiving federal grants, moreover, might well be the preparation of a state public health plan that provided for the coverage of every area of the state with full-time public health services within 5 or 10 years after a specified date.

The amount of money needed to support a good public health program depends, of course, on the limits by which public health is defined. In terms of conventional public health activities, about $2 per capita would be a minimum annual expenditure — a figure considerably higher than the present rural average. If more newly conceived activities such as cancer control or mental hygiene are included, $2.50 per capita would be a conservative estimate of the necessary annual minimum. If public health nursing is broadened to include the bedside care of the sick, the per capita annual cost might become $3 or $3.50. In any event, it is clear that few rural communities could support adequate public health services, even by the more conservative definition. If the local annual contribution to the support of the program could approximate $1 per capita, nevertheless, it would be a token of local interest that would stimulate the extension of maximum state and federal assistance. In some areas, local support is at an enforced low level because of outdated state laws limiting county taxing powers, and these statutes should obviously be amended.

A satisfactory level of public health performance requires a well-rounded staff of trained personnel, under the direction of a competent health officer.[3] The personnel lacks in public health are relatively even greater than those in clinical medicine. To meet the

[3] The composition of the optimal public health staff is discussed in Chap. 19.

needs of rural districts for proper staffs, there must be an extensive program of training. Not only are hundreds of trained medical officers of health needed, but also thousands of other public health workers such as sanitary engineers and sanitarians, public health nurses, health educators, statisticians, and laboratory technicians. The facilities for training these personnel are simply not at hand today. Only nine accredited schools of public health are to be found in the United States, clearly an insufficient number.[4] In addition to the need for more first-rate training schools, more funds are needed with which to subsidize the education of public health workers. Current federal grant-in-aid funds, though supplemented by training fellowships like those of the Kellogg Foundation and the National Foundation for Infantile Paralysis, fall far short of the needs.

If competent physicians and other personnel are to be attracted to rural public health work, more generous salaries are certainly needed. Selection and promotion, furthermore, must be placed on a merit basis. Merit systems are being widely installed in public health organizations, but they must have active local support.[5] Another prerequisite to better public health — as suggested earlier — is the vast improvement of physical facilities for health departments through the construction of appropriate health centers of various kinds.

Even with all these measures, public health organization cannot with certainty be assured to every rural community unless an additional step is taken. This is the one taken long ago in the field of public education — the mandatory establishment of functional agencies in every local jurisdiction of a state. Today there are many fairly prosperous rural communities that have not organized full-fledged departments of health merely because county political leadership does not regard the matter as important. While the processes of

[4] American Public Health Association, Committee on Professional Education, "Institutions Accredited by the American Public Health Association to Give the Degree of Master of Public Health (Diploma of Public Health in Canada) for the Academic Year 1946-1947," *American Journal of Public Health*, 36:244-247, March, 1946. This report cited eight accredited schools and one has been added since then.

[5] MOUNTIN, JOSEPH W., "The Evolving Pattern of Tomorrow's Health: Prerequisites to Improved Public Health," *American Journal of Public Health*, 33:1401-1407, December, 1943.

education and exhortation might eventually succeed in getting public health coverage of the entire nation in 50 or 100 years, we must ask whether it is in the interest of the individual, the community, or the nation to wait this long. Mandatory state legislation seems to be the only forthright approach.[6] At the same time, financial support must be forthcoming from the state and federal governments to assist local jurisdictions in abiding by any mandatory public health requirements.

Special Public Health Programs

Discussion of the specific public health measures requiring energetic action in rural areas has filled many volumes.[7] There is no segment of public health work, from elementary functions like vital statistics to newly developed ones like mental hygiene, which does not require vast extension and improvement. A few of the high lights may simply be mentioned.

As fundamental a need as any is the need for public health attention to rural sanitation. If the construction of necessary facilities is to achieve permanent benefits, there must be a program of continual education on sanitary maintenance. Sanitary codes should be enforced and new ones enacted, especially with regard to housing and sanitation for hired farm workers. Farm families must be educated about the control of mosquitoes and other insect pests to avoid such hazards as malaria. Hookworm disease must be attacked through education as well as the improvement of facilities. There should be adequate and systematic inspections of typically lax rural food-handling establishments and food handlers. The standard milk ordinance advised by the United States Public Health Service should be put into effect everywhere.[8] The control of stream pollution would benefit many rural, as well as urban, communities, and legislation on this matter, recently introduced in Congress, should be passed. Through all these measures to promote a sanitary environ-

[6] MUSTARD, HARRY S., *Government in Public Health*. New York: The Commonwealth Fund, 1945, pp. 193-196.

[7] See, for example, MUSTARD, HARRY S., *Rural Health Practice*. New York: The Commonwealth Fund, 1936.

[8] FUCHS, A. W., *The Need for Uniform Dairy Sanitation Legislation* (Midwest Regional Conference on Dairy Problems Called by the Council of State Governments, Chicago, Oct. 6, 1939). U. S. Public Health Service, Processed.

ment on the farm and in the village runs the need for constant health education.

With the high birth rate and the high proportion of children in rural areas, there are special needs for intensive programs of maternal and child health. Facilities for prenatal and postpartum care and for infant hygiene are desperately needed in most rural communities. Special attention must be devoted to such problems as the premature infant, rheumatic fever, and cerebral palsies. More intensive case finding is necessary in programs for crippled children, and consultation services should be made more widely available. To accomplish these aims, greatly augmented federal grants will be required.[9] The action of Congress in August, 1946, substantially increasing federal funds for grants-in-aid to the states, under Title V (maternal and child health services) of the Social Security Act, was an encouraging recognition of this need.

In 1945 there was introduced in Congress a bill that would provide a comprehensive program of public health as well as medical care services for all maternity cases and for children up to the age of 21 years.[10] This program would be financed through federal grants to the states. While the medical care aspects of this bill, confined as they were to certain segments of the population, fell far short of what would be desirable in a national medical care program, the public health aspects were well conceived. In the absence of a medical care program for the general population, there can be no quarrel with the objective of assuring comprehensive services at least to mothers and children. Nevertheless, the prior enactment of such partial-coverage legislation on a tax-supported, grant-in-aid basis rather than a social insurance basis might thwart the prospects of nation-wide health insurance; otherwise its passage would be a boon to rural people.

The rural school offers a special opportunity for preventive health work.[11] The child can be educated about healthful living and keeping fit, he can be examined periodically, and arrangements can be

[9] U. S. Children's Bureau, *Building the Future for Children and Youth: Next Steps Proposed by the National Commission in Wartime.* Washington: U. S. Department of Labor (Pub. 310), April, 1945.

[10] Proposed "Maternal and Child Welfare Act of 1945," 79th Cong., 1st Sess., S. 1318, July, 1945. A modified version of this bill was introduced again in 1947.

[11] WARBURTON, EMBER A., and ALICE H. KIESSLING, "Organizing a Health Program in a Rural School," *The Child,* 8:26-30, August, 1943.

made for the correction of any physical defects. The last element
has been the weakest in the average school program, but this need
not be the case if public health efforts come to be complemented
by a nation-wide medical care program. The school, moreover, offers
a convenient avenue for mass immunization of children and for
mass case finding of various kinds. Many possible achievements in
school hygiene are not reached because of administrative conflicts
between boards of education and departments of public health.
If a clear line is drawn between educational functions and health
service functions and if the work of the two agencies is coordinated
intelligently, this conflict can be obviated.

Expanded programs for the control of tuberculosis, venereal disease, and acute communicable diseases are as necessary in rural
areas as in the cities. The record of immunization against smallpox,
diphtheria, and other diseases is far from perfect. With veterans
returned from overseas, the hazard of certain tropical diseases
must be faced and rural health departments and physicians must
be vigilant to detect and control them.

The importance of nutrition education is widely recognized by
rural leaders.[12] In farming areas a nutrition program should include
not only education about the content and importance of a well-
balanced diet, but also guidance in the application of diversified
farming practices. The current program of federal subsidy for school
lunches acquires special importance for the nutrition of the rural
child, who can rarely get home for lunch. This federal-state cooperative program, which is of benefit to the agricultural economy as well
as to the public health, should be continued and expanded.

Dental hygiene is unquestionably one of the greatest public
health needs in rural sections. There is general agreement that a
long-range program for improving dental health must start with
the child. This calls for dental health education, the establishment
of good dental habits, and the early treatment of dental caries. Our
goal should be a dental chair in every rural school of any size, with
a dentist trained in children's dentistry in periodic attendance. In
the absence of permanent facilities in rural schools and health centers, mobile units should be used, which can be particularly help-

[12] U. S. Department of Agriculture, "Human Nutrition," *Food and Life*
(*Yearbook of Agriculture,* 1939). Washington: Government Printing Office,
pp. 97-380.

ful in sparsely settled districts. The use of fluorine applied topically or in the water supply, for the prevention of dental caries, should be promulgated if the results of present experimentation prove as promising as they now seem. The whole field of dental health and basic research in dental disease would be advanced through enactment of legislative proposals recently under consideration in Congress.[13]

Perhaps the greatest lack in rural public health services is in the field of mental hygiene. Child guidance and other mental hygiene services should be extended widely in rural sections.[14] With the return of millions of rural veterans, whose adjustments to war and now to peace will leave a residue of mental problems, the importance of these services is accentuated. The enactment of the National Mental Health Act in 1946 should make possible far-reaching developments in mental hygiene.[15] Under this act, the ceiling for federal Public Health Service grants to the states is elevated by 10 million dollars to encourage the development of mental hygiene clinics, the training of psychiatric personnel, and the extension of research in mental disease.

There are other special programs requiring expansion in the arena of rural public health. Laboratory services are deficient in most rural health departments. Vital statistics need constant improvement. Farm safety, first aid courses, and home nursing courses need promotion. Public health educational efforts to achieve the early diagnosis and care of cancer and heart disease are important new challenges. Earmarked Public Health Service grants for cancer control, recently authorized, are an important step forward. Exploratory programs by the Public Health Service in the early detection of diabetes and heart disease, on a mass basis, may point the way to effective attacks on these and other chronic, degenerative diseases.

Running across the lines of all these special programs is the need for greatly expanded public health nursing services. In rural sec-

[13] Hearings before a Subcommittee of the Committee on Education and Labor, U. S. Senate, 79th Cong., 1st Sess., S. 190 and S. 1099, *Dental Research and Dental Care*. Washington: Government Printing Office, 1945. New legislation along the same lines was introduced again in 1947.

[14] LOTT, GEORGE M., "Mental Hygiene Services in Rural Areas," *Public Health Reports*, 57:1115-1126, July 31, 1942.

[15] "National Mental Health Act," 79th Cong., 2d Sess., enacted August, 1946.

tions, more than the cities, there is need for a generalized — as distinguished from a specialized — public health nursing approach, since the factor of travel plays so large a part in the nurse's time.[16] To meet growing requirements for rural public health nurses, it is essential that more graduate nurses be given fellowships for special training in public health, and that many more be attracted into the rural health field.

Also cutting across the lines of every phase of public health work is the need for expanding efforts in health education.[17] It is clear that education plays a key role in sanitation, school hygiene, communicable disease control, nutrition, and virtually every other public health activity. Special importance attaches to education of the rural family regarding the entire role of the health department if support for its program is to be obtained from government.[18] It should be emphasized, too, that many of the special health problems afflicting the rural Negro can be attacked through intensive educational efforts.

An entirely new and vitally important kind of health education, moreover, is being demanded today. Rural families are eager to size up the medical care needs of their communities, to study ways in which such problems can be met, and to take whatever actions lie within their power to acquire better health and medical services. Health departments can play a key role in providing facts and figures and channeling these grass roots efforts along effective lines.

In health education, as well as certain other aspects of a well-rounded public health program, the activities of the health department can be effectively complemented by those of voluntary agencies.[19] There are enough tasks to be done in public health to make full use of assistance from every source. At the same time, for maximum benefit to be obtained from the efforts of voluntary agencies, there should be coordination of their activities in the community by the health department. The voluntary agency can often do its

[16] GARDNER, M. S., *Public Health Nursing*, 3d ed. New York: The Macmillan Company, 1936.

[17] DERRYBERRY, MAYHEW, "Health Education in the Public Health Program," *Public Health Reports*, 60:1394-1402, Nov. 23, 1945.

[18] DEARING, W. PALMER, "Improving Our Health Facilities," *Journal of Home Economics*, 36:621-625, December, 1944.

[19] GUNN, SELSKAR M., and PHILIP S. PLATT, *Voluntary Health Agencies: An Interpretative Study*. New York: The Ronald Press Company, 1945.

best work by raising funds for the promotion of special programs that are administered under the direction of the official health agency.

Unified Health Administration

Beyond the specific preventive programs included in the growing province of the health departments, there is another public responsibility more far-reaching than all others. This is the task of unifying the administration of all types of health services in a given area.

Through the years, there has developed in the United States at all levels of administration — federal, state, and local — a great multiplicity of agencies responsible for different aspects of public health and medical care.[20] This wide scope of services in such fields as welfare medicine, vocational rehabilitation, workmen's compensation, food and drug control, industrial hygiene, tuberculosis and mental disease hospitalization, visiting nurses' services, school hygiene, and a dozen other categories is in desperate need not only of coordination but of administrative supervision under a single agency. A step in the direction of unification was taken at the federal level in 1946, when the health and welfare functions of the Children's Bureau were transferred from the Department of Labor to the Federal Security Agency.[21] In some of the states, like Maine and Missouri, forward steps have been taken by the organization of over-all departments of health and welfare. The task is large and complex, but as the health responsibilities of government expand, it becomes the more necessary to coordinate them under a single agency. The logical nucleus of such an agency is the department of public health.

The most important aspect of the problem, by far, is the need for a competent agency to administer a national program of medical care. If diagnostic and treatment services are to be closely coordi-

[20] MOUNTIN, JOSEPH W., and EVELYN FLOOK, "The Administration of Health Services in the Structure of State Government: I. The Composite Pattern of State Health Services," *Public Health Reports*, 56:1673-1698, Aug. 22, 1941.

[21] U. S. House of Representatives, *Reorganization Plan No. 2 of 1946* (Message of the President of the United States Transmitting Reorganization Plan No. 2, 79th Cong., 2d Sess., Document 595). Washington, May 16, 1946.

nated with preventive services, as widely advocated, the assignment of medical care responsibilities to public health agencies becomes essential. As suggested earlier, moreover, the administration of nation-wide compulsory health insurance must be decentralized, and the nation's state and local public health agencies provide the framework for delegation of central authorities to meet varying local situations.[21a]

It is generally acknowledged that at present health departments are far from prepared to assume this new type of responsibility. It is not merely that public health coverage is still lacking in hundreds of counties, but existing departments of health are simply not oriented in the field. In the interest of maintaining amicable relations with the medical profession, most public health officials have done little to eliminate the artificial barrier between government-sponsored preventive services and privately sponsored treatment services. The American Public Health Association, professional organization of public health workers throughout the nation, has nevertheless recognized the essentiality of a new perspective.[22] In an official statement adopted in October, 1944, this Association affirmed:

A single responsible agency is a fundamental requisite to effective administration at all levels — federal, state, and local. The public health agencies — federal, state, and local — should carry major responsibilities in administering the health services of the future. Because of administrative experience, and accustomed responsibility for a public trust, they are uniquely fitted among public agencies to assume larger responsibilities and to discharge their duties to the public with integrity and skill.[23]

To acquire the know-how necessary for a job that is almost sure to come, there is much that the public health agency in rural areas

[21a] This is good reason for assigning major administrative responsibility for a nation-wide medical care program to the federal Public Health Service. This was done in the proposed National Health Bill of 1945, but in the 1947 National Health Insurance and Public Health Bill, major responsibility was vested with a board of five persons, of which the Surgeon General of the Public Health Service was to be one member.

[22] To help carry out its point of view among the public health workers of the nation, the American Public Health Association established in 1945 a special Subcommittee on Medical Care, with a full-time technical staff.

[23] American Public Health Association, "Medical Care in a National Health Program," *American Journal of Public Health*, 34:1252-1256, December, 1944.

as well as urban can do today. Its officials can become acquainted with the field of medical care administration through an abundant literature.[24] They can gain valuable experience by participating in operating medical care programs, which are to be found in all jurisdictions of the nation. The most widespread opportunities are in programs for the medical care of the indigent. In addition, there are the medical aspects of vocational rehabilitation programs, the administration of community hospitals, the special prepayment plans for Farmers Home Administration borrowers, and a wide variety of voluntary medical care projects in which the health department might play a role in either an advisory or a direct administrative capacity. Formal training in medical care administration, moreover, can be obtained at certain of the schools of public health.[25]

Fortunately, there is evidence of a tendency toward assumption of this kind of responsibility by health departments. Impetus to it was given by wartime duties under the Emergency Maternity and Infant Care program, in which health departments arranged for maternity and pediatric service to the wives and babies of servicemen. In addition, most health departments are becoming involved in state-wide hospital planning. In a few states, the state health officer must designate communities of doctor shortage where medical fellowship recipients will practice for an assigned period. The medical aspects of public welfare administration have been delegated to state health departments in a few states.[26] Some state public health agencies are launching educational programs on certain aspects of medical care, such as Mississippi on its shortage of doc-

[24] See, for example, HOLLINGSWORTH, HELEN, and MARGARET C. KLEM, *Selected Bibliography on Medical Economics* (U. S. Social Security Board, Bureau of Research and Statistics, Mem. 60). Washington: Government Printing Office, 1944.

[25] SINAI, NATHAN, "Content and Administration of a Medical Care Program. A National Health Service—Scope, Financing, and Administration," *American Journal of Public Health,* 84:1231-1233, December, 1944.

[26] Maryland, for example, took such steps in 1945 (ROBERTS, DEAN, "The Program for Medical Care of the Medical Indigent in the Counties of Maryland," *Journal of Pediatrics,* 27:384-388, October, 1945); Virginia in 1946. Missouri has had unified public health and welfare medical services in some of its rural counties for years (WILLIAMS, J. W. JR., "Integration of Medical Care into the Health Program in Rural Missouri," *American Journal of Public Health,* 33:499-504, May, 1943).

tors,[27] or Indiana on the general problems of geriatric medicine.[28] Only a beginning has been made, however, in this vast new field.

If health departments do not rally to the challenge of medical care, we face several possible alternatives. The main responsibility for over-all health insurance administration might be assigned to departments of public welfare. If this were done, it would be in the hands of agencies which traditionally have shown a deep concern for the common good but which are generally lacking in technical competence in the field of medical care. Responsibilities, on the other hand, might fall mainly to private medical societies. In this event, they would be in the hands of groups which are technically competent in the field of professional service but which are not especially qualified in administrative techniques nor characterized by any impressive record of concern for the public interest. Still another possibility would be the assumption of responsibility by a totally new type of health agency. If this were done, it seems clear that present administrative complexities would simply be enhanced. In none of these alternatives would there be the opportunity for effective coordination of medical care with public health services. Only through the health department can the essential unity of preventive and therapeutic medicine be achieved.[28a]

A word should be said about the qualifications of medical care administrators. While the importance of professional leadership in many aspects of medical administration cannot be gainsaid, there are many tasks that do not require the skill of the technically trained physician. Certainly the experience in the rural health programs of the Department of Agriculture has demonstrated that lay personnel can serve effectively in many phases of medical administration. If a comprehensive medical care program is to be launched throughout the length and breadth of this nation, in the mountain sections and the plains, in the river valleys, in the cutover areas, in hamlets and villages, it is essential that nonmedical adminis-

[27] Mississippi State Department of Health, *The Mississippi Doctor Shortage.* Jackson, 1936.

[28] Indiana State Board of Health, *Adult Hygiene and Geriatrics.* Indianapolis, 1946.

[28a] American Public Health Association, *The Health Department and Medical Care.* New York, 1947. See also ROEMER, MILTON I., "Trends in Medical Care, Medical Education, and Public Health," *Proceedings of the Southern Branch, American Public Health Association.* Miami, 1946.

trators be trained to do much of the work. There is no reason why many of the organizational, fiscal, budgetary, and related administrative problems cannot be handled as effectively, or more so, by lay personnel as by physicians.

In the ideal health program of the future one can envisage several administrative features. General policies and standards would be nationally determined but they would be interpreted and put into effect, with appropriate adjustments, in the local health service areas. Each local administrative area, defined by a minimum population and maximum traveling distance, would be centered typically around the local hospital. Its boundaries would serve as the outlines for administration of all classes of public health and medical services. In close relation, if not directly combined, with the hospital would be the health center housing the department of health — encompassing all official health functions — and also providing space for voluntary health agencies and for physical facilities for the diagnosis and treatment as well as the prevention of disease.

The unity of public health and medical care administration would extend up the line to higher levels of organization. At the state level or the level of the "hospital region" the administrative health agency would be closely related to the principal medical center. In states with medical schools there would be close integration of the state health department and the school.[29] At the federal level also, there would be unity. All health agencies of the Federal Government would be united under single direction. They would be embodied in an over-all department, with cabinet status, combining all federal services in the fields of health, welfare, and education. At all levels of administration, official actions would be guided by democratically appointed advisory councils representing both the consumers and providers of health services.

In such a framework the day-to-day program of public health would be intimately related to day-to-day clinical medicine. Maternal and infant hygiene programs would be tied in closely with the clinical practice of obstetrics and pediatrics. Tuberculosis control would be intimately related to the practice of internal medicine, cancer control

    [29] NEWDORP, JOHN, "Planning for Medical Care in the Postwar Period, with Particular Reference to Alabama," *Journal of the Medical Association of the State of Alabama*, 14:183-189, 213-219, 239-247, February, March, and April, 1945.

to the practice of surgery and radiology. Clinical psychiatry and mental hygiene would be coordinate techniques. Venereal disease control would be integrated with the clinical practice of gynecology, urology, and dermatology. Community clinics for the management of many conditions of high occurrence would be centers for the most specialized care of high quality, handling patients according to the classification of their medical needs rather than the size of their bank accounts. General medicine would be one of the principal channels of the community program of health education. No aspect of clinical medical practice would be unrelated to active community-wide efforts to prevent or control disease.[30]

With this broadened scope, the entire field of public health would acquire a stature far greater than it holds today. The field might better be defined as "social medicine," in so far as it would direct its attention toward all matters concerning the health of society. Artificial barriers, which were never based on rational understanding so much as on vested interests, would be broken down. The marshaling and application of all the techniques of medical and sanitary science would become a high responsibility of government, and nothing need stand in the way of the organized promotion of the highest levels of positive health.[31]

[30] MILLER, JAMES ALEXANDER, GEORGE BAEHR, and E. H. L. CORWIN, editors, *Preventive Medicine in Modern Practice* (New York Academy of Medicine, Committee on Public Relations). New York: Paul B. Hoeber, Inc., 1942.

[31] PARRAN, THOMAS, "Over the Horizon in Public Health," *Public Health Reports*, 60:457-464, Apr. 27, 1945.

CHAPTER 32

THE GOAL IN SIGHT

THE PEOPLE of the United States — the farm people, villagers, industrial workers, businessmen, church leaders, educators, the health professions — are rapidly learning that health security is attainable. They are rising up against inertia and inaction. They are setting their course forward and there will be no turning back. Among rural people — leaders and dirt farmers alike — interest was never so high in the right to good health. Planning was never so intensive and steps toward fundamental solutions were never so determined.

Health Planning

The ferment is at work from the lonely farm to Capitol Hill. The farmer's wife writes a heartfelt letter about the medical needs of her neighborhood. A Home Demonstration Club of farm women features health in its discussions. Farmers' Union education leaders distribute volumes of discussion material on medical care. Granges inquire about war surplus medical equipment. Farm Bureaus call for better care for babies and mothers. County health committees organize and map their programs. District meetings of rural leaders on health status and medical care are held all over Nebraska and throughout Idaho and Washington. Agricultural Extension Service leaders from every section of Ohio meet to discuss rural health conditions and what to do about them. The Texas Rural Health Committee sponsors democratized state hospital legislation — and wins. In Georgia 22 consumer organizations sponsor a "rural health conference." Alabama holds its health conference, and so does Utah and Washington, and Arkansas and Wisconsin and New Mexico. Out of rural health planning emerges a State Health Council in Virginia and a Health Planning Council representing 53 organizations in New Mexico. Mississippi's Rural Life Council explores paths to better medical care. The North Dakota Health Planning Committee surveys in detail the supply of physicians and hospital beds on its thinly settled plains.[1]

Governors and state legislatures are tackling the problem. Postwar planning commissions are taking special cognizance of rural health needs. North Carolina's Commission on Hospitals and Medical Care makes proposals on hospitals, rural medical fellowships, better care for the needy — and part of the program is enacted into state law.[2] Georgia has its plans, featuring adequate health facilities.[3] Virginia's planning efforts point up acute rural needs[4] and bear fruit in the enactment of an unprecedented volume of positive state health legislation.[5] Alabama surveys her resources and draws a master plan for hospitals and health centers.[6] New York sets two commissions to work on health planning. Driving forward, almost all the states have hospital surveys under way. The ferment is at work from border to border. For the first time, health is in competition with farm-to-market roads in winning the attention of the county commissioner and the rural state assemblyman.

Regional planning is uniting the interests of groups of states and stimulating further state action. The Northern Great Plains Council has set up a multistate rural health committee and furnished a planning coordinator.[7] The state agricultural colleges have cooperated with the federal Department of Agriculture in sponsoring re-

[1] North Dakota Health Planning Committee, *Medical Care and Health Facilities in North Dakota.* Fargo: North Dakota Agricultural College, March, 1945.

[2] Committee on Hospitals and Medical Care for Rural People, *Medical Care and Hospital Facilities for Rural People in North Carolina.* Raleigh, Oct. 11, 1944.

[3] Agricultural and Industrial Development Board of Georgia, *A Public Health Program for Georgia.* Atlanta, May, 1945.

[4] GARNETT, W. E., "Rural Medical Care on the March," *Bulletin of the Virginia Polytechnic Institute,* Vol. 38, No. 4, February, 1945.

[5] GARNETT, W. E., *Medical Care for Rural Virginia: A Progress Report.* Blacksburg: Virginia Council on Health and Medical Care and Virginia Polytechnic Institute, April, 1946.

[6] Alabama State Planning Board, in cooperation with the Postwar Planning Commission of the Medical Association of the State of Alabama and the Alabama Department of Health, *Health and Medical Care in Alabama: An Inventory of Conditions and a Proposed Hospital Plan,* May, 1945.

[7] Northern Great Plains Council, Subcommittee on Health, *Medical Care and Health Services for Farm Families of the Northern Great Plains.* Lincoln, 1945.

gional rural health committees. Productive regional conferences dealing with the many facets of rural health and medical care have been held in Dallas, in San Francisco, in Atlanta, in Lincoln, and in Washington, D. C. A broad-scale Southern Rural Health Conference was held in Chattanooga.[8] Farm and labor leaders from several near-by states joined in workshop conferences on health services in St. Paul, Minnesota, and at Jamestown, North Dakota, linking their efforts in recognition of their common aims. The momentum of local, state, and regional rural action has increased day by day.[9]

National health planning is more spirited than ever. Some is devoted almost solely to rural health; other general health planning points up rural needs as the most acute of all. The Department of Agriculture's Interbureau Committee on Post-War Programs has promoted state and regional planning and served as a clearing house of current information.[10] The Farm Foundation is extending its medical care activities into new regions, stimulating state and local thinking and action. The Commonwealth Fund is fostering a new demonstration in regionalized hospital planning.[11] The major farm organizations are featuring health in their educational and political programs. The American Medical Association has set up a Committee on Rural Medical Service [12] and sponsors its annual rural health conferences. Consumer-sponsored prepayment health plans meet at Two Harbors, Minnesota, and launch a national Cooperative Health Federation to promote their interests. For the first time, the American Institute of Cooperation — an organization chiefly of

[8] "The South's Health: A Picture with Promise" (Leland B. Tate, ed.), Hearings before Special Subcommittee on Cotton of the Committee on Agriculture, House of Representatives, 80th Cong., 1st Sess., *Study of Agricultural and Economic Problems of the Cotton Belt*. Washington: Government Printing Office, 1947, pp. 808-876.

[9] See, for example, University of Michigan, School of Public Health, *Public Health Economics: A Monthly Compilation of Events and Opinions*, 1945, 1946, and 1947 issues.

[10] *Report of the Secretary of Agriculture*, 1944. Washington: Government Printing Office, 1944, pp. 57-59; *Ibid.*, 1945, pp. 85-87.

[11] The Commonwealth Fund, *Twenty-Seventh Annual Report*, 1945, New York, pp. 21-23.

[12] "Report of Committee on Rural Medical Service," *Journal of the American Medical Association*, 129:1187-1189, Dec. 22, 1945.

agricultural marketing and production cooperatives — includes in its annual meeting a special session on rural health.[13] The debate subject of the year chosen by the National University Extension Association is on government's responsibility in medical care.[14] A call for improved general health services, particularly in rural areas, has come from a number of national voluntary organizations — the National Planning Association,[15] the American Association of University Women, the United States Chamber of Commerce, the National Board of the Y.W.C.A., the Southern Conference for Human Welfare,[16] the American Public Health Association, and many others. A significant national committee has sprung into action, its goal implicit in its name — the Committee for the Nation's Health.[17]

Throughout the world, bold plans are carried out for improving rural health services. Great Britain, under the Labor government, enacts a National Health Service Act, extending comprehensive medical services to its entire population as a public responsibility. Several Canadian provinces proceed in their development of rural medical services at public expense.[18] New Zealand, Chile, and European nations still bleeding from the war continue the expansion of their health insurance programs.[19] A World Health Organization is established under the United Nations, having as its objective not merely limitation of the spread of epidemic disease or the control of narcotics but "the attainment by all peoples of the highest possible level of health."[20]

[13] American Institute of Cooperation, *American Cooperation* 1946. Washington, 1947.

[14] National University Extension Association, *Medical Care: The Twentieth Annual Debate Handbook* (Bower Aly, ed.). Columbia, 1946. Vols. I and II.

[15] National Planning Association, *For a Better Post-war Agriculture.* Washington, May, 1942.

[16] *The Southern Patriot* (Southern Conference for Human Welfare), May, 1945, "Good Health Issue."

[17] "New Group Backs Health Insurance," *New York Times,* Apr. 2, 1946, p. C-21.

[18] For example, see SHEPS, MINDEL C., "Saskatchewan Plans Health Services," *Canadian Journal of Public Health.* 36:175-180, May, 1945.

[19] ROEMER, MILTON I., "Rural Health Programs in Different Nations," *The Milbank Memorial Fund Quarterly,* January, 1948.

[20] U. S. Public Health Service, "Constitution of the World Health Organization," *Public Health Reports,* 61:1268-1279, Aug. 30, 1946.

Public Opinion

Against a background of unmet medical needs and burdensome medical costs, people are thinking things through and seeking solutions. The majority have lost faith in palliatives; they want concrete results through bold action. Hospital and health center construction through federal aid has the wholehearted support of rural people. The nation-wide extension of local public health organization has their full backing. Over four-fifths of all farmers favor an increase of public clinics.[21]

Nation-wide polls covering both rural and urban people show a ground swell of support for national health insurance legislation. A Gallup Poll in 1943 showed 59 per cent in favor of expanding the social security program to include "payment of benefits for sickness, disability, doctor and hospital bills."[22] In 1944, a National Opinion Research Center poll revealed that 68 per cent favored having the social security law broadened to provide "paying for the doctor and hospital care," and the vote held at 58 per cent when those polled were apprised that this would increase periodic contributions by 1.5 per cent of income.[23] These results, reported by the two leading opinion-testing organizations, do not even reflect the opinion which was doubtless further mobilized by President Truman's open backing of compulsory health insurance in 1945 and widespread discussion of the proposed legislation implementing his program. Of the scores of organizations of the general public testifying on this legislation in 1946 before the Senate Committee on Education and Labor, only the spokesmen of the United States Chamber of Commerce and the Farm Bureau Federation clearly opposed it; all others favored it.[24]

Although farm and rural groups have not been polled specifically on the issue of national compulsory health insurance, there is ample

[21] RAPER, ARTHUR, and U. T. SUMMERS, "What Do Farmers Expect after the War?" *The Agricultural Situation* (U. S. Department of Agriculture), 28:22, October, 1944.

[22] American Institute of Public Opinion (Gallup Poll), Princeton, New Jersey, Release of Aug. 14, 1943.

[23] National Opinion Research Center, Denver, Colorado, Special Report on Federal Health Insurance, October, 1944.

[24] Committee for the Nation's Health, *Hearing Highlights: Final Report of Hearings on S. 1606.* Washington, July 8, 1946, Processed.

evidence of their recognition of need for an organized attack on the payment problem. A Department of Agriculture poll in 1944 showed that over three-fourths of all farmers want some flat-rate, prepayment plan to cover bills for doctors' and nurses' services as well as hospital care.[25] Asked for opinions in 1944 regarding "health cooperatives" with prepayment plans, as opposed to all-out "socialized medicine," leading farmers of the state of Washington voted 59 per cent for the former, but 24 per cent actually voted that "all needed medical services be made available to people free of charge and paid for out of tax funds, just as public schools are freely available to all children."[26] There has been virtually no opposition among local farmers, it will be recalled, to direct federal financial support in the Department of Agriculture's experimental prepayment plans.[27] The prepayment idea found almost universal acceptance among state agricultural postwar planning committees, and about one-fourth of a series of state reports spoke directly in terms of including medical service for farm people in federal social security legislation.[28] A constantly recurring thought underlying today's swing in farm opinion was succinctly expressed in rural Wisconsin, "If a farmer has a sick sow in the dirtiest pen imaginable, he can get expert advice free of charge, but if his children are sick, he cannot get medical care for them unless he has the money."[29]

Medical professional groups are far from holding a single-track view on fundamental solutions to the medical care problem. A poll of physicians in 1945 showed that 65 per cent feel the need for something to be done to make it easier for people to meet medical care expenses. That some good might accrue to the public from the Wagner-Murray-Dingell Bill was recognized by 23 per cent of phy-

[25] RAPER and SUMMERS, op. cit.

[26] REUSS, CARL F., Farmer Views on the Medical Situation. Pullman: State College of Washington Experiment Station (V Circ. 20), September, 1944.

[27] The Experimental Health Program of the United States Department of Agriculture, a Study Made for the Subcommittee on Wartime Health and Education, U. S. Senate, S. Res. 74 (78th Cong.) and S. Res. 62 (79th Cong.) (Subcommittee Monograph 1). Washington: Government Printing Office, 1946, p. 17.

[28] Report of the Secretary of Agriculture, 1944. Washington: Government Printing Office, 1944, pp. 57-59.

[29] Wisconsin Public Welfare Department, Medical Relief in Three Wisconsin Counties. Madison, June, 1937, p. 9.

sicians, and nearly the same proportion saw some good in it for the medical profession.[30] Among younger medical men — a sample of medical students, interns, and medical officers in the armed forces — as many as 30 percent favor national health insurance.[31] The American Medical Association, reacting to national trends, supplanted its platform of recent years with its "Constructive Program for Medical Care" in June, 1945,[32] and discarded this in turn for the "National Health Program of the American Medical Association" announced in February, 1946.[33] While ostensibly backing most other features of the over-all program urged by the President, the A.M.A. clings to the voluntary approach on the payment issue. Strongly behind compulsory health insurance, on the other hand, are the organizations of progressive physicians — the Physicians Forum and the Committee of Physicians for the Improvement of Medical Care[34] — and the professional body of Negro doctors, the National Medical Association.

It is no surprise that the *American Magazine's* "Poll of Experts" in 1946 showed a 99 to 1 ratio in favor of some kind of health insurance. Three-fifths of these medical care authorities backed a compulsory system. Care of high quality was a prominent consideration, for again 99 out of 100 favored group medical practice.[35]

Plans into Programs

As planning matures and as opinions crystallize, there is an accelerating trend toward concrete legislative proposals. During the

[30] Opinion Research Corporation, *Survey on Medical Care.* New York, May, 1944.

[31] "Straws in the Post-war Wind," *The Interne,* 10:147-149, July, 1944.

[32] American Medical Association, "Constructive Program for Medical Care," *Journal of the American Medical Association,* 128:883, July 21, 1945.

[33] "The American Medical Association Health Program and Prepayment Sickness Insurance Plans," editorial, *Journal of the American Medical Association,* 130:494-496, Feb. 23, 1946.

[34] Boas, Ernst P., Testimony before the Committee on Education and Labor, U. S. Senate, 79th Cong., 2d Sess., S. 1606, *National Health Program.* Washington: Government Printing Office, 1946, Part 2, pp. 735-783. Also Peters, John P., Testimony before the Committee on Education and Labor, U.S. Senate, 79th Cong., 2d Sess., S. 1606, *National Health Program.* Part 2, pp. 981-1016.

[35] "Should We Have Health Insurance?" (Poll of experts conducted by Arthur Kornhauser, Bureau of Applied Social Research, Columbia University), *The American Magazine,* 141:40-41, 116, January, 1946.

1945 sessions, 36 measures were introduced in 12 state legislatures calling for compulsory health insurance or cash benefits during sickness, whereas the previous 10 years had seen only six or seven bills a year introduced in all the states.[36] As for federal legislation, we have noted proposals on public health, maternal and child health, mental hygiene, dental care, medical care for the needy, aid for professional education and research, construction of hospitals and health centers, and national compulsory health insurance.[36a] These bills — while fundamental — were only a fraction of the 121 measures involving health and medical care which had been introduced in the 79th session of Congress by October, 1945.[37]

The road to better rural health, nevertheless, cannot take its origin solely from the legislative hall. The thinking and desires of an informed public must be embodied in legislation if it is to be wisely conceived and have prospect of enactment. A gratifying beginning has been made by rural health planning groups, but much remains to be done. The base of planning must be broadened. Agricultural and rural leaders must link their efforts with those of other groups working toward realization of the right to good health. Only through such unity can they reach the common goal.

The full application of medical science to meet the needs of all individuals in every section of the country is an endeavor in which everyone has some part. The common man has an intimate interest in the organization of health services in his community, as do the farm, labor, or civic leaders who are his spokesmen. The social scientist has a weighty responsibility as he helps to mold new medical relationships. The physician, with his hard-won skills and the obligation he has assumed to serve people, has a unique role to play. He and his associates in all the health professions are the providers of service and the guarantors of its high quality — and here their greatest contribution can be made.[38]

[36] STROW, CARL W., and GERHARD HIRSCHFELD, "Health Insurance," *Journal of the American Medical Association,* 128:870-878, July 21, 1945.

[36a] ROEMER, MILTON I., "Recent National Health Legislation," *Journal of the National Medical Association,* 39:117-121, May, 1947.

[37] PARRAN, THOMAS, "Public Health in the Reconversion Period," *American Journal of Public Health,* 35:987-993, October, 1945.

[38] BERGE, WENDELL, "Justice and the Future of Medicine," *Public Health Reports,* 60:1-16, Jan. 5, 1945.

There are tasks also at every level of our political structure. It is no more sensible to sit back and let the Federal Government worry about the whole job than to oppose federal action blindly as an encroachment on state or local rights. In rural counties and districts there are public health agencies to be organized or given increased support. There are hospitals and health centers to be planned and group practice clinics to be organized. Pending nation-wide health insurance, there are prepayment plans to be set up and directed. At the state level, the same general types of action are needed and many more. There are steps to be taken to attract doctors to rural sections. There are training schools to be strengthened, new ones to be established, and fellowships to be provided. Licensure barriers may need to be lowered. Democratic legislation promoting the unfettered organization of prepayment plans can be helpful. Various state health activities can be coordinated under a single, strong state health agency. In the absence of a nation-wide program, compulsory health insurance on a state-wide basis might be launched in some states.

State and local planning and action, to be effective in meeting needs, must be carried on within a broad framework of federal action. It is evident from all we have considered that rural states and rural communities cannot pick themselves up by their bootstraps. There cannot be an entirely separate rural health program if parity in medical care is to be achieved. So long as rural areas try to solve their problems by themselves, the quality of the service they will obtain will remain below optimal standards, commensurate with lower rural economic levels.

It is because of the disadvantaged circumstances of rural America, as much as for any other reason, that national planning and action are essential. The inequities across the nation in health facilities, personnel, and services can be corrected only by federal action. If a priority were to be assigned, putting first things first, national compulsory health insurance would surely head the agenda. Not only is the solution to the problem of medical purchasing power basic to the over-all improvement of medical resources and the quality of service. It is likewise the central pillar in the structure of preventive services for the future, in that early and adequate medical care is the best approach known to the major disease problems of current years.

In the absence of national health insurance, rural needs could be met only by vast claims on the general revenues of the national treasury. Even with insurance to spread medical costs, a comprehensive health program will require a greater share of tax support in rural areas than in the cities, so long as rural people hold a disadvantaged position in the national economy. Such greater support, however, will partially correct relative inequities to agriculture that have followed upon urbanization of our society.

Rural people are astir. They want better health services but they do not always know how to get them. Of fears and fancies about the threadbare shibboleths brought forward to stem the tides of social progress, they have perhaps had more than their share. Rural people need information, they want facts and figures, and if they get them they will choose the road to better rural medical care, undiscouraged by the counselors of hesitation and compromise.

There is reason for confidence in the future of rural medicine. There is no question about the progress made in rural health services if, withholding comparisons with the urban situation, we look at the rural scene in the perspective of a century. In all nations the economic problems of medical care have been faced and the development of social insurance has become almost historically inevitable in the path toward their solution. With this central economic measure, other steps toward a total health program will be on firm ground. The goal of the plain people on the farms and in the villages of America will cease to be a vision and will be attained. When the steps clearly within our power are taken, we can be certain that the gap between the technology of modern medicine and its social application will be closed. First-rate medical care and optimal health will be an everyday experience across the stretches of rural America.

NAME INDEX

563

SUBJECT INDEX

A

Abnormalities, of body weight, 123
(*See also* Obesity; Weight)
of the heart, 130
Accidents, causing death, 61
disabling, 91
in farm life, 98, 105, 281
in home, 61
hospitalization for, 223
livestock, 99
occupational, 61
in mining, 61, 110
in petroleum industry, 61
Actinomycosis, 98
Administrators, hospital, 166, 515
medical care, need for, 515
qualifications of, 550
need for, 515
nonmedical, training of, 550–551
in public health, 515
training of, 528
Adults, farm, physical defects in, 125
(*See also* Defects)
Age levels, median, of physicians, 171
(*See also* Population)
Agricultural agencies, Federal, 39
(*See also* names of agencies)
state (*see* names of states)
Agricultural colleges, state, public health research by, 387
and regional health plans, 554–555
Agricultural credit, extension of, 476
Agricultural distribution, by voluntary endeavor, 39
Agricultural experiment stations, state scientific research by, 391
studies made by, 391
Agricultural extension service, 37, 391
in Ohio, 553
(*See also* United States Department of Agriculture)
Agricultural markets, competition for, 16
Agricultural production (*see* Farm production)
Agricultural Research Administration (*see* United States Department of Agriculture)
Agricultural Workers Health and Medical Association, for migratory farm workers, 423
Agriculture, and better farm income, by balanced farming, 476
by curbing land prices, 476
through extension of credit, 476
through farmers' cooperatives, 476

Agriculture, and better farm income, through improved techniques, 476
by modernization of marketing methods, 476
through off-farm employment opportunities, 476
through soil, forest, and water conservation, 476
differences in, between and within regions, 21
economic opportunities in, 13, 15
occupational diseases of, 108–110
(*See also* Diseases)
in transition, 15–17
(*See also* Farms and farming, U. S. Department of Agriculture)
Ailments, functional, 86
ill-defined, 86
serious, 91–92
(*See also* Diseases; Illness)
Alabama, health conference in, 553
health education for rural Negroes in, 463
"movable school" project for rural Negroes in, 463
rural health units in, 465
rural physicians in, postgraduate training of, 458
prospective scholarships for, 382–383
survey of health resources in, 554
(*See also* Birmingham; Gadsden; Macon County; Montgomery County; Tuskegee)
Alberta, Canada, hospital bed ratio in, 224n.
Albuminuria, 130
Alcoholism, chronic, 112, 141
Alpha Kappa Alpha, 462
Ambulance service, 501
airplane, 234–235, 505
private, 235
helicopter, 505
in regional hospital service, 504
for rural areas, 234, 504
American Academy of Pediatrics, 181
American Association of Public Health Dentists, 460
American Association for Social Security, 461
American Association of Social Workers, 461
American Association of University Women, and health services, 556
American Cancer Society, 461
American College of Surgeons, and standards of performance of hospitals, 457
system of approval of, 237
American Dental Association, and professional standards, 457

571